THE COMMUNICATION DISCIPLINES IN HIGHER EDUCATION:

A Guide to Academic Programs in the United States and Canada

Compiled and Edited
by

Garland C. Elmore
Indiana University - Purdue University
at Indianapolis

ASSOCIATION FOR
COMMUNICATION ADMINISTRATION

ASSOCIATION OF
SCHOOLS OF JOURNALISM AND
MASS COMMUNICATION

Editorial inquiries, suggestions, corrections, and
updated information should be addressed to:

Garland C. Elmore
Office of Learning Technologies
Indiana University - Purdue University at Indianapolis
902 West New York Street
Indianapolis, Indiana 46202-5154
(317) 274-4507

Publication inquiries and book orders
should be addressed to:

Vernon W. Gantt
Association for Communication Administration
311 Wilson Hall
Murray State University
Murray, Kentucky 42071
(502) 762-3411

Composition and design by the Office of Learning Technologies,
Indiana University - Purdue University at Indianapolis.

ISBN 0-929506-01-4

Printed in the United States of America.

FOREWORD

Take a moment, if you will, and scan through this extraordinary volume. Extraordinary in that it is the first truly comprehensive guide to college and university programs in communication, speech, media studies, journalism, radio, television, film, advertising, public relations, and new technologies. It also represents the combined effort of two professional organizations, the Association for Communication Administration and the Association of Schools of Journalism and Mass Communication. The volume contains detailed information on 1,164 departments and programs, description of curricula and facilities, and other valuable information.

We are all aware of the phenomenal growth of students majoring and taking courses in communication and related disciplines in recent years. This has been both a blessing and curse. A blessing in that it has compelled everyone in higher education to understand communication in our global culture and economy. A curse in that it compels us to constantly stay in touch with what is going on in our own institutions and to what is changing in the myriad industries which require the services of our graduates. It is a task which we in the field have gladly undertaken, for in many ways we are unique in the American university system in that we have the dual responsibility for educating our students in the liberal arts yet recognize that there are specific skills and knowledge which our students need for their professional lives.

Recent developments in Europe, changes in Africa, Latin America and Asia, and the recognition of our own diverse society in the United States make our task even more important. Sharing of knowledge and information is also part of our mandate. This reference guide provides many different audiences with needed information. For educators and scholars in the field, the volume gives us the opportunity to compare and contrast how individual institutions define and manage their programs. Those advising students, whether entering programs or already studying on the undergraduate or graduate level, now have the most complete updated information available. Students themselves should be encouraged to use the volume and to take the opportunity to correspond directly with institutions which can benefit them. As mentioned earlier, it is essential for us to maintain our relationship with the communication industry. For those working in the field and charged with the responsibility of locating qualified, entry-level personnel, this guide will serve as a source of finding appropriate candidates. Finally, it should be recognized that this volume is an essential reference for all administrators. Understanding the growth, changes and direction of communication departments is essential for everyone in university life. Our society requires the understanding of the roles that communication and communication technologies play in almost every aspect of our day-to-day lives.

The Association of Schools of Journalism and Mass Communication and the Association for Communication Administration would like to commend and thank Garland C. Elmore for the passion and professionalism he gave to this difficult task. Our field is indebted to his effort.

Peter L. Haratonik, President
Association for Communication
Administration

Will Norton Jr., President
Association of Schools of Journalism
and Mass Communication

June, 1990

TABLE OF CONTENTS

Foreword

Introduction

Guide to the United States

Guide to Canada

Appendix

INTRODUCTION

Background

The research which led to this publication was based on an earlier project which resulted in the first edition of the Association for Communication Administration's *Communication Media in Higher Education*. *Communication Media* was a comprehensive guide to academic programs in radio, television, broadcasting, telecommunications, and film. It built upon the previous contributions of several professional organizations which are interested in media education and publish member directories, including the Association of Schools of Journalism and Mass Communication (ASJMC), the Association for Education in Journalism and Mass Communication (AEJMC), the Broadcast Education Association (BEA), the American Film Institute (AFI), the Speech Communication Association (SCA), and others. *Communication Media,* consequently, attempted to update, synthesize, and expand upon earlier efforts: *update* because many of the published listings were over a decade old; *synthesize* because the administration of media education evolves in several types of departments and schools which have different academic perspectives and cultures; and, *expand* because an exhaustive national survey across association affiliation (or without regard for association affiliation) had not been attempted previously.

Communication Media was published in January, 1987. Of the 2,994 colleges, universities, professional schools, and institutes listed in the *Yearbook of Higher Education* which were surveyed, 591 academic units were included in the database because they were found to offer at least one college-level course in media. For each qualified academic unit, the publication described selected aspects of the curriculum, including its focus and several important statistics, listed degrees offered, summarized available facilities, and provided mailing and administrative information. Additionally, the rank, highest degree earned, specialty, and research interests were described for each full-time faculty member. Data were included on a total of 1,706 full-time media faculty members.

The need to expand the media education database project to include other communication fields and specialties was considered in a summit meeting of the presidents of three professional associations (ACA, ASJMC, and BEA) in 1989. After discussing the project with their respective executive committees and boards, the Association for Communication Administration and the Association of Schools of Journalism and Mass Communication decided to jointly fund and develop the project in cooperation with Indiana University - Purdue University at

Indianapolis, where the first edition of *Communication Media* was compiled and edited. The new project was initiated in September, 1989 and completed in June, 1990. This publication, *The Communication Disciplines in Higher Education*, is printed from the resulting database. It replaces the more narrowly focused earlier edition. Updated editions are anticipated biannually.

Objectives

This project was undertaken by the Association for Communication Administration and the Association of Schools of Journalism and Mass Communication to 1) help define the discipline by identifying its institutions, administrators, program emphases and specializations, organization, resources, and facilities, 2) provide a mechanism to determine and document trends, growth patterns, and changes in communication education, 3) encourage intra-disciplinary communication, scholarship, research and professional development, 4) assist high school, undergraduate, and graduate students and their advisors in making decisions about communication study, and 5) help those outside the discipline identify programs and professionals in the field.

Method

The computer archive from which this reference guide was printed was developed from information submitted by college and university administrators and from data supplied by professional associations. Copies of the letter and questionnaire which appear in the appendix were mailed, along with pre-addressed postage-paid envelopes, to all institutions listed in the *Yearbook of Higher Education*. Institution names and addresses were checked against lists of undergraduate and graduate majors as determined in Barron's *Profiles of American Colleges*, Sixteenth Edition, and Peterson's *Guide to Four-Year Colleges*, Nineteenth Edition. Approximately 3,000 colleges, universities, professional schools, and institutes were included in this mailing list, but only a fraction were known to offer course work in communication.

A second and unquestionably more useful mailing list was compiled by examining data from academic programs in communication which had been previously collected by professional associations and through the *Communication Media* project. Especially helpful were member lists and other mailing lists supplied by the Association for Communication Administration, the Association of Schools of Journalism and Mass Communication, the Association for Education in Journalism and Mass Communication, and the Broadcast Education Association. The information from each of these sources was cross-referenced to verify data and to delete duplicate entries. This second list was then compared to the *Yearbook* list, taking special care to ensure that separately organized communication units within the same institution were identified and all were included in the mailing.

In September, 1989, 3,307 questionnaires were sent to academic programs throughout the United States and Canada. After 10 weeks a second mailing was processed for programs which had not responded but which had been earlier identified by one of the previously mentioned sources. A limited third mailing was processed in January, 1990, targeted to known communication-related units for which data had still not been received. In addition to the scheduled mailings, individual questionnaires were mailed as new units were identified by respondents. That is, one item on the questionnaire asked that respondents provide the names and addresses of other program administrators at their institutions who were responsible for areas of the communication curriculum outside their own academic unit. Ninety-six new programs were identified by administrators in this way. In sum, 3,403 unique addresses were included in the mailings.

Summary of Results

This reference guide lists 1,508 programs which offer communication courses or degrees in the United States or in Canada. A table at the end of this section lists the number of entries and responses for each state and Canada. Detailed information about the 1,164 academic units responding to the survey is provided in the individual listings beginning on page 1.

Sixty-three percent (n=723) of the responses were from public institutions, while 37 percent (n=421) were private. The curricula offered by the 1,164 programs included Advertising, Communication, Film, Information Science, Journalism and Mass Communication, Public Relations, Telecommunications, and Speech. Journalism and Mass Communication (69.1%), Telecommunications (67.4%), Communication (65.9%) and Speech (59.8%) were most commonly included in the curricula of the reporting institutions. Table I illustrates the number of administrators who indicated that their program included each area.

The total number of full-time faculty members teaching in the curriculum areas represented above was 11,661. The average (mean) unit size was 10. There were about an equal number of part-time faculty members and/or graduate teaching assistants who were teaching half-time or less. The part-time faculty totalled 11,406 or 9.8 per reporting unit. Additionally, the administrators reported 2,224 full-time professional, non-clerical staff members employed in their academic programs.

Table I
Communication Specialities Included in the Curriculum

Number	Percent	Content Areas or Specialties*
448	38.5%	Advertising
747	65.9%	Communication
381	32.7%	Film, Cinema
53	04.6%	Information Science
804	69.1%	Journalism, Mass Communication
552	47.4%	Public Relations
784	67.4%	Radio, TV, Broadcasting, Telecommunications
696	59.8%	Speech

*Excludes theatre, dance and other performing arts which are included in another ACA publication.

The number of students reported to be majoring in the communication disciplines was over 200,000. The majority of these were pursuing the Bachelor of Science or the Bachelor of Arts degree: 149,998 juniors and seniors. Students enrolled in Associate's Degree programs totalled 13,617. Other sums were: Bachelor of Fine Arts, 6,112; Masters Degree Programs, 13,431; Master of Fine Arts, 1,037. The number of Doctoral Degree students who were *in residence* during the 1989-1990 academic year totalled 2,161. There were 716 additional Ph.D. students who were involved in their studies but who were not in residence at the time of the survey.

A mean of 201 Bachelor of Arts or Sciences majors was determined from the data reported by the programs which offer that degree. The average number of Bachelor of Fine Arts majors was 130. Only juniors and seniors were included in these calculations. Seventy-four was the mean for associate's degree majors. At the Master's level the mean was 49 among MA and MS programs and 38 in MFA programs. The average number of doctoral students studying in residence where those programs were available was 27.

The facilities and services that administrators said were available to students through their academic programs are summarized in Table II. It is clear that many opportunities for professional experience are well established in communication education. Over half of the programs responded that they provide video editing facilities (n=783), work experience through a local commercial newspaper (n=762), experience on a campus newspaper published independently of the academic unit (n=762), darkroom facilities for photography (n=755), desktop publishing facilities (n=708), audio recording laboratories (n=659), electronic field production equipment used in classes (n=637), video laboratories or television simulation studios (n=632), and experience through a local commercial television station (n=621). The administrators reported 545 FM radio stations, 177 AM radio stations, and 210 TV stations operated by their institutions. Satellite uplink facilities were reported at 158 institutions; 63 specified Ku-Band and 51 indicated C-Band capability.

Table II
Facilities and Services Available

Num	%	Code	Facility or Service Available
399	34.3	AdA	Advertising Agency provides work experience.
177	15.2	AM	AM Radio Station operated by institution.
316	27.1	AP	Associated Press Feed.
659	56.6	AUD	Audio Recording Laboratory.
513	44.1	CATV	Local Community Cable TV uses student's work.
200	17.2	CCAud	Carrier Current or Land Line Audio System.
408	35.1	CCTV	Closed Circuit TV Facility for classroom or campus.
762	65.5	CN	Campus Newspaper published independently.
762	65.5	ComN	Local Commercial Newspaper provides experience.
621	53.4	ComTV	Local Commercial TV Station provides experience.
10	0.9	CP	Canadian Press Feed.
708	60.8	DESK	Desktop Publishing Facilities.
755	64.9	DR	Darkroom Facilities for photography.
783	67.3	EDIT	Video Editing Facility.
637	54.7	EFP	Electronic Field Production equipment.
210	18.0	ETV	TV Station operated by educational institution.
382	32.8	FILM	Film or Cinema Studio and Laboratories.
545	46.8	FM	FM Radio Station operated by institution.
148	12.7	ITFS	Instructional Television Fixed Service distribution.
274	23.5	JM	Journalism or other program publishes Magazine.
409	35.1	JN	Journalism or other program publishes Newspaper.
13	1.1	NYTS	New York Times Service Feed.
443	38.1	PRA	Public Relations Agency provides work experience.
8	0.7	RNA	Reuters News Agency Feed.
158	13.6	SAT	Satellite Uplink: [63] Ku Band [51] C Band.
103	8.8	UPI	United Press International Feed.
267	22.9	VDT	Electronic News and Data Processing used in classes.
632	54.3	VID	Video Laboratory or Television Simulation Studio.

Organization

In this publication, institutions in the United States are organized alphabetically by state and in Canada by province. Program titles within the same institution are listed alphabetically, except higher level organizations are listed first whenever structure could be determined from the response. Information about curriculum and instruction, as well as information about facilities and services, is included for the 1,164 programs which provided data.

Additions, Deletions, and Corrections

Editorial inquiries, additions, deletions, and corrections should be sent directly to the compiler, whose address appears following the inside title page. A copy of the questionnaire and cover letter used in this survey are included in the appendix. Although changes to the survey instrument may occur before the next edition, it is important that the computer archive from which this guide was printed be accurately maintained as a central discipline-wide resource. Program administrators are encouraged to send changes and suggestions for improving the utility of *Communication Disciplines in Higher Education.*

Publication Inquiries

Publication inquiries may be directed to the Association for Communication Administration or the Association of Schools of Journalism and Mass Communication. The address for publication inquires appears following the inside title page. Copies of *Communication Disciplines in Higher Education* may be ordered directly from the ACA.

Acknowledgement

This project was funded by the Association for Communication Administration, the Association of Schools of Journalism and Mass Communication, and Indiana University - Purdue University at Indianapolis (IUPUI). Those who undertook this work are thankful for the unique contributions of Karen Coffman, who processed the survey mailings and who entered information into the computer database, of Irene Ledeboer, who proofread the first drafts, of Patricia Van Noy, who assisted in project management, and of Vincent Cannon, who designed the cover and offered helpful advice on page formats. These individuals are affiliated with the Office of Learning Technologies at IUPUI, where the final copy was printed using standard desktop publishing tools.

Table III
Number of Entries and
Questionnaire Responses by Location

Location	Entries	Percent	Responses	Percent
United States				
Alabama	22	1.5	14	1.2
Alaska	7	0.5	5	0.4
Arizona	8	0.5	7	0.6
Arkansas	22	1.5	17	1.5
California	122	8.0	90	7.7
Colorado	23	1.5	18	1.5
Connecticut	12	0.8	10	0.9
Delaware	3	0.2	2	0.2
District of Columbia	11	0.7	6	0.5
Florida	38	2.5	31	2.7
Georgia	26	1.7	17	1.5
Hawaii	9	0.6	7	0.6
Idaho	6	0.4	6	0.5
Illinois	79	5.2	60	5.2
Indiana	49	3.2	37	3.2
Iowa	34	2.3	29	2.5
Kansas	32	2.1	23	2.0
Kentucky	36	2.4	31	2.7
Louisiana	21	1.4	16	1.4
Maine	7	0.5	7	0.6
Maryland	26	1.7	17	1.5
Massachusetts	41	2.7	29	2.5
Michigan	57	3.8	43	3.7
Minnesota	30	2.0	24	2.1
Mississippi	21	1.4	17	1.5
Missouri	44	2.9	39	3.4
Montana	6	0.4	5	0.4

Table III, Continued
Number of Entries and
Questionnaire Responses by Location

Location	Entries	Percent	Responses	Percent
United States, Cont.				
Nebraska	22	1.5	19	1.6
Nevada	3	0.2	0	0.0
New Hampshire	9	0.6	7	0.6
New Jersey	21	1.4	18	1.5
New Mexico	9	0.6	8	0.7
New York	96	6.7	74	6.4
North Carolina	34	2.3	30	2.6
North Dakota	5	0.3	4	0.3
Ohio	71	4.7	59	5.1
Oklahoma	24	1.6	21	1.8
Oregon	20	1.3	16	1.4
Pennsylvania	79	5.2	60	5.2
Rhode Island	7	0.5	5	0.4
South Carolina	17	1.1	10	0.9
South Dakota	9	0.6	7	0.6
Tennessee	31	2.1	25	2.1
Texas	88	5.8	66	5.7
Utah	6	0.4	6	0.5
Vermont	5	0.3	4	0.3
Virginia	40	2.7	25	2.1
Washington	30	2.0	22	1.9
West Virginia	19	1.3	14	1.2
Wisconsin	38	2.5	29	2.5
Wyoming	7	0.5	4	0.3
Canada	26	1.7	24	2.1

A Guide to
Academic Programs in
the United States and Canada

Alabama State University (Public)

Department of Communications Media
915 South Jackson
Montgomery, Alabama 36195
Telephone: (205) 293-4493

Katrina K. Covington, Chair
Robert P. Thomson, Dean, College of Arts and Science

CURRICULUM AND INSTRUCTION
Courses or Concentrations Available: Journalism or Mass Communication; Public Relations; Radio, Television, Broadcasting, or Telecommunications; *Undergraduate Objectives or Program Emphases*: To train and prepare students for professional careers in one of the three major areas: print, broadcasting (Radio-Television), or public relations; *Bachelor's Degree Majors*: 103; *Full-Time Faculty*: 3; *Part-Time Faculty*: 4; *Full-Time Professional (non-clerical) Staff Members*: 2.

FACILITIES AND SERVICES
Practical experiences available through: Advertising Agency; Audio Recording Laboratory; Campus Newspaper (Published Independently); Local Commercial Television Station; Desktop Publishing Facility; Photographic Darkrooms; Video Editing; Electronic Field Production (Video); FM Radio Station (Institutional); Institutional Magazine; Institutional Newspaper; Public Relations Agency; Satellite Uplink Facility (Ku Band Transmitter) (C Band Transmitter); United Press International Feed; Video Production Laboratory or Television Studio.

Auburn University (Public)

Speech Communication
6030 Haley Center
Auburn, Alabama 36849

Don Richardson, Administrator

Auburn University (Public)

Department of Communication
Montgomery, Alabama 36193

George L. Grice, Administrator

Auburn University (Public)

Department of Journalism
Auburn, Alabama 36849
Telephone: (205) 844-4000

Jack Simms, Chair
Mary P. Richards, Dean, College of Liberal Arts

CURRICULUM AND INSTRUCTION
Courses or Concentrations Available: Journalism or Mass Communication; Public Relations; *Undergraduate Objectives or Program Emphases*: Reporting, writing, interviewing, editing. Applied journalism courses; *Bachelor's Degree Majors*: 108; *Full-Time Faculty*: 7.

FACILITIES AND SERVICES
Practical experiences available through: AM Radio Station (Institutional); Audio Recording Laboratory; Closed Circuit Television Facility; Campus Newspaper (Published Independently); Local Commercial Newspaper; Desktop Publishing Facility; Photographic Darkrooms; Video Editing; Electronic Field Production (Video); Film or Cinema Laboratory; FM Radio Station (Institutional); Institutional Newspaper; Video News and Data Processing; Video Production Laboratory or Television Studio.

Chattahoochee Valley Community College (Public)

Program of Radio and Television Broadcasting
2602 Savage Drive
Phenix City, Alabama 36867
Telephone: (205) 291-4986

Robert W. Cunningham, Director
Michael Williams, Head, Department of Language and Fine Arts

CURRICULUM AND INSTRUCTION
Courses or Concentrations Available: Advertising; Communication; Journalism or Mass Communication; Public Relations; Radio, Television, Broadcasting, or Telecommunications; *Program Coordinator*: George Chard (Speech); *Undergraduate Objectives or Program Emphases*: To provide the basic skills training necessary for undergraduate Radio-Television majors to obtain employment in Broadcasting and related fields; *Associate's Degree Majors*: 80; *Full-Time Faculty*: 1; *Full-Time Professional (non-clerical) Staff Members*: 1.

FACILITIES AND SERVICES
Practical experiences available through: Advertising Agency; Audio Recording Laboratory; Community Antenna (Cable) Television Origination; Closed Circuit Television Facility; Local Commercial Television Station; Photographic Darkrooms; Video Editing; Electronic Field Production (Video); Public Relations Agency; Satellite Uplink Facility (C Band Transmitter); Video News and Data Processing; Video Production Laboratory or Television Studio.

Enterprise State Junior College (Public)

Program of Communication
U. S. 84 East
Enterprise, Alabama 36331
Telephone: (205) 347-3752

Richard C. Emanuel, Instructor
Scott R. Smith, Chair, Division of English, Foreign Languages and Communication

CURRICULUM AND INSTRUCTION
Courses or Concentrations Available: Communication; Journalism or Mass Communication; Speech; *Undergraduate Objectives or Program Emphases*: Provide basic communications preparation for further study at senior institutions; *Associate's Degree Majors*: 20; *Full-Time Faculty*: 1; *Part-Time Faculty*: 1.

FACILITIES AND SERVICES
Practical experiences available through: Institutional Newspaper.

Faulkner University

Communication
5345 Atlanta Highway Box 138
Montgomery, Alabama 36193-4601

David Spiceland, Administrator

Gadsden State Community College

Department of Radio-Television
Post Office Box 227
Gadsden, Alabama 35999-0227

Neil D. Mullin, Administrator

Huntingdon College

Department of Visual and Performing Arts
1500 East Fairview Avenue
Montgomery, Alabama 36106

Jeanne E. Shaffer, Administrator

Jacksonville State University (Public)

Department of Communication
Jacksonville, Alabama 36265
Telephone: (205) 231-5300

Ralph E. Carmode, Head
Dan Marsengill, Dean

CURRICULUM AND INSTRUCTION
Courses or Concentrations Available: Communication; Journalism or Mass Communication; Radio, Television, Broadcasting, or Telecommunications; *Undergraduate Objectives or Program*

Emphases: Professional orientation, including emphasis on writing and oral communication skills. Substantial background in liberal arts education; *Bachelor's Degree Majors*: 90; *Full-Time Faculty*: 5; *Full-Time Professional (non-clerical) Staff Members*: 3.

FACILITIES AND SERVICES
Practical experiences available through: Associated Press Wire Service Feed; Audio Recording Laboratory; Closed Circuit Television Facility; Local Commercial Television Station; Photographic Darkrooms; Video Editing; Electronic Field Production (Video); FM Radio Station (Institutional); Institutional Newspaper; Video Production Laboratory or Television Studio.

Jefferson Davis State Junior College (Public)

Broadcast/Journalism
P. O. Box 958
Brewton, Alabama 36247

Bo Ward, Administrator

John C. Calhoun College

Department of Radio-Television
Box 2216
Decatur, Alabama 35602

Bill Kling, Administrator

Mobile College (Private)

Program of Communications
P. O. Box 13220-346
College Parkway
Mobile, Alabama 36613
Telephone: (205) 675-5990

Billy N. Wolfe, Jr., Head
Frances Garner, Chair

CURRICULUM AND INSTRUCTION
Courses or Concentrations
Available: Advertising; Communication; Journalism or Mass Communication; Public Relations; Radio, Television, Broadcasting, or Telecommunications; *Bachelor's Degree*

Majors: 19; *Full-Time Faculty*: 1; *Part-Time Faculty*: 7.

FACILITIES AND SERVICES
Practical experiences available through: Advertising Agency; Audio Recording Laboratory; Community Antenna (Cable) Television Origination; Local Commercial Newspaper; Local Commercial Television Station; Desktop Publishing Facility; Photographic Darkrooms; Video Editing; Electronic Field Production (Video); Public Relations Agency; Video News and Data Processing; Video Production Laboratory or Television Studio.

Spring Hill College (Private)

Discipline of Communication Arts
4000 Dauphin Street
Mobile, Alabama 36608
Telephone: (205) 460-2392

Michele Hilmes, Director
Ruth Belasco, Head, Division of Communication and Fine Arts

CURRICULUM AND INSTRUCTION
Courses or Concentrations
Available: Advertising; Communication; Film or Cinema; Journalism or Mass Communication; Public Relations; Radio, Television, Broadcasting, or Telecommunications; Speech; Photography; *Undergraduate Objectives or Program Emphases*: To provide both critical knowledge and applied skills in communication areas, within the context of a liberal arts education; *Bachelor's Degree Majors*: 60; *Full-Time Faculty*: 3; *Part-Time Faculty*: 3.

FACILITIES AND SERVICES
Practical experiences available through: Advertising Agency; Audio Recording Laboratory; Local Commercial Newspaper; Local Commercial Television Station; Desktop Publishing Facility; Photographic Darkrooms; Video Editing; Electronic Field Production (Video); FM Radio Station (Institutional); Institutional Newspaper; Public Relations Agency; Video Production Laboratory or Television Studio.

Troy State University (Public)

School of Journalism
Troy, Alabama 36082
Telephone: (205) 566-8112

Merrill Bankester, Dean
Edward F. Barnett, Vice President,
Academic Affairs

CURRICULUM AND INSTRUCTION
*Courses or Concentrations
Available*: Journalism or Mass
Communication; Radio, Television,
Broadcasting, or Telecommunications;
Bachelor's Degree Majors: 230; *Full-Time
Faculty*: 3; *Part-Time Faculty*: 2; *Full-Time
Professional (non-clerical) Staff Members*: 2.

FACILITIES AND SERVICES
Practical experiences available through:
Associated Press Wire Service Feed; Audio
Recording Laboratory; Community Antenna
(Cable) Television Origination; Campus
Newspaper (Published Independently);
Local Commercial Newspaper; Desktop
Publishing Facility; Video Editing;
Electronic Field Production (Video);
Television Broadcast Station (Institutional);
FM Radio Station (Institutional).

University of Alabama - Tuscaloosa (Public)

College of Communication
P. O. Box 870172
Tuscaloosa, Alabama 35487-0172
Telephone: (205) 348-5520

Edward Mullins, Dean
Douglas E. Jones, Acting Academic Vice
President

CURRICULUM AND INSTRUCTION
*Courses or Concentrations
Available*: Advertising; Communication; Film
or Cinema; Journalism or Mass
Communication; Public Relations; Radio,
Television, Broadcasting, or
Telecommunications; Speech; *Program
Coordinators*: Dolf Zillmann (Graduate
Studies and Research); John Eighmey
(Advertising and Public Relations); Loy
Singleton (Broadcast and Film
Communication); Jay Black (Journalism);
Culpepper Clark (Speech Communication);
*Undergraduate Objectives or Program
Emphases*: Education for careers in mass

media and related areas in a liberal arts
context; communication as a liberal arts
discipline; *Graduate Objectives or Program
Emphases*: MA--Professional education for
careers in mass media and related areas;
research; entry to Ph.D. Ph.D.--Mass
communication research for itself and for
careers in teaching, business, and
government; *Bachelor's Degree Majors*: 1673;
Master's Degree Majors: 60; *Doctoral Degree
Majors Currently in Residence*: 9; *Full-Time
Faculty*: 45; *Part-Time Faculty*: 45;
*Full-Time Professional (non-clerical) Staff
Members*: 7. Also, see following entry.

FACILITIES AND SERVICES
Practical experiences available through:
Associated Press Wire Service Feed; Audio
Recording Laboratory; Community Antenna
(Cable) Television Origination; Campus
Newspaper (Published Independently);
Local Commercial Newspaper; Local
Commercial Television Station; Desktop
Publishing Facility; Photographic
Darkrooms; Video Editing; Electronic Field
Production (Video); Film or Cinema
Laboratory; FM Radio Station
(Institutional); ITFS Distribution System;
Institutional Magazine; Institutional
Newspaper; Satellite Uplink Facility; Video
News and Data Processing; Video
Production Laboratory or Television Studio.

University of Alabama - Tuscaloosa (Public)

Department of Speech Communication
Box 870240
Tuscaloosa, Alabama 35487-0240
Telephone: (205) 348-5995

E. Culpepper Clark, Chair
Edward Mullins, Dean

CURRICULUM AND INSTRUCTION
Courses or Concentrations Available: Speech;
*Undergraduate Objectives or Program
Emphases*: Instruction in Rhetoric,
Communication Theory, Political
Communication, Organizational
Communication, and Forensics; *Graduate
Objectives or Program Emphases*: Research
and seminars in Rhetoric, Communication
Theory, Political Communication,
Organizational Communication, and
Forensics; *Bachelor's Degree Majors*: 35;
Master's Degree Majors: 13; *Full-Time

Faculty: 9; *Part-Time Faculty*: 10; *Full-Time Professional (non-clerical) Staff Members*: 2.

University of Alabama - Birmingham (Public)

Department of Communication Studies
414 Humanities Building
Birmingham, Alabama 35294
Telephone: (205) 934-3877

Mark L. Hickson III, Chair
Theodore M. Benditt, Dean

CURRICULUM AND INSTRUCTION
Courses or Concentrations Available: Communication; Journalism or Mass Communication; Public Relations; Radio, Television, Broadcasting, or Telecommunications; *Undergraduate Objectives or Program Emphases*: Communication Arts; Mass Communication: Broadcasting, Journalism, Public Relations; *Full-Time Faculty*: 10; *Part-Time Faculty*: 4; *Full-Time Professional (non-clerical) Staff Members*: 2.

FACILITIES AND SERVICES
Practical experiences available through: Advertising Agency; Audio Recording Laboratory; Campus Newspaper (Published Independently); Local Commercial Newspaper; Local Commercial Television Station; Video Editing; Electronic Field Production (Video); FM Radio Station (Institutional); Institutional Magazine; Institutional Newspaper; Public Relations Agency.

University of Montevallo

Communication Arts Department
Station 305
Montevallo, Alabama 35115

Charles C. Harbour, Chair

University of Montevallo (Public)

Division of Mass Communications
Montevallo, Alabama 35115
Telephone: (205) 665-6625

Karl A. Perkins, Director
Charles Harbour, Chair, Department of Communication Arts

CURRICULUM AND INSTRUCTION
Courses or Concentrations Available: Film or Cinema; Journalism or Mass Communication; Radio, Television, Broadcasting, or Telecommunications; *Undergraduate Objectives or Program Emphases*: Hands on experience at all levels of program production; *Graduate Objectives or Program Emphases*: General professional upgrading; *Bachelor's Degree Majors*: 55; *Master's Degree Majors*: 4; *Other Degree Majors*: 70; *Full-Time Faculty*: 4; *Full-Time Professional (non-clerical) Staff Members*: 1.

FACILITIES AND SERVICES
Practical experiences available through: Advertising Agency; Audio Recording Laboratory; Community Antenna (Cable) Television Origination; Campus Newspaper (Published Independently); Local Commercial Newspaper; Local Commercial Television Station; Desktop Publishing Facility; Photographic Darkrooms; Video Editing; Electronic Field Production (Video); Public Relations Agency; Video Production Laboratory or Television Studio.

University of North Alabama (Public)

Department of Speech Communication Theatre
Florence, Alabama 35674
Telephone: (205) 760-4358

Eugene H. Balof, Head
Jack Moore, Dean, School of Arts and Sciences

CURRICULUM AND INSTRUCTION
Courses or Concentrations Available: Communication; Film or Cinema; Journalism or Mass Communication; Public Relations; Radio, Television, Broadcasting, or Telecommunications; Speech; Theatre; *Bachelor's Degree Majors*: 100; *Full-Time Faculty*: 8; *Full-Time Professional (non-clerical) Staff Members*: 2.

FACILITIES AND SERVICES
Practical experiences available through: Community Antenna (Cable) Television Origination; Campus Newspaper (Published Independently); Local Commercial Newspaper; Local Commercial Television Station; Desktop Publishing Facility; Photographic Darkrooms; Video Editing; Electronic Field Production (Video); Film or Cinema Laboratory; Public Relations Agency; Video Production Laboratory or Television Studio.

University of South Alabama (Public)

Department of Communication
Mobile, Alabama 36688
Telephone: (205) 460-6301

Donald K. Wright, Chair
S.G. Crossley, Dean, College of Arts and Sciences

CURRICULUM AND INSTRUCTION
Courses or Concentrations Available: Advertising; Communication; Film or Cinema; Journalism or Mass Communication; Public Relations; Radio, Television, Broadcasting, or Telecommunications; Speech; Organizational Communication; *Undergraduate Objectives or Program Emphases*: Speech, general communication, organizational communication, public relations, print journalism, broadcast journalism, general radio-television; *Graduate Objectives or Program Emphases*: MA program with an emphasis in corporate and public communication. Combines the faculty's strengths in public relations and organizational communication; *Bachelor's Degree Majors*: 250; *Master's Degree Majors*: 17; *Full-Time Faculty*: 14; *Part-Time Faculty*: 12; *Full-Time Professional (non-clerical) Staff Members*: 2.

FACILITIES AND SERVICES
Practical experiences available through: Advertising Agency; Audio Recording Laboratory; Community Antenna (Cable) Television Origination; Closed Circuit Television Facility; Campus Newspaper (Published Independently); Local Commercial Newspaper; Local Commercial Television Station; Desktop Publishing Facility; Video Editing; Electronic Field Production (Video); Public Relations Agency; Video Production Laboratory or Television Studio.

ALASKA

Matanuska-Susitna College - University of Alaska (Public)

Department of English/Speech
P. O. Box 2889
Palmer, Alaska 99645
Telephone: (907) 745-4255

Elizabeth J. Fallon, Coordinator
Glenn Massay, Chief Administrator

CURRICULUM AND INSTRUCTION
Courses or Concentrations Available: Speech;
*Undergraduate Objectives or Program
Emphases*: Our major emphasis is providing
the required speech class for both associate
and bachelor degrees. We occasionally offer
elective classes in interpersonal
communication, interviewing, magazine
article writing and video production;
Full-Time Faculty: 2; *Part-Time Faculty*: 6.

FACILITIES AND SERVICES
*Practical experiences available
through*: Desktop Publishing Facility;
Photographic Darkrooms; Video Editing.

Northwest Community College

Media Center
Pouch 400
Nome, Alaska 99762

Cary Bolling, Administrator

Sheldon Jackson College (Private)

Division of Liberal Arts
801 Lincoln Street
Sitka, Alaska 99835
Telephone: (907) 747-5243

Jan O. Craddick, Chair
Lowell Jornquist, Vice President, Academic
Programs

CURRICULUM AND INSTRUCTION
*Courses or Concentrations
Available*: Communication; Speech; Theatre;

*Undergraduate Objectives or Program
Emphases*: Covers following academic
objectives for students: to communicate
effectively; to apply principles of logic; to
recognize contributions of arts and
humanities to humankind; *Full-Time
Faculty*: 1.

FACILITIES AND SERVICES
*Practical experiences available
through*: Campus Newspaper (Published
Independently); Local Commercial
Television Station; Desktop Publishing
Facility; Photographic Darkrooms; Video
Editing.

University of Alaska - Anchorage (Public)

Telecommunications
2561 Providence Avenue
Anchorage, Alaska 99508

University of Alaska - Anchorage (Public)

Department of Journalism and Public
Communication
3211 Providence Drive
Anchorage, Alaska 99508
Telephone: (907) 786-1329

Sylvia C. Broady, Chair
Stan Johnson, Dean

CURRICULUM AND INSTRUCTION
*Courses or Concentrations
Available*: Advertising; Communication; Film
or Cinema; Information Science; Journalism
or Mass Communication; Public Relations;
Radio, Television, Broadcasting, or
Telecommunications; Photography;
*Undergraduate Objectives or Program
Emphases*: Preparation for careers in print
and broadcast journalism, advertising, public
relations, and radio-television production
through an integrated approach that
emphasizes the communication needs of
Alaska while meeting national standards;

Bachelor's Degree Majors: 78; *Full-Time Faculty*: 4; *Part-Time Faculty*: 2.

FACILITIES AND SERVICES
Practical experiences available through: Advertising Agency; Audio Recording Laboratory; Closed Circuit Television Facility; Campus Newspaper (Published Independently); Local Commercial Newspaper; Local Commercial Television Station; Desktop Publishing Facility; Photographic Darkrooms; Video Editing; Electronic Field Production (Video); Film or Cinema Laboratory; FM Radio Station (Institutional); Institutional Magazine; Public Relations Agency; Satellite Uplink Facility; Video Production Laboratory or Television Studio.

University of Alaska - Fairbanks (Public)

Department of Journalism and Broadcasting
Fairbanks, Alaska 99775-0940
Telephone: (907) 474-7761

Bruce L. Smith, Head

CURRICULUM AND INSTRUCTION
Courses or Concentrations Available: Journalism or Mass Communication; Radio, Television, Broadcasting, or Telecommunications; *Undergraduate Objectives or Program Emphases*: The department offers two sequences: News/Editorial and Broadcast; *Bachelor's Degree Majors*: 120; *Full-Time Faculty*: 6; *Part-Time Faculty*: 1; *Full-Time Professional (non-clerical) Staff Members*: 1.

FACILITIES AND SERVICES
Practical experiences available through: Advertising Agency; Associated Press Wire Service Feed; Community Antenna (Cable) Television Origination; Campus Newspaper (Published Independently); Local Commercial Newspaper; Local Commercial Television Station; Desktop Publishing Facility; Photographic Darkrooms; Video Editing; Electronic Field Production (Video); Television Broadcast Station (Institutional); FM Radio Station (Institutional); Institutional Magazine; Public Relations Agency; Video News and Data Processing; Video Production Laboratory or Television Studio.

University of Alaska - Southeast (Public)

Department of Communications
11120 Glacier Highway
Juneau, Alaska 99801
Telephone: (907) 789-4406

Susan H. Koester, Chair
John Pugh, Dean

CURRICULUM AND INSTRUCTION
Courses or Concentrations Available: Communication; Journalism or Mass Communication; Radio, Television, Broadcasting, or Telecommunications; Speech; English; Theatre; Languages; *Program Coordinators*: Joey Wauters (Writing); *Undergraduate Objectives or Program Emphases*: Though no major is offered a student may select an emphasis area within the communications department for their BA; *Associate's Degree Majors*: 30; *Bachelor's Degree Majors*: 10; *Full-Time Faculty*: 4; *Part-Time Faculty*: 20.

FACILITIES AND SERVICES
Practical experiences available through: Community Antenna (Cable) Television Origination; Closed Circuit Television Facility; Campus Newspaper (Published Independently); Local Commercial Newspaper; Local Commercial Television Station; Desktop Publishing Facility; Photographic Darkrooms; Video Editing; Institutional Magazine; Institutional Newspaper; Video Production Laboratory or Television Studio.

Arizona State University (Public)

Walter Cronkite School of Journalism and Telecommunication
Tempe, Arizona 85287-1305
Telephone: (602) 965-5011

Douglas A. Anderson, Director
Anne Schneider, Dean, College of Public Programs

CURRICULUM AND INSTRUCTION
Courses or Concentrations
Available: Journalism or Mass Communication; Public Relations; Radio, Television, Broadcasting, or Telecommunications;Photojournalism; Cable;; *Undergraduate Objectives or Program Emphases*: To prepare students to enter positions in media fields by teaching them what to communicate as well as how to communicate. The School's curriculum provides students with a practical component as well as a liberal education; *Graduate Objectives or Program Emphases*: The graduate program's M.M.C. degree is professionally-oriented. The purpose of the program is to help students achieve intellectual and professional growth; *Bachelor's Degree Majors*: 500; *Other Degree Majors*: 36; *Full-Time Faculty*: 19; *Part-Time Faculty*: 26; *Full-Time Professional (non-clerical) Staff Members*: 2.5.

FACILITIES AND SERVICES
Practical experiences available through: Associated Press Wire Service Feed; Audio Recording Laboratory; Community Antenna (Cable) Television Origination; Carrier Current Audio Distribution System; Closed Circuit Television Facility; Campus Newspaper (Published Independently); Local Commercial Newspaper; Local Commercial Television Station; Desktop Publishing Facility; Photographic Darkrooms; Video Editing; Electronic Field Production (Video); Television Broadcast Station (Institutional); ITFS Distribution System; Public Relations Agency; Satellite Uplink Facility (Ku Band Transmitter); Video News and Data Processing; Video Production Laboratory or Television Studio.

Arizona State University (Public)

Department of Communication
Tempe, Arizona 85287-1205
Telephone: (602) 965-5095

Charles R. Bantz, Chair
Anne L. Schneider, Dean, College of Public Programs

CURRICULUM AND INSTRUCTION
Courses or Concentrations
Available: Communication; Speech; *Undergraduate Objectives or Program Emphases*: Interpersonal communication; organizational communication; oral interpretation; rhetoric/public address; intercultural communication; *Graduate Objectives or Program Emphases*: Interpersonal communication; organizational communication; oral interpretation; rhetoric/public address; intercultural communication; *Bachelor's Degree Majors*: 600; *Master's Degree Majors*: 50; *Doctoral Degree Majors Currently in Residence*: 15; *Full-Time Faculty*: 22; *Part-Time Faculty*: 30; *Full-Time Professional (non-clerical) Staff Members*: 3.

FACILITIES AND SERVICES
Practical experiences available through: Video Production Laboratory or Television Studio.

Arizona Western College (Public)

Division of Communications
Yuma, Arizona 85364
Telephone: (415) 344-7639

Cecilia Lim, Chair
Millicent Valek, Dean of Instruction

CURRICULUM AND INSTRUCTION
Courses or Concentrations
Available: Journalism or Mass Communication; Radio, Television, Broadcasting, or Telecommunications; *Program Coordinators*: Robert Hardy (Broadcasting); *Undergraduate Objectives or Program Emphases*: The college offers a two year career program in radio broadcasting culminating in the A.A.S. degree. Courses

offered in journalism provide students with training necessary to work on the student newspaper. Future plans are to offer A.A. journalism degree; *Associate's Degree Majors*: 30; *Full-Time Faculty*: 13; *Part-Time Faculty*: 20; *Full-Time Professional (non-clerical) Staff Members*: 6.

FACILITIES AND SERVICES
Practical experiences available through: AM Radio Station (Institutional); Associated Press Wire Service Feed; Audio Recording Laboratory; Photographic Darkrooms; Institutional Newspaper.

Mesa Community College (Public)

Program of Telecommunication
1833 West Southern Avenue
Mesa, Arizona 85202
Telephone: (602) 461-7532

Ron L. McIntyre, Head

CURRICULUM AND INSTRUCTION
Courses or Concentrations Available: Communication; Journalism or Mass Communication; Public Relations; Radio, Television, Broadcasting, or Telecommunications; Speech; *Associate's Degree Majors*: 85; *Full-Time Faculty*: 1; *Part-Time Faculty*: 2.

FACILITIES AND SERVICES
Practical experiences available through: Audio Recording Laboratory; Local Commercial Television Station; Video Editing; Electronic Field Production (Video); Institutional Newspaper; Video Production Laboratory or Television Studio.

Northern Arizona University (Public)

School of Communication
Box 5619
Flagstaff, Arizona 86011
Telephone: (602) 523-2062

Norman J. Medoff, Director
Edward M. Groenhout, Dean

CURRICULUM AND INSTRUCTION
Courses or Concentrations

Available: Advertising; Communication; Journalism or Mass Communication; Public Relations; Radio, Television, Broadcasting, or Telecommunications; Speech; *Full-Time Faculty*: 22; *Part-Time Faculty*: 30.

FACILITIES AND SERVICES
Practical experiences available through: AM Radio Station (Institutional); Associated Press Wire Service Feed; Audio Recording Laboratory; Community Antenna (Cable) Television Origination; Campus Newspaper (Published Independently); Local Commercial Newspaper; Local Commercial Television Station; Desktop Publishing Facility; Photographic Darkrooms; Video Editing; Electronic Field Production (Video); FM Radio Station (Institutional); ITFS Distribution System; Institutional Newspaper; Satellite Uplink Facility; Video Production Laboratory or Television Studio.

Scottsdale Community College

Television
9000 East Chaparral Road
Scottsdale, Arizona 85253

Mary Kay Platte, Administrator

University of Arizona (Public)

Department of Media Arts
Modern Languages Building 265
Tucson, Arizona 85721
Telephone: (602) 621-7352

Caren J. Deming, Head
Pat Van Metre, Acting Dean

CURRICULUM AND INSTRUCTION
Courses or Concentrations Available: Advertising; Communication; Film or Cinema; Journalism or Mass Communication; Radio, Television, Broadcasting, or Telecommunications; *Bachelor's Degree Majors*: 450; *BFA Degree Majors*: 300; *Master's Degree Majors*: 15; *Full-Time Faculty*: 11; *Part-Time Faculty*: 16; *Full-Time Professional (non-clerical) Staff Members*: 1.

FACILITIES AND SERVICES
Practical experiences available through: Advertising Agency; Community Antenna (Cable) Television Origination;

Local Commercial Television Station; Video Editing; Electronic Field Production (Video); Film or Cinema Laboratory; Public Relations Agency; Video Production Laboratory or Television Studio.

University of Arizona (Public)

Department of Journalism
Tucson, Arizona 85721
Telephone: (602) 621-7556

George W. Ridge, Head
Lee Sigelman, Dean, Social Sciences

CURRICULUM AND INSTRUCTION
Courses or Concentrations Available: Journalism or Mass Communication; *Undergraduate Objectives or Program Emphases*: Professional training; *Graduate Objectives or Program Emphases*: Professional training; *Bachelor's Degree Majors*: 400; *Master's Degree Majors*: 50; *Full-Time Faculty*: 11; *Part-Time Faculty*: varies; *Full-Time Professional (non-clerical) Staff Members*: 2.

FACILITIES AND SERVICES
Practical experiences available through: AM Radio Station (Institutional); Associated Press Wire Service Feed; Community Antenna (Cable) Television Origination; Closed Circuit Television Facility; Campus Newspaper (Published Independently); Local Commercial Newspaper; Local Commercial Television Station; Desktop Publishing Facility; Photographic Darkrooms; Video Editing; Television Broadcast Station (Institutional); Film and Cinema Laboratory;FM Radio Station (Institutional); Institutional Newspaper; Public Relations Agency; Video Production Laboratory or Television Studio.

Arkansas College

Media Arts
P. O. Box 2317
Batesville, Arkansas 72503

L. J. Summers, Administrator

Arkansas State University (Public)

College of Communications
P. O. Box 24
Jonesboro, Arkansas 72467
Telephone: (501) 972-2468

Robert L. Hoskins, Dean

CURRICULUM AND INSTRUCTION
Courses or Concentrations
Available: Advertising; Journalism or Mass Communication; Public Relations; Radio, Television, Broadcasting, or Telecommunications; Photojournalism; Printing; *Program Coordinators*: Joel Gambill (Journalism and Printing); Richard Carvell (Radio-Television); *Undergraduate Objectives or Program Emphases*: To prepare men and women for productive roles in the various fields of mass communication; to provide a rich cultural background against which men and women can build rewarding lives; to provide a foundation for future research in mass communications; *Graduate Objectives or Program Emphases*: To provide advanced education and training for careers in mass communications and higher education; *Other Degree Majors*: 258; *Full-Time Faculty*: 19; *Part-Time Faculty*: 1; *Full-Time Professional (non-clerical) Staff Members*: 6. One or more additional entries follow.

FACILITIES AND SERVICES
Practical experiences available through: Associated Press Wire Service Feed; Audio Recording Laboratory; Community Antenna (Cable) Television Origination; Desktop Publishing Facility; Photographic Darkrooms; Video Editing; Electronic Field Production (Video); FM Radio Station (Institutional); Institutional Newspaper;

United Press International Feed; Video Production Laboratory or Television Studio.

Arkansas State University (Public)

Department of Radio-Television
P. O. Box 2160
Jonesboro, Arkansas 72467
Telephone: (501) 972-3070

Richard A Carvell, Chair
Robert L. Hoskins, Dean

CURRICULUM AND INSTRUCTION
Courses or Concentrations
Available: Advertising; Communication; Journalism or Mass Communication; Radio, Television, Broadcasting, or Telecommunications; *Undergraduate Objectives or Program Emphases*: Broadcast News; Management and Sales; Production and Performance; Cable and Alternate Technologies; *Graduate Objectives or Program Emphases*: Research; Broadcast News; Management; Production; *Other Degree Majors*: 383; *Full-Time Faculty*: 8; *Full-Time Professional (non-clerical) Staff Members*: 10.

FACILITIES AND SERVICES
Practical experiences available through: Associated Press Wire Service Feed; Audio Recording Laboratory; Community Antenna (Cable) Television Origination; Closed Circuit Television Facility; Local Commercial Television Station; Video Editing; Electronic Field Production (Video); FM Radio Station (Institutional); United Press International Feed; Video Production Laboratory or Television Studio.

Arkansas State University (Public)

Department of Speech Communication and Theatre
P. O. Box 369
Jonesboro, Arkansas 72467
Telephone: (501) 972-3091

O. L. Bayless, Chair
William Allen, Dean

CURRICULUM AND INSTRUCTION
Courses or Concentrations
Available: Communication; Speech;
Bachelor's Degree Majors: 17; *BFA Degree Majors*: 38; *Master's Degree Majors*: 23;
Other Degree Majors: 24; *Full-Time Faculty*: 9; *Part-Time Faculty*: 7.

Arkansas Tech University

Speech, Theatre and Journalism
Russellville, Arkansas 72801

Van A. Tyson, Administrator

Harding University (Private)

Department of Communication
Station A
Searcy, Arkansas 72143
Telephone: (501) 279-4000

John H. Ryan, Chair
Dean Priest, Dean, College of Arts and Sciences

CURRICULUM AND INSTRUCTION
Courses or Concentrations
Available: Advertising; Communication;
Journalism or Mass Communication; Public
Relations; Radio, Television, Broadcasting,
or Telecommunications; Speech;
Communication Disorders; Communication
Education; *Bachelor's Degree Majors*: 97;
Full-Time Faculty: 10; *Part-Time Faculty*: 3;
*Full-Time Professional (non-clerical) Staff
Members*: 1.

FACILITIES AND SERVICES
*Practical experiences available
through*: Advertising Agency; AM Radio
Station (Institutional); Associated Press
Wire Service Feed; Closed Circuit Television
Facility; Campus Newspaper (Published

Independently); Local Commercial
Newspaper; Desktop Publishing Facility;
Photographic Darkrooms; Video Editing;
Electronic Field Production (Video);
Television Broadcast Station (Institutional);
Public Relations Agency; Satellite Uplink
Facility; United Press International Feed;
Video Production Laboratory or Television
Studio.

Henderson State University (Public)

Department of Communication Arts and Sciences
1100 Henderson Street
Arkadelphia, Arkansas 71923
Telephone: (501) 246-5511

R. Randolph Duncan, Chair
Norman Bregman, Dean, Arts and Sciences

CURRICULUM AND INSTRUCTION
Courses or Concentrations
Available: Communication; Film or Cinema;
Journalism or Mass Communication; Radio,
Television, Broadcasting, or
Telecommunications; Speech; *Undergraduate
Objectives or Program
Emphases*: Understanding of human
communication theory and practice
combined with applied communication in a
variety of media and settings. Preparation of
students to become professional
communicators; *Bachelor's Degree
Majors*: 34; *Other Degree Majors*: 14;
Full-Time Faculty: 7; *Part-Time Faculty*: 4.

FACILITIES AND SERVICES
Practical experiences available through: Audio
Recording Laboratory; Local Commercial
Newspaper; Local Commercial Television
Station; Desktop Publishing Facility;
Photographic Darkrooms; FM Radio Station
(Institutional); Institutional Magazine;
Institutional Newspaper.

John Brown University (Private)

Division of Communication
West University Street
Siloam Springs, Arkansas 72761
Telephone: (501) 524-3131

Michael T. Flynn, Chair
A. J. Anglin, Vice President, Academic Affairs

CURRICULUM AND INSTRUCTION
Courses or Concentrations
Available: Advertising; Journalism or Mass Communication; Public Relations; Radio, Television, Broadcasting, or Telecommunications; Speech; Advertising Design; *Program Coordinators*: Fred P. Lollar (Journalism); *Undergraduate Objectives or Program Emphases*: Prepare students for careers in media; *Bachelor's Degree Majors*: 110; *Full-Time Faculty*: 4; *Part-Time Faculty*: 3; *Full-Time Professional (non-clerical) Staff Members*: 1.

FACILITIES AND SERVICES
Practical experiences available through: AM Radio Station (Institutional); Audio Recording Laboratory; Community Antenna (Cable) Television Origination; Carrier Current Audio Distribution System; Closed Circuit Television Facility; Desktop Publishing Facility; Photographic Darkrooms; Video Editing; Electronic Field Production (Video); FM Radio Station (Institutional); Institutional Magazine; Institutional Newspaper; United Press International Feed; Video News and Data Processing; Video Production Laboratory or Television Studio.

Ouachita Baptist University (Private)

Department of Communications
Box 791
Arkadelphia, Arkansas 71923

Bill Downs, Administrator

Phillips County Community College (Public)

Journalism Class
P. O. Box 785
Helena, Arkansas 72342
Telephone: (501) 338-6474

Carolyn Pittman, Instructor
Robin Bryant, Department Chair

CURRICULUM AND INSTRUCTION
Courses or Concentrations
Available: Journalism or Mass Communication; *Program Coordinators*: Kirk Whiteside (Speech); *Undergraduate Objectives or Program Emphases*: The objectives of journalism courses are to teach basic principles of news gathering and newswriting and to produce the school newspaper; *Associate's Degree Majors*: 2; *Full-Time Faculty*: 1.

FACILITIES AND SERVICES
Practical experiences available through: Desktop Publishing Facility; Photographic Darkrooms; Institutional Newspaper.

Southern Arkansas University

Department of Theatre and Communication
Magnolia, Arkansas 71753

Jerry Cortez, Administrator

Southern Baptist College (Private)

Division of Humanities
Fulbright Avenue
College City, Arkansas 72476
Telephone: (501) 886-6741

Jerry Gibbens, Chair
Jerol Swaim, Executive Vice-President and Academic Dean

CURRICULUM AND INSTRUCTION
Courses or Concentrations
Available: Journalism or Mass Communication; Speech; English Composition and Literature; Intercultural Communication; *Program Coordinators*: Melinda S. Williams (Speech and Journalism); *Associate's Degree*

Majors: 2; *Full-Time Faculty*: 8; *Part-Time Faculty*: 3.

FACILITIES AND SERVICES
Practical experiences available through: Photographic Darkrooms; Institutional Newspaper.

University of Arkansas - Fayetteville (Public)

Department of Journalism
116 Kimpel Hall
Fayetteville, Arkansas 72701
Telephone: (501) 575-3601

Louise F. Montgomery, Chair
Bernard L. Madison, Dean

CURRICULUM AND INSTRUCTION
Courses or Concentrations Available: Advertising; Communication; Film or Cinema; Journalism or Mass Communication; Public Relations; Radio, Television, Broadcasting, or Telecommunications; Speech; *Undergraduate Objectives or Program Emphases*: News; Community Journalism; Broadcast News; Public Relations; Advertising; *Graduate Objectives or Program Emphases*: News; Community Journalism; Broadcast News; Public Relations; Advertising; Political Communication; History of Communication; The Business of Communication; *Bachelor's Degree Majors*: 400; *Master's Degree Majors*: 15; *Full-Time Faculty*: 10; *Part-Time Faculty*: 6; *Full-Time Professional (non-clerical) Staff Members*: 2.

FACILITIES AND SERVICES
Practical experiences available through: Advertising Agency; Associated Press Wire Service Feed; Audio Recording Laboratory; Community Antenna (Cable) Television Origination; Carrier Current Audio Distribution System; Campus Newspaper (Published Independently); Local Commercial Newspaper; Local Commercial Television Station; Desktop Publishing Facility; Photographic Darkrooms; Video Editing; Electronic Field Production (Video); FM Radio Station (Institutional); Institutional Magazine; Public Relations Agency; Video News and Data Processing; Video Production Laboratory or Television Studio.

University of Arkansas - Fayetteville (Public)

Communication Department
417 Kimpel Hall
Fayetteville, Arkansas 72701

Jimmie N. Rogers, Administrator

University of Arkansas - Little Rock (Public)

College of Professional Studies
2801 S. University Avenue
Little Rock, Arkansas 72204
Telephone: (501) 569-3244

John W. Gray, Dean

CURRICULUM AND INSTRUCTION
Courses or Concentrations Available: Communication; Film or Cinema; Journalism or Mass Communication; Public Relations; Radio, Television, Broadcasting, or Telecommunications; Speech; Organizational Communication; *Program Coordinators*: Jerry Butler (Speech, Communication); Lynn Wilson (Radio, Television, Broadcasting, Telecommunications, Film); Jay Freidlander (Journalism, Public Relations); *Undergraduate Objectives or Program Emphases*: To train professionals in the various communication disciplines; *Graduate Objectives or Program Emphases*: To train professionals in the various communication disciplines; *Bachelor's Degree Majors*: 330; *Master's Degree Majors*: 60; *Full-Time Faculty*: 58; *Part-Time Faculty*: 46; *Full-Time Professional (non-clerical) Staff Members*: 5. One or more additional entries follow.

FACILITIES AND SERVICES
Practical experiences available through: Advertising Agency; AM Radio Station (Institutional); Associated Press Wire Service Feed; Audio Recording Laboratory; Community Antenna (Cable) Television Origination; Carrier Current Audio Distribution System; Closed Circuit Television Facility; Campus Newspaper (Published Independently); Local Commercial Newspaper; Local Commercial Television Station; Desktop Publishing Facility; Photographic Darkrooms; Video Editing; Electronic Field Production (Video); FM Radio Station (Institutional);

New York Times Service Feed; Public Relations Agency; Reuters News Agency; United Press International Feed; Video News and Data Processing; Video Production Laboratory or Television Studio.

University of Arkansas - Little Rock (Public)

Department of Radio-Television-Film
2801 S. University
Little Rock, Arkansas 72204
Telephone: (501) 569-3164

Lynda Wahl-Wilson, Chair
John Gray, Dean, College of Professional and Public Affairs

CURRICULUM AND INSTRUCTION
Courses or Concentrations Available: Film or Cinema; Radio, Television, Broadcasting, or Telecommunications; Broadcast Journalism; *Undergraduate Objectives or Program Emphases*: Prepare students to work in the field; increase knowledge of importance of media in society; *Bachelor's Degree Majors*: 200; *Full-Time Faculty*: 5; *Part-Time Faculty*: 2; *Full-Time Professional (non-clerical) Staff Members*: 2.

FACILITIES AND SERVICES
Practical experiences available through: Audio Recording Laboratory; Community Antenna (Cable) Television Origination; Campus Newspaper (Published Independently); Local Commercial Newspaper; Photographic Darkrooms; Video Editing; Electronic Field Production (Video); FM Radio Station (Institutional); Video Production Laboratory or Television Studio.

University of Arkansas - Little Rock (Public)

Department of Journalism
2801 S. University Avenue
Little Rock, Arkansas 72204
Telephone: (501) 569-3250

Edward J. Freidlander, Chair
John W. Gray, Dean

CURRICULUM AND INSTRUCTION
Courses or Concentrations Available: Journalism or Mass

Communication; Broadcast Journalism; Public Information; Professional and Technical Writing; *Undergraduate Objectives or Program Emphases*: To prepare liberally educated students to become successful writers, reporters and editors for print and broadcast media, as well as successful public information specialists for industry and government; *Graduate Objectives or Program Emphases*: To provide an understanding and appreciation of the mass media's social role, as well as the professional skills and research tools for career enhancement and for further study at the doctoral level. Thesis, non-thesis, and professional options; *Bachelor's Degree Majors*: 99; *Master's Degree Majors*: 20; *Full-Time Faculty*: 5; *Part-Time Faculty*: 7; *Full-Time Professional (non-clerical) Staff Members*: 3.

FACILITIES AND SERVICES
Practical experiences available through: Advertising Agency; Associated Press Wire Service Feed; Audio Recording Laboratory; Community Antenna (Cable) Television Origination; Closed Circuit Television Facility; Campus Newspaper (Published Independently); Local Commercial Newspaper; Local Commercial Television Station; Desktop Publishing Facility; Photographic Darkrooms; Video Editing; FM Radio Station (Institutional); Public Relations Agency; Video News and Data Processing.

University of Arkansas - Little Rock (Public)

Department of Speech Communication
2801 S. University Avenue
Little Rock, Arkansas 72201
Telephone: (501) 569-3158

Jerry P. Butler, Chair
John W. Gray, Dean

CURRICULUM AND INSTRUCTION
Courses or Concentrations Available: Communication; Speech; Speech Pathology, Audiology; *Graduate Objectives or Program Emphases*: Organizational and Interpersonal Communication; *Bachelor's Degree Majors*: 70; *Master's Degree Majors*: 40; *Full-Time Faculty*: 10; *Part-Time Faculty*: 15; *Full-Time Professional (non-clerical) Staff Members*: 26.

FACILITIES AND SERVICES
*Practical experiences available
through*: Desktop Publishing Facility.

University of Arkansas - Monticello (Public)

Department of English/Communication Arts
P. O. Box 3598
Monticello, Arkansas 71655
Telephone: (501) 460-1078

Gale H. Long, Head
Robert Gowdy, Vice Chancellor for Academic Affairs

CURRICULUM AND INSTRUCTION
*Courses or Concentrations
Available*: Communication; Journalism or
Mass Communication; Speech; English;
French; Philosophy; *Undergraduate Objectives
or Program Emphases*: Primarily education
majors in English and Speech. Secondarily
Communication Arts majors with collaterals
in business; *Bachelor's Degree Majors*: 30;
Full-Time Faculty: 15.

FACILITIES AND SERVICES
*Practical experiences available
through*: Closed Circuit Television Facility;
Desktop Publishing Facility; Photographic
Darkrooms; Video Editing; Video
Production Laboratory or Television Studio.

University of Central Arkansas (Public)

Department of Speech, Theatre, and Journalism
Conway, Arkansas 72032
Telephone: (501) 450-3162

Glenn D. Smith, Chair
James Dean Dombek, Administrator

CURRICULUM AND INSTRUCTION
*Courses or Concentrations
Available*: Communication; Film or Cinema;
Journalism or Mass Communication; Radio,
Television, Broadcasting, or
Telecommunications; Speech; *Undergraduate
Objectives or Program Emphases*: Prepare
students for careers in teaching,
broadcasting, public relations and corporate
communications; *Bachelor's Degree
Majors*: 120; *Full-Time Faculty*: 9;

Part-Time Faculty: 3; *Full-Time Professional
(non-clerical) Staff Members*: 2.

FACILITIES AND SERVICES
*Practical experiences available
through*: Advertising Agency; Associated
Press Wire Service Feed; Audio Recording
Laboratory; Community Antenna (Cable)
Television Origination; Closed Circuit
Television Facility; Campus Newspaper
(Published Independently); Local
Commercial Newspaper; Local Commercial
Television Station; Desktop Publishing
Facility; Photographic Darkrooms; Video
Editing; Electronic Field Production
(Video); Television Broadcast Station
(Institutional); FM Radio Station
(Institutional); Public Relations Agency;
Video News and Data Processing; Video
Production Laboratory or Television Studio.

University of the Ozarks (Private)

Division of Fine Arts and Humanities
415 College Avenue
Clarksville, Arkansas 72830
Telephone: (501) 754-3839

F. H. Mitchell, Chair

CURRICULUM AND INSTRUCTION
*Courses or Concentrations
Available*: Communication; Film or Cinema;
Journalism or Mass Communication; Radio,
Television, Broadcasting, or
Telecommunications; Speech; *Program
Coordinators*: Jane Cater (Mass
Communications); Patrick Farmer
(Theater/Drama); *Undergraduate Objectives
or Program Emphases*: Mass
Communications with emphasis on
broadcasting and video production.
Theater/Drama with emphasis on theater
production and study of drama; *Bachelor's
Degree Majors*: 50; *Full-Time Faculty*: 2;
Part-Time Faculty: 1.

FACILITIES AND SERVICES
Practical experiences available through: AM
Radio Station (Institutional); Audio
Recording Laboratory; Community Antenna
(Cable) Television Origination; Carrier
Current Audio Distribution System; Closed
Circuit Television Facility; Campus
Newspaper (Published Independently);
Local Commercial Newspaper; Local
Commercial Television Station; Desktop
Publishing Facility; Photographic

Darkrooms; Video Editing; Electronic Field
Production (Video); Institutional Magazine;
Institutional Newspaper; Video Production
Laboratory or Television Studio.

Westark Community College (Public)

Student Publications
P. O. Box 3649
Fort Smith, Arkansas 72913
Telephone: (501) 785-7150

Thomas H. Walton, Director
Stacey Jones, Director of Student Activities

CURRICULUM AND INSTRUCTION
Courses or Concentrations
Available: Communication; Journalism or
Mass Communication; Speech;
Undergraduate Objectives or Program
Emphases: Job training; *Associate's Degree*
Majors: 45; *Full-Time Faculty*: 1.

FACILITIES AND SERVICES
Practical experiences available
through: Advertising Agency; Campus
Newspaper (Published Independently);
Photographic Darkrooms; Institutional
Newspaper.

Academy of Art College (Private)

540 Powell Street
San Francisco, California 94108
Telephone: (415) 765-4200

Barbara L. Bradley, Dean
Andrew Jameson, President

CURRICULUM AND INSTRUCTION
Courses or Concentrations
Available: Advertising; Graphic Design;
Illustration; Photography; Interior Design;
Fashion; Fine Arts; *Undergraduate Objectives*
or Program Emphases: Highest quality of
professionalism upon graduation plus a good
general education, usually demonstrated by
portfolio; *BFA Degree Majors*: 800; *Other*
Degree Majors: 100; *Full-Time Faculty*: 31;
Part-Time Faculty: 160.

FACILITIES AND SERVICES
Practical experiences available
through: Advertising Agency; Campus
Newspaper (Published Independently);
Desktop Publishing Facility; Photographic
Darkrooms.

Academy of Art College (Private)

Department of Advertising Design
2300 Stockton
San Francisco, California 94133
Telephone: (415) 765-4238

Cummings G. Walker, Director
Barbara Bradley, Dean

CURRICULUM AND INSTRUCTION
Courses or Concentrations
Available: Advertising; Advertising Art
Direction; *Undergraduate Objectives or*
Program Emphases: To fully comprehend the
elements of advertising and promotion of
commercial creativity; *Graduate Objectives or*
Program Emphases: Further emphasis of the
elements of advertising and promotion of
commercial creativity; *BFA Degree*
Majors: 50; *Full-Time Faculty*: 2; *Part-Time*
Faculty: 19; *Full-Time Professional*
(non-clerical) Staff Members: 1.

FACILITIES AND SERVICES
Practical experiences available
through: Advertising Agency; Campus
Newspaper (Published Independently);
Desktop Publishing Facility; Photographic
Darkrooms.

Academy of Art College (Private)

Department of Graphic Design
540 Powell Street
San Francisco, California 94108
Telephone: (415) 765-4200

William H. Dunn, Director
Barbara Bradley, Dean

CURRICULUM AND INSTRUCTION
Courses or Concentrations
Available: Advertising; Communication;
Public Relations; Speech; Fashion Design
and Illustration; Photography; Illustration;
Fine Art; Liberal Arts; *Program*
Coordinators: Cummings Walker (Public
Relations, Advertising); Mary Fitzpatrick
(Speech, ESL); Ralph Reed (Fine Art);
Justine Parrish (Fashion); Melissa Marshall
(Illustration); Lynn Ingersol (Photography);
Undergraduate Objectives or Program
Emphases: Development of hand, technical
and design skills used creatively to solve
visual communication problems; *Graduate*
Objectives or Program Emphases: Provide the
Masters level student with guidance in
personal expression in the area of interest to
the student; *Full-Time Faculty*: 2; *Part-Time*
Faculty: 20.

FACILITIES AND SERVICES
Practical experiences available
through: Advertising Agency; Campus
Newspaper (Published Independently);
Local Commercial Television Station;
Desktop Publishing Facility; Photographic
Darkrooms; Public Relations Agency.

Ambassador College

College Publications
300 West Green Street
Pasadena, California 91129

Dennis Robertson, Administrator

Barstow College (Public)

Division of Liberal Arts
2700 Barstow Road
Barstow, California 92311
Telephone: (619) 252-2411 Extension: 266

Richard H. Reeb Jr., Chair
Ted Baca, Dean of Instruction

CURRICULUM AND INSTRUCTION
*Courses or Concentrations
Available*: Communication; Journalism or
Mass Communication; Speech;
*Undergraduate Objectives or Program
Emphases*: First two years college level
transfer; general education; remedial
education; special programs; *Associate's
Degree Majors*: 45; *Full-Time Faculty*: 12;
Part-Time Faculty: 19.

FACILITIES AND SERVICES
Practical experiences available through: ITFS
Distribution System; Institutional
Newspaper.

Barstow College (Public)

Department of Computer Science
2700 Barstow Road
Barstow, California 92311
Telephone: (619) 252-2411

Lori L. Gaskin, Division Chair
Ted Baca, Executive Dean of Instruction

CURRICULUM AND INSTRUCTION
*Courses or Concentrations
Available*: Information Science; Journalism
or Mass Communication; *Undergraduate
Objectives or Program Emphases*: Computer
science; *Part-Time Faculty*: 4.

FACILITIES AND SERVICES
*Practical experiences available
through*: Campus Newspaper; Desktop
Publishing Facility; Institutional Newspaper.

Biola University (Private)

Department of Communication
13800 Biola Avenue
La Mirada, California 90639
Telephone: (213) 903-6000

C. Diane Shanebeck, Chair
D. Jessup, Dean

CURRICULUM AND INSTRUCTION
*Courses or Concentrations
Available*: Communication; Film or Cinema;
Journalism or Mass Communication; Public
Relations; Radio, Television, Broadcasting,
or Telecommunications; Speech;
Speech/Drama; Communication Disorders;
Program Coordinators: Tom Nash (Radio,
Television, Film); Dean Rea (Journalism);
John Cochran (Speech, Drama); Carrie
Peirce (Public Relations); Todd Lewis
(Speech Communication); *Bachelor's Degree
Majors*: 150; *Full-Time Faculty*: 6;
Part-Time Faculty: 12.

FACILITIES AND SERVICES
*Practical experiences available
through*: Advertising Agency; AM Radio
Station (Institutional); Audio Recording
Laboratory; Community Antenna (Cable)
Television Origination; Campus Newspaper
(Published Independently); Local
Commercial Newspaper; Local Commercial
Television Station; Desktop Publishing
Facility; Photographic Darkrooms; Video
Editing; Film or Cinema Laboratory; Public
Relations Agency; Video Production
Laboratory or Television Studio.

Brooks Institute of Photography (Private)

Department of Motion Picture/Video
801 Alston Road
Santa Barbara, California 93108
Telephone: (805) 966-3888

William D. Johnson, Chair
Mike Verbois, Chief Administrator

CURRICULUM AND INSTRUCTION
Courses or Concentrations Available: Film or
Cinema; Radio, Television, Broadcasting, or
Telecommunications; *Undergraduate
Objectives or Program Emphases*: Teaches all
aspects of film and video production, writing,
directing, cinematography, editing,

animation; *Bachelor's Degree Majors*: 110; *Full-Time Faculty*: 5; *Part-Time Faculty*: 1.

FACILITIES AND SERVICES
Practical experiences available through: Audio Recording Laboratory; Community Antenna (Cable) Television Origination; Local Commercial Television Station; Photographic Darkrooms; Video Editing; Electronic Field Production (Video); Film or Cinema Laboratory; Video Production Laboratory or Television Studio.

Butte College (Public)

Department of Telecommunications
3536 Butte Campus Drive
Oroville, California 95965
Telephone: (916) 895-2288

Mark Hall, Coordinator
Milt Boyer, Chief Administrator

CURRICULUM AND INSTRUCTION
Courses or Concentrations Available: Advertising; Communication; Film or Cinema; Journalism or Mass Communication; Radio, Television, Broadcasting, or Telecommunications; *Associate's Degree Majors*: 200; *Full-Time Faculty*: 2; *Part-Time Faculty*: 5; *Full-Time Professional (non-clerical) Staff Members*: 10.

FACILITIES AND SERVICES
Practical experiences available through: Advertising Agency; Audio Recording Laboratory; Community Antenna (Cable) Television Origination; Closed Circuit Television Facility; Local Commercial Newspaper; Local Commercial Television Station; Desktop Publishing Facility; Photographic Darkrooms; Video Editing; Electronic Field Production (Video); Television Broadcast Station (Institutional); ITFS Distribution System; Institutional Newspaper; Public Relations Agency; Video Production Laboratory or Television Studio.

California Institute of the Arts (Private)

School of Film/Video
24700 McBean Parkway
Valencia, California 91355
Telephone: (805) 255-1050

Ed Emshwiller, Dean
Beverly O'Neal, Provost

CURRICULUM AND INSTRUCTION
Courses or Concentrations Available: Film or Cinema; *Undergraduate Objectives or Program Emphases*: Hands-on independent production of films and videotapes in three departments: Live Action; Motion Graphics; Character Animation; *BFA Degree Majors*: 179; *MFA Degree Majors*: 79; *Other Degree Majors*: 17; *Full-Time Faculty*: 18; *Part-Time Faculty*: 22; *Full-Time Professional (non-clerical) Staff Members*: 3.

FACILITIES AND SERVICES
Practical experiences available through: Audio Recording Laboratory; Closed Circuit Television Facility; Desktop Publishing Facility; Photographic Darkrooms; Video Editing; Electronic Field Production (Video); Film or Cinema Laboratory; FM Radio Station (Institutional); Video Production Laboratory or Television Studio.

California Polytechnic State University (Public)

Department of Speech Communication
San Luis Obispo, California 93407
Telephone: (805) 756-2553

Bernard K. Duffy, Chair
Glenn Irvin, Dean

CURRICULUM AND INSTRUCTION
Courses or Concentrations Available: Communication; Speech; *Full-Time Faculty*: 15; *Part-Time Faculty*: 3.

FACILITIES AND SERVICES
Practical experiences available through: Audio Recording Laboratory; Campus Newspaper (Published Independently); Photographic Darkrooms; Institutional Magazine; Institutional Newspaper; Video Production Laboratory or Television Studio.

California Polytechnic State University (Public)

Department of Journalism
San Luis Obispo, California 93407
Telephone: (805) 756-2508

Nishan Havandjian, Head
Glenn Irvin, Interim Dean

CURRICULUM AND INSTRUCTION
Courses or Concentrations
Available: Advertising; Journalism or Mass Communication; Public Relations; Radio, Television, Broadcasting, or Telecommunications; Agricultural Journalism; *Undergraduate Objectives or Program Emphases*: Practical and theoretical training in four journalism areas: News editing, broadcasting, public relations and agricultural journalism; *Degree Majors*: 260; *Full-Time Faculty*: 6; *Part-Time Faculty*: 1.

FACILITIES AND SERVICES
Practical experiences available through: Associated Press Wire Service Feed; Audio Recording Laboratory; Closed Circuit Television Facility; Local Commercial Newspaper; Local Commercial Television Station; Photographic Darkrooms; Video Editing; Electronic Field Production (Video); FM Radio Station (Institutional); Institutional Newspaper; Video News and Data Processing.

California State College - Bakersfield

Communication Department
9001 Stockdale Highway
Bakersfield, California 93311-1099

Charles B. Ewing, Administrator

California State College - Bakersfield

Fine Arts Department
9001 Stockdale Highway
Bakersfield, California 93311

Anita DuPratt, Administrator

California State Polytechnic University (Public)

Department of Communication
3801 West Temple Avenue
Pomona, California 91768-4007
Telephone: (714) 869-3520

Prudence Faxon, Assistant Professor
T. Harrell Allen, Chair

CURRICULUM AND INSTRUCTION
Courses or Concentrations
Available: Communication; Journalism or Mass Communication; Public Relations; Radio, Television, Broadcasting, or Telecommunications; Speech; *Undergraduate Objectives or Program Emphases*: The Communication major prepares students to fill communication positions in the mass media, business, government and education; *Degree Majors*: 500; *Full-Time Faculty*: 20; *Part-Time Faculty*: 10; *Full-Time Professional (non-clerical) Staff Members*: 2.

FACILITIES AND SERVICES
Practical experiences available through: Audio Recording Laboratory; Local Commercial Television Station; Photographic Darkrooms; Video Editing; Electronic Field Production (Video); ITFS Distribution System; Institutional Magazine; Institutional Newspaper; Public Relations Agency; Video Production Laboratory or Television Studio.

California State University - Chico (Public)

Department of Communication Design
Chico, California 95929-0504
Telephone: (916) 895-4048

Terry Curtis, Chair
Stephen King, Dean, College of Communication

CURRICULUM AND INSTRUCTION
Courses or Concentrations
Available: Communication; Information Science; Journalism or Mass Communication; Public Relations; Radio, Television, Broadcasting, or Telecommunications; Speech; Instructional Technology; Visual Communication (Graphics, Illustration); *Undergraduate Objectives or Program Emphases*: Graphic Design; Graphic Arts (Print and Publishing Technologies); Illustration; Instructional

Technology; Broadcasting; Information and Communication Systems; *Graduate Objectives or Program Emphases*: Instructional Technology; *Bachelor's Degree Majors*: 514; *Master's Degree Majors*: 27; *Full-Time Faculty*: 19; *Part-Time Faculty*: 6; *Full-Time Professional (non-clerical) Staff Members*: 1.

FACILITIES AND SERVICES
Practical experiences available through: Advertising Agency; Associated Press Wire Service Feed; Audio Recording Laboratory; Community Antenna (Cable) Television Origination; Carrier Current Audio Distribution System; Closed Circuit Television Facility; Local Commercial Newspaper; Local Commercial Television Station; Desktop Publishing Facility; Photographic Darkrooms; Video Editing; Electronic Field Production (Video); FM Radio Station (Institutional); ITFS Distribution System; Institutional Magazine; Institutional Newspaper; Public Relations Agency; Satellite Uplink Facility (Ku Band Transmitter) (C Band Transmitter); Video News and Data Processing; Video Production Laboratory or Television Studio.

California State University - Chico

Department of Information and Communication Studies
Chico, California 95929

James Chu, Administrator

California State University - Chico (Public)

College of Communication
Chico, California 95929-0502
Telephone: (916) 895-4015

Stephen W. King, Dean
Gerald Stairs, Provost

CURRICULUM AND INSTRUCTION
Courses or Concentrations Available: Communication; Information Science; Journalism or Mass Communication; Public Relations; Radio, Television, Broadcasting, or Telecommunications; Speech; Visual Communication; Organizational

Communication; Instructional Technology; *Program Coordinators*: Isaac Catt (Human Communication Studies); Jim Gregg (Journalism); Terry Curtis (Communication Design); *Bachelor's Degree Majors*: 1600; *Master's Degree Majors*: 80; *Full-Time Faculty*: 45; *Part-Time Faculty*: 80; *Full-Time Professional (non-clerical) Staff Members*: 12.

FACILITIES AND SERVICES
Practical experiences available through: Advertising Agency; Associated Press Wire Service Feed; Audio Recording Laboratory; Closed Circuit Television Facility; Campus Newspaper (Published Independently); Local Commercial Newspaper; Local Commercial Television Station; Desktop Publishing Facility; Photographic Darkrooms; Video Editing; Electronic Field Production (Video); FM Radio Station (Institutional); ITFS Distribution System; Public Relations Agency; Satellite Uplink Facility (Ku Band Transmitter) (C Band Transmitter); United Press International Feed; Video Production Laboratory or Television Studio.

California State University - Dominguez Hills (Public)

Department of Communication
1000 East Victoria Street
Carson, California 90747
Telephone: (213) 516-3313

W. Leonard Lee, Chair
Hansonia Caldwell, Dean

CURRICULUM AND INSTRUCTION
Courses or Concentrations Available: Advertising; Journalism or Mass Communication; Public Relations; Radio, Television, Broadcasting, or Telecommunications; *Undergraduate Objectives or Program Emphases*: Acquisition of specialized knowledge, writing proficiency, awareness of professional responsibilities, knowledge of ethical practices, and understanding the relationships between the media and the societies served. Print and electronic media proficiency; *Bachelor's Degree Majors*: 276; *Full-Time Faculty*: 5; *Part-Time Faculty*: 3.

FACILITIES AND SERVICES
Practical experiences available through: Advertising Agency; Audio

Recording Laboratory; Community Antenna (Cable) Television Origination; Local Commercial Newspaper; Local Commercial Television Station; Desktop Publishing Facility; Photographic Darkrooms; Video Editing; Electronic Field Production (Video); ITFS Distribution System; Institutional Magazine; Institutional Newspaper; Public Relations Agency; Satellite Uplink Facility (Ku Band Transmitter); Video Production Laboratory or Television Studio.

California State University - Fresno (Public)

Department of Telecommunications
Fresno, California 93740-0046
Telephone: (209) 294-2628

R.C. Adams, Chair
Phyllis Irwin, Acting Dean

CURRICULUM AND INSTRUCTION
Courses or Concentrations Available: Radio, Television, Broadcasting, or Telecommunications; *Program Coordinators*: Philip J. Lane (Mass Communications Graduate Program); *Undergraduate Objectives or Program Emphases*: Major includes four options. Creative: writers and performers. Management: media programers. News, public affairs, and documentary production. Production: studio techniques; *Bachelor's Degree Majors*: 175; *Master's Degree Majors*: 40; *Full-Time Faculty*: 7; *Part-Time Faculty*: 2.

FACILITIES AND SERVICES
Practical experiences available through: Associated Press Wire Service Feed; Audio Recording Laboratory; Community Antenna (Cable) Television Origination; Closed Circuit Television Facility; Local Commercial Television Station; Desktop Publishing Facility; Video Editing; Electronic Field Production (Video); FM Radio Station (Institutional); ITFS Distribution System; Video Production Laboratory or Television Studio.

California State University - Fresno

Department of Journalism
Fresno, California 93740

James B. Tucker, Administrator

California State University - Fresno (Public)

Department of Speech Communication
Fresno, California 93740-0046
Telephone: (209) 278-2826

John A. Cagle, Chair

CURRICULUM AND INSTRUCTION
Courses or Concentrations Available: Communication; Information Science; Speech; *Undergraduate Objectives or Program Emphases*: Comprehensive liberal arts program with strong applied and organizational communication options; *Graduate Objectives or Program Emphases*: Comprehensive speech communication MA with balanced emphases in rhetorical, public address, communication, and applied sciences; *Bachelor's Degree Majors*: 200; *Master's Degree Majors*: 10; *Full-Time Faculty*: 14; *Part-Time Faculty*: 12.

California State University - Fullerton (Public)

Department of Communications
Fullerton, California 92634-9450
Telephone: (714) 773-3517

Terry Hynes, Chair
David B. Sachsman, Dean, School of Communications

CURRICULUM AND INSTRUCTION
Courses or Concentrations Available: Advertising; Film or Cinema; Journalism or Mass Communication; Public Relations; Radio, Television, Broadcasting, or Telecommunications; Photocommunications; *Program Coordinators*: Larry Ward (Radio, Television, Film); David Pincus (Public Relations); Fred Zandpour (Advertising); Rack Pullen (Journalism); David Devries (Photocommunication); *Undergraduate*

Objectives or Program Emphases: Advertising, Journalism, Photocommunications, Public Relations, Radio, Television, Film; *Bachelor's Degree Majors*: 2152; *Master's Degree Majors*: 58; *Full-Time Faculty*: 29; *Part-Time Faculty*: 20; *Full-Time Professional (non-clerical) Staff Members*: 3.

FACILITIES AND SERVICES
Practical experiences available through: Associated Press Wire Service Feed; Audio Recording Laboratory; Community Antenna (Cable) Television Origination; Closed Circuit Television Facility; Desktop Publishing Facility; Photographic Darkrooms; Video Editing; Electronic Field Production (Video); Film or Cinema Laboratory; ITFS Distribution System; Institutional Newspaper; Public Relations Agency; Video News and Data Processing; Video Production Laboratory or Television Studio.

California State University - Fullerton (Public)

Department of Speech Communication
800 N. State College Boulevard
Fullerton, California 92634
Telephone: (714) 773-3617

Joyce M. Flocken, Chair
David B. Sachsman, Dean, School of Communication

CURRICULUM AND INSTRUCTION
Courses or Concentrations Available: Communication; Speech; Communicative Disorders; *Undergraduate Objectives or Program Emphases*: Organizational communication; interpersonal communication; intercultural communication; advocacy; rhetorical theory and criticism; communicative disorders; *Graduate Objectives or Program Emphases*: Speech communication; communicative disorders; *Bachelor's Degree Majors*: 275; *Master's Degree Majors*: 90; *Full-Time Faculty*: 20; *Part-Time Faculty*: 30; *Full-Time Professional (non-clerical) Staff Members*: 1.

California State University - Hayward (Public)

Department of Mass Communication
Hayward, California 94542
Telephone: (415) 881-3292

Mary E. Trapp, Chair
Alan M. Smith, Dean

CURRICULUM AND INSTRUCTION
Courses or Concentrations Available: Advertising; Film or Cinema; Journalism or Mass Communication; Public Relations; Radio, Television, Broadcasting, or Telecommunications; *Undergraduate Objectives or Program Emphases*: To prepare people for graduate work in mass communication, for an entry-level position in mass communication, or to be critical consumers of mass communication; *Bachelor's Degree Majors*: 220; *Full-Time Faculty*: 5; *Part-Time Faculty*: 5.

FACILITIES AND SERVICES
Practical experiences available through: Advertising Agency; Audio Recording Laboratory; Community Antenna (Cable) Television Origination; Closed Circuit Television Facility; Local Commercial Newspaper; Local Commercial Television Station; Desktop Publishing Facility; Photographic Darkrooms; Video Editing; Electronic Field Production (Video); Television Broadcast Station (Institutional); FM Radio Station (Institutional); Institutional Magazine; Institutional Newspaper; Public Relations Agency; Video Production Laboratory or Television Studio.

California State University - Hayward (Public)

Department of Speech Communication
Hayward, California 94542
Telephone: (415) 881-3118

Jack A. Samosky, Chair
Alan Smith, Dean

CURRICULUM AND INSTRUCTION
Courses or Concentrations Available: Communication; Speech; *Undergraduate Objectives or Program Emphases*: A liberal education; knowledge and training for careers in education, business and industry, law, and the ministry;

preparation for graduate study; *Graduate Objectives or Program Emphases*: To provide greater understanding of rhetorical interaction. By so doing we can discover how communication affects understanding and behavior, and why beings are human; *Bachelor's Degree Majors*: 60; *Master's Degree Majors*: 18; *Full-Time Faculty*: 9; *Part-Time Faculty*: 6.

California State University - Long Beach (Public)

Department of Radio-Television-Film
1250 Bellflower Boulevard
Long Beach, California 90840-2803
Telephone: (213) 985-5404

Robert G. Finney, Chair
Karl W. E. Anatol, Dean

CURRICULUM AND INSTRUCTION
Courses or Concentrations Available: Film or Cinema; Radio, Television, Broadcasting, or Telecommunications; *Undergraduate Objectives or Program Emphases*: Electronic media theory studies; film theory and critical studies; audio, video, and film production; telecommunication management; *Bachelor's Degree Majors*: 300; *Full-Time Faculty*: 10; *Part-Time Faculty*: 12; *Full-Time Professional (non-clerical) Staff Members*: 3.

FACILITIES AND SERVICES
Practical experiences available through: Audio Recording Laboratory; Community Antenna (Cable) Television Origination; Carrier Current Audio Distribution System; Video Editing; Electronic Field Production (Video); Film or Cinema Laboratory; FM Radio Station (Institutional); ITFS Distribution System; Video Production Laboratory or Television Studio.

California State University - Long Beach (Public)

Department of Journalism
1250 Bellflower Boulevard
Long Beach, California 90840
Telephone: (213) 985-4981

Wayne F. Kelly, Chair
Karl Anatol, Dean, School of Humanities

CURRICULUM AND INSTRUCTION
Courses or Concentrations Available: Communication; Journalism or Mass Communication; Public Relations; Radio, Television, Broadcasting, or Telecommunications; Photojournalism; Magazine; Education; *Undergraduate Objectives or Program Emphases*: Prepare for entry level positions in communication industry; *Bachelor's Degree Majors*: 650; *Full-Time Faculty*: 11; *Part-Time Faculty*: 4; *Full-Time Professional (non-clerical) Staff Members*: 1.

FACILITIES AND SERVICES
Practical experiences available through: AM Radio Station (Institutional); Audio Recording Laboratory; Local Commercial Newspaper; Public Relations Agency; Local Commercial Television Station; Desktop Publishing Facility; Photographic Darkrooms; Video Editing; Institutional Magazine; Institutional Newspaper; United Press International Feed; Video News and Data Processing.

California State University - Long Beach (Public)

Department of Speech Communication
1250 Bellflower Boulevard
Long Beach, California 90840-2407
Telephone: (213) 985-4301

Richard E. Porter, Chair
Virginia Warren, Acting Dean, School of Humanities

CURRICULUM AND INSTRUCTION
Courses or Concentrations Available: Communication; Speech; *Undergraduate Objectives or Program Emphases*: BA in Speech Communication with emphasis in rhetorical studies or in interpersonal and organizational communication; *Graduate Objectives or Program Emphases*: MA degree in speech communication with emphasis either in speech communication or an option in communication and human information systems; *Bachelor's Degree Majors*: 600; *Master's Degree Majors*: 40; *Full-Time Faculty*: 23; *Part-Time Faculty*: 12.

California State University - Los Angeles (Public)

Department of Communication Studies
5151 State University Drive
Los Angeles, California 90032
Telephone: (213) 343-4200

Howard P. Holladay, Chair
Bobby Patton, Dean, School of Arts and Letters

CURRICULUM AND INSTRUCTION
Courses or Concentrations
Available: Advertising; Communication; Film or Cinema; Journalism or Mass Communication; Public Relations; Radio, Television, Broadcasting, or Telecommunications; Speech; *Program Coordinators:* Suzanne Regan (Broadcasting, Film); Leslie DiMarc (Speech, Communication Theory); *Undergraduate Objectives or Program Emphases*: Broadcasting emphasizes theoretical understanding and practical application of mass media; Journalism prepares students for careers in editorial, advertising, public relations, etc. Speech Communication emphasizes the nature and functions of human symbolic communication; *Graduate Objectives or Program Emphases*: Speech Communication provides advanced study in fields of organizational and interpersonal communication, communication theory, language and behavior, oral interpretation, public address, argumentation, intercultural communication, and rhetorical theory; *Bachelor's Degree Majors*: 723; *Master's Degree Majors*: 68; *Full-Time Faculty*: 21; *Part-Time Faculty*: 23; *Full-Time Professional (non-clerical) Staff Members*: 8.

FACILITIES AND SERVICES
Practical experiences available through: Associated Press Wire Service Feed; Audio Recording Laboratory; Community Antenna (Cable) Television Origination; Closed Circuit Television Facility; Campus Newspaper (Published Independently); Local Commercial Newspaper; Local Commercial Television Station; Desktop Publishing Facility; Photographic Darkrooms; Video Editing; Electronic Field Production (Video); Film or Cinema Laboratory; Institutional Magazine; Institutional Newspaper; Public Relations Agency; Video News and Data Processing; Video Production Laboratory or Television Studio.

California State University - Northridge (Public)

Department of Radio-Television-Film
18111 Nordhoff Street
Northridge, California 91330
Telephone: (818) 885-3192
Alternate: 885-3444

Judith Marlane, Chair
Linda Bain, Dean

CURRICULUM AND INSTRUCTION
Courses or Concentrations
Available: Advertising; Communication; Film or Cinema; Journalism or Mass Communication; Radio, Television, Broadcasting, or Telecommunications; *Program Coordinators*: Michael Stanton (Radio-Television); Fred Kuretski (Film); *Undergraduate Objectives or Program Emphases*: Theory and Criticism, Media Management, Screenwriting, Film Production, Radio-Television Production, Corporate and Educational Media; *Graduate Objectives or Program Emphases*: Screenwriting, Theory and Criticism, Media Management, Corporate and Educational Media; *Bachelor's Degree Majors*: 148; *Master's Degree Majors*: 32; *Full-Time Faculty*: 16; *Part-Time Faculty*: 16; *Full-Time Professional (non-clerical) Staff Members*: 3.

FACILITIES AND SERVICES
Practical experiences available through: Audio Recording Laboratory; Community Antenna (Cable) Television Origination; Closed Circuit Television Facility; Campus Newspaper (Published Independently); Local Commercial Television Station; Desktop Publishing Facility; Video Editing; Electronic Field Production (Video); Television Broadcast Station (Institutional); FM Radio Station (Institutional); Satellite Uplink Facility; Video Production Laboratory or Television Studio.

California State University - Northridge (Public)

Department of Journalism
Northridge, California 91330
Telephone: (818) 885-3135

Tom Reilly, Chair
Linda Bain, Dean

CURRICULUM AND INSTRUCTION
Courses or Concentrations
Available: Journalism or Mass
Communication; *Undergraduate Objectives or Program Emphases*: News Print; Public Relations; Broadcast News; Photography; Magazine; *Graduate Objectives or Program Emphases*: Mass Communication; *Bachelor's Degree Majors*: 570; *Master's Degree Majors*: 40; *Full-Time Faculty*: 11; *Part-Time Faculty*: 20; *Full-Time Professional (non-clerical) Staff Members*: 5.

FACILITIES AND SERVICES
Practical experiences available through: Associated Press Wire Service Feed; Audio Recording Laboratory; Community Antenna (Cable) Television Origination; Closed Circuit Television Facility; Local Commercial Newspaper; Local Commercial Television Station; Desktop Publishing Facility; Photographic Darkrooms; Video Editing; Electronic Field Production (Video); FM Radio Station (Institutional); ITFS Distribution System; Institutional Magazine; Institutional Newspaper; Public Relations Agency.

California State University - Northridge (Public)

Department of Speech Communication
Northridge, California 91330
Telephone: (818) 885-2853

William F. Eadie, Chair
Linda L. Bain, Dean, School of Communication and Professional Studies

CURRICULUM AND INSTRUCTION
Courses or Concentrations
Available: Communication; Speech; Rhetoric; Performance of Literature; *Undergraduate Objectives or Program Emphases*: General speech communication, specializations in communication, rhetoric, and performance of literature, an interdisciplinary program in communication studies (including the mass communication departments), and a secondary credential major in English/Speech.; *Graduate Objectives or Program Emphases*: The graduate program is general, with required course work in communication, rhetoric and performance of literature, and provisions to allow students to specialize; *Bachelor's Degree Majors*: 700; *Master's Degree Majors*: 40; *Full-Time Faculty*: 14; *Part-Time Faculty*: 17.

FACILITIES AND SERVICES
Practical experiences available through: Advertising Agency; Desktop Publishing Facility; Public Relations Agency.

California State University - Sacramento (Public)

Department of Communication Studies
Sacramento, California 95819
Telephone: (916) 278-6688

David C. Martin, Chair
William Sullivan, Dean, Arts and Sciences

CURRICULUM AND INSTRUCTION
Courses or Concentrations
Available: Communication; Film or Cinema; Information Science; Journalism or Mass Communication; Public Relations; Radio, Television, Broadcasting, or Telecommunications; Speech; Organizational Communication; Instructional Communication; *Undergraduate Objectives or Program Emphases*: To provide a strong Liberal Arts education for majors and, in some areas, a pre-professional experience for students; *Graduate Objectives or Program Emphases*: A broadly based graduate curriculum; *Bachelor's Degree Majors*: 1200; *Master's Degree Majors*: 80; *Full-Time Faculty*: 28; *Part-Time Faculty*: 33; *Full-Time Professional (non-clerical) Staff Members*: 6.

FACILITIES AND SERVICES
Practical experiences available through: Audio Recording Laboratory; Closed Circuit Television Facility; Local Commercial Newspaper; Local Commercial Television Station; Desktop Publishing Facility; Photographic Darkrooms; Video Editing; Electronic Field Production (Video); Film or Cinema Laboratory; FM Radio Station (Institutional); ITFS Distribution System; Institutional Newspaper; Public Relations Agency; Satellite Uplink Facility (Ku Band Transmitter); Video News and Data Processing; Video Production Laboratory or Television Studio.

California State University - Sacramento

Department of Journalism
Sacramento, California 95819

Shirley Biagi, Administrator

California State University - San Bernardino (Public)

School of Humanities
5500 University Parkway
San Bernardino, California 92407-2397
Telephone: (714) 880-5800

Beverly L. Hendricks, Dean
Amer El-Ahraf, Acting ViceáPresident,
Academic Affairs

CURRICULUM AND INSTRUCTION
Courses or Concentrations
Available: Advertising; Communication; Film or Cinema; Journalism or Mass Communication; Public Relations; Radio, Television, Broadcasting, or Telecommunications; Speech; *Undergraduate Objectives or Program Emphases*: Generalist program to help students understand relationships between symbols and culture, discover information from its sources, understand how messages are transmitted and appreciate the ethics involved; *Bachelor's Degree Majors*: 150; *Full-Time Faculty*: 8; *Part-Time Faculty*: 5.

FACILITIES AND SERVICES
Practical experiences available through: AM Radio Station (Institutional); Campus Newspaper (Published Independently); Desktop Publishing Facility; Photographic Darkrooms; ITFS Distribution System.

California State University - Stanislaus (Public)

Department of Communication Studies
801 W. Monte Vista Avenue
Turlock, California 95380
Telephone: (209) 667-3371

Fred P. Hilpert, Jr., Chair
Horace A. Judson, Dean, College of Arts, Letters, and Sciences

CURRICULUM AND INSTRUCTION
Courses or Concentrations
Available: Communication; Journalism or Mass Communication; Public Relations; Speech; *Undergraduate Objectives or Program Emphases*: To provide students with an understanding of theories and processes of human communication, prepare students for graduate study, and to provide specialized knowledge and proficiencies in the communicative arts and science for various professions; *Bachelor's Degree Majors*: 100; *Full-Time Faculty*: 5; *Part-Time Faculty*: 5.

FACILITIES AND SERVICES
Practical experiences available through: Community Antenna (Cable) Television Origination; Closed Circuit Television Facility; Campus Newspaper (Published Independently); Local Commercial Newspaper; Local Commercial Television Station; FM Radio Station (Institutional); ITFS Distribution System; Public Relations Agency; Satellite Uplink Facility.

Canada College

4200 Farm Hill Boulevard
Redwood City, California 94601
Telephone: (415) 364-1212

Robert J. Glessing, Head
John Friesen, Administrator

CURRICULUM AND INSTRUCTION
Courses or Concentrations
Available: Advertising; Communication; Film or Cinema; Journalism or Mass Communication; Public Relations; Newswriting; *Full-Time Faculty*: 1.

Chabot College (Public)

Mass Communications -- Area of Language Arts
25555 Hesperian Boulevard
Hayward, California 94545
Telephone: (415) 786-6954

Stanley Lichtenstein, Chair
Leland Kent, Administrator

CURRICULUM AND INSTRUCTION
Courses or Concentrations
Available: Advertising; Communication; Journalism or Mass Communication; Radio,

Television, Broadcasting, or Telecommunications; *Program Coordinators*: G. Gropetti (Photography); D. Eaton (Graphics, Design); *Undergraduate Objectives or Program Emphases*: Training students for entry level mass communication positions; preparing students for four year colleges; *Associate's Degree Majors*: 50; *Full-Time Faculty*: 3; *Part-Time Faculty*: 2; *Full-Time Professional (non-clerical) Staff Members*: 1.

FACILITIES AND SERVICES
Practical experiences available through: Advertising Agency; AM Radio Station (Institutional); Associated Press Wire Service Feed; Audio Recording Laboratory; Community Antenna (Cable) Television Origination; Carrier Current Audio Distribution System; Closed Circuit Television Facility; Campus Newspaper (Published Independently); Local Commercial Newspaper; Local Commercial Television Station; Desktop Publishing Facility; Photographic Darkrooms; Video Editing; FM Radio Station (Institutional).

Chaffey Community College

Department of Communication Studies
5885 Haven Avenue
Alta Loma, California 91701

Chapman College (Private)

Department of Communications
333 North Glassell Street
Orange, California 92666
Telephone: (714) 997-6856

Jay Boylan, Chair
Barbara Mulch, Dean

CURRICULUM AND INSTRUCTION
Courses or Concentrations Available: Communication; Film or Cinema; Journalism or Mass Communication; Public Relations; Radio, Television, Broadcasting, or Telecommunications; Theatre; Dance; *Undergraduate Objectives or Program Emphases*: Primarily interested in pre-professional development in all programs; *Bachelor's Degree Majors*: 100; *BFA Degree Majors*: 200; *Full-Time Faculty*: 11; *Part-Time Faculty*: 10;

Full-Time Professional (non-clerical) Staff Members: 7.

FACILITIES AND SERVICES
Practical experiences available through: Advertising Agency; AM Radio Station (Institutional); Audio Recording Laboratory; Community Antenna (Cable) Television Origination; Closed Circuit Television Facility; Campus Newspaper (Published Independently); Local Commercial Newspaper; Local Commercial Television Station; Desktop Publishing Facility; Photographic Darkrooms; Video Editing; Electronic Field Production (Video); Television Broadcast Station (Institutional); Film or Cinema Laboratory; FM Radio Station (Institutional); Institutional Magazine; Institutional Newspaper; Public Relations Agency; Video News and Data Processing; Video Production Laboratory or Television Studio.

Christian Heritage College (Public)

Program of Communications
2100 Greenfield Drive
El Cajon, California 92019
Telephone: (619) 440-3043

Robert L. Arend, Chair
Steve Preacher, Administrator

CURRICULUM AND INSTRUCTION
Courses or Concentrations Available: Communication; Journalism or Mass Communication; Speech; *Undergraduate Objectives or Program Emphases*: Practice in speech communication with emphasis on delivery and style; understanding of mass media and its application; *Bachelor's Degree Majors*: 4; *Full-Time Faculty*: 2; *Part-Time Faculty*: 1; *Full-Time Professional (non-clerical) Staff Members*: 1.

FACILITIES AND SERVICES
Practical experiences available through: Audio Recording Laboratory; Campus Newspaper (Published Independently); Photographic Darkrooms; Institutional Magazine; Institutional Newspaper.

City College of San Francisco (Public)

Department of Journalism
50 Phelan Avenue
San Francisco, California 94112
Telephone: (415) 239-3446

Juan Gonzales, Chair
Keith Kerr, Dean of Instruction

CURRICULUM AND INSTRUCTION
Courses or Concentrations
Available: Communication; Journalism or
Mass Communication; Public Relations;
Undergraduate Objectives or Program
Emphases: Fundamental understanding and
practical skills training in print journalism;
Associate's Degree Majors: 35; *Full-Time*
Faculty: 1; *Part-Time Faculty*: 2; *Full-Time*
Professional (non-clerical) Staff Members: 1.

FACILITIES AND SERVICES
Practical experiences available
through: Campus Newspaper (Published
Independently); Desktop Publishing Facility;
Photographic Darkrooms.

City College of San Francisco (Public)

Department of Broadcasting
50 Phelan Avenues
San Francisco, California 94112
Telephone: (415) 239-3525

Phillip K. Brown, Chair
Linda Grohe, Dean

CURRICULUM AND INSTRUCTION
Courses or Concentrations
Available: Communication; Film or Cinema;
Journalism or Mass Communication; Radio,
Television, Broadcasting, or
Telecommunications; *Undergraduate*
Objectives or Program Emphases: First two
years of a college course in broadcasting;
Associate's Degree Majors: 250; *Full-Time*
Faculty: 4; *Part-Time Faculty*: 6; *Full-Time*
Professional (non-clerical) Staff Members: 3.

FACILITIES AND SERVICES
Practical experiences available through: Audio
Recording Laboratory; Community Antenna
(Cable) Television Origination; Carrier
Current Audio Distribution System; Closed
Circuit Television Facility; Campus
Newspaper (Published Independently);
Local Commercial Television Station;
Photographic Darkrooms; Video Editing;
Electronic Field Production (Video); Film
or Cinema Laboratory; FM Radio Station
(Institutional); Institutional Newspaper;
United Press International Feed; Video
Production Laboratory or Television Studio.

City College of San Francisco (Public)

Department of Film
50 Phelan Avenue
San Francisco, California 94112
Telephone: (415) 239-3651

Dick Ham, Film Coordinator
Linda Grohe, Dean

CURRICULUM AND INSTRUCTION
Courses or Concentrations Available: Film or
Cinema; *Undergraduate Objectives or Program*
Emphases: A two year hands-on course in
professional motion picture production, from
contracts and scripts through shooting,
editing and working with the laboratory to
produce a final print; *Associate's Degree*
Majors: 10; *Full-Time Faculty*: 1; *Part-Time*
Faculty: 8; *Full-Time Professional*
(non-clerical) Staff Members: 1.

FACILITIES AND SERVICES
Practical experiences available through: Audio
Recording Laboratory; Local Commercial
Television Station; Video Editing; Film or
Cinema Laboratory.

College of Notre Dame (Private)

Communication Major
1500 Ralston Avenue
Belmont, California 94002
Telephone: (415) 593-1601

Nancy Lee Jalonen, Director
Marc Wolterbeek, Chair, English
Department

CURRICULUM AND INSTRUCTION
Courses or Concentrations
Available: Advertising; Communication; Film
or Cinema; Journalism or Mass
Communication; Public Relations; Radio,
Television, Broadcasting, or
Telecommunications; Speech; Corporate
Communications; Media Law; *Program*

Coordinators: Oscar Cornejo (Advertising, Business Department); *Undergraduate Objectives or Program Emphases*: To provide a broad background in the theory and practice of communications to enable students to enter the fields of print and broadcast journalism and corporate communication; *Bachelor's Degree Majors*: 20; *Full-Time Faculty*: 1; *Part-Time Faculty*: 4.

FACILITIES AND SERVICES
Practical experiences available through: Audio Recording Laboratory; Campus Newspaper (Published Independently); Desktop Publishing Facility; Photographic Darkrooms; Institutional Magazine; Institutional Newspaper.

College of the Canyons (Public)

Department of Journalism
26455 North Rockwell Canyon Road
Valencia, California 91355
Telephone: (805) 259-7800

Susan A. Cornner, Lead Instructor

CURRICULUM AND INSTRUCTION
Courses or Concentrations Available: Advertising; Film or Cinema; Journalism or Mass Communication; Public Relations; Radio, Television, Broadcasting, or Telecommunications; Photography; Photojournalism; *Undergraduate Objectives or Program Emphases*: Journalism major, AA degree objective or transfer with BA objective; *Full-Time Faculty*: 2; *Part-Time Faculty*: 8; *Full-Time Professional (non-clerical) Staff Members*: 1.

FACILITIES AND SERVICES
Practical experiences available through: Audio Recording Laboratory; Community Antenna (Cable) Television Origination; Closed Circuit Television Facility; Local Commercial Newspaper; Desktop Publishing Facility; Photographic Darkrooms; Video Editing; Institutional Magazine; Institutional Newspaper; Video Production Laboratory or Television Studio.

College of the Desert (Public)

Division of Communication
43-500 Monterey Avenue
Palm Desert, California 92260
Telephone: (619) 346-8041

Douglas Garrison, Administrator
William R. Kroonen, Dean

CURRICULUM AND INSTRUCTION
Courses or Concentrations Available: Communication; Journalism or Mass Communication; Public Relations; Radio, Television, Broadcasting, or Telecommunications; Speech; *Program Coordinators*: S. Roy Wilson (Mass Communication, Journalism, Broadcasting); Buford Crites (Speech); *Undergraduate Objectives or Program Emphases*: Lower division transfer courses; *Associate's Degree Majors*: 30; *Full-Time Faculty*: 8; *Part-Time Faculty*: 50; *Full-Time Professional (non-clerical) Staff Members*: 3.

FACILITIES AND SERVICES
Practical experiences available through: Closed Circuit Television Facility; Local Commercial Newspaper; Local Commercial Television Station; Desktop Publishing Facility; Photographic Darkrooms; Video Editing; Electronic Field Production (Video); Institutional Newspaper.

Columbia College - Hollywood

Departments of Cinema and Broadcasting
925 LaBrea Avenue
Los Angeles, California 90038

Bruce H. Shoemaker, Administrator

Cosumnes River College (Public)

Department of Journalism
8401 Center Parkway
Sacramento, California 95823
Telephone: (916) 688-7251

Rick E. Boeck, Chair
Janis Caston, Assistant Dean, Business/Communications

CURRICULUM AND INSTRUCTION
Courses or Concentrations Available: Journalism or Mass

Communication; Public Relations;
*Undergraduate Objectives or Program
Emphases*: The journalism major is designed
to train students in the writing, reporting and
critical thinking skills required for jobs in the
news media or for transfer to a journalism
program at a four-year institution;
Associate's Degree Majors: 10; *Full-Time
Faculty*: 1; *Part-Time Faculty*: 1.

FACILITIES AND SERVICES
Practical experiences available through: Local
Commercial Newspaper; Local Commercial
Television Station; Desktop Publishing
Facility; Photographic Darkrooms;
Institutional Newspaper.

Diablo Valley College (Public)

Department of Performing Arts
321 Golf Club Road
Pleasant Hill, California 94523
Telephone: (415) 685-1230

Robert G. Hambelton, Chair
Bruce Watson, Chief Administrator

CURRICULUM AND INSTRUCTION
*Courses or Concentrations
Available*: Communication; Film or Cinema;
Radio, Television, Broadcasting, or
Telecommunications; Speech; *Undergraduate
Objectives or Program Emphases*: Increase
skills and knowledge in the particular
program; *Associate's Degree Majors*: 200;
Full-Time Faculty: 12; *Part-Time Faculty*: 8.

FACILITIES AND SERVICES
Practical experiences available through: Audio
Recording Laboratory; Closed Circuit
Television Facility; Campus Newspaper
(Published Independently); Photographic
Darkrooms; Video Editing; Electronic Field
Production (Video); Film or Cinema
Laboratory; Institutional Magazine;
Institutional Newspaper; Video Production
Laboratory or Television Studio.

El Camino College (Public)

Department of Journalism
16007 Crenshaw Boulevard
Torrance, California 90506
Telephone: (213) 715-3328

Jolene Combs, Chair
Thomas Lew, Dean, Humanities

CURRICULUM AND INSTRUCTION
*Courses or Concentrations
Available*: Journalism or Mass
Communication; Public Relations;
*Undergraduate Objectives or Program
Emphases*: Two year journalism program,
primarily print; *Associate's Degree
Majors*: 240; *Full-Time Faculty*: 2;
*Full-Time Professional (non-clerical) Staff
Members*: 1.

FACILITIES AND SERVICES
*Practical experiences available
through*: Campus Newspaper (Published
Independently); Local Commercial
Newspaper; Desktop Publishing Facility;
Photographic Darkrooms; Video Editing;
Institutional Magazine; Institutional
Newspaper; Public Relations Agency.

Fullerton College (Public)

Division of Communications
321 East Chapman Avenue
Fullerton, California 92634
Telephone: (714) 992-7161

Paul W. Kelly, Dean
Jane Armstrong, Vice President

CURRICULUM AND INSTRUCTION
*Courses or Concentrations
Available*: Advertising; Journalism or Mass
Communication; Public Relations; Radio,
Television, Broadcasting, or
Telecommunications; *Associate's Degree
Majors*: 525; *Full-Time Faculty*: 9;
Part-Time Faculty: 22; *Full-Time
Professional (non-clerical) Staff Members*: 3.

FACILITIES AND SERVICES
*Practical experiences available
through*: Advertising Agency; Associated
Press Wire Service Feed; Audio Recording
Laboratory; Community Antenna (Cable)
Television Origination; Closed Circuit
Television Facility; Local Commercial
Newspaper; Local Commercial Television

Station; Desktop Publishing Facility; Photographic Darkrooms; Video Editing; Electronic Field Production (Video); FM Radio Station (Institutional); Institutional Magazine; Institutional Newspaper; Public Relations Agency; Video News and Data Processing; Video Production Laboratory or Television Studio.

Fullerton College (Public)

Division of Humanities
321 E. Chapman Avenue
Fullerton, California 92634
Telephone: (714) 992-7168

Janet S. Portolan, Dean

CURRICULUM AND INSTRUCTION
Courses or Concentrations Available: Film or Cinema; Speech; *Program Coordinators*: Lois Powers (Film); Richard Kirkham (Speech); *Undergraduate Objectives or Program Emphases*: General Education; *Associate's Degree Majors*: 8; *Full-Time Faculty*: 45; *Part-Time Faculty*: 60; *Full-Time Professional (non-clerical) Staff Members*: 6.

Grossmont College (Public)

Department of Communication Arts,
Journalism, Telecommunications
8800 Grossmont College Drive
El Cajon, California 92020
Telephone: (619) 465-1700

Keith H. Bryden, Chair
Sharon Yaap, Dean, Communication and
Fine Arts Division

CURRICULUM AND INSTRUCTION
Courses or Concentrations Available: Journalism or Mass Communication; Public Relations; Radio, Television, Broadcasting, or Telecommunications; *Program Coordinator*: Pat Higgins (Journalism); *Undergraduate Objectives or Program Emphases*: Audio and video areas designed to meet lower division transfer or job entry requirements. Journalism courses are designed to develop competency in the numerous skills demanded of today's journalists. Mass Communications and Public Relations courses; *Associate's Degree*

Majors: 150; *Full-Time Faculty*: 5; *Part-Time Faculty*: 14; *Full-Time Professional (non-clerical) Staff Members*: 1.

FACILITIES AND SERVICES
Practical experiences available through: Audio Recording Laboratory; Community Antenna (Cable) Television Origination; Carrier Current Audio Distribution System; Local Commercial Newspaper; Local Commercial Television Station; Desktop Publishing Facility; Photographic Darkrooms; Video Editing; Electronic Field Production (Video); Institutional Newspaper; Satellite Uplink Facility (Ku Band Transmitter) (C Band Transmitter); United Press International Feed; Video Production Laboratory or Television Studio.

Holy Names College

Special Programs Department
3500 Mountain Boulevard
Oakland, California 94619

John T. Neavill, Administrator

Humboldt State University (Public)

Department of Speech Communication
Arcata, California 95521
Telephone: (707) 826-3261

Stephen W. Littlejohn, Chair
Ronald R. Young, Dean

CURRICULUM AND INSTRUCTION
Courses or Concentrations Available: Communication; Radio, Television, Broadcasting, or Telecommunications; Speech; *Undergraduate Objectives or Program Emphases*: General communication studies and speech, including public address, interpersonal, group and organizational, rhetoric, communication theory, and broadcasting; *Bachelor's Degree Majors*: 40; *Full-Time Faculty*: 12; *Part-Time Faculty*: 3.

FACILITIES AND SERVICES
Practical experiences available through: AM Radio Station (Institutional); Audio Recording Laboratory; Carrier Current Audio Distribution System; Campus Newspaper (Published Independently);

Local Commercial Television Station; Electronic Field Production (Video); FM Radio Station (Institutional).

Humboldt State University (Public)

Department of Journalism
Arcata, California 95521
Telephone: (707) 826-4775

Mark A. Larson, Chair
Ron Young, Dean, College of Humanities

CURRICULUM AND INSTRUCTION
Courses or Concentrations Available: Journalism or Mass Communication; Public Relations; Radio, Television, Broadcasting, or Telecommunications; *Undergraduate Objectives or Program Emphases*: News-editorial; Public Relations; Broadcast News; *Bachelor's Degree Majors*: 90; *Full-Time Faculty*: 5; *Part-Time Faculty*: 4.

FACILITIES AND SERVICES
Practical experiences available through: Associated Press Wire Service Feed; Community Antenna (Cable) Television Origination; Carrier Current Audio Distribution System; Local Commercial Newspaper; Local Commercial Television Station; Desktop Publishing Facility; Photographic Darkrooms; Video Editing; FM Radio Station (Institutional); Institutional Magazine; Institutional Newspaper.

Humboldt State University (Public)

Department of Theatre Arts
Arcata, California 95521
Telephone: (707) 826-3566

Richard Rothrock, Chair
Robert Everding, Dean, College of Visual and Performing Arts

CURRICULUM AND INSTRUCTION
Courses or Concentrations Available: Film or Cinema; *Undergraduate Objectives or Program Emphases*: Liberal Arts education with study in both film and theatre; *Graduate Objectives or Program Emphases*: Experience in advanced film production; *Bachelor's Degree Majors*: 40; *Master's Degree Majors*: 9; *Full-Time Faculty*: 14; *Part-Time Faculty*: 4; *Full-Time Professional (non-clerical) Staff Members*: 4.

FACILITIES AND SERVICES
Practical experiences available through: Audio Recording Laboratory; Community Antenna (Cable) Television Origination; Campus Newspaper (Published Independently); Local Commercial Television Station; Desktop Publishing Facility; Photographic Darkrooms; Film or Cinema Laboratory.

Loma Linda University

Department of Communication
4700 Pierce Street
Riverside, California 92515

Larry Arany, Administrator

Long Beach College

Department of Telecommunications
4901 East Carson Street
Long Beach, California 90808

Alan Heywood, Administrator

Los Angeles City College (Public)

Department of Radio-Television-Film
855 North Vermont Avenue
Los Angeles, California 90029
Telephone: (213) 669-5545

Robert Stahley, Chair
Robert Wilkinson, Administrator

CURRICULUM AND INSTRUCTION
Courses or Concentrations Available: Film or Cinema; Radio, Television, Broadcasting, or Telecommunications; *Program Coordinators*: Vaughn Obers (Film, Cinema); George Bowden (Television); Robert Stahley (Radio); *Undergraduate Objectives or Program Emphases*: Film and Television production; *Associate's Degree Majors*: 300; *Full-Time Faculty*: 10; *Part-Time Faculty*: 8; *Full-Time Professional (non-clerical) Staff Members*: 7.

FACILITIES AND SERVICES
Practical experiences available through: Audio Recording Laboratory; Community Antenna (Cable) Television Origination; Carrier Current Audio Distribution System; Local Commercial Television Station; Video Editing; Electronic Field Production (Video); Film or Cinema Laboratory; United Press International Feed; Video Production Laboratory or Television Studio.

Los Angeles City College (Public)

Department of Speech
855 N. Vermont Avenue
Los Angeles, California 90029
Telephone: (213) 669-4000

James G. Luter, Jr., Chair
Robert Wilkenson, Dean

CURRICULUM AND INSTRUCTION
Courses or Concentrations Available: Speech; English as a second language; *Undergraduate Objectives or Program Emphases*: To understand and apply the principles of effective oral communication. ESL students use standard American English pronunciation and then to enter mainstream classes; students gain interpersonal skills and learn to express ideas effectively in groups; *Associate's Degree Majors*: 5; *Full-Time Faculty*: 8; *Part-Time Faculty*: 12; *Full-Time Professional (non-clerical) Staff Members*: 1.

Los Angeles Harbor College (Public)

Division of Communications
1111 Figueroa Place
Wilmington, California 90744
Telephone: (213) 518-1000

J. Christopher McCarthy, Chair
Cal Garvin, Dean

CURRICULUM AND INSTRUCTION
Courses or Concentrations Available: Communication; Film or Cinema; Journalism or Mass Communication; Public Relations; Radio, Television, Broadcasting, or Telecommunications; Speech; *Full-Time Faculty*: 25; *Part-Time Faculty*: 28; *Full-Time Professional (non-clerical) Staff Members*: 1.

FACILITIES AND SERVICES
Practical experiences available through: Desktop Publishing Facility; Photographic Darkrooms; Institutional Newspaper.

Los Angeles Pierce College (Public)

Department of Speech Communication
6201 Winnetka Avenue
Woodland Hills, California 91371
Telephone: (818) 719-6460

James R. Lagerstrom, Chair
Paul Whalen, Chief Administrator

CURRICULUM AND INSTRUCTION
Courses or Concentrations Available: Communication; Speech; *Undergraduate Objectives or Program Emphases*: Provide general education requirement courses for the oral communication component; provide lower division courses for speech communication majors; offer skills courses for vocational programs; *Associate's Degree Majors*: 70; *Full-Time Faculty*: 4; *Part-Time Faculty*: 8.

FACILITIES AND SERVICES
Practical experiences available through: Closed Circuit Television Facility; Campus Newspaper (Published Independently).

Los Angeles Trade-Technical College (Public)

Program of Journalism
400 West Washington Boulevard
Los Angeles, California 90015
Telephone: (213) 744-9046

J. N. Draznin, Chair
Ray Garay, Dean

CURRICULUM AND INSTRUCTION
Courses or Concentrations Available: Communication; Journalism or Mass Communication; Public Relations; Speech; *Undergraduate Objectives or Program Emphases*: Prepare transfer students to four-year institutions, award AA degrees and certificates of completion; *Associate's Degree Majors*: 50; *Full-Time Faculty*: 1; *Part-Time Faculty*: 1.

FACILITIES AND SERVICES
*Practical experiences available
through*: Campus Newspaper (Published
Independently); Local Commercial
Newspaper; Photographic Darkrooms;
Institutional Magazine; Institutional
Newspaper; Video Production Laboratory or
Television Studio.

Loyola Marymount University (Private)

Department of Communication Arts
Loyola Boulevard
Los Angeles, California 90045
Telephone: (213) 645-3033

Donald J. Zirpola, Chair
A. Bloom, Dean

CURRICULUM AND INSTRUCTION
*Courses or Concentrations
Available*: Communication; Film or Cinema;
Mass Communication; Television and
Broadcasting; Speech; Screenwriting;
Recording Arts; *Undergraduate Objectives or
Program Emphases*: Information and
entertainment industries; *Graduate Objectives
or Program Emphases*: Information and
entertainment industries; *Bachelor's Degree
Majors*: 450; *Master's Degree Majors*: 55;
Full-Time Faculty: 19; *Part-Time
Faculty*: 20; *Full-Time Professional
(non-clerical) Staff Members*: 6.

FACILITIES AND SERVICES
*Practical experiences available
through*: Advertising Agency; Audio
Recording Laboratory; Campus Newspaper
(Published Independently); Local
Commercial Newspaper; Local Commercial
Television Station; Photographic
Darkrooms; Video Editing; Film or Cinema
Laboratory; FM Radio Station
(Institutional); Institutional Newspaper;
Public Relations Agency; Video Production
Laboratory or Television Studio.

Marymount Palos Verdes College

Department of Communication
30800 Palos Verdes Drive East
Rancho Palos Verdes, California 90274

Master's College

Department of Communication
21726 West Placerita Canyon Road
Newhall, California 91322-0878

Julie M. Larson, Administrator

Menlo College (Private)

Department of Communication
1000 El Camino Real
Atherton, California 94027-4185
Telephone: (415) 323-6141

Susannah R. Barber, Chair
David Butler, Acting Academic Dean and
President of the College

CURRICULUM AND INSTRUCTION
*Courses or Concentrations
Available*: Advertising; Communication; Film
or Cinema; Journalism or Mass
Communication; Radio, Television,
Broadcasting, or Telecommunications;
Corporate Media; *Undergraduate Objectives
or Program Emphases*: The program focuses
on evaluating, managing and producing the
contents of newspapers, magazines, motion
pictures, radio, television, advertising and
corporate communication. Interdisciplinary
programs tailored to personal interests and
career aspirations; *Bachelor's Degree
Majors*: 96; *Full-Time Faculty*: 3; *Part-Time
Faculty*: 6.

FACILITIES AND SERVICES
*Practical experiences available
through*: Advertising Agency; AM Radio
Station (Institutional); Carrier Current
Audio Distribution System; Local
Commercial Newspaper; Local Commercial
Television Station; Desktop Publishing
Facility; Photographic Darkrooms;
Electronic Field Production (Video);
Institutional Magazine; Institutional
Newspaper.

Mills College

Department of Communication
5000 MacArthur Boulevard
Oakland, California 94613

Philip S. Kipper, Administrator

Modesto Junior College (Public)

Division of Arts, Humanities and
Communication
435 College Avenue
Modesto, California 95350
Telephone: (209) 575-6081

Robert G. Gauvreau, Dean
Ron Manzani, Dean of Instruction

CURRICULUM AND INSTRUCTION
*Courses or Concentrations
Available*: Communication; Film or Cinema;
Journalism or Mass Communication; Radio,
Television, Broadcasting, or
Telecommunications; Speech; *Undergraduate
Objectives or Program Emphases*: Speech;
Radio-Television; Film (Video); *Associate's
Degree Majors*: 100; *Full-Time Faculty*: 19;
Part-Time Faculty: 25; *Full-Time
Professional (non-clerical) Staff Members*: 5.

FACILITIES AND SERVICES
Practical experiences available through: AM
Radio Station (Institutional); Audio
Recording Laboratory; Community Antenna
(Cable) Television Origination; Carrier
Current Audio Distribution System; Desktop
Publishing Facility; Photographic
Darkrooms; Video Editing; Electronic Field
Production (Video); Film or Cinema
Laboratory; Institutional Newspaper; Video
Production Laboratory or Television Studio.

Moorpark College

Department of Telecommunications
7075 Campus Road
Moorpark, California 93021

Al Miller, Administrator

Mount San Antonio College

Speech Communication/Broadcasting
1100 North Grand Avenue
Walnut, California 91789

Carter Doran, Administrator

Napa Valley Community College (Public)

Program of Telecommunications Technology
Napa, California 94558
Telephone: (707) 253-3258

Gary Vann, Coordinator

CURRICULUM AND INSTRUCTION
Courses or Concentrations Available: Radio,
Television, Broadcasting, or
Telecommunications; *Undergraduate
Objectives or Program Emphases*: Television
engineer, technical emphasis, electronics
requirement; *Graduate Objectives or Program
Emphases*: Telecommunications technology,
vocational preparation; *Full-Time Faculty*: 1;
*Full-Time Professional (non-clerical) Staff
Members*: 1.

FACILITIES AND SERVICES
*Practical experiences available
through*: Community Antenna (Cable)
Television Origination; Closed Circuit
Television Facility; Video Editing; Video
Production Laboratory or Television Studio.

Orange Coast College

Department of Broadcast Arts
2701 Fairview Road
Costa Mesa, California 92626

Pete Scarpello, Administrator

Oxnard College

Department of Telecommunications
4000 South Rose Avenue
Oxnard, California 93033

Winston Sarafian, Administrator

Pacific Christian College (Private)

Department of Speech
2500 East Nutwood Avenue
Fullerton, California 92631
Telephone: (714) 879-3901

John D. Webb, Chair
Gerald L. Tiffin, Academic Dean

CURRICULUM AND INSTRUCTION
Courses or Concentrations
Available: Communication; Journalism or Mass Communication; Speech; Preaching; *Undergraduate Objectives or Program Emphases*: Combined with classes at California State University, Fullerton, a series of communication degrees in Communication is offered in conjunction with a Bible major; *Bachelor's Degree Majors*: 6; *Full-Time Faculty*: 1; *Part-Time Faculty*: 2.

FACILITIES AND SERVICES
Practical experiences available through: Closed Circuit Television Facility; Campus Newspaper (Published Independently).

Pacific Union College

Communication Department
Angwin, California 94508

James D. Chase, Administrator

Palomar College (Public)

Department of Communication
1140 West Mission Road
San Marcos, California 92069

Dana Hawkes, Chair
LuAnn Poulsen, Dean

CURRICULUM AND INSTRUCTION
Courses or Concentrations
Available: Communication; Film or Cinema; Journalism or Mass Communication; Radio, Television, Broadcasting, or Telecommunications; Photography; *Associate's Degree Majors*: 300; *Other Degree Majors*: 150; *Full-Time Faculty*: 8; *Part-Time Faculty*: 25; *Full-Time Professional (non-clerical) Staff Members*: 3.

FACILITIES AND SERVICES
Practical experiences available through: Audio Recording Laboratory; Community Antenna (Cable) Television Origination; Carrier Current Audio Distribution System; Closed Circuit Television Facility; Campus Newspaper (Published Independently); Local Commercial Newspaper; Local Commercial Television Station; Desktop Publishing Facility; Photographic Darkrooms; Video Editing; Electronic Field Production (Video); Television Broadcast Station (Institutional); Film or Cinema Laboratory; FM Radio Station (Institutional); ITFS Distribution System; Institutional Magazine; Institutional Newspaper; United Press International Feed; Video News and Data Processing; Video Production Laboratory or Television Studio.

Pasadena City College (Public)

Department of Communications
1570 East Colorado Boulevard
Pasadena, California 91106
Telephone: (818) 578-7216

Lane M. Bloebaum, Chair
David Ledbetter, Assistant Superintendent

CURRICULUM AND INSTRUCTION
Courses or Concentrations
Available: Communication; Film or Cinema; Journalism or Mass Communication; Public Relations; Radio, Television, Broadcasting, or Telecommunications; Speech; *Undergraduate Objectives or Program Emphases*: Preprofessional training oriented towards either students continuing on to four year institutions, or students going directly into the job market; *Full-Time Faculty*: 20; *Part-Time Faculty*: 51; *Full-Time Professional (non-clerical) Staff Members*: 5.

FACILITIES AND SERVICES
Practical experiences available through: Associated Press Wire Service Feed; Audio Recording Laboratory; Community Antenna (Cable) Television Origination; Carrier Current Audio Distribution System; Campus Newspaper (Published Independently); Local Commercial Newspaper; Local Commercial Television Station; Desktop Publishing Facility; Photographic Darkrooms; Video Editing; Electronic Field Production (Video); Television Broadcast Station (Institutional); Film or Cinema Laboratory; FM Radio Station (Institutional); Institutional Newspaper; Public Relations Agency; Reuters News Agency; Satellite Uplink Facility; United Press International Feed; Video News and Data Processing; Video Production Laboratory or Television Studio.

Pepperdine University (Private)

Division of Communication
24255 Pacific Coast Highway
Malibu, California 90263
Telephone: (213) 456-4211

Donald L. Shores, Chair
John Wilson, Dean

CURRICULUM AND INSTRUCTION
*Courses or Concentrations
Available*: Advertising; Communication;
Journalism or Mass Communication; Public
Relations; Radio, Television, Broadcasting,
or Telecommunications; Speech; *Program
Coordinators*: David N. Lowry
(Broadcasting); Michael Casey (Basic Public
Speaking); *Undergraduate Objectives or
Program Emphases*: To provide both a
theoretical and practical approach to the
study of human communication; *Graduate
Objectives or Program Emphases*: To provide
a theoretical base for professionals and those
wishing more advanced studies; *Bachelor's
Degree Majors*: 500; *Master's Degree
Majors*: 21; *Full-Time Faculty*: 22;
Part-Time Faculty: 25; *Full-Time
Professional (non-clerical) Staff Members*: 6.

FACILITIES AND SERVICES
*Practical experiences available
through*: Associated Press Wire Service Feed;
Audio Recording Laboratory; Community
Antenna (Cable) Television Origination;
Closed Circuit Television Facility; Desktop
Publishing Facility; Photographic
Darkrooms; Video Editing; Electronic Field
Production (Video); Television Broadcast
Station (Institutional); FM Radio Station
(Institutional); Institutional Magazine;
Institutional Newspaper; Video Production
Laboratory or Television Studio.

Porterville College (Public)

Program of Speech
900 South Main Street
Porterville, California 93257
Telephone: (209) 781-3130

Phil Simons, Instructor
Ron Kean, Administrator

CURRICULUM AND INSTRUCTION
*Courses or Concentrations
Available*: Communication; Speech;
Undergraduate Objectives or Program

Emphases: To provide instruction and
practice in the process of oral
communication; *Full-Time Faculty*: 1;
Part-Time Faculty: 1.

Rancho Santiago College (Public)

Department of Telecommunications and
Journalism
17th at Bristol Streets
Santa Anna, California 92706
Telephone: (714) 667-3266

Terry W. Bales, Chair
Marie Pooler, Interim Dean

CURRICULUM AND INSTRUCTION
*Courses or Concentrations
Available*: Communication; Film or Cinema;
Journalism or Mass Communication; Public
Relations; Radio, Television, Broadcasting,
or Telecommunications; Speech;
*Undergraduate Objectives or Program
Emphases*: AA degree and certificates in
print journalism, broadcast journalism,
television production, television scriptwriting;
Associate's Degree Majors: 50; *Full-Time
Faculty*: 2; *Part-Time Faculty*: 7; *Full-Time
Professional (non-clerical) Staff Members*: 2.

FACILITIES AND SERVICES
Practical experiences available through: Audio
Recording Laboratory; Community Antenna
(Cable) Television Origination; Desktop
Publishing Facility; Photographic
Darkrooms; Video Editing; Electronic Field
Production (Video); Institutional Magazine;
Institutional Newspaper; Satellite Uplink
Facility (C Band Transmitter); Video News
and Data Processing; Video Production
Laboratory or Television Studio.

Rio Hondo College

Department of Communications
3600 Workman Mill Road
Whittier, California 90608

Carolyn Russel, Administrator

Saddleback College (Public)

Department of Fine Arts and Communications
28000 Marguerite Parkway
Mission Viejo, California 92692
Telephone: (714) 582-4882

Mark W. Schiffelbein, Director
Greg Bishopp, Dean, Fine Arts

CURRICULUM AND INSTRUCTION
Courses or Concentrations
Available: Communication; Film or Cinema;
Radio, Television, Broadcasting, or
Telecommunications; *Undergraduate*
Objectives or Program Emphases: Production
skills and hands-on learning; *Associate's*
Degree Majors: 25; *Full-Time Faculty*: 3;
Part-Time Faculty: 3; *Full-Time Professional*
(non-clerical) Staff Members: 6.

FACILITIES AND SERVICES
Practical experiences available
through: Associated Press Wire Service Feed;
Audio Recording Laboratory; Community
Antenna (Cable) Television Origination;
Campus Newspaper (Published
Independently); Desktop Publishing Facility;
Photographic Darkrooms; Video Editing;
Electronic Field Production (Video); FM
Radio Station (Institutional); ITFS
Distribution System; Institutional Magazine;
Institutional Newspaper; Video Production
Laboratory or Television Studio.

San Diego State University (Public)

Department of Speech Communication
5300 Companile Drive
San Diego, California 92182
Telephone: (619) 594-6051

Janis Andersen, Chair
Joyce Gattan, Dean

CURRICULUM AND INSTRUCTION
Courses or Concentrations
Available: Communication; Speech;
Undergraduate Objectives or Program
Emphases: Instruction in communication
theory and practice; forensic program,
speakers bureau, community speaking
referral; *Graduate Objectives or Program*
Emphases: Instruction in communication
theory; understanding of and capability to
conduct communication research; *Bachelor's*

Degree Majors: 500; *Master's Degree*
Majors: 80; *Full-Time Faculty*: 10;
Part-Time Faculty: 40.

San Diego State University (Public)

Department of Journalism
PSFA 325
San Diego, California 92182
Telephone: (619) 594-6635

Glenn M. Broom, Chair

CURRICULUM AND INSTRUCTION
Courses or Concentrations
Available: Advertising; Journalism or Mass
Communication; Public Relations;
Radio-Television News; *Program*
Coordinator: David Dozier (Graduate
Program in Mass Communication);
Undergraduate Objectives or Program
Emphases: Professional orientation for
careers in journalism and mass
communication; *Graduate Objectives or*
Program Emphases: Graduate education in
theory, research and advanced study;
Bachelor's Degree Majors: 690; *Other Degree*
Majors: 25; *Full-Time Faculty*: 12;
Part-Time Faculty: 16; *Full-Time*
Professional (non-clerical) Staff Members: 2.

FACILITIES AND SERVICES
Practical experiences available
through: Advertising Agency; Community
Antenna (Cable) Television Origination;
Campus Newspaper (Published
Independently); Local Commercial
Newspaper; Local Commercial Television
Station; Desktop Publishing Facility;
Photographic Darkrooms; Video Editing;
Electronic Field Production (Video);
Television Broadcast Station (Institutional);
Film or Cinema Laboratory; FM Radio
Station (Institutional); Institutional
Magazine; Public Relations Agency.

San Diego State University

Telecommunications and Film
San Diego, California 92182

Michael R. Real, Administrator

San Francisco Art Institute

Film Department
800 Chestnut Street
San Francisco, California 94133

Janis Crystal Lipzin, Administrator

San Francisco State University (Public)

Department of Broadcast Communication Arts
1600 Holloway Avenue
San Francisco, California 94132
Telephone: (415) 338-1787

Ronald J. Compesi, Chair
Warren Rasmussen, Associate Dean

CURRICULUM AND INSTRUCTION
Courses or Concentrations Available: Communication; Journalism or Mass Communication; Radio, Television, Broadcasting, or Telecommunications; *Undergraduate Objectives or Program Emphases*: Audio Production; Broadcast News; Business aspects of and writing for electronic media; educational, instructional media; mass communication theory and criticism; media performance; radio production and programming; television and video producing and directing; *Graduate Objectives or Program Emphases*: Mass communication theory and criticism, media aesthetics, writing and production for electronic media; *Bachelor's Degree Majors*: 900; *Master's Degree Majors*: 100; *Full-Time Faculty*: 21; *Part-Time Faculty*: 15; *Full-Time Professional (non-clerical) Staff Members*: 4.

FACILITIES AND SERVICES
Practical experiences available through: Audio Recording Laboratory; Community Antenna (Cable) Television Origination; Carrier Current Audio Distribution System; Closed Circuit Television Facility; Desktop Publishing Facility; Video Editing; Electronic Field Production (Video); Satellite Uplink Facility (Ku Band Transmitter) (C Band Transmitter); Video News and Data Processing; Video Production Laboratory or Television Studio.

San Francisco State University (Public)

Department of Journalism
1600 Holloway Avenue
San Francisco, California 94132

Betty Medsger, Administrator

San Francisco State University (Public)

Department of Cinema
1600 Holloway Avenue
San Francisco, California 94132
Telephone: (415) 338-1649

Bill Nichols, Chair
August Coppola, Dean

CURRICULUM AND INSTRUCTION
Courses or Concentrations Available: Film or Cinema; *Program Coordinator*: R. Compesi (Broadcasting); *Undergraduate Objectives or Program Emphases*: Studies and production in cinema; *Graduate Objectives or Program Emphases*: Studies and production in cinema; *Bachelor's Degree Majors*: 300; *Master's Degree Majors*: 90; *Full-Time Faculty*: 14; *Part-Time Faculty*: 23; *Full-Time Professional (non-clerical) Staff Members*: 2.

FACILITIES AND SERVICES
Practical experiences available through: Community Antenna (Cable) Television Origination; Closed Circuit Television Facility; Campus Newspaper (Published Independently); Local Commercial Television Station; Video Editing; Film or Cinema Laboratory.

San Francisco State University (Public)

Department of Speech and Communication Studies
1600 Holloway Avenue
San Francisco, California 94132
Telephone: (415) 338-1597

Nancy G. McDermid, Dean, School of Humanities

CURRICULUM AND INSTRUCTION
Courses or Concentrations Available: Communication; Speech;

Undergraduate Objectives or Program Emphases: Three areas: Speech Communication, Intercultural Communication, and Organizational Communication; *Graduate Objectives or Program Emphases*: Speech Communication; *Bachelor's Degree Majors*: 450; *Master's Degree Majors*: 40; *Full-Time Faculty*: 20; *Part-Time Faculty*: 20.

FACILITIES AND SERVICES
Practical experiences available through: Desktop Publishing Facility.

San Joaquin Delta College (Public)

Department of Journalism
5151 Pacific Avenue
Stockton, California 95207
Telephone: (209) 474-5286

William P. Davis, Head
Mary Ann Cox, Chair

CURRICULUM AND INSTRUCTION
Courses or Concentrations Available: Journalism or Mass Communication; Radio, Television, Broadcasting, or Telecommunications; Speech; *Undergraduate Objectives or Program Emphases*: Two-year program in journalism leading to Associate degree or transfer to four year school; *Associate's Degree Majors*: 50; *Full-Time Faculty*: 1.

FACILITIES AND SERVICES
Practical experiences available through: Associated Press Wire Service Feed; Community Antenna (Cable) Television Origination; Desktop Publishing Facility; Photographic Darkrooms; Institutional Newspaper.

San Jose City College

Humanities and Social Sciences Division
2100 Moorpark Avenue
San Jose, California 95128

William Kester, Administrator

San Jose State University (Public)

Department of Journalism and Mass Communications
One Washington Square
San Jose, California 95192
Telephone: (408) 924-3240

Kenneth W. Blase, Chair
Rose Tseng, Dean

CURRICULUM AND INSTRUCTION
Courses or Concentrations Available: Advertising; Communication; Film or Cinema; Journalism or Mass Communication; Public Relations; Radio, Television, Broadcasting, or Telecommunications; Speech; *Program Coordinators*: Marshall Raines (Advertising); Bill Tillinghast (Journalism); Darla Belshe (Radio-Television News); Harvey Cotliffe (Magazine Journalism); James McNay (Photojournalism); Dennis Wilcox (Public Relations); *Undergraduate Objectives or Program Emphases*: BS in Advertising, Public Relations; BS in Journalism: Reporting and editing, broadcast, photojournalism, magazine journalism; *Graduate Objectives or Program Emphases*: MS in Mass Communications; *Other Degree Majors*: 1480; *Full-Time Faculty*: 21; *Part-Time Faculty*: 28; *Full-Time Professional (non-clerical) Staff Members*: 2.

FACILITIES AND SERVICES
Practical experiences available through: Advertising Agency; Associated Press Wire Service Feed; Audio Recording Laboratory; Community Antenna (Cable) Television Origination; Closed Circuit Television Facility; Local Commercial Newspaper; Local Commercial Television Station; Desktop Publishing Facility; Photographic Darkrooms; Video Editing; Electronic Field Production (Video); FM Radio Station (Institutional); ITFS Distribution System; Institutional Magazine; Institutional Newspaper; Public Relations Agency; United Press International Feed; Video News and Data Processing; Video Production Laboratory or Television Studio.

San Jose State University (Public)

Program of Radio-Television-Film
One Washington Square
San Jose, California 95192
Telephone: (408) 924-4543

Charles L. Chess, Director
Stanly Boran, Administrator

CURRICULUM AND INSTRUCTION
*Courses or Concentrations
Available*: Communication; Film or Cinema;
Radio, Television, Broadcasting, or
Telecommunications; *Undergraduate
Objectives or Program Emphases*: General
background and study in radio, television,
film; production, history, writing, aesthetics,
communication theory, leading to a BA; a
strong liberal arts education; *Full-Time
Faculty*: 7; *Part-Time Faculty*: 3; *Full-Time
Professional (non-clerical) Staff Members*: 3.

FACILITIES AND SERVICES
Practical experiences available through: Audio
Recording Laboratory; Closed Circuit
Television Facility; Campus Newspaper
(Published Independently); Local
Commercial Newspaper; Local Commercial
Television Station; Desktop Publishing
Facility; Video Editing; Electronic Field
Production (Video); Television Broadcast
Station (Institutional); Film or Cinema
Laboratory; FM Radio Station
(Institutional); ITFS Distribution System;
Video Production Laboratory or Television
Studio.

San Jose State University

Communication Studies Department
One Washington Square
San Jose, California 95192

David H. Elliott, Administrator

Santa Barbara City College

Inter-Departmental Program of Television
Production
721 Cliff Drive
Santa Barbara, California 93109

Kenneth Berry, Administrator

Santa Barbara City College

Speech Communication Department
721 Cliff Drive
Santa Barbara, California 93109

Ronald B. Adler, Administrator

Santa Clara University

Department of Communication
St. Joseph's 209
Santa Clara, California 95053

Thomas E. Shanks, Administrator

Santa Monica College

Broadcasting Department
1900 Pico Boulevard
Santa Monica, California 90405

Furnell William, Administrator

Santa Rosa Junior College (Public)

Media Program, Communication Studies
Department
1501 Mendocino Avenue
Santa Rosa, California 95401
Telephone: (707) 527-4398

John W. Bigby, Director
Alberta S. Hart, Administrator

CURRICULUM AND INSTRUCTION
*Courses or Concentrations
Available*: Communication; Film or Cinema;
Journalism or Mass Communication; Radio,
Television, Broadcasting, or
Telecommunications; *Undergraduate
Objectives or Program Emphases*: Both
practical and theoretical experience for
majors and critical skills for general
education students; *Associate's Degree
Majors*: 30; *Full-Time Faculty*: 2; *Part-Time
Faculty*: 3; *Full-Time Professional
(non-clerical) Staff Members*: 1.

FACILITIES AND SERVICES
Practical experiences available through: Audio
Recording Laboratory; Local Commercial
Television Station; Desktop Publishing
Facility; Photographic Darkrooms; Video

Editing; Electronic Field Production (Video); Film or Cinema Laboratory; Video Production Laboratory or Television Studio.

Solano College (Public)

Division of Fine and Applied Arts
4000 Suisun Valley Road
Suisun City, California 94585
Telephone: (707) 864-7000

Carol W. Bishop, Chair
June Elioff, Dean of Instruction

CURRICULUM AND INSTRUCTION
Courses or Concentrations Available: Communication; Film or Cinema; Radio, Television, Broadcasting, or Telecommunications; Speech; *Program Coordinators*: Thomas Kuehbiel (Communication, Speech); Maile Ornellas (Film, Cinema, Radio, Telecommunications); *Undergraduate Objectives or Program Emphases*: Transfer and vocational: television, telecommunications, cinema. Transfer: general education in speech, communications; *Associate's Degree Majors*: 40; *Full-Time Faculty*: 18; *Part-Time Faculty*: 45; *Full-Time Professional (non-clerical) Staff Members*: 4.

FACILITIES AND SERVICES
Practical experiences available through: Audio Recording Laboratory; Community Antenna (Cable) Television Origination; Closed Circuit Television Facility; Local Commercial Television Station; Photographic Darkrooms; Video Editing; Electronic Field Production (Video); Film or Cinema Laboratory; ITFS Distribution System; Satellite Uplink Facility; Video Production Laboratory or Television Studio.

Sonoma State University (Public)

Program of Communication Studies
Rohnert Park, California 94928
Telephone: (707) 664-2149

Michael G. Litle, Coordinator
William Babula, Dean

CURRICULUM AND INSTRUCTION
Courses or Concentrations Available: Film or Cinema; Journalism or Mass Communication; Public Relations; Radio,

Television, Broadcasting, or Telecommunications; Mass Media Criticism; Project Censored; *Program Coordinators*: Bill Gayn (Film Minor); Arthur Hills (Music Recording); Marsha Adams (Photography); *Undergraduate Objectives or Program Emphases*: A small and innovative program that integrates practical experience with historical study and a critical approach to the mass media. Internships are required. Home of Project Censored, all faculty with extensive, real world experiences; *Bachelor's Degree Majors*: 120; *Full-Time Faculty*: 3; *Part-Time Faculty*: 4; *Full-Time Professional (non-clerical) Staff Members*: 2.

FACILITIES AND SERVICES
Practical experiences available through: Advertising Agency; Audio Recording Laboratory; Closed Circuit Television Facility; Campus Newspaper (Published Independently); Local Commercial Newspaper; Local Commercial Television Station; Desktop Publishing Facility; Photographic Darkrooms; Video Editing; Electronic Field Production (Video); FM Radio Station (Institutional); Institutional Magazine; Public Relations Agency; Video Production Laboratory or Television Studio.

Southern California College (Private)

Department of Communication
55 Fair Drive
Costa Mesa, California 92626
Telephone: (714) 556-3610

Morris Pike, Chair
Shirley Felt, Chief Administrator

CURRICULUM AND INSTRUCTION
Courses or Concentrations Available: Journalism or Mass Communication; Radio, Television, Broadcasting, or Telecommunications; Speech; *Program Coordinators*: Gerald Fisher (Television); Richard Hardy (Broadcast, Journalism); *Undergraduate Objectives or Program Emphases*: Technical knowledge and hands-on experience through classes and internships; *Bachelor's Degree Majors*: 20; *Full-Time Faculty*: 3; *Part-Time Faculty*: 3.

FACILITIES AND SERVICES
Practical experiences available through: Desktop Publishing Facility; Video

Editing; Electronic Field Production (Video); Video Production Laboratory or Television Studio.

Southwestern College (Public)

Division of Communication Arts
900 Otay Lakes Road
Chula Vista, California 92010
Telephone: (619) 421-6700

Christina Chiriboga, Dean

CURRICULUM AND INSTRUCTION
Courses or Concentrations Available: Speech; *Program Coordinator*: John Caufal (Speech); *Full-Time Faculty*: 6; *Part-Time Faculty*: 3.

FACILITIES AND SERVICES
Practical experiences available through: Audio Recording Laboratory; Desktop Publishing Facility; ITFS Distribution System.

Southwestern College (Public)

Division of Arts and Humanities
900 Otay Lakes Road
Chula Vista, California 92041
Telephone: (619) 421-6700

Sara Megling, Coordinator
Patricia Caldwell, Dean

CURRICULUM AND INSTRUCTION
Courses or Concentrations Available: Journalism or Mass Communication; *Undergraduate Objectives or Program Emphases*: To provide general education requirements for transfer students; to satisfy lower-division requirements to transfer students seeking a degree in journalism; to provide skills for students seeking entry-level jobs in journalism; *Associate's Degree Majors*: 118; *Full-Time Faculty*: 2.

FACILITIES AND SERVICES
Practical experiences available through: Desktop Publishing Facility; Photographic Darkrooms; Institutional Magazine; Institutional Newspaper.

St. Mary's College of California (Private)

Department of Communications
Moraga, California 94575
Telephone: (415) 631-4000

Michael A. Russo, Chair
Paul Zingg, Dean, School of Liberal Arts

CURRICULUM AND INSTRUCTION
Courses or Concentrations Available: Advertising; Communication; Film or Cinema; Journalism or Mass Communication; Public Relations; Radio, Television, Broadcasting, or Telecommunications; Speech; *Undergraduate Objectives or Program Emphases*: Theory driven, liberal arts program for undergraduate major; exposure to media of radio, television, news writing and corporate communication; *Bachelor's Degree Majors*: 200; *Full-Time Faculty*: 6; *Part-Time Faculty*: 5; *Full-Time Professional (non-clerical) Staff Members*: 2.

FACILITIES AND SERVICES
Practical experiences available through: Community Antenna (Cable) Television Origination; Closed Circuit Television Facility; Campus Newspaper (Published Independently); Desktop Publishing Facility; Video Editing; Electronic Field Production (Video); FM Radio Station (Institutional).

Stanford University (Private)

Department of Communication
Building 120
Stanford, California 94305-2050
Telephone: (415) 723-0440

Steven H. Chaffee, Chair
Ewart Thomas, Dean, Humanities and Sciences

CURRICULUM AND INSTRUCTION
Courses or Concentrations Available: Communication; Film or Cinema; Journalism or Mass Communication; Radio, Television, Broadcasting, or Telecommunications; Communication Science; *Undergraduate Objectives or Program Emphases*: A liberal arts major introducing students to the field of mass communication. Combines academic courses with introductory skills training in all media;

Graduate Objectives or Program Emphases: MA entry-level skills in journalism or documentary film-making (two separate programs). Ph.D. program prepares students for academic research and teaching careers, with emphasis on social science theories and methodology; *Bachelor's Degree Majors*: 100; *Master's Degree Majors*: 30; *Doctoral Degree Majors Currently in Residence*: 21; *Additional Doctoral Degree Majors*: 5; *Other Degree Majors*: 18; *Full-Time Faculty*: 10; *Part-Time Faculty*: 8; *Full-Time Professional (non-clerical) Staff Members*: 1.

FACILITIES AND SERVICES
Practical experiences available through: Campus Newspaper (Published Independently); Local Commercial Newspaper; Local Commercial Television Station; Desktop Publishing Facility; Video Editing; Electronic Field Production (Video); Film or Cinema Laboratory; Reuters News Agency; Video News and Data Processing; Video Production Laboratory or Television Studio.

University of California - Berkeley

Department of Broadcast
Graduate School of Journalism
Berkeley, California 94720

Andrew A. Stern, Administrator

University of California - Davis (Public)

Department of Rhetoric and Communication
Davis, California 95616
Telephone: (916) 752-1221

Michael T. Motley, Chair
Robert Crummey, Dean, Liberal Arts and Sciences

CURRICULUM AND INSTRUCTION
Courses or Concentrations Available: Communication; Speech; *Undergraduate Objectives or Program Emphases*: Balanced curriculum in interpersonal communication, rhetoric, and mass communication; *Graduate Objectives or Program Emphases*: M.A. thesis and

non-thesis options in interpersonal communication, rhetoric, and mass communication; *Bachelor's Degree Majors*: 400; *Master's Degree Majors*: 22; *Full-Time Faculty*: 13; *Part-Time Faculty*: 20.

FACILITIES AND SERVICES
Practical experiences available through: Closed Circuit Television Facility; Campus Newspaper (Published Independently); Local Commercial Television Station; Desktop Publishing Facility; Video Editing; FM Radio Station (Institutional); Public Relations Agency.

University of La Verne

Department of Television/Radio
1950 Third Street
La Verne, California 91750

Sara LaRiviere, Administrator

University of San Francisco (Private)

Department of Communication Arts
Ignatian Heights
San Francisco, California 94117-1080
Telephone: (415) 666-6421;
Alternate: 666-6680

Richard E. Davis, Chair
Larry Wenner, Associate Dean, Arts

CURRICULUM AND INSTRUCTION
Courses or Concentrations Available: Advertising; Communication; Film or Cinema; Information Science; Journalism or Mass Communication; Public Relations; Radio, Television, Broadcasting, or Telecommunications; Speech; *Program Coordinators*: Steve Runyon (Mass Media); Paula Campbell (Communication Theory); *Undergraduate Objectives or Program Emphases*: Mass Media: professional preparation for careers in mass media particularly broadcasting and journalism. Communication Theory: diversified area with a number of concentrations, including organizational, human communication law and society, information science, fine and performing arts; *Bachelor's Degree Majors*: 190; *Full-Time Faculty*: 8; *Part-Time Faculty*: 11.

FACILITIES AND SERVICES
*Practical experiences available
through*: Advertising Agency; Carrier
Current Audio Distribution System; Campus
Newspaper (Published Independently);
Local Commercial Newspaper; Local
Commercial Television Station; Video
Editing; FM Radio Station (Institutional);
ITFS Distribution System; Institutional
Magazine; Public Relations Agency.

University of Southern California (Private)

**Department of Communication Arts and
Sciences**
GFS 344
Los Angeles, California 90089-1694
Telephone: (213) 743-2490

Thomas A. Hollihan, Chair
**Sylvester Whitaker, Dean, Social Sciences
and Communications**

CURRICULUM AND INSTRUCTION
*Courses or Concentrations
Available*: Communication; Speech;
*Undergraduate Objectives or Program
Emphases*: Communication Arts and
Sciences; *Graduate Objectives or Program
Emphases*: Communication Theory; Rhetoric
and Public Address; *Bachelor's Degree
Majors*: 500; *Master's Degree Majors*: 7;
*Doctoral Degree Majors Currently in
Residence*: 28; *Additional Doctoral Degree
Majors*: 10; *Full-Time Faculty*: 13;
Part-Time Faculty: 28; *Full-Time
Professional (non-clerical) Staff Members*: 1.

University of Southern California (Private)

School of Journalism
GFS 315, University Park
Los Angeles, California 90089-1695
Telephone: (213) 743-7622

William J. Woestendiek, Director
**C. Sylvester Whitaker, Dean, Social Science
Division**

CURRICULUM AND INSTRUCTION
*Courses or Concentrations
Available*: Advertising; Journalism or Mass
Communication; Public Relations; Radio,
Television, Broadcasting, or
Telecommunications; *Program*

Coordinators: Ed Cray (Print); Joe Saltzman
(Broadcast); Bill Faith (Public Relations);
*Undergraduate Objectives or Program
Emphases*: Best possible education in all
aspects of journalism with strong emphasis
on writing and ethics. Strong internship
program and job placement; *Graduate
Objectives or Program Emphases*: Best
possible education in all aspects of
journalism with strong emphasis on writing
and ethics. Strong internship program and
job placement; *Bachelor's Degree Majors*: 578;
Master's Degree Majors: 77; *Full-Time
Faculty*: 15; *Part-Time Faculty*: 62;
*Full-Time Professional (non-clerical) Staff
Members*: 8.

FACILITIES AND SERVICES
*Practical experiences available
through*: Associated Press Wire Service Feed;
Audio Recording Laboratory; Campus
Newspaper (Published Independently);
Local Commercial Newspaper; Local
Commercial Television Station; Desktop
Publishing Facility; Photographic
Darkrooms; Video Editing; FM Radio
Station (Institutional); Public Relations
Agency; Video News and Data Processing;
Video Production Laboratory or Television
Studio.

University of the Pacific

Department of Communication
3601 Pacific Avenue
Stockton, California 95211

Jon F. Schamber, Administrator

Victor Valley College (Public)

**Department of Speech Communication and
Theatre Arts**
18422 Bear Valley Road
Victorville, California 92392
Telephone: (619) 245-4271

Marjorie L. Milroy, Chair
Sameniego, Dean

CURRICULUM AND INSTRUCTION
*Courses or Concentrations
Available*: Communication; Speech;
*Undergraduate Objectives or Program
Emphases*: To provide courses that meet
general education requirements. To help

students develop basic communication skills and interpersonal awareness.

Westmont College (Private)

Department of Communication Studies
955 La Paz Road
Santa Barbara, California 93108
Telephone: (805) 565-6000

Greg Spencer, Chair
Bud Blankenbaker, Academic Dean

CURRICULUM AND INSTRUCTION
Courses or Concentrations
Available: Communication; Journalism or Mass Communication; Speech; Rhetorical Studies; *Undergraduate Objectives or Program Emphases*: Overview of communication discipline in a Christian liberal arts perspective. Emphasize rhetorical theory, media ethics, and interpersonal communication; *Bachelor's Degree Majors*: 75; *Full-Time Faculty*: 3; *Part-Time Faculty*: 2.

FACILITIES AND SERVICES
Practical experiences available through: Advertising Agency; Campus Newspaper (Published Independently); Local Commercial Newspaper; Local Commercial Television Station; Television Broadcast Station (Institutional); Institutional Magazine; Institutional Newspaper; Public Relations Agency.

World College West (Private)

Video Communication Track
101 S. San Antonio Road
Petaluma, California 94952
Telephone: (707) 765-4500

Gerry Courtney, Director
Deborah Merola, Chief Administrator

CURRICULUM AND INSTRUCTION
Courses or Concentrations Available: Video; *Undergraduate Objectives or Program Emphases*: To educate students about the uses of video as an educational tool; to provide hands-on experience with equipment; to encourage experimentation, exploration and to emphasize content over form; *Bachelor's Degree Majors*: 6; *Full-Time Faculty*: 1; *Part-Time Faculty*: 1.

FACILITIES AND SERVICES
Practical experiences available through: Campus Newspaper (Published Independently); Local Commercial Television Station; Photographic Darkrooms.

Yuba College (Public)

Division of Language Arts, Media Services, Academic Skills Center
2088 North Beale Road
Marysville, California 95901
Telephone: (916) 741-6761

George Shaw, Dean
Annette Lambson, Dean of Instruction

CURRICULUM AND INSTRUCTION
Courses or Concentrations
Available: Advertising; Communication; Film or Cinema; Journalism or Mass Communication; Radio, Television, Broadcasting, or Telecommunications; Speech; Stephen Cato (Media Services); *Undergraduate Objectives or Program Emphases*: Transfer and job skills; *Associate's Degree Majors*: 150; *Full-Time Faculty*: 19; *Part-Time Faculty*: 37; *Full-Time Professional (non-clerical) Staff Members*: 4.

FACILITIES AND SERVICES
Practical experiences available through: Audio Recording Laboratory; Community Antenna (Cable) Television Origination; Closed Circuit Television Facility; Photographic Darkrooms; Video Editing; Electronic Field Production (Video); Television Broadcast Station (Institutional); Film or Cinema Laboratory; Video Production Laboratory or Television Studio.

Adams State College

Department of Communications
Alamosa, Colorado 81102

Jodine Ryan, Administrator

Adams State College (Public)

Program of Journalism
Education and Social Studies Building
Alamosa, Colorado 81102
Telephone: (719) 589-7427

John L. Morris, Instructor
Jodine Ryan, Head, Communications
Department

CURRICULUM AND INSTRUCTION
Courses or Concentrations
Available: Journalism or Mass
Communication; Radio, Television,
Broadcasting, or Telecommunications;
*Undergraduate Objectives or Program
Emphases*: To prepare students to enter a
career as a newspaper or radio news
journalist; *Bachelor's Degree Majors*: 30;
Full-Time Faculty: 1; *Part-Time Faculty*: 1.

FACILITIES AND SERVICES
*Practical experiences available
through*: Campus Newspaper (Published
Independently); Local Commercial
Newspaper; Desktop Publishing Facility;
Photographic Darkrooms; Video Editing;
FM Radio Station (Institutional);
Institutional Magazine; Video News and
Data Processing.

Adams State College (Public)

School of Business
Alamosa, Colorado 81102
Telephone: (719) 589-7161

J. Thomas Gilmore, Dean
Gary Peer, Academic Vice President

CURRICULUM AND INSTRUCTION
Courses or Concentrations

Available: Advertising; *Undergraduate
Objectives or Program Emphases*: Prepare
students for a career in advertising;
Bachelor's Degree Majors: 375; *Full-Time
Faculty*: 13; *Full-Time Professional
(non-clerical) Staff Members*: 1.

FACILITIES AND SERVICES
Practical experiences available through: Audio
Recording Laboratory; Closed Circuit
Television Facility; Campus Newspaper
(Published Independently); Local
Commercial Newspaper; Desktop Publishing
Facility; Photographic Darkrooms; Video
Editing; Electronic Field Production
(Video); Film or Cinema Laboratory; FM
Radio Station (Institutional); Institutional
Magazine; Institutional Newspaper; Video
News and Data Processing; Video
Production Laboratory or Television Studio.

Aims Community College (Public)

Department of Communications Media
4801 West 20th Street
Greeley, Colorado 80631
Telephone: (303) 330-8008

Kenneth F. Sauer, Director
Dwane Raile, Dean, Arts and Sciences

CURRICULUM AND INSTRUCTION
Courses or Concentrations
Available: Advertising; Communication; Film
or Cinema; Journalism or Mass
Communication; Public Relations; Radio,
Television, Broadcasting, or
Telecommunications; Speech; Computer
Graphics; Photography; Audio Engineering;
*Undergraduate Objectives or Program
Emphases*: Functional literacy in all forms of
mass media resulting from a largely
hands-on curriculum; *Associate's Degree
Majors*: 100; *Full-Time Faculty*: 1;
Part-Time Faculty: 2; *Full-Time Professional
(non-clerical) Staff Members*: 5.

Arapahoe Community College (Public)

Program of Speech Communication
5900 S. Santa Fe Drive, P.O. Box 9002
Littlejohn, Colorado 80160-9002
Telephone: (303) 797-5822

Polly C. Rogers, Coordinator
Herman R. Jantzen, Division Director

CURRICULUM AND INSTRUCTION
Courses or Concentrations
Available: Communication; Speech;
Undergraduate Objectives or Program Emphases: To fulfill the core curriculum to transfer to a four-year college or university; *Full-Time Faculty*: 2; *Part-Time Faculty*: 7.

FACILITIES AND SERVICES
Practical experiences available through: Campus Newspaper (Published Independently).

Blair Junior College (Private)

Department of General Education
828 Wooten Road
Colorado Springs, Colorado 80915
Telephone: (719) 574-1082

Judith M. Trzeciak, Chair
Rebecca B. Farenback, Administrator

CURRICULUM AND INSTRUCTION
Courses or Concentrations
Available: Communication; Speech;
Full-Time Faculty: 2; *Part-Time Faculty*: 12; *Full-Time Professional (non-clerical) Staff Members*: 4.

Colorado State University (Public)

Department of Speech Communication
Fort Collins, Colorado 80523
Telephone: (303) 491-6858

G. Jack Gravlee, Chair
Thomas Knight, Dean

CURRICULUM AND INSTRUCTION
Courses or Concentrations
Available: Communication; Film or Cinema; Radio, Television, Broadcasting, or Telecommunications; Speech; Rhetorical Theory and Criticism; *Undergraduate Objectives or Program Emphases*: Speech communication and broadcasting; *Graduate Objectives or Program Emphases*: Rhetorical theory and criticism; communication theory; broadcasting; *Bachelor's Degree Majors*: 280; *Master's Degree Majors*: 19; *Full-Time Faculty*: 16; *Part-Time Faculty*: 17.

FACILITIES AND SERVICES
Practical experiences available through: Community Antenna (Cable) Television Origination; Closed Circuit Television Facility; FM Radio Station (Institutional); Video Production Laboratory or Television Studio.

Colorado State University (Public)

Department of Technical Journalism
Fort Collins, Colorado 80523
Telephone: (303) 491-6310

David G. Clark, Chair
Thomas J. Knight, Dean, College of Arts, Humanities and Social Science

CURRICULUM AND INSTRUCTION
Courses or Concentrations
Available: Advertising; Communication; Journalism or Mass Communication; Public Relations; Radio, Television, Broadcasting, or Telecommunications; Technical-Specialized Communication; *Undergraduate Objectives or Program Emphases*: To prepare news editing, electronic reporting, public relations, and technical-specialized communication students for careers in those fields, while giving them a basic liberal arts education; *Graduate Objectives or Program Emphases*: Prepare graduates for communication management positions in technical communication and public relations; *Bachelor's Degree Majors*: 175; *Other Degree Majors*: 31; *Full-Time Faculty*: 13; *Part-Time Faculty*: 6; *Full-Time Professional (non-clerical) Staff Members*: 2.

FACILITIES AND SERVICES
Practical experiences available through: Advertising Agency; Community Antenna (Cable) Television Origination; Closed Circuit Television Facility; Campus Newspaper (Published Independently); Local Commercial Newspaper; Local Commercial Television Station; Desktop

Publishing Facility; Photographic Darkrooms; Video Editing; Electronic Field Production (Video); FM Radio Station (Institutional); ITFS Distribution System; Institutional Magazine; Institutional Newspaper; Public Relations Agency; Satellite Uplink Facility (Ku Band Transmitter) (C Band Transmitter); Video News and Data Processing; Video Production Laboratory or Television Studio.

Denver Seminary (Private)

Department of Homiletics and Speech
P. O. Box 10,000
Denver, Colorado 80210
Telephone: (303) 761-2482

Paul D. Borden, Chair
Ralph Covell, Academic Dean

CURRICULUM AND INSTRUCTION
Courses or Concentrations
Available: Communication; Speech; Homiletics; Oral Reading; *Graduate Objectives or Program Emphases*: To prepare people to be Biblically relevant communicators; To integrate ethological work in the original Biblical languages with the communication of sermons; *Degree Majors*: 35; *Full-Time Faculty*: 2; *Part-Time Faculty*: 6.

FACILITIES AND SERVICES
Practical experiences available through: Closed Circuit Television Facility; Desktop Publishing Facility; Video Editing; Video Production Laboratory or Television Studio.

Fort Lewis College (Public)

Department of English/Communications
College Heights
Durango, Colorado 81301
Telephone: (303) 247-7496

Leonard Bird, Chair

CURRICULUM AND INSTRUCTION
Courses or Concentrations
Available: Advertising; Communication; Film or Cinema; Journalism or Mass Communication; Public Relations; Radio, Television, Broadcasting, or Telecommunications; *Program*

Coordinators: Larry Hartsfield (Journalism, Mass Communication, Film, Cinema); Gordon Cheesewright (Radio, Television, Broadcast); *Undergraduate Objectives or Program Emphases*: To provide a liberal arts, humanities-based approach to communications studies; mass-communication in the context of analysis, textual studies, and literature, with additional stress on professional skills; *Bachelor's Degree Majors*: 200; *Full-Time Faculty*: 12; *Part-Time Faculty*: 5; *Full-Time Professional (non-clerical) Staff Members*: 2.

FACILITIES AND SERVICES
Practical experiences available through: Advertising Agency; Associated Press Wire Service Feed; Audio Recording Laboratory; Community Antenna (Cable) Television Origination; Campus Newspaper (Published Independently); Local Commercial Newspaper; Local Commercial Television Station; Desktop Publishing Facility; Photographic Darkrooms; Video Editing; Electronic Field Production (Video); Television Broadcast Station (Institutional); Film or Cinema Laboratory; FM Radio Station (Institutional); ITFS Distribution System; Institutional Magazine; Institutional Newspaper; Public Relations Agency; Satellite Uplink Facility; United Press International Feed; Video News and Data Processing; Video Production Laboratory or Television Studio.

Metropolitan State College

Speech Department Box 34
1006 11th Street
Denver, Colorado 80204

W. Thomas Cook, Administrator

Northeastern Junior College (Public)

Division of Humanities and Human Sciences
100 College Drive
Sterling, Colorado 80751
Telephone: (303) 522-6600

Bud Christian, Instructor/Advisor
Peter Youngers, Chief Administrator

CURRICULUM AND INSTRUCTION
Courses or Concentrations

Available: Advertising; Journalism or Mass Communication; Speech; *Undergraduate Objectives or Program Emphases*: To provide introductory level courses in journalism, advertising and mass communication. Speech courses also function as part of required core curriculum for transfer students; *Associate's Degree Majors*: 40; *Full-Time Faculty*: 2; *Part-Time Faculty*: 2.

FACILITIES AND SERVICES
Practical experiences available through: Campus Newspaper (Published Independently); Local Commercial Television Station; Desktop Publishing Facility; Photographic Darkrooms.

United States Air Force Academy

Department of Communication
Colorado Springs, Colorado 80840

University of Colorado - Boulder (Public)

School of Journalism and Mass Communication
Campus Box 287
Boulder, Colorado 80309
Telephone: (303) 492-4364

Willard D. Rowland, Jr., Dean
Bruce Ekstrand, Vice Chancellor for Academic Affairs

CURRICULUM AND INSTRUCTION
Courses or Concentrations Available: Advertising; Communication; Journalism or Mass Communication; Public Relations; Radio, Television, Broadcasting, or Telecommunications; *Program Coordinators*: Tom Duncan (Advertising); Lee Wilkins (News-Editorial); Steve Jones (Broadcast Production Management, Broadcast News); Jo Arnold (Master's Program); Bob Trager (Doctoral Program); *Undergraduate Objectives or Program Emphases*: Print (news-editorial) journalism; advertising; broadcast news; broadcast production and management; *Graduate Objectives or Program Emphases*: Masters in advanced professional skills; Masters in media studies and the fundamentals of graduate level communication research; Ph.D. in media studies track (institutions, policy, media processes and international

communications); *Bachelor's Degree Majors*: 387; *Master's Degree Majors*: 68; *Doctoral Degree Majors Currently in Residence*: 3; *Full-Time Faculty*: 23; *Part-Time Faculty*: 11.

FACILITIES AND SERVICES
Practical experiences available through: Advertising Agency; Associated Press Wire Service Feed; Audio Recording Laboratory; Community Antenna (Cable) Television Origination; Carrier Current Audio Distribution System; Closed Circuit Television Facility; Campus Newspaper (Published Independently); Local Commercial Newspaper; Local Commercial Television Station; Desktop Publishing Facility; Photographic Darkrooms; Video Editing; Electronic Field Production (Video); Television Broadcast Station (Institutional); ITFS Distribution System; Institutional Newspaper; Public Relations Agency; Satellite Uplink Facility; Video News and Data Processing; Video Production Laboratory or Television Studio.

University of Colorado - Colorado Springs (Public)

Department of Communication
1420 Austin Bluffs Parkway
Colorado Springs, Colorado 80933-7150
Telephone: (719) 593-3279

Kim B. Walker, Director
Pamela Shockley, Chair

CURRICULUM AND INSTRUCTION
Courses or Concentrations Available: Advertising; Communication; Journalism or Mass Communication; Radio, Television, Broadcasting, or Telecommunications; Speech; Media Management; Photography; *Undergraduate Objectives or Program Emphases*: General Communication; Organizational Communication; Industrial Media; Management; *Graduate Objectives or Program Emphases*: Organizational Communication; *Bachelor's Degree Majors*: 234; *Master's Degree Majors*: 10; *Full-Time Faculty*: 8; *Part-Time Faculty*: 7; *Full-Time Professional (non-clerical) Staff Members*: 5.

FACILITIES AND SERVICES
Practical experiences available through: Advertising Agency; Audio

Recording Laboratory; Closed Circuit Television Facility; Campus Newspaper (Published Independently); Local Commercial Newspaper; Local Commercial Television Station; Desktop Publishing Facility; Photographic Darkrooms; Video Editing; Electronic Field Production (Video); ITFS Distribution System; Institutional Magazine; Institutional Newspaper; Public Relations Agency; Satellite Uplink Facility (Ku Band Transmitter) (C Band Transmitter); Video Production Laboratory or Television Studio.

University of Colorado - Denver (Public)

Department of Communication
Denver, Colorado 80204
Telephone: (303) 556-2888

Samuel A. Betty, Chair
Marvin Loflin, Dean

CURRICULUM AND INSTRUCTION
Courses or Concentrations Available: Communication; Public Relations; Speech; *Undergraduate Objectives or Program Emphases*: Interpersonal Communication; Organizational Communication; *Graduate Objectives or Program Emphases*: Interpersonal Communication; Organizational Communication; Rhetorical Theory; *Bachelor's Degree Majors*: 100; *Master's Degree Majors*: 30; *Full-Time Faculty*: 4; *Part-Time Faculty*: 17.

FACILITIES AND SERVICES
Practical experiences available through: Campus Newspaper (Published Independently); Local Commercial Television Station; Public Relations Agency.

University of Denver (Private)

Department of Mass Communication
2490 South Gaylord
Denver, Colorado 80208
Telephone: (303) 871-2166

Michael O. Wirth, Chair
William Zaranka, Dean, Division of Social Sciences

CURRICULUM AND INSTRUCTION
Courses or Concentrations Available: Film or

Cinema; Journalism or Mass Communication; Public Relations; Radio, Television, Broadcasting, or Telecommunications; *Program Coordinator*: Connie Roser (Graduate Studies); *Undergraduate Objectives or Program Emphases*: To provide a liberal education based on an examination of the role and operations of mass media in society. Courses in video production, journalism and public relations are also offered; *Graduate Objectives or Program Emphases*: To provide students with a broad-based understanding of the role and operations of the mass media in contemporary society. Law, criticism, media effects, audience research, media management, and policy formulation are emphasized; *Bachelor's Degree Majors*: 90; *Master's Degree Majors*: 20; *Other Degree Majors*: 5; *Full-Time Faculty*: 10; *Part-Time Faculty*: 9; *Full-Time Professional (non-clerical) Staff Members*: 1.

FACILITIES AND SERVICES
Practical experiences available through: Advertising Agency; Carrier Current Audio Distribution System; Campus Newspaper (Published Independently); Local Commercial Newspaper; Local Commercial Television Station; Desktop Publishing Facility; Photographic Darkrooms; Video Editing; Electronic Field Production (Video); Public Relations Agency; Video News and Data Processing; Video Production Laboratory or Television Studio.

University of Denver (Private)

Department of Speech Communication
Denver, Colorado 80208
Telephone: (303) 871-2385

Alton Barbour, Chair
William Zaranka, Dean, Division of Social Sciences

CURRICULUM AND INSTRUCTION
Courses or Concentrations Available: Communication; Speech; *Undergraduate Objectives or Program Emphases*: Communication Theory; Interpersonal and Group Communication; Organizational Communication; Rhetoric; *Graduate Objectives or Program Emphases*: Communication Theory; Interpersonal and Group Communication; Organizational Communication; Rhetoric;

Bachelor's Degree Majors: 35; *Master's Degree Majors*: 15; *Doctoral Degree Majors Currently in Residence*: 45; *Additional Doctoral Degree Majors*: 30; *Full-Time Faculty*: 8; *Part-Time Faculty*: 17.

FACILITIES AND SERVICES
Practical experiences available through: Advertising Agency; Campus Newspaper (Published Independently); Local Commercial Newspaper; Local Commercial Television Station; Desktop Publishing Facility.

University of Northern Colorado (Public)

Department of Journalism and Mass Communication
Greeley, Colorado 80639
Telephone: (303) 351-2726

Mort Stern, Chair
Roger Kovar, Dean, College of Arts and Sciences

CURRICULUM AND INSTRUCTION
Courses or Concentrations Available: Advertising; Film or Cinema; Journalism or Mass Communication; Public Relations; Radio, Television, Broadcasting, or Telecommunications; *Program Coordinators*: Charles Ingold (Telecommunications); Wayne Melanson (Advertising); Donna Logan (Public Relations); David Anderson (Journalism--News-editorial); *Undergraduate Objectives or Program Emphases*: Introduction, impact on society, law and basic writing; news-editorial (Journalism); telecommunications (radio, television, film); advertising; public relations; *Graduate Objectives or Program Emphases*: Master of Arts with emphasis is one of the above areas; *Bachelor's Degree Majors*: 150; *Master's Degree Majors*: 30; *Full-Time Faculty*: 8; *Part-Time Faculty*: 2.

FACILITIES AND SERVICES
Practical experiences available through: Advertising Agency; Audio Recording Laboratory; Community Antenna (Cable) Television Origination; Carrier Current Audio Distribution System; Campus Newspaper (Published Independently); Local Commercial Newspaper; Local Commercial Television Station; Photographic Darkrooms; Video Editing;

Electronic Field Production (Video); FM Radio Station (Institutional); Public Relations Agency; Video News and Data Processing; Video Production Laboratory or Television Studio.

University of Northern Colorado (Public)

Department of Speech Communication Arts and Science
Greeley, Colorado 80639
Telephone: (303) 351-2045

Robert F. Ross, Chair
Roger Kovar, Dean, College of Arts and Sciences

CURRICULUM AND INSTRUCTION
Courses or Concentrations Available: Communication; Speech; Forensics; Speech Communication; *Undergraduate Objectives or Program Emphases*: Understanding of effective communication; understanding of research for context; preparation for career; preparation for Masters degree; *Graduate Objectives or Program Emphases*: Mastery of content for effective human communication; preparation for career or doctoral program; *Bachelor's Degree Majors*: 200; *Master's Degree Majors*: 30; *Full-Time Faculty*: 6; *Part-Time Faculty*: 6; *Full-Time Professional (non-clerical) Staff Members*: 1.

University of Southern Colorado

Department of Mass Communication
2200 Bonforte Boulevard
Pueblo, Colorado 81001-4901

Richard E. Pavlik, Administrator

University of Southern Colorado

Speech Communication and Theatre Department
2200 N. Bonforte Boulevard
Pueblo, Colorado 81001

John R. Sherman, Administrator

Western State College of Colorado (Public)

Program of Communication
Gunnison, Colorado 81231
Telephone: (303) 943-2025

James M. Gelwicks, Head
Frank Venturo, Chair, Communication, Theatre and Sociology

CURRICULUM AND INSTRUCTION
Courses or Concentrations Available: Communication; Journalism or Mass Communication; Radio, Television, Broadcasting, or Telecommunications; Speech; *Undergraduate Objectives or Program Emphases*: General overview with emphasis in either speech communication, mass media, organizational, or information specialist; *Bachelor's Degree Majors*: 100; *Full-Time Faculty*: 5; *Part-Time Faculty*: 1.

FACILITIES AND SERVICES
Practical experiences available through: Associated Press Wire Service Feed; Community Antenna (Cable) Television Origination; Campus Newspaper (Published Independently); Local Commercial Newspaper; Desktop Publishing Facility; Photographic Darkrooms; Video Editing; FM Radio Station (Institutional); Video Production Laboratory or Television Studio.

CONNECTICUT

Central Connecticut State University (Public)

Department of Communication
1615 Stanley Street
New Britain, Connecticut 06050
Telephone: (203) 827-7492

Sarah S. King, Chair
George Clarke, Dean

CURRICULUM AND INSTRUCTION
*Courses or Concentrations
Available*: Communication; Information Science; Journalism or Mass Communication; Public Relations; Radio, Television, Broadcasting, or Telecommunications; *Program Coordinators*: Ross Baiera (English); Clifford L. Pelletier (Computer Science); *Undergraduate Objectives or Program Emphases*: To provide students with communication competencies sufficient for them to act as leaders in modern society; *Graduate Objectives or Program Emphases*: To give professional training useful in the business world as well as for those wishing to pursue doctoral programs in Communication or Business; *Bachelor's Degree Majors*: 472; *Other Degree Majors*: 23; *Full-Time Faculty*: 10; *Part-Time Faculty*: 13; *Full-Time Professional (non-clerical) Staff Members*: 1.

FACILITIES AND SERVICES
Practical experiences available through: Advertising Agency; AM Radio Station (Institutional); Audio Recording Laboratory; Community Antenna (Cable) Television Origination; Campus Newspaper (Published Independently); Local Commercial Television Station; Desktop Publishing Facility; Video Editing; Electronic Field Production (Video); FM Radio Station (Institutional); Public Relations Agency; Video Production Laboratory or Television Studio.

Eastern Connecticut State University (Public)

Department of Communication
83 Windham Street
Willimantic, Connecticut 06226
Telephone: (203) 456-5368

Charles A. Herrick, Chair
Kelvie Comer, Dean, School of Professional Studies

CURRICULUM AND INSTRUCTION
*Courses or Concentrations
Available*: Communication; Journalism or Mass Communication; Public Relations; Radio, Television, Broadcasting, or Telecommunications; Speech; Photography; *Undergraduate Objectives or Program Emphases*: To prepare students for leadership in audio, video, and related communication oriented enterprises; *Degree Majors*: 50; *Full-Time Faculty*: 6.

FACILITIES AND SERVICES
Practical experiences available through: Advertising Agency; Associated Press Wire Service Feed; Audio Recording Laboratory; Community Antenna (Cable) Television Origination; Closed Circuit Television Facility; Campus Newspaper (Published Independently); Local Commercial Newspaper; Local Commercial Television Station; Desktop Publishing Facility; Photographic Darkrooms; Video Editing; Electronic Field Production (Video); FM Radio Station (Institutional); Public Relations Agency.

Mohegan Community College (Public)

Department of Languages and Arts
Mahan Drive
Norwich, Connecticut 06360
Telephone: (203) 889-1413

Linda M. Crootof, Head
James Coleman, Chair

CURRICULUM AND INSTRUCTION
Courses or Concentrations

Available: Advertising; Journalism or Mass Communication; English; Desktop publishing; *Undergraduate Objectives or Program Emphases*: To prepare students to work in the print media; *Degree Majors*: 3; *Full-Time Faculty*: 8; *Part-Time Faculty*: 36.

FACILITIES AND SERVICES
Practical experiences available through: Local Commercial Newspaper; Desktop Publishing Facility; Photographic Darkrooms; Institutional Newspaper; Video News and Data Processing.

Quinnipiac College (Private)

Department of Communications
Hamden, Connecticut 06518-0569
Telephone: (203) 288-5251

Raymond Foery, Chair

CURRICULUM AND INSTRUCTION
Courses or Concentrations
Available: Communication; Film or Cinema; Journalism or Mass Communication; Radio, Television, Broadcasting, or Telecommunications; Speech; *Undergraduate Objectives or Program Emphases*: General education in media studies within the tradition of Liberal Arts.; *Bachelor's Degree Majors*: 75; *Full-Time Faculty*: 5; *Part-Time Faculty*: 4; *Full-Time Professional (non-clerical) Staff Members*: 1.

FACILITIES AND SERVICES
Practical experiences available through: AM Radio Station (Institutional); Audio Recording Laboratory; Community Antenna (Cable) Television Origination; Campus Newspaper (Published Independently); Desktop Publishing Facility; Photographic Darkrooms; Video Editing; Electronic Field Production (Video); Film or Cinema Laboratory; FM Radio Station (Institutional); Video Production Laboratory or Television Studio.

Sacred Heart University (Private)

Communication Studies
5151 Park Avenue
Fairfield, Connecticut 06432
Telephone: (203) 371-7810

Angela DiPace Fritz, Chair

CURRICULUM AND INSTRUCTION
Courses or Concentrations
Available: Communication; Film or Cinema; Journalism or Mass Communication; Public Relations; Radio, Television, Broadcasting, or Telecommunications; Speech; Photography; Video Production; *Undergraduate Objectives or Program Emphases*: English, modern foreign languages, media studies; *Bachelor's Degree Majors*: 200; *Full-Time Faculty*: 16; *Part-Time Faculty*: 50; *Full-Time Professional (non-clerical) Staff Members*: 1.

FACILITIES AND SERVICES
Practical experiences available through: Advertising Agency; AM Radio Station (Institutional); Audio Recording Laboratory; Campus Newspaper (Published Independently); Local Commercial Newspaper; Photographic Darkrooms; Video Editing; Film or Cinema Laboratory; FM Radio Station (Institutional).

Southern Connecticut State University (Public)

Department of Communication
501 Crescent Street
New Haven, Connecticut 06515

B. P. McCabe, Administrator

Southern Connecticut State University (Public)

Department of Journalism
501 Crescent Street
New Haven, Connecticut 06515
Telephone: (203) 397-4311

Robin M. Glassman, Chair
J. Philip Smith, Dean, School of Arts and Sciences

CURRICULUM AND INSTRUCTION
Courses or Concentrations
Available: Journalism or Mass Communication; Public Relations; Radio, Television, Broadcasting, or Telecommunications; *Program Coordinators*: Jerry Dunklee (Broadcasting); *Undergraduate Objectives or Program Emphases*: Newswriting and reporting; media studies; *Bachelor's Degree Majors*: 10; *Other Degree Majors*: 40; *Full-Time Faculty*: 4;

Part-Time Faculty: 1; *Full-Time Professional (non-clerical) Staff Members*: 1.

FACILITIES AND SERVICES
Practical experiences available through: Advertising Agency; AM Radio Station (Institutional); Associated Press Wire Service Feed; Audio Recording Laboratory; Community Antenna (Cable) Television Origination; Campus Newspaper (Published Independently); Local Commercial Newspaper; Local Commercial Television Station; Desktop Publishing Facility; Photographic Darkrooms; Video Editing; Electronic Field Production (Video); Public Relations Agency.

University of Bridgeport (Private)

Department of Mass Communication
Bridgeport, Connecticut 06601
Telephone: (203) 576-4292

Jerry L. Allen, Chair
Robert Regan, Administrator

CURRICULUM AND INSTRUCTION
Courses or Concentrations Available: Advertising; Communication; Journalism or Mass Communication; Public Relations; Radio, Television, Broadcasting, or Telecommunications; *Undergraduate Objectives or Program Emphases*: Communication, advertising, public relations, journalism, radio and television; *Bachelor's Degree Majors*: 87; *Full-Time Faculty*: 7; *Part-Time Faculty*: 8.

FACILITIES AND SERVICES
Practical experiences available through: AM Radio Station (Institutional); Community Antenna (Cable) Television Origination; Campus Newspaper (Published Independently); Local Commercial Newspaper; Desktop Publishing Facility; Photographic Darkrooms; FM Radio Station (Institutional); Institutional Newspaper.

University of Connecticut (Public)

Department of Journalism
337 Mansfield Road
Storrs, Connecticut 06269-1129
Telephone: (203) 486-4221

Maureen E. Croteau, Head
Frank Vasington, Dean

CURRICULUM AND INSTRUCTION
Courses or Concentrations Available: Journalism or Mass Communication; *Undergraduate Objectives or Program Emphases*: Professional education for print and broadcast reporters and editors, within a strong liberal arts context; *Bachelor's Degree Majors*: 70; *Full-Time Faculty*: 4; *Part-Time Faculty*: 12.

FACILITIES AND SERVICES
Practical experiences available through: Associated Press Wire Service Feed; Campus Newspaper (Published Independently); Local Commercial Newspaper; Local Commercial Television Station; Desktop Publishing Facility; FM Radio Station (Institutional); ITFS Distribution System; Institutional Newspaper; Video News and Data Processing.

University of Hartford

Department of Communication
200 Bloomfield Avenue
West Hartford, Connecticut 06117

Donald Ellis, Administrator

Western Connecticut State University (Public)

Department of Communication and Theatre Arts
181 White Street
Danbury, Connecticut 06810
Telephone: (203) 797-4383

Connie Hellmann, Chair
Carol Hawices, Administrator

CURRICULUM AND INSTRUCTION
Courses or Concentrations Available: Communication; Film or Cinema; Journalism or Mass Communication; Radio,

Television, Broadcasting, or Telecommunications; Speech; Human Relations; Communication Disorders; Theatre Arts; *Program Coordinators*: Hugh McCarney (Media Arts); Richard Reimold (Theatre Arts); *Undergraduate Objectives or Program Emphases*: To provide students with a broad based understanding of communication processes, and specific understanding and experience in a particular area of communication; *Bachelor's Degree Majors*: 318; *Full-Time Faculty*: 11; *Part-Time Faculty*: 18.

FACILITIES AND SERVICES
Practical experiences available through: Associated Press Wire Service Feed; Community Antenna (Cable) Television Origination; Campus Newspaper (Published Independently); Local Commercial Newspaper; Video Editing; Electronic Field Production (Video); FM Radio Station (Institutional); Institutional Magazine; Institutional Newspaper; Video Production Laboratory or Television Studio.

Western Connecticut State University (Public)

Journalism Program
English Department
181 White Street
Danbury, Connecticut 06810
Telephone: (203) 797-4365

John Briggs, Head
Edward Hagan, Chair, English Department

CURRICULUM AND INSTRUCTION
Courses or Concentrations Available: Advertising; Journalism or Mass Communication; Public Relations; *Undergraduate Objectives or Program Emphases*: Journalism minor is part of English Department Writing option and hence is focused on training writing, practical journalists; *Bachelor's Degree Majors*: 20; *Full-Time Faculty*: 1; *Part-Time Faculty*: 1.

FACILITIES AND SERVICES
Practical experiences available through: Associated Press Wire Service Feed; Campus Newspaper (Published Independently); Local Commercial Newspaper; Desktop Publishing Facility; Photographic Darkrooms; Institutional Magazine; Institutional Newspaper.

DELAWARE

University of Delaware (Public)

Department of Communication
250 Newark Hall
Newark, Delaware 19716
Telephone: (302) 451-8041

John A. Courtright, Chair
Helen Gouldner, Dean, College of Arts and Sciences

CURRICULUM AND INSTRUCTION
Courses or Concentrations
Available: Communication; Journalism or Mass Communication; Public Relations; Radio, Television, Broadcasting, or Telecommunications; Speech; *Undergraduate Objectives or Program Emphases*: Social-Behaviorial Science approach to study of human communication, emphasizing critical thinking, reading, and writing which is consistent with a broadly based liberal arts education; *Graduate Objectives or Program Emphases*: Prepare MA students to become critical consumers of the professional, research-oriented literature in the discipline of communication; *Bachelor's Degree Majors*: 300; *Master's Degree Majors*: 35; *Full-Time Faculty*: 12; *Part-Time Faculty*: 12.

FACILITIES AND SERVICES
Practical experiences available through: AM Radio Station (Institutional); Associated Press Wire Service Feed; Closed Circuit Television Facility; Campus Newspaper (Published Independently); Desktop Publishing Facility; Video Editing; Electronic Field Production (Video); Public Relations Agency; Video Production Laboratory or Television Studio.

University of Delaware (Public)

Journalism Program
Newark, Delaware 19716

Edward A. Nickerson, Administrator

Wesley College (Private)

Department of Speech Communication
120 North State Street
Dover, Delaware 19901
Telephone: (302) 736-2366

Samuel R. Johnson, Chair

CURRICULUM AND INSTRUCTION
Courses or Concentrations
Available: Communication; Journalism or Mass Communication; Public Relations; Radio, Television, Broadcasting, or Telecommunications; Speech; *Program Coordinator*: Michael Nielsen; *Undergraduate Objectives or Program Emphases*: Generalist program; *Associate's Degree Majors*: 3; *Bachelor's Degree Majors*: 72; *Full-Time Faculty*: 2; *Part-Time Faculty*: 7.

FACILITIES AND SERVICES
Practical experiences available through: Advertising Agency; Audio Recording Laboratory; Carrier Current Audio Distribution System; Closed Circuit Television Facility; Campus Newspaper (Published Independently); Local Commercial Newspaper; Local Commercial Television Station; Desktop Publishing Facility; Photographic Darkrooms; Video Editing; Electronic Field Production (Video); Institutional Newspaper; Public Relations Agency; Video Production Laboratory or Television Studio.

American University

School of Communication
4400 Massachusetts and Nebraska Avenues, Northwest
Washington, District of Columbia 20016

John C. Doolittle, Administrator

Catholic University of America

Radio Station WCUA
Box 184 Cardinal Station CUA
Washington, District of Columbia 20064

Christopher Monetta, Administrator

Gallaudet University (Public)

Department of Television-Film and Photography
800 Florida Avenue NE
Washington, District of Columbia 20002
Telephone: (202) 651-5115

Marin Pearson Allen, Chair
Njeri Nuru, Dean, School of Communication

CURRICULUM AND INSTRUCTION
Courses or Concentrations Available: Film or Cinema; Television, Broadcasting, or Telecommunications; *Undergraduate Objectives or Program Emphases*: To train deaf and hard of hearing undergraduate students inside a liberal arts framework to produce professional television film and photographic products with a firm theoretical base; *Bachelor's Degree Majors*: 25; *Full-Time Faculty*: 3; *Part-Time Faculty*: 2; *Full-Time Professional (non-clerical) Staff Members*: 25.

FACILITIES AND SERVICES
Practical experiences available through: Advertising Agency; Audio Recording Laboratory; Community Antenna (Cable) Television Origination; Closed Circuit Television Facility; Campus Newspaper (Published Independently); Local Commercial Newspaper; Local Commercial Television Station; Desktop Publishing Facility; Photographic Darkrooms; Video Editing; Electronic File Production; ITFS Distribution System; Video Production Laboratory or Television Studio.

Gallaudet University (Public)

Department of Communication Arts
800 Florida Avenue NE
Washington, District of Columbia 20002
Telephone: (202) 651-5420

Paul Siegel, Chair
Njeri Nuru, Dean, School of Communication

CURRICULUM AND INSTRUCTION
Courses or Concentrations Available: Communication; Journalism or Mass Communication; Speech; *Undergraduate Objectives or Program Emphases*: Prepare students with a broad base of knowledge of communication in various contexts, offering classes in interpersonal, group, organizational and mass communication as well as persuasion, non-verbal, family, humor, etc.; *Bachelor's Degree Majors*: 25; *Full-Time Faculty*: 7; *Part-Time Faculty*: 2.

FACILITIES AND SERVICES
Practical experiences available through: Closed Circuit Television Facility; Campus Newspaper (Published Independently).

George Washington University (Private)

Department of Communication
Washington, District of Columbia 20052
Telephone: (202) 994-6350

Christopher H. Sterling, Acting Chair
Robert Kenny, Dean

CURRICULUM AND INSTRUCTION
Courses or Concentrations

Available: Communication; Film or Cinema; Radio, Television, Broadcasting, or Telecommunications; Speech; *Undergraduate Objectives or Program Emphases*: Broad Liberal Arts context for electronic media; *Bachelor's Degree Majors*: 120; *Full-Time Faculty*: 9; *Part-Time Faculty*: 6; *Full-Time Professional (non-clerical) Staff Members*: 6.

FACILITIES AND SERVICES
Practical experiences available through: Audio Recording Laboratory; Community Antenna (Cable) Television Origination; Carrier Current Audio Distribution System; Closed Circuit Television Facility; Campus Newspaper (Published Independently); Local Commercial Television Station; Electronic Field Production (Video); ITFS Distribution System; Video Production Laboratory or Television Studio.

George Washington University (Private)

Department of Journalism
Washington, District of Columbia 20052
Telephone: (202) 994-6225

Robert C. Willson, Chair
Robert W. Kenny, Dean, Columbia College of Arts and Sciences

CURRICULUM AND INSTRUCTION
Courses or Concentrations
Available: Journalism or Mass Communication; Public Relations; Radio, Television, Broadcasting, or Telecommunications; *Undergraduate Objectives or Program Emphases*: News-editorial, primarily print; *Bachelor's Degree Majors*: 62; *Full-Time Faculty*: 3; *Part-Time Faculty*: 14.

FACILITIES AND SERVICES
Practical experiences available through: Associated Press Wire Service Feed; Carrier Current Audio Distribution System; Closed Circuit Television Facility; Campus Newspaper (Published Independently); Local Commercial Newspaper; Local Commercial Television Station; Photographic Darkrooms.

Georgetown University

Department of Fine Arts
37th and O Streets, NW
Washington, District of Columbia 20057

Alison Hilton, Administrator

Howard University (Private)

School of Communications
2400 6th Street, NW
Washington, District of Columbia 20059
Telephone: (202) 636-7690

Orlando L. Taylor, Dean

CURRICULUM AND INSTRUCTION
Courses or Concentrations
Available: Communication; Film or Cinema; Journalism or Mass Communication; Public Relations; Radio, Television, Broadcasting, or Telecommunications; Speech; Communication Disorders; *Program Coordinators*: Lawrence Kaggwa (Journalism [Print and Broadcast], Public Relations); Bishetta Merritt (Radio, Television, Film); Noma Anderson (Communication Disorders); Lyndrey Niles (Speech, Mass Communication); *Undergraduate Objectives or Program Emphases*: Preprofessional preparation in non media fields; professional preparation in media fields; *Graduate Objectives or Program Emphases*: Professional film preparation; research; *Bachelor's Degree Majors*: 400; *Master's Degree Majors*: 90; *MFA Degree Majors*: 25; *Doctoral Degree Majors Currently in Residence*: 50; *Additional Doctoral Degree Majors*: 10; *Full-Time Faculty*: 48; *Part-Time Faculty*: 20; *Full-Time Professional (non-clerical) Staff Members*: 23.

FACILITIES AND SERVICES
Practical experiences available through: Associated Press Wire Service Feed; Audio Recording Laboratory; Carrier Current Audio Distribution System; Campus Newspaper (Published Independently); Local Commercial Newspaper; Local Commercial Television Station; Desktop Publishing Facility; Photographic Darkrooms; Video Editing; Electronic Field Production (Video); Television Broadcast Station (Institutional); Film or Cinema Laboratory; FM Radio Station (Institutional); Institutional Newspaper; New York Times Service Feed; Public Relations Agency; Reuters News Agency;

Satellite Uplink Facility (Ku Band Transmitter); United Press International Feed; Video News and Data Processing; Video Production Laboratory or Television Studio.

Howard University (Private)

Department of Journalism
525 Bryant Street, NW
Washington, District of Columbia 20059
Telephone: (202) 636-7855

Lawrence N. Kaggwa, Chair
Orlando L. Taylor, Dean

CURRICULUM AND INSTRUCTION
Courses or Concentrations
Available: Advertising; Journalism or Mass Communication; Public Relations; *Program Coordinators*: Lee Thornton (Broadcast Journalism); *Undergraduate Objectives or Program Emphases*: Print Journalism Sequence; Broadcast Journalism Sequence; Advertising Sequence; Public Relations Sequence; Editing and Management Sequence; *Bachelor's Degree Majors*: 350; *Full-Time Faculty*: 9; *Part-Time Faculty*: 6; *Full-Time Professional (non-clerical) Staff Members*: 4.

FACILITIES AND SERVICES
Practical experiences available through: Audio Recording Laboratory; Carrier Current Audio Distribution System; Campus Newspaper (Published Independently); Local Commercial Newspaper; Local Commercial Television Station; Desktop Publishing Facility; Photographic Darkrooms; Video Editing; Electronic Field Production (Video); Television Broadcast Station (Institutional); Film or Cinema Laboratory; FM Radio Station (Institutional); Institutional Newspaper; Public Relations Agency; United Press International Feed; Video News and Data Processing.

Mount Vernon College

Department of Communication
2100 Foxhall Road, NW
Washington, District of Columbia 20007

Jean Folkerts, Administrator

University of the District of Columbia

Department of Mass Media and Performing Arts
4200 Connecticut Avenue, NW
Washington, District of Columbia 20008

Joseph Gathings, Administrator

Barry University (Private)

Department of Communication
11300 NE 111 Street
Miami Shores, Florida 33161
Telephone: (305) 899-3456

Robert T. Jones, Chair
Shirley Paolini, Dean, Arts and Sciences

CURRICULUM AND INSTRUCTION
Courses or Concentrations
Available: Communication; Film or Cinema;
Journalism or Mass Communication; Public
Relations; Radio, Television, Broadcasting,
or Telecommunications; Speech;
Telecommunication (Voice and Data);
Bachelor's Degree Majors: 60; *Master's
Degree Majors*: 40; *Other Degree Majors*: 20;
Full-Time Faculty: 7; *Part-Time Faculty*: 3;
*Full-Time Professional (non-clerical) Staff
Members*: 1.

FACILITIES AND SERVICES
*Practical experiences available
through*: Advertising Agency; Audio
Recording Laboratory; Community Antenna
(Cable) Television Origination; Carrier
Current Audio Distribution System; Closed
Circuit Television Facility; Campus
Newspaper (Published Independently);
Local Commercial Newspaper; Local
Commercial Television Station; Desktop
Publishing Facility; Photographic
Darkrooms; Video Editing; Electronic Field
Production (Video); ITFS Distribution
System; Institutional Magazine; Institutional
Newspaper; Public Relations Agency;
Satellite Uplink Facility (C Band
Transmitter); Video Production Laboratory
or Television Studio.

Bethune-Cookman College

Division of Humanities
640 Second Avenue
Daytona Beach, Florida 32015

S. Louise Rosemond, Administrator

Broward Community College - North

Division of Speech
Pompano Beach, Florida 33066

Central Florida Community College (Public)

Division of Communication
P.O. Box 1388
Ocala, Florida 32678
**Telephone: (904) 237-2111 Extension or
Alternate: 235**

Orlando J. Moreno, Chair
Ike Williams, Vice President of Instruction

CURRICULUM AND INSTRUCTION
Courses or Concentrations
Available: Advertising; Communication; Film
or Cinema; Journalism or Mass
Communication; Public Relations; Speech;
*Undergraduate Objectives or Program
Emphases*: Introductory and/or survey
courses in all areas mentioned; *Full-Time
Faculty*: 17; *Part-Time Faculty*: 15.

FACILITIES AND SERVICES
*Practical experiences available
through*: Associated Press Feed; Closed
Circuit Television Facility; Local
Commercial Newspaper; Desktop Publishing
Facility; Photographic Darkrooms;
Institutional Newspaper; New York Times
Service Feed; Satellite Uplink Facility (C
Band Transmitter); United Press
International Feed.

Edison Community College (Public)

Division of Humanities
8099 College Parkway, S.W.
Fort Myers, Florida 33906-6210
Telephone: (813) 489-9300

Vern Denning, Dean
**Dorothy Lord, Vice President, Academic
Affairs**

CURRICULUM AND INSTRUCTION
Courses or Concentrations Available: Journalism or Mass Communication; Radio, Television, Broadcasting, or Telecommunications; Speech; *Associate's Degree Majors*: 10; *Full-Time Faculty*: 1; *Part-Time Faculty*: 2.

FACILITIES AND SERVICES
Practical experiences available through: Closed Circuit Television Facility; Local Commercial Television Station; Photographic Darkrooms; Video Editing; Electronic Field Production (Video); Institutional Newspaper; Video Production Laboratory or Television Studio.

Edward Waters College (Private)

Division of Arts and Sciences
1658 Kings Road
Jacksonville, Florida 32208
Telephone: (904) 366-2502

Dale Shaw, Chair

CURRICULUM AND INSTRUCTION
Courses or Concentrations Available: Journalism or Mass Communication; Speech; *Undergraduate Objectives or Program Emphases*: To provide students with training to find employment in print and broadcast media; *Bachelor's Degree Majors*: 15; *Full-Time Faculty*: 10; *Part-Time Faculty*: 2.

FACILITIES AND SERVICES
Practical experiences available through: Audio Recording Laboratory; Carrier Current Audio Distribution System; Desktop Publishing Facility; Photographic Darkrooms; Electronic Field Production (Video); Institutional Newspaper; Satellite Uplink Facility (Ku Band Transmitter)

Florida Atlantic University (Public)

Department of Communication
P.O. Box 3091
Boca Raton, Florida 33431
Telephone: (407) 367-3850

Dorothy Guinn, Chair
Sandra Norton, Chief Administrator

CURRICULUM AND INSTRUCTION
Courses or Concentrations Available: Communication; Film or Cinema; Journalism or Mass Communication; Radio, Television, Broadcasting, or Telecommunications; Speech; Cultural Studies; Gender Studies; Rhetoric; *Undergraduate Objectives or Program Emphases*: Broad liberal arts education plus opportunities for professional specialization in journalism, television and other fields; *Graduate Objectives or Program Emphases*: Broad liberal arts program plus flexible curriculum for those with professional goals; *Bachelor's Degree Majors*: 281; *Master's Degree Majors*: 16; *Full-Time Faculty*: 9; *Part-Time Faculty*: 12.

FACILITIES AND SERVICES
Practical experiences available through: Community Antenna (Cable) Television Origination; Campus Newspaper (Published Independently); Local Commercial Newspaper; Local Commercial Television Station; Video Editing; Electronic Field Production (Video); Public Relations Agency.

Florida Community College (Public)

101 West State Street
Jacksonville, Florida 32202
Telephone: (904) 633-8262

Kevin L. Kirk, Dean
Carol Miner, Provost

CURRICULUM AND INSTRUCTION
Courses or Concentrations Available: Communication; Film or Cinema; Journalism or Mass Communication; Radio, Television, Broadcasting, or Telecommunications; Speech; *Program Coordinators*: Ron Morriseau (Radio-Television); *Undergraduate Objectives or Program Emphases*: Radio and Television Broadcasting; *Full-Time Faculty*: 1; *Full-Time Professional (non-clerical) Staff Members*: 4.

FACILITIES AND SERVICES
Practical experiences available through: Community Antenna (Cable) Television Origination; Closed Circuit Television Facility; Campus Newspaper (Published Independently); Local Commercial Newspaper; Local Commercial Television Station; Desktop Publishing

Facility; Video Editing; Electronic Field Production (Video); Film or Cinema Laboratory; ITFS Distribution System; Institutional Newspaper; Video Production Laboratory or Television Studio.

Florida International University (Public)

School of Journalism and Mass Communication
North Miami, Florida 33181
Telephone: (305) 940-5625

J. Arthur Heise, Director
James A. Mau, Dean, College of Arts and Sciences

CURRICULUM AND INSTRUCTION
Courses or Concentrations
Available: Advertising; Journalism or Mass Communication; Public Relations; Radio, Television, Broadcasting, or Telecommunications; *Undergraduate Objectives or Program Emphases*: Provide a strong liberal arts background and a professionally oriented communication degree program; *Graduate Objectives or Program Emphases*: Provide a strong professionally oriented degree program; *Master's Degree Majors*: 26; *Full-Time Faculty*: 15; *Part-Time Faculty*: 10; *Full-Time Professional (non-clerical) Staff Members*: 2.

FACILITIES AND SERVICES
Practical experiences available through: AM Radio Station (Institutional); Campus Newspaper (Published Independently); Local Commercial Newspaper; Local Commercial Television Station; Desktop Publishing Facility; Photographic Darkrooms; Video Editing; Electronic Field Production (Video); Public Relations Agency; Video News and Data Processing; Video Production Laboratory or Television Studio.

Florida Southern College

Communications Department
111 Lake Hollingsworth Drive
Lakeland, Florida 33801-5698

John P. Obrecht, Administrator

Florida State University (Public)

Department of Communication
413 Diffenbaugh
Tallahassee, Florida 32306
Telephone: (904) 644-5034

Edward Forrest, Chair
Theodore Clevenger, Dean

CURRICULUM AND INSTRUCTION
Courses or Concentrations
Available: Advertising; Communication; Film or Cinema; Information Science; Journalism or Mass Communication; Public Relations; Radio, Television, Broadcasting, or Telecommunications; Speech; Political Communication; Organizational Communication; Marketing Communication; *Undergraduate Objectives or Program Emphases*: Applied professional communication course sequences; *Graduate Objectives or Program Emphases*: The masters level professional programs in Marketing Communication and New Technologies. Both Graduate Programs: Communication Theory and Research; *Bachelor's Degree Majors*: 500; *Master's Degree Majors*: 60; *Doctoral Degree Majors Currently in Residence*: 25; *Additional Doctoral Degree Majors*: 10; *Full-Time Faculty*: 20; *Part-Time Faculty*: 25; *Full-Time Professional (non-clerical) Staff Members*: 6.

FACILITIES AND SERVICES
Practical experiences available through: Advertising Agency; Audio Recording Laboratory; Community Antenna (Cable) Television Origination; Local Commercial Newspaper; Local Commercial Television Station; Desktop Publishing Facility; Video Editing; Electronic Field Production (Video); Television Broadcast Station (Institutional); Film or Cinema Laboratory; FM Radio Station (Institutional); Public Relations Agency; Video Production Laboratory or Television Studio.

Gulf Coast Community College (Public)

Department of Radio/Television Broadcasting
5230 West Highway 98
Panama City, Florida 32401
Telephone: (904) 769-5241

Lester Spencer, Station Manager
Robert Jones, Administrator

CURRICULUM AND INSTRUCTION
Courses or Concentrations
Available: Advertising; Communication; Journalism or Mass Communication; Speech; *Program Coordinators*: Janice Lucas (Journalism); Ann Higgins (Language Arts); Joyce Buttermore (Speech); *Undergraduate Objectives or Program Emphases*: Freshman, Sophomore level instruction; *Associate's Degree Majors*: 15; *Other Degree Majors*: 10; *Full-Time Faculty*: 4; *Part-Time Faculty*: 5; *Full-Time Professional (non-clerical) Staff Members*: 4.

FACILITIES AND SERVICES
Practical experiences available through: AM Radio Station (Institutional); Associated Press Wire Service Feed; Audio Recording Laboratory; Closed Circuit Television Facility; Campus Newspaper (Published Independently); Photographic Darkrooms; Video Editing; FM Radio Station (Institutional); ITFS Distribution System; United Press International Feed; Video Production Laboratory or Television Studio.

Jacksonville University (Private)

Program of Mass Communication
2800 University Boulevard North
Jacksonville, Florida 32211
Telephone: (904) 744-3950 Extension or Alternate: 3480

Dennis K. Stouse, Coordinator

CURRICULUM AND INSTRUCTION
Courses or Concentrations
Available: Advertising; Communication; Film or Cinema; Journalism or Mass Communication; Public Relations; Radio, Television, Broadcasting, or Telecommunications; Speech; *Undergraduate Objectives or Program Emphases*: Prepare students for careers in mass media; prepare students for graduate school. Offers core of skills-oriented communication courses based on firm foundation in Arts and Sciences. There are three sequences: Newspaper and Magazine; Radio, Television, Film; Public Relations and Advertising; *Bachelor's Degree Majors*: 175; *Full-Time Faculty*: 3; *Part-Time Faculty*: 3.

FACILITIES AND SERVICES
Practical experiences available through: Advertising Agency; AM Radio Station (Institutional); Audio Recording Laboratory; Campus Newspaper (Published Independently); Local Commercial Newspaper; Local Commercial Television Station; Desktop Publishing Facility; Photographic Darkrooms; Institutional Magazine; Public Relations Agency.

Lake-Sumter Community College

Humanities Division
5900 South Highway 441
Leesburg, Florida 32788

Ken Tolliver, Administrator

Miami-Dade Community College

Department of Communication Arts
11011 Southwest 104th Street
Miami, Florida 33176
Telephone: (305) 347-2365

Edward A. Anderson, Chair
Alexandra Holloway, Associate Dean

CURRICULUM AND INSTRUCTION
Courses or Concentrations
Available: Communication; Journalism or Mass Communication; Radio, Television, Broadcasting, or Telecommunications; Speech; Drama; Dance; Philosophy; *Program Coordinator*: David Gravel (Broadcasting); *Associate's Degree Majors*: 40; *Full-Time Faculty*: 15; *Part-Time Faculty*: 8; *Full-Time Professional (non-clerical) Staff Members*: 2.

FACILITIES AND SERVICES
Practical experiences available through: Campus Newspaper (Published Independently); Institutional Newspaper; United Press International Feed.

North Florida Junior College (Public)

Department of Arts and Humanities
1000 Turner Davis Drive
Madison, Florida 32340
Telephone: (904) 973-2288

William F. Gardner, Chair
John MaGuire, Administrator

CURRICULUM AND INSTRUCTION
Courses or Concentrations
Available: Journalism or Mass
Communication; Speech; *Undergraduate*
Objectives or Program Emphases: Prepare
students for transfer to four year institutions;
Full-Time Faculty: 11; *Part-Time Faculty*: 9.

FACILITIES AND SERVICES
Practical experiences available
through: Institutional Newspaper.

Palm Beach Atlantic College (Private)

Department of Speech and Drama
P.O. Box 3353
West Palm Beach, Florida 33402-3353
Telephone: (407) 650-7603

H. Herbert Sennett, Chair
Michael Simoneawx, Chair, Fine Arts
Division

CURRICULUM AND INSTRUCTION
Courses or Concentrations
Available: Communication; Film or Cinema;
Radio, Television, Broadcasting, or
Telecommunications; Speech; Theatre Arts;
Undergraduate Objectives or Program
Emphases: To provide a broad-based
educational experience with both theoretical
and practical training in the communication
arts and sciences; *Bachelor's Degree*
Majors: 60; *Full-Time Faculty*: 2; *Part-Time*
Faculty: 4.

FACILITIES AND SERVICES
Practical experiences available
through: Advertising Agency; Community
Antenna (Cable) Television Origination;
Campus Newspaper (Published
Independently); Local Commercial
Newspaper; Local Commercial Television
Station; Photographic Darkrooms;
Television Broadcast Station (Institutional);
Public Relations Agency.

Palm Beach Atlantic College (Private)

Department of English
901 S. Flagler Drive
West Palm Beach, Florida 33402-3353
Telephone: (407) 650-7662

Jo M. Turk, Chair
L. Foster Harwell, Administrator

CURRICULUM AND INSTRUCTION
Courses or Concentrations
Available: Communication; Journalism or
Mass Communication; Writing, Literature,
Foreign Language; *Undergraduate Objectives*
or Program Emphases: 1) to provide
preprofessional study for graduate and
professional schooling, 2) to provide the
foundation for graduate study in English,
linguistics, and English/education, and 3) to
train the English major for teaching service
at the pre-college levels; *Bachelor's Degree*
Majors: 20; *Full-Time Faculty*: 5; *Part-Time*
Faculty: 5.

FACILITIES AND SERVICES
Practical experiences available
through: Institutional Magazine; Institutional
Newspaper.

Pensacola Junior College

Department of Broadcasting
1000 College Boulevard
Pensacola, Florida 32504

Donald E. Dorin, Administrator

Rollins College (Private)

Department of Organizational
Communication
Winter Park, Florida 32789
Telephone: (407) 646-2000

Greg H. Gardner, Chair
Joan Straumanis, Dean

CURRICULUM AND INSTRUCTION
Courses or Concentrations
Available: Communication; Public Relations;
Speech; *Bachelor's Degree Majors*: 159;
Full-Time Faculty: 5; *Part-Time Faculty*: 5.

FACILITIES AND SERVICES
Practical experiences available through: FM
Radio Station (Institutional).

St. Vincent De Paul Regional Seminary (Private)

Program of Homiletics
10701 South Military Trail
Boynton Beach, Florida 33436
Telephone: (407) 432-4424

John O'Leary, Lecturer
Joseph Cunningham, Rector

CURRICULUM AND INSTRUCTION
Courses or Concentrations
Available: Communication; Speech;
Preaching; *Graduate Objectives or Program*
Emphases: To preach effectively in the
liturgy; *Master's Degree Majors*: 20; *Other*
Degree Majors: 30; *Full-Time Faculty*: 1;
Part-Time Faculty: 1.

FACILITIES AND SERVICES
Practical experiences available
through: Desktop Publishing Facility; Video
Production Laboratory or Television Studio.

Santa Fe Community College (Public)

Graphics Design Technology
3000 N.W. 83rd Street
Gainesville, Florida 32606
Telephone: (904) 395-5347

Elizabeth T. Grant, Director
Jim Humphries, Chief Administrator

CURRICULUM AND INSTRUCTION
Courses or Concentrations
Available: Advertising; Communication;
Speech; Commercial Design; Marketing;
Computer Graphics; Graphic Arts
Production; *Undergraduate Objectives or*
Program Emphases: The AS in Graphic
Design Technology trains students in skills
and theory to be graphic designers and
encompasses many facets of communications;
Degree Majors: 106; *Full-Time Faculty*: 1;
Part-Time Faculty: 7; *Full-Time Professional*
(non-clerical) Staff Members: 1.

FACILITIES AND SERVICES
Practical experiences available

through: Advertising Agency; Community
Antenna (Cable) Television Origination;
Closed Circuit Television Facility; Local
Commercial Newspaper; Local Commercial
Television Station; Desktop Publishing
Facility; Photographic Darkrooms; Video
Editing; Electronic Field Production
(Video); Television Broadcast Station
(Institutional); Public Relations Agency;
Satellite Uplink Facility; Advertising
Agencies.

Seminole Community College (Public)

Division of Arts and Sciences
100 Weldon Boulevard
Sanford, Florida 32773
Telephone: (407) 323-1450

Robert L. Levin, Dean
Keith Samuels, Administrator

CURRICULUM AND INSTRUCTION
Courses or Concentrations
Available: Communication; Film or Cinema;
Journalism or Mass Communication; Speech;
Undergraduate Objectives or Program
Emphases: Basic training and fundamentals;
Associate's Degree Majors: 25; *Full-Time*
Faculty: 60; *Part-Time Faculty*: 58;
Full-Time Professional (non-clerical) Staff
Members: 10.

FACILITIES AND SERVICES
Practical experiences available
through: Advertising Agency; Audio
Recording Laboratory; Local Commercial
Newspaper; Desktop Publishing Facility;
Photographic Darkrooms; Electronic Field
Production (Video); ITFS Distribution
System; Institutional Magazine; Satellite
Uplink Facility; Video News and Data
Processing.

Stetson University

Speech and Theatre Department
Box 8377
DeLand, Florida 32720

James C. Wright, Administrator

University of Central Florida (Public)

School of Communication
P.O. Box 25000
Orlando, Florida 32816
Telephone: (407) 275-2681

James W. Welke, Director
Stuart Lilie, Dean, Arts and Sciences

CURRICULUM AND INSTRUCTION
Courses or Concentrations Available: Advertising; Communication; Film or Cinema; Journalism or Mass Communication; Public Relations; Radio, Television, Broadcasting, or Telecommunications; Speech; *Program Coordinators*: Frederic Fedler (Journalism); Milan Meeske (Radio, Television); K. Phillip Taylor (Interpersonal, Organizational Communication); Charles Harpole (Film); *Graduate Objectives or Program Emphases*: Communication Theory and Research; *Bachelor's Degree Majors*: 964; *MFA Degree Majors*: 32; *Full-Time Faculty*: 22; *Part-Time Faculty*: 18; *Full-Time Professional (non-clerical) Staff Members*: 2.

FACILITIES AND SERVICES
Practical experiences available through: Advertising Agency; Associated Press Wire Service Feed; Audio Recording Laboratory; Community Antenna (Cable) Television Origination; Carrier Current Audio Distribution System; Closed Circuit Television Facility; Campus Newspaper (Published Independently); Local Commercial Newspaper; Local Commercial Television Station; Desktop Publishing Facility; Photographic Darkrooms; Video Editing; Electronic Field Production (Video); Film or Cinema Laboratory; FM Radio Station (Institutional); ITFS Distribution System; Public Relations Agency; Satellite Uplink Facility (C Band Transmitter); Video Production Laboratory or Television Studio.

University of Central Florida (Public)

Division of Film
Alfaya Road
Orlando, Florida 32816

Charles H. Harpole, Head
James Welke, Director

CURRICULUM AND INSTRUCTION
Courses or Concentrations Available: Film or Cinema; *Undergraduate Objectives or Program Emphases*: BA preparation in filmmaking and cinema history; *Bachelor's Degree Majors*: 30; *Full-Time Faculty*: 5; *Part-Time Faculty*: 4; *Full-Time Professional (non-clerical) Staff Members*: 2.

FACILITIES AND SERVICES
Practical experiences available through: Audio Recording Laboratory; Community Antenna (Cable) Television Origination; Campus Newspaper (Published Independently); Local Commercial Newspaper; Local Commercial Television Station; Desktop Publishing Facility; Photographic Darkrooms; Video Editing; Film or Cinema Laboratory; FM Radio Station (Institutional).

University of Florida (Public)

Department of Telecommunications
Wiemer Hall
Gainesville, Florida 32601
Telephone: (904) 392-0463

G. Paul Smeyak, Chair
Ralph Lowenstein, Dean

CURRICULUM AND INSTRUCTION
Courses or Concentrations Available: Film or Cinema; Radio, Television, Broadcasting, or Telecommunications; Broadcast Journalism; *Undergraduate Objectives or Program Emphases*: Professional education balanced with theory to provide communicators with areas of emphasis in: Broadcast News and Public Affairs; Production (film, television, industrial); and Operations (sales, research, management); *Graduate Objectives or Program Emphases*: A mass communication program with a theoretical and research emphasis; *Bachelor's Degree Majors*: 377; *Master's Degree Majors*: 7; *MFA Degree Majors*: 22; *Full-Time Faculty*: 13; *Part-Time Faculty*: 2.

FACILITIES AND SERVICES
Practical experiences available through: AM Radio Station (Institutional); Associated Press Wire Service Feed; Audio Recording Laboratory; Desktop Publishing Facility; Photographic Darkrooms; Video Editing; Electronic Field Production (Video); Television Broadcast Station (Institutional); Film or Cinema Laboratory; FM Radio Station (Institutional); Satellite Uplink Facility (Ku Band Transmitter); Video News and Data Processing; Video Production Laboratory or Television Studio.

University of Florida (Public)

Department of Journalism
Gainesville, Florida 32611
Telephone: (904) 392-0500

Jon A. Roosenraad, Chair
Ralph L. Lowenstein, Dean, College of Journalism and Communications

CURRICULUM AND INSTRUCTION
Courses or Concentrations Available: Journalism or Mass Communication; *Program Coordinators*: Joe Pisani (Advertising); Paul Smeyak (Broadcasting); Jack Detweiler (Public Relations); *Undergraduate Objectives or Program Emphases*: Professional education in print journalism (newspaper and magazine) in areas of reporting, editing, photos and graphics; *Bachelor's Degree Majors*: 340; *Full-Time Faculty*: 14; *Part-Time Faculty*: 14; *Full-Time Professional (non-clerical) Staff Members*: 2.

FACILITIES AND SERVICES
Practical experiences available through: Associated Press Wire Service Feed; Campus Newspaper (Published Independently); Local Commercial Newspaper; Desktop Publishing Facility; Photographic Darkrooms; Institutional Magazine; Satellite Uplink Facility (Ku Band Transmitter); United Press International Feed; Video News and Data Processing; Video Production Laboratory or Television Studio.

University of Florida (Public)

Department of Public Relations
College of Journalism and Communications
Gainesville, Florida 32611
Telephone: (904) 392-0466

John S. Detweiler, Chair
Ralph L. Lowenstein, Dean

CURRICULUM AND INSTRUCTION
Courses or Concentrations Available: Public Relations; *Undergraduate Objectives or Program Emphases*: Public relations, research, planning, writing, cases and campaigns, ethics; *Graduate Objectives or Program Emphases*: Management and research principles in public relations; relevant communications theory; *Bachelor's Degree Majors*: 260; *Master's Degree Majors*: 25; *Doctoral Degree Majors Currently in Residence*: 1; *Full-Time Faculty*: 8; *Part-Time Faculty*: 8.

FACILITIES AND SERVICES
Practical experiences available through: Community Antenna (Cable) Television Origination; Campus Newspaper (Published Independently); Desktop Publishing Facility; Photographic Darkrooms; Video Editing; Television Broadcast Station (Institutional); FM Radio Station (Institutional); Institutional Magazine; Public Relations Agency.

University of Florida (Public)

Division of Communication
335 Dauer Hall
Gainesville, Florida 32611
Telephone: (904) 392-2035

Rebecca J. Cline, Director
Kenneth J. Gerhardt, Chair, Department of Communication Proccesses and Disorders

CURRICULUM AND INSTRUCTION
Courses or Concentrations Available: Communication; Speech; *Undergraduate Objectives or Program Emphases*: Communication Studies; Interpersonal Communication; Health Communication; *Graduate Objectives or Program Emphases*: Communication Studies; Interpersonal Communication; Health Communication; *Bachelor's Degree Majors*: 100; *Master's Degree Majors*: 3; *Doctoral Degree Majors Currently in*

Residence: 7; *Full-Time Faculty*: 7; *Part-Time Faculty*: 7.

University of Miami (Private)

School of Communication
Box 248127
Coral Gables, Florida 33124
Telephone: (305) 284-2265

Edward J. Pfister, Dean

CURRICULUM AND INSTRUCTION
Courses or Concentrations Available: Advertising; Film or Cinema; Journalism or Mass Communication; Public Relations; Radio, Television, Broadcasting, or Telecommunications; Speech; *Program Coordinators*: Stanley Harrison (Advertising, Public Relations); Mitchell Shapiro (Broadcasting, Broadcast Journalism); Bruce Garrison (News-Editorial, Photography); Paul Lazarus (Motion Pictures); Thomas Steinfatt (Speech); *Undergraduate Objectives or Program Emphases*: To develop understanding and appreciation of communication theory, art, and science; to improve awareness of the pervasive role of communication in society; and to enhance communication skills; *Graduate Objectives or Program Emphases*: The School of Communication offers both academic and professional programs leading to the Master of Arts in communication studies, journalism, and film studies, and the Master of Fine Arts in motion pictures, with academic and professional perspectives; *BFA Degree Majors*: 30; *Master's Degree Majors*: 34; *MFA Degree Majors*: 7; *Other Degree Majors*: 932; *Full-Time Faculty*: 30; *Part-Time Faculty*: 15. One or more additional entries follow.

FACILITIES AND SERVICES
Practical experiences available through: Advertising Agency; Associated Press Wire Service Feed; Audio Recording Laboratory; Community Antenna (Cable) Television Origination; Closed Circuit Television Facility; Campus Newspaper (Published Independently); Local Commercial Newspaper; Local Commercial Television Station; Desktop Publishing Facility; Photographic Darkrooms; Video Editing; Electronic Field Production (Video); Film or Cinema Laboratory; FM Radio Station (Institutional); Institutional Newspaper; Public Relations Agency; Video News and Data Processing; Video Production Laboratory or Television Studio.

University of Miami (Private)

Program of Broadcasting and Broadcast Journalism
P. O. Box 248127
Coral Gables, Florida 33124
Telephone: (305) 284-2265

Mitchell E. Shapiro, Director
Edward Pfister, Dean

CURRICULUM AND INSTRUCTION
Courses or Concentrations Available: Journalism or Mass Communication; Radio, Television, Broadcasting, or Telecommunications; *Program Coordinators*: Stanley Harrison (Advertising, Public Relations); Bruce Garrison (News-Editorial, Photography); Paul Lazarus (Film); Tom Steinfatt (Speech); *Undergraduate Objectives or Program Emphases*: Combination of liberal arts and pre-professional; *Degree Majors*: 100; *Full-Time Faculty*: 7; *Part-Time Faculty*: 2; *Full-Time Professional (non-clerical) Staff Members*: 1.

FACILITIES AND SERVICES
Practical experiences available through: Advertising Agency; Audio Recording Laboratory; Community Antenna (Cable) Television Origination; Closed Circuit Television Facility; Campus Newspaper (Published Independently); Local Commercial Newspaper; Local Commercial Television Station; Photographic Darkrooms; Video Editing; Electronic Field Production (Video); Film or Cinem Laboratory; FM Radio Station (Institutional); Public Relations Agency; Video News and Data Processing; Video Production Laboratory or Television Studio.

University of North Florida (Public)

Department of Communication and Visual Arts
4567 St. Johns Bluff Road, S.
Jacksonville, Florida 32216
Telephone: (904) 646-2650

Shirley Staples Carter, Chair
Afesa Adams, Dean

CURRICULUM AND INSTRUCTION
Courses or Concentrations
Available: Advertising; Journalism or Mass Communication; Public Relations; Radio, Television, Broadcasting, or Telecommunications; Speech; Graphic Design; Photojournalism; *Undergraduate Objectives or Program Emphases*: The comprehensive, multi-faceted curriculum is designed to produce a visually and verbally sophisticated graduate with realistic expectations to compete in the job market or pursue graduate study; *Bachelor's Degree Majors*: 235; *BFA Degree Majors*: 57; *Full-Time Faculty*: 11; *Part-Time Faculty*: 5; *Full-Time Professional (non-clerical) Staff Members*: 2.

FACILITIES AND SERVICES
Practical experiences available through: Advertising Agency; Audio Recording Laboratory; Community Antenna (Cable) Television Origination; Closed Circuit Television Facility; Campus Newspaper (Published Independently); Local Commercial Newspaper; Local Commercial Television Station; Desktop Publishing Facility; Photographic Darkrooms; Video Editing; Electronic Field Production (Video); Public Relations Agency; Video Production Laboratory or Television Studio.

University of South Florida (Public)

Department of Mass Communication
Cooper Hall 107
Tampa, Florida 33620-5550
Telephone: (813) 974-2591

Donna L. Dickerson, Chair
William J. Heim, Dean, College of Arts and Letters

CURRICULUM AND INSTRUCTION
Courses or Concentrations
Available: Advertising; Film or Cinema; Journalism or Mass Communication; Public Relations; Radio, Television, Broadcasting, or Telecommunications; Visual Communications; *Undergraduate Objectives or Program Emphases*: Pre-professional education for students planning careers in mass communications; *Graduate Objectives or Program Emphases*: Research and theory of mass media systems; *Bachelor's Degree Majors*: 622; *Master's Degree Majors*: 35; *Full-Time Faculty*: 18; *Part-Time Faculty*: 10; *Full-Time Professional (non-clerical) Staff Members*: 3.

FACILITIES AND SERVICES
Practical experiences available through: Associated Press Wire Service Feed; Audio Recording Laboratory; Carrier Current Audio Distribution System; Closed Circuit Television Facility; Campus Newspaper (Published Independently); Local Commercial Newspaper; Local Commercial Television Station; Desktop Publishing Facility; Photographic Darkrooms; Video Editing; Electronic Field Production (Video); Television Broadcast Station (Institutional); Film or Cinema Laboratory; FM Radio Station (Institutional); ITFS Distribution System; Institutional Newspaper; Video Production Laboratory or Television Studio.

University of South Florida (Public)

Department of Communication
Cooper Hall Room 443, 4202 E. Fowler Avenue
Tampa, Florida 33620-5550
Telephone: (813) 974-2145

Arthur P. Bochner, Chair
William J. Heim, Acting Dean

CURRICULUM AND INSTRUCTION
Courses or Concentrations
Available: Communication; *Undergraduate Objectives or Program Emphases*: Rhetorical and communication studies; performance studies; *Graduate Objectives or Program Emphases*: Rhetorical and communication studies; performance studies; *Bachelor's Degree Majors*: 250; *Master's Degree Majors*: 15; *Full-Time Faculty*: 11; *Part-Time Faculty*: 16; *Full-Time Professional (non-clerical) Staff Members*: 1.

University of West Florida
(Public)

Department of Communication Arts
Building 76 Room 208
Pensacola, Florida 32514-5751
Telephone: (904) 474-2874

Churchill L. Roberts, Chair
John D. Fulton, Dean

CURRICULUM AND INSTRUCTION
*Courses or Concentrations
Available*: Advertising; Communication; Film
or Cinema; Journalism or Mass
Communication; Public Relations; Radio,
Television, Broadcasting, or
Telecommunications; Speech; *Undergraduate
Objectives or Program Emphases*: A
professionally oriented program which
combines a broad liberal arts foundation with
theory and practice in a variety of
communication specialties; *Graduate
Objectives or Program Emphases*: A
broad-based research oriented program
designed for communication practitioners
and students planning to pursue their
doctorates; *Bachelor's Degree Majors*: 260;
Master's Degree Majors: 30; *Full-Time
Faculty*: 9; *Part-Time Faculty*: 12; *Full-Time
Professional (non-clerical) Staff Members*: 3.

FACILITIES AND SERVICES
*Practical experiences available
through*: Advertising Agency; Audio
Recording Laboratory; Closed Circuit
Television Facility; Local Commercial
Newspaper; Local Commercial Television
Station; Desktop Publishing Facility;
Photographic Darkrooms; Video Editing;
Electronic Field Production (Video);
Television Broadcast Station (Institutional);
Film or Cinema Laboratory; FM Radio
Station (Institutional); Institutional
Newspaper; Public Relations Agency;
United Press International Feed; Video
News and Data Processing; Video
Production Laboratory or Television Studio.

Valencia Community College

Department of Communication
1800 South Kirkman Road
Orlando, Florida 32802

Warner Southern College
(Private)

Department of Communication Arts
Highway 27 South
Lake Wales, Florida 33853
Telephone: (813) 638-1426

Howard Othoson, Chair
Ronald Jack, Academic Dean

CURRICULUM AND INSTRUCTION
*Courses or Concentrations
Available*: Journalism or Mass
Communication; Radio, Television,
Broadcasting, or Telecommunications;
Speech; English; Photography; *Undergraduate
Objectives or Program Emphases*: Develop
job-entry level skills for journalism, radio
and television, instructional television, and
education (English, Speech, Media); develop
awareness of current legal, ethical, moral and
social issues; *Bachelor's Degree Majors*: 17;
Full-Time Faculty: 2; *Part-Time Faculty*: 4.

FACILITIES AND SERVICES
Practical experiences available through: Local
Commercial Newspaper; Desktop Publishing
Facility; Photographic Darkrooms; Video
Editing; Electronic Field Production
(Video); FM Radio Station (Institutional);
Institutional Magazine; Institutional
Newspaper.

Abraham Baldwin College (Public)

Division of Humanities
P.O. Box 20, ABAC Station
Tifton, Georgia 31793
Telephone: (912) 386-3250

Lew S. Akin, Chair

CURRICULUM AND INSTRUCTION
*Courses or Concentrations
Available*: Journalism or Mass
Communication; Radio, Television,
Broadcasting, or Telecommunications;
Speech; *Program Coordinator*: Helen L.
Strickland (Journalism); *Undergraduate
Objectives or Program Emphases*: College
panelled program to prepare for senior
college program; *Full-Time Faculty*: 2.

FACILITIES AND SERVICES
*Practical experiences available
through*: Closed Circuit Television Facility;
Campus Newspaper (Published
Independently); Local Commercial
Newspaper; Desktop Publishing Facility;
Photographic Darkrooms; FM Radio Station
(Institutional); Institutional Magazine.

Art Institute of Atlanta

Photography
3376 Peachtree Road, Northeast
Atlanta, Georgia 30326

Michael Lawsky, Administrator

Augusta College (Public)

Department of Languages and Literature
Augusta, Georgia 30910
Telephone: (404) 737-1500 Extension or
Alternate: 737-1400

Fred Wharton, Chair
Ronald Tallman, Dean

CURRICULUM AND INSTRUCTION
Courses or Concentrations

Available: Advertising; Communication; Film
or Cinema; Journalism or Mass
Communication; Public Relations; Radio,
Television, Broadcasting, or
Telecommunications; Speech; Drama;
Program Coordinators: Eugene Muto
(Drama); *Undergraduate Objectives or
Program Emphases*: To equip students with
critical and analytical skills, and with basic
technical skills in their chosen professional
concentration; *Bachelor's Degree Majors*: 154;
Full-Time Faculty: 4; *Part-Time Faculty*: 4.

FACILITIES AND SERVICES
*Practical experiences available
through*: Advertising Agency; Audio
Recording Laboratory; Closed Circuit
Television Facility; Campus Newspaper
(Published Independently); Local
Commercial Newspaper; Local Commercial
Television Station; Photographic
Darkrooms; Video Editing; Electronic Field
Production (Video); FM Radio Station
(Institutional); Public Relations Agency;
Satellite Uplink Facility (Ku Band
Transmitter); Video Production Laboratory
or Television Studio.

Augusta College

Communications Department
2500 Walton Way
Augusta, Georgia 30910

Randall Salzman, Administrator

Berry College (Private)

Division of Communication Arts
Box 5010 Berry College
Mount Berry, Georgia 30149
Telephone: (404) 232-5374

Robert L. Frank, Coordinator
Mack Smith, Department Head

CURRICULUM AND INSTRUCTION
*Courses or Concentrations
Available*: Communication; Journalism or
Mass Communication; Public Relations;

Radio, Television, Broadcasting, or Telecommunications; Speech; *Undergraduate Objectives or Program Emphases*: Teach students to write, speak well; acquaint students with a basic knowledge of their field (journalism, public relations, or broadcasting), including its history, institutions, theory and literature; *Bachelor's Degree Majors*: 70; *Full-Time Faculty*: 5.

FACILITIES AND SERVICES
Practical experiences available through: Community Antenna (Cable) Television Origination; Campus Newspaper (Published Independently); Local Commercial Newspaper; Local Commercial Television Station; Photographic Darkrooms; Video Editing; Electronic Field Production (Video); Institutional Magazine; Public Relations Agency; Video Production Laboratory or Television Studio.

Brenau College

Department of Humanities and Communication Arts
One Centennial Drive
Gainesville, Georgia 30501

Calvin Hanrahan, Administrator

Clark Atlanta University (Private)

Department of Mass Media Arts
James P. Brewley Drive at Fair Street, S.W.
Atlanta, Georgia 30314
Telephone: (404) 880-8304

James D. McJunkins, Chair
Harry Amanz, Division Director

CURRICULUM AND INSTRUCTION
Courses or Concentrations Available: Advertising; Communication; Film or Cinema; Journalism or Mass Communication; Public Relations; Radio, Television, Broadcasting, or Telecommunications; *Undergraduate Objectives or Program Emphases*: To prepare students for careers in public relations, journalism, radio, film; *Bachelor's Degree Majors*: 300; *Full-Time Faculty*: 5; *Part-Time Faculty*: 6; *Full-Time Professional (non-clerical) Staff Members*: 4.

FACILITIES AND SERVICES
Practical experiences available through: Advertising Agency; Community Antenna (Cable) Television Origination; Closed Circuit Television Facility; Campus Newspaper (Published Independently); Local Commercial Newspaper; Local Commercial Television Station; Desktop Publishing Facility; Photographic Darkrooms; Video Editing; Electronic Field Production (Video); Television Broadcast Station (Institutional); Film or Cinema Laboratory; FM Radio Station (Institutional); Institutional Newspaper; Public Relations Agency; Satellite Uplink Facility; United Press International Feed; Video News and Data Processing.

Clark College

Department of Mass Communication
240 Chestnut Street, Southwest
Atlanta, Georgia 30314

Lenora C. Stephens, Administrator

Columbus College

Speech/Drama
Columbus, Georgia 31933

Hazel Hall, Administrator

DeKalb College

Fine Arts Division
555 North Indian Creek Drive
Clarkston, Georgia 30021

Louis L. Wells, Administrator

Fort Valley State College (Public)

Program of Mass Communication
1005 State College Drive
Fort Valley, Georgia 31030
Telephone: (912) 825-6212

Louise W. Hermanson, Director
Joyce D. Jenkins, Head, Department of Languages and Mass Communication

CURRICULUM AND INSTRUCTION
Courses or Concentrations

Available: Advertising; Communication; Journalism or Mass Communication; Public Relations; Radio, Television, Broadcasting, or Telecommunications; *Undergraduate Objectives or Program Emphases*: To provide quality education in Mass Communication areas of broadcasting, public relations and print. Strong liberal arts requirements; *Bachelor's Degree Majors*: 87; *Full-Time Faculty*: 5; *Full-Time Professional (non-clerical) Staff Members*: 3.

FACILITIES AND SERVICES
Practical experiences available through: Audio Recording Laboratory; Community Antenna (Cable) Television Origination; Closed Circuit Television Facility; Campus Newspaper (Published Independently); Local Commercial Newspaper; Local Commercial Television Station; Desktop Publishing Facility; Photographic Darkrooms; Video Editing; Electronic Field Production (Video); Institutional Newspaper; Public Relations Agency; Satellite Uplink Facility (Ku Band Transmitter) (C Band Transmitter); Video News and Data Processing; Video Production Laboratory or Television Studio.

Georgia Southern College (Public)

Department of Communication Arts
Statesboro, Georgia 30460
Telephone: (912) 681-5138

David W. Addington, Head
Warren F. Jones, Dean, School of Arts and Science

CURRICULUM AND INSTRUCTION
Courses or Concentrations
Available: Communication; Film or Cinema; Information Science; Journalism or Mass Communication; Public Relations; Radio, Television, Broadcasting, or Telecommunications; Speech; Theatre; *Undergraduate Objectives or Program Emphases*: To provide a liberal arts education with emphasis in practical instruction; *Bachelor's Degree Majors*: 12; *Other Degree Majors*: 400; *Full-Time Faculty*: 16; *Part-Time Faculty*: 3; *Full-Time Professional (non-clerical) Staff Members*: 1.

FACILITIES AND SERVICES
Practical experiences available through: AM Radio Station (Institutional); Audio

Recording Laboratory; Community Antenna (Cable) Television Origination; Campus Newspaper (Published Independently); Local Commercial Television Station; Photographic Darkrooms; Video Editing; Public Relations Agency.

Georgia State University (Public)

Department of Communication
University Plaza
Atlanta, Georgia 30303
Telephone: (404) 651-3200 Extension or Alternate: 651-2000

Marsha H. Stanback, Chair
Clyde W. Faulkner, Dean, College of Arts and Sciences

CURRICULUM AND INSTRUCTION
Courses or Concentrations
Available: Communication; Film or Cinema; Journalism or Mass Communication; Public Relations; Radio, Television, Broadcasting, or Telecommunications; Speech; *Undergraduate Objectives or Program Emphases*: To develop knowledge and skills in communication, knowledge about the nature and functions of the mass media and the skills necessary for careers in mass communication; *Graduate Objectives or Program Emphases*: To provide a multi-disciplinary practical degree based on courses offered by the programs in film, journalism, public relations, speech and theatre; *Bachelor's Degree Majors*: 600; *Master's Degree Majors*: 100; *Full-Time Faculty*: 19; *Part-Time Faculty*: 13.

FACILITIES AND SERVICES
Practical experiences available through: Audio Recording Laboratory; Community Antenna (Cable) Television Origination; Closed Circuit Television Facility; Campus Newspaper (Published Independently); Local Commercial Newspaper; Local Commercial Television Station; Video Editing; Electronic Field Production (Video);

Film or Cinema Laboratory; FM Radio Station (Institutional); Public Relations Agency; Video Production Laboratory or Television Studio.

Macon College (Public)

Division of Humanities
College Station Road
Macon, Georgia 31204
Telephone: (912) 474-2793

Charles J. Pecor, Chair
Robert Trammell, Dean of the College

CURRICULUM AND INSTRUCTION
Courses or Concentrations
Available: Journalism or Mass
Communication; Speech; *Undergraduate
Objectives or Program Emphases*: To expose
students to the basics of public speaking and
journalism; *Associate's Degree Majors*: 15;
Full-Time Faculty: 1; *Part-Time Faculty*: 2.

FACILITIES AND SERVICES
*Practical experiences available
through*: Campus Newspaper (Published
Independently); Local Commercial
Television Station; Institutional Magazine.

Mercer University - Macon (Private)

Department of Speech and Dramatic Art
1400 Coleman Avenue
Macon, Georgia 31207
Telephone: (912) 752-2974

John J. Chalfa, Jr., Chair
Sammye Greer, Dean

CURRICULUM AND INSTRUCTION
Courses or Concentrations
Available: Communication; Film or Cinema;
Journalism or Mass Communication; Radio,
Television, Broadcasting, or
Telecommunications; Speech; *Undergraduate
Objectives or Program Emphases*: To prepare
students to demonstrate a critical frame of
reference, an appreciation and capacity for
critical and creative thinking, an
understanding and appreciation of historical
roots and ethical foundations of the field, and
to communicate effectively; *Bachelor's Degree
Majors*: 35; *Full-Time Faculty*: 7; *Part-Time
Faculty*: 1.

FACILITIES AND SERVICES
*Practical experiences available
through*: Advertising Agency; Audio
Recording Laboratory; Community Antenna
(Cable) Television Origination; Closed
Circuit Television Facility; Campus

Newspaper (Published Independently);
Local Commercial Newspaper; Local
Commercial Television Station; Desktop
Publishing Facility; Video Editing;
Electronic Field Production (Video); Public
Relations Agency; Video Production
Laboratory or Television Studio.

Mercer University - Macon

Journalism Department
Macon, Georgia 31207

Harlan S. Stensaas, Administrator

Mercer University - Macon

Broadcast/Film Department
Macon, Georgia 31207

John Chalfa, Administrator

Morehouse College

Department of English and Linguistics
223 Chestnut Street, Southwest
Atlanta, Georgia 30314

Oglethorpe University (Private)

Program of Writing
4484 Peachtree Road NE
Atlanta, Georgia 30319
Telephone: (404) 261-1441

Madeleine Picciotto, Director
William Brightman, Administrator

CURRICULUM AND INSTRUCTION
Courses or Concentrations
Available: Journalism or Mass
Communication; *Undergraduate Objectives or
Program Emphases*: An undergraduate minor
in Writing that prepares students to enter a
variety of communications fields, especially
journalism and public relations; *Bachelor's
Degree Majors*: 18; *Full-Time Faculty*: 1;
Part-Time Faculty: 8.

FACILITIES AND SERVICES
Practical experiences available through: Audio
Recording Laboratory; Campus Newspaper
(Published Independently).

Reinhardt College (Private)

Public Relations
Development Department
P. O. Box 128
Waleska, Georgia 30183
Telephone: (404) 479-1454

Marsha D. Snow, Director
McDonald Willis, Administrator

CURRICULUM AND INSTRUCTION
Courses or Concentrations
Available: Journalism or Mass
Communication; Speech; *Undergraduate
Objectives or Program Emphases*: Establish
firm educational background that will be
further developed in the students' final years
of college; *Full-Time Faculty*: 1.

FACILITIES AND SERVICES
*Practical experiences available
through*: Institutional Magazine; Institutional
Newspaper.

Savannah State College (Public)

Department of Humanities
Savannah, Georgia 31404
Telephone: (912) 356-2368

Luetta C. Milledge, Head
J. A. Jahannes, Dean

CURRICULUM AND INSTRUCTION
Courses or Concentrations
Available: Journalism or Mass
Communication; Radio, Television,
Broadcasting, or Telecommunications;
Program Coordinator: Novella C. Holmes
(Journalism, Mass Communications, Radio,
TV, Broadcast, Telecommunications);
*Undergraduate Objectives or Program
Emphases*: To prepare students for careers
and/or advanced study in electronic and print
media; *Bachelor's Degree Majors*: 50;
Full-Time Faculty: 14; *Part-Time Faculty*: 4;
*Full-Time Professional (non-clerical) Staff
Members*: 1.

FACILITIES AND SERVICES
*Practical experiences available
through*: Advertising Agency; Audio
Recording Laboratory; Community Antenna
(Cable) Television Origination; Campus
Newspaper (Published Independently);
Local Commercial Newspaper; Local
Commercial Television Station; Desktop

Publishing Facility; Photographic
Darkrooms; Video Editing; Electronic Field
Production (Video); FM Radio Station
(Institutional); Public Relations Agency;
Satellite Uplink Facility (Ku Band
Transmitter); Video News and Data
Processing; Video Production Laboratory or
Television Studio.

Shorter College (Private)

Division of Communication Arts
315 Shorter Avenue
Rome, Georgia 30161-4298
Telephone: (404) 291-2121

Betty Z. Morris, Chair
Harold E. Newman, Vice President,
Academic Affairs and Dean of College

CURRICULUM AND INSTRUCTION
Courses or Concentrations
Available: Communication; Film or Cinema;
Journalism or Mass Communication; Public
Relations; Radio, Television, Broadcasting,
or Telecommunications; Speech; *Program
Coordinators*: William Steis (Broadcasting);
Mona Oppenheim (Journalism);
*Undergraduate Objectives or Program
Emphases*: Radio and Television, Electronic
Media; Print Journalism; Speech
Communication; Public Relations; *Bachelor's
Degree Majors*: 15; *Full-Time Faculty*: 3;
Part-Time Faculty: 1.

FACILITIES AND SERVICES
*Practical experiences available
through*: Advertising Agency; Audio
Recording Laboratory; Community Antenna
(Cable) Television Origination; Local
Commercial Newspaper; Local Commercial
Television Station; Photographic
Darkrooms; Video Editing; Electronic Field
Production (Video); Film or Cinema
Laboratory; FM Radio Station
(Institutional); Institutional Newspaper;
Public Relations Agency; Video Production
Laboratory or Television Studio.

University of Georgia (Public)

School of Journalism and Mass
Communication
Athens, Georgia 30602
Telephone: (404) 542-1704

J. Thomas Russell, Dean
William F. Peokasy, Vice President,
Academic Affairs

CURRICULUM AND INSTRUCTION
Courses or Concentrations
Available: Advertising; Film or Cinema;
Journalism or Mass Communication; Public
Relations; Radio, Television, Broadcasting,
or Telecommunications; Broadcast News,
Magazines; *Program Coordinators*: Al Hester
(Journalism); Barry Sherman
(Telecommunications); Len Reid
(Advertising, Public Relations);
*Undergraduate Objectives or Program
Emphases*: To prepare for careers within the
mass communication industries and to
understand and appreciate the operation,
function, and significance of mass media in
contemporary society; *Graduate Objectives or
Program Emphases*: Instruction leading to
Ph.D., MA, or MMC degrees; experience in
practice, management and evaluation;
Bachelor's Degree Majors: 715; *Master's
Degree Majors*: 60; *Doctoral Degree Majors
Currently in Residence*: 12; *Additional
Doctoral Degree Majors*: 3; *Full-Time
Faculty*: 40; *Part-Time Faculty*: 3; *Full-Time
Professional (non-clerical) Staff Members*: 4.

FACILITIES AND SERVICES
*Practical experiences available
through*: Associated Press Wire Service Feed;
Audio Recording Laboratory; Community
Antenna (Cable) Television Origination;
Closed Circuit Television Facility; Campus
Newspaper (Published Independently);
Local Commercial Newspaper; Local
Commercial Television Station; Desktop
Publishing Facility; Photographic
Darkrooms; Video Editing; Electronic Field
Production (Video); Film or Cinema
Laboratory; FM Radio Station
(Institutional); Institutional Magazine;
Public Relations Agency; Video News and
Data Processing; Video Production
Laboratory or Television Studio.

University of Georgia (Public)

Department of Speech Communication
Athens, Georgia 30602
Telephone: (404) 542-4893

Dale G. Leathers, Head
John J. Kozak, Dean

CURRICULUM AND INSTRUCTION
*Courses or Concentrations
Available*: Communication; Speech;
*Undergraduate Objectives or Program
Emphases*: To provide in-depth knowledge of
major concepts and competencies in public
and interpersonal communication; *Graduate
Objectives or Program Emphases*: To develop
competencies needed to be a publishing
scholar; *Bachelor's Degree Majors*: 400;
Master's Degree Majors: 20; *Doctoral Degree
Majors Currently in Residence*: 6; *Full-Time
Faculty*: 12.

FACILITIES AND SERVICES
*Practical experiences available
through*: Closed Circuit Television Facility;
Television Broadcast Station (Institutional).

Valdosta State College (Public)

Department of Communication Arts
Valdosta, Georgia 31698
Telephone: (912) 333-5820

Charles F. Beadle, Jr., Head
Robert B. Welch, Dean

CURRICULUM AND INSTRUCTION
*Courses or Concentrations
Available*: Communication; Public Relations;
Radio, Television, Broadcasting, or
Telecommunications; Speech; *BFA Degree
Majors*: 350; *Full-Time Faculty*: 13;
Part-Time Faculty: 3; *Full-Time Professional
(non-clerical) Staff Members*: 3.

FACILITIES AND SERVICES
Practical experiences available through: Audio
Recording Laboratory; Community Antenna
(Cable) Television Origination; Video
Editing; Electronic Field Production
(Video); FM Radio Station (Institutional);
Video Production Laboratory or Television
Studio.

West Georgia College (Public)

Department of Mass Communication and Theatre Arts
Maple Street
Carrollton, Georgia 30118
Telephone: (404) 836-6518

Chester Gibson, Chair
Richard Dangle, Dean, School of Arts and Sciences

CURRICULUM AND INSTRUCTION
Courses or Concentrations
Available: Communication; Journalism or Mass Communication; Public Relations; Radio, Television, Broadcasting, or Telecommunications; Speech; Theatre Arts; *Undergraduate Objectives or Program Emphases*: To provide, within a context of a liberal arts education, training in both the theory and practice of mass communication and theatre; *Bachelor's Degree Majors*: 300; *Full-Time Faculty*: 8; *Part-Time Faculty*: 2; *Full-Time Professional (non-clerical) Staff Members*: 1.

FACILITIES AND SERVICES
Practical experiences available through: Associated Press Wire Service Feed; Audio Recording Laboratory; Community Antenna (Cable) Television Origination; Closed Circuit Television Facility; Campus Newspaper (Published Independently); Local Commercial Newspaper; Desktop Publishing Facility; Photographic Darkrooms; Video Editing; Electronic Field Production (Video); FM Radio Station (Institutional); Institutional Newspaper; Public Relations Agency; Video News and Data Processing; Video Production Laboratory or Television Studio.

Brigham Young University - Hawaii

Speech Communication Department
55-220 Kulanui Avenue
Laie, Hawaii 96762

James Ludlow, Administrator

Chaminade University of Honolulu (Private)

Department of Communication
3140 Waialae Avenue
Honolulu, Hawaii 96816
Telephone: (808) 735-4711

Jude Yablonsky, Chair

CURRICULUM AND INSTRUCTION
Courses or Concentrations Available: Communication; Journalism or Mass Communication; Public Relations; Radio, Television, Broadcasting, or Telecommunications; Speech; *Undergraduate Objectives or Program Emphases*: Effective communication; *Bachelor's Degree Majors*: 27; *Full-Time Faculty*: 2; *Part-Time Faculty*: 4.

FACILITIES AND SERVICES
Practical experiences available through: Advertising Agency; Closed Circuit Television Facility; Local Commercial Newspaper; Local Commercial Television Station; Desktop Publishing Facility; Video Editing; Institutional Newspaper; Public Relations Agency.

Honolulu Community College (Public)

Educational Media Center
874 Dillingham Boulevard
Honolulu, Hawaii 96817
Telephone: (808) 845-9126

Jon H. Blumhardt, Director
Ramsey Pederson, Dean of Instruction

CURRICULUM AND INSTRUCTION
Courses or Concentrations Available: Radio, Television, Broadcasting, or Telecommunications; Printing; Graphic Arts; *Undergraduate Objectives or Program Emphases*: Basic studio production; vocational press operations; vocational graphics arts production; *Full-Time Faculty*: 1; *Full-Time Professional (non-clerical) Staff Members*: 10.

FACILITIES AND SERVICES
Practical experiences available through: Audio Recording Laboratory; Community Antenna (Cable) Television Origination; Closed Circuit Television Facility; Campus Newspaper (Published Independently); Desktop Publishing Facility; Photographic Darkrooms; Video Editing; Electronic Field Production (Video); Television Broadcast Station (Institutional); ITFS Distribution System; Institutional Magazine; Institutional Newspaper; Satellite Uplink Facility; Video Production Laboratory or Television Studio.

Leeward Community College (Public)

Division of Language Arts
96-045 Ala Ike
Pearl City, Hawaii 96782
Telephone: (808) 455-0331

Kay M. Yamada, Coordinator
Douglas Kaya, Division Chair

CURRICULUM AND INSTRUCTION
Courses or Concentrations Available: Communication; Journalism or Mass Communication; Speech; Television News Reporting; *Undergraduate Objectives or Program Emphases*: Writing and speaking skills; *Associate's Degree Majors*: 50; *Full-Time Faculty*: 3; *Part-Time Faculty*: 3.

FACILITIES AND SERVICES
Practical experiences available through: Audio Recording Laboratory; Closed Circuit Television Facility; Local Commercial Television Station; Desktop Publishing Facility; Institutional Magazine;

Institutional Newspaper; Video Production Laboratory or Television Studio.

Leeward Community College (Public)

Division of Business Education and Advertising
96-045 Ala Ike
Pearl City, Hawaii 96701
Telephone: (808) 455-0345

Elena Bumanglag, Chair
Kathi Hiyane-Brown, Administrator

CURRICULUM AND INSTRUCTION
Courses or Concentrations
Available: Advertising; Speech;
Undergraduate Objectives or Program
Emphases: Provide training for entry-level jobs in management accounting and office administration technology; to provide lower division transfer courses; to provide for upward mobility training; *Degree Majors*: 300; *Full-Time Faculty*: 18; *Part-Time Faculty*: 15; *Full-Time Professional (non-clerical) Staff Members*: 1.

Leeward Community College (Public)

Program of Television Production
96-045 Ala Ike
Pearl City, Hawaii 96782
Telephone: (808) 455-0302

Robert W. Hochstein, Coordinator and Instructor

CURRICULUM AND INSTRUCTION
Courses or Concentrations
Available: Television, Broadcasting;
Undergraduate Objectives or Program
Emphases: To provide vocational training for entry level Television Production positions; *Degree Majors*: 40; *Full-Time Faculty*: 1; *Part-Time Faculty*: 4; *Full-Time Professional (non-clerical) Staff Members*: 3.

FACILITIES AND SERVICES
Practical experiences available through: Advertising Agency; Audio Recording Laboratory; Community Antenna (Cable) Television Origination; Closed Circuit Television Facility; Campus Newspaper (Published Independently);

Local Commercial Television Station; Desktop Publishing Facility; Photographic Darkrooms; Video Editing; Electronic Field Production (Video); ITFS Distribution System; Institutional Magazine; Institutional Newspaper; Video Production Laboratory or Television Studio.

University of Hawaii (Public)

Department of Communication
2650 Campus Road
Honolulu, Hawaii 96822
Telephone: (808) 948-8715

L.S. Harms, Chair
Richard Dubanoski, Dean, Social Sciences

CURRICULUM AND INSTRUCTION
Courses or Concentrations
Available: Communication; *Undergraduate Objectives or Program*
Emphases: Telecommunication, management communication, world communication;
Graduate Objectives or Program
Emphases: Telecommunication, management communication, world communication;
Bachelor's Degree Majors: 240; *Master's Degree Majors*: 60; *Doctoral Degree Majors Currently in Residence*: 10; *Full-Time Faculty*: 12; *Part-Time Faculty*: 10; *Full-Time Professional (non-clerical) Staff Members*: 1.

FACILITIES AND SERVICES
Practical experiences available through: Advertising Agency; AM Radio Station (Institutional); Audio Recording Laboratory; Community Antenna (Cable) Television Origination; Carrier Current Audio Distribution System; Closed Circuit Television Facility; Campus Newspaper (Published Independently); Local Commercial Television Station; Desktop Publishing Facility; Video Editing; Electronic Field Production (Video); Television Broadcast Station (Institutional); Film or Cinema Laboratory; ITFS Distribution System; Public Relations Agency; Video Production Laboratory or Television Studio.

University of Hawaii (Public)

Department of Journalism
Honolulu, Hawaii 96822

John Luter, Administrator

University of Hawaii (Public)

Department of Speech
2560 Campus Road
Honolulu, Hawaii 96822
Telephone: (808) 948-8202

Ronald E. Cambra, Chair
Robert S. Hines, Dean

CURRICULUM AND INSTRUCTION
Courses or Concentrations
Available: Communication; Speech;
Undergraduate Objectives or Program
Emphases: A quality curricular instruction at
undergraduate and graduate levels; engage in
and publish research, and to conduct
program of co-curricular training and
community service; *Graduate Objectives or*
Program Emphases: Message processing and
relational influences; *Bachelor's Degree*
Majors: 150; *Master's Degree Majors*: 7;
Full-Time Faculty: 12; *Part-Time*
Faculty: 14; *Full-Time Professional*
(non-clerical) Staff Members: 2.

Boise State University (Public)

Department of Communication
1910 University Boulevard
Boise, Idaho 83725
Telephone: (208) 385-3320

Robert R. Boren, Chair
Robert Sims, Dean, School of Social
Sciences and Public Affairs

CURRICULUM AND INSTRUCTION
Courses or Concentrations
Available: Communication; Journalism or
Mass Communication; Public Relations;
Radio, Television, Broadcasting, or
Telecommunications; Speech;
Communication Education; Communication
Training and Development; *Undergraduate
Objectives or Program
Emphases*: Communication; Mass
Communication; Broadcasting; Journalism;
Interpersonal Communication;
Communication Education; Communication
Training and Development; Communication
and English; *Graduate Objectives or Program
Emphases*: Public Affairs (Reporting and
Public Relations); Communication Education
(both secondary schools and training and
development); *Bachelor's Degree Majors*: 475;
Full-Time Faculty: 14; *Part-Time
Faculty*: 15.

FACILITIES AND SERVICES
*Practical experiences available
through*: Advertising Agency; Associated
Press Wire Service Feed; Audio Recording
Laboratory; Community Antenna (Cable)
Television Origination; Closed Circuit
Television Facility; Campus Newspaper
(Published Independently); Local
Commercial Newspaper; Local Commercial
Television Station; Desktop Publishing
Facility; Photographic Darkrooms; Video
Editing; Electronic Field Production
(Video); Television Broadcast Station
(Institutional); FM Radio Station
(Institutional); ITFS Distribution System;
Public Relations Agency; Satellite Uplink
Facility; United Press International Feed;
Video Production Laboratory or Television
Studio.

Idaho State University (Public)

Program of Mass Communication
Box 8242
Pocatello, Idaho 83201
Telephone: (208) 236-3295

Mike Trinklein, Director
Bruce Loebs, Administrator

CURRICULUM AND INSTRUCTION
*Courses or Concentrations
Available*: Advertising; Journalism or Mass
Communication; Public Relations; Radio,
Television, Broadcasting, or
Telecommunications; *Undergraduate
Objectives or Program Emphases*: Journalism,
Public Relations; Television; Photography;
Media Studies. All programs are hands-on
and professionally-oriented; *Bachelor's
Degree Majors*: 100; *Full-Time Faculty*: 4;
Part-Time Faculty: 1; *Full-Time Professional
(non-clerical) Staff Members*: 2.

FACILITIES AND SERVICES
*Practical experiences available
through*: Advertising Agency; Community
Antenna (Cable) Television Origination;
Closed Circuit Television Facility; Campus
Newspaper (Published Independently);
Local Commercial Newspaper; Local
Commercial Television Station; Desktop
Publishing Facility; Photographic
Darkrooms; Video Editing; Electronic Field
Production (Video); Institutional
Newspaper; Public Relations Agency;
Satellite Uplink Facility; Video Production
Laboratory or Television Studio.

North Idaho College (Public)

Division of Communication Arts
1000 West Garden Avenue
Coeur d'Alene, Idaho 83814
Telephone: (208) 769-3423

Mona Klinger, Chair
Dennis Conners, Dean, Academic Affairs

CURRICULUM AND INSTRUCTION
*Courses or Concentrations
Available*: Communication; Journalism or

Mass Communication; Radio, Television, Broadcasting, or Telecommunications; Speech; Interpersonal Communication; Photography; Small Group; *Program Coordinators*: Michael J. Miller (Radio, Television); Phil Corlis (Photography); Nils Rosdahl (Journalism); *Undergraduate Objectives or Program Emphases*: Transfer program; *Associate's Degree Majors*: 25; *Full-Time Faculty*: 6; *Part-Time Faculty*: 4.

FACILITIES AND SERVICES
Practical experiences available through: Associated Press Wire Service Feed; Audio Recording Laboratory; Community Antenna (Cable) Television Origination; Desktop Publishing Facility; Photographic Darkrooms; Video Editing; Television Broadcast Station (Institutional); Institutional Magazine; Institutional Newspaper; Satellite Uplink Facility; United Press International Feed; Video Production Laboratory or Television Studio.

Northwest Nazarene College (Private)

Division of Language and Literature
Nampa, Idaho 98686
Telephone: (208) 467-8100

Earl R. Owens, Chair
Merilyn Thompson, Head, Department of Speech Communication

CURRICULUM AND INSTRUCTION
Courses or Concentrations Available: Advertising; Communication; Journalism or Mass Communication; Public Relations; Speech; *Undergraduate Objectives or Program Emphases*: To provide understanding of the role that communication plays in contemporary society. Students can use their training to assume leadership positions in public administration, the behavioral sciences, the media, or as a basis for graduate study in communication; *Full-Time Faculty*: 15; *Part-Time Faculty*: 1.

FACILITIES AND SERVICES
Practical experiences available through: Local Commercial Newspaper; Local Commercial Television Station; Photographic Darkrooms; Video Editing; Institutional Newspaper; Public Relations Agency.

Ricks College (Private)

Department of Communication
Rexburg, Idaho 83460-0105
Telephone: (208) 356-2921

David Hillier, Chair
Kay Wilkins, Administrator

CURRICULUM AND INSTRUCTION
Courses or Concentrations Available: Advertising; Communication; Journalism or Mass Communication; Radio, Television, Broadcasting, or Telecommunications; Speech; *Undergraduate Objectives or Program Emphases*: To prepare students for productive transfers to four-year institutions; *Associate's Degree Majors*: 45; *Full-Time Faculty*: 7; *Part-Time Faculty*: 1; *Full-Time Professional (non-clerical) Staff Members*: 1.

FACILITIES AND SERVICES
Practical experiences available through: Associated Press Wire Service Feed; Audio Recording Laboratory; Carrier Current Audio Distribution System; Closed Circuit Television Facility; Campus Newspaper (Published Independently); Desktop Publishing Facility; Photographic Darkrooms; Video Editing; Electronic Field Production (Video); FM Radio Station (Institutional); Institutional Newspaper; Video Production Laboratory or Television Studio.

University of Idaho (Public)

Department of Communication
Moscow, Idaho 83843
Telephone: (208) 885-6458

Peter A. Haggart, Director
Kurt Olsson, Acting Dean

CURRICULUM AND INSTRUCTION
Courses or Concentrations Available: Advertising; Communication; Journalism or Mass Communication; Public Relations; Radio, Television, Broadcasting, or Telecommunications; Photography, Film; Organizational Communication; *Undergraduate Objectives or Program Emphases*: Solid Liberal Arts university education combined with career training in the professional areas of the curriculum; *Bachelor's Degree Majors*: 200; *Full-Time Faculty*: 11; *Part-Time Faculty*: 15;

*Full-Time Professional (non-clerical) Staff
Members*: 1.

FACILITIES AND SERVICES
*Practical experiences available
through*: Advertising Agency; Audio
Recording Laboratory; Community Antenna
(Cable) Television Origination; Closed
Circuit Television Facility; Campus
Newspaper (Published Independently);
Local Commercial Newspaper; Local
Commercial Television Station;
Photographic Darkrooms; Video Editing;
Electronic Field Production (Video);
Television Broadcast Station (Institutional);
FM Radio Station (Institutional); Satellite
Uplink Facility (Ku Band Transmitter) (C
Band Transmitter); Video Production
Laboratory or Television Studio.

ILLINOIS

Augustana College (Private)

Department of Speech Communication and Theatre Arts
639 38th Street
Rock Island, Illinois 61201
Telephone: (309) 794-7581

W. David Snowball, Chair
Tom Robin Harris, Division Chair

CURRICULUM AND INSTRUCTION
Courses or Concentrations
Available: Advertising; Communication; Journalism or Mass Communication; Speech; Speech Pathology and Audiology; *Undergraduate Objectives or Program Emphases*: A Liberal Arts department with internship placements in media and public relation; *Bachelor's Degree Majors*: 40; *Full-Time Faculty*: 14; *Part-Time Faculty*: 1.

FACILITIES AND SERVICES
Practical experiences available through: Associated Press Wire Service Feed; Campus Newspaper (Published Independently); Photographic Darkrooms; FM Radio Station (Institutional); Institutional Magazine.

Augustana College (Private)

Program of Journalism
639 38th Street
Rock Island, Illinois 61201
Telephone: (309) 794-7460

Lisa D. Norton, Director
Karin Youngberg, Administrator

CURRICULUM AND INSTRUCTION
Courses or Concentrations
Available: Journalism or Mass Communication; *Undergraduate Objectives or Program Emphases*: Critical thinking combined with basic journalistic skills such as reporting, writing, interviewing and editing; *Full-Time Faculty*: 1.

FACILITIES AND SERVICES
Practical experiences available through: Campus Newspaper (Published Independently); Desktop Publishing Facility; Photographic Darkrooms; Institutional Magazine; Video News and Data Processing.

Aurora University (Private)

Department of Communication
347 Gladstone
Aurora, Illinois 60506
Telephone: (708) 892-6431

Laurel M. Church, Chair

CURRICULUM AND INSTRUCTION
Courses or Concentrations
Available: Advertising; Communication; Public Relations; Television Production; *Undergraduate Objectives or Program Emphases*: Corporate Professional Communication, Public Relations and Promotion; Media Studies, including Television Production; *Bachelor's Degree Majors*: 75; *Full-Time Faculty*: 3; *Part-Time Faculty*: 5; *Full-Time Professional (non-clerical) Staff Members*: 1.

FACILITIES AND SERVICES
Practical experiences available through: Advertising Agency; Community Antenna (Cable) Television Origination; Local Commercial Newspaper; Local Commercial Television Station; Desktop Publishing Facility; Photographic Darkrooms; Video Editing; Electronic Field Production (Video); Television Broadcast Station (Institutional); Institutional Magazine; Public Relations Agency; Video Production Laboratory or Television Studio.

Black Hawk College

Creative Arts
6600 34th Avenue
Moline, Illinois 61265

Phillip Johnson, Administrator

Blackburn College (Private)

Department of Speech Communication
Carlinville, Illinois 62626
Telephone: (217) 854-2805

Rusalyn H. Andrews, Chair
Ann Barnard, Chair, English Department

CURRICULUM AND INSTRUCTION
Courses or Concentrations
Available: Communication; Journalism or
Mass Communication; Speech; Theory;
Research; Oral Interpretation; Group
Process; *Undergraduate Objectives or Program
Emphases*: To provide a broad understanding
of theories, issues, and ethical issues relevant
to communication in addition to advancing
practical expertise and critical awareness;
Bachelor's Degree Majors: 12; *Full-Time
Faculty*: 1; *Part-Time Faculty*: 2.

FACILITIES AND SERVICES
*Practical experiences available
through*: Desktop Publishing Facility.

Bradley University (Private)

Division of Communication
Bradley Hall
Peoria, Illinois 61625
Telephone: (309) 677-2354

Joe Misiewicz, Director
**Jim Ballowe, Dean, College of
Communication and Fine Arts**

CURRICULUM AND INSTRUCTION
Courses or Concentrations
Available: Advertising; Communication;
Public Relations; Radio, Television,
Broadcasting, or Telecommunications;
Speech; Photography; News; *Undergraduate
Objectives or Program Emphases*: Split theory
and professional curriculum with a
communication core; *Bachelor's Degree
Majors*: 94; *Other Degree Majors*: 400;
Full-Time Faculty: 22; *Part-Time Faculty*: 7.

FACILITIES AND SERVICES
*Practical experiences available
through*: Advertising Agency; Audio
Recording Laboratory; Community Antenna
(Cable) Television Origination; Carrier
Current Audio Distribution System; Closed
Circuit Television Facility; Campus
Newspaper (Published Independently);
Local Commercial Newspaper; Local
Commercial Television Station; Desktop
Publishing Facility; Photographic
Darkrooms; Video Editing; Electronic Field
Production (Video); Television Broadcast
Station (Institutional); FM Radio Station
(Institutional); ITFS Distribution System;
Public Relations Agency; Satellite Uplink
Facility (C Band Transmitter); Video
Production Laboratory or Television Studio.

Chicago State University (Public)

Division of Speech
95th Street at King Drive
Chicago, Illinois 60628
Telephone: (312) 995-2189

Caryn Lynn Cleeland, Speech Coordinator
Michael Miller, Administrator

CURRICULUM AND INSTRUCTION
Courses or Concentrations
Available: Communication; Journalism or
Mass Communication; Radio, Television,
Broadcasting, or Telecommunications;
Speech; *Undergraduate Objectives or Program
Emphases*: The Bachelor of Arts degree in
speech is a broadly based program to prepare
students for entry level positions in radio and
television. The department also offers
minors in theatre and speech
communications; *Bachelor's Degree
Majors*: 45; *Full-Time Faculty*: 5; *Part-Time
Faculty*: 2.

FACILITIES AND SERVICES
Practical experiences available through: Audio
Recording Laboratory; Community Antenna
(Cable) Television Origination; Campus
Newspaper (Published Independently);
Local Commercial Television Station;
Desktop Publishing Facility; Photographic
Darkrooms; Video Editing; Electronic Field
Production (Video); Video Production
Laboratory or Television Studio.

College of Dupage

Vocational Technology
22nd and Lambert Road
Glen Ellyn, Illinois 60137

Mary Lou Lockerby, Administrator

College of St. Francis (Private)

Department of Journalism/Communications
500 Wilcox Street
Joliet, Illinois 60435
Telephone: (815) 740-3696

Richard E. Lorenc, Chair
Jim Doppke, Dean

CURRICULUM AND INSTRUCTION
Courses or Concentrations
Available: Advertising; Communication;
Journalism or Mass Communication; Public
Relations; Radio, Television, Broadcasting,
or Telecommunications; Speech; *Program
Coordinators*: Rita Travis (Newspaper);
Walter Hamilton (Radio); *Full-Time
Faculty*: 4; *Part-Time Faculty*: 1.

FACILITIES AND SERVICES
*Practical experiences available
through*: Community Antenna (Cable)
Television Origination; Campus Newspaper
(Published Independently); Photographic
Darkrooms; Video Editing; Electronic Field
Production (Video); Television Broadcast
Station (Institutional); FM Radio Station
(Institutional); Institutional Newspaper;
Video Production Laboratory or Television
Studio.

Columbia College - Chicago (Private)

Department of Journalism
600 S. Michigan
Chicago, Illinois 60605
Telephone: (312) 663-1600

Nat Lehrmann, Chair
Lya Rosenblum, Dean

CURRICULUM AND INSTRUCTION
Courses or Concentrations
Available: Journalism or Mass
Communication; Radio, Television,
Broadcasting, or Telecommunications;
Magazine editing; *Undergraduate Objectives
or Program Emphases*: Train students for
professional careers in news reporting;
broadcast news; magazine editing and
writing; *Graduate Objectives or Program
Emphases*: Public affairs journalism;
Bachelor's Degree Majors: 80; *Master's
Degree Majors*: 8; *Full-Time Faculty*: 7;
Part-Time Faculty: 30.

FACILITIES AND SERVICES
*Practical experiences available
through*: Community Antenna (Cable)
Television Origination; Closed Circuit
Television Facility; Campus Newspaper
(Published Independently); Local
Commercial Newspaper; Local Commercial
Television Station; Desktop Publishing
Facility; Photographic Darkrooms; Video
Editing; Electronic Field Production
(Video); Film or Cinema Laboratory; FM
Radio Station (Institutional); Institutional
Magazine; Institutional Newspaper; Public
Relations Agency.

Columbia College - Chicago (Private)

Department of Television
600 South Michigan Avenue
Chicago, Illinois 60605
Telephone: (312) 663-1600

Edward L. Morris, Chair
Lucas Palermo, Administrator

CURRICULUM AND INSTRUCTION
Courses or Concentrations
Available: Advertising; Communication; Film
or Cinema; Journalism or Mass
Communication; Public Relations; Radio,
Television, Broadcasting, or
Telecommunications; Dance; Theatre;
Bachelor's Degree Majors: 658; *Full-Time
Faculty*: 8; *Part-Time Faculty*: 58; *Full-Time
Professional (non-clerical) Staff Members*: 5.

FACILITIES AND SERVICES
Practical experiences available through: Audio
Recording Laboratory; Community Antenna
(Cable) Television Origination; Closed
Circuit Television Facility; Campus
Newspaper (Published Independently);
Local Commercial Television Station;
Desktop Publishing Facility; Photographic
Darkrooms; Video Editing.

Columbia College - Chicago (Private)

Department of Marketing Communication
600 S. Michigan Avenue
Chicago, Illinois 60605
Telephone: (312) 663-1600

John H. Tarini, Chair
Lya Rosenblum, Dean

CURRICULUM AND INSTRUCTION
Courses or Concentrations
Available: Advertising; Communication; Public Relations; Marketing; *Program Coordinators*: Phil Kaplan (Marketing Program); Margaret Sullivan (Advertising Program); Mort Kaplan (Public Relations Program); *Bachelor's Degree Majors*: 400; *Full-Time Faculty*: 5; *Part-Time Faculty*: 36.

FACILITIES AND SERVICES
Practical experiences available through: Advertising Agency; AM Radio Station (Institutional); Local Commercial Newspaper; Local Commercial Television Station.

Columbia College - Chicago (Private)

Program of Public Relations Studies
600 S. Michigan
Chicago, Illinois 60605
Telephone: (312) 663-1600

Morton H. Kaplan, Director
John Tarini, Chair

CURRICULUM AND INSTRUCTION
Courses or Concentrations
Available: Advertising; Communication; Journalism or Mass Communication; Public Relations; Speech; *Program Coordinators*: Margaret Sullivan (Advertising); Nat Lehrman (Journalism); *Undergraduate Objectives or Program Emphases*: To develop an understanding of the planned management function of public relations. To learn and perfect those skills which help organizations reach, educate and influence their target audiences; *Bachelor's Degree Majors*: 150; *Full-Time Faculty*: 1; *Part-Time Faculty*: 8; *Full-Time Professional (non-clerical) Staff Members*: 2.

FACILITIES AND SERVICES
Practical experiences available through: Advertising Agency; AM Radio Station (Institutional); Campus Newspaper (Published Independently); Local Commercial Newspaper; Local Commercial Television Station; Public Relations Agency.

Concordia College (Private)

Department of Communication and Theatre
7400 Augusta
River Forest, Illinois 60305
Telephone: (312) 771-8300

Eunice R. Eifert, Chair
R. Allen Zimmer, Administrator

CURRICULUM AND INSTRUCTION
Courses or Concentrations
Available: Communication; Film or Cinema; Journalism or Mass Communication; Radio, Television, Broadcasting, or Telecommunications; Speech; *Undergraduate Objectives or Program Emphases*: Interdisciplinary communication major and a secondary education major; *Bachelor's Degree Majors*: 30; *Full-Time Faculty*: 4; *Part-Time Faculty*: 1.

FACILITIES AND SERVICES
Practical experiences available through: Advertising Agency; Closed Circuit Television Facility; Campus Newspaper (Published Independently); Desktop Publishing Facility; Photographic Darkrooms; Video Editing; Electronic Field Production (Video); Video Production Laboratory or Television Studio.

DePaul University (Private)

Department of Communication
2323 N. Seminary
Chicago, Illinois 60614
Telephone: (312) 341-6881

Richard A. Katula, Chair

CURRICULUM AND INSTRUCTION
Courses or Concentrations
Available: Advertising; Communication; Film or Cinema; Journalism or Mass Communication; Radio, Television, Broadcasting, or Telecommunications; Speech; Debate; *Program Coordinators*: Rick Garlick (Internship Director); Dennis Condon (Debate Coach); Sarah Wortman (Radio Director); *Undergraduate Objectives or Program Emphases*: To give students a humanities based, professionally-oriented understanding of communication in interpersonal, group, public and institutional contexts; *Bachelor's Degree Majors*: 400; *Full-Time Faculty*: 9; *Part-Time Faculty*: 10.

FACILITIES AND SERVICES
Practical experiences available
through: Advertising Agency; AM Radio
Station (Institutional); Campus Newspaper
(Published Independently); Local
Commercial Newspaper; Local Commercial
Television Station; Film or Cinema
Laboratory; Public Relations Agency.

Eastern Illinois University (Public)

Department of Speech Communication
Charleston, Illinois 61920
Telephone: (217) 581-2016

Douglas G. Bock, Chair
Jon Laible, Administrator

CURRICULUM AND INSTRUCTION
Courses or Concentrations
Available: Communication; Public Relations;
Radio, Television, Broadcasting, or
Telecommunications; Speech; Interpersonal
Communication; *Undergraduate Objectives or
Program Emphases*: Mass Communication;
Interpersonal Communication; Public
Relations; Rhetoric; *Graduate Objectives or
Program Emphases*: Mass Communication;
Rhetoric; Interpersonal Communication;
Public Relations; *Bachelor's Degree
Majors*: 321; *Full-Time Faculty*: 23;
Part-Time Faculty: 12; *Full-Time
Professional (non-clerical) Staff Members*: 2.

FACILITIES AND SERVICES
Practical experiences available
through: Advertising Agency; AM Radio
Station (Institutional); Associated Press
Wire Service Feed; Audio Recording
Laboratory; Community Antenna (Cable)
Television Origination; Campus Newspaper
(Published Independently); Local
Commercial Newspaper; Desktop Publishing
Facility; Photographic Darkrooms; Video
Editing; Electronic Field Production
(Video); Television Broadcast Station
(Institutional); FM Radio Station
(Institutional); Institutional Magazine;
Institutional Newspaper; Public Relations
Agency; United Press International Feed;
Video News and Data Processing.

Eastern Illinois University (Public)

Department of Journalism
Charleston, Illinois 61920
Telephone: (217) 581-6003 Extension or
Alternate: 581-5000

John David Reed, Chair
**Jon Laible, Dean, College of Liberal Arts
and Sciences**

CURRICULUM AND INSTRUCTION
Courses or Concentrations
Available: Advertising; Journalism; Public
Relations; Radio, Television, Broadcasting,
or Telecommunications; *Bachelor's Degree
Majors*: 170; *Full-Time Faculty*: 12;
Part-Time Faculty: 4; *Full-Time Professional
(non-clerical) Staff Members*: 1.

FACILITIES AND SERVICES
Practical experiences available
through: Advertising Agency; Associated
Press Wire Service Feed; Audio Recording
Laboratory; Closed Circuit Television
Facility; Campus Newspaper (Published
Independently); Local Commercial
Newspaper; Desktop Publishing Facility;
Photographic Darkrooms; Video Editing;
Electronic Field Production (Video);
Television Broadcast Station (Institutional);
FM Radio Station (Institutional);
Institutional Magazine; Institutional
Newspaper; Public Relations Agency;
Satellite Uplink Facility; United Press
International Feed; Video News and Data
Processing; Video Production Laboratory or
Television Studio.

Elgin Community College (Public)

Department of Speech
1700 Spartan Drive
Elgin, Illinois 60123
Telephone: (708) 697-1000

D. Gail Shadwell, Instructional Coordinator
Polly Nash-Wright, Administrator

CURRICULUM AND INSTRUCTION
Courses or Concentrations Available: Film or
Cinema; Radio, Television, Broadcasting, or
Telecommunications; Speech; *Undergraduate
Objectives or Program Emphases*: To provide
courses equivalent to Freshman-Sophomore
level for transfer students; to provide

required speech class for technical programs; to provide drama and forensics co-curricular programs; *Full-Time Faculty*: 4; *Part-Time Faculty*: 5.

FACILITIES AND SERVICES
Practical experiences available through: Community Antenna (Cable) Television Origination; Local Commercial Television Station; Video Production Laboratory or Television Studio.

Eureka College (Private)

Department of Speech Communication and Theatre Arts
300 College Avenue
Eureka, Illinois 61530
Telephone: (309) 467-3721

William A. Davis, Head
Gary Gammon, Dean

CURRICULUM AND INSTRUCTION
Courses or Concentrations Available: Communication; Information Science; Journalism or Mass Communication; Radio, Television, Broadcasting, or Telecommunications; Speech; *Undergraduate Objectives or Program Emphases*: Introductory course in a liberal arts setting; *Bachelor's Degree Majors*: 10; *Full-Time Faculty*: 2; *Part-Time Faculty*: 1.

FACILITIES AND SERVICES
Practical experiences available through: Audio Recording Laboratory; Closed Circuit Television Facility; Campus Newspaper (Published Independently); Local Commercial Newspaper; Photographic Darkrooms; Institutional Magazine; Public Relations Agency; Video Production Laboratory or Television Studio.

Governors State University (Public)

Division of Communication
University Park, Illinois 60466
Telephone: (708) 534-5000

Michael W. Purdy, Chair
Joyce Verrett, Dean

CURRICULUM AND INSTRUCTION
Courses or Concentrations

Available: Advertising; Communication; Film or Cinema; Journalism or Mass Communication; Public Relations; Radio, Television, Broadcasting, or Telecommunications; Speech; Instructional and Training Technology; *Undergraduate Objectives or Program Emphases*: To provide a liberal arts degree in communication with a core of communication theory and applications, while offering students career specific options and preparation for graduate degrees; *Graduate Objectives or Program Emphases*: To provide a core of communication theory and application for students preparing for communication professions or a Ph.D. program; *Bachelor's Degree Majors*: 55; *Master's Degree Majors*: 110; *Full-Time Faculty*: 10; *Part-Time Faculty*: 6; *Full-Time Professional (non-clerical) Staff Members*: 2.

FACILITIES AND SERVICES
Practical experiences available through: Advertising Agency; Audio Recording Laboratory; Community Antenna (Cable) Television Origination; Closed Circuit Television Facility; Campus Newspaper (Published Independently); Local Commercial Newspaper; Local Commercial Television Station; Desktop Publishing Facility; Photographic Darkrooms; Video Editing; Electronic Field Production (Video); ITFS Distribution System; Public Relations Agency; Satellite Uplink Facility; Video Production Laboratory or Television Studio.

Highland Community College (Public)

Division of Humanities/Social Sciences
Pearl City Road
Freeport, Illinois 61032
Telephone: (815) 235-6121

Tom Myers, Chair
John Raner, Dean of Instruction

CURRICULUM AND INSTRUCTION
Courses or Concentrations Available: Communication; Film or Cinema; Journalism or Mass Communication; Radio, Television, Broadcasting, or Telecommunications; Speech; Theatre; *Undergraduate Objectives or Program Emphases*: Provide the lower level course offerings for all majors; *Full-Time Faculty*: 17; *Part-Time Faculty*: 25;

Full-Time Professional (non-clerical) Staff
Members: 1.

FACILITIES AND SERVICES
Practical experiences available through: AM
Radio Station (Institutional); Audio
Recording Laboratory; Closed Circuit
Television Facility; Desktop Publishing
Facility; Photographic Darkrooms; Video
Editing; ITFS Distribution System;
Institutional Newspaper.

Illinois Benedictine College (Private)

**Department of Literature and
Communications
5700 College Road
Lisle, Illinois 60532
Telephone: (708) 960-1500 Extension or
Alternate: 603**

Peter B. Seely, Head

CURRICULUM AND INSTRUCTION
*Courses or Concentrations
Available*: Advertising; Communication; Film
or Cinema; Journalism or Mass
Communication; Public Relations; Radio,
Television, Broadcasting, or
Telecommunications; Speech; *Undergraduate
Objectives or Program Emphases*: To provide
a broad-based, yet career-oriented liberal
arts education for students interested in
broadcasting, cable, advertising, public
relations, publishing, literature, or English
education; *Bachelor's Degree Majors*: 70;
Full-Time Faculty: 6; *Part-Time Faculty*: 5.

FACILITIES AND SERVICES
*Practical experiences available
through*: Advertising Agency; AM Radio
Station (Institutional); Audio Recording
Laboratory; Community Antenna (Cable)
Television Origination; Campus Newspaper
(Published Independently); Local
Commercial Newspaper; Local Commercial
Television Station; Video Editing; Public
Relations Agency; Video Production
Laboratory or Television Studio.

Illinois Central College

**Fine Arts Department
East Peoria, Illinois 61635**

Kenneth Camp, Administrator

Illinois Institute of Technology (Private)

**Program of Technical and Professional
Communication
3101 S. Dearborn
Chicago, Illinois 60616
Telephone: (312) 567-3465**

Susan Feinberg, Director

CURRICULUM AND INSTRUCTION
*Courses or Concentrations
Available*: Communication; Information
Science; Speech; *Undergraduate Objectives or
Program Emphases*: Technical
communication and communication for
management, professional communication;
*Graduate Objectives or Program
Emphases*: Technical communication;
Bachelor's Degree Majors: 14; *Other Degree
Majors*: 55; *Full-Time Faculty*: 6; *Part-Time
Faculty*: 2.

FACILITIES AND SERVICES
*Practical experiences available
through*: Advertising Agency; Associated
Press Wire Service Feed; Audio Recording
Laboratory; Closed Circuit Television
Facility; Campus Newspaper (Published
Independently); Local Commercial
Newspaper; Canadian Press Feed; Desktop
Publishing Facility; Photographic
Darkrooms; Video Editing; Television
Broadcast Station (Institutional);
Institutional Newspaper; New York Times
Service Feed; Public Relations Agency;
Reuters News Agency; Satellite Uplink
Facility; United Press International Feed;
Video News and Data Processing; Video
Production Laboratory or Television Studio.

Illinois State University (Public)

Department of Mass Communication
Normal, Illinois 61761
Telephone: (309) 438-3671

Vincent Hazleton, Chair
Virginia Owen, Dean, Arts and Sciences

CURRICULUM AND INSTRUCTION
Courses or Concentrations
Available: Communication; Journalism or
Mass Communication; Public Relations;
Radio, Television, Broadcasting, or
Telecommunications; Speech; *Undergraduate
Objectives or Program Emphases*: Degree
programs in speech communication, public
relations and mass communication with
sequences in journalism and broadcasting;
*Graduate Objectives or Program
Emphases*: Masters program in
communication, theory oriented; *Master's
Degree Majors*: 63; *Full-Time Faculty*: 42;
Part-Time Faculty: 43.

FACILITIES AND SERVICES
*Practical experiences available
through*: Associated Press Wire Service Feed;
Audio Recording Laboratory; Community
Antenna (Cable) Television Origination;
Carrier Current Audio Distribution System;
Campus Newspaper (Published
Independently); Local Commercial
Newspaper; Local Commercial Television
Station; Desktop Publishing Facility;
Photographic Darkrooms; Video Editing;
Electronic Field Production (Video); FM
Radio Station (Institutional); Public
Relations Agency; Video News and Data
Processing; Video Production Laboratory or
Television Studio.

Illinois State University

Department of Communication
Normal, Illinois 60611

George Tuttle, Administrator

Illinois Valley Community College (Public)

Division of Humanities
2578 E. 350th Road
Oglesby, Illinois 61348
Telephone: (815) 224-2720

Samuel Rogal, Chair

CURRICULUM AND INSTRUCTION
Courses or Concentrations
Available: Communication; Film or Cinema;
Journalism or Mass Communication; Radio,
Television, Broadcasting, or
Telecommunications; Speech; *Undergraduate
Objectives or Program Emphases*: Preparing
students for transfer into communication
programs; *Full-Time Faculty*: 17.

FACILITIES AND SERVICES
*Practical experiences available
through*: Campus Newspaper (Published
Independently); Desktop Publishing Facility;
Photographic Darkrooms; Video Production
Laboratory or Television Studio.

John Wood Community College (Public)

Department of Communication
150 South 48th Street
Quincy, Illinois 62301-9990
Telephone: (217) 224-6500

Stephen Herald, Coordinator
Evert Boissell, OLC Director

CURRICULUM AND INSTRUCTION
Courses or Concentrations
Available: Communication; Journalism or
Mass Communication; Public Relations;
Radio, Television, Broadcasting, or
Telecommunications; Speech; *Undergraduate
Objectives or Program Emphases*: General
education courses for AA/AS students.

FACILITIES AND SERVICES
Practical experiences available through: Audio
Recording Laboratory; Community Antenna
(Cable) Television Origination; Desktop
Publishing Facility; Photographic
Darkrooms; Video Editing; Electronic Field
Production (Video); FM Radio Station
(Institutional); ITFS Distribution System;
Institutional Magazine; Satellite Uplink
Facility.

Joliet Junior College

Department of Fine Arts
1216 Houbolt Avenue
Joliet, Illinois 60436

Judson College (Private)

Concentration of Mass Communication
1151 North State Street
Elgin, Illinois 60123
Telephone: (708) 695-2500

Ronald I. Stotyn, Coordinator
Stuart Ryder, Chair, Communication Arts
Division

CURRICULUM AND INSTRUCTION
*Courses or Concentrations
Available*: Advertising; Communication; Film
or Cinema; Journalism or Mass
Communication; Public Relations; Radio and
Broadcasting; Popular Culture; *Program
Coordinators*: Stuart Ryder; *Undergraduate
Objectives or Program Emphases*: A broadly
based foundational program within a
Christian Liberal Arts degree program
intended to produce well trained and flexible
skilled communicators for the
communications industry; *Bachelor's Degree
Majors*: 25; *Full-Time Faculty*: 4; *Part-Time
Faculty*: 4.

FACILITIES AND SERVICES
*Practical experiences available
through*: Advertising Agency; Audio
Recording Laboratory; Carrier Current
Audio Distribution System; Campus
Newspaper (Published Independently);
Local Commercial Newspaper; Photographic
Darkrooms; Public Relations Agency.

Judson College (Private)

Division of Communication Arts
1151 North State Street
Elgin, Illinois 60123
Telephone: (708) 695-2500

Stuart Ryder, Chair
Harold Harper, Academic Dean

CURRICULUM AND INSTRUCTION
*Courses or Concentrations
Available*: Communication; Journalism or
Mass Communication; Public Relations;
Radio, Television, Broadcasting, or
Telecommunications; Speech; *Undergraduate
Objectives or Program Emphases*: Language
and literature, mass media, speech, general
communications; *Bachelor's Degree
Majors*: 30; *Full-Time Faculty*: 3; *Part-Time
Faculty*: 3.

FACILITIES AND SERVICES
*Practical experiences available
through*: Carrier Current Audio Distribution
System.

Kennedy-King College (Public)

Department of Speech, Theatre,
Broadcasting
6800 S. Wentworth Avenue
Chicago, Illinois 60621
Telephone: (312) 962-3200 Extension or
Alternate: 325

Frank Hayashida, Assistant Professor
Philip L. Williams, Administrator

CURRICULUM AND INSTRUCTION
*Courses or Concentrations
Available*: Communication; Radio,
Television, Broadcasting, or
Telecommunications; Speech; *Program
Coordinators*: Margaret Stubbs (Speech);
Philip Williams (Theatre); Virgil Hemphill
(Broadcasting); *Undergraduate Objectives or
Program Emphases*: To provide classroom
instruction and practical laboratory
experiences for students interested in speech
communication, broadcasting technology and
theatre technology; *Associate's Degree
Majors*: 50; *Full-Time Faculty*: 9; *Full-Time
Professional (non-clerical) Staff Members*: 5.

FACILITIES AND SERVICES
*Practical experiences available
through*: Community Antenna (Cable)
Television Origination; Video Editing;
Electronic Field Production (Video); FM
Radio Station (Institutional); ITFS
Distribution System; Satellite Uplink
Facility.

Lake Land College (Public)

Department of Radio-Television
South Route 45
Mattoon, Illinois 61938
Telephone: (217) 235-3231

Ed Moore, Director

CURRICULUM AND INSTRUCTION
Courses or Concentrations
Available: Advertising; Radio, Television, Broadcasting, or Telecommunications; Speech; *Undergraduate Objectives or Program Emphases*: The curriculum is geared to employment after completing the two year program. Some students transfer to four year schools, but acceptance is limited at a few in-state schools; *Associate's Degree Majors*: 34; *Full-Time Faculty*: 1.

FACILITIES AND SERVICES
Practical experiences available through: Campus Newspaper (Published Independently); Photographic Darkrooms; Video Editing; Electronic Field Production (Video); FM Radio Station (Institutional).

Lewis University (Private)

Department of Communications and Theatre
Route 53
Romeoville, Illinois 60441
Telephone: (815) 838-0500

Chet Kondratowicz, Chair

CURRICULUM AND INSTRUCTION
Courses or Concentrations
Available: Communication; Journalism or Mass Communication; Radio, Television, Broadcasting, or Telecommunications; Speech; Theatre; *Program Coordinators*: Collette Pollard (Journalism); Tom Lyzenga (Radio, Television); *Undergraduate Objectives or Program Emphases*: Career and/or graduate school preparation in broadcasting, print media, education or theatre; *Bachelor's Degree Majors*: 45; *Full-Time Faculty*: 5; *Full-Time Professional (non-clerical) Staff Members*: 2.

FACILITIES AND SERVICES
Practical experiences available through: Associated Press Wire Service Feed; Community Antenna (Cable) Television Origination; Closed Circuit Television Facility; Local Commercial Newspaper; Desktop Publishing Facility; Photographic Darkrooms; Video Editing; Television Broadcast Station (Institutional); FM Radio Station (Institutional); Institutional Newspaper.

Lewis and Clark College

Radio Broadcasting Department
5800 Godfrey Street
Godfrey, Illinois 62035

Stepehen Jankowski, Administrator

Lincoln College (Private)

Department of Broadcasting
300 Keokuk Street
Lincoln, Illinois 62656
Telephone: (217) 732-3155 Extension or Alternate: 213

Lloyd R. Kirby, General Manager
Thomas Zurkammer, Dean

CURRICULUM AND INSTRUCTION
Courses or Concentrations
Available: Communication; Journalism or Mass Communication; Public Relations; Radio, Television, Broadcasting, or Telecommunications; *Program Coordinator*: Lynn Spellman (Newspaper Journalism); *Undergraduate Objectives or Program Emphases*: Basic operating procedures at radio station, log keeping, format programming, broadcast journalism, remote broadcasting, editorials, history of radio, first amendment privileges; *Associate's Degree Majors*: 17; *Full-Time Faculty*: 1.

FACILITIES AND SERVICES
Practical experiences available through: Photographic Darkrooms; FM Radio Station (Institutional); Institutional Newspaper.

Loyola University of Chicago

Department of Communication
820 North Michigan Avenue
Chicago, Illinois 60611

Elaine Bruggemeir, Administrator

MacCormac Junior College

Speech, Communication, Journalism or Media Program
327 South LaSalle Street
Chicago, Illinois 60604

MacMurray College (Private)

Program of Journalism
Jacksonville, Illinois 62650
Telephone: (217) 479-7049

Allan A. Metcalf, Director
Betty Youngblood, Dean

CURRICULUM AND INSTRUCTION
Courses or Concentrations
Available: Journalism or Mass
Communication; *Undergraduate Objectives or Program Emphases*: Training in news writing and editing for newspapers; *Full-Time Faculty*: 1.

FACILITIES AND SERVICES
Practical experiences available through: Institutional Newspaper; Public Relations Agency; Video News and Data Processing.

McHenry County College (Public)

Division of Humanities and Social Sciences
Route 14 and Lucas Road
Crystal Lake, Illinois 60012
Telephone: (815) 455-3700

Robert M. Riner, Associate Dean
John Adelmann, Dean of Instruction

CURRICULUM AND INSTRUCTION
Courses or Concentrations
Available: Communication; Journalism or Mass Communication; Speech; *Program Coordinator*: Dora Tippens (English); *Undergraduate Objectives or Program Emphases*: Primarily general and specific education requirements and electives for transfer to a four year university or college; *Full-Time Faculty*: 24; *Part-Time Faculty*: 35.

FACILITIES AND SERVICES
Practical experiences available through: Campus Newspaper (Published Independently); Photographic Darkrooms;

Video Editing; Institutional Magazine; Video Production Laboratory or Television Studio.

Millikin University (Private)

Department of Communications
1182 West Main Street
Decatur, Illinois 62522
Telephone: (217) 424-6225

Hazel J. Rozema, Chair
Gerald Redford, Dean, Arts and Sciences

CURRICULUM AND INSTRUCTION
Courses or Concentrations
Available: Communication; Journalism or Mass Communication; Public Relations; Radio, Television, Broadcasting, or Telecommunications; Speech; *Program Coordinators*: Jimm Seaney (Radio-Television Broadcasting; Mass Media); *Undergraduate Objectives or Program Emphases*: Mass Communication, Radio, Television; Public Relations; Interpersonal and Organizational Communication; Public Speaking; Communication Theory; *Bachelor's Degree Majors*: 60; *Full-Time Faculty*: 4; *Part-Time Faculty*: 5.

FACILITIES AND SERVICES
Practical experiences available through: AM Radio Station (Institutional); Associated Press Wire Service Feed; Audio Recording Laboratory; Community Antenna (Cable) Television Origination; Closed Circuit Television Facility; Campus Newspaper (Published Independently); Local Commercial Newspaper; Local Commercial Television Station; Photographic Darkrooms; FM Radio Station (Institutional); Institutional Magazine; Institutional Newspaper; Satellite Uplink Facility (C Band Transmitter).

Monmouth College (Private)

Department of Speech Communication and Theatre Arts
700 East Broadway
Monmouth, Illinois 61462
Telephone: (309) 457-2397

William J. Wallace, Chair
William B. Julian, Dean of the College

CURRICULUM AND INSTRUCTION
Courses or Concentrations
Available: Communication; Journalism or Mass Communication; Public Relations; Radio, Television, Broadcasting, or Telecommunications; Speech; *Undergraduate Objectives or Program Emphases*: Preparation for entry level jobs and for graduate study; *Bachelor's Degree Majors*: 22; *Full-Time Faculty*: 4; *Part-Time Faculty*: 1.

FACILITIES AND SERVICES
Practical experiences available through: Audio Recording Laboratory; Carrier Current Audio Distribution System; Campus Newspaper (Published Independently); Local Commercial Newspaper; Canadian Press Feed; Video Editing; Electronic Field Production (Video); Institutional Newspaper; Video News and Data Processing; Video Production Laboratory or Television Studio.

Moody Bible Institute (Private)

Department of Communication
820 North LaSalle Drive
Chicago, Illinois 60610
Telephone: (312) 329-4000

Charles N. Christensen, Chair
Robert W. Woodburn, Administrator

CURRICULUM AND INSTRUCTION
Courses or Concentrations
Available: Communication; Journalism or Mass Communication; Radio, Television, Broadcasting, or Telecommunications; Speech; Audiovisual; English Composition; *Undergraduate Objectives or Program Emphases*: To develop an understanding of the principles of communication and enlarge abilities and skills in media arts to serve in church related organizations; *Bachelor's Degree Majors*: 57; *Other Degree Majors*: 13; *Full-Time Faculty*: 11; *Part-Time Faculty*: 5; *Full-Time Professional (non-clerical) Staff Members*: 3.

FACILITIES AND SERVICES
Practical experiences available through: AM Radio Station (Institutional); Audio Recording Laboratory; Carrier Current Audio Distribution System; Campus Newspaper (Published Independently); Photographic Darkrooms; Video Editing; Electronic Field Production (Video); FM Radio Station (Institutional); Institutional Newspaper; Video Production Laboratory or Television Studio.

Morton College (Public)

Division of Transfer Studies
3801 South Central Avenue
Cicero, Illinois 60650
Telephone: (708) 656-8000

Robert C. Ericson, Dean
T. G. Ludwig, Vice President, Academic Affairs

CURRICULUM AND INSTRUCTION
Courses or Concentrations
Available: Advertising; Communication; Film or Cinema; Journalism or Mass Communication; Speech; Drama; *Undergraduate Objectives or Program Emphases*: The English and Speech Curricula introduce the student to the components and interrelationships among English, speech and theatre; *Full-Time Faculty*: 8; *Part-Time Faculty*: 7.

FACILITIES AND SERVICES
Practical experiences available through: Campus Newspaper (Published Independently); Desktop Publishing Facility; Photographic Darkrooms.

Mundelein College (Private)

Department of Communications
6363 N. Sheridan Road
Chicago, Illinois 60660
Telephone: (312) 262-8100

Mary P. Haley, Chair
Mary Murphy, Vice President, Academic Affairs

CURRICULUM AND INSTRUCTION
Courses or Concentrations
Available: Communication; Film or Cinema; Journalism or Mass Communication; Public Relations; Radio, Television, Broadcasting, or Telecommunications; *Undergraduate Objectives or Program Emphases*: Broad overview of communications disciplines, visual literacy; knowledge of uses, techniques and effects of media technologies; knowledge of history, methods, issues of communications systems; professional production, especially in journalism and

public relations; *BFA Degree Majors*: 55;
Full-Time Faculty: 3; *Part-Time Faculty*: 2.

FACILITIES AND SERVICES
Practical experiences available
through: Campus Newspaper (Published
Independently); Desktop Publishing Facility;
Photographic Darkrooms.

North Central College (Private)

Department of Speech Communication,
Broadcasting Track
30 North Brainard Street
Naperville, Illinois 60566
Telephone: (708) 420-3438

Mary Ann Cunningham, Instructor
William G. Berberet, Vice President,
Academic Affairs

CURRICULUM AND INSTRUCTION
Courses or Concentrations
Available: Communication; Mass
Communication; Radio, Television,
Broadcasting, or Telecommunications;
Speech; *Undergraduate Objectives or Program*
Emphases: Preparing students for careers in
broadcasting through a liberal arts approach;
Bachelor's Degree Majors: 50; *Full-Time*
Faculty: 6; *Part-Time Faculty*: 3.

FACILITIES AND SERVICES
Practical experiences available
through: Associated Press Wire Service Feed;
Audio Recording Laboratory; Campus
Newspaper (Published Independently); FM
Radio Station (Institutional); Institutional
Newspaper.

North Park College

Department of Speech/Communications
5125 North Spaulding Avenue
Chicago, Illinois 60625-4987

Craig Stewart, Administrator

Northeastern Illinois University (Public)

Department of Speech and Performing Arts
5500 North St. Louis Avenue
Chicago, Illinois 60625
Telephone: (312) 583-4050

David F. Unumb, Chair
Battista Galassi, Dean, College of Arts and
Sciences

CURRICULUM AND INSTRUCTION
Courses or Concentrations
Available: Communication; Public Relations;
Radio, Television, Broadcasting, or
Telecommunications; Speech; *Undergraduate*
Objectives or Program Emphases: Broad
liberal arts program culminating in an
internship or capstone experience; *Graduate*
Objectives or Program Emphases: Research
oriented program designed to increase
students' understanding and skills; *Bachelor's*
Degree Majors: 155; *Master's Degree*
Majors: 56; *Full-Time Faculty*: 13;
Part-Time Faculty: 3; *Full-Time Professional*
(non-clerical) Staff Members: 1.

FACILITIES AND SERVICES
Practical experiences available
through: Advertising Agency; Campus
Newspaper (Published Independently);
Local Commercial Television Station; Video
Editing; FM Radio Station (Institutional);
Public Relations Agency.

Northern Illinois University (Public)

Department of Communication Studies
DeKalb, Illinois 60115
Telephone: (815) 753-1563

Richard L. Johannesen, Chair
James D. Norris, Dean, Liberal Arts and
Sciences

CURRICULUM AND INSTRUCTION
Courses or Concentrations
Available: Advertising; Communication; Film
or Cinema; Radio, Television, Broadcasting,
or Telecommunications; Speech; Rhetoric;
Organizational Communication; *Program*
Coordinators: Martha Cooper (Rhetoric);
Charles Larson (Communication Theory);
Robert Miller (Media studies);
Undergraduate Objectives or Program
Emphases: Interpersonal and Public

Communication; Communication Education; Media Studies; Organizational and Corporate Communication; *Graduate Objectives or Program Emphases*: Rhetorical Studies; Media Studies; Communication Theory and Organizational Communication; *Bachelor's Degree Majors*: 450; *Master's Degree Majors*: 50; *Other Degree Majors*: 500; *Full-Time Faculty*: 34; *Part-Time Faculty*: 27.

FACILITIES AND SERVICES
Practical experiences available through: AM Radio Station (Institutional); Audio Recording Laboratory; Community Antenna (Cable) Television Origination; Carrier Current Audio Distribution System; Campus Newspaper (Published Independently); Video Editing; Electronic Field Production (Video); FM Radio Station (Institutional); Video Production Laboratory or Television Studio.

Northern Illinois University (Public)

Department of Journalism
DeKalb, Illinois 60115
Telephone: (815) 753-1925

Donald F. Brod, Chair
James D. Norris, Dean

CURRICULUM AND INSTRUCTION
Courses or Concentrations Available: Journalism or Mass Communication; Public Relations; Radio, Television, Broadcasting, or Telecommunications; Photojournalism; *Undergraduate Objectives or Program Emphases*: To prepare communicators and an educated public by providing a professional program in a liberal arts context; *Graduate Objectives or Program Emphases*: To prepare communicators, scholars, and teachers to understand and deal with the mass media; *Bachelor's Degree Majors*: 200; *Master's Degree Majors*: 10; *Full-Time Faculty*: 11; *Full-Time Professional (non-clerical) Staff Members*: 3.

FACILITIES AND SERVICES
Practical experiences available through: Associated Press Wire Service Feed; Community Antenna (Cable) Television Origination; Campus Newspaper (Published Independently); Local Commercial Newspaper; Desktop Publishing Facility;

Photographic Darkrooms; Video Editing; Electronic Field Production (Video); Television Broadcast Station (Institutional); FM Radio Station (Institutional); Public Relations Agency; United Press International Feed; Video News and Data Processing.

Northwestern University (Private)

School of Speech
633 Clark Street
Evanston, Illinois 60208-2260
Telephone: (708) 491-7023

David Zarefsky, Dean

CURRICULUM AND INSTRUCTION
Courses or Concentrations Available: Communication; Film or Cinema; Radio, Television, Broadcasting, or Telecommunications; Speech; Communication Sciences and Disorders; *Program Coordinators*: Carol Simpson Stern (Performance); Paul Arntson (Communication); Mimi White (Radio, Television, and Film); Jerilyn Logemann (Communication Sciences, Disorders); Dean Garstecki (Audiology); Doris Johnson (Learning Disabilities); Charles Larson (Speech, Language Pathology); Pamela Cooper (Speech Education); Susan Lee (Theatre); *Undergraduate Objectives or Program Emphases*: To provide a liberal arts education with a particular focus on one of the speech disciplines, which students may also use for pre-professional purposes; *Graduate Objectives or Program Emphases*: To educate scholars, teachers, clinicians, and practitioners who are particularly oriented to research and theory; *Master's Degree Majors*: 153; *MFA Degree Majors*: 30; *Doctoral Degree Majors Currently in Residence*: 148; *Other Degree Majors*: 526; *Full-Time Faculty*: 89; *Part-Time Faculty*: 84; *Full-Time Professional (non-clerical) Staff Members*: 6. See one or more additional entries below.

FACILITIES AND SERVICES
Practical experiences available through: Audio Recording Laboratory; Local Commercial Television Station; Video Editing; Electronic Field Production (Video); Film or Cinema Laboratory; FM Radio Station (Institutional); Video Production Laboratory or Television Studio.

Northwestern University (Private)

Department of Radio/Television/Film
1905 Sheridan Road
Evanston, Illinois 60208
Telephone: (708) 491-7315

Miriam White, Chair
David Zarefsky, Dean, School of Speech

CURRICULUM AND INSTRUCTION
Courses or Concentrations Available: Film or Cinema; Radio, Television, Broadcasting, or Telecommunications; *Master's Degree Majors*: 10; *MFA Degree Majors*: 10; *Doctoral Degree Majors Currently in Residence*: 15; *Additional Doctoral Degree Majors*: 10; *Other Degree Majors*: 139; *Full-Time Faculty*: 13; *Part-Time Faculty*: 14; *Full-Time Professional (non-clerical) Staff Members*: 4.

FACILITIES AND SERVICES
Practical experiences available through: Associated Press Wire Service Feed; Audio Recording Laboratory; Community Antenna (Cable) Television Origination; Campus Newspaper (Published Independently); Desktop Publishing Facility; Video Editing; Electronic Field Production (Video); FM Radio Station (Institutional); Video Production Laboratory or Television Studio.

Northwestern University (Private)

Medill School of Journalism
1845 Sheridan Road
Evanston, Illinois 60208-2101
Telephone: (708) 491-5597

Michael C. Janeway, Dean
Arnold R. Weber, President

CURRICULUM AND INSTRUCTION
Courses or Concentrations Available: Advertising; Journalism or Mass Communication; Public Relations; Radio, Television, Broadcasting, or Telecommunications; *Undergraduate Objectives or Program Emphases*: Heavy emphasis in hands-on training in professional journalism practice and policies with specialties in newspaper, magazine, and broadcasting, within a context of a traditional liberal arts education; *Graduate Objectives or Program Emphases*: Heavy emphasis in hands-on training in terminal professional degree programs. Advertising takes an interdisciplinary approach; two programs include paid internships. Journalism emphasizes practice, policies, and offers coursework in Evanston, Chicago, and the District of Columbia; *Degree Majors*: 535; *Full-Time Faculty*: 51; *Part-Time Faculty*: 25.

FACILITIES AND SERVICES
Practical experiences available through: Advertising Agency; Associated Press Wire Service Feed; Community Antenna (Cable) Television Origination; Closed Circuit Television Facility; Campus Newspaper (Published Independently); Local Commercial Newspaper; Local Commercial Television Station; Desktop Publishing Facility; Video Editing; Electronic Field Production (Video); FM Radio Station (Institutional); Institutional Magazine; Public Relations Agency; Video Production Laboratory or Television Studio.

Oakton Community College

Audiovisual Services
1600 East Golf Road
Des Plaines, Illinois 60016

Robert Burton, Administrator

Olivet Nazarene University (Private)

Department of Speech Communication
Kankakee, Illinois 60901
Telephone: (815) 939-5287

Henry L. Smith, Director/Head
David Kale, Chair, Division of Communication

CURRICULUM AND INSTRUCTION
Courses or Concentrations Available: Communication; Journalism or Mass Communication; Radio, Television, Broadcasting, or Telecommunications; Speech; *Bachelor's Degree Majors*: 40; *Full-Time Faculty*: 4; *Part-Time Faculty*: 1; *Full-Time Professional (non-clerical) Staff Members*: 2.

FACILITIES AND SERVICES
Practical experiences available through: Audio Recording Laboratory; Carrier Current

Audio Distribution System; Desktop Publishing Facility; Photographic Darkrooms; FM Radio Station (Institutional); Institutional Newspaper; United Press International Feed.

Parkland College

Broadcasting Department
2400 West Bradley Avenue
Champaign, Illinois 61820

Steven Brown, Administrator

Principia College (Private)

Program of Mass Communication
Elsah, Illinois 62028
Telephone: (618) 374-2131

Richard Dearborn, Chair
Judy McCreary Felch, Unit Head

CURRICULUM AND INSTRUCTION
Courses or Concentrations
Available: Advertising; Journalism or Mass Communication; Public Relations; Radio, Television, Broadcasting, or Telecommunications; Speech; *Program Coordinator*: John W. Williams (Journalism and Mass Communication); *Undergraduate Objectives or Program Emphases*: Broadcasting (Television and Radio); Journalism; Mass Communication; *Bachelor's Degree Majors*: 25; *Full-Time Faculty*: 3; *Part-Time Faculty*: 2; *Full-Time Professional (non-clerical) Staff Members*: 1.

FACILITIES AND SERVICES
Practical experiences available through: Advertising Agency; Audio Recording Laboratory; Campus Newspaper (Published Independently); Local Commercial Newspaper; Local Commercial Television Station; Desktop Publishing Facility; Photographic Darkrooms; Video Editing; Electronic Field Production (Video); FM Radio Station (Institutional); Public Relations Agency; Video News and Data Processing; Video Production Laboratory or Television Studio.

Rend Lake College

Arts and Communications Department
Rural Route 1
Ina, Illinois 62846

Joseph H. Rust, Administrator

Roosevelt University

Journalism Department
430 South Michigan Avenue
Chicago, Illinois 60605

Charles Gene McDaniel, Administrator

St. Xavier College

Program Mass Communications
3700 West 103rd Street
Chicago, Illinois 60655

Don Pukala, Administrator

Sangamon State University (Public)

Program of Communication
Springfield, Illinois 62794-9243
Telephone: (217) 786-6790

Henry E. Nicholson, Convenor
William Bloemer, Dean, Liberal Arts and Science

CURRICULUM AND INSTRUCTION
Courses or Concentrations
Available: Communication; Journalism or Mass Communication; Public Relations; Radio, Television, Broadcasting, or Telecommunications; Speech; Semantics; *Undergraduate Objectives or Program Emphases*: Meaning; Intepersonal and Organizational Systems; Mass Media Systems; *Graduate Objectives or Program Emphases*: Meaning; Interpersonal and Organizational Systems; Mass Media Systems; *Bachelor's Degree Majors*: 109; *Master's Degree Majors*: 85; *Full-Time Faculty*: 6; *Part-Time Faculty*: 3.

FACILITIES AND SERVICES
Practical experiences available through: Associated Press Wire Service Feed; Audio Recording Laboratory; Community

Antenna (Cable) Television Origination; Closed Circuit Television Facility; Campus Newspaper (Published Independently); Desktop Publishing Facility; Photographic Darkrooms; Video Editing; Electronic Field Production (Video); FM Radio Station (Institutional); Institutional Magazine; Satellite Uplink Facility (Ku Band Transmitter); Video Production Laboratory or Television Studio.

Southern Illinois University - Carbondale (Public)

College of Communication and Fine Arts
Carbondale, Illinois 62901-6605
Telephone: (618) 453-4308

Marvin D. Kleinau, Acting Dean
Benjamin Shepherd, Vice President, Academic Affairs and Research

CURRICULUM AND INSTRUCTION
Courses or Concentrations Available: Advertising; Communication; Film or Cinema; Information Science; Journalism or Mass Communication; Public Relations; Radio, Television, Broadcasting, or Telecommunications; Speech; *Program Coordinators*: Joe Foote (Radio, Television); David Gilmore (Cinema and Photography); James VanOosting (Speech Communication); Walter Jaehnig (Journalism); *Undergraduate Objectives or Program Emphases*: Sales management, news and public affairs, production, news-editorial, performance studies, public relations, organizational, interpersonal, and persuasive communication, communication education; *Graduate Objectives or Program Emphases*: MA in management, policy and new technologies; Ph.D. in journalism with emphases in history, law, mass communication, political and international communication; Also, Ph.D. in Speech with emphasis in performance, philosophy, interpersonal communication; *Bachelor's Degree Majors*: 300; *Master's Degree Majors*: 56; *Doctoral Degree Majors Currently in Residence*: 50; *Additional Doctoral Degree Majors*: 25; *Other Degree Majors*: 705; *Full-Time Faculty*: 42; *Part-Time Faculty*: 67; *Full-Time Professional (non-clerical) Staff Members*: 7. See one or more additional entries below.

FACILITIES AND SERVICES
Practical experiences available through: Advertising Agency; AM Radio Station (Institutional); Audio Recording Laboratory; Community Antenna (Cable) Television Origination; Carrier Current Audio Distribution System; Local Commercial Newspaper; Local Commercial Television Station; Desktop Publishing Facility; Photographic Darkrooms; Video Editing; Electronic Field Production (Video); Television Broadcast Station (Institutional); Film or Cinema Laboratory; FM Radio Station (Institutional); ITFS Distribution System; Institutional Newspaper; Public Relations Agency; United Press International Feed.

Southern Illinois University - Carbondale (Public)

Department of Radio and Television
1056 Communications Building
Carbondale, Illinois 62901
Telephone: (618) 536-7555

Joe S. Foote, Chair
Marvin Kleineau, Acting Dean

CURRICULUM AND INSTRUCTION
Courses or Concentrations Available: Radio, Television, Broadcasting, or Telecommunications; *Undergraduate Objectives or Program Emphases*: BA in Radio and Television; Sales and Management; News and Public Affairs; Production; *Bachelor's Degree Majors*: 400; *Master's Degree Majors*: 30; *Full-Time Faculty*: 12; *Part-Time Faculty*: 2; *Full-Time Professional (non-clerical) Staff Members*: 3.

FACILITIES AND SERVICES
Practical experiences available through: AM Radio Station (Institutional); Associated Press Wire Service Feed; Carrier Current Audio Distribution System; Local Commercial Television Station; Video Editing; Television Broadcast Station (Institutional); United Press International Feed.

Southern Illinois University - Carbondale (Public)

School of Journalism
College of Communication and Fine Arts
Carbondale, Illinois 62901
Telephone: (618) 536-3361

Walter B. Jaehnig, Director
Marvin D. Kleinau, Acting Dean

CURRICULUM AND INSTRUCTION
*Courses or Concentrations
Available*: Advertising; Journalism or Mass
Communication; *Undergraduate Objectives or
Program Emphases*: News-editorial degree
program; advertising degree program;
*Graduate Objectives or Program
Emphases*: MS: Professional; MA: Academic;
Ph.D.: Journalism, emphases in history, law
or Mass Communication, Political
Communication; *Bachelor's Degree
Majors*: 380; *Master's Degree Majors: 5;
Doctoral Degree Majors Currently in
Residence*: 10; *Additional Doctoral Degree
Majors*: 5; *Other Degree Majors*: 15;
Full-Time Faculty: 13; *Part-Time
Faculty*: 17; *Full-Time Professional
(non-clerical) Staff Members*: 6.

FACILITIES AND SERVICES
*Practical experiences available
through*: Advertising Agency; AM Radio
Station (Institutional); Carrier Current
Audio Distribution System; Local
Commercial Newspaper; Local Commercial
Television Station; Desktop Publishing
Facility; Photographic Darkrooms; Video
Editing; Television Broadcast Station
(Institutional); Film and Cinema
Laboratory; FM Radio Station
(Institutional); Institutional Newspaper;
Public Relations Agency; United Press
International Feed.

Southern Illinois University - Carbondale (Public)

Department of Cinema and Photography
College of Communication and Fine Arts
Carbondale, Illinois 62901
Telephone: (618) 453-2365

David A Gilmore, Chair
Marvin Kleinau, Dean

CURRICULUM AND INSTRUCTION
Courses or Concentrations Available: Film or
Cinema; Photography; *Undergraduate
Objectives or Program Emphases*: Film,
photography production; film criticism,
theory, history; photography theory, history;
*Graduate Objectives or Program
Emphases*: Film, photography production;
film criticism, theory, history; photography
theory, history; *Bachelor's Degree
Majors*: 300; *MFA Degree Majors*: 20;
Full-Time Faculty: 10; *Full-Time
Professional (non-clerical) Staff Members*: 2.

FACILITIES AND SERVICES
*Practical experiences available
through*: Photographic Darkrooms; Film or
Cinema Laboratory.

Southern Illinois University - Edwardsville (Public)

School of Fine Arts and Communication
Campus Box 1770
Edwardsville, Illinois 62025
Telephone: (618) 692-2771

William H. Tarwater, Acting Dean
David J. Werner, Provost and Vice President

CURRICULUM AND INSTRUCTION
*Courses or Concentrations
Available*: Advertising; Communication; Film
or Cinema; Journalism or Mass
Communication; Public Relations; Radio,
Television, Broadcasting, or
Telecommunications; Speech; *Program
Coordinators*: David Valley (Speech
Communication); William Ward
(Journalism); Barbara Regnell (Television,
Radio and Mass Communication);
*Undergraduate Objectives or Program
Emphases*: To provide General Education to
all University students; to provide
pre-professional training in art, music,
journalism, radio and television, speech
communication, and theatre and dance;
*Graduate Objectives or Program
Emphases*: To provide professional training
in art, music, mass communications, and
speech communication; *Bachelor's Degree
Majors*: 346; *BFA Degree Majors*: 259;
Master's Degree Majors: 90; *MFA Degree
Majors*: 67; *Other Degree Majors*: 323;
Full-Time Faculty: 80; *Part-Time
Faculty*: 69; *Full-Time Professional
(non-clerical) Staff Members*: 6.

FACILITIES AND SERVICES
Practical experiences available

through: Associated Press Wire Service Feed; Audio Recording Laboratory; Community Antenna (Cable) Television Origination; Campus Newspaper (Published Independently); Photographic Darkrooms; Video Editing; Electronic Field Production (Video); Film or Cinema Laboratory; FM Radio Station (Institutional); Institutional Magazine; Video Production Laboratory or Television Studio.

Southern Illinois University - Edwardsville (Public)

Department of Speech Communication
Edwardsville, Illinois 62026-1772
Telephone: (618) 692-3090

David B. Valley, Chair
William Tarwater, Dean

CURRICULUM AND INSTRUCTION
Courses or Concentrations
Available: Communication; Public Relations; Speech; *Undergraduate Objectives or Program Emphases*: Interpersonal, public address, rhetorical criticism, teaching education, public relations, organizational; *Graduate Objectives or Program Emphases*: Interpersonal, organizational, and general communication; *Bachelor's Degree Majors*: 75; *Master's Degree Majors*: 35; *Full-Time Faculty*: 9; *Part-Time Faculty*: 9.

FACILITIES AND SERVICES
Practical experiences available through: Campus Newspaper (Published Independently); Desktop Publishing Facility; FM Radio Station (Institutional); Public Relations Agency; Video Production Laboratory or Television Studio.

Southern Illinois University - Edwardsville (Public)

Department of Mass Communication
Box 1775
Edwardsville, Illinois 62026
Telephone: (618) 692-2230

Barbara C. Regnell, Chair
William H. Tarwater, Dean, School of Fine Arts and Communications

CURRICULUM AND INSTRUCTION
Courses or Concentrations
Available: Journalism or Mass Communication; Radio, Television, Broadcasting, or Telecommunications; *Undergraduate Objectives or Program Emphases*: Professional; *Graduate Objectives or Program Emphases*: Problem oriented; *Bachelor's Degree Majors*: 250; *Master's Degree Majors*: 30; *Full-Time Faculty*: 9; *Part-Time Faculty*: 3; *Full-Time Professional (non-clerical) Staff Members*: 4.

FACILITIES AND SERVICES
Practical experiences available through: Associated Press Wire Service Feed; Audio Recording Laboratory; Campus Newspaper (Published Independently); Desktop Publishing Facility; Photographic Darkrooms; Video Editing; Electronic Field Production (Video); FM Radio Station (Institutional); Institutional Magazine; Video Production Laboratory or Television Studio.

Trinity Christian College (Private)

Department of Communication Arts
6601 West College Drive
Palos Heights, Illinois 60463
Telephone: (708) 597-3000

Annalee R. Ward, Chair
Burton Rozema, Administrator

CURRICULUM AND INSTRUCTION
Courses or Concentrations
Available: Advertising; Communication; Film or Cinema; Journalism or Mass Communication; Radio, Television, Broadcasting, or Telecommunications; Speech; *Undergraduate Objectives or Program Emphases*: Equip students to evaluate and communicate responsibly; to complement existing majors; to educate students about the breadth of communication studies; *Bachelor's Degree Majors*: 15; *Part-Time Faculty*: 4.

FACILITIES AND SERVICES
Practical experiences available through: Advertising Agency; Audio Recording Laboratory; Campus Newspaper (Published Independently); Photographic Darkrooms; Video Editing; Public Relations Agency; Video Production Laboratory or Television Studio.

University of Illinois - Chicago (Public)

Department of Communication and Theater
Box 4348
Chicago, Illinois 60680
Telephone: (312) 996-3187

Barbara Wood, Acting Head
Jay Levine, Dean, Liberal Arts and Sciences

CURRICULUM AND INSTRUCTION
*Courses or Concentrations
Available*: Communication; Journalism or
Mass Communication; Public Relations;
Radio, Television, Broadcasting, or
Telecommunications; Speech; *Undergraduate
Objectives or Program Emphases*: Ranges
from study of interpersonal communication
to the analysis of the communication process
in professional and social settings, using
various methods; a major chooses sequences
representing empirical, ethonographic, and
rhetorical-critical approaches; *Bachelor's
Degree Majors*: 260; *Master's Degree
Majors*: 58; *Full-Time Faculty*: 12;
Part-Time Faculty: 10; *Full-Time
Professional (non-clerical) Staff Members*: 2.

FACILITIES AND SERVICES
Practical experiences available through: Audio
Recording Laboratory; Campus Newspaper
(Published Independently); Local
Commercial Television Station; Video
Editing; Electronic Field Production
(Video); Institutional Newspaper; Video
Production Laboratory or Television Studio.

University of Illinois - Urbana (Public)

College of Communications
810 South Wright Street
Urbana, Illinois 61801
Telephone: (217) 333-2350

James W. Carey, Dean
Robert M. Berdahl, Administrator

CURRICULUM AND INSTRUCTION
*Courses or Concentrations
Available*: Advertising; Communication;
Journalism or Mass Communication; Radio,
Television, Broadcasting, or
Telecommunications; Media Studies;
Program Coordinators: Kim Rotzoll
(Advertising); Steven Helle (Journalism,
Radio, Television); Clifford Christians (Mass

Communication, Media Studies);
*Undergraduate Objectives or Program
Emphases*: These are professional programs
leading to the B.S. in Journalism, Advertising
and Broadcast Journalism. Media Studies is
an academic degree with a small component
of professional training in public
broadcasting; *Graduate Objectives or Program
Emphases*: Professional masters degrees in
Journalism and Advertising; Ph.D. is a
research degree in Communications;
Bachelor's Degree Majors: 437; *Master's
Degree Majors*: 75; *Doctoral Degree Majors
Currently in Residence*: 34; *Additional
Doctoral Degree Majors*: 10; *Full-Time
Faculty*: 43; *Part-Time Faculty*: 17;
*Full-Time Professional (non-clerical) Staff
Members*: 85.

FACILITIES AND SERVICES
Practical experiences available through: AM
Radio Station (Institutional); Associated
Press Wire Service Feed; Audio Recording
Laboratory; Community Antenna (Cable)
Television Origination; Campus Newspaper
(Published Independently); Desktop
Publishing Facility; Photographic
Darkrooms; Video Editing; Electronic Field
Production (Video); Television Broadcast
Station (Institutional); FM Radio Station
(Institutional); Video News and Data
Processing; Video Production Laboratory or
Television Studio.

University of Illinois - Urbana

Speech Communication Department
702 S. Wright St. #244
Urbana, Illinois 61801

Kenneth E. Anderson, Administrator

Wabash Valley College (Public)

Department of Broadcasting
2200 College Drive
Mount Carmel, Illinois 62863
Telephone: (618) 262-8641

James L. Cox, Director
Harry Benson, President

CURRICULUM AND INSTRUCTION
Courses or Concentrations Available: Radio,
Television, Broadcasting, or
Telecommunications; *Undergraduate*

Objectives or Program Emphases: The Radio and Television Broadcasting Program is a two year technical program offering an Associate in Applied Science Degree and emphasizing practical production and broadcast experiences in professional audio and video; *Associate's Degree Majors*: 28; *Full-Time Faculty*: 1; *Part-Time Faculty*: 3; *Full-Time Professional (non-clerical) Staff Members*: 3.

FACILITIES AND SERVICES
Practical experiences available through: Associated Press Wire Service Feed; Audio Recording Laboratory; Community Antenna (Cable) Television Origination; Campus Newspaper (Published Independently); Desktop Publishing Facility; Photographic Darkrooms; Video Editing; Electronic Field Production (Video); Television Broadcast Station (Institutional); FM Radio Station (Institutional); Video Production Laboratory or Television Studio.

Waubonsee Community College (Public)

Department of Speech, Journalism
Sugar Grove, Illinois 60554
Telephone: (708) 466-4811

Robert L. Gage, Dean of Instruction
Donald Foster, Vice President, Academic Affairs

CURRICULUM AND INSTRUCTION
Courses or Concentrations Available: Journalism or Mass Communication; Speech; *Associate's Degree Majors*: 10; *Full-Time Faculty*: 3; *Part-Time Faculty*: 6.

FACILITIES AND SERVICES
Practical experiences available through: Audio Recording Laboratory; Community Antenna (Cable) Television Origination; Closed Circuit Television Facility; Campus Newspaper (Published Independently); ITFS Distribution System; Video Production Laboratory or Television Studio.

Western Illinois University (Public)

Department of Communication Arts and Sciences
Macomb, Illinois 61455
Telephone: (309) 298-1507

Carolyn S. Collins, Chair
Richard Schaefer, Dean, College of Arts and Sciences

CURRICULUM AND INSTRUCTION
Courses or Concentrations Available: Communication; Radio, Television, Broadcasting, or Telecommunications; Speech; *Undergraduate Objectives or Program Emphases*: The program offers a BA degree in Communication Arts and Sciences with four options: Communication Arts and Sciences, Teacher Education, Public Communication and Human Relations, and Broadcasting; *Graduate Objectives or Program Emphases*: The program offers a comprehensive degree in communication and broadcasting; *Full-Time Faculty*: 20; *Part-Time Faculty*: 1; *Full-Time Professional (non-clerical) Staff Members*: 1.

FACILITIES AND SERVICES
Practical experiences available through: AM Radio Station (Institutional); Community Antenna (Cable) Television Origination.

Western Illinois University

Department of English and Journalism
Simpkins Hall
Macomb, Illinois 61455

Ronald Walker, Administrator

Wheaton College

Department of Communication
501 East Seminary
Wheaton, Illinois 60187

Paul Mark Fackler, Administrator

Wilbur Wright College

Speech Communication Department
3400 N. Austin Avenue
Chicago, Illinois 60634

Ronald H. Subeck, Administrator

William Rainey Harper College

Learning Resource Center
Algonquin and Roselle Roads
Palatine, Illinois 60067

Al Dunikoski, Administrator

Anderson University (Private)

Department of Communication
1100 East 5th Street
Anderson, Indiana 46012
Telephone: (317) 641-4340

Donald G. Boggs, Chair
Darlove Millor, Dean, School of Professional and Social Studies

CURRICULUM AND INSTRUCTION
Courses or Concentrations
Available: Communication; Journalism or Mass Communication; Public Relations; Radio, Television, Broadcasting, or Telecommunications; Speech; *Undergraduate Objectives or Program Emphases*: Preparation of students for life-long learning through theoretical and practical experiences; *Bachelor's Degree Majors*: 40; *Full-Time Faculty*: 5; *Part-Time Faculty*: 6; *Full-Time Professional (non-clerical) Staff Members*: 1.

FACILITIES AND SERVICES
Practical experiences available through: Associated Press Wire Service Feed; Audio Recording Laboratory; Carrier Current Audio Distribution System; Local Commercial Newspaper; Local Commercial Television Station; Desktop Publishing Facility; Photographic Darkrooms; Video Editing; Electronic Field Production (Video); Institutional Newspaper; Public Relations Agency; Video News and Data Processing; Video Production Laboratory or Television Studio.

Ball State University (Public)

Center for Information and Communication Sciences - BC 213
Muncie, Indiana 47306
Telephone: (317) 285-1889

Ray L. Steele, Chair
Marjorie Smelator, Dean

CURRICULUM AND INSTRUCTION
Courses or Concentrations
Available: Communication; Information Science; Radio, Television, Broadcasting, or Telecommunications; *Graduate Objectives or Program Emphases*: An interdisciplinary degree program which offers educational and laboratory experiences for people who wish to work with voice, data, and video imagining technologies in the business, government, health-care and education sectors of society.; *Other Degree Majors*: 150; *Full-Time Faculty*: 6; *Part-Time Faculty*: 12.

FACILITIES AND SERVICES
Practical experiences available through: Audio Recording Laboratory; Carrier Current Audio Distribution System; Closed Circuit Television Facility; Desktop Publishing Facility; Video Editing; Electronic Field Production (Video); Television Broadcast Station (Institutional); FM Radio Station (Institutional); ITFS Distribution System; Video Production Laboratory or Television Studio.

Ball State University (Public)

Department of Telecommunications
2000 University Avenue
Muncie, Indiana 47306

John Kurtz, Administrator

Ball State University (Public)

Department of Journalism
Muncie, Indiana 47306
Telephone: (317) 285-8200

Earl L. Conn, Chair
Marjorie Smelstor, Dean

CURRICULUM AND INSTRUCTION
Courses or Concentrations
Available: Advertising; Journalism or Mass Communication; Public Relations; *Undergraduate Objectives or Program Emphases*: To prepare students for media careers and to offer all campus students useful work in gathering, writing, and processing information; *Graduate Objectives or Program Emphases*: Offer students professional improvement work plus

acquisition of research tools; *Associate's Degree Majors*: 3; *Bachelor's Degree Majors*: 452; *Master's Degree Majors*: 69; *Full-Time Faculty*: 20; *Part-Time Faculty*: 10; *Full-Time Professional (non-clerical) Staff Members*: 5.

FACILITIES AND SERVICES
Practical experiences available through: Advertising Agency; Desktop Publishing Facility; Photographic Darkrooms; Television Broadcast Station (Institutional); Institutional Magazine; Institutional Newspaper; Public Relations Agency; Video News and Data Processing.

Ball State University (Public)

Speech Communication Department
Muncie, Indiana 47306

Richard G. Nitcavic, Administrator

Butler University (Private)

Department of Journalism
Indianapolis, Indiana 46208

James T. Neal, Administrator

Butler University - Jordan College of Fine Arts (Private)

Department of Radio/Television
4600 Sunset Avenue
Indianapolis, Indiana 46208
Telephone: (317) 283-9231

Kenneth C. Creech, Chair
Jack L. Eaton, Dean

CURRICULUM AND INSTRUCTION
Courses or Concentrations Available: Film or Cinema; Radio, Television, Broadcasting, or Telecommunications; *Undergraduate Objectives or Program Emphases*: Advanced broadcasting as an art and an industry; provide hands-on experience; allow for study outside the major (24 hours) and for a strong Liberal Arts core curriculum at the university; *Graduate Objectives or Program Emphases*: Advanced study in broadcasting; study in an outside area; opportunity for creative pursuits and research; *Degree*

Majors: 140; *Full-Time Faculty*: 3; *Part-Time Faculty*: 10; *Full-Time Professional (non-clerical) Staff Members*: 5.

FACILITIES AND SERVICES
Practical experiences available through: Associated Press Wire Service Feed; Community Antenna (Cable) Television Origination; Carrier Current Audio Distribution System; Campus Newspaper (Published Independently); Desktop Publishing Facility; Video Editing; Electronic Field Production (Video); FM Radio Station (Institutional); United Press International Feed; Video News and Data Processing; Video Production Laboratory or Television Studio.

Calumet College

Division of Communication and Fine Arts
2400 New York Avenue
Whiting, Indiana 46394

Robert Anderson, Administrator

DePauw University (Private)

Department of English
Greencastle, Indiana 46135
Telephone: (317) 658-4800

Martha Rainbolt, Chair
Fred Silander, Academic Vice President

CURRICULUM AND INSTRUCTION
Courses or Concentrations Available: Film or Cinema; Journalism or Mass Communication; *Bachelor's Degree Majors*: 100; *Full-Time Faculty*: 15; *Part-Time Faculty*: 10.

FACILITIES AND SERVICES
Practical experiences available through: AM Radio Station (Institutional); Campus Newspaper (Published Independently); Local Commercial Newspaper; Desktop Publishing Facility; Photographic Darkrooms; Video Editing.

DePauw University (Private)

Department of Communication Arts and Sciences
Greencastle, Indiana 46135
Telephone: (317) 658-4800

Larry G. Sutton, Chair
Fred Silander, Vice President, Academic Affairs

CURRICULUM AND INSTRUCTION
Courses or Concentrations
Available: Communication; Journalism or Mass Communication; Public Relations; Radio, Television, Broadcasting, or Telecommunications; Speech; Theatre; *Undergraduate Objectives or Program Emphases*: Areas of specialties within a framework of liberal arts; program emphasizes substantive course work; *Bachelor's Degree Majors*: 160; *Full-Time Faculty*: 9; *Part-Time Faculty*: 2.

FACILITIES AND SERVICES
Practical experiences available through: Associated Press Wire Service Feed; Closed Circuit Television Facility; Campus Newspaper (Published Independently); Desktop Publishing Facility; Photographic Darkrooms; Video Editing; Electronic Field Production (Video); FM Radio Station (Institutional); Video Production Laboratory or Television Studio.

Defense Information School (Military)

Journalism, Broadcasting and Public Administration Department
Building 400, Room 171
Fort Benjamin Harrison
Indianapolis, Indiana 46216-6200

Jack Rubak, Administrator

Earlham College (Private)

Department of English
Richmond, Indiana 47374
Telephone: (317) 983-1200

Lincoln C. Blake, Convener
Leonard Clark, Dean of the Faculty

CURRICULUM AND INSTRUCTION
Courses or Concentrations Available: Journalism or Mass Communication; Speech; *Undergraduate Objectives or Program Emphases*: Introduction to techniques of newswriting and the proper handling of news copy; *Full-Time Faculty*: 7.

FACILITIES AND SERVICES
Practical experiences available through: Associated Press Wire Service Feed; Campus Newspaper (Published Independently); Local Commercial Newspaper; Desktop Publishing Facility; Photographic Darkrooms; Video Editing; FM Radio Station (Institutional); Public Relations Agency.

Fort Wayne Bible College

1025 West Rudisill Boulevard
Fort Wayne, Indiana 46807

Jon Swanson, Administrator

Franklin College (Private)

Pulliam School of Journalism
501 East Monroe Street
Franklin, Indiana 46131
Telephone: (317) 736-8441

Jerry Miller, Chair
Lawrence Bryan, Dean

CURRICULUM AND INSTRUCTION
Courses or Concentrations Available: Advertising; Journalism or Mass Communication; Public Relations; Radio, Television, Broadcasting, or Telecommunications; *Undergraduate Objectives or Program Emphases*: To provide a balanced journalism education and a well-rounded mix of theory and practice, all within a liberal-arts context; *Bachelor's Degree Majors*: 50; *Full-Time Faculty*: 5; *Part-Time Faculty*: 1; *Full-Time Professional (non-clerical) Staff Members*: 1.

FACILITIES AND SERVICES
Practical experiences available through: Associated Press Wire Service Feed; Audio Recording Laboratory; Photographic Darkrooms; Video Editing; FM Radio Station (Institutional); Institutional Magazine; Institutional Newspaper; Video

News and Data Processing; Video Production Laboratory or Television Studio.

Goshen College (Private)

Department of Communication
1700 South Main Street
Goshen, Indiana 46526
Telephone: (219) 535-7000

Stuart W. Showalter, Chair
John W. Eby, Dean of the College

CURRICULUM AND INSTRUCTION
Courses or Concentrations
Available: Communication; Film or Cinema; Journalism or Mass Communication; Public Relations; Radio, Television, Broadcasting, or Telecommunications; Speech; *Undergraduate Objectives or Program Emphases*: To teach fundamental skills in speaking and writing while emphasizing an understanding of the history, structures, and functions of communication systems. Students study in the liberal arts context with a 14-week international study-service term; *Bachelor's Degree Majors*: 32; *Full-Time Faculty*: 4; *Part-Time Faculty*: 2; *Full-Time Professional (non-clerical) Staff Members*: 1.

FACILITIES AND SERVICES
Practical experiences available through: Associated Press Wire Service Feed; Audio Recording Laboratory; Local Commercial Newspaper; Local Commercial Television Station; Desktop Publishing Facility; Photographic Darkrooms; Video Editing; Electronic Field Production (Video); FM Radio Station (Institutional); Institutional Newspaper; Video News and Data Processing.

Grace College

Department of Communication
200 Seminary Drive
Winona Lake, Indiana 46590

Stephen A. Grill, Administrator

Hanover College

Department of Communication
206 Garritt Street
Hanover, Indiana 47243

Barbara Oney Garvey, Administrator

Huntington College (Private)

Department of Speech Communication
2303 College Avenue
Huntington, Indiana 46750
Telephone: (219) 356-6000

William G. Covington Jr., Head
Chaney R. Bergdall, Division Chair

CURRICULUM AND INSTRUCTION
Courses or Concentrations
Available: Communication; Radio, Television, Broadcasting, or Telecommunications; Speech; *Undergraduate Objectives or Program Emphases*: The major is a preprofessional program designed to provide an adequate foundation for professional education or careers in the mass communication media; *Bachelor's Degree Majors*: 20; *Full-Time Faculty*: 1.

FACILITIES AND SERVICES
Practical experiences available through: Campus Newspaper (Published Independently); Local Commercial Newspaper; Local Commercial Television Station; Television Broadcast Station (Institutional); Institutional Newspaper; Video Production Laboratory or Television Studio.

Indiana State University (Public)

Department of Communication
Stalker Hall, Room 213
Terre Haute, Indiana 47809
Telephone: (812) 237-3245

Dan P. Millar, Chair
Judy Hample, Dean, College of Arts and Sciences

CURRICULUM AND INSTRUCTION
Courses or Concentrations
Available: Advertising; Communication; Film or Cinema; Journalism or Mass Communication; Public Relations; Radio, Television, Broadcasting, or

Telecommunications; Speech; Theatre; *Program Coordinators*: Warren Barnard (Journalism); Joe Duncan (Radio, Television, Film); Donald Shields (Speech Communication); *Undergraduate Objectives or Program Emphases*: Several special areas and programs constitute the department: Journalism; Radio, Television, and Film; Speech Communication; Public Relations; Oral Interpretation of Literature; and Communication Education; *Graduate Objectives or Program Emphases*: Journalism; Radio, Television, and Film; Speech Communication; Public Relations; Oral Interpretation of Literature; and Communication Education; *Bachelor's Degree Majors*: 430; *Master's Degree Majors*: 50; *Full-Time Faculty*: 21; *Part-Time Faculty*: 29; *Full-Time Professional (non-clerical) Staff Members*: 2.

FACILITIES AND SERVICES
Practical experiences available through: Associated Press Wire Service Feed; Audio Recording Laboratory; Carrier Current Audio Distribution System; Campus Newspaper (Published Independently); Local Commercial Newspaper; Local Commercial Television Station; Desktop Publishing Facility; Photographic Darkrooms; Video Editing; Electronic Field Production (Video); Film or Cinema Laboratory; FM Radio Station (Institutional); ITFS Distribution System; Institutional Magazine; Public Relations Agency; Satellite Uplink Facility; Video Production Laboratory or Television Studio.

Indiana University - Bloomington (Public)

School of Library and Information Science
Bloomington, Indiana 47405
Telephone: (812) 855-2848

Herbert S. White, Dean
Kenneth R. R. Gros Louis, Vice President and Chancellor

CURRICULUM AND INSTRUCTION
Courses or Concentrations Available: Information Science; Library Science; Information Center Administration; *Graduate Objectives or Program Emphases*: Prepare students to work as information and library professionals. Academic preparation includes nine dual degree programs; *Doctoral Degree Majors*

Currently in Residence: 45; *Additional Doctoral Degree Majors*: 15; *Other Degree Majors*: 550; *Full-Time Faculty*: 16; *Part-Time Faculty*: 40; *Full-Time Professional (non-clerical) Staff Members*: 3.

FACILITIES AND SERVICES
Practical experiences available through: Audio Recording Laboratory.

Indiana University - Bloomington (Public)

Department of Speech Communication
809 East 7th Street
Bloomington, Indiana 47405
Telephone: (812) 855-6467

James R. Andrews, Chair
Morton Lowengrub, Dean, College of Arts and Sciences

CURRICULUM AND INSTRUCTION
Courses or Concentrations Available: Communication; Speech; Rhetorical Studies; *Undergraduate Objectives or Program Emphases*: To provide an understanding of the nature and processes of communication and to development abilities needed to apply concepts; *Graduate Objectives or Program Emphases*: Development of scholars, teachers and professionals in rhetoric and communication; *Bachelor's Degree Majors*: 136; *Master's Degree Majors*: 15; *Doctoral Degree Majors Currently in Residence*: 25; *Additional Doctoral Degree Majors*: 21; *Full-Time Faculty*: 12; *Part-Time Faculty*: 34.

Indiana University - Bloomington (Public)

Department of Telecommunications
Radio-Television Building Room 101
Bloomington, Indiana 47405
Telephone: (812) 855-6895

Donald E. Agostino, Chair

CURRICULUM AND INSTRUCTION
Courses or Concentrations Available: Radio, Television, Broadcasting, or Telecommunications; *Program Coordinators*: Chris Anderson (Honors);

Michael McGregor (Voice, Data, Imaging); *Undergraduate Objectives or Program Emphases*: The curriculum is designed for students who desire knowledge of the structures, economics, and effects of electronic media and their place in contemporary society, who plan to enter the media industries, and who plan careers in related areas; Preparation for advance study; *Graduate Objectives or Program Emphases*: MA, MS, and Ph.D. programs prepare students for research, teaching, or administrative positions at intermediate or advanced levels in careers related to the mass media; *Bachelor's Degree Majors*: 538; *Master's Degree Majors*: 8; *Doctoral Degree Majors Currently in Residence*: 13; *Additional Doctoral Degree Majors*: 6; *Other Degree Majors*: 3; *Full-Time Faculty*: 15; *Part-Time Faculty*: 22; *Full-Time Professional (non-clerical) Staff Members*: 1.

FACILITIES AND SERVICES
Practical experiences available through: Associated Press Wire Service Feed; Audio Recording Laboratory; Community Antenna (Cable) Television Origination; Carrier Current Audio Distribution System; Closed Circuit Television Facility; Campus Newspaper (Published Independently); Video Editing; Electronic Field Production (Video); Television Broadcast Station (Institutional); FM Radio Station (Institutional); ITFS Distribution System; Institutional Magazine; Institutional Newspaper; Satellite Uplink Facility (C Band Transmitter); Video News and Data Processing.

Indiana University - Bloomington (Public)

School of Journalism
Bloomington, Indiana 47405

Trevor R. Brown, Dean

Indiana University - South Bend (Public)

Department of Communication Arts
1700 Mishawaka Avenue
P. O. Box 7111
South Bend, Indiana 46634
Telephone: (219) 237-4268

Warren Pepperdine, Chair
Paul Hern, Administrator

CURRICULUM AND INSTRUCTION
Courses or Concentrations Available: Communication; Film or Cinema; Journalism or Mass Communication; Radio, Television, Broadcasting, or Telecommunications; Speech; *Undergraduate Objectives or Program Emphases*: To provide a liberal arts background; theatre emphasis on production; *Bachelor's Degree Majors*: 55; *Full-Time Faculty*: 6; *Part-Time Faculty*: 12.

FACILITIES AND SERVICES
Practical experiences available through: Advertising Agency; Audio Recording Laboratory; Closed Circuit Television Facility; Campus Newspaper (Published Independently); Local Commercial Newspaper; Local Commercial Television Station; Desktop Publishing Facility; Photographic Darkrooms; Video Editing.

Indiana University - Purdue University - Indianapolis (Public)

Department of Communication and Theatre
525 North Blackford Street
Indianapolis, Indiana 46202-3120
Telephone: (317) 274-0566

Robert C. Dick, Chair
John Barlow, Dean, School of Liberal Arts

CURRICULUM AND INSTRUCTION
Courses or Concentrations Available: Communication; Radio, Television, Broadcasting, or Telecommunications; Speech; Organizational Communication; *Program Coordinators*: Michael E. Balmert (Organizational Communication); Stan Denski, Acting (Telecommunications); *Undergraduate Objectives or Program Emphases*: Tracks are offered in Organizational Communication, Speech,

Telecommunications, and Theatre Arts; *Associate's Degree Majors*: 3; *Bachelor's Degree Majors*: 169; *Full-Time Faculty*: 12; *Part-Time Faculty*: 47; *Full-Time Professional (non-clerical) Staff Members*: 1.

FACILITIES AND SERVICES
Practical experiences available through: Audio Recording Laboratory; Community Antenna (Cable) Television Origination; Closed Circuit Television Facility; Campus Newspaper (Published Independently); Local Commercial Television Station; Video Editing; Electronic Field Production (Video); Institutional Newspaper; Public Relations Agency; Desktop Publishing; Video Production Laboratory or Television Studio.

Indiana University - Purdue University - Indianapolis (Public)

Department of English
425 University Boulevard
Indianapolis, Indiana 46202-5140
Telephone: (317) 274-0080

Marian Brock, Administrator
Richard Turner, Chair
John Barlow, Dean, School of Liberal Arts

CURRICULUM AND INSTRUCTION
Courses or Concentrations Available: Film or Cinema; English-Composition; *Undergraduate Objectives or Program Emphases*: Film Criticism, History of Film, Film Aesthetics; *Full-Time Faculty*: 2.

Indiana University - Purdue University - Indianapolis (Public)

School of Journalism
Indianapolis, Indiana 46223

James W. Brown, Associate Dean

Indiana University - Purdue University - Fort Wayne (Public)

Department of Communication
2101 Coliseum Boulevard East
Fort Wayne, Indiana 46805
Telephone: (219) 481-6825

David E. Switzer, Acting Chair
David Cox, Dean, Arts and Sciences

CURRICULUM AND INSTRUCTION
Courses or Concentrations Available: Communication; Film or Cinema; Journalism or Mass Communication; Public Relations; Radio, Television, Broadcasting, or Telecommunications; Speech; *Undergraduate Objectives or Program Emphases*: Interpersonal and Public Relations; Radio-Television; *Graduate Objectives or Program Emphases*: Professional Communication Studies (pending); *Bachelor's Degree Majors*: 300; *Full-Time Faculty*: 11; *Part-Time Faculty*: 9; *Full-Time Professional (non-clerical) Staff Members*: 1.

FACILITIES AND SERVICES
Practical experiences available through: Audio Recording Laboratory; Community Antenna (Cable) Television Origination; Closed Circuit Television Facility; Local Commercial Newspaper; Local Commercial Television Station; Video Editing; Electronic Field Production (Video); Public Relations Agency; Video Production Laboratory or Television Studio.

Indiana Vocational Technical College

Electronics
3501 Fist Avenue
Evansville, Indiana 47710

Jerome Schultheis, Administrator

Manchester College (Private)

Department of Communication Studies
North Manchester, Indiana 46962
Telephone: (219) 982-5000

Scott K. Strode, Chair
Ronald Arnett, Academic Dean

CURRICULUM AND INSTRUCTION
*Courses or Concentrations
Available*: Communication; Journalism or
Mass Communication; Radio, Television,
Broadcasting, or Telecommunications;
Speech; Organizational, Interpersonal;
Rhetoric, Public Address; *Program
Coordinators*: Marcia Benjamin
(Organizational, Interpersonal); Sam Davis
(Broadcast Media); Larry Underberg
(Rhetoric, Public Address); *Undergraduate
Objectives or Program Emphases*: To assess
impact of communication through an
audience centered perspective; to illustrate
basic variables in oral communication; to
equip students for responsible
decision-making; to study theories and
practices of the various communication
fields; *Associate's Degree Majors*: 6;
Bachelor's Degree Majors: 19; *Full-Time
Faculty*: 4.

FACILITIES AND SERVICES
*Practical experiences available
through*: Advertising Agency; Campus
Newspaper (Published Independently);
Local Commercial Newspaper; Local
Commercial Television Station; FM Radio
Station (Institutional); Public Relations
Agency; United Press International Feed;
Video Production Laboratory or Television
Studio.

Marian College (Private)

**Department of English
3200 Coldspring Road
Indianapolis, Indiana 46222
Telephone: (317) 929-0123**

**Brian U. Adler, Head
Raymond C. Craig, Administrator**

CURRICULUM AND INSTRUCTION
*Courses or Concentrations
Available*: Communication; Film or Cinema;
Journalism or Mass Communication;
Rhetoric; *Program Coordinators*: James
Goebel (Film, Cinema); *Undergraduate
Objectives or Program Emphases*: English
Major; English Education Major; Journalism
and Mass Communication Minor; *Bachelor's
Degree Majors*: 30; *Full-Time Faculty*: 5;
Part-Time Faculty: 5.

FACILITIES AND SERVICES
*Practical experiences available
through*: Advertising Agency; Campus
Newspaper (Published Independently);

Desktop Publishing Facility; Photographic
Darkrooms; Film or Cinema Laboratory;
Institutional Newspaper.

Marian College (Private)

**Department of Theatre/Speech
Communications
3200 Cold Spring Road
Indianapolis, Indiana 46222
Telephone: (317) 929-0292**

**David P. Edgecombe, Chair
Sr. Clair Whalen, Dean**

CURRICULUM AND INSTRUCTION
*Courses or Concentrations
Available*: Communication; Film or Cinema;
Public Relations; Radio, Television,
Broadcasting, or Telecommunications;
Speech; Arts Administration; *Undergraduate
Objectives or Program Emphases*: To provide
a general knowledge of communication field.
To integrate theatre, broadcasting and
communication into a liberal arts context;
Bachelor's Degree Majors: 9; *Full-Time
Faculty*: 2; *Part-Time Faculty*: 4.

FACILITIES AND SERVICES
Practical experiences available through: Audio
Recording Laboratory; Campus Newspaper
(Published Independently); Local
Commercial Television Station; Desktop
Publishing Facility; Photographic
Darkrooms; Electronic Field Production
(Video); Institutional Magazine;
Institutional Newspaper.

Martin Center College (Private)

**Division of Communication Arts
P.O. Box 18567
Indianapolis, Indiana 46218
Telephone: (317) 543-3235**

**Roberta H. Kimble, Chair
Sr. Jane Schilling, Academic Dean**

CURRICULUM AND INSTRUCTION
*Courses or Concentrations
Available*: Communication; Journalism or
Mass Communication; Public Relations;
Speech; Composition, Literature, Foreign
Language; *Undergraduate Objectives or
Program Emphases*: Interdisciplinary
approach to developing oral and written

communication skills with focus in composition and speech, language skills, appreciation of literature as a form of communication, and practical applications for today's society in mass media.; *Bachelor's Degree Majors*: 15; *Full-Time Faculty*: 3; *Part-Time Faculty*: 8.

FACILITIES AND SERVICES
Practical experiences available through: Community Antenna (Cable) Television Origination; Campus Newspaper (Published Independently); Local Commercial Newspaper; Desktop Publishing Facility; Photographic Darkrooms; Institutional Magazine.

Purdue University - North Central (Public)

Program of Communication
1401 South U. S. Highway 421
Westville, Indiana 46391-9528
Telephone: (219) 785-5202

Scott Smithson, Coordinator
Thomas Young, Administrator

CURRICULUM AND INSTRUCTION
Courses or Concentrations Available: Communication; Speech; *Undergraduate Objectives or Program Emphases*: Prepare area students for transfer to other Purdue campuses to complete communication degrees in specialty areas; *Associate's Degree Majors*: 35; *Other Degree Majors*: 35; *Full-Time Faculty*: 2; *Part-Time Faculty*: 6; *Full-Time Professional (non-clerical) Staff Members*: 1.

FACILITIES AND SERVICES
Practical experiences available through: Campus Newspaper (Published Independently); Video Editing; Electronic Field Production (Video); Video Production Laboratory or Television Studio.

Purdue University - West Lafayette (Public)

Department of Communication
West Lafayette, Indiana 47907
Telephone: (317) 494-3304

Charles J. Stewart, Head
David A. Caputo, Dean

CURRICULUM AND INSTRUCTION
Courses or Concentrations Available: Advertising; Communication; Journalism or Mass Communication; Public Relations; Radio, Television, Broadcasting, or Telecommunications; Speech; *Undergraduate Objectives or Program Emphases*: Theory, principles and application; *Graduate Objectives or Program Emphases*: Theory; Research; Criticism; *Bachelor's Degree Majors*: 750; *Master's Degree Majors*: 40; *Doctoral Degree Majors Currently in Residence*: 30; *Full-Time Faculty*: 32; *Part-Time Faculty*: 70; *Full-Time Professional (non-clerical) Staff Members*: 1.

FACILITIES AND SERVICES
Practical experiences available through: AM Radio Station (Institutional); Audio Recording Laboratory; Community Antenna (Cable) Television Origination; Campus Newspaper (Published Independently); Local Commercial Newspaper; Local Commercial Television Station; Desktop Publishing Facility; Video Editing; Electronic Field Production (Video); Video Production Laboratory or Television Studio.

Purdue University - Calumet (Public)

Department of Communication and Creative Arts
Hammond, Indiana 46323
Telephone: (219) 989-2393

Michael R. Moore, Head
Carol B. Gartner, Dean, School of Liberal Arts and Sciences

CURRICULUM AND INSTRUCTION
Courses or Concentrations Available: Advertising; Communication; Journalism or Mass Communication; Public Relations; Radio, Television, Broadcasting, or Telecommunications; Speech; Art; Music; Theatre; *Undergraduate Objectives or*

Program Emphases: To guide students in developing competency in one or more areas within communication or the creative arts while receiving a strong liberal arts education; *Graduate Objectives or Program Emphases*: To provide advanced study in communication commensurate with the student's professional or academic needs; *Bachelor's Degree Majors*: 170; *Master's Degree Majors*: 51; *Full-Time Faculty*: 14; *Part-Time Faculty*: 20.

FACILITIES AND SERVICES
Practical experiences available through: Advertising Agency; Audio Recording Laboratory; Community Antenna (Cable) Television Origination; Campus Newspaper (Published Independently); Local Commercial Newspaper; Local Commercial Television Station; Desktop Publishing Facility; Photographic Darkrooms; Video Editing; Electronic Field Production (Video); ITFS Distribution System; Institutional Magazine; Public Relations Agency; Satellite Uplink Facility; Video News and Data Processing; Video Production Laboratory or Television Studio.

St. Francis College (Private)

Department of English/Communications
2701 Spring Street
Fort Wayne, Indiana 46808
Telephone: (219) 434-3100

Randyll K. Yoder, Director
Sister Elise Kriss, Vice President, Academic Affairs

CURRICULUM AND INSTRUCTION
Courses or Concentrations Available: Communication; Journalism or Mass Communication; Public Relations; Radio, Television, Broadcasting, or Telecommunications; Speech; *Program Coordinators*: Hal Gunderson (Speech); *Undergraduate Objectives or Program Emphases*: Four year traditional liberal arts program with emphasis in electronic media and communications. Fusion of professional work experience with educational background and training for majors and minors; *Bachelor's Degree Majors*: 20; *Full-Time Faculty*: 2.

FACILITIES AND SERVICES
Practical experiences available through: Audio Recording Laboratory; Community Antenna

(Cable) Television Origination; Local Commercial Television Station; Photographic Darkrooms; Video Editing; Electronic Field Production (Video); Public Relations Agency; Video Production Laboratory or Television Studio.

St. Mary's College (Private)

Department of Communication and Theatre
Notre Dame, Indiana 46556

A. L. Plamondon, Administrator

St. Mary-of-the-Woods College (Private)

Department of Communication Arts
Le Far Hall
Saint Mary-of-the-Woods,
Indiana 47876
Telephone: (812) 535-5151

Janice Dukes, Chair
Suzanne Dailey, Vice President, Academic Affairs

CURRICULUM AND INSTRUCTION
Courses or Concentrations Available: Advertising; Communication; Film or Cinema; Journalism or Mass Communication; Public Relations; Speech; English; Foreign Languages; *Program Coordinators*: T. Jean Harrison (Journalism); Patrick Harkins (Communication, Film); Janice Dakes (Speech); Peggy Berry (Foreign Languages); *Undergraduate Objectives or Program Emphases*: The department is committed to a developmental process in the curricular and co-curricular functions. Such development is extended both in time and in depth in connections between facts, feelings, and philosophy; *Bachelor's Degree Majors*: 40; *Full-Time Faculty*: 15; *Part-Time Faculty*: 5; *Full-Time Professional (non-clerical) Staff Members*: 1.

FACILITIES AND SERVICES
Practical experiences available through: Advertising Agency; Audio Recording Laboratory; Local Commercial Newspaper; Local Commercial Television Station; Desktop Publishing Facility; Photographic Darkrooms; Video Editing; Institutional Magazine; Public Relations Agency; Video News and Data Processing.

Taylor University (Private)

Department of Communication Arts
Upland, Indiana 46989
Telephone: (317) 998-5262

Dale M. Jackson, Chair
Richard Stanislaw, Vice President, Academic Affairs

CURRICULUM AND INSTRUCTION
Courses or Concentrations Available: Communication; Journalism or Mass Communication; Public Relations; Radio, Television, Broadcasting, or Telecommunications; Speech; *Undergraduate Objectives or Program Emphases*: Help students understand how communication works in various contexts; help students develop communication skills that can benefit their relationships as well as their vocation; *Bachelor's Degree Majors*: 54; *Other Degree Majors*: 4; *Full-Time Faculty*: 5; *Part-Time Faculty*: 6; *Full-Time Professional (non-clerical) Staff Members*: 1.

FACILITIES AND SERVICES
Practical experiences available through: Audio Recording Laboratory; Carrier Current Audio Distribution System; Closed Circuit Television Facility; Campus Newspaper (Published Independently); Desktop Publishing Facility; Photographic Darkrooms; Video Editing; Electronic Field Production (Video); ITFS Distribution System; Satellite Uplink Facility; Video Production Laboratory or Television Studio.

University of Evansville (Private)

Department of Communications
1800 Lincoln Avenue
Evansville, Indiana 47722
Telephone: (812) 479-2377

T. Dean Thomlinson, Chair
Erik Nielson, Vice President, Academic Affairs

CURRICULUM AND INSTRUCTION
Courses or Concentrations Available: Advertising; Communication; Journalism or Mass Communication; Public Relations; Radio, Television, Broadcasting, or Telecommunications; Speech; Interpersonal Communication, Organizational Communication; *Program Coordinators*: Caroline Dow (Journalism);

Robert West (Telecommunications, Advertising); Doug Covert (Public Relations); Hope Bock (Interpersonal Communication); *Undergraduate Objectives or Program Emphases*: To offer a broadly-based, liberal arts education which blends communication theory and application to provide multiple career opportunities; *Bachelor's Degree Majors*: 15; *Other Degree Majors*: 120; *Full-Time Faculty*: 7; *Part-Time Faculty*: 1; *Full-Time Professional (non-clerical) Staff Members*: 2.

FACILITIES AND SERVICES
Practical experiences available through: Advertising Agency; Audio Recording Laboratory; Campus Newspaper (Published Independently); Local Commercial Newspaper; Local Commercial Television Station; Desktop Publishing Facility; Photographic Darkrooms; Video Editing; Electronic Field Production (Video); FM Radio Station (Institutional); Public Relations Agency; United Press International Feed; Video Production Laboratory or Television Studio.

University of Indianapolis (Private)

Department of Communications
1400 East Hanna Avenue
Indianapolis, Indiana 46227
Telephone: (317) 788-3368

Patricia A. Jefferson-Bilby, Chair
Mary Moore, Dean, College of Arts and Sciences

CURRICULUM AND INSTRUCTION
Courses or Concentrations Available: Communication; Journalism or Mass Communication; Public Relations; Radio, Television, Broadcasting, or Telecommunications; Speech; Sports Information; *Program Coordinators*: Terri Johnson (Journalism, Sports Information); Billy Catchings (Communications in Business-Public Relations); Wilfred Trembley (Radio, Television); Journalism program publishes yearbook; *Degree Majors*: 70; *Full-Time Faculty*: 5; *Part-Time Faculty*: 10; *Full-Time Professional (non-clerical) Staff Members*: 1.

FACILITIES AND SERVICES
Practical experiences available through: Audio Recording Laboratory; Community Antenna

(Cable) Television Origination; Local Commercial Newspaper; Local Commercial Television Station; Desktop Publishing Facility; Photographic Darkrooms; Video Editing; Electronic Field Production (Video); Television Broadcast Station (Institutional); FM Radio Station (Institutional); Institutional Newspaper; Public Relations Agency; United Press International Feed; Video Production Laboratory or Television Studio.

University of Notre Dame (Private)

Department of Communication and Theatre
Notre Dame, Indiana 46556
Telephone: (219) 239-5134

Mark C. Pilkinton, Chair
Michael J. Loux, Dean

CURRICULUM AND INSTRUCTION
Courses or Concentrations
Available: Advertising; Communication; Film or Cinema; Journalism or Mass Communication; Public Relations; Radio, Television, Broadcasting, or Telecommunications; *Bachelor's Degree Majors*: 50; *Master's Degree Majors*: 15; *Full-Time Faculty*: 9; *Part-Time Faculty*: 1; *Full-Time Professional (non-clerical) Staff Members*: 1.

FACILITIES AND SERVICES
Practical experiences available through: Advertising Agency; AM Radio Station (Institutional); Local Commercial Television Station; Desktop Publishing Facility; Photographic Darkrooms; Video Editing; Electronic Field Production (Video); Television Broadcast Station (Institutional); Film or Cinema Laboratory; FM Radio Station (Institutional); Public Relations Agency; Satellite Uplink Facility; Video Production Laboratory or Television Studio.

University of Southern Indiana (Public)

Department of Communications
8600 University Boulevard
Evansville, Indiana 47712
Telephone: (812) 464-1741

Helen Sands, Acting Chair
James Blevins, Dean

CURRICULUM AND INSTRUCTION
Courses or Concentrations
Available: Communication; Journalism or Mass Communication; Public Relations; Radio, Television, Broadcasting, or Telecommunications; Speech; Theatre; *Bachelor's Degree Majors*: 175; *Full-Time Faculty*: 10; *Part-Time Faculty*: 15; *Full-Time Professional (non-clerical) Staff Members*: 1.

FACILITIES AND SERVICES
Practical experiences available through: AM Radio Station (Institutional); Associated Press Wire Service Feed; Audio Recording Laboratory; Community Antenna (Cable) Television Origination; Closed Circuit Television Facility; Campus Newspaper (Published Independently); Local Commercial Television Station; Desktop Publishing Facility; Photographic Darkrooms; Video Editing; Electronic Field Production (Video); Institutional Magazine; Institutional Newspaper.

Valparaiso University (Private)

Department of Communication
Valparaiso, Indiana 46383
Telephone: (219) 464-5271

Douglas J. Kocher, Chair
Philip Gilbertson, Dean

CURRICULUM AND INSTRUCTION
Courses or Concentrations
Available: Advertising; Communication; Journalism or Mass Communication; Public Relations; Radio, Television, Broadcasting, or Telecommunications; *Undergraduate Objectives or Program Emphases*: Training in communication fields within the context of a strong liberal arts background. The department emphasizes understanding of skills as part of the larger social context of communication; *Bachelor's Degree*

Majors: 200; *Full-Time Faculty*: 8; *Part-Time Faculty*: 5.

FACILITIES AND SERVICES
Practical experiences available through: Advertising Agency; Audio Recording Laboratory; Closed Circuit Television Facility; Campus Newspaper (Published Independently); Local Commercial Newspaper; Local Commercial Television Station; Desktop Publishing Facility; Video Editing; Electronic Field Production (Video); FM Radio Station (Institutional); Public Relations Agency; Video News and Data Processing; Video Production Laboratory or Television Studio.

Vincennes University (Public)

Program of Journalism
1002 N. First Street
Vincennes, Indiana 47591
Telephone: (812) 885-4551
Alternate: (812) 882-3350

Frederic J. Walker Jr., Director

CURRICULUM AND INSTRUCTION
Courses or Concentrations Available: Journalism or Mass Communication; *Undergraduate Objectives or Program Emphases*: Print media; The program prepares students to perform and compete successfully in upper divisions of the universities to which they transfer and/or to succeed as reporters, copy editors, and photographers of daily or weekly newspapers; *Associate's Degree Majors*: 15; *Full-Time Faculty*: 1; *Part-Time Faculty*: 1; *Full-Time Professional (non-clerical) Staff Members*: 1.

FACILITIES AND SERVICES
Practical experiences available through: Desktop Publishing Facility; Photographic Darkrooms; Video Editing; Institutional Newspaper.

Vincennes University (Public)

Department of Broadcasting
1002 N. 1st Street
Vincennes, Indiana 47591
Telephone: (812) 885-4135

Jack A. Hanes, Chair
Jack Eads, Division Chair

CURRICULUM AND INSTRUCTION
Courses or Concentrations Available: Advertising; Communication; Journalism or Mass Communication; Radio, Television, Broadcasting, or Telecommunications; Promotions; *Undergraduate Objectives or Program Emphases*: Hands-on production and operations, news, management, sales, and promotions; *Degree Majors*: 197; *Full-Time Faculty*: 9; *Full-Time Professional (non-clerical) Staff Members*: 24.

FACILITIES AND SERVICES
Practical experiences available through: Associated Press Wire Service Feed; Audio Recording Laboratory; Carrier Current Audio Distribution System; Desktop Publishing Facility; Video Editing; Electronic Field Production (Video); FM Radio Station (Institutional); Video News and Data Processing; Video Production Laboratory or Television Studio.

Vincennes University (Public)

Department of Speech and Theatre
Department
Shircliff Humanities
Vincennes, Indiana 47591
Telephone: (812) 885-4480

Mary J. Trimbo, Chair
Phillip Pierpont, Administrator

CURRICULUM AND INSTRUCTION
Courses or Concentrations Available: Public Relations; Speech; *Undergraduate Objectives or Program Emphases*: Offer the first two years of instruction and prepare the student to transfer as well as provide a general education speech function; *Associate's Degree Majors*: 30; *Full-Time Faculty*: 10; *Part-Time Faculty*: 2.

FACILITIES AND SERVICES
Practical experiences available through: Photographic Darkrooms; Institutional Newspaper; Public Relations Agency.

Wabash College (Private)

Department of Communication
301 West Wabash
Crawfordsville, Indiana 47933
Telephone: (317) 362-1400

Joseph O'Rourke, Chair
P. Donald Herring, Administrator

CURRICULUM AND INSTRUCTION
Courses or Concentrations Available: Communication; Speech; *Undergraduate Objectives or Program Emphases*: Rhetoric, public speaking, persuasion, discussion, debate, classical rhetoric, history and criticism of public address, communication theory; *Bachelor's Degree Majors*: 14; *Full-Time Faculty*: 3.

FACILITIES AND SERVICES
Practical experiences available through: Advertising Agency; Campus Newspaper (Published Independently); Desktop Publishing Facility; Photographic Darkrooms; FM Radio Station (Institutional); Public Relations Agency.

Briar Cliff College (Private)

Department of Mass Communications
3303 Rebecca Street
Sioux City, Iowa 51104-2100
Telephone: (712) 279-5321

Ralph A. Swain, Chair
Jeffrey Willens, Academic Dean

CURRICULUM AND INSTRUCTION
Courses or Concentrations
Available: Advertising; Communication;
Journalism or Mass Communication; Public
Relations; Radio, Television, Broadcasting,
or Telecommunications; Photography;
Publications; *Undergraduate Objectives or
Program Emphases*: Requirement that all
majors engage in both print and non-print
areas as well as campus and off-campus
internships in order to be multi-faceted for
media careers; *Bachelor's Degree Majors*: 30;
Full-Time Faculty: 2; *Part-Time Faculty*: 2;
*Full-Time Professional (non-clerical) Staff
Members*: 1.

FACILITIES AND SERVICES
*Practical experiences available
through*: Advertising Agency; AM Radio
Station (Institutional); Audio Recording
Laboratory; Community Antenna (Cable)
Television Origination; Carrier Current
Audio Distribution System; Closed Circuit
Television Facility; Campus Newspaper
(Published Independently); Local
Commercial Newspaper; Local Commercial
Television Station; Desktop Publishing
Facility; Photographic Darkrooms; Video
Editing; Electronic Field Production
(Video); Institutional Magazine;
Institutional Newspaper; Public Relations
Agency; United Press International Feed;
Video Production Laboratory or Television
Studio.

Buena Vista College

School of Communication
Storm Lake, Iowa 50588

David Diamond, Administrator

Clarke College

Communication Department
1550 Clarke Drive
Dubuque, Iowa 52004-3198

Michael R. Acton, Administrator

Clinton Community College (Public)

Program of Humanities/Social Sciences
1000 Lincoln Boulevard
Clinton, Iowa 52732
Telephone: (319) 242-6841

Herman C. Eichmeier, Coordinator
Jim Arneson, Associate Dean

CURRICULUM AND INSTRUCTION
Courses or Concentrations
Available: Advertising; Communication; Film
or Cinema; Journalism or Mass
Communication; Speech; *Program
Coordinators*: Melvin Erickson (Journalism);
Dan Leighton (Film); Curt Pefferman
(Advertising); *Undergraduate Objectives or
Program Emphases*: Two year program for
transfer; *Associate's Degree Majors*: 1;
Full-Time Faculty: 8; *Part-Time Faculty*: 12.

FACILITIES AND SERVICES
*Practical experiences available
through*: Closed Circuit Television Facility;
Campus Newspaper (Published
Independently); Local Commercial
Newspaper; Desktop Publishing Facility;
Photographic Darkrooms; Video Editing;
ITFS Distribution System; Institutional
Newspaper; Satellite Uplink Facility (Ku
Band Transmitter) (C Band Transmitter).

Des Moines Area Community College - Ankeny (Public)

Department of Communication and Humanities
2006 S. Ankeny Boulevard, Building 2
Ankeny, Iowa 50310
Telephone: (515) 964-6213 Extension or Alternate: 964-6200

Ruth H. Aurelius, Instructor
Jim Stick, Chair

CURRICULUM AND INSTRUCTION
Courses or Concentrations
Available: Advertising; Communication; Film or Cinema; Journalism or Mass Communication; Speech; Language Arts; Art; Music; Philosophy; *Program Coordinators*: Sharon Hann (Art); Virginia Bennett (Music); Curt Wiberg (Philosophy); Lloyd Miller (Language); Rick Chapman (Film); *Undergraduate Objectives or Program Emphases*: To help students understand the importance of communication in academic, career, civic, and recreational contexts; to understand and use all components of communication; and to help students think creatively and problem solve; *Associate's Degree Majors*: 2; *Full-Time Faculty*: 9; *Part-Time Faculty*: 10.

FACILITIES AND SERVICES
Practical experiences available through: Audio Recording Laboratory; Desktop Publishing Facility; Photographic Darkrooms; Video Editing; Institutional Magazine; Institutional Newspaper; Satellite Uplink Facility

Dordt College (Private)

Department of Communication
Sioux Center, Iowa 51250
Telephone: (712) 722-3771

Daryl J. Vander Kooi, Chair
R. McCarthy, Dean, Social Sciences

CURRICULUM AND INSTRUCTION
Courses or Concentrations
Available: Communication; Journalism or Mass Communication; Public Relations; Radio, Television, Broadcasting, or Telecommunications; Speech; *Undergraduate Objectives or Program Emphases*: Development of perspective, general knowledge of communication, handle issues, provide skills; *Bachelor's Degree Majors*: 20; *Full-Time Faculty*: 3; *Part-Time Faculty*: 2.

FACILITIES AND SERVICES
Practical experiences available through: Audio Recording Laboratory; Campus Newspaper (Published Independently); Local Commercial Newspaper; Local Commercial Television Station; Desktop Publishing Facility; Photographic Darkrooms; FM Radio Station (Institutional); Institutional Newspaper; Public Relations Agency; Video Production Laboratory or Television Studio.

Drake University (Private)

School of Journalism and Mass Communication
25th and University Avenue
Des Moines, Iowa 50311
Telephone: (515) 271-3194

Michael R. Cheney, Dean
Richard Hersh, Provost

CURRICULUM AND INSTRUCTION
Courses or Concentrations
Available: Advertising; Journalism or Mass Communication; Public Relations; Radio, Television, Broadcasting, or Telecommunications; Media Graphics; Broadcast News; Magazines; *Undergraduate Objectives or Program Emphases*: Professional journalism and mass communication education; *Graduate Objectives or Program Emphases*: Professional journalism and mass communication education; *Bachelor's Degree Majors*: 290; *Master's Degree Majors*: 50; *Full-Time Faculty*: 12; *Part-Time Faculty*: 5.

FACILITIES AND SERVICES
Practical experiences available through: Advertising Agency; Audio Recording Laboratory; Community Antenna (Cable) Television Origination; Carrier Current Audio Distribution System; Closed Circuit Television Facility; Campus Newspaper (Published Independently); Local Commercial Newspaper; Local Commercial Television Station; Desktop Publishing Facility; Photographic Darkrooms; Video Editing; Electronic Field Production (Video); Institutional Magazine; Public Relations Agency; Video News and Data Processing; Video Production Laboratory or Television Studio.

Ellsworth Community College (Public)

Department of Speech/Drama
1100 College Avenue
Iowa Falls, Iowa 50126
Telephone: (515) 648-4611

Dennis M. Peer, Chair
Gary Passer, Administrator

CURRICULUM AND INSTRUCTION
Courses or Concentrations
Available: Journalism or Mass
Communication; Speech; *Undergraduate
Objectives or Program Emphases*: To provide
required speech curriculum; *Associate's
Degree Majors*: 5; *Full-Time Faculty*: 2.

FACILITIES AND SERVICES
*Practical experiences available
through*: Photographic Darkrooms;
Institutional Newspaper.

Ellsworth Community College (Public)

Department of Language and Literature
1100 College Avenue
Iowa Falls, Iowa 50126
Telephone: (515) 648-3623

Patrice Coleman, Instructor
Karen Dhar, Department Head

CURRICULUM AND INSTRUCTION
Courses or Concentrations
Available: Advertising; Communication;
Information Science; Journalism or Mass
Communication; Public Relations; Speech;
Program Coordinators: Dennis Peer (Speech);
Greg Snere (Marketing); *Undergraduate
Objectives or Program Emphases*: To instill
the importance of effective communication
and a variety of strategies to achieve this
outcome; *Associate's Degree Majors*: 6;
Full-Time Faculty: 5; *Part-Time Faculty*: 2;
*Full-Time Professional (non-clerical) Staff
Members*: 5.

FACILITIES AND SERVICES
*Practical experiences available
through*: Desktop Publishing Facility;
Photographic Darkrooms; Institutional
Newspaper.

Grand View College (Private)

Department of Mass Communication
1200 Grand View Avenue
Des Moines, Iowa 50316
Telephone: (515) 263-2931

William J. Schaefer, Chair
Tom Fischer, Provost

CURRICULUM AND INSTRUCTION
Courses or Concentrations
Available: Journalism or Mass
Communication; Radio, Television,
Broadcasting, or Telecommunications; Still
Photography; *Undergraduate Objectives or
Program Emphases*: To develop basic
communication skills in Journalism,
Radio-Television, Photography and Public
Relations with a liberal arts foundation in
order to obtain entry level jobs in the mass
communication industry; *Associate's Degree
Majors*: 3; *Bachelor's Degree Majors*: 60;
Full-Time Faculty: 5; *Part-Time Faculty*: 6;
*Full-Time Professional (non-clerical) Staff
Members*: 2.

FACILITIES AND SERVICES
Practical experiences available through: Audio
Recording Laboratory; Community Antenna
(Cable) Television Origination; Campus
Newspaper (Published Independently);
Local Commercial Newspaper; Local
Commercial Television Station; Desktop
Publishing Facility; Photographic
Darkrooms; Video Editing; Electronic Field
Production (Video); FM Radio Station
(Institutional); Institutional Newspaper;
Public Relations Agency; United Press
International Feed.

Hawkeye Institute of Technology (Public)

Department of Graphic and Applied Arts
1501 East Orange Road
Waterloo, Iowa 50701
Telephone: (319) 296-2320

John W. Sorenson, Chair
Glen Peterson, Administrator

CURRICULUM AND INSTRUCTION
Courses or Concentrations
Available: Advertising; Communication; Film
or Cinema; Radio, Television, Broadcasting,
or Telecommunications; Speech; *Program
Coordinators*: Richard Kitemer

(Photography); Patricia Willoughby (Commercial Art); *Undergraduate Objectives or Program Emphases*: To prepare individuals for career entry positions in the photography and commercial art fields; *Associate's Degree Majors*: 200; *Full-Time Faculty*: 14; *Part-Time Faculty*: 6; *Full-Time Professional (non-clerical) Staff Members*: 1.

FACILITIES AND SERVICES
Practical experiences available through: Audio Recording Laboratory; Desktop Publishing Facility; Photographic Darkrooms; Video Editing; Film or Cinema Laboratory; Video Production Laboratory or Television Studio.

Iowa Central Community College (Public)

Program of Broadcasting
330 Avenue M
Fort Dodge, Iowa 50501
Telephone: (515) 576-7201

Ray Gales, Coordinator
Ray Beets, Administrator

CURRICULUM AND INSTRUCTION
Courses or Concentrations Available: Advertising; Communication; Information Science; Journalism or Mass Communication; Radio, Television, Broadcasting, or Telecommunications; Speech; *Undergraduate Objectives or Program Emphases*: Provide skills necessary to obtain entry level radio broadcast position; *Associate's Degree Majors*: 44; *Full-Time Faculty*: 2.

FACILITIES AND SERVICES
Practical experiences available through: AM Radio Station (Institutional); Associated Press Wire Service Feed; Audio Recording Laboratory; Campus Newspaper (Published Independently); Desktop Publishing Facility; Electronic Field Production (Video); FM Radio Station (Institutional); Video News and Data Processing.

Iowa State University (Public)

Department of Journalism and Mass Communication
114 Hamilton Hall
Ames, Iowa 50011
Telephone: (515) 294=4340

J. Thomas Emmerson, Chair
David Bright, Dean, College of Science and Humanities

CURRICULUM AND INSTRUCTION
Courses or Concentrations Available: Advertising; Journalism or Mass Communication; Public Relations; Radio, Television, Broadcasting, or Telecommunications; *Undergraduate Objectives or Program Emphases:* Advertising, Broadcast, Magazine, Newspaper, Public Relations/Public Information, Science Writing and Journalism Education. Beginning in 1990, Telecommunicative Arts will provide a new Electronic Media Studies Emphasis; *Graduate Objectives:* Mass Communication in Science and Technology and Mass Communication as a Social Force; *Program Coordinators*: Veryl Fritz (Advertising); Stephen Coon (Broadcast News); Jane Peterson (Journalism Education); Marcia Prior-Miller (Magazine); Giles Fowler (Newspaper); Karl Friederich (Public Relations/Public Information); Richard Kraemer (Telecommunicative Arts); Kim Smith (Graduate Program); *Bachelor's Degree Majors*: 655 (BS and BA); *Master's Degree Majors*: 95; *Full-Time Faculty*: 23; *Part-Time Faculty*: 10.

FACILITIES AND SERVICES
Practical experiences available through: Advertising Agency; AM Radio Station (Institutional); Associated Press Wire Service Feed; Community Antenna (Cable) Television Origination; Closed Circuit Television Facility; Campus Newspaper (Published Independently); Local Commercial Newspaper; Desktop Publishing Facility; Photographic Darkrooms; Video Editing; Film or Cinema Laboratory; FM Radio Station (Institutional); Institutional Magazine; Public Relations Agency; Video Production Laboratory or Television Studio.

Iowa State University of Science and Technology (Public)

Department of Speech Communication
Ames, Iowa 50011
Telephone: (515) 294-7670

Claudia L. Hale, Chair
David F. Bright, Dean

CURRICULUM AND INSTRUCTION
Courses or Concentrations
Available: Communication; Film or Cinema; Radio, Television, Broadcasting, or Telecommunications; Speech; Theatre; Communication Disorders; *Program Coordinators*: Mark Redmond (Interpersonal and Rhetorical Communication); Richard Kraemer (Telecommunications Arts); H. S. Venkatagiri (Communication Disorders); David Hirvela (Theatre); *Undergraduate Objectives or Program Emphases*: IRC (Speech)--Interpersonal and Rhetorical Communication Theory; Applied and Organizational Communication; TCA--Radio, Television, Video, Film; CM DIS--pre-professional program; Theatre--acting, directing, production, arts management; *Bachelor's Degree Majors*: 400; *Full-Time Faculty*: 40; *Part-Time Faculty*: 4; *Full-Time Professional (non-clerical) Staff Members*: 6.

FACILITIES AND SERVICES
Practical experiences available through: Local Commercial Television Station; Video Editing; Electronic Field Production (Video); Film or Cinema Laboratory.

Iowa Western Community College - Council Bluffs (Public)

Department of Communication Arts
2700 College Road
Council Bluffs, Iowa 51502
Telephone: (712) 325-3276

Bonnie R. Miley, Director
Martin Wolf, Vice President

CURRICULUM AND INSTRUCTION
Courses or Concentrations
Available: Communication; Journalism or Mass Communication; Radio, Television, Broadcasting, or Telecommunications; Speech; English; Creative Writing; *Program Coordinators*: Steve Stone (Journalism);

David Hufford (English Composition, Speech); *Associate's Degree Majors*: 40; *Full-Time Faculty*: 7; *Part-Time Faculty*: 8.

FACILITIES AND SERVICES
Practical experiences available through: Associated Press Wire Service Feed; Audio Recording Laboratory; Community Antenna (Cable) Television Origination; Campus Newspaper (Published Independently); Local Commercial Newspaper; Local Commercial Television Station; Desktop Publishing Facility; Photographic Darkrooms; FM Radio Station (Institutional); Institutional Magazine; Institutional Newspaper; Satellite Uplink Facility; Video News and Data Processing; Video Production Laboratory or Television Studio.

Kirkwood Community College (Public)

Department of Communication Media/Public Relations
6301 Kirkwood Boulevard, SW
Cedar Rapids, Iowa 52406
Telephone: (319) 398-5411

Rose K. Kodet, Coordinator
Kathy Collison, Administrator

CURRICULUM AND INSTRUCTION
Courses or Concentrations
Available: Advertising; Communication; Journalism or Mass Communication; Public Relations; Radio, Television, Broadcasting, or Telecommunications; *Full-Time Faculty*: 3; *Part-Time Faculty*: 3.

FACILITIES AND SERVICES
Practical experiences available through: Audio Recording Laboratory; Community Antenna (Cable) Television Origination; Closed Circuit Television Facility; Campus Newspaper (Published Independently); Local Commercial Television Station; Photographic Darkrooms; Video Editing; Electronic Field Production (Video); FM Radio Station (Institutional); ITFS Distribution System; Video Production Laboratory or Television Studio.

Loras College (Private)

Department of Speech Communication
1450 Alta Vista
Dubuque, Iowa 52001
Telephone: (319) 588-7400

Donald W. Stribling, Chair

CURRICULUM AND INSTRUCTION
Courses or Concentrations
Available: Communication; Journalism or
Mass Communication; Public Relations;
Radio, Television, Broadcasting, or
Telecommunications; Speech; *Undergraduate
Objectives or Program Emphases*: To prepare
students with sound theoretical and practical
knowledge. Preparation for a job, but more
importantly, for life; *Bachelor's Degree
Majors*: 65; *Full-Time Faculty*: 10;
Part-Time Faculty: 3.

FACILITIES AND SERVICES
*Practical experiences available
through*: Carrier Current Audio Distribution
System; Closed Circuit Television Facility;
Local Commercial Television Station;
Photographic Darkrooms; Video Editing;
Electronic Field Production (Video);
Institutional Newspaper; Public Relations
Agency; Video Production Laboratory or
Television Studio.

Marycrest College

**Department of Communication and
Performing Arts**
1607 West 12th Street
Davenport, Iowa 52804

J. T. Jacobs, Administrator

Morningside College (Private)

Department of Communicative Arts
1501 Morningside Avenue
Sioux City, Iowa 51106
Telephone: (712) 274-5299

David Diamond, Chair
Frank Breneisen, Administrator

CURRICULUM AND INSTRUCTION
Courses or Concentrations
Available: Advertising; Communication; Film
or Cinema; Journalism or Mass
Communication; Public Relations; Radio,

Television, Broadcasting, or
Telecommunications; Speech; Corporate
Communication; Sportscasting/Writing;
Professional writing; *Bachelor's Degree
Majors*: 31; *Other Degree Majors*: 30;
Full-Time Faculty: 4; *Part-Time Faculty*: 2;
*Full-Time Professional (non-clerical) Staff
Members*: 2.

FACILITIES AND SERVICES
*Practical experiences available
through*: Advertising Agency; Associated
Press Wire Service Feed; Audio Recording
Laboratory; Community Antenna (Cable)
Television Origination; Closed Circuit
Television Facility; Campus Newspaper
(Published Independently); Local
Commercial Newspaper; Local Commercial
Television Station; Photographic
Darkrooms; Video Editing; Electronic Field
Production (Video); Television Broadcast
Station (Institutional); Film or Cinema
Laboratory; FM Radio Station
(Institutional); ITFS Distribution System;
Institutional Newspaper; Public Relations
Agency; Video News and Data Processing.

St. Ambrose College

**Department of Speech/Theatre and Mass
Communication**
518 W. Locust
Davenport, Iowa 52803

Daniel Bozik, Administrator

Scott Community College (Public)

Communications Media
500 Belmont Road
Bettendorf, Iowa 52722
Telephone: (319) 359-7531

Tami S. Seitz Parkin, Head
Victoria Welch, Administrator

CURRICULUM AND INSTRUCTION
Courses or Concentrations
Available: Communication; Journalism or
Mass Communication; Radio, Television,
Broadcasting, or Telecommunications;
*Undergraduate Objectives or Program
Emphases*: Television Production, Radio
Production, Broadcast Sales, Broadcast
Performance; *Associate's Degree Majors*: 15;
Full-Time Faculty: 1; *Part-Time Faculty*: 2.

FACILITIES AND SERVICES

Practical experiences available through: Audio Recording Laboratory; Community Antenna (Cable) Television Origination; Closed Circuit Television Facility; Photographic Darkrooms; Video Editing; Electronic Field Production (Video); ITFS Distribution System; Video Production Laboratory or Television Studio.

University of Dubuque (Private)

Department of Speech
2000 University Avenue
Dubuque, Iowa 52001
Telephone: (319) 589-3564

Mary Carol C. Harris, Chair
William Gould, Division Chair

CURRICULUM AND INSTRUCTION
Courses or Concentrations Available: Communication; Speech; *Undergraduate Objectives or Program Emphases*: Speech major: Interpersonal Communication emphasis; Intercultural communication emphasis; *Bachelor's Degree Majors*: 20; *Full-Time Faculty*: 1; *Full-Time Professional (non-clerical) Staff Members*: 1.

FACILITIES AND SERVICES
Practical experiences available through: Advertising Agency; Community Antenna (Cable) Television Origination; Campus Newspaper (Published Independently); Local Commercial Newspaper; Local Commercial Television Station.

University of Iowa (Public)

Department of Communication Studies
105 Communication Studies Building
Iowa City, Iowa 52242
Telephone: (319) 335-0575

Bruce E. Gronbeck, Chair
G. Loewenberg, Dean, College of Liberal Arts

CURRICULUM AND INSTRUCTION
Courses or Concentrations Available: Communication; Film or Cinema; Radio, Television, Broadcasting, or Telecommunications; Speech; *Program Coordinators*: Samuel Becker (Broadcasting Studies); John Lyne (Rhetorical Studies);

Steve Duck (Communication Research); Lauren Rabinovitz (Film Studies); Franklin Miller (Production); Randy Hirokawa (Communication); *Undergraduate Objectives or Program Emphases*: Instruct students in the theory, history, criticism, and science of communication in society; provide students with training in oral communication, radio, audio, television, video, and filmmaking skills; *Graduate Objectives or Program Emphases*: Training principinary Doctoral students in broadcast, film, communication, and rhetorical studies; offering a scholastic and practicum production studies (MA); *Associate's Degree Majors*: 42; *Bachelor's Degree Majors*: 526; *Master's Degree Majors*: 49; *Doctoral Degree Majors Currently in Residence*: 70; *Additional Doctoral Degree Majors*: 20; *Full-Time Faculty*: 16; *Part-Time Faculty*: 32; *Full-Time Professional (non-clerical) Staff Members*: 5.

FACILITIES AND SERVICES
Practical experiences available through: AM Radio Station (Institutional); Audio Recording Laboratory; Community Antenna (Cable) Television Origination; Closed Circuit Television Facility; Photographic Darkrooms; Video Editing; Electronic Field Production (Video); Film or Cinema Laboratory; FM Radio Station (Institutional); Video Production Laboratory or Television Studio.

University of Iowa (Public)

Department of Rhetoric
Iowa City, Iowa 52242
Telephone: (319) 335-3786

Douglas M. Trank, Chair
Gerhard Loewenberg, Dean

CURRICULUM AND INSTRUCTION
Courses or Concentrations Available: Basic Communication-writing, speaking, critical reading; *Undergraduate Objectives or Program Emphases*: Fulfill general education requirements in writing, speaking, reading; *Full-Time Faculty*: 12; *Part-Time Faculty*: 125.

University of Iowa (Public)

School of Journalism and Mass Communication
Iowa City, Iowa 52242
Telephone: (319) 335-5821

Don D. Smith, Director
Gerhard Loewenberg, Dean

CURRICULUM AND INSTRUCTION
Courses or Concentrations Available: Communication; Journalism or Mass Communication; Public Relations; Radio, Television, Broadcasting, or Telecommunications; *Undergraduate Objectives or Program Emphases*: To prepare students for professional positions in Journalism and for other careers in the broad field of mass communication; *Graduate Objectives or Program Emphases*: MA professional--To improve students' technical and analytical skills. Ph.D.--Interdisciplinary inquiry into mass communication phenomena; *Bachelor's Degree Majors*: 196; *Master's Degree Majors*: 60; *Doctoral Degree Majors Currently in Residence*: 30; *Full-Time Faculty*: 14; *Part-Time Faculty*: 8; *Full-Time Professional (non-clerical) Staff Members*: 2.

FACILITIES AND SERVICES
Practical experiences available through: Audio Recording Laboratory; Community Antenna (Cable) Television Origination; Campus Newspaper (Published Independently); Local Commercial Newspaper; Desktop Publishing Facility; Photographic Darkrooms; Video Editing; Electronic Field Production (Video); FM Radio Station (Institutional); Institutional Newspaper; Public Relations Agency; Video News and Data Processing.

University of Northern Iowa (Public)

Department of Communication and Theatre Arts
Cedar Falls, Iowa 50614
Telephone: (319) 273-2217

G. Jon Hall, Head
Tom Thompson, Dean, College of Humanities and Fine Arts

CURRICULUM AND INSTRUCTION
Courses or Concentrations Available: Communication; Public Relations; Radio, Television, Broadcasting, or Telecommunications; Speech; Theatre; Oral Interpretation; *Program Coordinators*: Charles Scholz (Radio-Television); Dean Kruckeberg (Public Relations); *Bachelor's Degree Majors*: 400; *Master's Degree Majors*: 35; *Full-Time Faculty*: 40; *Part-Time Faculty*: 12; *Full-Time Professional (non-clerical) Staff Members*: 2.

FACILITIES AND SERVICES
Practical experiences available through: Advertising Agency; Audio Recording Laboratory; Community Antenna (Cable) Television Origination; Carrier Current Audio Distribution System; Closed Circuit Television Facility; Campus Newspaper (Published Independently); Local Commercial Newspaper; Local Commercial Television Station; Desktop Publishing Facility; Video Editing; Electronic Field Production (Video); FM Radio Station (Institutional); Public Relations Agency; Video News and Data Processing; Video Production Laboratory or Television Studio.

University of Northern Iowa (Public)

Division of Broadcast
Auditorium 138
Cedar Falls, Iowa 50614-0139
Telephone: (319) 273-6209

Charles B. Scholz, Coordinator
Jon Hall, Head, Communication and Theatre Arts

CURRICULUM AND INSTRUCTION
Courses or Concentrations Available: Radio, Television, Broadcasting, or Telecommunications; *Program Coordinators*: Dean Kruckeberg (Public Relations); Jon Hall (Communication); *Undergraduate Objectives or Program Emphases*: To provide students with technical skills, knowledge necessary for career in the broadcasting industry. To prepare students as future decision-makers in the field. Focus student interest into more specific areas (Journalism, Business, Performance, Production); *Bachelor's Degree Majors*: 85; *Full-Time Faculty*: 4; *Part-Time Faculty*: 3.

FACILITIES AND SERVICES
Practical experiences available

through: Advertising Agency; AM Radio Station (Institutional); Associated Press Wire Service Feed; Audio Recording Laboratory; Community Antenna (Cable) Television Origination; Campus Newspaper (Published Independently); Local Commercial Television Station; Photographic Darkrooms; Video Editing; Electronic Field Production (Video); FM Radio Station (Institutional); ITFS Distribution System; Institutional Newspaper; Public Relations Agency; Video News and Data Processing; Video Production Laboratory or Television Studio.

Waldorf College (Private)

Department of Telecommunications Systems
106 South 6th Street
Forest City, Iowa 50436
Telephone: (515) 582-8153

Rita DuCharme, Director
John Robinson, Chair, Business and Economics Division

CURRICULUM AND INSTRUCTION
Courses or Concentrations
Available: Communication; Journalism or Mass Communication; Radio, Television, Broadcasting, or Telecommunications; Telephony and HDTV and Video Systems; *Undergraduate Objectives or Program Emphases*: To gain a good understanding of terminology and concepts of voice, data and video systems. To understand how information is distributed from one point to another; *Associate's Degree Majors*: 550; *Full-Time Faculty*: 2; *Part-Time Faculty*: 4; *Full-Time Professional (non-clerical) Staff Members*: 2.

FACILITIES AND SERVICES
Practical experiences available through: AM Radio Station (Institutional); Carrier Current Audio Distribution System; Closed Circuit Television Facility; Campus Newspaper (Published Independently); Local Commercial Newspaper; Local Commercial Television Station; Desktop Publishing Facility; Photographic Darkrooms; Video Editing; Electronic Field Production (Video); Film or Cinema Laboratory; FM Radio Station (Institutional); Satellite Uplink Facility (Ku Band Transmitter) (C Band Transmitter); Video Production Laboratory or Television Studio.

Wartburg College (Private)

Department of Communication Arts
222 9th Street, NW
Waverly, Iowa 50677
Telephone: (319) 352-8200

Robert C. Gremmels, Chair

CURRICULUM AND INSTRUCTION
Courses or Concentrations
Available: Advertising; Film or Cinema; Journalism or Mass Communication; Public Relations; Radio, Television, Broadcasting, or Telecommunications; Speech; *Program Coordinator*: Kenneth J. Nordstrom (Broadcasting, Speech); *Undergraduate Objectives or Program Emphases*: To prepare students for jobs in mass communication and, to some degree, for graduate work in mass communication; *Bachelor's Degree Majors*: 50; *Full-Time Faculty*: 2; *Part-Time Faculty*: 2.

FACILITIES AND SERVICES
Practical experiences available through: Community Antenna (Cable) Television Origination; Campus Newspaper (Published Independently); Local Commercial Newspaper; Desktop Publishing Facility; Photographic Darkrooms; Film or Cinema Laboratory; Film or Cinema Laboratory; FM Radio Station (Institutional); United Press International Feed.

Wartburg College (Private)

Department of Business Administration and Economics
222 Ninth Street NW
Waverly, Iowa 50677
Telephone: (319) 352-8200

Gloria L. Campbell, Chair
Carlyle Haaland, Administrator

CURRICULUM AND INSTRUCTION
Courses or Concentrations
Available: Advertising; *Undergraduate Objectives or Program Emphases*: Business Administration; *Bachelor's Degree Majors*: 150; *Full-Time Faculty*: 8; *Part-Time Faculty*: 1.

Wartburg Theological Seminary

Division of Ministry
333 Wartburg Place
Dubuque, Iowa 52001

Burton Everist, Administrator

Western Iowa Tech Community College (Public)

Department of English and Humanities
4647 Stone Avenue
Sioux City, Iowa 51102
Telephone: (712) 274-6400

Terrence N. Lane, Chair
Robert J. Rice, Vice President

CURRICULUM AND INSTRUCTION
Courses or Concentrations
Available: Communication; Speech; Foreign
language; *Undergraduate Objectives or*
Program Emphases: Programs for first two
years of undergraduate transfer to other four
year institutions; *Full-Time Faculty*: 1;
Part-Time Faculty: 6.

FACILITIES AND SERVICES
Practical experiences available through: FM
Radio Station (Institutional).

Westmar College (Private)

Program of Speech and
Drama/Broadcasting
1002 3rd Avenue, S.E.
LeMars, Iowa 51031
Telephone: (712) 546-7081

Harry B. Parker, Director
Frank Summerside, Division Director

CURRICULUM AND INSTRUCTION
Courses or Concentrations
Available: Advertising; Communication;
Journalism or Mass Communication; Public
Relations; Radio, Television, Broadcasting,
or Telecommunications; Speech;
Undergraduate Objectives or Program
Emphases: Broadcasting degree consists of
three years of liberal arts training at
Westmar, one year of broadcasting training
at Brown Institute in Minneapolis; *Bachelor's*
Degree Majors: 5; *Full-Time Faculty*: 1;
Part-Time Faculty: 1.

FACILITIES AND SERVICES
Practical experiences available
through: Campus Newspaper (Published
Independently); Photographic Darkrooms;
Institutional Newspaper.

William Penn College (Private)

Speech Division of English Department
Oskaloosa, Iowa 52577
Telephone: (515) 673-8311

James A. Pearce, Administrator
Marcella Ward, Administrator

CURRICULUM AND INSTRUCTION
Courses or Concentrations
Available: Communication; Journalism or
Mass Communication; Radio, Television,
Broadcasting, or Telecommunications;
Speech; *Undergraduate Objectives or Program*
Emphases: Teacher education; Public
Relations; Professional Broadcasting;
Bachelor's Degree Majors: 40; *Full-Time*
Faculty: 5; *Part-Time Faculty*: 1; *Full-Time*
Professional (non-clerical) Staff Members: 1.

FACILITIES AND SERVICES
Practical experiences available through: AM
Radio Station (Institutional); Campus
Newspaper (Published Independently);
Local Commercial Newspaper; Local
Commercial Television Station;
Photographic Darkrooms; Public Relations
Agency.

Allen County Community College (Public)

Division of Communication and Fine Arts
1801 North Cottonwood
Iola, Kansas 66749
Telephone: (316) 365-5116

Tosca D. Bryant, Chair
Jerrilee Mosier, Vice President for
Instruction

CURRICULUM AND INSTRUCTION
*Courses or Concentrations
Available*: Advertising; Communication;
Journalism or Mass Communication; Speech;
Desktop Publishing; *Undergraduate
Objectives or Program Emphases*: The goal
for our undergraduate programs is to
prepare students for either the university or
the work place depending on the individual
student's goals; *Associate's Degree
Majors*: 150; *Full-Time Faculty*: 7;
Part-Time Faculty: 5.

FACILITIES AND SERVICES
*Practical experiences available
through*: Desktop Publishing Facility;
Photographic Darkrooms; Institutional
Magazine; Institutional Newspaper; Satellite
Uplink Facility.

Baker University (Private)

Department of Communication
Pulliam Center for Journalism and Mass
Communication
Baldwin City, Kansas 66006
Telephone: (913) 594-6451

Kenneth V. Sibert, Chair
Keith Keeling, Academic Dean and Provost

CURRICULUM AND INSTRUCTION
*Courses or Concentrations
Available*: Advertising; Communication;
Journalism or Mass Communication; Public
Relations; Radio, Television, Broadcasting,
or Telecommunications; Speech; *Program
Coordinators*: Ron Sheafer (Broadcasting);
Steven Brooks (Speech Communication);
Undergraduate Objectives or Program

Emphases: Both practical and theoretical
aspects of communication within a broad
liberal arts curriculum. Writing and research
skills are emphasized in every course. All
students intern within their chosen sequence
and acquire practical experience; *Bachelor's
Degree Majors*: 60; *Full-Time Faculty*: 4;
Part-Time Faculty: 1.

FACILITIES AND SERVICES
*Practical experiences available
through*: Associated Press Wire Service Feed;
Audio Recording Laboratory; Community
Antenna (Cable) Television Origination;
Local Commercial Newspaper; Desktop
Publishing Facility; Photographic
Darkrooms; Video Editing; Electronic Field
Production (Video); FM Radio Station
(Institutional); ITFS Distribution System;
Institutional Magazine; Institutional
Newspaper; Satellite Uplink Facility (Ku
Band Transmitter) (C Band Transmitter);
Video News and Data Processing; Video
Production Laboratory or Television Studio.

Benedictine College

Journalism Department
South Campus
Atchison, Kansas 66002

Donna Ullrich-Eaton, Administrator

Bethel College

Communications Department
300 East 27th
North Newton, Kansas 67117

Thane Chastain, Administrator

Cloud County Community College (Public)

College of Communications
2221 Campus Drive
Concordia, Kansas 66901
Telephone: (913) 243-1435

Thelma Workman, Instructor
James Douglass, Dean of Instruction

CURRICULUM AND INSTRUCTION
Courses or Concentrations
Available: Communication; Journalism or Mass Communication; French and English Composition; *Program Coordinators*: David Norlin (Radio Broadcasting); *Undergraduate Objectives or Program Emphases*: Print journalism: Newspaper and Yearbook; *Associate's Degree Majors*: 4; *Full-Time Faculty*: 6.

FACILITIES AND SERVICES
Practical experiences available through: Local Commercial Newspaper; Desktop Publishing Facility; Photographic Darkrooms; FM Radio Station (Institutional); Institutional Newspaper.

Cloud County Community College (Public)

Department of Broadcasting
2221 Campus Drive
Concordia, Kansas 66901
Telephone: (913) 283-1935

David A. Norlin, Head
James Douglas, Dean of Instruction

CURRICULUM AND INSTRUCTION
Courses or Concentrations
Available: Advertising; Journalism or Mass Communication; Radio, Television, Broadcasting, or Telecommunications; Speech; *Undergraduate Objectives or Program Emphases*: Overview of broadcast industry, news reporting, television reporting, sales/employment; *Associate's Degree Majors*: 20; *Full-Time Faculty*: 1.

FACILITIES AND SERVICES
Practical experiences available through: Audio Recording Laboratory; Campus Newspaper (Published Independently); Local Commercial Newspaper; Desktop Publishing Facility; Photographic Darkrooms; FM Radio Station (Institutional); Institutional Newspaper.

Colby Community College (Public)

Department of Radio Broadcasting
1255 South Range
Colby, Kansas 67701
Telephone: (913) 462-3984

Jon Burlew, Director
Deborah Castrop, Administrator

CURRICULUM AND INSTRUCTION
Courses or Concentrations
Available: Advertising; Communication; Journalism or Mass Communication; Radio, Television, Broadcasting, or Telecommunications; Speech; *Undergraduate Objectives or Program Emphases*: To train students and develop those skills which will enable graduates to secure a position in the broadcast industry upon completion of curriculum; *Associate's Degree Majors*: 25; *Full-Time Faculty*: 4; *Full-Time Professional (non-clerical) Staff Members*: 1.

FACILITIES AND SERVICES
Practical experiences available through: Associated Press Wire Service Feed; Audio Recording Laboratory; Community Antenna (Cable) Television Origination; Carrier Current Audio Distribution System; Closed Circuit Television Facility; Campus Newspaper (Published Independently); Local Commercial Newspaper; Local Commercial Television Station; Photographic Darkrooms; Video Editing; Electronic Field Production (Video); Television Broadcast Station (Institutional); FM Radio Station (Institutional); Institutional Newspaper; Satellite Uplink Facility; Video Production Laboratory or Television Studio.

Emporia State University

Administration, Curriculum and Instruction
12th and Commercial Street
Emporia, Kansas 66801

Gene Werner, Administrator

Emporia State University (Public)

Division of Communication and Theatre
Arts
1200 Commercial Street
Emporia, Kansas 66801
Telephone: (316) 343-1200

Virginia H. Higgins, Chair
Kendall Blanchard, Dean, Liberal Arts and
Sciences

CURRICULUM AND INSTRUCTION
*Courses or Concentrations
Available*: Communication; Public Relations;
Speech; *Undergraduate Objectives or Program
Emphases*: Public communication,
interpersonal communication, organizational
communication, secondary school teaching,
acting and directing, interpretation, and
technical theatre; *Graduate Objectives or
Program Emphases*: M.A.T. degree
encompasses speech, debate and forensics,
theatre, and communication theory;
Bachelor's Degree Majors: 6; *BFA Degree
Majors*: 90; *Other Degree Majors*: 6;
Full-Time Faculty: 12; *Part-Time Faculty*: 2.

FACILITIES AND SERVICES
Practical experiences available through: Audio
Recording Laboratory; Campus Newspaper
(Published Independently); Local
Commercial Television Station; Television
Broadcast Station (Institutional); FM Radio
Station (Institutional); Satellite Uplink
Facility.

Emporia State University (Public)

Program of Journalism
1200 Commercial
Emporia, Kansas 66801
Telephone: (316) 343-5216

Kay Lingenfelter, Head
James Hoy, Chair, English Division

CURRICULUM AND INSTRUCTION
*Courses or Concentrations
Available*: Journalism or Mass
Communication; *Undergraduate Objectives or
Program Emphases*: To provide secondary
education certification; to provide an
English/journalism dual degree; to prepare
students to enter a journalism school;
Full-Time Faculty: 1.

FACILITIES AND SERVICES
*Practical experiences available
through*: Campus Newspaper (Published
Independently); Local Commercial
Newspaper; Local Commercial Television
Station; Desktop Publishing Facility;
Photographic Darkrooms; Television
Broadcast Station (Institutional).

Emporia State University (Public)

School of Library and Information
Management
1200 Commercial
Emporia, Kansas 66801
Telephone: (316) 343-5203

Martha L. Hale, Dean
David Payne, Vice President, Academic
Affairs

CURRICULUM AND INSTRUCTION
*Courses or Concentrations
Available*: Information Science; Library and
Information Management; *Graduate
Objectives or Program Emphases*: Master of
Library Science in Library and Information
Management; *Full-Time Faculty*: 11;
Part-Time Faculty: 6.

FACILITIES AND SERVICES
*Practical experiences available
through*: Advertising Agency; Carrier
Current Audio Distribution System; Campus
Newspaper (Published Independently);
Video Editing; Electronic Field Production
(Video); Television Broadcast Station
(Institutional); ITFS Distribution System;
Video News and Data Processing.

Fort Hays State University (Public)

Department of Communication
600 Park Street
Hays, Kansas 67601
Telephone: (913) 628-5365

James I. Costigan, Chair
Reland Bartholomew, Dean

CURRICULUM AND INSTRUCTION
*Courses or Concentrations
Available*: Advertising; Communication; Film
or Cinema; Journalism or Mass
Communication; Public Relations; Radio,
Television, Broadcasting, or

Telecommunications; Speech; *Program Coordinators*: M. Ke Lei Kam (Radio-Television); Robert Hanson (Journalism); *Bachelor's Degree Majors*: 200; *Master's Degree Majors*: 40; *Full-Time Faculty*: 12; *Part-Time Faculty*: 8; *Full-Time Professional (non-clerical) Staff Members*: 4.

FACILITIES AND SERVICES
Practical experiences available through: Advertising Agency; Community Antenna (Cable) Television Origination; Carrier Current Audio Distribution System; Closed Circuit Television Facility; Campus Newspaper (Published Independently); Local Commercial Newspaper; Local Commercial Television Station; Desktop Publishing Facility; Photographic Darkrooms; Video Editing; Electronic Field Production (Video); Institutional Newspaper; Public Relations Agency; Satellite Uplink Facility; Video Production Laboratory or Television Studio.

Fort Hays State University (Public)

Radio-Television-Film
600 Park Street
Hays, Kansas 67601-4099

Jack R. Heather, Administrator

Fort Scott Community College (Public)

Department of Journalism
2108 South Horton
Fort Scott, Kansas 66701
Telephone: (316) 223-2700

John W. Beal, Instructor
Robert Shores, Dean of Instruction

CURRICULUM AND INSTRUCTION
Courses or Concentrations Available: Journalism or Mass Communication; *Undergraduate Objectives or Program Emphases*: Provide transfer credit for students planning to major in journalism at a university; *Associate's Degree Majors*: 8; *Full-Time Faculty*: 1.

FACILITIES AND SERVICES
Practical experiences available

through: Desktop Publishing Facility; Photographic Darkrooms; Institutional Newspaper.

Friends University

Language and Literature
2100 University Avenue
Wichita, Kansas 67213

Raymond Nelson, Administrator

Friends University

Mass Communication
2100 University
Wichita, Kansas 67213

Billy G. Brant, Administrator

Garden City Community College (Public)

Department of Speech and Forensics Activities
801 Campus Drive
Garden City, Kansas 67846
Telephone: (316) 276-7611 Extension or Alternate: 541

Lee Tiberghien, Director
Larry Walker, Administrator

CURRICULUM AND INSTRUCTION
Courses or Concentrations Available: Communication; Speech; Forensics; *Undergraduate Objectives or Program Emphases*: To satisfy an associate of arts or science degree; *Associate's Degree Majors*: 15; *Full-Time Faculty*: 3; *Full-Time Professional (non-clerical) Staff Members*: 2.

FACILITIES AND SERVICES
Practical experiences available through: Local Commercial Newspaper; Local Commercial Television Station.

Hutchinson Community College

Department of Literature and Language
1300 North Plum Street
Hutchinson, Kansas 67501

Janice Tyrell, Administrator

Johnson County Community College (Public)

Program of Speech, Language and Academic Enhancement
12345 College Boulevard at Quivira Road
Overland Park, Kansas 66210-1299
Telephone: (913) 469-8500 Extension or Alternate: 3904

Richard W. Scott, Program Director
James Williams, Assistant Dean

CURRICULUM AND INSTRUCTION
Courses or Concentrations
Available: Communication; Speech; Foreign Languages; Hearing Impaired Interpreter; *Program Coordinators*: Bill Lamb (Journalism, Public Relations, Film); *Undergraduate Objectives or Program Emphases*: High quality freshman and sophomore transfer courses and in Interpreter Training; career training to become professional interpreter for the hearing impaired; *Associate's Degree Majors*: 28; *Full-Time Faculty*: 15; *Part-Time Faculty*: 50.

FACILITIES AND SERVICES
Practical experiences available through: ITFS Distribution System.

Kansas City Kansas Community College (Public)

Division of Humanities
7250 State Avenue
Kansas City, Kansas 66112
Telephone: (913) 334-1100

James L. Brown, Chair
Charles Johnson, Dean of Instruction

CURRICULUM AND INSTRUCTION
Courses or Concentrations
Available: Communication; Journalism or Mass Communication; Speech; *Program Coordinators*: Jo Ann Haen (Journalism and Mass Communication); Barbara Morrison and Evelyn Huffman (Speech); *Undergraduate Objectives or Program Emphases*: Transfer courses aimed at preparing students to enter the two state schools of journalism (Kansas University and Kansas State University). Speech classes are general education requirements at Kansas Regents Schools; *Associate's Degree Majors*: 13; *Full-Time Faculty*: 22; *Part-Time Faculty*: 15.

FACILITIES AND SERVICES
Practical experiences available through: Closed Circuit Television Facility; Campus Newspaper (Published Independently); Local Commercial Newspaper; Local Commercial Television Station; Photographic Darkrooms; Institutional Newspaper; Video Production Laboratory or Television Studio.

Kansas State University (Public)

A. Q. Miller School of Journalism and Mass Communications
Manhattan, Kansas 66506-1501
Telephone: (913) 532-6890

Carol E. Oukrop, Director
Thomas L. Isenhour, Dean, College of Arts and Sciences

CURRICULUM AND INSTRUCTION
Courses or Concentrations
Available: Advertising; Journalism or Mass Communication; Public Relations; Radio, Television, Broadcasting, or Telecommunications; *Program Coordinators*: Charles Pearce (Advertising); Harry Marsh (Journalism); Richard Nelson (Public Relations); Paul Prince (Radio-Television); *Undergraduate Objectives or Program Emphases*: To prepare students for entry-level positions in mass communications professions, with tools needed to advance in their careers and participate in society as informed citizens; *Graduate Objectives or Program Emphases*: To prepare students for advanced positions in mass communication; *Bachelor's Degree Majors*: 400; *Other Degree Majors*: 23; *Full-Time Faculty*: 19; *Part-Time Faculty*: 5; *Full-Time Professional (non-clerical) Staff Members*: 1.

FACILITIES AND SERVICES
Practical experiences available

through: Associated Press Wire Service Feed;
Audio Recording Laboratory; Campus
Newspaper (Published Independently);
Desktop Publishing Facility; Photographic
Darkrooms; Video Editing; Electronic Field
Production (Video); FM Radio Station
(Institutional); Institutional Magazine;
Video News and Data Processing; Video
Production Laboratory or Television Studio.

Kansas State University (Public)

Department of Speech
Manhattan, Kansas 66506
Telephone: (913) 532-6875

Harold J. Nichols, Head
Thomas Isenhour, Dean, College of Arts and
Sciences

CURRICULUM AND INSTRUCTION
Courses or Concentrations
Available: Communication; Film or Cinema;
Speech; Rhetoric; Speech Pathology,
Audiology; Linguistics; *Program
Coordinators*: Bill Schenck-Hamlin
(Rhetoric, Communication); *Undergraduate
Objectives or Program Emphases*: General
communication studies; *Graduate Objectives
or Program Emphases*: Rhetorical theory and
criticism, political communication, research
methodology, social influence; *Bachelor's
Degree Majors*: 17; *Master's Degree
Majors*: 12; *Full-Time Faculty*: 32;
Part-Time Faculty: 25.

McPherson College

Audiovisual Communications
407 South Grand
McPherson, Kansas 67460

Herbert Johnson, Administrator

Mid-America Nazarene College (Private)

Speech Communication in the Division of
Humanities
College Way
Olathe, Kansas 66062
Telephone: (913) 782-3750

Harry D. Russell, Chair

CURRICULUM AND INSTRUCTION
Courses or Concentrations
Available: Communication; Speech;
Bachelor's Degree Majors: 25; *Full-Time
Faculty*: 2; *Part-Time Faculty*: 1; *Full-Time
Professional (non-clerical) Staff Members*: 1.

FACILITIES AND SERVICES
Practical experiences available
through: Closed Circuit Television Facility;
Campus Newspaper (Published
Independently).

Pittsburg State University (Public)

Department of Communication
Pittsburg, Kansas 66762
Telephone: (316) 231-7000 Extension or
Alternate: 4715

Peter K. Hamilton, Chair
Richard C. Welty, Dean, College of Arts and
Sciences

CURRICULUM AND INSTRUCTION
Courses or Concentrations
Available: Advertising; Communication;
Journalism or Mass Communication; Public
Relations; Radio, Television, Broadcasting,
or Telecommunications; Speech; Theatre;
Communication Education; Photojournalism;
*Undergraduate Objectives or Program
Emphases*: Preparation for careers in
communication, secondary education or
theatre; *Graduate Objectives or Program
Emphases*: Preparation for Ph.D. work,
develop understanding of theory and practice
in communication. Research emphasis;
Bachelor's Degree Majors: 120; *Master's
Degree Majors*: 25; *Full-Time Faculty*: 10;
Part-Time Faculty: 7.

FACILITIES AND SERVICES
Practical experiences available
through: Advertising Agency; AM Radio
Station (Institutional); Audio Recording
Laboratory; Community Antenna (Cable)
Television Origination; Campus Newspaper
(Published Independently); Local
Commercial Newspaper; Local Commercial
Television Station; Desktop Publishing
Facility; Photographic Darkrooms; Video
Editing; Electronic Field Production
(Video); Television Broadcast Station
(Institutional); FM Radio Station
(Institutional); ITFS Distribution System;
Institutional Newspaper; Public Relations
Agency; Video News and Data Processing;

Video Production Laboratory or Television Studio.

St. Mary of the Plains College (Private)

Department of Mass Communication
240 San Jose Drive
Dodge City, Kansas 67801
Telephone: (316) 225-4171

Margaret M. Butcher, Chair
Pamela Young, Interim Vice President,
Academic Affairs

CURRICULUM AND INSTRUCTION
Courses or Concentrations
Available: Advertising; Communication; Journalism or Mass Communication; Public Relations; Radio, Television, Broadcasting, or Telecommunications; *Undergraduate Objectives or Program Emphases*: The department of Mass Communication prepares a student in the areas of radio-television and journalism through a very broad Liberal Arts education, supplemented by writing, editing, speaking and camera skills; *Bachelor's Degree Majors*: 12; *Full-Time Faculty*: 2; *Part-Time Faculty*: 1.

FACILITIES AND SERVICES
Practical experiences available through: Advertising Agency; Audio Recording Laboratory; Campus Newspaper (Published Independently); Local Commercial Newspaper; Local Commercial Television Station; Desktop Publishing Facility; Photographic Darkrooms; Video Editing; Electronic Field Production (Video); Institutional Newspaper; Video News and Data Processing; Video Production Laboratory or Television Studio.

Seward County Community College (Public)

Program of Journalism
1801 North Kansas
Liberal, Kansas 67901
Telephone: (316) 624-1951

Andrea G. Yoxall, Instructor
Jon Ulm, Division Chair

CURRICULUM AND INSTRUCTION
Courses or Concentrations
Available: Advertising; Communication; Journalism or Mass Communication; Radio, Television, Broadcasting, or Telecommunications; Speech; *Undergraduate Objectives or Program Emphases*: First two years of a transfer degree offered; *Associate's Degree Majors*: 5; *Full-Time Faculty*: 1; *Part-Time Faculty*: 1.

FACILITIES AND SERVICES
Practical experiences available through: Desktop Publishing Facility; Photographic Darkrooms; Institutional Magazine; Institutional Newspaper.

Southwestern College (Private)

Department of Communication
100 College Street
Winfield, Kansas 67156
Telephone: (316) 221-4150

Bill DeArmord, Head
Marguerite Hessini, Administrator

CURRICULUM AND INSTRUCTION
Courses or Concentrations
Available: Advertising; Communication; Film or Cinema; Journalism or Mass Communication; Public Relations; Radio, Television, Broadcasting, or Telecommunications; Speech; Visual Media; *Program Coordinators*: Roger Moon (Theatre); Jennifer Morgan (Forensics); *Undergraduate Objectives or Program Emphases*: Developing communication skills and preparing students for professional careers; *Bachelor's Degree Majors*: 25; *Full-Time Faculty*: 3; *Part-Time Faculty*: 4.

FACILITIES AND SERVICES
Practical experiences available through: Community Antenna (Cable) Television Origination; Photographic Darkrooms; Video Editing; Electronic Field Production (Video); Film or Cinema Laboratory; FM Radio Station (Institutional); Institutional Magazine; Institutional Newspaper; Video Production Laboratory or Television Studio.

University of Kansas (Public)

Wm. A. White School of Journalism and Mass Communication
Lawrence, Kansas 66045
Telephone: (913) 864-4755

M. A. Kautsch, Dean
Del Brinkman, Vice Chancellor, Academic Affairs

CURRICULUM AND INSTRUCTION
Courses or Concentrations Available: Advertising; Journalism or Mass Communication; Radio, Television, Broadcasting, or Telecommunications; Business Communication; Magazine; *Undergraduate Objectives or Program Emphases*: To prepare students for careers in journalism or other fields in mass communications. The school offers a professional program; *Graduate Objectives or Program Emphases*: Advanced professional program; *Other Degree Majors*: 1170; *Full-Time Faculty*: 31; *Part-Time Faculty*: 10; *Full-Time Professional (non-clerical) Staff Members*: 10. See one or more additional entries below.

FACILITIES AND SERVICES
Practical experiences available through: Advertising Agency; Associated Press Wire Service Feed; Audio Recording Laboratory; Community Antenna (Cable) Television Origination; Campus Newspaper (Published Independently); Local Commercial Newspaper; Desktop Publishing Facility; Photographic Darkrooms; Video Editing; Electronic Field Production (Video); FM Radio Station (Institutional); Institutional Magazine; Institutional Newspaper; Public Relations Agency; United Press International Feed; Video News and Data Processing; Video Production Laboratory or Television Studio.

University of Kansas (Public)

Department of Radio-Television
200 Stauffer-Flint
Lawrence, Kansas 66045
Telephone: (913) 864-3991

Max Utsler, Chair
Mike Kautsch, Dean, School of Journalism

CURRICULUM AND INSTRUCTION
Courses or Concentrations

Available: Advertising; Journalism or Mass Communication; Public Relations; *Undergraduate Objectives or Program Emphases*: Professional preparation in: News, sales, business communication; *Graduate Objectives or Program Emphases*: Professional preparation in news, sales, business communication; also a mid-career program that emphasizes management; *Bachelor's Degree Majors*: 125; *Other Degree Majors*: 15; *Full-Time Faculty*: 7; *Part-Time Faculty*: 2; *Full-Time Professional (non-clerical) Staff Members*: 3.

FACILITIES AND SERVICES
Practical experiences available through: Associated Press Wire Service Feed; Audio Recording Laboratory; Campus Newspaper (Published Independently); Local Commercial Television Station; Desktop Publishing Facility; Video Editing; Electronic Field Production (Video); FM Radio Station (Institutional); Institutional Magazine; Public Relations Agency; Video Production Laboratory or Television Studio.

Washburn University of Topeka

Center for Media and Communication Studies
1700 College
Topeka, Kansas 66621

Frank J. Chorba, Administrator

Wichita State University (Public)

Elliott School of Communication
1845 North Fairmount, Box 31
Wichita, Kansas 67208
Telephone: (316) 689-3185

Vernon A. Keel, Director
Phillip Thomas, Dean, Liberal Arts and Sciences

CURRICULUM AND INSTRUCTION
Courses or Concentrations Available: Advertising; Journalism or Mass Communication; Public Relations; Radio, Television, Broadcasting, or Telecommunications; Speech; *Undergraduate Objectives or Program Emphases*: An integrated communication program providing professional education in advertising, broadcasting, journalism, public relations and

speech communication; *Graduate Objectives or Program Emphases*: MA with emphasis in communication theory, cross-cultural communication, general communication, mass communication, theatre and drama; *Bachelor's Degree Majors*: 223; *Master's Degree Majors*: 42; *Full-Time Faculty*: 15; *Part-Time Faculty*: 22; *Full-Time Professional (non-clerical) Staff Members*: 5.

FACILITIES AND SERVICES
Practical experiences available through: Advertising Agency; Audio Recording Laboratory; Community Antenna (Cable) Television Origination; Closed Circuit Television Facility; Campus Newspaper (Published Independently); Local Commercial Newspaper; Local Commercial Television Station; Desktop Publishing Facility; Photographic Darkrooms; Video Editing; Electronic Field Production (Video); Television Broadcast Station (Institutional); Film or Cinema Laboratory; FM Radio Station (Institutional); ITFS Distribution System; Institutional Magazine; Public Relations Agency; Video News and Data Processing; Video Production Laboratory or Television Studio.

Asbury College (Private)

Department of Communication Arts
201 N. Lexington Avenue
Wilmore, Kentucky 40390
Telephone: (606) 858-3511

Donald B. Simmons, Head
Paul Vincent, Division Chair

CURRICULUM AND INSTRUCTION
*Courses or Concentrations
Available*: Communication; Film or Cinema;
Journalism or Mass Communication; Radio,
Television, Broadcasting, or
Telecommunications; *Undergraduate
Objectives or Program Emphases*: To prepare
students for professionally oriented positions
in media and other communication related
positions; *Bachelor's Degree Majors*: 35;
Full-Time Faculty: 1; *Part-Time Faculty*: 4;
*Full-Time Professional (non-clerical) Staff
Members*: 1.

FACILITIES AND SERVICES
*Practical experiences available
through*: Advertising Agency; Audio
Recording Laboratory; Community Antenna
(Cable) Television Origination; Carrier
Current Audio Distribution System; Closed
Circuit Television Facility; Campus
Newspaper (Published Independently);
Desktop Publishing Facility; Video Editing;
Television Broadcast Station (Institutional);
Institutional Newspaper; Video Production
Laboratory or Television Studio.

Campbellsville College (Private)

Division of Humanities
200 West College Street
Campbellsville, Kentucky 42718
Telephone: (502) 465-8158

Virginia P. Flanagan, Director
Shirley B. Meece, Administrator

CURRICULUM AND INSTRUCTION
*Courses or Concentrations
Available*: Journalism or Mass
Communication; Radio, Television,
Broadcasting, or Telecommunications;
Speech; *Program Coordinators*: Russell G.
Mobley (Speech); *Undergraduate Objectives
or Program Emphases*: Speech, journalism,
television production; *Bachelor's Degree
Majors*: 5; *Full-Time Faculty*: 1; *Part-Time
Faculty*: 3.

FACILITIES AND SERVICES
*Practical experiences available
through*: Campus Newspaper (Published
Independently); Photographic Darkrooms;
Television Broadcast Station (Institutional);
Institutional Newspaper.

Eastern Kentucky University

Department of Mass Communication
DONAX 102
Richmond, Kentucky 40475
Telephone: (606) 622-1871

Glen A. W. Kleine, Chair
Kenneth Hansson, Dean

Eastern Kentucky University (Public)

**Department of Speech Communication and
Theatre Arts**
Campbell 306
Richmond, Kentucky 40475
Telephone: (606) 622-1315

Dan R. Robinette, Chair
John M. Long, Dean, Arts and Humanities

CURRICULUM AND INSTRUCTION
Courses or Concentrations Available: Speech;
*Undergraduate Objectives or Program
Emphases*: We offer a liberal arts degree in
Human Services communication and
organizational communication; *Bachelor's
Degree Majors*: 40; *Full-Time Faculty*: 8.

FACILITIES AND SERVICES
Practical experiences available through: AM
Radio Station (Institutional); Community
Antenna (Cable) Television Origination;
Closed Circuit Television Facility; Campus

Newspaper (Published Independently);
Local Commercial Newspaper; Local
Commercial Television Station; Desktop
Publishing Facility; Photographic
Darkrooms; Video Production Laboratory
or Television Studio.

Elizabethtown Community College

Department of Humanities
College Street Road
Elizabethtown, Kentucky 42701

Jean Dudgeon, Administrator

Jefferson Community College (Public)

Department of Commercial Art Technology
109 East Broadway
Louisville, Kentucky 40202
Telephone: (502) 584-0181

L. R. Anderson, Head
Gerald Riedling, Administrator

CURRICULUM AND INSTRUCTION
Courses or Concentrations
Available: Advertising; Film or Cinema;
*Undergraduate Objectives or Program
Emphases*: Understand principles of
advertising design and illustration; *Associate's
Degree Majors*: 185; *Full-Time Faculty*: 3;
Part-Time Faculty: 5; *Full-Time Professional
(non-clerical) Staff Members*: 2.

FACILITIES AND SERVICES
*Practical experiences available
through*: Advertising Agency; Photographic
Darkrooms; Public Relations Agency.

Georgetown College (Private)

Division of Fine Arts
100 East College
Georgetown, Kentucky 40324-1696
**Telephone: (502) 863-8011 Extension or
Alternate: 863-8161**

Margaret T. Greynolds, Chair
**Joe O. Lewis, Vice President, Academic
Affairs**

CURRICULUM AND INSTRUCTION
Courses or Concentrations
Available: Advertising; Communication; Film
or Cinema; Journalism or Mass
Communication; Public Relations; Radio,
Television, Broadcasting, or
Telecommunications; Speech; Interpretation;
Theatre; Rhetoric; Debate; Persuasion;
Program Coordinators: E. Eugene Hall
(Communication Arts); R. Patrick Lergh
(Radio Activities); George McGee
(Theatre); *Undergraduate Objectives or
Program Emphases*: A general broad-based
liberal arts approach that is performance
rather than theory based. Students are
required to take one course in each of the
following: theatre, interpretation,
broadcasting, and public address. Then they
may specialize; *Bachelor's Degree Majors*: 35;
Full-Time Faculty: 4; *Part-Time Faculty*: 1.

FACILITIES AND SERVICES
*Practical experiences available
through*: Advertising Agency; Audio
Recording Laboratory; Community Antenna
(Cable) Television Origination; Campus
Newspaper (Published Independently);
Local Commercial Newspaper; Local
Commercial Television Station; Canadian
Press Feed; Desktop Publishing Facility;
Photographic Darkrooms; Video Editing;
FM Radio Station (Institutional);
Institutional Magazine; Public Relations
Agency.

Henderson Community College (Public)

**Arts and Humanities - Communications
Technology Program**
2660 S. Green Street
Henderson, Kentucky 42420
Telephone: (502) 827-1867

Tony A. Strawn, Chair
David Brauer, Academic Dean

CURRICULUM AND INSTRUCTION
Courses or Concentrations
Available: Advertising; Communication;
Journalism or Mass Communication; Radio,
Television, Broadcasting, or
Telecommunications; Speech; *Undergraduate
Objectives or Program Emphases*: Prepare
students as reporters and photographers for
all media. Also give students first two years
of a four year degree; *Associate's Degree
Majors*: 25; *Full-Time Faculty*: 2; *Part-Time

Faculty: 4; *Full-Time Professional (non-clerical) Staff Members*: 2.

FACILITIES AND SERVICES
Practical experiences available through: Audio Recording Laboratory; Community Antenna (Cable) Television Origination; Closed Circuit Television Facility; Local Commercial Newspaper; Local Commercial Television Station; Desktop Publishing Facility; Photographic Darkrooms; Video Editing; Electronic Field Production (Video); Institutional Newspaper; Video News and Data Processing; Video Production Laboratory or Television Studio.

Jefferson Community College (Public)

Department of Speech Communication
109 East Broadway
Louisville, Kentucky 40202
Telephone: (502) 584-0181

Maria B. Miller, Coordinator
G. L. Reidling, Chair, Humanities Division

CURRICULUM AND INSTRUCTION
Courses or Concentrations
Available: Communication; Mass Communication; Television, Broadcasting, or Telecommunications; Speech; *Full-Time Faculty*: 5; *Part-Time Faculty*: 5.

Kentucky Wesleyan College (Private)

Department of English and Journalism
3000 Frederica Street
Owensboro, Kentucky 42301
Telephone: (502) 926-3111 Extension or Alternate: 271

C. B. (Bob) Darrell, Chair
Ray Purdom, Academic Dean

CURRICULUM AND INSTRUCTION
Courses or Concentrations
Available: Advertising; Communication; Film or Cinema; Information Science; Journalism or Mass Communication; Public Relations; Radio, Television, Broadcasting, or Telecommunications; Speech; *Undergraduate Objectives or Program Emphases*: Literature (preparation for professional or graduate school); journalism (preparation for gateway

journalism job or MA studies) technical and professional writing; modern languages (preparation for government service, mission field, international business); *Bachelor's Degree Majors*: 30; *Full-Time Faculty*: 4; *Part-Time Faculty*: 4; *Full-Time Professional (non-clerical) Staff Members*: 1.

FACILITIES AND SERVICES
Practical experiences available through: Advertising Agency; AM Radio Station (Institutional); Audio Recording Laboratory; Community Antenna (Cable) Television Origination; Closed Circuit Television Facility; Campus Newspaper (Published Independently); Local Commercial Newspaper; Local Commercial Television Station; Desktop Publishing Facility; Photographic Darkrooms; Video Editing; Electronic Field Production (Video); FM Radio Station (Institutional); ITFS Distribution System; Institutional Magazine; Institutional Newspaper; Public Relations Agency; United Press International Feed; Video Production Laboratory or Television Studio.

Kentucky Wesleyan College (Private)

Program of Mass Communications
3000 Frederica Street, Box 1039
Owensboro, Kentucky 42302-1039
Telephone: (502) 685-5937

Gary R. Drum, Director
William Kolok, Chair, Communications and Fine Arts

CURRICULUM AND INSTRUCTION
Courses or Concentrations
Available: Advertising; Communication; Public Relations; Radio, Television, Broadcasting, or Telecommunications; *Undergraduate Objectives or Program Emphases*: Four year 43 semester hour major has three emphases. Students take 25 hours of core courses, then 15-18 hours in one of three areas: Management/Sales (includes programming); Creative (audio and video production); Advertising/Public Relations; *Bachelor's Degree Majors*: 30; *Full-Time Faculty*: 2; *Part-Time Faculty*: 2; *Full-Time Professional (non-clerical) Staff Members*: 1.

FACILITIES AND SERVICES
Practical experiences available through: Advertising Agency; Audio

Recording Laboratory; Community Antenna (Cable) Television Origination; Closed Circuit Television Facility; Campus Newspaper (Published Independently); Local Commercial Newspaper; Local Commercial Television Station; Photographic Darkrooms; Video Editing; Electronic Field Production (Video); FM Radio Station (Institutional); Public Relations Agency; United Press International Feed; Video Production Laboratory or Television Studio.

Lees College (Private)

Oral Communications
601 Jefferson Avenue
Jackson, Kentucky 41339
Telephone: (606) 666-7521

Basil B. Clark, Instructor
Mary Smith, Chair, Humanities Division

CURRICULUM AND INSTRUCTION
Courses or Concentrations Available: Speech; *Undergraduate Objectives or Program Emphases*: Instill confidence in basic speaking skills in front of others; *Full-Time Faculty*: 1.

FACILITIES AND SERVICES
Practical experiences available through: Campus Newspaper (Published Independently).

Lexington Baptist College

Christian Education Communications
163 North Ashland Avenue
Lexington, Kentucky 40502

Jim Jeffries, Administrator

Lindsey Wilson College (Private)

Department of Speech
210 Lindsey Wilson Street
Columbia, Kentucky 42728
Telephone: (502) 384-2126

Mary E. Blakeman, Instructor
David Moore, Administrator

CURRICULUM AND INSTRUCTION
Courses or Concentrations Available: Communication; Speech; Performance of Literature; *Undergraduate Objectives or Program Emphases*: We offer public speaking, advanced speech and performance of literature; *Full-Time Faculty*: 1; *Part-Time Faculty*: 3.

Maysville Community College

U.S. Route 68
Maysville, Kentucky 41056

John Crockett, Administrator

Mid-Continent College (Private)

Department of English
P.O. Box 7010
Mayfield, Kentucky 42066
Telephone: (502) 247-8521

Paula Brown, Instructor
Robert Vann, Dean

CURRICULUM AND INSTRUCTION
Courses or Concentrations Available: Communication; Speech; *Undergraduate Objectives or Program Emphases*: Religion; *Part-Time Faculty*: 1.

Morehead State University (Public)

Department of Communications
Breckinridge Hall
Morehead, Kentucky 40351
Telephone: (606) 783-2134

Richard J. Dandeneau, Chair
John C. Philley, Dean, College of Arts and Sciences

CURRICULUM AND INSTRUCTION
Courses or Concentrations Available: Advertising; Communication; Journalism or Mass Communication; Public Relations; Radio, Television, Broadcasting, or Telecommunications; Speech; *Undergraduate Objectives or Program Emphases*: Provide career preparation for jobs in journalism, radio-television, advertising, public relations and theatre; *Graduate Objectives or Program*

Emphases: Pre Ph.D. and career tracks in journalism, radio, television and theatre; *Associate's Degree Majors*: 6; *Bachelor's Degree Majors*: 50; *Master's Degree Majors*: 20; *Full-Time Faculty*: 25; *Part-Time Faculty*: 10.

FACILITIES AND SERVICES
Practical experiences available through: Audio Recording Laboratory; Community Antenna (Cable) Television Origination; Closed Circuit Television Facility; Campus Newspaper (Published Independently); Local Commercial Newspaper; Desktop Publishing Facility; Photographic Darkrooms; Video Editing; Electronic Field Production (Video); Television Broadcast Station (Institutional); FM Radio Station (Institutional).

Morehead State University (Public)

Area of Journalism
Department of Communication
U.P.O. 882
Morehead, Kentucky 40351
Telephone: (606) 783-2694

William D. Brown, Coordinator
Richard Dandeneau, Head, Department of Communications

CURRICULUM AND INSTRUCTION
Courses or Concentrations
Available: Advertising; Communication; Journalism or Mass Communication; Public Relations; *Undergraduate Objectives or Program Emphases*: News editorial, advertising, public relations, photojournalism, teaching, community newspaper emphases; *Bachelor's Degree Majors*: 98; *Master's Degree Majors*: 7; *Full-Time Faculty*: 4; *Part-Time Faculty*: 3.

FACILITIES AND SERVICES
Practical experiences available through: Advertising Agency; Associated Press Wire Service Feed; Audio Recording Laboratory; Community Antenna (Cable) Television Origination; Closed Circuit Television Facility; Local Commercial Newspaper; Desktop Publishing Facility; Photographic Darkrooms; Video Editing; FM Radio Station (Institutional); Institutional Newspaper; Video Production Laboratory or Television Studio.

Murray State University (Public)

College of Fine Arts and Communication
Murray, Kentucky 42071
Telephone: (502) 762-4516

Gary T. Hunt, Dean
James L. Booth, Vice President, Academic Affairs

CURRICULUM AND INSTRUCTION
Courses or Concentrations
Available: Advertising; Communication; Journalism or Mass Communication; Public Relations; Radio, Television, Broadcasting, or Telecommunications; Organizational Communication; *Undergraduate Objectives or Program Emphases*: Provide broad liberal arts education; provide career preparation in liberal arts context; provide service as comprehensive state regional university; *Graduate Objectives or Program Emphases*: Provide graduate program to support mission of university; *Bachelor's Degree Majors*: 500; *Master's Degree Majors*: 100; *Full-Time Faculty*: 20; *Part-Time Faculty*: 10; *Full-Time Professional (non-clerical) Staff Members*: 10.

FACILITIES AND SERVICES
Practical experiences available through: Advertising Agency; Associated Press Wire Service Feed; Audio Recording Laboratory; Community Antenna (Cable) Television Origination; Closed Circuit Television Facility; Local Commercial Television Station; Desktop Publishing Facility; Photographic Darkrooms; Video Editing; Electronic Field Production (Video); Television Broadcast Station (Institutional); FM Radio Station (Institutional); Institutional Newspaper; Video News and Data Processing; Video Production Laboratory or Television Studio.

Murray State University (Public)

Department of Journalism and Radio-Television
Box 2456 University Station
Murray, Kentucky 42071
Telephone: (502) 753-5083

Robert H. McGaughey III, Chair
Gary Hunt, Dean

CURRICULUM AND INSTRUCTION
Courses or Concentrations

Available: Advertising; Journalism or Mass Communication; Public Relations; Radio, Television, Broadcasting, or Telecommunications; *Undergraduate Objectives or Program Emphases*: Majors are offered in journalism, radio-television, public relations and advertising; *Bachelor's Degree Majors*: 206; *Master's Degree Majors*: 17; *Other Degree Majors*: 106; *Full-Time Faculty*: 8; *Part-Time Faculty*: 8; *Full-Time Professional (non-clerical) Staff Members*: 3.

FACILITIES AND SERVICES
Practical experiences available through: Associated Press Wire Service Feed; Audio Recording Laboratory; Community Antenna (Cable) Television Origination; Campus Newspaper (Published Independently); Desktop Publishing Facility; Photographic Darkrooms; Video Editing; Electronic Field Production (Video); FM Radio Station (Institutional); Institutional Magazine; Institutional Newspaper; Video Production Laboratory or Television Studio.

Murray State University (Public)

Department of Speech Communication and Theatre
Fine Arts Building
Murray, Kentucky 42071
Telephone: (502) 762-4483

Jerry W. Mayes, Chair
Gary Hunt, Dean

CURRICULUM AND INSTRUCTION
Courses or Concentrations
Available: Communication; Speech; Theatre; *Undergraduate Objectives or Program Emphases*: Organizational Communication, Speech Communication, and Theatre/Dance; *Graduate Objectives or Program Emphases*: Organizational Communication; *Bachelor's Degree Majors*: 105; *Master's Degree Majors*: 48; *Full-Time Faculty*: 9; *Part-Time Faculty*: 6; *Full-Time Professional (non-clerical) Staff Members*: 1.

FACILITIES AND SERVICES
Practical experiences available through: Desktop Publishing Facility.

Northern Kentucky University (Public)

Department of Communications
Highland Heights, Kentucky 41076
Telephone: (606) 572-5435

Michael L. Turney, Chair
John Johnson, Dean, College of Professional Studies

CURRICULUM AND INSTRUCTION
Courses or Concentrations
Available: Advertising; Communication; Journalism or Mass Communication; Public Relations; Radio, Television, Broadcasting, or Telecommunications; Speech; *Undergraduate Objectives or Program Emphases*: Communication programs combine broad general studies coursework with an academic foundation in theory and extensive hands-on production experience to prepare students for careers in communication; *Bachelor's Degree Majors*: 380; *Full-Time Faculty*: 15; *Part-Time Faculty*: 24; *Full-Time Professional (non-clerical) Staff Members*: 2.

FACILITIES AND SERVICES
Practical experiences available through: Audio Recording Laboratory; Community Antenna (Cable) Television Origination; Carrier Current Audio Distribution System; Closed Circuit Television Facility; Campus Newspaper (Published Independently); Video Editing; Electronic Field Production (Video); FM Radio Station (Institutional); Public Relations Agency; Video News and Data Processing; Video Production Laboratory or Television Studio.

Paducah Community College (Public)

Program of Television and Theatre
Box 7380
Paducah, Kentucky 42001
Telephone: (502) 554-9200

Bob C. Shy, Coordinator
Kathy Wood, Administrator

CURRICULUM AND INSTRUCTION
Courses or Concentrations
Available: Advertising; Communication; Journalism or Mass Communication; Public Relations; Radio, Television, Broadcasting, or Telecommunications; Speech;

Introduction to theatre, acting, stage craft, interpersonal; *Program Coordinator*: John Stewart (Communications Technology Program); *Undergraduate Objectives or Program Emphases*: Introductory level classes in communications; *Associate's Degree Majors*: 40; *Full-Time Faculty*: 5; *Part-Time Faculty*: 3; *Full-Time Professional (non-clerical) Staff Members*: 7.

FACILITIES AND SERVICES
Practical experiences available through: Audio Recording Laboratory; Community Antenna (Cable) Television Origination; Closed Circuit Television Facility; Campus Newspaper (Published Independently); Local Commercial Television Station; Photographic Darkrooms; Video Editing; Electronic Field Production (Video); Television Broadcast Station (Institutional); Institutional Newspaper; Satellite Uplink Facility (C Band Transmitter); Video Production Laboratory or Television Studio.

Prestonsburg Community College

Division of Humanities
Bert Combs Drive
Prestonburg, Kentucky 41653

Somerset Community College

Department of Communications
808 South Monticello Road
Somerset, Kentucky 42501

Donald F. Orwin, Administrator

Southern Baptist Theological Seminary (Private)

Program of Vocational Major in Communication
2825 Lexington Road
Louisville, Kentucky 40280
Telephone: (502) 897-4011

Robert D. Hughes, Director
William Rogers, Dean, School of Christian Education

CURRICULUM AND INSTRUCTION
Courses or Concentrations Available: Communication; Journalism or

Mass Communication; Public Relations; Radio, Television, Broadcasting, or Telecommunications; Speech; *Graduate Objectives or Program Emphases*: To prepare ministers to make effective use of the mass media; *Master's Degree Majors*: 20; *Full-Time Faculty*: 1; *Part-Time Faculty*: 4.

FACILITIES AND SERVICES
Practical experiences available through: Audio Recording Laboratory; Community Antenna (Cable) Television Origination; Carrier Current Audio Distribution System; Campus Newspaper (Published Independently); Local Commercial Television Station; Photographic Darkrooms; Video Editing; Electronic Field Production (Video); Public Relations Agency; Video Production Laboratory or Television Studio.

Spalding University (Private)

Program of Communications
851 S. Fourth Street
Louisville, Kentucky 40203
Telephone: (502) 585-9911

Iverson L. Warinner, Director
Phyllis Passafiume, Administrator

CURRICULUM AND INSTRUCTION
Courses or Concentrations Available: Advertising; Communication; Film or Cinema; Public Relations; Radio, Television, Broadcasting, or Telecommunications; Speech; Theatre; *Undergraduate Objectives or Program Emphases*: A broad program of study complemented by internships to develop theoretical understanding and skills required for working effectively in the various areas of communications; *Bachelor's Degree Majors*: 30; *Other Degree Majors*: 15; *Full-Time Faculty*: 21; *Part-Time Faculty*: 9.

FACILITIES AND SERVICES
Practical experiences available through: Advertising Agency; Audio Recording Laboratory; Community Antenna (Cable) Television Origination; Campus Newspaper (Published Independently); Local Commercial Television Station; Photographic Darkrooms; Video Editing; Electronic Field Production (Video); Public Relations Agency; Video Production Laboratory or Television Studio.

Transylvania University (Private)

Program of Speech
300 North Broadway
Lexington, Kentucky 40508
Telephone: (606) 233-8201

Gary Deaton, Director
Gary Anderson, Chair, Division of Fine Arts

CURRICULUM AND INSTRUCTION
Courses or Concentrations
Available: Communication; Film or Cinema;
Journalism or Mass Communication; Speech;
*Undergraduate Objectives or Program
Emphases*: Exposing students to a broad
knowledge of communication concepts with
focus on organizing and influencing
functions; *Full-Time Faculty*: 1.

FACILITIES AND SERVICES
Practical experiences available through: AM
Radio Station (Institutional); Campus
Newspaper (Published Independently);
Photographic Darkrooms; Institutional
Magazine; Institutional Newspaper.

Union College (Private)

Program of Journalism
310 College Street
Barbourville, Kentucky 40906
Telephone: (606) 546-4151

Debra R. van Tuyll, Coordinator
Candy Wood, Head, English, Journalism,
and Foreign Language Department

CURRICULUM AND INSTRUCTION
Courses or Concentrations
Available: Communication; Journalism or
Mass Communication; English; *Program
Coordinators*: Candy Wood (English);
*Undergraduate Objectives or Program
Emphases*: To produce a well-educated
communicator who has a well-rounded
background in a variety of subjects and who
has studied writing from both a scholarly and
a commercial perspective; *Bachelor's Degree
Majors*: 8; *Full-Time Faculty*: 1; *Part-Time
Faculty*: 1.

FACILITIES AND SERVICES
Practical experiences available through: Local
Commercial Newspaper; Local Commercial
Television Station; Desktop Publishing
Facility; Photographic Darkrooms;
Institutional Newspaper.

University of Kentucky (Public)

College of Communication
Greham Building
Lexington, Kentucky 40506-0042
Telephone: (606) 257-3874

Douglas A. Boyd, Dean
Robert E. Hemenway, Chancellor

CURRICULUM AND INSTRUCTION
Courses or Concentrations
Available: Advertising; Communication;
Journalism or Mass Communication; Public
Relations; Radio, Television, Broadcasting,
or Telecommunications; *Program
Coordinators*: James Applegate
(Communication); Tom Lindlof
(Telecommunications); David Dick
(Journalism); *Undergraduate Objectives or
Program Emphases*: The undergraduate
programs in the department of
Communication and Telecommunications
are theory based. In Telecommunications it
is possible for a student to emphasize
production. The School of Journalism is
accredited and there is a professional
orientation within the major; *Graduate
Objectives or Program Emphases*: The MA
and Ph.D. programs are administered on a
college-wide basis from the Dean's office.
The curriculum is theory and research
oriented; *Bachelor's Degree Majors*: 1000;
Master's Degree Majors: 42; *Doctoral Degree
Majors Currently in Residence*: 40; *Full-Time
Faculty*: 29; *Part-Time Faculty*: 30;
*Full-Time Professional (non-clerical) Staff
Members*: 2.

FACILITIES AND SERVICES
*Practical experiences available
through*: Advertising Agency; AM Radio
Station (Institutional); Associated Press
Wire Service Feed; Audio Recording
Laboratory; Closed Circuit Television
Facility; Campus Newspaper (Published
Independently); Local Commercial
Newspaper; Local Commercial Television
Station; Desktop Publishing Facility;
Photographic Darkrooms; Video Editing;
FM Radio Station (Institutional); Public
Relations Agency; Satellite Uplink Facility
(Ku Band Transmitter) (C Band
Transmitter); Video News and Data
Processing; Video Production Laboratory or
Television Studio.

University of Kentucky (Public)

Department of Telecommunications
218 Grehan Building
Lexington, Kentucky 40506-0042
Telephone: (606) 257-1730

Thomas R. Lindlof, Chair
Douglas A. Boyd, Dean, College of Communications

CURRICULUM AND INSTRUCTION
Courses or Concentrations Available: Radio, Television, Broadcasting, or Telecommunications; *Undergraduate Objectives or Program Emphases*: The program emphasizes societal effects, public and private policy, and managerial processes of information produced and distributed by electronic media; to prepare students with the professional and critical thinking skills necessary for telecommunications; *Graduate Objectives or Program Emphases*: The graduate program in Communication is designed to serve the needs of students whose goals may include teaching and academic research, professional research, or careers in the media or other organizations; *Bachelor's Degree Majors*: 90; *Full-Time Faculty*: 5; *Part-Time Faculty*: 7.

FACILITIES AND SERVICES
Practical experiences available through: Advertising Agency; Audio Recording Laboratory; Community Antenna (Cable) Television Origination; Closed Circuit Television Facility; Campus Newspaper (Published Independently); Local Commercial Television Station; Video Editing; Electronic Field Production (Video); FM Radio Station (Institutional); Video Production Laboratory or Television Studio.

University of Kentucky (Public)

Department of Communication and Theatre
227 Orehan Building
Lexington, Kentucky 40506
Telephone: (606) 257-3621

James L. Applegate, Chair
Douglas Boyd, Dean, College of Communications

CURRICULUM AND INSTRUCTION
Courses or Concentrations Available: Communication; Information Science; Public Relations; Speech; *Undergraduate Objectives or Program Emphases*: Interpersonal, organizational, intercultural-international, media studies, public relations; *Bachelor's Degree Majors*: 420; *Master's Degree Majors*: 30; *Doctoral Degree Majors Currently in Residence*: 20; *Additional Doctoral Degree Majors*: 30; *Full-Time Faculty*: 13; *Part-Time Faculty*: 25; *Full-Time Professional (non-clerical) Staff Members*: 2.

FACILITIES AND SERVICES
Practical experiences available through: Advertising Agency; Audio Recording Laboratory; Campus Newspaper (Published Independently); Local Commercial Newspaper; Local Commercial Television Station; Desktop Publishing Facility; Photographic Darkrooms; Video Editing; FM Radio Station (Institutional); New York Times Service Feed; Public Relations Agency.

University of Kentucky (Public)

School of Journalism
Lexington, Kentucky 40506-0042
Telephone: (606) 257-7811

David B. Dick, Director
Douglas Boyd, Dean

CURRICULUM AND INSTRUCTION
Courses or Concentrations Available: Advertising; Public Relations; Radio, Television, Broadcasting, or Telecommunications; General Editorial; *Undergraduate Objectives or Program Emphases*: To provide a quality liberal arts education with sequences of study in advertising and general editorial; *Bachelor's Degree Majors*: 4; *Full-Time Faculty*: 9; *Part-Time Faculty*: 7; *Full-Time Professional (non-clerical) Staff Members*: 2.

FACILITIES AND SERVICES
Practical experiences available through: Associated Press Wire Service Feed; Community Antenna (Cable) Television Origination; Closed Circuit Television Facility; Campus Newspaper (Published Independently); Local Commercial Newspaper; Local Commercial Television Station; Desktop Publishing Facility; Photographic Darkrooms; Video Editing; FM Radio Station (Institutional).

University of Louisville (Public)

Department of Communication
Louisville, Kentucky 40292
Telephone: (502) 588-6976

Charles A. Willard, Chair
Victor A. Olorunsola, Dean, Arts and
Sciences

CURRICULUM AND INSTRUCTION
*Courses or Concentrations
Available*: Advertising; Communication;
Journalism or Mass Communication; Public
Relations; Radio, Television, Broadcasting,
or Telecommunications; Speech; *Bachelor's
Degree Majors*: 600; *Full-Time Faculty*: 12;
Part-Time Faculty: 25.

FACILITIES AND SERVICES
*Practical experiences available
through*: Campus Newspaper (Published
Independently); Local Commercial
Newspaper; Local Commercial Television
Station; FM Radio Station (Institutional).

Western Kentucky University (Public)

Department of Communication and
Broadcasting
Fine Arts Center 130
Bowling Green, Kentucky 42101
Telephone: (502) 745-0111

Randall H. Capps, Head
Ward Hellstrom, Dean

CURRICULUM AND INSTRUCTION
*Courses or Concentrations
Available*: Communication; Journalism or
Mass Communication; Radio, Television,
Broadcasting, or Telecommunications;
Speech; *Undergraduate Objectives or Program
Emphases*: Liberal arts basis for career
studies in speech, broadcasting, and
corporate communication; comprehensive
preparation for graduate studies; *Graduate
Objectives or Program
Emphases*: Communication careers in
business, health-care, and government;
comprehensive preparation for doctoral
studies; *Bachelor's Degree Majors*: 274;
Master's Degree Majors: 80; *Full-Time
Faculty*: 17; *Part-Time Faculty*: 30.

FACILITIES AND SERVICES
*Practical experiences available
through*: Associated Press Wire Service Feed;
Audio Recording Laboratory; Community
Antenna (Cable) Television Origination;
Carrier Current Audio Distribution System;
Closed Circuit Television Facility; Campus
Newspaper (Published Independently);
Local Commercial Newspaper; Local
Commercial Television Station; Desktop
Publishing Facility; Photographic
Darkrooms; Video Editing; Electronic Field
Production (Video); Television Broadcast
Station (Institutional); Film and Cinema
Laboratory; FM Radio Station
(Institutional); ITFS Distribution System;
Video Production Laboratory or Television
Studio.

Western Kentucky University (Public)

Department of Journalism
Gordon Wilson Hall
Bowling Green, Kentucky 45201
Telephone: (502) 745-4143

Jo-Ann Huff Albers, Head
Ward Hellstrom, Dean Potter College

CURRICULUM AND INSTRUCTION
*Courses or Concentrations
Available*: Advertising; Journalism or Mass
Communication; Public Relations;
Photojournalism; *Undergraduate Objectives or
Program Emphases*: Advertising,
Photojournalism, Print Journalism, and
Public Relations. Minor available in
Journalism Education; *Bachelor's Degree
Majors*: 317; *Full-Time Faculty*: 14;
Part-Time Faculty: 9.

FACILITIES AND SERVICES
*Practical experiences available
through*: Advertising Agency; Community
Antenna (Cable) Television Origination;
Campus Newspaper (Published
Independently); Local Commercial
Newspaper; Local Commercial Television
Station; Desktop Publishing Facility;
Photographic Darkrooms; Public Relations
Agency.

Grambling State University (Public)

Department of Mass Communication
P.O. Box 45
Grambling, Louisiana 71245

Rama M. Tunuguntla, Head
Dardanella Ennis, Dean

CURRICULUM AND INSTRUCTION
Courses or Concentrations
Available: Advertising; Journalism or Mass
Communication; Public Relations; Radio,
Television, Broadcasting, or
Telecommunications; Speech; Visual
Communication, Technical Communication;
Undergraduate Objectives or Program
Emphases: To prepare students for
professional careers in mass communication;
Bachelor's Degree Majors: 80; *Full-Time*
Faculty: 9; *Part-Time Faculty*: 2.

FACILITIES AND SERVICES
Practical experiences available
through: Associated Press Wire Service Feed;
Audio Recording Laboratory; Community
Antenna (Cable) Television Origination;
Closed Circuit Television Facility; Desktop
Publishing Facility; Photographic
Darkrooms; Video Editing; Electronic Field
Production (Video); FM Radio Station
(Institutional); Institutional Newspaper.

Louisiana Tech University

Journalism Department
Ruston, Louisiana 71272

Wiley W. Hilburn Jr., Administrator

Louisiana College (Private)

Department of Communication Arts
College Station
Pineville, Louisiana 71359-0560
Telephone: (318) 487-7598

Thomas N. Tift, Chair
Stanley Lott, Vice President, Academic
Affairs

CURRICULUM AND INSTRUCTION
Courses or Concentrations
Available: Advertising; Communication;
Journalism or Mass Communication; Radio,
Television, Broadcasting, or
Telecommunications; Speech; Theatre;
Bachelor's Degree Majors: 15; *Full-Time*
Faculty: 3.

FACILITIES AND SERVICES
Practical experiences available
through: Campus Newspaper (Published
Independently); Local Commercial
Television Station; Photographic
Darkrooms; Video Editing; Institutional
Newspaper.

Louisiana State University - Baton Rouge (Public)

Department of Speech Communication,
Communication Disorders, Theatre
Baton Rouge, Louisiana 70803
Telephone: (504) 388-4172

Mary Frances Hopkins, Chair
David B. Harned, Dean, Arts and Sciences

CURRICULUM AND INSTRUCTION
Courses or Concentrations Available: Speech;
Theatre; Communication Disorders; *Program*
Coordinators: Gresdna Doty (Theatre); Ray
Daniloff (Communication Disorders);
Undergraduate Objectives or Program
Emphases: Communication Theory
(Interpersonal and Organizational),
Performance Studies, Rhetoric and Public
Address; *Graduate Objectives or Program*
Emphases: Communication Theory
(Interpersonal and Organizational),
Performance Studies, Rhetoric and Public

Address; *Bachelor's Degree Majors*: 100; *Master's Degree Majors*: 12; *Doctoral Degree Majors Currently in Residence*: 25; *Additional Doctoral Degree Majors*: 10; *Full-Time Faculty*: 41; *Part-Time Faculty*: 35.

Louisiana State University - Baton Rouge (Public)

Manship School of Journalism
222 Journalism Building
Baton Rouge, Louisiana 70802
Telephone: (504) 388-2336

William E. Giles, Director
David Harned, Dean, College of Arts and Sciences

CURRICULUM AND INSTRUCTION
Courses or Concentrations Available: Advertising; Journalism or Mass Communication; Public Relations; Radio, Television, Broadcasting, or Telecommunications; News Editorial; *Undergraduate Objectives or Program Emphases*: Advertising, News-editorial, Broadcasting; *Graduate Objectives or Program Emphases*: Masters of Journalism; *Bachelor's Degree Majors*: 450; *Master's Degree Majors*: 50; *Full-Time Faculty*: 19; *Part-Time Faculty*: 6.

FACILITIES AND SERVICES
Practical experiences available through: Advertising Agency; AM Radio Station (Institutional); Associated Press Wire Service Feed; Audio Recording Laboratory; Campus Newspaper (Published Independently); Local Commercial Newspaper; Desktop Publishing Facility; Photographic Darkrooms; Television Broadcast Station (Institutional); Public Relations Agency.

Louisiana State University - Shreveport (Public)

Department of Communication
One University Place
Shreveport, Louisiana 71115
Telephone: (318) 797-5375

Dalton L. Cloud, Chair
Mary G. McBride, Dean, Liberal Arts

CURRICULUM AND INSTRUCTION
Courses or Concentrations Available: Communication; Journalism or Mass Communication; Public Relations; Speech; Speech Pathology; *Undergraduate Objectives or Program Emphases*: A basic undergraduate program in speech, public relations and journalism to provide an excellent general education with undergraduate level coursework in each of the specific areas cited above, including speech pathology; *Full-Time Faculty*: 10; *Part-Time Faculty*: 3.

FACILITIES AND SERVICES
Practical experiences available through: Advertising Agency; Community Antenna (Cable) Television Origination; Campus Newspaper (Published Independently); Local Commercial Newspaper; Local Commercial Television Station; Photographic Darkrooms; FM Radio Station (Institutional); Public Relations Agency.

Louisiana Tech University (Public)

Department of Speech
P.O. Box 3165
Ruston, Louisiana 71272
Telephone: (318) 257-4764

Guy D. Leake, Jr., Head
John C. Trisler, Dean, College of Arts and Sciences

CURRICULUM AND INSTRUCTION
Courses or Concentrations Available: Communication; Radio, Television, Broadcasting, or Telecommunications; Speech; *Undergraduate Objectives or Program Emphases*: Theatre, speech communication, and speech language pathology and audiology; *Graduate Objectives or Program Emphases*: Theatre, speech communication, and speech language pathology and audiology; *Bachelor's Degree Majors*: 53; *Master's Degree Majors*: 15; *Part-Time Faculty*: 4.

FACILITIES AND SERVICES
Practical experiences available through: FM Radio Station (Institutional); Video Production Laboratory or Television Studio.

Loyola University (Private)

Department of Communications
6363 St. Charles Avenue
New Orleans, Louisiana 70118
Telephone: (504) 865-3430

Alfred L. Lorenz, Chair
William W. Eidson, Dean, Arts and Sciences

CURRICULUM AND INSTRUCTION
Courses or Concentrations
Available: Advertising; Journalism; Public
Relations; Radio, Television, Broadcasting,
or Telecommunications; Film Studies,
Communications Studies; *Program
Coordinators*: William Kelly (Advertising);
William Huey (Public Relations); Michael
Cremedas (Broadcast Journalism); Tom Bell
(Print Journalism); William Hammel (Film
Studies); David Myers (Graduate
Coordinator); *Undergraduate Objectives or
Program Emphases*: Balance of theory and
practice in eight sequences; *Graduate
Objectives or Program Emphases*: Mass
Communications, with emphasis on ethical
practice; *Bachelor's Degree Majors*: 240;
Master's Degree Majors: 21; *Other Degree
Majors*: 466; *Full-Time Faculty*: 13;
Part-Time Faculty: 8; *Full-Time Professional
(non-clerical) Staff Members*: 4.

FACILITIES AND SERVICES
*Practical experiences available
through*: Advertising Agency; Associated
Press Wire Service Feed; Audio Recording
Laboratory; Community Antenna (Cable)
Television Origination; Carrier Current
Audio Distribution System; Campus
Newspaper (Published Independently);
Local Commercial Newspaper; Local
Commercial Television Station; Desktop
Publishing Facility; Photographic
Darkrooms; Video Editing; Electronic Field
Production (Video); Institutional Magazine;
Public Relations Agency; Video News and
Data Processing; Video Production
Laboratory or Television Studio.

McNeese State University (Public)

Department of Communication and Theatre
Ryan Street
Lake Charles, Louisiana 70609
Telephone: (318) 475-5040

Charles V. Roberts, Head
Millard Jones, Dean

CURRICULUM AND INSTRUCTION
Courses or Concentrations
Available: Advertising; Communication;
Journalism or Mass Communication; Public
Relations; Radio, Television, Broadcasting,
or Telecommunications; Speech;
*Undergraduate Objectives or Program
Emphases*: Prepare professional mass
communication majors, prepare students for
graduate school, and provide liberal arts
preparation for general majors in other areas
of curriculum; *Degree Majors*: 200;
Full-Time Faculty: 12; *Full-Time
Professional (non-clerical) Staff Members*: 2.

FACILITIES AND SERVICES
*Practical experiences available
through*: Advertising Agency; Audio
Recording Laboratory; Closed Circuit
Television Facility; Campus Newspaper
(Published Independently); Local
Commercial Newspaper; Local Commercial
Television Station; Desktop Publishing
Facility; Photographic Darkrooms; Video
Editing; Electronic Field Production
(Video); Public Relations Agency; Video
Production Laboratory or Television Studio.

New Orleans Baptist Theological Seminary

Division of Pastoral Ministries
3939 Gentilly Boulevard
New Orleans, Louisiana 70126
Telephone: (504) 282-4455

Harold T. Bryson, Chair
Joe Cothen, Academic Dean

FACILITIES AND SERVICES
Practical experiences available through: Audio
Recording Laboratory; Campus Newspaper
(Published Independently); FM Radio
Station (Institutional); Video Production
Laboratory or Television Studio.

Nicholls State University

Communication Arts Program
Thibodaux, Louisiana 70301

Alfred N. Delahaye, Administrator

Northeast Louisiana University (Public)

School of Communication
700 University Avenue
Monroe, Louisiana 71209-0320
Telephone: (318) 342-2144

William R. Rambin, Director
Frank Morgan, Jr., Dean, College of Liberal Arts

CURRICULUM AND INSTRUCTION
Courses or Concentrations Available: Communication; Film or Cinema; Journalism or Mass Communication; Public Relations; Radio, Television, Broadcasting, or Telecommunications; Speech; Communication Disorders; Photojournalism; Broadcast News; *Program Coordinators*: David L. Irwin (Communicative Disorders); James D. Whitfield (Journalism); Edwin H. Ryland (Radio-TV-Film); Patrick J. Hebert (Speech Communication); *Undergraduate Objectives or Program Emphases*: To provide a comprehensive Liberal Arts education as well as specific career preparation in a wide range of fields within the broad area of communication. Those fields are represented by a total of twelve discrete undergraduate degrees; *Graduate Objectives or Program Emphases*: To allow a student, working with a major advisor, to tailor a specific degree plan to meet the individual student's career plans in academic or other professional fields; *Associate's Degree Majors*: 38; *Bachelor's Degree Majors*: 453; *Master's Degree Majors*: 57; *Full-Time Faculty*: 18; *Part-Time Faculty*: 14; *Full-Time Professional (non-clerical) Staff Members*: 1.

FACILITIES AND SERVICES
Practical experiences available through: Advertising Agency; Associated Press Wire Service Feed; Audio Recording Laboratory; Closed Circuit Television Facility; Campus Newspaper (Published Independently); Local Commercial Newspaper; Local Commercial Television Station; Desktop Publishing Facility; Photographic Darkrooms; Video Editing; Electronic Field Production (Video); Film or Cinema Laboratory; FM Radio Station (Institutional); Public Relations Agency; Video News and Data Processing; Video Production Laboratory or Television Studio.

Northwestern State University (Public)

Division of Journalism
103 Kyser Hall
Natchitoches, Louisiana 71497
Telephone: (318) 357-5213

Thomas N. Whitehead, Coordinator
Sara Burroughs, Administrator

CURRICULUM AND INSTRUCTION
Courses or Concentrations Available: Journalism or Mass Communication; Public Relations; Radio, Television, Broadcasting, or Telecommunications; *Undergraduate Objectives or Program Emphases*: News editorial, public relations, and broadcasting; *Bachelor's Degree Majors*: 79; *Full-Time Faculty*: 3; *Part-Time Faculty*: 1.

FACILITIES AND SERVICES
Practical experiences available through: Advertising Agency; Associated Press Wire Service Feed; Audio Recording Laboratory; Closed Circuit Television Facility; Campus Newspaper (Published Independently); Desktop Publishing Facility; Photographic Darkrooms; Video Editing; Electronic Field Production (Video); FM Radio Station (Institutional); Public Relations Agency; Satellite Uplink Facility (Ku Band Transmitter).

Southeastern Louisiana University (Public)

Department of Communication and Theatre
P.O. Box 451, SLU
Hammond, Louisiana 70402
Telephone: (504) 549-2105

Win Welford, Head

CURRICULUM AND INSTRUCTION
Courses or Concentrations

Available: Communication; Film or Cinema; Radio, Television, Broadcasting, or Telecommunications; Speech; Dance/Performing Arts; *Undergraduate Objectives or Program Emphases*: Training in the intelligent consumption and use of oral communication; *Bachelor's Degree Majors*: 200; *Full-Time Faculty*: 8; *Part-Time Faculty*: 3; *Full-Time Professional (non-clerical) Staff Members*: 1.

FACILITIES AND SERVICES
Practical experiences available through: Audio Recording Laboratory; Video Editing; Electronic Field Production (Video); FM Radio Station (Institutional); Video Production Laboratory or Television Studio.

Southeastern Louisiana University

Department of English
Hammond, Louisiana 70402
Telephone: (504) 549-2000

Parrill A. Sue, Head
David Watts, Dean, College of Arts and Sciences

CURRICULUM AND INSTRUCTION
Courses or Concentrations Available: Film or Cinema; Journalism or Mass Communication; *Other Degree Majors*: 11; *Full-Time Faculty*: 35; *Part-Time Faculty*: 18; *Full-Time Professional (non-clerical) Staff Members*: 1.

FACILITIES AND SERVICES
Practical experiences available through: Campus Newspaper (Published Independently); Desktop Publishing Facility; FM Radio Station (Institutional); Institutional Magazine.

Southern University

Department of Speech and Theatre
Baton Rouge, Louisiana 70813

Tulane University (Private)

Department of Communication
Newcomb Hall 1229 Broadway
New Orleans, Louisiana 70118
Telephone: (504) 865-5730
Alternate: 865-5830

John H. Patton, Chair
James K Kilroy, Dean, Liberal Arts and Sciences Faculty

CURRICULUM AND INSTRUCTION
Courses or Concentrations Available: Communication; Film or Cinema; Journalism or Mass Communication; Rhetoric and Public Communication; *Undergraduate Objectives or Program Emphases*: To provide historical, theoretical, and critical understanding of human communication as a basic liberal art. The program offers three concentration areas: Rhetoric/Public Communication; Interpersonal and Communication Theory; Mass Communication and Film Studies; *Graduate Objectives or Program Emphases*: MA in planning stages; *Bachelor's Degree Majors*: 168; *Full-Time Faculty*: 9; *Part-Time Faculty*: 4.

FACILITIES AND SERVICES
Practical experiences available through: Advertising Agency; AM Radio Station (Institutional); Community Antenna (Cable) Television Origination; Campus Newspaper (Published Independently); Local Commercial Television Station; FM Radio Station (Institutional); Public Relations Agency.

University of New Orleans

Journalism Area
English Department
New Orleans, Louisiana 70148

Laurence B. Alexander, Administrator

University of New Orleans (Public)

Department of Drama and Communications
Lakefront
New Orleans, Louisiana 70148
Telephone: (504) 286-6317

George A. Wood, Chair
Dennis R. McSeveney, Dean, Liberal Arts

CURRICULUM AND INSTRUCTION
Courses or Concentrations
Available: Advertising; Communication; Film
or Cinema; Journalism or Mass
Communication; Radio, Television,
Broadcasting, or Telecommunications;
Speech; All areas of Theatre; *Program
Coordinators*: Stephen Hank (Film); Barbara
Coleman (Television); H. Wayne Smith
(Cinema, Speech); Mona Brooks
(Advertising, Public Relations);
*Undergraduate Objectives or Program
Emphases*: To provide a general introduction
to mass media within the structure of a
liberal arts curriculum. Sufficient
specialization is available at the senior level
to allow for individual emphasis. Internships
are encouraged; *Graduate Objectives or
Program Emphases*: Masters candidates are
required to write a scholarly thesis in
preparation for further graduate study. MFA
students pursue a pre-professional program
culminating in a film, television or
inter-media production and thesis; *Bachelor's
Degree Majors*: 365; *Master's Degree
Majors*: 31; *MFA Degree Majors*: 17;
Full-Time Faculty: 12; *Part-Time
Faculty*: 19; *Full-Time Professional
(non-clerical) Staff Members*: 1.

FACILITIES AND SERVICES
*Practical experiences available
through*: Advertising Agency; Community
Antenna (Cable) Television Origination;
Closed Circuit Television Facility; Campus
Newspaper (Published Independently);
Local Commercial Newspaper; Local
Commercial Television Station; Desktop
Publishing Facility; Video Editing;
Electronic Field Production (Video); Film
or Cinema Laboratory; FM Radio Station
(Institutional); Institutional Newspaper;
Public Relations Agency; Video Production
Laboratory or Television Studio.

University of Southwestern Louisiana (Public)

Department of Communication
P.O. Box 43650 USL
Lafayette, Louisiana 70504
Telephone: (318) 231-6104

E. Joseph Broussard, Head
Richard Cusimano, Dean

CURRICULUM AND INSTRUCTION
Courses or Concentrations
Available: Advertising; Communication;
Journalism or Mass Communication; Public
Relations; Radio, Television, Broadcasting,
or Telecommunications; Speech; *Bachelor's
Degree Majors*: 590; *Other Degree Majors*: 43;
Full-Time Faculty: 15; *Part-Time
Faculty*: 30; *Full-Time Professional
(non-clerical) Staff Members*: 2.

FACILITIES AND SERVICES
*Practical experiences available
through*: Advertising Agency; Associated
Press Wire Service Feed; Audio Recording
Laboratory; Community Antenna (Cable)
Television Origination; Campus Newspaper
(Published Independently); Local
Commercial Newspaper; Local Commercial
Television Station; Desktop Publishing
Facility; Photographic Darkrooms; Video
Editing; Electronic Field Production
(Video); FM Radio Station (Institutional);
Institutional Newspaper; Public Relations
Agency; Video News and Data Processing;
Video Production Laboratory or Television
Studio.

Xavier University of Louisiana

Mass Communications Department
7325 Palmetto Street
New Orleans, Louisiana 70125

Elizabeth Ann Barron, Administrator

Bowdoin College (Private)

Department of Theater Arts
Brunswick, Maine 04011
Telephone: (207) 725-3341

A. Raymond Rutan, Chair/Director
A. LeRoy Greason, President

CURRICULUM AND INSTRUCTION
*Courses or Concentrations
Available*: Communication; Film or Cinema;
Radio, Television, Broadcasting, or
Telecommunications; Speech; *Undergraduate
Objectives or Program Emphases*: Self
designed majors only. Major or principal
emphasis is extracurricular; *Bachelor's Degree
Majors*: 3; *Full-Time Faculty*: 3; *Full-Time
Professional (non-clerical) Staff Members*: 1.

FACILITIES AND SERVICES
*Practical experiences available
through*: Campus Newspaper (Published
Independently); Photographic Darkrooms;
Video Editing; Electronic Field Production
(Video); FM Radio Station (Institutional);
Satellite Uplink Facility; Video Production
Laboratory or Television Studio.

Husson College (Private)

School of Broadcasting
One College Circle
Bangor, Maine 04401
Telephone: (207) 947-6083

George E. Wildey, Director

CURRICULUM AND INSTRUCTION
*Courses or Concentrations
Available*: Advertising; Communication;
Journalism or Mass Communication; Public
Relations; Radio, Television, Broadcasting,
or Telecommunications; Speech; Sound
Recording; *Undergraduate Objectives or
Program Emphases*: Emphasis is placed on a
practical application in all areas of
broadcasting, designed for the entry level
position. Extensive hands on laboratory
work; *Associate's Degree Majors*: 60;
Full-Time Faculty: 3; *Part-Time Faculty*: 14;

*Full-Time Professional (non-clerical) Staff
Members*: 2.

FACILITIES AND SERVICES
*Practical experiences available
through*: Advertising Agency; Associated
Press Wire Service Feed; Audio Recording
Laboratory; Community Antenna (Cable)
Television Origination; Closed Circuit
Television Facility; Local Commercial
Television Station; Video Editing;
Electronic Field Production (Video); FM
Radio Station (Institutional); Public
Relations Agency; Video News and Data
Processing.

University of Maine - Augusta (Public)

Division of Science, Math and Social Science
Augusta, Maine 04330
Telephone: (207) 622-7131

Rodney M. Cole, Professor
Charles Danforth, Dean, Arts and Sciences

CURRICULUM AND INSTRUCTION
*Courses or Concentrations
Available*: Communication; Journalism or
Mass Communication; Speech;
*Undergraduate Objectives or Program
Emphases*: Service courses and
communication requirements; *Full-Time
Faculty*: 2; *Part-Time Faculty*: 3.

FACILITIES AND SERVICES
Practical experiences available through: ITFS
Distribution System.

University of Maine - Orono (Public)

Department of Journalism and Mass Communication
107 Lord Hall
Orono, Maine 04469
Telephone: (207) 581-1283

Stuart J. Bullion, Chair
Julia Watkins, Dean

CURRICULUM AND INSTRUCTION
Courses or Concentrations
Available: Advertising; Journalism or Mass Communication; Radio, Television, Broadcasting, or Telecommunications; *Undergraduate Objectives or Program Emphases*: News-editorial, broadcast news, advertising, and broadcasting; *Bachelor's Degree Majors*: 170; *Full-Time Faculty*: 8; *Part-Time Faculty*: 4.

FACILITIES AND SERVICES
Practical experiences available through: Associated Press Wire Service Feed; Closed Circuit Television Facility; Campus Newspaper (Published Independently); Video Editing; Electronic Field Production (Video); Television Broadcast Station (Institutional); FM Radio Station (Institutional); ITFS Distribution System; Video News and Data Processing; Video Production Laboratory or Television Studio.

University of Maine - Orono (Public)

Department of Speech Communication
315 Stevens Hall
Orono, Maine 04469
Telephone: (207) 581-1935

Eric E. Peterson, Chair
Julia Watkins, Dean

CURRICULUM AND INSTRUCTION
Courses or Concentrations
Available: Communication; Public Relations; Speech; *Undergraduate Objectives or Program Emphases*: To develop a broad understanding of communication; how people communicate in a variety of contexts. Students are encouraged to explore the diversity of perspectives on communication and to concentrate on areas of interest; *Graduate Objectives or Program Emphases*: To develop a broad understanding of historical and contemporary theories of communication, the research skills necessary to explore the nature of communication, and the ability to apply their knowledge of communication in varied settings; *Bachelor's Degree Majors*: 75; *Master's Degree Majors*: 15; *Full-Time Faculty*: 8; *Part-Time Faculty*: 14; *Full-Time Professional (non-clerical) Staff Members*: 1.

University of Southern Maine (Public)

Department of Communication
96 Falmouth Street
Portland, Maine 04103
Telephone: (207) 780-5387

Leonard J. Shedletsky, Chair
Dave Davis, Dean

CURRICULUM AND INSTRUCTION
Courses or Concentrations
Available: Communication; Film or Cinema; Information Science; Journalism or Mass Communication; Radio, Television, Broadcasting, or Telecommunications; *Undergraduate Objectives or Program Emphases*: Liberal arts, theoretically based communication major with a strong social science perspective. The television production option is currently intended largely to produce television programs for local access TV although there are some courses on aesthetics and editing; *Bachelor's Degree Majors*: 300; *Full-Time Faculty*: 7; *Part-Time Faculty*: 3.

FACILITIES AND SERVICES
Practical experiences available through: Advertising Agency; AM Radio Station (Institutional); Community Antenna (Cable) Television Origination; Campus Newspaper (Published Independently); Local Commercial Television Station; Video Editing; Television Broadcast Station (Institutional).

University of Southern Maine (Public)

Department of USM Television
96 Falmouth Street
Portland, Maine 04103
Telephone: (207) 874-6540

Caroline L. Hendry, Coordinator
John W. Bay, Director

CURRICULUM AND INSTRUCTION
Courses or Concentrations Available: Advertising; Communication; Film or Cinema; Information Science; Journalism or Mass Communication; Public Relations; Radio, Television, Broadcasting, or Telecommunications; *Undergraduate Objectives or Program Emphases*: We offer three practica (hands on basic television experience) to undergraduate students. Credit does not apply toward major; only general elective credit; *Bachelor's Degree Majors*: 350; *Full-Time Professional (non-clerical) Staff Members*: 2.

FACILITIES AND SERVICES
Practical experiences available through: Community Antenna (Cable) Television Origination; Closed Circuit Television Facility; Local Commercial Television Station; Video Editing; Electronic Field Production (Video); Television Broadcast Station (Institutional).

Alleghany Community College

Media Technology
Willow Brook Road
Cumberland, Maryland 21502

Terry Feck, Administrator

Anne Arundel Community College (Public)

Department of Communication Arts
Technology
101 College Parkway
Arnold, Maryland 21012
Telephone: (301) 541-2433

James Privitera, Chair
Mumford Will, Administrator

CURRICULUM AND INSTRUCTION
Courses or Concentrations
Available: Communication; Radio,
Television, Broadcasting, or
Telecommunications; Photography, Graphic
Arts; *Undergraduate Objectives or Program*
Emphases: To prepare students for transfer
to four year colleges or entry level jobs in
video, photography or graphic arts;
Associate's Degree Majors: 150; *Full-Time*
Faculty: 4; *Part-Time Faculty*: 4.

FACILITIES AND SERVICES
Practical experiences available
through: Photographic Darkrooms; Video
Editing; Electronic Field Production
(Video); Video Production Laboratory or
Television Studio.

Bowie State College

Department of Communications
Jericho Park Road
Bowie, Maryland 20715

Elaine Bourne-Heath, Administrator

Catonsville Community College

Department of Communication
800 South Rolling Road
Catoonsville, Maryland 21228

College of Notre Dame of Maryland

Communication Arts Department
4701 North Charles Street
Baltimore, Maryland 21210

Karen M. Stoddard, Administrator

Community College of Baltimore (Public)

Division of Applied Technologies
2901 Liberty Heights Avenue
Baltimore, Maryland 21215
Telephone: (301) 396-1833

Dennis E. Mackowski, Assistant Dean
Ron Wright, Vice President, Academic and
Student Affairs

CURRICULUM AND INSTRUCTION
Courses or Concentrations
Available: Communication; Film or Cinema;
Journalism or Mass Communication; Radio,
Television, Broadcasting, or
Telecommunications; Speech; *Program*
Coordinators: Charles Fox (Mass
Communication); Jeanne Lowinger (Graphic
Design); *Undergraduate Objectives or*
Program Emphases: Mass
Communication--transfer and employment
in broadcasting, educational and industrial
communications. Graphic Design--transfer
and employment in photography, computer
graphics, publications; *Other Degree*
Majors: 120; *Full-Time Faculty*: 8;
Part-Time Faculty: 4; *Full-Time Professional*
(non-clerical) Staff Members: 1.

FACILITIES AND SERVICES
Practical experiences available
through: Associated Press Wire Service Feed;
Community Antenna (Cable) Television

Origination; Carrier Current Audio Distribution System; Campus Newspaper (Published Independently); Local Commercial Television Station; Desktop Publishing Facility; Photographic Darkrooms; Video Editing; Electronic Field Production (Video); Video Production Laboratory or Television Studio.

Dundalk Community College (Public)

Division of Humanities and Arts
7200 Sollers Point Road
Baltimore, Maryland 21222
Telephone: (301) 285-9876

Steven O. Tanner, Chair
Tom Sepe, Dean of Instruction

CURRICULUM AND INSTRUCTION
*Courses or Concentrations
Available*: Communication; Speech;
*Undergraduate Objectives or Program
Emphases*: Fundamentals of Human
Communication; *Full-Time Faculty*: 13;
Part-Time Faculty: 20.

FACILITIES AND SERVICES
Practical experiences available through: Audio
Recording Laboratory; Community Antenna
(Cable) Television Origination; Campus
Newspaper (Published Independently);
Desktop Publishing Facility; Photographic
Darkrooms; Electronic Field Production
(Video).

Essex Community College (Public)

**Department of Speech, Mass
Communication and Theatre**
Rossville Boulevard
Baltimore County, Maryland 21237
Telephone: (301) 522-1420

Beverly C. Reynolds, Head
**W. P. Ellis, Chair, Division of Humanities
and Arts**

CURRICULUM AND INSTRUCTION
*Courses or Concentrations
Available*: Communication; Film or Cinema;
Journalism or Mass Communication; Radio,
Television, Broadcasting, or

Telecommunications; Speech; Film and
Television Story Board Graphics; Film and
Television Script Writing; *Program
Coordinators*: Mitchell Perkins (Mass
Communication); *Associate's Degree
Majors*: 130; *Full-Time Faculty*: 8;
Part-Time Faculty: 5.

FACILITIES AND SERVICES
*Practical experiences available
through*: Community Antenna (Cable)
Television Origination; Campus Newspaper
(Published Independently); Local
Commercial Newspaper; Local Commercial
Television Station; Video Editing; FM
Radio Station (Institutional).

Frederick Community College

Humanities Division
7932 Opossumtown Pike
Frederick, Maryland 21701

Joyce D. Meeks, Administrator

Frostburg State College

**Department of Communication and Theatre
Arts**
Frostburg, Maryland 21532

Gary D. Cook, Administrator

Goucher College (Private)

Department of Communication
Dulaney Valley Road
Towson, Maryland 21204
Telephone: (301) 337-6277

Gary R. Edgerton, Chair

CURRICULUM AND INSTRUCTION
*Courses or Concentrations
Available*: Advertising; Communication; Film
or Cinema; Journalism or Mass
Communication; Public Relations; Radio,
Television, Broadcasting, or
Telecommunications; Speech; *Undergraduate
Objectives or Program Emphases*: The
Communication Department is an integral
part of Goucher's liberal arts tradition.
Students develop a sense of communication
history and a critical view to make ethical

judgements. A means is provided for mastery of the grammar of the mass media; *Bachelor's Degree Majors*: 50; *Full-Time Faculty*: 5; *Part-Time Faculty*: 5; *Full-Time Professional (non-clerical) Staff Members*: 1.

FACILITIES AND SERVICES
Practical experiences available through: Advertising Agency; Audio Recording Laboratory; Campus Newspaper (Published Independently); Local Commercial Newspaper; Local Commercial Television Station; Desktop Publishing Facility; Photographic Darkrooms; Video Editing; Electronic Field Production (Video); Film or Cinema Laboratory; Public Relations Agency; Satellite Uplink Facility (Ku Band Transmitter); Video Production Laboratory or Television Studio.

Hagerstown Junior College (Public)

Division of Humanities - AV Services
751 Robinwood Drive
Hagerstown, Maryland 21740
Telephone: (301) 790-2800

Ralph Chapin, Coordinator
Margaret Nirpourfard, Administrator

CURRICULUM AND INSTRUCTION
Courses or Concentrations Available: Journalism or Mass Communication; Radio, Television, Broadcasting, or Telecommunications; *Part-Time Faculty*: 5.

FACILITIES AND SERVICES
Practical experiences available through: Community Antenna (Cable) Television Origination; Local Commercial Television Station; Desktop Publishing Facility; Photographic Darkrooms; Video Editing; Electronic Field Production (Video); Video Production Laboratory or Television Studio.

Harford Community College (Public)

Program of Mass Communication
401 Thomas Run Road
Bel Air, Maryland 21014
Telephone: (301) 836-4358

John A. Davlin, Head
Ronald Upperman, Associate Dean, Career Studies Division

CURRICULUM AND INSTRUCTION
Courses or Concentrations Available: Advertising; Communication; Journalism or Mass Communication; Public Relations; Radio, Television, Broadcasting, or Telecommunications; Speech; Business; *Undergraduate Objectives or Program Emphases*: To provide terminal and transfer education toward an ultimate goal of employment in the mass media of radio, television, cable, advertising, public relations; *Associate's Degree Majors*: 85; *Full-Time Faculty*: 1; *Part-Time Faculty*: 3; *Full-Time Professional (non-clerical) Staff Members*: 1.

FACILITIES AND SERVICES
Practical experiences available through: Advertising Agency; Associated Press Wire Service Feed; Audio Recording Laboratory; Community Antenna (Cable) Television Origination; Local Commercial Newspaper; Local Commercial Television Station; Video Editing; Electronic Field Production (Video); FM Radio Station (Institutional); Public Relations Agency; Video Production Laboratory or Television Studio.

Loyola College (Private)

Department of Writing and Media
4501 North Charles Street
Baltimore, Maryland 21210
Telephone: (301) 323-1010

Andrew Ciofalo, Coordinator
Barbara Mallonee, Chair

CURRICULUM AND INSTRUCTION
Courses or Concentrations Available: Advertising; Journalism or Mass Communication; Public Relations; Publishing (magazine and book); *Undergraduate Objectives or Program Emphases*: A writing oriented professional program that requires mastery of the written word in both media

and non-media writing courses. No mass communication theory is offered; *Bachelor's Degree Majors*: 324; *Full-Time Faculty*: 11; *Part-Time Faculty*: 6.

FACILITIES AND SERVICES
Practical experiences available through: Advertising Agency; Campus Newspaper (Published Independently); Desktop Publishing Facility; Photographic Darkrooms; Institutional Magazine; Public Relations Agency.

Morgan State University (Public)

Program of Speech Communication
Coldspring Lane and Hillen Road
Baltimore, Maryland 21239
Telephone: (301) 444-3363

Lucia S. Hawthorne, Coordinator
Jean F. Turpin, Administrator

CURRICULUM AND INSTRUCTION
Courses or Concentrations Available: Speech; *Undergraduate Objectives or Program Emphases*: To prepare students in general speech, in speech education or in rhetoric and public address; *Bachelor's Degree Majors*: 10; *Full-Time Faculty*: 1; *Part-Time Faculty*: 1.

FACILITIES AND SERVICES
Practical experiences available through: Carrier Current Audio Distribution System; Campus Newspaper (Published Independently); FM Radio Station (Institutional).

Peabody Institute of Johns Hopkins University (Private)

Department of Recording Arts and Sciences
1 East Mount Vernon Place
Baltimore, Maryland 21202
Telephone: (301) 659-8136

Alan P. Kefauver, Director
Robert O. Pierce, Director of Conservatory

CURRICULUM AND INSTRUCTION
Courses or Concentrations Available: Audio Recording; *Undergraduate Objectives or Program Emphases*: Train recording engineers; *Degree Majors*: 25; *Full-Time*

Faculty: 1; *Part-Time Faculty*: 15; *Full-Time Professional (non-clerical) Staff Members*: 2.

FACILITIES AND SERVICES
Practical experiences available through: Audio Recording Laboratory; Campus Newspaper (Published Independently); FM Radio Station (Institutional).

Prince George's Community College

Speech Communication and Theatre Department
301 Largo Road
Largo, Maryland 20772

Darlyn R. Wolvin, Administrator

Salisbury State College

Department of Communication Arts
Salisbury, Maryland 21801

Lou Ann Daly, Administrator

Towson State University (Public)

Department of Speech and Mass Communication
Van Bokkelen Hall, Room 109
Towson, Maryland 21131
Telephone: (301) 830-2890

Ronald J. Matlon, Chair
Gilbert A. Brungardt, Dean, Fine Arts and Communication

CURRICULUM AND INSTRUCTION
Courses or Concentrations Available: Advertising; Communication; Film or Cinema; Journalism or Mass Communication; Public Relations; Radio, Television, Broadcasting, or Telecommunications; Speech; *Undergraduate Objectives or Program Emphases*: Undergraduate majors are offered in Communication Studies and in Mass Communication. These allow students to develop skills as a method of inquiry and advocacy and to provide a broad understanding of processes, functions, and responsibilities of Mass Communication; *Graduate Objectives or Program*

Emphases: The Master of Arts Degree in Mass Communication is structured to integrate communicology, film, journalism, public relations, radio and television. This holistic approach is the strength of the program; *Bachelor's Degree Majors*: 950; *Master's Degree Majors*: 100; *Full-Time Faculty*: 27; *Part-Time Faculty*: 43; *Full-Time Professional (non-clerical) Staff Members*: 8.

FACILITIES AND SERVICES
Practical experiences available through: Advertising Agency; Associated Press Wire Service Feed; Audio Recording Laboratory; Campus Newspaper (Published Independently); Local Commercial Newspaper; Local Commercial Television Station; Photographic Darkrooms; Video Editing; Electronic Field Production (Video); Television Broadcast Station (Institutional); Film or Cinema Laboratory; FM Radio Station (Institutional); ITFS Distribution System; Institutional Newspaper; Public Relations Agency; Satellite Uplink Facility (Ku Band Transmitter) (C Band Transmitter); United Press International Feed; Video News and Data Processing; Video Production Laboratory or Television Studio.

United States Naval Academy (Public)

Department of English
Annapolis, Maryland 21402
Telephone: (301) 267-2836

Charles J. Nolan, Jr., Chair
Colonel F. T. Fagan, USMC, Administrator

CURRICULUM AND INSTRUCTION
Courses or Concentrations Available: Communication; Journalism or Mass Communication; Public Relations; *Program Coordinator*: Timothy Mennoti (Mass Communications, Media); *Undergraduate Objectives or Program Emphases*: Introduction to Mass Media history, responsibilities, operation, and effects; *Full-Time Faculty*: 1.

FACILITIES AND SERVICES
Practical experiences available through: Closed Circuit Television Facility; Video Editing; Satellite Uplink Facility.

University of Baltimore (Public)

Program of Corporate Communication
1420 N. Charles Street
Baltimore, Maryland 21201
Telephone: (301) 625-3285

Jonathan L. Shorr, Director
Carol M. Pierce, Chair, English and Communication Design

CURRICULUM AND INSTRUCTION
Courses or Concentrations Available: Communication; Journalism or Mass Communication; Radio, Television, Broadcasting, or Telecommunications; *Undergraduate Objectives or Program Emphases*: Prepare students to work in communication departments of businesses and nonprofit agencies. Corporate communication major comprises writing, graphic design, media production, oral communication and management; *Graduate Objectives or Program Emphases*: Currently applying for M.A. in Communication Design; *Other Degree Majors*: 100; *Full-Time Faculty*: 3; *Part-Time Faculty*: 4; *Full-Time Professional (non-clerical) Staff Members*: 1.

FACILITIES AND SERVICES
Practical experiences available through: Audio Recording Laboratory; Campus Newspaper (Published Independently); Desktop Publishing Facility; Video Editing; Electronic Field Production (Video); Video Production Laboratory or Television Studio.

University of Baltimore (Public)

Master's Program in Publications Design
1420 N. Charles Street
Baltimore, Maryland 21201
Telephone: (301) 625-3000

Virginia K-S Carruthers, Director
Carol M. Pierce, Chair, English and Communication Design

CURRICULUM AND INSTRUCTION
Courses or Concentrations Available: Advertising; Communication; Public Relations; Publications Design (writing and graphics); *Graduate Objectives or Program Emphases*: The integration of writing and graphics in the process of publications design; *MFA Degree Majors*: 140; *Full-Time Faculty*: 10; *Part-Time Faculty*: 9.

FACILITIES AND SERVICES
*Practical experiences available
through*: Campus Newspaper (Published
Independently); Desktop Publishing Facility.

University of Maryland (Public)

**College of Journalism
Journalism Building
College Park, Maryland 20742
Telephone: (301) 454-5715**

**Reese Cleghorn, Dean
J. Robert Dorfman, Provost**

CURRICULUM AND INSTRUCTION
*Courses or Concentrations
Available*: Advertising; Communication;
Journalism or Mass Communication; Public
Relations; Mass Communication;
Communication Research; *Undergraduate
Objectives or Program
Emphases*: Professional training in
journalism and related fields with a public
affairs emphases; *Graduate Objectives or
Program Emphases*: Professional training in
journalism and related fields with a public
affairs emphases; *Bachelor's Degree
Majors*: 650; *Master's Degree Majors*: 135;
*Doctoral Degree Majors Currently in
Residence*: 70; *Full-Time Faculty*: 24;
Part-Time Faculty: 30; *Full-Time
Professional (non-clerical) Staff Members*: 2.

FACILITIES AND SERVICES
*Practical experiences available
through*: Advertising Agency; AM Radio
Station (Institutional); Audio Recording
Laboratory; Community Antenna (Cable)
Television Origination; Closed Circuit
Television Facility; Campus Newspaper
(Published Independently); Local
Commercial Newspaper; Local Commercial
Television Station; Desktop Publishing
Facility; Photographic Darkrooms; Video
Editing; Electronic Field Production
(Video); FM Radio Station (Institutional);
Institutional Magazine; Public Relations
Agency; Video News and Data Processing;
Video Production Laboratory or Television
Studio.

University of Maryland (Public)

**Communication Arts and Theatre
Department
1146 Tawes Fine Arts Building
College Park, Maryland 20742**

Patti P. Gillespie, Administrator

Villa Julie College (Private)

**Communication Arts: Television/Theatre
Greenspring Valley Road
Stevenson, Maryland 21153
Telephone: (301) 486-7000**

**Sally Harris, Chair
Rose Dawson, Dean**

CURRICULUM AND INSTRUCTION
*Courses or Concentrations
Available*: Communication; Radio,
Television, Broadcasting, or
Telecommunications; Speech; Theatre;
Video; *Undergraduate Objectives or Program
Emphases*: Production; *Associate's Degree
Majors*: 25; *Full-Time Faculty*: 3; *Part-Time
Faculty*: 10.

FACILITIES AND SERVICES
*Practical experiences available
through*: Desktop Publishing Facility;
Photographic Darkrooms; Video Editing;
Electronic Field Production (Video);
Institutional Newspaper; Video Production
Laboratory or Television Studio.

Western Maryland College (Private)

**Department of Communication and Theatre
Arts
Westminster, Maryland 21157
Telephone: (301) 848-7000**

**Pamela T. Regis, Chair
M. Delmar Palmer, Dean and Vice
President, Academic Affairs**

CURRICULUM AND INSTRUCTION
*Courses or Concentrations
Available*: Communication; Film or Cinema;
Information Science; Journalism or Mass
Communication; Radio, Television,
Broadcasting, or Telecommunications;
Speech; History of Human Communication;

Undergraduate Objectives or Program Emphases: To acquaint students with communication theory and provide an overview of practice, with special attention to film and video; *Bachelor's Degree Majors*: 120; *Full-Time Faculty*: 3; *Part-Time Faculty*: 2.

FACILITIES AND SERVICES
Practical experiences available through: Carrier Current Audio Distribution System; Closed Circuit Television Facility; Campus Newspaper (Published Independently); Local Commercial Newspaper; Local Commercial Television Station; Desktop Publishing Facility; Photographic Darkrooms; Video Editing; Public Relations Agency; Video Production Laboratory or Television Studio.

Anna Maria College (Private)

Department of English
Sunset Lane
Paxton, Massachusetts 01612-1198
Telephone: (508) 757-4586

Louise N. Soldani, Head
Ann M. McMorrow, Academic Dean

CURRICULUM AND INSTRUCTION
Courses or Concentrations Available: Print
Communication with experience in
Broadcasting; *Undergraduate Objectives or
Program Emphases*: To offer a career path to
the English major. Focus is on print
communication but opportunity is offered
through internships to gain experience in
some aspects of Broadcast Communication;
Bachelor's Degree Majors: 6; *Full-Time
Faculty*: 2; *Part-Time Faculty*: 2.

FACILITIES AND SERVICES
*Practical experiences available
through*: Advertising Agency; Community
Antenna (Cable) Television Origination;
Local Commercial Newspaper; Public
Relations Agency.

Bay Path College (Private)

588 Longmeadow Street
Longmeadow, Massachusetts 01106
Telephone: (413) 567-0621

Ralph J. Shirley, Dean
Jeannette T. Wright, President

CURRICULUM AND INSTRUCTION
*Courses or Concentrations
Available*: Communication; Public Relations;
Associate's Degree Majors: 4; *Full-Time
Faculty*: 18; *Part-Time Faculty*: 5.

FACILITIES AND SERVICES
*Practical experiences available
through*: Advertising Agency; Desktop
Publishing Facility; Photographic
Darkrooms.

Boston College

**Speech Communication and Theatre
Department**
215 Lyons Hall
Chestnut Hill, Massachusetts 02167

Dorman Picklesimer Jr., Administrator

Boston University (Private)

College of Communication
640 Commonwealth Avenue
Boston, Massachusetts 02215
Telephone: (617) 353-3488

H. Joachim Maitre, Dean
Dennis Berkey, Provost

CURRICULUM AND INSTRUCTION
*Courses or Concentrations
Available*: Advertising; Communication; Film
or Cinema; Journalism or Mass
Communication; Public Relations; Radio,
Television, Broadcasting, or
Telecommunications; Speech;
Photojournalism; Reporting on Science and
Medicine; *Program Coordinators*: Jasper K.
Smith (Broadcasting and Film); David
Anable (Journalism); Walter Lubars (Mass
Communication and Public Relations);
*Undergraduate Objectives or Program
Emphases*: BS degrees offered in
Broadcasting, Film (Television Studies, Film,
Video), Journalism (News Editorial,
Photojournalism, Magazine, Broadcast
Journalism), Communication, Advertising,
Advanced Practices (Writing Studies, Public
and International Communication, Public
Relations); *Graduate Objectives or Program
Emphases*: MS degrees offered in
Broadcasting, Broadcast Administration.
Film, Journalism, Broadcast Journalism,
Reporting on Science and Medicine, Mass
Communication, and Public Relations.
Other dual degrees and joint degrees,
including the MBA and JD, are offered;
Other Degree Majors: 1580; *Full-Time
Faculty*: 57; *Part-Time Faculty*: 63;
*Full-Time Professional (non-clerical) Staff
Members*: 15.

FACILITIES AND SERVICES
*Practical experiences available
through*: Advertising Agency; Associated
Press Wire Service Feed; Audio Recording
Laboratory; Community Antenna (Cable)
Television Origination; Carrier Current
Audio Distribution System; Campus
Newspaper (Published Independently);
Local Commercial Newspaper; Local
Commercial Television Station; Desktop
Publishing Facility; Photographic
Darkrooms; Video Editing; Electronic Field
Production (Video); Film or Cinema
Laboratory; FM Radio Station
(Institutional); Institutional Magazine;
Public Relations Agency; Satellite Uplink
Facility; United Press International Feed;
Video News and Data Processing; Video
Production Laboratory or Television Studio.

Bridgewater State College (Public)

**Department of Speech Communication,
Theatre Arts and Communication Disorders
Bridgewater, Massachusetts 02324
Telephone: (508) 697-1348**

**Susan A. Holton, Chair
Jacquelyn Madry-Taylor, Vice President,
Academic Affairs**

CURRICULUM AND INSTRUCTION
*Courses or Concentrations
Available*: Communication; Journalism or
Mass Communication; Public Relations;
Radio, Television, Broadcasting, or
Telecommunications; Speech; *Undergraduate
Objectives or Program Emphases*: The
theoretical component of mass
communication rather than production;
Bachelor's Degree Majors: 150; *Full-Time
Faculty*: 16; *Part-Time Faculty*: 15;
*Full-Time Professional (non-clerical) Staff
Members*: 2.

FACILITIES AND SERVICES
*Practical experiences available
through*: Advertising Agency; AM Radio
Station (Institutional); Community Antenna
(Cable) Television Origination; Closed
Circuit Television Facility; Campus
Newspaper (Published Independently);
Local Commercial Newspaper; Local
Commercial Television Station; Desktop
Publishing Facility; Photographic
Darkrooms; Video Editing; Electronic Field
Production (Video); Television Broadcast
Station (Institutional); Film and Cinema

Laboratory; FM Radio Station
(Institutional); ITFS Distribution System;
Institutional Newspaper; Public Relations
Agency; Video Production Laboratory or
Television Studio.

Bristol Community College (Public)

**Program of Communications
777 Ellsbree Street
Fall River, Massachusetts 02720
Telephone: (508) 678-2811**

**Jules R. Ryckebusch, Director
Paul Fletcher, Division Chair**

CURRICULUM AND INSTRUCTION
*Courses or Concentrations
Available*: Marketing; Communication; Film
or Cinema; Journalism or Mass
Communication; Speech; Six credits of field
experience at local media outlets;
*Undergraduate Objectives or Program
Emphases*: Prepares students to transfer to a
four-year college or university
communications program. Students learn the
basics of journalism and receive a solid
background in the liberal arts and sciences
that gives them preparation they need to
work in the field; *Associate's Degree
Majors*: 68; *Full-Time Faculty*: 1; *Part-Time
Faculty*: 1.

FACILITIES AND SERVICES
*Practical experiences available
through*: Advertising Agency; Community
Antenna (Cable) Television Origination;
Closed Circuit Television Facility; Campus
Newspaper (Published Independently);
Local Commercial Newspaper; Local
Commercial Television Station; Desktop
Publishing Facility; Photographic
Darkrooms; Video Editing; Electronic Field
Production (Video); ITFS Distribution
System; Public Relations Agency; Video
Production Laboratory or Television Studio.

Cape Cod Community College (Public)

Department of Language Arts
Route 132
West Barnstable, Massachusetts 02668
Telephone: (508) 362-2131

Bruce Bell, Associate Dean, Humanities Division

CURRICULUM AND INSTRUCTION
Courses or Concentrations
Available: Advertising; Communication; Film or Cinema; Journalism or Mass Communication; Radio, Television, Broadcasting, or Telecommunications; Speech; *Program Coordinator*: Dale Lumsden (Radio, Television, Mass Media); *Undergraduate Objectives or Program Emphases*: To provide basic introductory courses to prepare for a major in Speech Communication; *Associate's Degree Majors*: 10; *Full-Time Faculty*: 23; *Part-Time Faculty*: 20.

FACILITIES AND SERVICES
Practical experiences available through: Advertising Agency; Community Antenna (Cable) Television Origination; Carrier Current Audio Distribution System; Campus Newspaper (Published Independently); Local Commercial Newspaper; Local Commercial Television Station; Video Editing; Electronic Field Production (Video); FM Radio Station (Institutional); ITFS Distribution System; Institutional Newspaper; Video Production Laboratory or Television Studio.

Curry College (Private)

Department of Communication
1071 Blue Hill Avenue
Milton, Massachusetts 02186
Telephone: (617) 333-0500

Alan H. Frank, Chair
George Wharton, Chair

CURRICULUM AND INSTRUCTION
Courses or Concentrations
Available: Communication; Journalism or Mass Communication; Public Relations; Radio, Television, Broadcasting, or Telecommunications; Speech; *Program Coordinators*: George Wharton (Speech); Lucille McLaughlon (Public Relations);

Undergraduate Objectives or Program Emphases: Radio Television Broadcast skill development; *Bachelor's Degree Majors*: 46; *Full-Time Faculty*: 4; *Part-Time Faculty*: 20.

FACILITIES AND SERVICES
Practical experiences available through: Advertising Agency; Associated Press Wire Service Feed; Audio Recording Laboratory; Community Antenna (Cable) Television Origination; Campus Newspaper (Published Independently); Local Commercial Television Station; Desktop Publishing Facility; Photographic Darkrooms; Video Editing; Film or Cinema Laboratory; FM Radio Station (Institutional); Institutional Newspaper; Public Relations Agency.

Dean Junior College (Private)

Program of Communication Arts
99 Main Street
Franklin, Massachusetts 02038
Telephone: (508) 528-9100

Michael C. Keith, Director
Sandy Courchesne, Administrator

CURRICULUM AND INSTRUCTION
Courses or Concentrations
Available: Communication; Journalism or Mass Communication; Radio, Television, Broadcasting, or Telecommunications; *Undergraduate Objectives or Program Emphases*: Transfer oriented; *Associate's Degree Majors*: 135; *Full-Time Faculty*: 5; *Part-Time Faculty*: 1; *Full-Time Professional (non-clerical) Staff Members*: 2.

FACILITIES AND SERVICES
Practical experiences available through: Audio Recording Laboratory; Community Antenna (Cable) Television Origination; Campus Newspaper (Published Independently); Local Commercial Newspaper; Photographic Darkrooms; Video Editing; Electronic Field Production (Video); FM Radio Station (Institutional); United Press International Feed; Video Production Laboratory or Television Studio.

Eastern Nazarene College (Private)

Department of Communication Arts
23 East Elm Avenue
Wollaston, Massachusetts 02170
Telephone: (617) 773-6350

Ronda R. Winderl, Head
Donald Young, Administrator

CURRICULUM AND INSTRUCTION
Courses or Concentrations
Available: Advertising; Communication;
Journalism or Mass Communication; Public
Relations; Radio, Television, Broadcasting,
or Telecommunications; Speech; Multi
Image, General Media; *Undergraduate
Objectives or Program
Emphases*: Broad-based liberal arts training
including speaking, listening, writing, analysis
and utilization of various media. Strong
individualization of program components and
emphasis on internship experiences;
Bachelor's Degree Majors: 25; *Full-Time
Faculty*: 3.

FACILITIES AND SERVICES
*Practical experiences available
through*: Advertising Agency; Audio
Recording Laboratory; Community Antenna
(Cable) Television Origination; Carrier
Current Audio Distribution System; Campus
Newspaper (Published Independently);
Local Commercial Newspaper; Local
Commercial Television Station; Desktop
Publishing Facility; Photographic
Darkrooms; Video Editing; Electronic Field
Production (Video); Public Relations
Agency.

Emerson College (Private)

Division of Communication Studies
100 Beacon Street
Boston, Massachusetts 02116
Telephone: (617) 578-8737
Alternate: 578-8736

J. Gregory Payne, Chair
Jacqueline Liebergott, Vice President and
Academic Dean

CURRICULUM AND INSTRUCTION
Courses or Concentrations
Available: Advertising; Communication;
Public Relations; Speech; Political
Communication; *Program*

Coordinators: Regina Sherard (Advertising);
Ted Hollingsworth (Public Relations);
Full-Time Faculty: 18; *Part-Time
Faculty*: 23; *Full-Time Professional
(non-clerical) Staff Members*: 15.

FACILITIES AND SERVICES
*Practical experiences available
through*: Advertising Agency; Audio
Recording Laboratory; Campus Newspaper
(Published Independently); Desktop
Publishing Facility; Photographic
Darkroom; Video Editing.

Emerson College (Private)

Division of Mass Communication
100 Beacon Street
Boston, Massachusetts 02116
Telephone: (617) 578-8800

A. David Gordon, Chair
Jacqueline Liebergott, Vice President,
Academic Affairs

CURRICULUM AND INSTRUCTION
Courses or Concentrations Available: Film or
Cinema; Journalism or Mass
Communication; Radio, Television,
Broadcasting, or Telecommunications;
Program Coordinators: Michael Bantell
(Film/Cinema); Marsha Della-Giusting
(Journalism); George Quenzel (Television);
Francine Berger (Audio); *Undergraduate
Objectives or Program Emphases*: To provide
a central, core Mass Communication
curriculum, and to allow students to
specialize and develop hands-on skills and
substantive, knowledge in one of four
areas: Audio, Film, Journalism and
Television; *Graduate Objectives or Program
Emphases*: To provide theoretical and
practical training, including a perspective on
emerging technologies, in Audio, Journalism,
Television, Media Management and general
Mass Communication; *Bachelor's Degree
Majors*: 437; *BFA Degree Majors*: 12;
Master's Degree Majors: 92; *Full-Time
Faculty*: 23; *Part-Time Faculty*: 32;
*Full-Time Professional (non-clerical) Staff
Members*: 9.

FACILITIES AND SERVICES
Practical experiences available through: Audio
Recording Laboratory; Carrier Current
Audio Distribution System; Campus
Newspaper (Published Independently);
Associated Press Wire Service Feed;

Desktop Publishing Facility; Video Editing; Electronic Field Production (Video); Film or Cinema Laboratory; FM Radio Station (Institutional); ITFS Distribution System; United Press International Feed; Video News and Data Processing; Video Production Laboratory or Television Studio.

Emerson College (Private)

Division of Graduate Studies
100 Beacon Street
Boston, Massachusetts 02116
Telephone: (617) 578-8612

William R. Elwood, Dean
Jacqueline Liebergott, Vice President, Academic Affairs

CURRICULUM AND INSTRUCTION
Courses or Concentrations Available: Advertising; Communication; Film or Cinema; Journalism or Mass Communication; Public Relations; Radio, Television, Broadcasting, or Telecommunications; Speech; Performing Arts; Communication Disorders; Writing, Literature and Publishing; *Program Coordinators*: Don Fry (Mass Communications); Andrew Rancer (Communication Studies); Suzanne Bennett (Communication Disorders); Robin Fast, Ted Weesner (Writing, Literature and Publishing); Bob Colby, Maureen Shea (Performing Arts); *Graduate Objectives or Program Emphases*: The divisions offer advanced work to train MA and MS students to work in the professions represented in the disciplines and to continue work at the doctoral level; *Master's Degree Majors*: 354; *MFA Degree Majors*: 66; *Full-Time Faculty*: 96; *Part-Time Faculty*: 138; *Full-Time Professional (non-clerical) Staff Members*: 125.

FACILITIES AND SERVICES
Practical experiences available through: Advertising Agency; Associated Press Wire Service Feed; Audio Recording Laboratory; Carrier Current Audio Distribution System; Campus Newspaper (Published Independently); Local Commercial Newspaper; Local Commercial Television Station; Desktop Publishing Facility; Photographic Darkrooms; Video Editing; Electronic Field Production (Video); Film or Cinema Laboratory; FM Radio Station (Institutional); ITFS

Distribution System; Public Relations Agency; United Press International Feed; Video Production Laboratory or Television Studio.

Emmanuel College (Private)

Department of English
400 The Fenway
Boston, Massachusetts 02115
Telephone: (617) 735-9823

Steven F. Bloom, Chair
Helen Trimble, Dean and Vice President, Academic Affairs

CURRICULUM AND INSTRUCTION
Courses or Concentrations Available: Advertising; Communication; Film or Cinema; Journalism or Mass Communication; Public Relations; Radio, Television, Broadcasting, or Telecommunications; Speech; Graphic Design; *Program Coordinators*: Louise Cash (Speech); David Thomas (Graphic Design); *Undergraduate Objectives or Program Emphases*: To teach writing and critical thinking skills within a liberal arts context as applied to various fields within Communications. To offer introduction to technical aspects; *Bachelor's Degree Majors*: 35; *Full-Time Faculty*: 5; *Part-Time Faculty*: 4.

FACILITIES AND SERVICES
Practical experiences available through: Campus Newspaper (Published Independently); Local Commercial Newspaper; Local Commercial Television Station; Photographic Darkrooms; Video Editing.

Endicott College (Private)

Department of Communications
Beverly, Massachusetts 01915
Telephone: (508) 927-0585

Thomas J. Healy, Chair

CURRICULUM AND INSTRUCTION
Courses or Concentrations Available: Advertising; Communication; Journalism or Mass Communication; Public Relations; Radio, Television, Broadcasting, or Telecommunications; *Undergraduate*

Objectives or Program Emphases: Associate degree program with heavy liberal arts emphasis and separate tracks for specific concentrations in Advertising, Media Production, General Communication; *Associate's Degree Majors*: 77; *Full-Time Faculty*: 3; *Part-Time Faculty*: 4; *Full-Time Professional (non-clerical) Staff Members*: 1.

FACILITIES AND SERVICES
Practical experiences available through: Audio Recording Laboratory; Community Antenna (Cable) Television Origination; Campus Newspaper (Published Independently); Desktop Publishing Facility; Video Editing; Electronic Field Production (Video); Institutional Newspaper; Video Production Laboratory or Television Studio.

Framingham State College (Public)

Department of Communication Arts
100 State Street
Framingham, Massachusetts 01701
Telephone: (508) 620-1220

Jeffrey J. Baker, Chair
Madeleine Adler, Academic Vice President

CURRICULUM AND INSTRUCTION
Courses or Concentrations Available: Communication; Journalism or Mass Communication; Radio, Television, Broadcasting, or Telecommunications; Speech; *Undergraduate Objectives or Program Emphases*: A mastery of Communication theory and the execution or performance of that theory; *Bachelor's Degree Majors*: 90; *Full-Time Faculty*: 8; *Part-Time Faculty*: 2; *Full-Time Professional (non-clerical) Staff Members*: 3.

FACILITIES AND SERVICES
Practical experiences available through: Audio Recording Laboratory; Community Antenna (Cable) Television Origination; Campus Newspaper (Published Independently); Desktop Publishing Facility; Photographic Darkrooms; Video Editing; Electronic Field Production (Video); FM Radio Station (Institutional); Institutional Newspaper; Video News and Data Processing; Video Production Laboratory or Television Studio.

Framington State College (Public)

Speech Department
Box 2000
Framington, Massachusetts 01701

Joan Horrigan, Administrator

Greenfield Community College (Public)

Program of Media Communication
1 College Drive
Greenfield, Massachusetts 01301
Telephone: (413) 774-3131

Robert R. Tracy, Director
Joan Ibish, Administrator

CURRICULUM AND INSTRUCTION
Courses or Concentrations Available: Communication; Information Science; Radio, Television, Broadcasting, or Telecommunications; *Undergraduate Objectives or Program Emphases*: Photography; Graphics; Computer Graphics; Video Production; *Degree Majors*: 30; *Full-Time Faculty*: 2; *Part-Time Faculty*: 1; *Full-Time Professional (non-clerical) Staff Members*: 2.

FACILITIES AND SERVICES
Practical experiences available through: Audio Recording Laboratory; Community Antenna (Cable) Television Origination; Closed Circuit Television Facility; Desktop Publishing Facility; Photographic Darkrooms; Video Editing; Electronic Field Production (Video); Video Production Laboratory or Television Studio.

Hampshire College

School of Communication and Cognitive Science
893 West Street
Amherst, Massachusetts 01002

Mark Feinstein, Administrator

Harvard University Business School

Department of Management Communication
Cambridge, Massachusetts 02163

Lasell College (Private)

Program of Communications
1844 Commonwealth Avenue
Newton, Massachusetts 02166
Telephone: (617) 243-2000

David M. Murphy, Director

CURRICULUM AND INSTRUCTION
Courses or Concentrations Available: Communication; Journalism or Mass Communication; *Undergraduate Objectives or Program Emphases*: Career option and a transfer option in a two year program; *Associate's Degree Majors*: 5; *Full-Time Faculty*: 1.

FACILITIES AND SERVICES
Practical experiences available through: Campus Newspaper (Published Independently); Desktop Publishing Facility.

Massasoit Community College (Public)

Department of Communicative Arts
1 Massasoit Boulevard
Brockton, Massachusetts 02402
Telephone: (508) 588-9100 Extension: 191

John R. Chase, Chair
Barbara Finklestein, Division Chair

CURRICULUM AND INSTRUCTION
Courses or Concentrations Available: Communication; Film or Cinema; Journalism or Mass Communication; Radio, Television, Broadcasting, or Telecommunications; Speech; *Program Coordinators*: Robert Bowers (Radio, Audio Production); Tim Trask (Television, Video Production); *Associate's Degree Majors*: 30; *Full-Time Faculty*: 3; *Part-Time Faculty*: 3; *Full-Time Professional (non-clerical) Staff Members*: 2.

FACILITIES AND SERVICES
Practical experiences available through: Audio

Recording Laboratory; Community Antenna (Cable) Television Origination; Carrier Current Audio Distribution System; Closed Circuit Television Facility; Campus Newspaper (Published Independently); Local Commercial Television Station; Photographic Darkrooms; Video Editing; Electronic Field Production (Video); FM Radio Station (Institutional); ITFS Distribution System; Video Production Laboratory or Television Studio.

Merrimack College (Private)

Department of Fine Arts
Turnpike Road
North Andover, Massachusetts 01845
Telephone: (518) 683-7111

Albert Brenner, Head
T. Long, Dean

CURRICULUM AND INSTRUCTION
Courses or Concentrations Available: Film or Cinema; Speech; *Undergraduate Objectives or Program Emphases*: General introductory courses; *Full-Time Faculty*: 1; *Part-Time Faculty*: 1.

FACILITIES AND SERVICES
Practical experiences available through: Community Antenna (Cable) Television Origination; Closed Circuit Television Facility; Photographic Darkrooms; Video Editing; Film or Cinema Laboratory; Video Production Laboratory or Television Studio.

Mt. Wachusett Community College (Public)

Department of Broadcasting and Telecommunications
444 Green Street
Gardner, Massachusetts 01440-1000
Telephone: (508) 632-6600

Vincent S. Ialenti, Chair
Frank Desorbo, Chair, Division of Social Sciences

CURRICULUM AND INSTRUCTION
Courses or Concentrations Available: Advertising; Communication; Radio, Television, Broadcasting, or Telecommunications; *Full-Time Faculty*: 3;

Part-Time Faculty: 2; Full-Time Professional (non-clerical) Staff Members: 5.

North Shore Community College

Department of Speech Communication
3 Essex Street
Beverly, Massachusetts 01915

Northeastern University (Private)

Department of Speech Communication
360 Huntington Avenue
Boston, Massachusetts 02115
Telephone: (617) 437-5517

Alan Zaremoa, Chair

CURRICULUM AND INSTRUCTION
Courses or Concentrations Available: Communication; Journalism or Mass Communication; Radio, Television, Broadcasting, or Telecommunications; Speech; *Undergraduate Objectives or Program Emphases*: Rhetoric, Interpersonal, Organizational, Mass Communication, Communication Theory; *Bachelor's Degree Majors*: 350; *Full-Time Faculty*: 8; *Part-Time Faculty*: 5; *Full-Time Professional (non-clerical) Staff Members*: 3.

FACILITIES AND SERVICES
Practical experiences available through: AM Radio Station (Institutional); Associated Press Wire Service Feed; Campus Newspaper (Published Independently); Desktop Publishing Facility.

Northeastern University

School of Journalism
Boston, Massachusetts 02115

LaRue W. Gilleland, Administrator

Pine Manor College

Division of Arts and Communication
400 Heath Street
Chestnut Hill, Massachusetts 02167

David M. Smith, Administrator

Quinsigamond Community College

Humanities Division
670 West Boylston Street
Worcester, Massachusetts 01606

Carl Sundell, Administrator

Salem State College (Public)

Department of Theatre and Speech Communication
Salem, Massachusetts 01970
Telephone: (508) 741-6000

Myrna Finn, Chair
Marion Kiljim, Dean

CURRICULUM AND INSTRUCTION
Courses or Concentrations Available: Speech; Theatre; *Undergraduate Objectives or Program Emphases*: Skill in organizing and presenting thoughts powerfully and logically; *BFA Degree Majors*: 20; *Full-Time Faculty*: 11; *Part-Time Faculty*: 4; *Full-Time Professional (non-clerical) Staff Members*: 2.

Salem State College (Public)

Department of English, Communications Program
352 Lafayette Street
Salem, Massachusetts 01970
Telephone: (508) 741-6270

Eileen G. Margerum, Coordinator
Clair J. Keyes, Chair, English Department

CURRICULUM AND INSTRUCTION
Courses or Concentrations Available: Advertising; Communication; Journalism or Mass Communication; Public Relations; Radio, Television, Broadcasting, or Telecommunications; *Undergraduate Objectives or Program Emphases*: Program has three major concentrations: Advertising, Public Relations and Professional Writing. Program objective is to provide students with the skills and the knowledge that will develop their abilities in written communication; *Degree Majors*: 84; *Full-Time Faculty*: 5; *Part-Time Faculty*: 2.

FACILITIES AND SERVICES
Practical experiences available

through: Advertising Agency; Associated Press Wire Service Feed; Campus Newspaper (Published Independently); Local Commercial Newspaper; Local Commercial Television Station; Desktop Publishing Facility; Video Editing; Electronic Field Production (Video); FM Radio Station (Institutional); Public Relations Agency; Reuters News Agency; United Press International Feed; Video Production Laboratory or Television Studio.

Simmons College

Department of Communication
300 The Fenway
Boston, Massachusetts 02115

Deborah Smiley, Administrator

Smith College

Department of Radio and Television
Northampton, Massachusetts 01063

Springfield College (Private)

Department of English
Alden Street
Springfield, Massachusetts 01109
Telephone: (413) 788-3186

Paul J. LeBlanc, Chair
Jan Eldridge, Vice President, Academic Affairs

CURRICULUM AND INSTRUCTION
Courses or Concentrations Available: Communication; Film or Cinema; Journalism or Mass Communication; Public Relations; Radio, Television, Broadcasting, or Telecommunications; Speech; *Undergraduate Objectives or Program Emphases*: Three major concentrations within the English BA: American Literature; British Literature; Professional Writing; *Bachelor's Degree Majors*: 60; *Full-Time Faculty*: 10; *Part-Time Faculty*: 9; *Full-Time Professional (non-clerical) Staff Members*: 2.

FACILITIES AND SERVICES
Practical experiences available through: Campus Newspaper (Published Independently); Local Commercial Newspaper; Local Commercial Television

Station; Desktop Publishing Facility; Photographic Darkrooms; FM Radio Station (Institutional); Institutional Magazine; Video News and Data Processing.

Springfield Technical Community College (Public)

Department of Telecommunications
1 Armory Square
Springfield, Massachusetts 01105
Telephone: (413) 781-7822

Kirk T. Smallman, Chair
Dick Warner, Chair, Engineering Technologies Division

CURRICULUM AND INSTRUCTION
Courses or Concentrations Available: Journalism or Mass Communication; Radio, Television, Broadcasting, or Telecommunications; *Undergraduate Objectives or Program Emphases*: Learning technical skills, which may be applied in task oriented small groups, and learning good judgement and cooperation through complex video production projects; *Associate's Degree Majors*: 60; *Full-Time Faculty*: 2; *Part-Time Faculty*: 1.

FACILITIES AND SERVICES
Practical experiences available through: Audio Recording Laboratory; Community Antenna (Cable) Television Origination; Closed Circuit Television Facility; Campus Newspaper (Published Independently); Local Commercial Newspaper; Local Commercial Television Station; Video Editing; Electronic Field Production (Video); Institutional Newspaper; Video Production Laboratory or Television Studio.

Stonehill College (Private)

Department of Communication
North Easton, Massachusetts 02357
Telephone: (508) 230-1249

Robert Trapp, Chair
Jo-Ann Flora, Academic Dean

CURRICULUM AND INSTRUCTION
Courses or Concentrations Available: Communication; Journalism or Mass Communication; Speech; *Bachelor's*

Degree Majors: 130; *Full-Time Faculty*: 6; *Part-Time Faculty*: 3.

FACILITIES AND SERVICES
Practical experiences available through: Campus Newspaper (Published Independently); Local Commercial Newspaper; Local Commercial Television Station; FM Radio Station (Institutional); Institutional Magazine.

Suffolk University

Department of Speech Communication
Beacon Hill
Boston, Massachusetts 02114

Edward Harris, Administrator

Suffolk University

Department of Journalism
Boston, Massachusetts 02108

Richard P. Preiss, Administrator

University of Massachusetts (Public)

Department of Journalism
108 Bartlett Hall
Amherst, Massachusetts 01003
Telephone: (413) 545-1376

Norman Sims, Chair
Murray Schwartz, Dean

CURRICULUM AND INSTRUCTION
Courses or Concentrations Available: Journalism or Mass Communication; *Undergraduate Objectives or Program Emphases*: Critical, historical, literary and cultural studies in journalism. Provides a liberal-arts grounding in the reporting, writing, and editing disciplines, and preparation for graduate school or careers in publishing, public relations and the media; *Bachelor's Degree Majors*: 239; *Full-Time Faculty*: 9; *Part-Time Faculty*: 4.

FACILITIES AND SERVICES
Practical experiences available through: Community Antenna (Cable) Television Origination; Campus Newspaper (Published Independently); Local Commercial Newspaper; Desktop Publishing Facility; FM Radio Station (Institutional); Video News and Data Processing.

University of Massachusetts (Public)

Department of Communication (Graduate Program)
Amherst, Massachusetts 01003
Telephone: (413) 545-1311

Jarice Hanson, Director
W. Barnett Pearce, Chair

CURRICULUM AND INSTRUCTION
Courses or Concentrations Available: Communication; Film or Cinema; Journalism or Mass Communication; Radio, Television, Broadcasting, or Telecommunications; Speech; *Undergraduate Objectives or Program Emphases*: Theory in Mass Communication, Rhetoric, Interpersonal; *Graduate Objectives or Program Emphases*: Theory and Research; Interpersonal, Rhetoric, Mass Communication, Critical and Cultural Studies, and Communication Theory; *Bachelor's Degree Majors*: 250; *Master's Degree Majors*: 18; *Doctoral Degree Majors Currently in Residence*: 42; *Additional Doctoral Degree Majors*: 19; *Full-Time Faculty*: 23; *Part-Time Faculty*: 45; *Full-Time Professional (non-clerical) Staff Members*: 2.

FACILITIES AND SERVICES
Practical experiences available through: Closed Circuit Television Facility; Campus Newspaper (Published Independently); Video Editing; Electronic Field Production (Video); Television Broadcast Station (Institutional); Film or Cinema Laboratory.

Worcester State College (Public)

College of Media, Arts and Philosophy
486 Chandler Street
Worcester, Massachusetts 01602
Telephone: (508) 793-8145

Donald Bullens, Chair
Kalyan Gosh, Academic Vice President

CURRICULUM AND INSTRUCTION

*Courses or Concentrations
Available*: Advertising; Communication; Film or Cinema; Radio, Television, Broadcasting, or Telecommunications; Speech; *Undergraduate Objectives or Program Emphases*: To provide students with skills in the communication processes that use vocal, mechanical, optical and electronic means. To prepare students for entry level positions in business, industry, health services and other fields in which communication skills are essential; *Bachelor's Degree Majors*: 200; *Full-Time Faculty*: 20; *Part-Time Faculty*: 8; *Full-Time Professional (non-clerical) Staff Members*: 1.

FACILITIES AND SERVICES

Practical experiences available through: Advertising Agency; AM Radio Station (Institutional); Audio Recording Laboratory; Community Antenna (Cable) Television Origination; Closed Circuit Television Facility; Campus Newspaper (Published Independently); Local Commercial Television Station; Photographic Darkrooms; Video Editing; Electronic Field Production (Video); Television Broadcast Station (Institutional); Film or Cinema Laboratory; Video Production Laboratory or Television Studio.

Adrian College (Private)

Department of Communication Arts and Sciences
110 South Madison Street
Adrian, Michigan 49221
Telephone: (517) 265-5161

Daniel W. Scully, Chair
Daniel W. Behring, Vice President, Academic Affairs

CURRICULUM AND INSTRUCTION
Courses or Concentrations Available: Communication; Radio, Television, Broadcasting, or Telecommunications; Speech; *Undergraduate Objectives or Program Emphases*: Common outcomes relative to all concentrations include 1) becoming a more effective communicator, 2) developing creative and imaginative attitudes and approaches, and 3) realizing that success is enhanced by cooperation within a team effort; *Bachelor's Degree Majors*: 30; *Full-Time Faculty*: 4; *Part-Time Faculty*: 5; *Full-Time Professional (non-clerical) Staff Members*: 2.

FACILITIES AND SERVICES
Practical experiences available through: Community Antenna (Cable) Television Origination; Campus Newspaper (Published Independently); Video Editing; Electronic Field Production (Video); FM Radio Station (Institutional).

Albion College (Private)

Department of Communication
Herrick Center
Albion, Michigan 49224
Telephone: (517) 629-0345

Bruce J. Weaver, Chair
Daniel Poteet, Administrator

CURRICULUM AND INSTRUCTION
Courses or Concentrations Available: Communication; Journalism or Mass Communication; Public Relations; Radio, Television, Broadcasting, or Telecommunications; Speech; *Bachelor's*

Degree Majors: 65; *Full-Time Faculty*: 5; *Part-Time Faculty*: 2; *Full-Time Professional (non-clerical) Staff Members*: 1.

FACILITIES AND SERVICES
Practical experiences available through: Audio Recording Laboratory; Carrier Current Audio Distribution System; Campus Newspaper (Published Independently); Local Commercial Newspaper; Photographic Darkrooms; Video Editing; FM Radio Station (Institutional); Institutional Magazine; Institutional Newspaper; United Press International Feed; Video News and Data Processing; Video Production Laboratory or Television Studio.

Albion College (Private)

Department of English
Herrick Center
Albion, Michigan 49224
Telephone: (517) 629-0232

Charles W. Crupi, Chair
D. Poteet, Provost

CURRICULUM AND INSTRUCTION
Courses or Concentrations Available: Journalism or Mass Communication; *Undergraduate Objectives or Program Emphases*: Print journalism; *Bachelor's Degree Majors*: 20; *Full-Time Faculty*: 1.

FACILITIES AND SERVICES
Practical experiences available through: Campus Newspaper (Published Independently); ITFS Distribution System; Institutional Magazine.

Alma College (Private)

Department of Speech Communication
Alma, Michigan 48801
Telephone: (517) 463-7238

Robert W. Smith, Chair
Ronald O. Kapp, Provost

CURRICULUM AND INSTRUCTION
*Courses or Concentrations
Available*: Communication; Journalism or
Mass Communication; Public Relations;
Radio, Television, Broadcasting, or
Telecommunications; Speech; *Undergraduate
Objectives or Program Emphases*: To
understand, appreciate and participate in
speech theory and practice, perhaps the
oldest of the academic disciplines. To make
students functional, literate members of
society; *Bachelor's Degree Majors*: 5;
Full-Time Faculty: 1; *Part-Time Faculty*: 2.

FACILITIES AND SERVICES
Practical experiences available through: Audio
Recording Laboratory; Carrier Current
Audio Distribution System; Campus
Newspaper (Published Independently);
Video Editing.

Alma College (Private)

Journalism Program
Alma, Michigan 48801

Eugene H. Pattison, Administrator

Andrews University

Communication Department
Berrien Springs, Michigan 49103

Luanne Bauer, Administrator

Calvin College (Private)

**Department of Communication Arts and
Sciences**
3233 Burton South East
Grand Rapids, Michigan 49546
Telephone: (616) 957-6286

Randall L. Bytwerk, Chair
Rodger R. Rice, Dean

CURRICULUM AND INSTRUCTION
*Courses or Concentrations
Available*: Communication; Mass
Communication; Radio, Television,
Broadcasting, or Telecommunications;
Speech; *Undergraduate Objectives or Program
Emphases*: To provide a liberal arts based
education in communication from a
Reformed Christian perspective; *Bachelor's*

Degree Majors: 70; *Full-Time Faculty*: 9;
Part-Time Faculty: 5; *Full-Time Professional
(non-clerical) Staff Members*: 2.

FACILITIES AND SERVICES
*Practical experiences available
through*: Carrier Current Audio Distribution
System; Closed Circuit Television Facility;
Campus Newspaper (Published
Independently); Local Commercial
Newspaper; Local Commercial Television;
Desktop Publishing Facility; Photographic
Darkrooms; Fm Radio Station; Satellite
Uplikn (Ku Band) (C Band).

Central Michigan University (Public)

**Department of Broadcast and Cinematic
Arts**
340 Moore Hall
Mt. Pleasant, Michigan 48859
Telephone: (517) 774-3851

B. R. Smith, Chair
**Ronald Johnstone, Dean, College of Arts
and Science**

CURRICULUM AND INSTRUCTION
Courses or Concentrations Available: Film or
Cinema; Radio, Television, Broadcasting, or
Telecommunications; *Undergraduate
Objectives or Program Emphases*: To educate
leaders and managers for broadcasting, cable
and video industries. To prepare students
with hands-on opportunities to develop entry
level skills; *Graduate Objectives or Program
Emphases*: To prepare students for careers in
electronic media management and education;
Bachelor's Degree Majors: 20; *BFA Degree
Majors*: 10; *Master's Degree Majors*: 12;
Other Degree Majors: 30; *Full-Time
Faculty*: 9; *Part-Time Faculty*: 2; *Full-Time
Professional (non-clerical) Staff Members*: 1.

FACILITIES AND SERVICES
*Practical experiences available
through*: Associated Press Wire Service Feed;
Audio Recording Laboratory; Community
Antenna (Cable) Television Origination;
Campus Newspaper (Published
Independently); Local Commercial
Television Station; Video Editing;
Electronic Field Production (Video);
Television Broadcast Station (Institutional);
Film or Cinema Laboratory; FM Radio
Station (Institutional); Institutional

Newspaper; Video Production Laboratory or Television Studio.

Central Michigan University (Public)

Department of Journalism
Anspach Hall
Mt. Pleasant, Michigan 48859
Telephone: (517) 774-3196

James Wieghart, Chair
Ronald Johnstone, Dean, College of Arts and Sciences

CURRICULUM AND INSTRUCTION
Courses or Concentrations Available: Advertising; Journalism or Mass Communication; Public Relations; Photojournalism; *Undergraduate Objectives or Program Emphases*: Advertising; Magazine Journalism; News-Editorial Journalism; Photojournalism; Public Relations; Secondary Education in Journalism; *Full-Time Faculty*: 11; *Part-Time Faculty*: 7.

FACILITIES AND SERVICES
Practical experiences available through: Advertising Agency; AM Radio Station (Institutional); Associated Press Wire Service Feed; Campus Newspaper (Published Independently); Local Commercial Newspaper; Desktop Publishing Facility; Photographic Darkrooms; Video Editing; Television Broadcast Station (Institutional); FM Radio Station (Institutional); Public Relations Agency.

Central Michigan University (Public)

Department of Speech Communication and Dramatic Arts
333 Moore Hall
Mt. Pleasant, Michigan 48859
Telephone: (517) 774-3177

Denny L. Bettisworth, Chair
Ronald Johnstone, Dean, College of Arts and Sciences

CURRICULUM AND INSTRUCTION
Courses or Concentrations Available: Communication; Speech; Theatre Arts; *Undergraduate Objectives or Program Emphases*: Offer BA, BS degrees in interpersonal and public communication. Offer BA, BS and BFA degrees in theatre and interpretation; *Graduate Objectives or Program Emphases*: Offer MA in interpersonal and public communication; *Bachelor's Degree Majors*: 550; *BFA Degree Majors*: 10; *Master's Degree Majors*: 30; *Full-Time Faculty*: 24; *Part-Time Faculty*: 5; *Full-Time Professional (non-clerical) Staff Members*: 3.

FACILITIES AND SERVICES
Practical experiences available through: Desktop Publishing Facility.

Delta College (Public)

Program of Broadcasting/Telecommunications
Delta Road
University Center, Michigan 48710
Telephone: (517) 686-9350

Presley D. Holmes, Director
Eugene Duckworth, Dean

CURRICULUM AND INSTRUCTION
Courses or Concentrations Available: Radio, Television, Broadcasting, or Telecommunications; *Undergraduate Objectives or Program Emphases*: Video/Television; Radio; Audio; *Associate's Degree Majors*: 103; *Part-Time Faculty*: 8.

FACILITIES AND SERVICES
Practical experiences available through: Associated Press Wire Service Feed; Audio Recording Laboratory; Community Antenna (Cable) Television Origination; Closed Circuit Television Facility; Local Commercial Television Station; Video Editing; Electronic Field Production (Video); Television Broadcast Station (Institutional); FM Radio Station (Institutional); ITFS Distribution System.

Eastern Michigan University (Public)

Program of Telecommunications and Film Area
Ypsilanti, Michigan 48197
Telephone: (313) 487-3131

Lucy A. Liggett, Head
Dennis Beager, Head, Department of Communication and Theatre Arts

CURRICULUM AND INSTRUCTION
Courses or Concentrations Available: Film or Cinema; Radio, Television, Broadcasting, or Telecommunications; *Undergraduate Objectives or Program Emphases*: To provide a liberal arts major balancing theoretical and practical courses that prepare students for entry level positions or advanced study; *Bachelor's Degree Majors*: 360; *Full-Time Faculty*: 5; *Part-Time Faculty*: 5; *Full-Time Professional (non-clerical) Staff Members*: 1.

FACILITIES AND SERVICES
Practical experiences available through: Audio Recording Laboratory; Community Antenna (Cable) Television Origination; Carrier Current Audio Distribution System; Campus Newspaper (Published Independently); Local Commercial Newspaper; Local Commercial Television Station; Video Editing; Electronic Field Production (Video); FM Radio Station (Institutional); Video Production Laboratory or Television Studio.

Eastern Michigan University (Public)

Department of English Language and Literature
Ypsilanti, Michigan 48104
Telephone: (313) 487-4220

Marcia A. Dalbey, Head
Barry Fish, Acting Dean

CURRICULUM AND INSTRUCTION
Courses or Concentrations Available: Journalism or Mass Communication; Public Relations; *Program Coordinators*: Elly Wright and Jean Dye (Advisors, Journalism and Public Relations); *Bachelor's Degree Majors*: 80; *Full-Time Faculty*: 50; *Part-Time Faculty*: 30.

FACILITIES AND SERVICES
Practical experiences available through: Campus Newspaper (Published Independently); Desktop Publishing Facility.

Ferris State University (Public)

Program of Television Production
I.R.C. #108
Big Rapids, Michigan 49307
Telephone: (616) 592-2717

Robert C. Hunter, Program Coordinator
Scott D. Whitener, Dean, School of Education

CURRICULUM AND INSTRUCTION
Courses or Concentrations Available: Film or Cinema; Radio, Television, Broadcasting, or Telecommunications; Television Production (not performance); *Undergraduate Objectives or Program Emphases*: Television production emphasis is on production skills in audio, video, cinematography and multi-images; *Bachelor's Degree Majors*: 90; *Full-Time Faculty*: 6; *Part-Time Faculty*: 2; *Full-Time Professional (non-clerical) Staff Members*: 3.

FACILITIES AND SERVICES
Practical experiences available through: Audio Recording Laboratory; Community Antenna (Cable) Television Origination; Campus Newspaper (Published Independently); Photographic Darkrooms; Video Editing; Electronic Field Production (Video); Film or Cinema Laboratory; Video Production Laboratory or Television Studio.

Grace Bible College (Private)

Department of Speech and Drama
1011 Aldon S.W.
Wyoming, Michigan 49509
Telephone: (616) 538-2330

Irvin Lister, Head
Martin Olson, Chief Administrator

CURRICULUM AND INSTRUCTION
Courses or Concentrations Available: Speech; *Undergraduate Objectives or Program Emphases*: Individual courses in speech and drama; *Full-Time Faculty*: 1.

FACILITIES AND SERVICES
Practical experiences available through: Closed Circuit Television Facility.

Grand Rapids Baptist College

Communications Department
1001 East Beltline Northeast
Grand Rapids, Michigan 49505

Timothy J. Detwiler, Administrator

Grand Rapids Junior College (Public)

Department of Journalism
143 Bostwick N.E.
Grand Rapids, Michigan 49503
Telephone: (616) 456-4869

Scott E. McNabb, Instructor/Advisor
Charles Chamberlain, Administrator

CURRICULUM AND INSTRUCTION
Courses or Concentrations Available: Journalism or Mass Communication; *Undergraduate Objectives or Program Emphases*: Introductory course work in news writing, newspaper production, and mass media; *Associate's Degree Majors*: 45; *Full-Time Faculty*: 1.

FACILITIES AND SERVICES
Practical experiences available through: Local Commercial Television Station; Desktop Publishing Facility; Photographic Darkrooms; Television Broadcast Station (Institutional); Institutional Newspaper.

Grand Valley State College

Department of Radio and Television
College Landing
Allendale, Michigan 49401

Grand Valley State College

School of Communication
Allendale, Michigan 49401

Alex Nesterenko, Administrator

Henry Ford Community College (Public)

Department of Performing Arts
5101 Evergreen Road
Dearborn, Michigan 48128
Telephone: (313) 845-9634

Aileen Sundstrom, Chair
Richard Hespen, Dean and Vice President

CURRICULUM AND INSTRUCTION
Courses or Concentrations Available: Communication; Film or Cinema; Radio, Television, Broadcasting, or Telecommunications; Speech; Interpretation Theatre; Technical Theatre; Debate; Music (choral, instrumental, keyboard); *Undergraduate Objectives or Program Emphases*: To help students prepare to major in their selected area; *Associate's Degree Majors*: 50; *Full-Time Faculty*: 9; *Part-Time Faculty*: 24.

FACILITIES AND SERVICES
Practical experiences available through: AM Radio Station (Institutional); Community Antenna (Cable) Television Origination; Local Commercial Newspaper; Local Commercial Television Station; Video Editing; Television Broadcast Station (Institutional); Film or Cinema Laboratory; FM Radio Station (Institutional).

Hope College (Private)

Department of Communication
Holland, Michigan 49423
Telephone: (616) 394-7595

Joseph W. MacDoniels, Chair
Nancy Miller, Dean, Social Science

CURRICULUM AND INSTRUCTION
Courses or Concentrations Available: Communication; Journalism or Mass Communication; Radio, Television, Broadcasting, or Telecommunications; Speech; *Undergraduate Objectives or Program Emphases*: Develop theoretical understanding of process of communication, gain knowledge and skills in particular areas of application such as interpersonal relations, group and organizations, mass media, and presentational situations; *Bachelor's Degree Majors*: 65; *Full-Time Faculty*: 4; *Part-Time Faculty*: 7.

FACILITIES AND SERVICES
Practical experiences available through: Audio Recording Laboratory; Community Antenna (Cable) Television Origination; Campus Newspaper (Published Independently); Local Commercial Newspaper; Video Editing; Electronic Field Production (Video); FM Radio Station (Institutional); Public Relations Agency; Video Production Laboratory or Television Studio.

Kellogg Community College

Visual and Performing Arts Department
450 North Avenue
Battle Creek, Michigan 49016

Maureen Moore, Administrator

Kendall College of Print Design

Division of Visual Communications
111 Division Avenue North
Grand Rapids, Michigan 49503

Theron P. Elliott, Administrator

Kirtland Community College (Public)

Department of Speech Communication
10375 N. St. Helen Rd.
Roscommon, Michigan 48653
Telephone: (517) 375-5121

Clay Horton, Head
Richard Silverman, Dean of Instruction

CURRICULUM AND INSTRUCTION
Courses or Concentrations Available: Communication; Speech; *Undergraduate Objectives or Program Emphases*: To develop skills in speech and communication for freshman and sophomores; *Part-Time Faculty*: 4.

FACILITIES AND SERVICES
Practical experiences available through: Closed Circuit Television Facility; ITFS Distribution System.

Lake Michigan College

Speech and Theatre Department
2755 East Napier
Benton Harbor, Michigan 49022

R. D. Williams, Administrator

Madonna College (Private)

Program of Journalism-Public Relations
36600 Schoolcraft
Livonia, Michigan 48150-1173
Telephone: (313) 591-5000

S. Jacqueline Anderson, Director
James Reilly, Chair, Communications Department

CURRICULUM AND INSTRUCTION
Courses or Concentrations Available: Communication; Journalism or Mass Communication; Public Relations; Radio, Television, Broadcasting, or Telecommunications; Speech; *Program Coordinators*: Chuck Derry (Video Communications); *Undergraduate Objectives or Program Emphases*: To help students think and perform as journalists. Students receive experience in writing, editing, photography, advertising and video while acquiring research skills and an understanding of legal issues; *Associate's Degree Majors*: 2; *Bachelor's Degree Majors*: 34; *Full-Time Faculty*: 4; *Part-Time Faculty*: 5; *Full-Time Professional (non-clerical) Staff Members*: 1.

FACILITIES AND SERVICES
Practical experiences available through: Advertising Agency; Community Antenna (Cable) Television Origination; Closed Circuit Television Facility; Local Commercial Newspaper; Local Commercial Television Station; Desktop Publishing Facility; Photographic Darkrooms; Video Editing; Electronic Field Production (Video); ITFS Distribution System; Institutional Newspaper; Public Relations Agency; Satellite Uplink Facility; Video Production Laboratory or Television Studio.

Michigan State University (Public)

College of Communication Arts and Sciences
287 Communication Arts Building
East Lansing, Michigan 48823
Telephone: (517) 355-3410

Erwin P. Bettinghaus, Dean
David K. Scott, Provost

CURRICULUM AND INSTRUCTION
Courses or Concentrations Available: Advertising; Communication; Film or Cinema; Journalism or Mass Communication; Public Relations; Radio, Television, Broadcasting, or Telecommunications; Audiology and Speech Sciences; *Program Coordinators*: Michael Casby (Audiology and Speech Science); Bruce Vanden Bergh (Advertising); Gerald R. Miller (Communication); Stanley R. Soffin (Journalism); Bradley S. Greenburg (Telecommunications); Thomas Baldwin (Mass Media Ph.D. Program); *Undergraduate Objectives or Program Emphases*: The College offers programs in five separate departments: Advertising, Communication, Journalism, Telecommunications, and Audiology and Speech Sciences; *Graduate Objectives or Program Emphases*: Advanced degree programs are available, including Ph.D. programs in Audiology and Speech Sciences, Communication, and Mass Media; *Bachelor's Degree Majors*: 2550; *Master's Degree Majors*: 201; *Doctoral Degree Majors Currently in Residence*: 62; *Full-Time Faculty*: 79; *Part-Time Faculty*: 108; *Full-Time Professional (non-clerical) Staff Members*: 9. See one or more additional entries below.

FACILITIES AND SERVICES
Practical experiences available through: AM Radio Station (Institutional); Associated Press Wire Service Feed; Audio Recording Laboratory; Community Antenna (Cable) Television Origination; Carrier Current Audio Distribution System; Closed Circuit Television Facility; Campus Newspaper (Published Independently); Local Commercial Newspaper; Local Commercial Television Station; Desktop Publishing Facility; Photographic Darkrooms; Video Editing; Electronic Field Production (Video); Television Broadcast Station (Institutional); FM Radio Station (Institutional); Institutional Newspaper; Satellite Uplink Facility (Ku Band Transmitter); United Press International Feed; Video News and Data Processing; Video Production Laboratory or Television Studio.

Michigan State University (Public)

Department of Telecommunication
409 Communication Arts Building
East Lansing, Michigan 48824-1212
Telephone: (517) 355-8372

Bradley S. Greenberg, Chair
Erwin P. Bettinghaus, Dean

CURRICULUM AND INSTRUCTION
Courses or Concentrations Available: Radio, Television, Broadcasting, or Telecommunications; *Undergraduate Objectives or Program Emphases*: Management; Policy; Production; Audience Research; *Graduate Objectives or Program Emphases*: Management, Social Effects, International, Production, Information Technologies; *Bachelor's Degree Majors*: 475; *Master's Degree Majors*: 80; *Doctoral Degree Majors Currently in Residence*: 29; *Full-Time Faculty*: 10; *Part-Time Faculty*: 31; *Full-Time Professional (non-clerical) Staff Members*: 1.

FACILITIES AND SERVICES
Practical experiences available through: AM Radio Station (Institutional); Audio Recording Laboratory; Community Antenna (Cable) Television Origination; Closed Circuit Television Facility; Campus Newspaper (Published Independently); Desktop Publishing Facility; Video Editing; Electronic Field Production (Video); Television Broadcast Station (Institutional); FM Radio Station (Institutional); Video Production Laboratory or Television Studio.

Michigan State University (Public)

School of Journalism
East Lansing, Michigan 48824-1212
Telephone: (517) 353-6430

Stanley I. Soffin, Chair
Erwin Bettinghaus, Dean

CURRICULUM AND INSTRUCTION
Courses or Concentrations
Available: Journalism or Mass Communication; Public Relations; Radio, Television, Broadcasting, or Telecommunications; *Undergraduate Objectives or Program Emphases*: To instill journalist skills, knowledge, and responsibilities necessary for successful careers in mass media; develop critical consumers of mass media; enlighten students to society's problems by requiring a liberal education in arts, sciences and humanities; *Graduate Objectives or Program Emphases*: To provide students with opportunity to acquire skills and knowledge for careers in mass media or for advanced graduate study; *Bachelor's Degree Majors*: 722; *Master's Degree Majors*: 46; *Full-Time Faculty*: 15; *Part-Time Faculty*: 11; *Full-Time Professional (non-clerical) Staff Members*: 3.

FACILITIES AND SERVICES
Practical experiences available through: AM Radio Station (Institutional); Associated Press Wire Service Feed; Audio Recording Laboratory; Community Antenna (Cable) Television Origination; Closed Circuit Television Facility; Campus Newspaper (Published Independently); Local Commercial Newspaper; Local Commercial Television Station; Canadian Press Feed; Desktop Publishing Facility; Photographic Darkrooms; Video Editing; Electronic Field Production (Video); Television Broadcast Station (Institutional); FM Radio Station (Institutional); ITFS Distribution System; Institutional Magazine; Institutional Newspaper; Reuters News Agency; Satellite Uplink Facility; United Press International Feed; Video News and Data Processing; Video Production Laboratory or Television Studio.

Michigan State University (Public)

Department of Advertising
309 Communication Arts and Sciences Building
East Lansing, Michigan 48824-1212
Telephone: (517) 355-2314

Bruce G. Vanden Bergh, Chair
Erwin Bettinghaus, Dean

CURRICULUM AND INSTRUCTION
Courses or Concentrations

Available: Advertising; Public Relations; *Undergraduate Objectives or Program Emphases*: Advertising with a strong liberal arts and business foundation; *Graduate Objectives or Program Emphases*: Advertising and Public Relations with a strong business and research focus; *Bachelor's Degree Majors*: 599; *Master's Degree Majors*: 150; *Doctoral Degree Majors Currently in Residence*: 11; *Additional Doctoral Degree Majors*: 2; *Full-Time Faculty*: 14; *Part-Time Faculty*: 10.

FACILITIES AND SERVICES
Practical experiences available through: Advertising Agency; Audio Recording Laboratory; Campus Newspaper (Published Independently); Desktop Publishing Facility; Public Relations Agency.

Michigan State University (Public)

Department of Communication
473 Communication Arts and Sciences
East Lansing, Michigan 48824
Telephone: (517) 355-3470

Gerald R. Miller, Chair
Erwin P. Bettinghaus, Dean

CURRICULUM AND INSTRUCTION
Courses or Concentrations
Available: Communication; Information Science; Speech; *Undergraduate Objectives or Program Emphases*: Provide students with a background of theoretical and empirical knowledge sufficient to ensure entry level positions or continuation in graduate or professional school; *Graduate Objectives or Program Emphases*: Develop skills sufficient to permit student to pursue research and scholarship independently; *Bachelor's Degree Majors*: 800; *Master's Degree Majors*: 65; *Doctoral Degree Majors Currently in Residence*: 21; *Additional Doctoral Degree Majors*: 8; *Full-Time Faculty*: 16; *Part-Time Faculty*: 21.

FACILITIES AND SERVICES
Practical experiences available through: Desktop Publishing Facility.

Michigan State University (Public)

Mass Media Ph.D. Program
Communication Arts and Sciences
East Lansing, Michigan 48824-1212
Telephone: (517) 353-6336

Thomas F. Baldwin, Chair
Erwin Bettinghaus, Dean

CURRICULUM AND INSTRUCTION
Courses or Concentrations
Available: Advertising; Film or Cinema;
Journalism or Mass Communication; Public
Relations; Radio, Television, Broadcasting,
or Telecommunications; *Graduate Objectives*
or Program Emphases: Mass Media,
including advertising, journalism, and
telecommunication; *Doctoral Degree Majors*
Currently in Residence: 32; *Additional*
Doctoral Degree Majors: 5; *Full-Time*
Faculty: 40; *Part-Time Faculty*: 40;
Full-Time Professional (non-clerical) Staff
Members: 20.

FACILITIES AND SERVICES
Practical experiences available
through: Advertising Agency; AM Radio
Station (Institutional); Associated Press
Wire Service Feed; Audio Recording
Laboratory; Community Antenna (Cable)
Television Origination; Closed Circuit
Television Facility; Campus Newspaper
(Published Independently); Local
Commercial Newspaper; Local Commercial
Television Station; Desktop Publishing
Facility; Photographic Darkrooms; Video
Editing; Electronic Field Production
(Video); Television Broadcast Station
(Institutional); FM Radio Station
(Institutional); Satellite Uplink Facility (Ku
Band Transmitter) (C Band Transmitter);
United Press International Feed; Video
News and Data Processing; Video
Production Laboratory or Television Studio.

Mid Michigan Community College (Public)

Division of Arts and Sciences
1375 South Clare Avenue
Harrison, Michigan 48625
Telephone: (517) 386-7792

Linda Loomis, Chair
Charles Dee, Dean of Instruction

CURRICULUM AND INSTRUCTION
Courses or Concentrations
Available: Communication; Speech;
Part-Time Faculty: 3; *Full-Time Professional*
(non-clerical) Staff Members: 16.

FACILITIES AND SERVICES
Practical experiences available
through: Desktop Publishing Facility;
Institutional Magazine; Institutional
Newspaper.

Mott Community College (Public)

School of Arts/Humanities
1401 East Court Street
Flint, Michigan 48503
Telephone: (313) 762-0470

Mary Pine, Dean
Mary Fifield, Vice President

CURRICULUM AND INSTRUCTION
Courses or Concentrations Available: Film or
Cinema; Journalism or Mass
Communication; Radio, Television,
Broadcasting, or Telecommunications;
Speech; Journalism Co-op Practicum;
Undergraduate Objectives or Program
Emphases: Introductory Courses; *Associate's*
Degree Majors: 20; *Full-Time Faculty*: 4.

FACILITIES AND SERVICES
Practical experiences available
through: Community Antenna (Cable)
Television Origination; Campus Newspaper
(Published Independently); Local
Commercial Television Station; Desktop
Publishing Facility; Photographic
Darkrooms.

Mt. Pleasant Vocational - Technical Center (Public)

Broadcasting Area
Trade and Industry Department
1155 S. Elizabeth
Mt. Pleasant, Michigan 48858
Telephone: (517) 773-5500

Jay S. Rouman, Director
Merrin Oberlender, Vocational Director

CURRICULUM AND INSTRUCTION
Courses or Concentrations
Available: Communication; Radio,
Television, Broadcasting, or

Telecommunications; *Undergraduate Objectives or Program Emphases*: This is a secondary education vocational/technical program which offers an emphasis on production skills for audio and video. Courses are also available in writing, editing, advertising and related subjects; *Other Degree Majors*: 70; *Full-Time Faculty*: 1.

FACILITIES AND SERVICES
Practical experiences available through: Audio Recording Laboratory; Community Antenna (Cable) Television Origination; Closed Circuit Television Facility; Video Editing; Electronic Field Production (Video); Video Production Laboratory or Television Studio.

Muskegon Community College

Program of Media
221 Quarterline Road
Muskegon, Michigan 49442
Telephone: (616) 777-0297

Kent M. DeYoung, Coordinator
Mark Gustafson, Chief Administrator

CURRICULUM AND INSTRUCTION
Courses or Concentrations
Available: Advertising; Communication; Film or Cinema; Journalism or Mass Communication; Radio, Television, Broadcasting, or Telecommunications; Speech; *Associate's Degree Majors*: 20; *Full-Time Faculty*: 3; *Part-Time Faculty*: 3; *Full-Time Professional (non-clerical) Staff Members*: 3.

FACILITIES AND SERVICES
Practical experiences available through: Advertising Agency; Audio Recording Laboratory; Community Antenna (Cable) Television Origination; Closed Circuit Television Facility; Local Commercial Newspaper; Desktop Publishing Facility; Photographic Darkrooms; Video Editing; Electronic Field Production (Video); Film or Cinema Laboratory; Video Production Laboratory or Television Studio.

Northern Michigan University (Public)

Department of Speech
Marquette, Michigan 49855
Telephone: (906) 226-2045

James L. Rapport, Head
Donald Heikkinen, Dean

CURRICULUM AND INSTRUCTION
Courses or Concentrations
Available: Communication; Journalism or Mass Communication; Public Relations; Radio, Television, Broadcasting, or Telecommunications; Speech; Theatre, Speech Education; *Undergraduate Objectives or Program Emphases*: BA/BS Degree in substantive areas; professional employment in specialty areas such as theatre, broadcasting, and public relations; graduate school preparation; *Graduate Objectives or Program Emphases*: MA in Education (secondary); *Bachelor's Degree Majors*: 320; *Master's Degree Majors*: 6; *Full-Time Faculty*: 13; *Part-Time Faculty*: 4.

FACILITIES AND SERVICES
Practical experiences available through: Audio Recording Laboratory; Community Antenna (Cable) Television Origination; Carrier Current Audio Distribution System; Closed Circuit Television Facility; Campus Newspaper (Published Independently); Local Commercial Newspaper; Local Commercial Television Station; Desktop Publishing Facility; Photographic Darkrooms; Video Editing; Electronic Field Production (Video); Television Broadcast Station (Institutional); Film and Cinema Laboratory; FM Radio Station (Institutional); ITFS Distribution System; Institutional Newspaper; United Press International Feed; Video News and Data Processing; Video Production Laboratory or Television Studio.

Northwestern Michigan College (Public)

Program of Broadcast Communication
Traverse City, Michigan 49684
Telephone: (616) 922-1191

M. G. Ross, Director
J. P. Pahl, Head, Division of Communication

CURRICULUM AND INSTRUCTION
Courses or Concentrations
Available: Advertising; Communication;
Information Science; Journalism or Mass
Communication; Public Relations; Radio,
Television, Broadcasting, or
Telecommunications; Speech; *Undergraduate
Objectives or Program Emphases*: Associate
of Applied Science includes basic
communication theory, broadcasting theory
and skills; Broadcasting as a business; *Other
Degree Majors*: 30; *Full-Time Faculty*: 3;
Part-Time Faculty: 2; *Full-Time Professional
(non-clerical) Staff Members*: 1.

FACILITIES AND SERVICES
Practical experiences available through: Audio
Recording Laboratory; Community Antenna
(Cable) Television Origination; Closed
Circuit Television Facility; Campus
Newspaper (Published Independently);
Local Commercial Newspaper; Local
Commercial Television Station; Desktop
Publishing Facility; Photographic
Darkrooms; Video Editing; Electronic Field
Production (Video); Television Broadcast
Station (Institutional); FM Radio Station
(Institutional); ITFS Distribution System;
Institutional Magazine; Video Production
Laboratory or Television Studio.

Oakland Community College

Department of Communication Arts
27055 Orchard Lake Road
Farmington Hills, Michigan 48018

William Stuart, Administrator

Oakland Community College

Department of English/Humanities
7350 Cooley Lake Road
Union Lake, Michigan 48085

Sr. Mary Van Guilder, Administrator

Oakland University (Public)

Film Aesthetics and History
Rochester, Michigan 48063

Brian F. Murphy, Coordinator/Director

Oakland University (Public)

Department of Rhetoric, Communication
and Journalism
Rochester, Michigan 48309-4401
Telephone: (313) 370-4120

Jane Briggs-Bunting, Chair/Director
John K. Urice, Dean, College of Arts and
Sciences

CURRICULUM AND INSTRUCTION
Courses or Concentrations
Available: Advertising; Communication;
Journalism or Mass Communication; Public
Relations; Radio, Television, Broadcasting,
or Telecommunications; Speech; *Program
Coordinator*: Donald C. Hildum
(Communication, Radio and Television,
Speech); *Undergraduate Objectives or
Program Emphases*: Skill level training in
Journalism to prepare students for entry level
jobs in newspapers, broadcasting, public
relations and advertising agencies; *Bachelor's
Degree Majors*: 50; *Other Degree Majors*: 400;
Full-Time Faculty: 15; *Part-Time
Faculty*: 54.

FACILITIES AND SERVICES
*Practical experiences available
through*: Advertising Agency; AM Radio
Station (Institutional); Community Antenna
(Cable) Television Origination; Campus
Newspaper (Published Independently);
Local Commercial Newspaper; Local
Commercial Television Station; Desktop
Publishing Facility; Photographic
Darkrooms; Video Editing; Public
Relations Agency; Video Production
Laboratory or Television Studio.

Olivet College

Department of Journalism
Main Street
Olivet, Michigan 49076

William Thomson, Administrator

Reformed Bible College (Private)

Department of Communications
1869 Robinson Road, Southeast
Grand Rapids, Michigan 49506
Telephone: (616) 458-0404

Harold J. Bruxvoort, Director
Paul Bremer, Vice President, Academic
Affairs

CURRICULUM AND INSTRUCTION
Courses or Concentrations
Available: Communication; Journalism or
Mass Communication; Radio, Television,
Broadcasting, or Telecommunications;
Speech; *Undergraduate Objectives or Program
Emphases*: To speak effectively; to write in
journalistic style; to work effectively as
announcer on radio; to operate radio control
board, obtain FCC license; *Associate's Degree
Majors*: 3; *Bachelor's Degree Majors*: 45;
Full-Time Faculty: 2.

FACILITIES AND SERVICES
*Practical experiences available
through*: Community Antenna (Cable)
Television Origination; Carrier Current
Audio Distribution System; Closed Circuit
Television Facility; Campus Newspaper
(Published Independently); Video
Production Laboratory or Television Studio.

Sacred Heart Seminary College (Private)

Division of Communication and Language
Arts
2701 Chicago Boulevard
Detroit, Michigan 48206
Telephone: (313) 883-8500

Robert W. Peckham, Head
Rev. Allen Vigneron, Dean of Studies

CURRICULUM AND INSTRUCTION
*Courses or Concentrations
Available*: Communication; Speech; Writing
and Developmental Reading; Foreign
Language Skills; *Undergraduate Objectives or
Program Emphases*: To master the basic
communication skills of reading, writing and
speaking in English and in relevant foreign
language; *Full-Time Faculty*: 1; *Part-Time
Faculty*: 4.

FACILITIES AND SERVICES
Practical experiences available

through: Closed Circuit Television Facility;
Photographic Darkrooms; Institutional
Magazine.

Saginaw Valley State University (Public)

Department of Communication and Theatre
2250 Pierce Road
University Center, Michigan 48710
Telephone: (517) 790-4306
Alternate: 790-4000

William Gourd, Chair
William K. Barnett, Dean, College of Arts
and Behavioral Sciences

CURRICULUM AND INSTRUCTION
*Courses or Concentrations
Available*: Communication; Speech; Theatre;
Program Coordinators: Janet E. Rubin
(Theatre); *Undergraduate Objectives or
Program Emphases*: To provide a generalist
major and/or minor course of study in each
of the disciplines of communication and
theatre, leading to the Bachelor of Arts
degree in each major; *Bachelor's Degree
Majors*: 80; *Full-Time Faculty*: 4; *Part-Time
Faculty*: 4.

Saginaw Valley State University (Public)

Department of English
7500 Pierce Road
University Center, Michigan 48710
Telephone: (517) 790-4000

Gary Thompson, Chair
William K. Barrett, Dean, Arts and
Behavioral Sciences

CURRICULUM AND INSTRUCTION
Courses or Concentrations Available: Film or
Cinema; Journalism or Mass
Communication; *Undergraduate Objectives or
Program Emphases*: English,
including American literature, writing
courses at beginning, advanced and
pre-college basic skills levels, reading
courses, etc.; *Bachelor's Degree Majors*: 62;
Other Degree Majors: 141; *Full-Time
Faculty*: 15; *Part-Time Faculty*: 21.

FACILITIES AND SERVICES
*Practical experiences available
through*: Institutional Newspaper.

Saint Clair County Community College (Public)

Division of Communication
323 Erie Street
Port Huron, Michigan 48060
Telephone: (313) 984-3881

James Voss, Director
Gail Johnson, Division Chair

CURRICULUM AND INSTRUCTION
*Courses or Concentrations
Available*: Communication; Journalism or
Mass Communication; Radio, Television,
Broadcasting, or Telecommunications;
Speech; *Undergraduate Objectives or Program
Emphases*: To offer a transfer program to a
four year school or a two year associate
degree; *Degree Majors*: 10; *Full-Time
Faculty*: 12; *Part-Time Faculty*: 15;
*Full-Time Professional (non-clerical) Staff
Members*: 7.

FACILITIES AND SERVICES
Practical experiences available through: AM
Radio Station (Institutional); Associated
Press Wire Service Feed; Audio Recording
Laboratory; Community Antenna (Cable)
Television Origination; Closed Circuit
Television Facility; Campus Newspaper
(Published Independently); Photographic
Darkrooms; Video Editing; Television
Broadcast Station (Institutional); Film and
Cinema Laboratory; FM Radio Station
(Institutional); Institutional Magazine;
Institutional Newspaper; Satellite Uplink
Facility; Video Production Laboratory or
Television Studio.

Spring Arbor College (Private)

Department of Communication
106 Main Street
Spring Arbor, Michigan 49283
Telephone: (517) 750-1200

Rev. Thomas M. Ball, Head
**Allen Carden, Vice President, Academic
Affairs**

CURRICULUM AND INSTRUCTION
Courses or Concentrations

Available: Advertising; Journalism or Mass
Communication; Public Relations; Radio,
Television, Broadcasting, or
Telecommunications; Speech; Graphic
Design; *Program Coordinators*: Margaret
O'Rourke (Advertising and Public
Relations); Wally Metts, Jr. (Professional
Writing); Esther Maddox (Oral
Performance); Bill Bippes (Graphic Design);
*Undergraduate Objectives or Program
Emphases*: To educate liberally and prepare
adequately serious Christian students who
already exhibit a solid Judeo-Christian work
ethic, for entry-level employment in various
mass-communication industries; *Bachelor's
Degree Majors*: 25; *Full-Time Faculty*: 4;
Part-Time Faculty: 5; *Full-Time Professional
(non-clerical) Staff Members*: 1.

FACILITIES AND SERVICES
Practical experiences available through: AM
Radio Station (Institutional); Associated
Press Wire Service Feed; Audio Recording
Laboratory; Community Antenna (Cable)
Television Origination; Campus Newspaper
(Published Independently); Local
Commercial Newspaper; Local Commercial
Television Station; Desktop Publishing
Facility; Photographic Darkrooms; Video
Editing; Electronic Field Production
(Video); FM Radio Station (Institutional);
Institutional Magazine; Video News and
Data Processing; Video Production
Laboratory or Television Studio.

University of Detroit (Private)

Department of Communication Studies
4001 West McNichols Road
Detroit, Michigan 48221-9987
Telephone: (313) 927-1173

Vivian I. Dicks, Chair
John Orr Dwyer, Dean

CURRICULUM AND INSTRUCTION
*Courses or Concentrations
Available*: Advertising; Communication;
Journalism or Mass Communication; Public
Relations; Radio, Television, Broadcasting,
or Telecommunications; Speech;
*Undergraduate Objectives or Program
Emphases*: To provide a broad framework
for understanding communication; to provide
skill and field related experience within
concentrations; *Degree Majors*: 150;
Full-Time Faculty: 7; *Part-Time Faculty*: 4;

Full-Time Professional (non-clerical) Staff Members: 3.

FACILITIES AND SERVICES
Practical experiences available through: Advertising Agency; Audio Recording Laboratory; Community Antenna (Cable) Television Origination; Carrier Current Audio Distribution System; Campus Newspaper (Published Independently); Local Commercial Newspaper; Local Commercial Television Station; Photographic Darkrooms; Video Editing; Electronic Field Production (Video); Institutional Magazine; Public Relations Agency; Video Production Laboratory or Television Studio.

University of Michigan (Public)

Department of Communication
2020 Frieze Building
Ann Arbor, Michigan 48109-1285
Telephone: (313) 764-0420

Frank E. Beaver, Chair
Edie Goldenberg, Dean, College of Literature, Science, and the Arts

CURRICULUM AND INSTRUCTION
Courses or Concentrations Available: Communication; Film or Cinema; Information Gathering; Journalism or Mass Communication; Radio, Television, Broadcasting, or Telecommunications; Seminars on wide variety of mass communication topics; *Program Coordinators*: Livingston Program for Young Journalists, director Charles Eisendrath; *Undergraduate Objectives or Program Emphases*: To develop a foundation of general knowledge pertaining to people, events, and issues in mass communication; to foster critical and analytical thinking and writing; to cultivate an intellectual ability in a minimum of three areas of mass communication; *Graduate Objectives or Program Emphases*: To master essential principles of instruction and practice pertinent to the program: For Telecommunication Arts: as producer, writer, director; for Journalism: as reporter, feature writer, editor; for Comm Studies and doctoral work: as researcher and writer; *Bachelor's Degree Majors*: 400; *Master's Degree Majors*: 100; *Doctoral Degree Majors Currently in Residence*: 15; *Additional Doctoral Degree Majors*: 10; *Full-Time*

Faculty: 19; *Part-Time Faculty*: 65; *Full-Time Professional (non-clerical) Staff Members*: 2.

FACILITIES AND SERVICES
Practical experiences available through: Advertising Agency; Associated Press Wire Service Feed; Audio Recording Laboratory; Community Antenna (Cable) Television Origination; Carrier Current Audio Distribution System; Campus Newspaper (Published Independently); Local Commercial Newspaper; Local Commercial Television Station; Video Editing; Electronic Field Production (Video); Television Broadcast Station (Institutional); Film or Cinema Laboratory; FM Radio Station (Institutional); Public Relations Agency; Video News and Data Processing; Video Production Laboratory or Television Studio.

Walsh College of Accountancy and Business Administration (Private)

Department of Communications
3838 Livernois Road, P.O. Box 7006
Troy, Michigan 48007-7006
Telephone: (313) 689-8282

Barbara E. Alpern, Chair
Thomas Courneya, Administrator

CURRICULUM AND INSTRUCTION
Courses or Concentrations Available: Advertising; Communication; Public Relations; Speech; *Undergraduate Objectives or Program Emphases*: To prepare students to become effective communicators. Written and oral communication opportunities are given throughout each communication class; *Degree Majors*: 1740; *Full-Time Faculty*: 2; *Part-Time Faculty*: 7; *Full-Time Professional (non-clerical) Staff Members*: 2.

FACILITIES AND SERVICES
Practical experiences available through: Community Antenna (Cable) Television Origination; Campus Newspaper (Published Independently); Desktop Publishing Facility; Video News and Data Processing.

Washtenaw Community College

Continuing Education/Community Services
P.O. Box D-1
4800 East Huron River Drive
Ann Arbor, Michigan 48106-0978

Edith Jacques, Administrator

Wayne State University (Public)

Department of Communication
585 Manoogian
Detroit, Michigan 48202
Telephone: (313) 577-2943

Edward J. Pappas, Chair

CURRICULUM AND INSTRUCTION
*Courses or Concentrations
Available*: Advertising; Communication; Film
or Cinema; Journalism or Mass
Communication; Public Relations; Radio,
Television, Broadcasting, or
Telecommunications; Speech; Oral
Interpretation; *Program Coordinators*: John
Spalding (Film, Broadcasting, Mass
Communication); Richard Wright
(Journalism, Advertising); George
Ziegelmueller (Speech Communication, Oral
Interpretation); James Measell (Public
Relations); *Undergraduate Objectives or
Program Emphases*: Programs are available
in Communication and Rhetorical Process,
Radio-Television-Film, and Journalism;
*Graduate Objectives or Program
Emphases*: Radio-Television-Film majors
leading to the M.A. or Ph.D. in the field are
available through the Department of Speech
Communication. There is no graduate
program in Journalism; *Bachelor's Degree
Majors*: 600; *Master's Degree Majors*: 100;
*Doctoral Degree Majors Currently in
Residence*: 60; *Full-Time Faculty*: 17;
Part-Time Faculty: 40; *Full-Time
Professional (non-clerical) Staff Members*: 1.

FACILITIES AND SERVICES
*Practical experiences available
through*: Advertising Agency; Closed Circuit
Television Facility; Campus Newspaper
(Published Independently); Local
Commercial Newspaper; Photographic
Darkrooms; Video Editing; Film or Cinema
Laboratory; FM Radio Station
(Institutional); Institutional Magazine;
Public Relations Agency; Video News and
Data Processing; Video Production
Laboratory or Television Studio.

Wayne State University (Public)

Program of Journalism
163 Manoogian
Detroit, Michigan 48202
Telephone: (313) 577-2627

Richard A. Wright, Acting Director
Edward J. Pappas, Chair, Department of
Communication

CURRICULUM AND INSTRUCTION
*Courses or Concentrations
Available*: Advertising; Journalism or Mass
Communication; *Undergraduate Objectives or
Program Emphases*: A BA in Journalism with
emphasis in print, broadcast or advertising;
Bachelor's Degree Majors: 350; *Full-Time
Faculty*: 4; *Part-Time Faculty*: 14.

FACILITIES AND SERVICES
*Practical experiences available
through*: Community Antenna (Cable)
Television Origination; Campus Newspaper
(Published Independently); Local
Commercial Newspaper; Local Commercial
Television Station; Desktop Publishing
Facility; Photographic Darkrooms; Video
Editing; Film and Cinema Laboratory; FM
Radio Station (Institutional); Public
Relations Agency; Video Production
Laboratory or Television Studio.

Western Michigan University
(Public)

Department of Communication
319 Sprau Tower
Kalamazoo, Michigan 49008
Telephone: (616) 387-3130

Richard J. Dieker, Chair
David Lyon, Dean

CURRICULUM AND INSTRUCTION
*Courses or Concentrations
Available*: Communication; Film or Cinema;
Public Relations; Radio, Television,
Broadcasting, or Telecommunications;
Speech; Creative Drama; Communication
Education; *Undergraduate Objectives or
Program Emphases*: Public Relations; Mass
Media; Organizational and Interpersonal
Communication; *Graduate Objectives or
Program Emphases*: Organizational
Communication; Interpersonal
Communication; General Communication;
Bachelor's Degree Majors: 440; *Master's*

Degree Majors: 150; *Full-Time Faculty*: 27; *Part-Time Faculty*: 7; *Full-Time Professional (non-clerical) Staff Members*: 2.

FACILITIES AND SERVICES
Practical experiences available through: AM Radio Station (Institutional); Associated Press Wire Service Feed; Audio Recording Laboratory; Community Antenna (Cable) Television Origination; Closed Circuit Television Facility; Campus Newspaper (Published Independently); Local Commercial Newspaper; Local Commercial Television Station; Desktop Publishing Facility; Video Editing; Electronic Field Production (Video); Film or Cinema Laboratory; FM Radio Station (Institutional); Public Relations Agency; Satellite Uplink Facility; United Press International Feed; Video News and Data Processing; Video Production Laboratory or Television Studio.

Western Michigan University (Public)

English Department
Kalamazoo, Michigan 49008

Nancy Y. Stone, Administrator

Austin Technical Institute (Public)

Program of Radio/Television Broadcasting
1900 8th Avenue NW
Austin, Minnesota 55912
Telephone: (507) 433-0641

John O'Rourke, Department Leader
John Gedker, Administrator

CURRICULUM AND INSTRUCTION
Courses or Concentrations Available: Radio, Television, Broadcasting, or Telecommunications; *Undergraduate Objectives or Program Emphases*: The basic program is one year. Students may take a second year, concentrating on Radio or Television. The second year is spent half-days at Austin Community College, a 2 year institution. Successful completion of the second year curriculum leads to an AAS from Community College; *Degree Majors*: 35; *Full-Time Faculty*: 2; *Part-Time Faculty*: 2; *Full-Time Professional (non-clerical) Staff Members*: 1.

FACILITIES AND SERVICES
Practical experiences available through: Associated Press Wire Service Feed; Audio Recording Laboratory; Community Antenna (Cable) Television Origination; Campus Newspaper (Published Independently); Local Commercial Television Station; Video Editing; Electronic Field Production (Video); Television Broadcast Station (Institutional); FM Radio Station (Institutional); Video Production Laboratory or Television Studio.

Bemidji State University (Public)

Department of Mass Communication
1500 Birchmont Avenue
Bemidji, Minnesota 56601
Telephone: (218) 755-3370

Lee Hawk, Chair
Judy McDonald, Dean

CURRICULUM AND INSTRUCTION
Courses or Concentrations

Available: Advertising; Journalism or Mass Communication; Public Relations; Radio, Television, Broadcasting, or Telecommunications; *Undergraduate Objectives or Program Emphases*: General mass communication curriculum with journalism and broadcast emphasis; *Bachelor's Degree Majors*: 160; *Full-Time Faculty*: 6.

FACILITIES AND SERVICES
Practical experiences available through: Audio Recording Laboratory; Carrier Current Audio Distribution System; Closed Circuit Television Facility; Campus Newspaper (Published Independently); Desktop Publishing Facility; Photographic Darkrooms; Video Editing; Electronic Field Production (Video); Television Broadcast Station (Institutional); FM Radio Station (Institutional); United Press International Feed.

Bethany Lutheran College (Private)

Division of Humanities
734 Marsh Street
Mankato, Minnesota 56001
Telephone: (507) 625-2977

Ron Younge, Academic Dean

CURRICULUM AND INSTRUCTION
Courses or Concentrations Available: Communication; Speech; *Undergraduate Objectives or Program Emphases*: Courses primarily to satisfy general education requirements leading to an AA degree; *Full-Time Faculty*: 5; *Part-Time Faculty*: 1.

FACILITIES AND SERVICES
Practical experiences available through: Campus Newspaper (Published Independently); Photographic Darkrooms; Institutional Magazine; Institutional Newspaper.

Bethel College (Private)

Department of Speech Communication
3900 Bethel Drive
St. Paul, Minnesota 55112
Telephone: (612) 638-6260

Leta J. Frazier, Chair
Dean Edner, Vice President

CURRICULUM AND INSTRUCTION
Courses or Concentrations
Available: Communication; Public Relations; Radio, Television, Broadcasting, or Telecommunications; Speech; *Undergraduate Objectives or Program Emphases*: To provide students a balanced educational experience between the theoretical and pragmatic aspects of speech communication and ethical framework for communication decisions; to offer opportunities for practical experience in communication related fields; *Bachelor's Degree Majors*: 70; *Full-Time Faculty*: 5; *Part-Time Faculty*: 2; *Full-Time Professional (non-clerical) Staff Members*: 1.

FACILITIES AND SERVICES
Practical experiences available through: Audio Recording Laboratory; Community Antenna (Cable) Television Origination; Campus Newspaper (Published Independently); Local Commercial Newspaper; Local Commercial Television Station; Desktop Publishing Facility; Photographic Darkrooms; Video Editing; FM Radio Station (Institutional); Institutional Magazine; Public Relations Agency.

College of St. Scholastica

Communication
1200 Kenwood Avenue
Duluth, Minnesota 55811

Dan Johnson, Administrator

College of St. Thomas (Private)

Department of Communication
2115 Summit Avenue
St. Paul, Minnesota 55105
Telephone: (612) 647-5499

Kevin O. Sauter, Chair
John Nemo, Dean of the College

CURRICULUM AND INSTRUCTION
Courses or Concentrations
Available: Communication; Radio, Television, Broadcasting, or Telecommunications; Speech; *Undergraduate Objectives or Program Emphases*: The study of human interaction and its effects in the forms and forums in which it occurs. The integration of Speech Communication and Telecommunication underlies the central focus on communication issues as occurs in face-to-face and mediated channels; *Bachelor's Degree Majors*: 125; *Full-Time Faculty*: 8; *Part-Time Faculty*: 16.

FACILITIES AND SERVICES
Practical experiences available through: Audio Recording Laboratory; Community Antenna (Cable) Television Origination; Closed Circuit Television Facility; Campus Newspaper (Published Independently); Local Commercial Newspaper; Local Commercial Television Station; Desktop Publishing Facility; Photographic Darkrooms; Video Editing; Electronic Field Production (Video); Television Broadcast Station (Institutional); Institutional Magazine; Institutional Newspaper; Satellite Uplink Facility.

College of St. Thomas (Private)

Department of Journalism and Mass Communication
MS #5013, 2115 Summitt Avenue
St. Paul, Minnesota 55105
Telephone: (612) 647-5637

Thomas B. Connery, Chair

CURRICULUM AND INSTRUCTION
Courses or Concentrations
Available: Advertising; Journalism or Mass Communication; Public Relations; Radio, Television, Broadcasting, or Telecommunications; *Bachelor's Degree Majors*: 112; *Full-Time Faculty*: 5; *Part-Time Faculty*: 15.

FACILITIES AND SERVICES
Practical experiences available through: Community Antenna (Cable) Television Origination; Closed Circuit Television Facility; Local Commercial Newspaper; Desktop Publishing Facility; Photographic Darkrooms; Video Editing; Electronic Field Production (Video); Institutional Newspaper; Video Production Laboratory or Television Studio.

Concordia College (Private)

Department of Speech Communication and Theatre Arts
901 South 8th Street
Moorhead, Minnesota 56560
Telephone: (218) 299-3725

Henry T. Tkachuk, Chair
H. Robert Homann, Dean

CURRICULUM AND INSTRUCTION
Courses or Concentrations
Available: Advertising; Communication; Film or Cinema; Journalism or Mass Communication; Public Relations; Radio, Television, Broadcasting, or Telecommunications; Speech; Theatre; *Program Coordinators*: Harold Casselton (Media Studies); *Undergraduate Objectives or Program Emphases*: Broad liberal arts preparation with some concentration in area of choice; *Bachelor's Degree Majors*: 175; *Full-Time Faculty*: 12; *Part-Time Faculty*: 3; *Full-Time Professional (non-clerical) Staff Members*: 3.

FACILITIES AND SERVICES
Practical experiences available through: Advertising Agency; Audio Recording Laboratory; Community Antenna (Cable) Television Origination; Carrier Current Audio Distribution System; Closed Circuit Television Facility; Campus Newspaper (Published Independently); Local Commercial Newspaper; Local Commercial Television Station; Desktop Publishing Facility; Photographic Darkrooms; Video Editing; Electronic Field Production (Video); ITFS Distribution System; Institutional Newspaper; Video Production Laboratory or Television Studio.

Fergus Falls Community College (Public)

Program of Speech Communication
1414 College Way
Fergus Falls, Minnesota 56537
Telephone: (218) 739-7474

Missy S. Goodman, Director
Marnie Fischer, Vice-Provost

CURRICULUM AND INSTRUCTION
Courses or Concentrations Available: Speech; *Undergraduate Objectives or Program Emphases*: Public address; interpersonal communication; small group communication; *Full-Time Faculty*: 1; *Part-Time Faculty*: 1.

Gustavus Adolphus College (Private)

Department of Speech and Communication Studies
St. Peter, Minnesota 56082
Telephone: (507) 931-7366

William Robertz, Chair

CURRICULUM AND INSTRUCTION
Courses or Concentrations
Available: Communication; Radio, Television, Broadcasting, or Telecommunications; Speech; *Undergraduate Objectives or Program Emphases*: To provide exposure to the three areas of rhetoric/public address, communication studies, and media studies in a liberal arts concentration; *Bachelor's Degree Majors*: 135; *Full-Time Faculty*: 5.

FACILITIES AND SERVICES
Practical experiences available through: Carrier Current Audio Distribution System; Campus Newspaper (Published Independently); Local Commercial Television Station; Video Editing; Electronic Field Production (Video); FM Radio Station (Institutional); Video Production Laboratory or Television Studio.

Hibbing Community College

Department of Television Production
1515 East 25th
Hibbing, Minnesota 55746

Robert T. Rutt, Administrator

Inver Hills Community College

Film, Video, and Audio Programs
8445 College Trail
Inver Grove Heights, Minnesota 55075

Bruce J. Mamer, Administrator

Mankato State University (Public)

Mass Communications Institute
Box 39 MSU
Mankato, Minnesota 56001
Telephone: (507) 389-6417

Ellen M. Mrja, Director
Jane F. Earley, Dean

CURRICULUM AND INSTRUCTION
*Courses or Concentrations
Available*: Journalism or Mass
Communication; Public Relations;
*Undergraduate Objectives or Program
Emphases*: To give students training for
entry-level communications positions, within
the context of a liberal arts education;
Bachelor's Degree Majors: 220; *Full-Time
Faculty*: 4; *Part-Time Faculty*: 3.

FACILITIES AND SERVICES
*Practical experiences available
through*: Associated Press Wire Service Feed;
Community Antenna (Cable) Television
Origination; Campus Newspaper (Published
Independently); Local Commercial
Newspaper; Local Commercial Television
Station; Desktop Publishing Facility;
Photographic Darkrooms.

Minneapolis College of Art and Design (Private)

Division of Media Arts
2501 Stevens Avenue S
Minneapolis, Minnesota 55404
Telephone: (612) 870-3238

Tom DeBiaso, Chair
Tom Morin, Dean, Academic Affairs

CURRICULUM AND INSTRUCTION
Courses or Concentrations Available: Film or
Cinema; Video; Photography; Art;
*Undergraduate Objectives or Program
Emphases*: Our objective is to teach the
understanding and practice of the media arts;
BFA Degree Majors: 85; *Full-Time
Faculty*: 8; *Part-Time Faculty*: 4.

FACILITIES AND SERVICES
*Practical experiences available
through*: Advertising Agency; Campus
Newspaper (Published Independently);
Desktop Publishing Facility; Photographic
Darkrooms; Video Editing; Electronic Field

Production (Video); Film or Cinema
Laboratory; Public Relations Agency; Video
Production Laboratory or Television Studio.

Minneapolis Community College (Public)

Department of English/Journalism
1501 Hennepin Avenue South
Minneapolis, Minnesota 55403
Telephone: (612) 341-7028

Mary Barwise, Instructor
Carol Brambl, Assistant Dean

CURRICULUM AND INSTRUCTION
*Courses or Concentrations
Available*: Communication; Journalism or
Mass Communication; *Undergraduate
Objectives or Program Emphases*: To
encourage a broadly-based liberal arts
foundation for transfer to a four year school
with a communication major; *Associate's
Degree Majors*: 100; *Full-Time Faculty*: 1.

FACILITIES AND SERVICES
*Practical experiences available
through*: Campus Newspaper (Published
Independently); Photographic Darkrooms.

Moorhead State University (Public)

Department of Speech Communication and
Theatre Art
Moorhead, Minnesota 56560

Delmar J. Hansen, Administrator

Moorhead State University (Public)

Department of Mass Communications
Moorhead, Minnesota 56560
Telephone: (218) 236-2985

Martin Grindeland, Chair
David C. Nelson, Dean, Business, Industry
and Applied Programs

CURRICULUM AND INSTRUCTION
*Courses or Concentrations
Available*: Advertising; Communication; Film

or Cinema; Journalism or Mass Communication; Public Relations; Radio, Television, Broadcasting, or Telecommunications; Speech; Dual major: English and Mass Communication; *Undergraduate Objectives or Program Emphases*: The major in mass communications is designed to balance the breadth of liberal education with the depth of a professional program; *Degree Majors*: 209; *Full-Time Faculty*: 8; *Part-Time Faculty*: 2; *Full-Time Professional (non-clerical) Staff Members*: 1.

FACILITIES AND SERVICES
Practical experiences available through: Advertising Agency; Audio Recording Laboratory; Community Antenna (Cable) Television Origination; Carrier Current Audio Distribution System; Closed Circuit Television Facility; Campus Newspaper (Published Independently); Local Commercial Newspaper; Local Commercial Television Station; Desktop Publishing Facility; Photographic Darkrooms; Video Editing; Electronic Field Production (Video); Public Relations Agency; Video News and Data Processing; Video Production Laboratory or Television Studio.

Northwestern College (Private)

Department of Communication
3003 North Snelling Avenue
St. Paul, Minnesota 55113
Telephone: (612) 631-5100

Timothy C. Tomlinson, Chair
David Onderein, Vice President for Academic Affairs

CURRICULUM AND INSTRUCTION
Courses or Concentrations Available: Advertising; Communication; Film or Cinema; Information Science; Journalism or Mass Communication; Public Relations; Radio, Television, Broadcasting, or Telecommunications; Speech; Foreign languages; *Program Coordinators*: Daniel Pawley (Journalism); Richard Tremaine (Speech); *Undergraduate Objectives or Program Emphases*: To prepare students to be effective and ethical communicators who can combine practical skills with theoretical understanding; *Associate's Degree Majors*: 1; *Bachelor's Degree Majors*: 43; *Full-Time Faculty*: 6; *Part-Time Faculty*: 5.

FACILITIES AND SERVICES
Practical experiences available through: Associated Press Wire Service Feed; Audio Recording Laboratory; Community Antenna (Cable) Television Origination; Carrier Current Audio Distribution System; Desktop Publishing Facility; Video Editing; Electronic Field Production (Video); Film or Cinema Laboratory; Institutional Magazine; Video Production Laboratory or Television Studio.

St. Cloud State University (Public)

Department of Mass Communications
St. Cloud, Minnesota 56301
Telephone: (612) 255-3295

Francis H. Voelker, Chair
Michael Counaughton, Dean

CURRICULUM AND INSTRUCTION
Courses or Concentrations Available: Advertising; Public Relations; News Editorial; Broadcasting; *Undergraduate Objectives or Program Emphases*: The BS degree program has a professional focus with blend of theory and practicum courses; *Graduate Objectives or Program Emphases*: In planning stages for MS in Communication Management; *Degree Majors*: 250; *Full-Time Faculty*: 10; *Part-Time Faculty*: 1; *Full-Time Professional (non-clerical) Staff Members*: 4.

FACILITIES AND SERVICES
Practical experiences available through: Advertising Agency; Associated Press Wire Service Feed; Audio Recording Laboratory; Community Antenna (Cable) Television Origination; Campus Newspaper (Published Independently); Desktop Publishing Facility; Photographic Darkrooms; Video Editing; Electronic Field Production (Video); FM Radio Station (Institutional); Institutional Newspaper; Public Relations Agency.

St. Cloud State University (Public)

Department of Speech Communication
St. Cloud, Minnesota 56301
Telephone: (612) 255-0121

Charles F. Vick, Chair
Michael Connaughton, Dean

CURRICULUM AND INSTRUCTION
*Courses or Concentrations
Available*: Communication; Speech;
*Undergraduate Objectives or Program
Emphases*: To offer a well rounded program
in Speech Communication to majors and
minors, to provide a required general
education course in speech to all students,
and to provide service courses for other
departments; *Bachelor's Degree Majors*: 56;
Other Degree Majors: 300; *Full-Time
Faculty*: 22; *Part-Time Faculty*: 3.

St. John's University (Private)

Department of Communication and Media
Collegeville, Minnesota 56321
Telephone: (612) 363-3147

Joan E. Steck, Chair
Dietrich Reinhart, Dean

CURRICULUM AND INSTRUCTION
*Courses or Concentrations
Available*: Communication; Journalism or
Mass Communication; Speech; Rhetorical
Theory and Criticism; Homiletics (graduate);
*Undergraduate Objectives or Program
Emphases*: Minors in Rhetoric and Public
Address, Journalism and Mass Media
Criticism, and Communication Theory;
Bachelor's Degree Majors: 101; *Full-Time
Faculty*: 3; *Part-Time Faculty*: 3.

FACILITIES AND SERVICES
*Practical experiences available
through*: Advertising Agency; Associated
Press Wire Service Feed; Closed Circuit
Television Facility; Campus Newspaper
(Published Independently); Local
Commercial Newspaper; Desktop Publishing
Facility; Photographic Darkrooms; Video
Editing; FM Radio Station (Institutional);
Institutional Newspaper; Public Relations
Agency; United Press International Feed.

St. Mary's College

Mass Communications Department
Winona, Minnesota 55987

Dom Caristi, Administrator

St. Olaf College (Private)

Department of Speech/Theater
Northfield, Minnesota 55057
Telephone: (507) 663-3240

Patrick J. Quade, Chair
Jon Moline, Vice President and Dean of the
College

CURRICULUM AND INSTRUCTION
*Courses or Concentrations
Available*: Communication; Journalism or
Mass Communication; Public Relations;
Speech; Theater; *Undergraduate Objectives or
Program Emphases*: BA in Liberal Arts;
Bachelor's Degree Majors: 82; *Full-Time
Faculty*: 10; *Full-Time Professional
(non-clerical) Staff Members*: 3.

FACILITIES AND SERVICES
*Practical experiences available
through*: Associated Press Wire Service Feed;
Community Antenna (Cable) Television
Origination; Campus Newspaper (Published
Independently); Photographic Darkrooms;
FM Radio Station (Institutional); Public
Relations Agency.

Thief River Falls Technical College (Public)

College of Radio-Television Broadcasting
Highway 1 East
Thief River Falls, Minnesota 56701
Telephone: (218) 681-6364

Howard M. Rokke, Head
Olley Gunderson, Administrator

CURRICULUM AND INSTRUCTION
*Courses or Concentrations
Available*: Advertising; Radio, Television,
Broadcasting, or Telecommunications;
*Undergraduate Objectives or Program
Emphases*: Train broadcasters for
announcing, sales and news; television
technicians; *Associate's Degree Majors*: 20;
Full-Time Faculty: 2.

FACILITIES AND SERVICES
*Practical experiences available
through*: Associated Press Wire Service Feed;
Community Antenna (Cable) Television
Origination; Closed Circuit Television
Facility; Video Editing; FM Radio Station
(Institutional); Video Production Laboratory
or Television Studio.

University of Minnesota - Duluth (Public)

Department of Communication
10 University Drive
Duluth, Minnesota 55812
Telephone: (218) 726-8576

Virginia T. Katz, Chair
Judith Gillespie, Dean

CURRICULUM AND INSTRUCTION
*Courses or Concentrations
Available*: Communication; Journalism or
Mass Communication; Speech;
*Undergraduate Objectives or Program
Emphases*: A broadly based liberal arts major
with strong emphasis on theory in rhetoric,
mass communication, interpersonal
communication. No production work in
radio or television, only theory and criticism.
Advanced public speaking and history of
rhetoric are required; *Bachelor's Degree
Majors*: 250; *Other Degree Majors*: 300;
Full-Time Faculty: 7; *Part-Time Faculty*: 3.

FACILITIES AND SERVICES
*Practical experiences available
through*: Campus Newspaper (Published
Independently).

University of Minnesota - Minneapolis (Public)

**School of Journalism and Mass
Communication**
111 Murphy Hall
206 Church Street, SE
Minneapolis, Minnesota 55455
Telephone: (612) 625-9824

Daniel B. Wackman, Director
**Craig Swan, Acting Dean, College of Liberal
Arts**

CURRICULUM AND INSTRUCTION
*Courses or Concentrations
Available*: Advertising; Journalism or Mass

Communication; Broadcast Journalism,
Visual Communication; *Undergraduate
Objectives or Program
Emphases*: Professional education in four
areas: News/editorial, broadcast, advertising,
visual communication, public relations. A
liberal arts major in mass communication
studies is also provided; *Graduate Objectives
or Program Emphases*: MA which combines
academic/professional emphasis or mass
communication styles; *Bachelor's Degree
Majors*: 350; *Master's Degree Majors*: 80;
*Doctoral Degree Majors Currently in
Residence*: 30; *Additional Doctoral Degree
Majors*: 15; *Full-Time Faculty*: 19;
Part-Time Faculty: 37; *Full-Time
Professional (non-clerical) Staff Members*: 2.

FACILITIES AND SERVICES
*Practical experiences available
through*: Associated Press Wire Service Feed;
Audio Recording Laboratory; Community
Antenna (Cable) Television Origination;
Closed Circuit Television Facility; Campus
Newspaper (Published Independently);
Local Commercial Newspaper; Local
Commercial Television Station; Desktop
Publishing Facility; Photographic
Darkrooms; Video Editing; Electronic Field
Production (Video); Television Broadcast
Station (Institutional); FM Radio Station
(Institutional); Institutional Magazine;
Public Relations Agency; Video News and
Data Processing; Video Production
Laboratory or Television Studio.

University of Minnesota - Minneapolis (Public)

Department of Speech Communication
317 Folwell Hall
9 Pleasant Street SE
Minneapolis, Minnesota 55455
Telephone: (612) 624-5800

Donald R. Browne, Chair
**Craig Swan, Acting Dean, College of Liberal
Arts**

CURRICULUM AND INSTRUCTION
Courses or Concentrations Available: Radio,
Television, Broadcasting, or
Telecommunications; Speech; *Undergraduate
Objectives or Program Emphases*: To provide
an understanding of the full range of verbal
and non-verbal (but not including print)
communications activities. To that end we
do not offer specializations within the

Department; *Graduate Objectives or Program Emphases*: Much the same as undergraduate, but students do tend to select areas of specialization from among rhetoric and public address, small group communication, organizational communication, communication theory, intercultural communication and electronic media; *Bachelor's Degree Majors*: 250; *Master's Degree Majors*: 40; *Doctoral Degree Majors Currently in Residence*: 40; *Additional Doctoral Degree Majors*: 20; *Full-Time Faculty*: 13; *Part-Time Faculty*: 30.

FACILITIES AND SERVICES
Practical experiences available through: AM Radio Station (Institutional); Audio Recording Laboratory; Local Commercial Television Station.

University of Minnesota - Morris (Public)

Division of Speech Communication
Morris, Minnesota 56267
Telephone: (612) 589-2211

Raymond J. Lammers, Coordinator
C. F. Farrell, Jr., Division Chair

CURRICULUM AND INSTRUCTION
Courses or Concentrations Available: Communication; Mass Communication; Radio, Television, Broadcasting, or Telecommunications; Speech; Rhetorical history and criticism; *Undergraduate Objectives or Program Emphases*: The speech communication curriculum provides instruction and experiences for those interested in the oral communication tradition. Courses explore principles and concepts from that tradition that have implications for the contemporary world; *Bachelor's Degree Majors*: 80; *Full-Time Faculty*: 5.

FACILITIES AND SERVICES
Practical experiences available through: AM Radio Station (Institutional); Community Antenna (Cable) Television Origination; Campus Newspaper (Published Independently).

Winona State University

Mass Communication Department
PAC 215
Winona, Minnesota 55987

Dennis Pack, Chair

Winona State University (Public)

Department of Communication and Theatre Arts
Winona, Minnesota 55987
Telephone: (507) 457-5241

David L. Bratt, Chair
James Reynolds, Dean, College of Liberal Arts

CURRICULUM AND INSTRUCTION
Courses or Concentrations Available: Communication; Speech; Theatre; *Undergraduate Objectives or Program Emphases*: Communication education in Public Affairs/Information, Human Resource Development, Communication Theory, Organizational Communication, and Cross-Cultural Communication; *Bachelor's Degree Majors*: 30; *Full-Time Faculty*: 12; *Part-Time Faculty*: 4; *Full-Time Professional (non-clerical) Staff Members*: 2.

Alcorn State University (Public)

Program of Communications
P.O. Box 269
Lorman, Mississippi 39096
Telephone: (601) 877-6612

David L. Crosby, Director
Norris A. Edney, Director, Division of Arts and Sciences

CURRICULUM AND INSTRUCTION
Courses or Concentrations
Available: Advertising; Communication; Film or Cinema; Journalism or Mass Communication; Public Relations; Radio, Television, Broadcasting, or Telecommunications; *Undergraduate Objectives or Program Emphases*: To prepare students for entry level positions in journalism, radio and television production, and communication management; *Bachelor's Degree Majors*: 40; *Full-Time Faculty*: 3; *Part-Time Faculty*: 3.

FACILITIES AND SERVICES
Practical experiences available through: Associated Press Wire Service Feed; Audio Recording Laboratory; Local Commercial Newspaper; Local Commercial Television Station; Desktop Publishing Facility; Photographic Darkrooms; Video Editing; Electronic Field Production (Video); FM Radio Station (Institutional); Institutional Magazine; Video News and Data Processing; Video Production Laboratory or Television Studio.

Alcorn State University (Public)

Area of Speech and Theatre
Lorman, Mississippi 39096
Telephone: (601) 877-6261

Jerry Bangham, Chair
Jo Ya Bolden, Chair, Department of Fine Arts

CURRICULUM AND INSTRUCTION
Courses or Concentrations
Available: Communication; Journalism or Mass Communication; Radio, Television, Broadcasting, or Telecommunications; *Undergraduate Objectives or Program Emphases*: Teach one oral communications course taken by all students. Stage plays and musicals; *Full-Time Faculty*: 2.

Belhaven College (Private)

Department of Speech and Drama
1500 Peachtree Street
Jackson, Mississippi 39202
Telephone: (601) 968-5928

Frances Tamboli, Director
Bill Durrett, Chair, English Department

CURRICULUM AND INSTRUCTION
Courses or Concentrations Available: Speech; Drama; *Undergraduate Objectives or Program Emphases*: Minor is offered, with the emphasis being in speech communication; *Part-Time Faculty*: 2.

Delta State University (Public)

Department of Speech Communication
3137 Delta State
Cleveland, Mississippi 38732
Telephone: (601) 846-4091

Willard C. Booth, Chair
Mardin Bond, Division Chair

CURRICULUM AND INSTRUCTION
Courses or Concentrations
Available: Communication; Film or Cinema; Radio, Television, Broadcasting, or Telecommunications; Speech; Drama; *Undergraduate Objectives or Program Emphases*: To provide basic foundations in the speech/communication arts; *Bachelor's Degree Majors*: 15; *Full-Time Faculty*: 5; *Part-Time Faculty*: 1.

FACILITIES AND SERVICES
Practical experiences available through: AM Radio Station (Institutional); Audio Recording Laboratory; Campus Newspaper (Published Independently); Photographic

Darkrooms; Video Production Laboratory or Television Studio.

Holmes Junior College

Vocational-Technical
Goodman, Mississippi 39079

Robert Irby, Administrator

Itawamba College

Department of Speech and Theatre
Fulton, Mississippi 38843

Jackson College of Ministries (Private)

Division of Christian Education
1555 Beasley Road
Jackson, Mississippi 39206
Telephone: (601) 981-1611

Sidney L. Poe, Dean
Thomas L. Craft, Administrator

CURRICULUM AND INSTRUCTION
Courses or Concentrations Available: Communication; Public Relations; Speech; *Undergraduate Objectives or Program Emphases*: To increase communication skills in writing and speaking; *Full-Time Faculty*: 3; *Part-Time Faculty*: 3.

FACILITIES AND SERVICES
Practical experiences available through: Audio Recording Laboratory; Desktop Publishing Facility.

Jackson State University (Public)

Department of Mass Communications
P. O. Box 18590
Jackson, Mississippi 39217-0990
Telephone: (601) 968-2151

Elayne Hayes-Anthony, Chair
Mary E. Benjamin, Dean

CURRICULUM AND INSTRUCTION
Courses or Concentrations Available: Advertising; Journalism or Mass Communication; Public Relations; Radio, Television, Broadcasting, or Telecommunications; *Undergraduate Objectives or Program Emphases*: Overall mission of the department is to educate and train students for entry level positions in mass communications; *Graduate Objectives or Program Emphases*: To begin Fall, 1992; *Degree Majors*: 185; *Full-Time Faculty*: 7; *Part-Time Faculty*: 2; *Full-Time Professional (non-clerical) Staff Members*: 2.

FACILITIES AND SERVICES
Practical experiences available through: Advertising Agency; Audio Recording Laboratory; Community Antenna (Cable) Television Origination; Campus Newspaper (Published Independently); Local Commercial Newspaper; Local Commercial Television Station; Desktop Publishing Facility; Photographic Darkrooms; Video Editing; Electronic Field Production (Video); Television Broadcast Station (Institutional); FM Radio Station (Institutional); ITFS Distribution System; Institutional Magazine; Public Relations Agency; United Press International Feed; Video News and Data Processing.

Mississippi College (Private)

Department of Communication
Box 4207
Clinton, Mississippi 39058
Telephone: (601) 925-3428

Billy D. Lytal, Head
Glen Eaves, Administrator

CURRICULUM AND INSTRUCTION
Courses or Concentrations Available: Communication; Journalism or Mass Communication; Public Relations; Radio, Television, Broadcasting, or Telecommunications; *Undergraduate Objectives or Program Emphases*: Areas within the department may be chosen to help prepare the student to function in such fields as business, law, the ministry, mass communication, government, education, or industrial settings; *Graduate Objectives or Program Emphases*: MS degree is designed for graduate study in field of communication; *Bachelor's Degree Majors*: 7; *Master's Degree Majors*: 15; *Other Degree Majors*: 50; *Full-Time Faculty*: 6; *Part-Time Faculty*: 5; *Full-Time Professional (non-clerical) Staff Members*: 1.

FACILITIES AND SERVICES
Practical experiences available through: Advertising Agency; Audio Recording Laboratory; Campus Newspaper (Published Independently); Local Commercial Newspaper; Local Commercial Television Station; Desktop Publishing Facility; Photographic Darkrooms; Video Editing; Electronic Field Production (Video); FM Radio Station (Institutional); Institutional Newspaper; Public Relations Agency; Video News and Data Processing; Video Production Laboratory or Television Studio.

Mississippi Gulf Coast Community College - Jefferson Davis (Public)

Program of Radio Broadcasting Technology
Courthouse Road Station
Gulfport, Mississippi 39501-3896
Telephone: (601) 896-3355 Extension: 251

Doug Hendon, Head
Ronnie Lee, Technical Director

CURRICULUM AND INSTRUCTION
Courses or Concentrations Available: Advertising; Speech; *Program Coordinators*: Ronnie Lee (Advertising-Marketing and Merchandising Management); *Undergraduate Objectives or Program Emphases*: Radio Broadcasting/Sales (local commercial radio station provides work experience); *Associate's Degree Majors*: 25; *Full-Time Faculty*: 1.

FACILITIES AND SERVICES
Practical experiences available through: Advertising Agency; AM Radio Station (Institutional); Audio Recording Laboratory; Carrier Current Audio Distribution System; Campus Newspaper (Published Independently); Local Commercial Newspaper; Local Commercial Television Station; Photographic Darkrooms; Video News and Data Processing.

Mississippi Gulf Coast Community College - Jefferson Davis (Public)

Department of Fine Arts
2226 Switzer Road
Gulfport, Mississippi 39507-3899
Telephone: (601) 896-3355

Wayne Catlett, Chair
Q. A. Long, Dean, Academic and General Instruction

CURRICULUM AND INSTRUCTION
Courses or Concentrations Available: Communication; Speech; Theatre; *Undergraduate Objectives or Program Emphases*: Speech--offer basic understanding of communication process generally and provide public speaking experiences specifically. Theatre--provide opportunities for production experience on all levels for majors and non-majors; *Associate's Degree Majors*: 25; *Full-Time Faculty*: 2; *Part-Time Faculty*: 2.

FACILITIES AND SERVICES
Practical experiences available through: AM Radio Station (Institutional).

Mississippi State University (Public)

Department of Communication
P. O. Drawer PF
Mississippi State, Mississippi 39762
Telephone: (601) 325-3320

Sidney R. Hill Jr., Head
Lida K. Barrett, Dean, College of Arts and Sciences

CURRICULUM AND INSTRUCTION
Courses or Concentrations Available: Communication; Journalism or Mass Communication; Public Relations; Radio, Television, Broadcasting, or Telecommunications; Speech; *Undergraduate Objectives or Program Emphases*: Professional training within the context of a high-quality liberal arts education; *Bachelor's Degree Majors*: 200; *Full-Time Faculty*: 19; *Part-Time Faculty*: 8; *Full-Time Professional (non-clerical) Staff Members*: 2.

FACILITIES AND SERVICES

Practical experiences available through: Audio Recording Laboratory; Community Antenna (Cable) Television Origination; Campus Newspaper (Published Independently); Local Commercial Newspaper; Local Commercial Television Station; Desktop Publishing Facility; Photographic Darkrooms; Video Editing; Electronic Field Production (Video); Institutional Newspaper; Public Relations Agency; Satellite Uplink Facility (Ku Band Transmitter); Video Production Laboratory or Television Studio.

Mississippi University for Women (Public)

Division of Communication
P. O. Box W-940
Columbus, Mississippi 39701
Telephone: (601) 329-7249

Barbara A. Hanners, Head
Dorothy Burdeshaw, Interim Vice President, Academic Affairs

CURRICULUM AND INSTRUCTION

Courses or Concentrations Available: Advertising; Communication; Journalism or Mass Communication; Public Relations; Radio, Television, Broadcasting, or Telecommunications; Speech; Speech - Language Pathology; *Undergraduate Objectives or Program Emphases*: To prepare students in broadcasting, journalism, and public relations to pursue careers in mass communication; to prepare students in speech pathology for graduate study; *Bachelor's Degree Majors*: 20; *Other Degree Majors*: 45; *Full-Time Faculty*: 7; *Part-Time Faculty*: 3; *Full-Time Professional (non-clerical) Staff Members*: 3.

FACILITIES AND SERVICES

Practical experiences available through: Advertising Agency; Audio Recording Laboratory; Carrier Current Audio Distribution System; Campus Newspaper (Published Independently); Local Commercial Newspaper; Local Commercial Television Station; Desktop Publishing Facility; Photographic Darkrooms; Video Editing; Electronic Field Production (Video); Television Broadcast Station (Institutional); FM Radio Station (Institutional); Institutional Newspaper; Public Relations Agency; Video Production Laboratory or Television Studio.

Mississippi Valley State University

Department of English and Speech
P. O. Box 372
Itta Bena, Mississippi 38941

Rust College (Private)

Department of Mass Communication
150 E. Rust Avenue
Holly Springs, Mississippi 38635
Telephone: (601) 252-4661

Sylvester W. Oliver, Jr., Chair
W. A. McMillan, Administrator

CURRICULUM AND INSTRUCTION

Courses or Concentrations Available: Journalism or Mass Communication; Radio, Television, Broadcasting, or Telecommunications; *Undergraduate Objectives or Program Emphases*: Journalism, Radio and Television; *Bachelor's Degree Majors*: 46; *Full-Time Faculty*: 3; *Part-Time Faculty*: 3; *Full-Time Professional (non-clerical) Staff Members*: 5.

FACILITIES AND SERVICES

Practical experiences available through: Associated Press Wire Service Feed; Audio Recording Laboratory; Community Antenna (Cable) Television Origination; Closed Circuit Television Facility; Campus Newspaper (Published Independently); Video Editing; Electronic Field Production (Video); Television Broadcast Station (Institutional); FM Radio Station (Institutional).

Tougaloo College

Department of Journalism
Tougaloo, Mississippi 39174

Lynette Johnson Shelton, Administrator

University of Mississippi (Public)

Department of Journalism
Farley Hall
University, Mississippi 38677
Telephone: (601) 232-7146

Will Norton, Chair
Dale Abadie, Dean

CURRICULUM AND INSTRUCTION
Courses or Concentrations
Available: Advertising; Journalism or Mass
Communication; Public Relations; Radio,
Television, Broadcasting, or
Telecommunications; Magazines;
*Undergraduate Objectives or Program
Emphases*: Preparation for media career
within a broad liberal arts education;
*Graduate Objectives or Program
Emphases*: Preparation for media career
within a broad liberal arts education;
Bachelor's Degree Majors: 400; *Master's
Degree Majors*: 50; *Full-Time Faculty*: 10;
Part-Time Faculty: 5.

FACILITIES AND SERVICES
*Practical experiences available
through*: Associated Press Wire Service Feed;
Audio Recording Laboratory; Community
Antenna (Cable) Television Origination;
Campus Newspaper (Published
Independently); Local Commercial
Newspaper; Desktop Publishing Facility;
Photographic Darkrooms; Video Editing;
Electronic Field Production (Video); Film
or Cinema Laboratory; Institutional
Magazine; Public Relations Agency.

University of Southern Mississippi (Public)

School of Communications
Southern Station, Box 5158
Hattiesburg, Mississippi 39406-5158
Telephone: (601) 266-5650

Robert G. Wiggins, Director
**Glenn T. Harper, Dean, College of Liberal
Arts**

CURRICULUM AND INSTRUCTION
Courses or Concentrations
Available: Advertising; Communication; Film
or Cinema; Journalism or Mass
Communication; Public Relations; Radio,
Television, Broadcasting, or
Telecommunications; Speech;

Photojournalism; *Program
Coordinators*: Arthur J. Kaul
(News-editorial, Public Relations,
Advertising, Photojournalism, Journalism
Education); David H. Goff (Radio Television
Production, Broadcast Journalism, Broadcast
Sales and Management, Film); Keith
Erickson (Speech Communication,
Communication, Speech Communication
Education); *Undergraduate Objectives or
Program Emphases*: News-editorial, public
relations, advertising, photojournalism,
journalism education, radio-television
production, broadcast journalism, broadcast
sales and management, film, speech
communication, communication, speech
communication education; *Graduate
Objectives or Program Emphases*: Offer MA,
MS in communication; MS in public
relations; Ph.D. in communication;
Bachelor's Degree Majors: 600; *Master's
Degree Majors*: 47; *Doctoral Degree Majors
Currently in Residence*: 18; *Additional
Doctoral Degree Majors*: 19; *Full-Time
Faculty*: 26; *Part-Time Faculty*: 7; *Full-Time
Professional (non-clerical) Staff Members*: 7.
See one or more additional entries below.

FACILITIES AND SERVICES
*Practical experiences available
through*: Associated Press Wire Service Feed;
Audio Recording Laboratory; Community
Antenna (Cable) Television Origination;
Local Commercial Newspaper; Local
Commercial Television Station; Desktop
Publishing Facility; Photographic
Darkrooms; Video Editing; Electronic Field
Production (Video); Film or Cinema
Laboratory; FM Radio Station
(Institutional); Institutional Newspaper;
Satellite Uplink Facility; Video News and
Data Processing; Video Production
Laboratory or Television Studio.

University of Southern Mississippi (Public)

Department of Journalism
Southern Station 5121
Hattiesburg, Mississippi 39406-5121
Telephone: (601) 266-4258

Arthur J. Kaul, Chair
**Robert G. Wiggins, Director, School of
Communication**

CURRICULUM AND INSTRUCTION
Courses or Concentrations

Available: Advertising; Journalism or Mass Communication; Public Relations; Photojournalism (Major Emphasis); *Undergraduate Objectives or Program Emphases*: The School of Communication is a separately organized entity within the College of Liberal Arts and is comprised of five programs and departments: Advertising, Communication, Journalism, Radio, Television, and Film, and Speech Communication; *Bachelor's Degree Majors*: 250; *Full-Time Faculty*: 9; *Part-Time Faculty*: 5; *Full-Time Professional (non-clerical) Staff Members*: 3.

FACILITIES AND SERVICES
Practical experiences available through: Local Commercial Newspaper; Photographic Darkrooms; FM Radio Station (Institutional); Institutional Newspaper.

University of Southern Mississippi (Public)

Department of Speech Communication
Southern Station Box 5131
Hattiesburg, Mississippi 39406
Telephone: (601) 266-4271

Keith V. Erickson, Chair
Robert G. Wiggins, Director, School of Communication

CURRICULUM AND INSTRUCTION
Courses or Concentrations Available: Speech; *Undergraduate Objectives or Program Emphases*: Speech Communication; *Graduate Objectives or Program Emphases*: Speech Communication; *Bachelor's Degree Majors*: 70; *Master's Degree Majors*: 10; *Doctoral Degree Majors Currently in Residence*: 5; *Additional Doctoral Degree Majors*: 5; *Full-Time Faculty*: 9; *Part-Time Faculty*: 7.

FACILITIES AND SERVICES
Practical experiences available through: Advertising Agency; AM Radio Station (Institutional); Associated Press Wire Service Feed; Audio Recording Laboratory; Campus Newspaper (Published Independently); Local Commercial Newspaper; Local Commercial Television Station; Desktop Publishing Facility; Photographic Darkrooms; Video Editing; Electronic Field Production (Video); Television Broadcast Station (Institutional); Film and Cinema Laboratory; Institutional Newspaper; Public Relations Agency; Satellite Uplink Facility; Video News and Data Processing; Video Production Laboratory or Television Studio.

Wood Junior College (Private)

Journalism Department
Communication Department
1 Weber Drive
Mathiston, Mississippi 39752
Telephone: (601) 263-4964

Sandra J. Grych, Instructor/Head
Barbara Crawford, Academic Dean

CURRICULUM AND INSTRUCTION
Courses or Concentrations Available: Communication; Journalism or Mass Communication; Speech; Theatre; *Program Coordinators*: Doyce Gunter (Speech); Frances Heller (Drama/Theatre); *Undergraduate Objectives or Program Emphases*: The college offers a basic liberal arts program with the Communication Department offering basic courses in speech, journalism and drama; *Associate's Degree Majors*: 100; *Part-Time Faculty*: 3; *Full-Time Professional (non-clerical) Staff Members*: 1.

FACILITIES AND SERVICES
Practical experiences available through: Campus Newspaper (Published Independently); Photographic Darkrooms; Institutional Newspaper.

Avila College (Private)

Division of Communication
11901 Wornall Road
Kansas City, Missouri 64145
Telephone: (816) 942-8400

Catherine Wickern, Coordinator
Daniel Paul Larson, Chair, Department of Humanities

CURRICULUM AND INSTRUCTION
Courses or Concentrations
Available: Advertising; Communication; Film or Cinema; Journalism or Mass Communication; Public Relations; Radio, Television, Broadcasting, or Telecommunications; Speech; *Undergraduate Objectives or Program Emphases*: Communication major with choice of concentrations in Business, Electronic Media, Public Relations, or Writing; *Bachelor's Degree Majors*: 46; *Full-Time Faculty*: 2; *Part-Time Faculty*: 7.

FACILITIES AND SERVICES
Practical experiences available through: Advertising Agency; Campus Newspaper (Published Independently); Local Commercial Newspaper; Local Commercial Television Station; Photographic Darkrooms; Video Editing; Electronic Field Production (Video); Film or Cinema Laboratory; Public Relations Agency; Video Production Laboratory or Television Studio.

Avila College (Private)

Department of Business Administration and Economics
11901 Wornall Road
Kansas City, Missouri 64145
Telephone: (816) 942-8400

Louis J. James, Chair
Sr. Marie Joan Harris, Vice President

CURRICULUM AND INSTRUCTION
Courses or Concentrations
Available: Communication; Business Communication; *Full-Time Faculty*: 10; *Part-Time Faculty*: 25.

Central Missouri State University (Public)

Department of Communication
Warrensburg, Missouri 64093
Telephone: (816) 429-4111

Dan B. Curtis, Chair
Robert Schwartz, Administrator

CURRICULUM AND INSTRUCTION
Courses or Concentrations
Available: Advertising; Communication; Film or Cinema; Journalism or Mass Communication; Public Relations; Radio, Television, Broadcasting, or Telecommunications; Speech; Organizational Communication; *Program Coordinators*: John Smead (Broadcasting, Film); Kuldip Rampal (Journalism); Steve Thomsen (Public Relations); Deems Brooks (Speech, Organizational Communication); *Undergraduate Objectives or Program Emphases*: BS: Journalism; Public Relations; Broadcasting and Film; Organizational Communication; Speech Communication. BA: Mass Communication; Speech Communication; *Graduate Objectives or Program Emphases*: MA: Communication options and Mass Communication; Speech Communication; *Full-Time Faculty*: 21; *Part-Time Faculty*: 18.

FACILITIES AND SERVICES
Practical experiences available through: Advertising Agency; Audio Recording Laboratory; Community Antenna (Cable) Television Origination; Desktop Publishing Facility; Photographic Darkrooms; Video Editing; Electronic Field Production (Video); Television Broadcast Station (Institutional); Film or Cinema Laboratory; FM Radio Station (Institutional); Institutional Magazine; Institutional Newspaper; Public Relations Agency; Video Production Laboratory or Television Studio.

Culver-Stockton College (Private)

Department of Journalism
1 College Hill
Canton, Missouri 63435
Telephone: (314) 288-5221

Cathy Johnson, Head
Ed Sawyer, Administrator

CURRICULUM AND INSTRUCTION
Courses or Concentrations
Available: Advertising; Journalism or Mass
Communication; Public Relations; Radio,
Television, Broadcasting, or
Telecommunications; *Undergraduate*
Objectives or Program Emphases: To prepare
students for print journalism; *Bachelor's*
Degree Majors: 15; *Full-Time Faculty*: 1;
Part-Time Faculty: 1.

FACILITIES AND SERVICES
Practical experiences available
through: Desktop Publishing Facility;
Photographic Darkrooms; Institutional
Newspaper.

DeVry Institute of Technology (Private)

Program of Speech Communication
11224 Holmes Road
Kansas City, Missouri 64131
Telephone: (816) 941-0430

Joel D. Patterson, Coordinator
Simon Maxwell, Administrator

CURRICULUM AND INSTRUCTION
Courses or Concentrations Available: Speech;
Undergraduate Objectives or Program
Emphases: A basic public speaking course;
Full-Time Faculty: 2.

FACILITIES AND SERVICES
Practical experiences available
through: Campus Newspaper (Published
Independently); Desktop Publishing Facility;
Photographic Darkrooms; Video Editing;
Electronic Field Production (Video).

Drury College

Communication Department
900 North Benton Avenue
Springfield, Missouri 65802

Joe McAdoo, Administrator

Evangel College (Private)

Department of Communications
1111 North Glenstone
Springfield, Missouri 65807
Telephone: (417) 865-2811

Shirley A. Shedd, Chair
Glenn Bernet, Academic Dean

CURRICULUM AND INSTRUCTION
Courses or Concentrations
Available: Advertising; Communication;
Journalism or Mass Communication; Public
Relations; Radio, Television, Broadcasting,
or Telecommunications; Speech;
Undergraduate Objectives or Program
Emphases: To provide students with a
well-rounded liberal arts education while
helping them to gain knowledge and skills in
the areas of journalism, broadcasting and
speech that will enable them to have
profitable careers; *Associate's Degree*
Majors: 5; *Bachelor's Degree Majors*: 100;
Full-Time Faculty: 4; *Part-Time Faculty*: 5.

FACILITIES AND SERVICES
Practical experiences available
through: Advertising Agency; Associated
Press Wire Service Feed; Community
Antenna (Cable) Television Origination;
Carrier Current Audio Distribution System;
Local Commercial Newspaper; Local
Commercial Television Station; Desktop
Publishing Facility; Photographic
Darkrooms; Video Editing; Electronic Field
Production (Video); Institutional
Newspaper; Video Production Laboratory or
Television Studio.

Jefferson College (Public)

Program of Television
North Highway 21
P. O. Box 1000
Hillsboro, Missouri 63050
Telephone: (314) 789-3951

Robert G. Harrison, General Manager
Dan Steadman, Dean, Arts and Sciences

CURRICULUM AND INSTRUCTION
Courses or Concentrations Available: Radio, Television, Broadcasting, or Telecommunications; Interpersonal Communication; *Undergraduate Objectives or Program Emphases*: Beginning courses in television production; preparation for transfer to four year institution; *Associate's Degree Majors*: 14; *Full-Time Faculty*: 2.

FACILITIES AND SERVICES
Practical experiences available through: Audio Recording Laboratory; Community Antenna (Cable) Television Origination; Campus Newspaper (Published Independently); Local Commercial Newspaper; Local Commercial Television Station; Desktop Publishing Facility; Photographic Darkrooms; Video Editing; Electronic Field Production (Video); Television Broadcast Station (Institutional); Video News and Data Processing; Video Production Laboratory or Television Studio.

Lincoln University

Department of Communications
Jefferson City, Missouri 65101

Thomas Pawley, Administrator

Lindenwood College (Private)

Department of Communications
1st Capitol and Kings Highway
Saint Charles, Missouri 63301
Telephone: (314) 949-2000

James A. Wilson, Chair

CURRICULUM AND INSTRUCTION
Courses or Concentrations Available: Communication; Journalism or Mass Communication; Public Relations; Radio, Television, Broadcasting, or Telecommunications; Speech; *Undergraduate*

Objectives or Program Emphases: Preparation for professional careers in the fields of communication and preparation for advanced study in communications law; *Graduate Objectives or Program Emphases*: Focused study in corporate communication; *Bachelor's Degree Majors*: 120; *Master's Degree Majors*: 20; *Full-Time Faculty*: 6; *Part-Time Faculty*: 5; *Full-Time Professional (non-clerical) Staff Members*: 3.

FACILITIES AND SERVICES
Practical experiences available through: Advertising Agency; Associated Press Wire Service Feed; Audio Recording Laboratory; Community Antenna (Cable) Television Origination; Carrier Current Audio Distribution System; Campus Newspaper (Published Independently); Local Commercial Newspaper; Desktop Publishing Facility; Photographic Darkrooms; Video Editing; Electronic Field Production (Video); FM Radio Station (Institutional); Institutional Magazine; Institutional Newspaper; Public Relations Agency; Video News and Data Processing; Video Production Laboratory or Television Studio.

Maryville College - Saint Louis (Private)

Department of Communications
13550 Conway Road
Saint Louis, Missouri 63141
Telephone: (314) 576-9300

Nancy Wahonick, Chair
Jerry Sherry, Administrator

CURRICULUM AND INSTRUCTION
Courses or Concentrations Available: Advertising; Communication; Film or Cinema; Journalism or Mass Communication; Public Relations; Radio, Television, Broadcasting, or Telecommunications; *Undergraduate Objectives or Program Emphases*: Business Communications; Print Journalism; Broadcasting; *Bachelor's Degree Majors*: 145; *Full-Time Faculty*: 3; *Part-Time Faculty*: 10.

FACILITIES AND SERVICES
Practical experiences available through: Advertising Agency; Local Commercial Newspaper; Local Commercial Television Station; Desktop Publishing Facility; Photographic Darkrooms; Video

Editing; FM Radio Station (Institutional);
Institutional Newspaper; Public Relations
Agency.

Missouri Southern State College (Public)

Department of Communications
3950 Newman Road
Joplin, Missouri 64801
Telephone: (417) 625-9300

Richard W. Massa, Head
Ray Malzahn, Dean, School of Arts and Science

CURRICULUM AND INSTRUCTION
Courses or Concentrations
Available: Communication; Journalism or
Mass Communication; Public Relations;
Radio, Television, Broadcasting, or
Telecommunications; Speech; Foreign
Languages; *Undergraduate Objectives or
Program Emphases*: A program based on
general communication skills with a liberal
arts background allowing a student a degree
of specialization in Mass Communication or
Speech Communication; *Bachelor's Degree
Majors*: 198; *Full-Time Faculty*: 13;
Part-Time Faculty: 7; *Full-Time Professional
(non-clerical) Staff Members*: 4.

FACILITIES AND SERVICES
Practical experiences available through: Audio
Recording Laboratory; Community Antenna
(Cable) Television Origination; Local
Commercial Newspaper; Local Commercial
Television Station; Desktop Publishing
Facility; Photographic Darkrooms; Video
Editing; Electronic Field Production
(Video); Television Broadcast Station
(Institutional); FM Radio Station
(Institutional); Institutional Newspaper;
Video Production Laboratory or Television
Studio.

Missouri Western State College (Public)

**Department of English, Foreign Languages
and Journalism**
4525 Downs Drive
St. Joseph, Missouri 64507
Telephone: (816) 271-4310

M. Jane Frick, Chair
**William H. Nunez, Dean, Liberal Arts and
Sciences**

CURRICULUM AND INSTRUCTION
Courses or Concentrations
Available: Communication; Film or Cinema;
Journalism or Mass Communication; Public
Relations; Technical Communication;
Full-Time Faculty: 16; *Part-Time
Faculty*: 10.

FACILITIES AND SERVICES
Practical experiences available through: Local
Commercial Newspaper; Local Commercial
Television Station; Desktop Publishing
Facility; Photographic Darkrooms; Video
Editing; Institutional Magazine;
Institutional Newspaper; Public Relations
Agency.

Missouri Western State College (Public)

**Department of Communication Studies,
Theatre and Humanities**
4525 Downs Drive
St. Joseph, Missouri 64507
Telephone: (816) 271-4385

C. Irwin Parmenter, Chair
**William J. Nunez, Dean, Liberal Arts and
Science**

CURRICULUM AND INSTRUCTION
Courses or Concentrations
Available: Communication; Public Relations;
Speech; *Bachelor's Degree Majors*: 45;
Full-Time Faculty: 5; *Part-Time Faculty*: 1.

FACILITIES AND SERVICES
*Practical experiences available
through*: Closed Circuit Television Facility;
Local Commercial Newspaper; Local
Commercial Television Station; Desktop
Publishing Facility; Photographic
Darkrooms; Institutional Newspaper; Video
Production Laboratory or Television Studio.

Northeast Missouri State University (Public)

Division of Languages and Literature
Kirksville, Missouri 63501
Telephone: (816) 785-4481

Edwin C. Carpenter, Head
Jack Magruder, Academic Dean

CURRICULUM AND INSTRUCTION
Courses or Concentrations
Available: Advertising; Communication;
Journalism or Mass Communication; Public
Relations; Radio, Television, Broadcasting,
or Telecommunications; Speech; English and
nine foreign languages; *Undergraduate
Objectives or Program Emphases*: Liberal
Arts and Science base with BA degrees in
Speech Communication, Journalism, English,
French, German, Spanish and three year
programs in Greek, Latin, Hebrew, Japanese,
Chinese, Russian; *Graduate Objectives or
Program Emphases*: MA in English;
Bachelor's Degree Majors: 400; *Full-Time
Faculty*: 68; *Part-Time Faculty*: 32;
*Full-Time Professional (non-clerical) Staff
Members*: 4.

FACILITIES AND SERVICES
*Practical experiences available
through*: Associated Press Wire Service Feed;
Carrier Current Audio Distribution System;
Campus Newspaper (Published
Independently); Local Commercial
Newspaper; Local Commercial Television
Station; Desktop Publishing Facility;
Photographic Darkrooms; Video Editing;
Institutional Magazine; Institutional
Newspaper; Video News and Data
Processing; Video Production Laboratory or
Television Studio.

Northwest Missouri State University (Public)

College of Arts and Humanities
Wells Hall 235
Maryville, Missouri 64468
Telephone: (816) 562-1617

Fred C. Lamer, Chair
Robert Sunkel, Dean

CURRICULUM AND INSTRUCTION
Courses or Concentrations
Available: Communication; Journalism or
Mass Communication; Radio, Television,

Broadcasting, or Telecommunications;
Bachelor's Degree Majors: 295; *Full-Time
Faculty*: 8; *Full-Time Professional
(non-clerical) Staff Members*: 1. See one or
more additional entries below.

FACILITIES AND SERVICES
Practical experiences available through: Audio
Recording Laboratory; Community Antenna
(Cable) Television Origination; Campus
Newspaper (Published Independently);
Desktop Publishing Facility; Photographic
Darkrooms; Video Editing; Electronic Field
Production (Video); FM Radio Station
(Institutional); Institutional Magazine;
Institutional Newspaper.

Northwest Missouri State University (Public)

Department of Speech
Maryville, Missouri 64468
Telephone: (816) 562-1212

Kathie A. Leeper, Chair
Robert Sunkel, Dean

CURRICULUM AND INSTRUCTION
Courses or Concentrations Available: Public
Relations; Speech; *Undergraduate Objectives
or Program Emphases*: Public Relations;
Speech Communication; Organizational
Communication; Speech Education;
*Graduate Objectives or Program
Emphases*: Education; *Bachelor's Degree
Majors*: 100; *Full-Time Faculty*: 9.

FACILITIES AND SERVICES
Practical experiences available through: Local
Commercial Newspaper; Public Relations
Agency.

Park College

Department of Communication Arts
8700 River Park Drive
Parkville, Missouri 64152

David E. Crowell, Administrator

Rockhurst College (Private)

Program of Broadcast Journalism
5225 Troost Avenue
Kansas City, Missouri 64110
Telephone: (816) 926-0000

William J. Ryan, Director
Weslynn Martin, Chair

CURRICULUM AND INSTRUCTION
Courses or Concentrations
Available: Advertising; Communication; Film
or Cinema; Journalism or Mass
Communication; Radio, Television,
Broadcasting, or Telecommunications;
Speech; *Bachelor's Degree Majors*: 18;
Full-Time Faculty: 1; *Part-Time Faculty*: 3.

FACILITIES AND SERVICES
Practical experiences available through: Audio
Recording Laboratory; Community Antenna
(Cable) Television Origination; Carrier
Current Audio Distribution System; Campus
Newspaper (Published Independently);
Local Commercial Newspaper; Local
Commercial Television Station; Desktop
Publishing Facility; Photographic
Darkrooms; Video Editing; Electronic Field
Production (Video); Institutional Magazine;
Public Relations Agency; Video Production
Laboratory or Television Studio.

Rockhurst College (Private)

Department of Communication and Fine
Arts
5225 Troost Avenue
Kansas City, Missouri 64110
Telephone: (816) 926-4000

Weslynn S. Martin, Chair
Tom Trebon, Dean, College of Arts and
Sciences

CURRICULUM AND INSTRUCTION
Courses or Concentrations
Available: Advertising; Communication; Film
or Cinema; Journalism or Mass
Communication; Public Relations; Radio,
Television, Broadcasting, or
Telecommunications; Speech; Business
Communication; Theatre; Broadcast
Journalism; Arts Management; Fine
Arts: Art, Music; *Program*
Coordinators: William Ryan (Broadcasting,
Broadcast Journalism); Janet Sheeran
(Theatre, Arts Management); John Green

(Music); Will Valk (Art); *Bachelor's Degree*
Majors: 40; *Full-Time Faculty*: 6; *Part-Time*
Faculty: 7.

FACILITIES AND SERVICES
Practical experiences available
through: Advertising Agency; Audio
Recording Laboratory; Community Antenna
(Cable) Television Origination; Campus
Newspaper (Published Independently);
Local Commercial Newspaper; Local
Commercial Television Station; Desktop
Publishing Facility; Photographic
Darkrooms; Video Editing; Electronic Field
Production (Video); FM Radio Station
(Institutional); Institutional Newspaper;
Public Relations Agency; Video Production
Laboratory or Television Studio.

School of the Ozarks

Speech Communication and Theatre
Department
Point Lookout, Missouri 65726

C. Darrell Langley, Administrator

Southeast Missouri State University (Public)

Department of Mass Communication
One University Plaza
Cape Girardeau, Missouri 63701
Telephone: (314) 651-2241

R. Ferrell Ervin, Chair
Martin Jones, Dean, College of Liberal Arts

CURRICULUM AND INSTRUCTION
Courses or Concentrations
Available: Advertising; Journalism; Public
Relations; Radio, Television; Corporate
Video; Community Journalism; Journalism
Education; *Program Coordinators*: Jim Dufek
(Television, Corporate Video); Bruce Mims
(Radio); Gil Welsch (Advertising); Gordon
Holland (Journalism, Community
Journalism); *Degree Majors*: 450; *Full-Time*
Faculty: 9; *Part-Time Faculty*: 7; *Full-Time*
Professional (non-clerical) Staff Members: 3.

FACILITIES AND SERVICES
Practical experiences available
through: Advertising Agency; Audio
Recording Laboratory; Closed Circuit
Television Facility; Local Commercial

Newspaper; Local Commercial Television Station; Desktop Publishing Facility; Photographic Darkrooms; Video Editing; Electronic Field Production (Video); FM Radio Station (Institutional); Institutional Magazine; Institutional Newspaper; Public Relations Agency; Video News and Data Processing; Video Production Laboratory or Television Studio.

Southwest Baptist University (Private)

Department of Communication
Bolivar, Missouri 65613
Telephone: (417) 326-1697

Bob R. Derryberry, Chair
Darrel Strait, Dean, Arts and Sciences

CURRICULUM AND INSTRUCTION
Courses or Concentrations
Available: Communication; Public Relations; Radio, Television, Broadcasting, or Telecommunications; Speech; *Program Coordinator*: Eric Moore (Communication Technology); *Undergraduate Objectives or Program Emphases*: General oral communication; speech-theatre education; public relations; pre-professional programs such as speech science-pathology; *Bachelor's Degree Majors*: 20; *Other Degree Majors*: 5; *Full-Time Faculty*: 3; *Part-Time Faculty*: 1.

FACILITIES AND SERVICES
Practical experiences available through: Advertising Agency; Associated Press Wire Service Feed; Campus Newspaper (Published Independently); Local Commercial Newspaper; Institutional Newspaper; Public Relations Agency; United Press International Feed.

Southwest Missouri State University (Public)

Department of Communications
901 South National Avenue
Springfield, Missouri 65804-0095
Telephone: (417) 836-5218

John I. Sisco, Head
Bethany Oberst, Dean

CURRICULUM AND INSTRUCTION
Courses or Concentrations
Available: Communication; Film or Cinema; Public Relations; Radio, Television, Broadcasting, or Telecommunications; Speech; *Undergraduate Objectives or Program Emphases*: Communication management, electronic media, organizational communication; *Graduate Objectives or Program Emphases*: Communication; *Master's Degree Majors*: 45; *Bachelor's Degree Majors*: 900; *Full-Time Faculty*: 35; *Part-Time Faculty*: 21.

FACILITIES AND SERVICES
Practical experiences available through: Audio Recording Laboratory; Campus Newspaper (Published Independently); Local Commercial Television Station; Desktop Publishing Facility; Video Editing; Electronic Field Production (Video); FM Radio Station (Institutional); Public Relations Agency; Video Production Laboratory or Television Studio.

Southwest Missouri State University (Public)

Program of Journalism
901 S. National Avenue
Springfield, Missouri 65804
Telephone: (417) 836-5107

Thomas V. Dickson, Coordinator
Ron Lunsford, Head, English Department

CURRICULUM AND INSTRUCTION
Courses or Concentrations
Available: Journalism or Mass Communication; *Undergraduate Objectives or Program Emphases*: News-editorial, writing for public relations, photojournalism; *Full-Time Faculty*: 4; *Part-Time Faculty*: 12; *Full-Time Professional (non-clerical) Staff Members*: 1.

FACILITIES AND SERVICES
Practical experiences available through: Campus Newspaper (Published Independently); Local Commercial Newspaper; Desktop Publishing Facility; Video Editing; Public Relations Agency.

St. Louis Community College

Communication Division
11333 Big Bend Boulevard
St. Louis, Missouri 63122

Robert T. Dixon, Administrator

St. Louis Community College - Florissant Valley (Public)

Department of Communication
3400 Pershall Road
St. Louis, Missouri 63135
Telephone: (314) 595-4477

Donna M. Spaulding, Chair
Roger Schnell, Acting Associate Dean of
Communication and Arts

CURRICULUM AND INSTRUCTION
*Courses or Concentrations
Available*: Advertising; Communication; Film
or Cinema; Journalism or Mass
Communication; Public Relations; Radio,
Television, Broadcasting, or
Telecommunications; Speech; Deaf
Communication Studies; *Program
Coordinators*: Roger Carlson (Journalism);
John Balas (Broadcasting); *Undergraduate
Objectives or Program Emphases*: To provide
students with the skills and knowledge to
proceed to four year institutions; *Associate's
Degree Majors*: 322; *Full-Time Faculty*: 5;
Part-Time Faculty: 12; *Full-Time
Professional (non-clerical) Staff Members*: 2.

FACILITIES AND SERVICES
*Practical experiences available
through*: Associated Press Wire Service Feed;
Audio Recording Laboratory; Community
Antenna (Cable) Television Origination;
Desktop Publishing Facility; Photographic
Darkrooms; Video Editing; Electronic Field
Production (Video); FM Radio Station
(Institutional); Satellite Uplink Facility (Ku
Band Transmitter); Institutional Newspaper;
Video Production Laboratory or Television
Studio.

St. Louis Community College - Forest Park (Public)

Department of Communications
5600 Oakland Avenue
St. Louis, Missouri 63108
Telephone: (314) 644-9388

M. Katherine Dunlop, Chair
Alice Warren, Associate Dean of Humanities

CURRICULUM AND INSTRUCTION
*Courses or Concentrations
Available*: Advertising; Communication; Film
or Cinema; Journalism or Mass
Communication; Public Relations; Radio,
Television, Broadcasting, or
Telecommunications; Speech; Desktop
Publishing; *Program Coordinators*: Lynn
Wilbur (Broadcast); John Coleman
(Broadcast Engineering); Evann Richards
(Computer-Aided Publications);
*Undergraduate Objectives or Program
Emphases*: Prepare students for transfer to
four year schools; teach specific skills in
Broadcast Engineering and Computer Aided
Publishing (certificates of proficiency) for
students already working in field; *Associate's
Degree Majors*: 100; *Full-Time Faculty*: 2;
Part-Time Faculty: 8.

FACILITIES AND SERVICES
*Practical experiences available
through*: Advertising Agency; Audio
Recording Laboratory; Community Antenna
(Cable) Television Origination; Closed
Circuit Television Facility; Local
Commercial Newspaper; Local Commercial
Television Station; Desktop Publishing
Facility; Photographic Darkrooms; Video
Editing; Electronic Field Production
(Video); Film or Cinema Laboratory; ITFS
Distribution System; Institutional
Newspaper; Public Relations Agency;
Satellite Uplink Facility (Ku Band
Transmitter); Video News and Data
Processing; Video Production Laboratory or
Television Studio.

St. Louis University (Private)

Department of Communication
221 N. Grand Boulevard
St. Louis, Missouri 62025
Telephone: (314) 658-3191

Noreen M. Carrocci, Chair
James E. Bundschuh, Dean, College of Arts and Sciences

CURRICULUM AND INSTRUCTION
Courses or Concentrations
Available: Advertising; Communication; Journalism or Mass Communication; Public Relations; Speech; Radio courses; *Program Coordinators*: Lawrence J. Baricevic (Advertising); Avis E. Meyer (Journalism); *Undergraduate Objectives or Program Emphases*: All students receive background in basic communication theory, speaking, and writing. Beyond that, three areas of emphasis are provided: communication studies, journalism and mass communication, and promotion; *Graduate Objectives or Program Emphases*: Currently not accepting MA students; proposal to reopen program is pending; *Bachelor's Degree Majors*: 120; *Full-Time Faculty*: 8; *Part-Time Faculty*: 9.

FACILITIES AND SERVICES
Practical experiences available through: Advertising Agency; Audio Recording Laboratory; Carrier Current Audio Distribution System; Campus Newspaper (Published Independently); Local Commercial Newspaper; Local Commercial Television Station; Desktop Publishing Facility; Photographic Darkrooms; Institutional Magazine; Public Relations Agency.

State Fair Community College (Public)

Division of Arts and Sciences
3201 West 16th
Sedalia, Missouri 65301
Telephone: (816) 826-7100

Robert L. Solomon, Dean
Marvin Fielding, President

CURRICULUM AND INSTRUCTION
Courses or Concentrations
Available: Journalism or Mass Communication; Public Relations; Radio, Television, Broadcasting, or Telecommunications; Speech; *Undergraduate Objectives or Program Emphases*: Provide general education and provide first two years designed to transfer to four year schools; *Associate's Degree Majors*: 20; *Full-Time Faculty*: 30; *Part-Time Faculty*: 10.

FACILITIES AND SERVICES
Practical experiences available through: Audio Recording Laboratory; Campus Newspaper (Published Independently); Local Commercial Newspaper; Photographic Darkrooms; Video Editing; Institutional Magazine; Institutional Newspaper.

Stephens College (Private)

Department of Communications
1200 E. Broadway
Columbia, Missouri 65215
Telephone: (314) 442-2211

Ben Andrews, Chair
Mary Kitterman, Dean

CURRICULUM AND INSTRUCTION
Courses or Concentrations
Available: Journalism or Mass Communication; Public Relations; Radio, Television, Broadcasting, or Telecommunications; Speech; *Bachelor's Degree Majors*: 37; *Other Degree Majors*: 69; *Full-Time Faculty*: 3; *Part-Time Faculty*: 3; *Full-Time Professional (non-clerical) Staff Members*: 4.

FACILITIES AND SERVICES
Practical experiences available through: Associated Press Wire Service Feed; Audio Recording Laboratory; Closed Circuit Television Facility; Local Commercial Television Station; Desktop Publishing Facility; Photographic Darkrooms; Video Editing; Electronic Field Production (Video); FM Radio Station (Institutional); Institutional Newspaper; Public Relations Agency; Video Production Laboratory or Television Studio.

University of Missouri - Columbia (Public)

Department of Communication
115 Switzler Hall
Columbia, Missouri 65211
Telephone: (314) 882-4431

James W. Gibson, Chair
Larry D. Clark, Dean, Arts and Sciences

CURRICULUM AND INSTRUCTION
Courses or Concentrations
Available: Communication; Radio, Television, Broadcasting, or Telecommunications; Speech; *Undergraduate Objectives or Program Emphases*: Radio and television programming and production; media studies; interpersonal, communication theory and rhetorical studies; *Graduate Objectives or Program Emphases*: Radio and television programming and production; media studies; interpersonal, communication theory and rhetorical studies; *Bachelor's Degree Majors*: 168; *Master's Degree Majors*: 24; *Doctoral Degree Majors Currently in Residence*: 14; *Additional Doctoral Degree Majors*: 3; *Full-Time Faculty*: 8; *Part-Time Faculty*: 24; *Full-Time Professional (non-clerical) Staff Members*: 2.

FACILITIES AND SERVICES
Practical experiences available through: Desktop Publishing Facility; FM Radio Station (Institutional).

University of Missouri - Columbia (Public)

School of Journalism
P. O. Box 838
Columbia, Missouri 65205
Telephone: (314) 882-4821

R. Mills, Dean
Lois DeFleur, Provost

CURRICULUM AND INSTRUCTION
Courses or Concentrations
Available: Advertising; Journalism; Public Relations; Radio, Television; Photojournalism; *Undergraduate Objectives or Program Emphases*: To prepare students for professional work in journalism or advertising; *Graduate Objectives or Program Emphases*: The MA also provides a professional education; the Ph.D. is the traditional scholarly degree; *Bachelor's*

Degree Majors: 600; *Master's Degree Majors*: 180; *Doctoral Degree Majors Currently in Residence*: 12; *Additional Doctoral Degree Majors*: 13; *Full-Time Faculty*: 67; *Part-Time Faculty*: 12; *Full-Time Professional (non-clerical) Staff Members*: 10.

FACILITIES AND SERVICES
Practical experiences available through: Advertising Agency; Associated Press Wire Service Feed; Audio Recording Laboratory; Campus Newspaper (Published Independently); Local Commercial Newspaper; Local Commercial Television Station; Desktop Publishing Facility; Photographic Darkrooms; Video Editing; Electronic Field Production (Video); Television Broadcast Station (Institutional); Film and Cinema Laboratory; FM Radio Station (Institutional); Institutional Magazine; Institutional Newspaper; New York Times Service Feed; Public Relations Agency; Satellite Uplink Facility; Video News and Data Processing; Video Production Laboratory or Television Studio.

University of Missouri - Columbia (Public)

Department of Broadcast News
P.O. Box 838
Columbia, Missouri 65205
Telephone: (314) 882-7377

Rod G. Gelatt, Chair
Dean Mills, Dean

CURRICULUM AND INSTRUCTION
Courses or Concentrations
Available: Journalism or Mass Communication; Radio, Television, Broadcasting, or Telecommunications; Videotape Shooting, Editing, News Producing; *Undergraduate Objectives or Program Emphases*: To help prepare better educated people for a complex society and to prepare them for entry level positions in radio or television journalism; *Graduate Objectives or Program Emphases*: The professional aspects are parallel for graduate and undergraduate students. Graduate students, in addition, may select a professional project or a more traditional thesis; *Bachelor's Degree Majors*: 135; *Master's Degree Majors*: 30; *Full-Time Faculty*: 12; *Part-Time Faculty*: 20;

Full-Time Professional (non-clerical) Staff Members: 6.

FACILITIES AND SERVICES
Practical experiences available through: Associated Press Wire Service Feed; Audio Recording Laboratory; Campus Newspaper (Published Independently); Local Commercial Newspaper; Local Commercial Television Station; FM Radio Station (Institutional); Institutional Magazine; New York Times Service Feed.

University of Missouri - Columbia (Public)

Department of Extension and Agricultural Information
1-98 Agriculture Building
Columbia, Missouri 65211
Telephone: (314) 882-6637

Robert L. Thomas, Director
Roger Mitchell and Don Swoboda, Administrators

CURRICULUM AND INSTRUCTION
Courses or Concentrations Available: Communication; Journalism or Mass Communication; Radio, Television, Broadcasting, or Telecommunications; *Undergraduate Objectives or Program Emphases*: Prepare students for careers in agricultural journalism. This includes sequences in photojournalism, newspapers, magazines, and broadcasting; *Bachelor's Degree Majors*: 35; *Full-Time Faculty*: 18; *Part-Time Faculty*: 1; *Full-Time Professional (non-clerical) Staff Members*: 5.

FACILITIES AND SERVICES
Practical experiences available through: Associated Press Wire Service Feed; Audio Recording Laboratory; Campus Newspaper (Published Independently); Local Commercial Newspaper; Local Commercial Television Station; Desktop Publishing Facility; Photographic Darkrooms; Television Broadcast Station (Institutional); FM Radio Station (Institutional); Institutional Newspaper; Satellite Uplink Facility (Ku Band Transmitter); United Press International Feed; Video News and Data Processing.

University of Missouri - Rolla (Public)

Section of Speech and Media Studies
211 H-SS
Rolla, Missouri 65401
Telephone: (314) 341-4803

W. Lance Haynes, Assistant Professor
Wayne C. Cognell, Chair, Department of Philosophy and Liberal Art

CURRICULUM AND INSTRUCTION
Courses or Concentrations Available: Communication; Film or Cinema; Radio, Television, Broadcasting, or Telecommunications; Speech; Technical Writing; Photography; *Program Coordinators*: James Bogan (Film Program); *Undergraduate Objectives or Program Emphases*: A minor in speech and media studies with an objective to prepare engineering students for careers in management; *Full-Time Faculty*: 2; *Part-Time Faculty*: 2.

FACILITIES AND SERVICES
Practical experiences available through: Associated Press Wire Service Feed; Audio Recording Laboratory; Campus Newspaper (Published Independently); Desktop Publishing Facility; Photographic Darkrooms; Video Editing; FM Radio Station (Institutional); Satellite Uplink Facility (Ku Band Transmitter);

University of Missouri - Rolla (Public)

Department of English
225 Humanities-Social Sciences
Rolla, Missouri 65401
Telephone: (314) 341-4687

James N. Wise, Chair
Marvin W. Barker, Dean, College of Arts and Sciences

CURRICULUM AND INSTRUCTION
Courses or Concentrations Available: Composition courses, Technical Writing; *Undergraduate Objectives or Program Emphases*: BA in English with three minor programs: writing, or literature, or interdisciplinary; also, a cooperative secondary teaching certificate in English with UM-Columbia and general education courses in writing and humanities for

engineering and science majors; *Bachelor's Degree Majors*: 20; *Full-Time Faculty*: 13; *Part-Time Faculty*: 2.

FACILITIES AND SERVICES
Practical experiences available through: Associated Press Wire Service Feed; Audio Recording Laboratory; Campus Newspaper (Published Independently); Local Commercial Newspaper; Desktop Publishing Facility; FM Radio Station (Institutional); Public Relations Agency; Satellite Uplink Facility (Ku Band Transmitter);

University of Missouri - St. Louis (Public)

Department of Communication
8001 Natural Bridge
St. Louis, Missouri 63121
Telephone: (314) 553-5485

Elizabeth J. Kizer, Chair
E. Terrence Jones, Administrator

CURRICULUM AND INSTRUCTION
Courses or Concentrations Available: Advertising; Communication; Film or Cinema; Information Science; Journalism or Mass Communication; Public Relations; Radio, Television, Broadcasting, or Telecommunications; Speech; Oral interpretation; Theatre; *Undergraduate Objectives or Program Emphases*: Prepare students for careers and/or graduate school. Emphasis on: Mass Communication (Radio, Television, Film); Communication Theory and Rhetoric); Applied Communication, Public Relations, and general; *Bachelor's Degree Majors*: 150; *Full-Time Faculty*: 12; *Part-Time Faculty*: 6. See one or more additional entries below.

FACILITIES AND SERVICES
Practical experiences available through: Advertising Agency; Associated Press Wire Service Feed; Audio Recording Laboratory; Community Antenna (Cable) Television Origination; Closed Circuit Television Facility; Campus Newspaper (Published Independently); Local Commercial Newspaper; Local Commercial Television Station; Video Editing; Electronic Field Production (Video); FM Radio Station (Institutional); ITFS Distribution System; Public Relations

Agency; Video Production Laboratory or Television Studio.

University of Missouri - St. Louis (Public)

Program of Mass Communication
570 Lucas Hall
St. Louis, Missouri 63121
Telephone: (314) 553-5496

Michael D. Murray, Director
E. J. Kizer, Chair

CURRICULUM AND INSTRUCTION
Courses or Concentrations Available: Advertising; Film or Cinema; Journalism or Mass Communication; Radio, Television, Broadcasting, or Telecommunications; *Undergraduate Objectives or Program Emphases*: Mass communication. Minor in public affairs reporting; *Bachelor's Degree Majors*: 150; *Full-Time Faculty*: 6; *Part-Time Faculty*: 3; *Full-Time Professional (non-clerical) Staff Members*: 3.

FACILITIES AND SERVICES
Practical experiences available through: Associated Press Wire Service Feed; Community Antenna (Cable) Television Origination; Local Commercial Television Station; FM Radio Station (Institutional).

Webster University (Private)

Department of Media Communications
470 East Lockwood Boulevard
St. Louis, Missouri 63119
Telephone: (314) 968-6925

Arthur M. Silverblatt, Chair
James Staley, Associate Dean, Liberal Arts

CURRICULUM AND INSTRUCTION
Courses or Concentrations Available: Advertising; Film or Cinema; Journalism or Mass Communication; Public Relations; Radio, Television, Broadcasting, or Telecommunications; Photography; Audio Production; Broadcast TV; *Undergraduate Objectives or Program Emphases*: A comprehensive program providing a balance of theory/history courses in conjunction with production classes; *Graduate Objectives or Program Emphases*: A program focusing on

effective management of media systems, including corporate communications, advertising, and public relations; *Bachelor's Degree Majors*: 115; *Master's Degree Majors*: 110; *Other Degree Majors*: 175; *Full-Time Faculty*: 8; *Part-Time Faculty*: 40; *Full-Time Professional (non-clerical) Staff Members*: 12.

FACILITIES AND SERVICES
Practical experiences available through: Advertising Agency; Audio Recording Laboratory; Community Antenna (Cable) Television Origination; Carrier Current Audio Distribution System; Campus Newspaper (Published Independently); Local Commercial Newspaper; Local Commercial Television Station; Desktop Publishing Facility; Photographic Darkrooms; Video Editing; Electronic Field Production (Video); Film or Cinema Laboratory; Institutional Newspaper; Public Relations Agency; Satellite Uplink Facility (Ku Band Transmitter) (C Band Transmitter).

Webster University (Private)

Department of Journalism
470 E. Lockwood
St. Louis, Missouri 63119
Telephone: (314) 968-6975

Don H. Corrigan, Associate Professor
Arthur Silverblatt, Administrator

CURRICULUM AND INSTRUCTION
Courses or Concentrations Available: Film or Cinema; Journalism or Mass Communication; Public Relations; Radio, Television, Broadcasting, or Telecommunications; Photojournalism; *Program Coordinators*: Michael Burks (Film); Kathy Corley (Video); Debby Carpenter (Public Relations); Barry Hufkee (Audio, Radio); Susan Hacker (Photojournalism); *Bachelor's Degree Majors*: 200; *Master's Degree Majors*: 80; *Full-Time Faculty*: 8; *Part-Time Faculty*: 30; *Full-Time Professional (non-clerical) Staff Members*: 3.

FACILITIES AND SERVICES
Practical experiences available through: Audio Recording Laboratory; Community Antenna (Cable) Television Origination; Carrier Current Audio Distribution System; Local Commercial Newspaper; Desktop Publishing Facility; Photographic Darkrooms; Video

Editing; Electronic Field Production (Video); Institutional Newspaper; Public Relations Agency; Satellite Uplink Facility (Ku Band Transmitter) (C Band Transmitter); Video News and Data Processing.

Westminster College (Private)

Department of Speech
501 Westminster Avenue
Fulton, Missouri 65251-1299
Telephone: (314) 642-3361

Tammy M. Ostrander, Chair
Richard Mattingly, Dean

CURRICULUM AND INSTRUCTION
Courses or Concentrations Available: Communication; Speech; *Undergraduate Objectives or Program Emphases*: To provide a broad base of both theory and practice in speech communication; *Bachelor's Degree Majors*: 1; *BFA Degree Majors*: 6; *Full-Time Faculty*: 1.

FACILITIES AND SERVICES
Practical experiences available through: Campus Newspaper (Published Independently); Local Commercial Newspaper; Desktop Publishing Facility; Photographic Darkrooms; Institutional Magazine.

William Jewel College (Private)

Program of KWJC Radio/William Jewell Broadcasting
Liberty, Missouri 64068
Telephone: (816) 781-7700

Philip A. Thompsen, General Manager
Tom Willett, Chair

CURRICULUM AND INSTRUCTION
Courses or Concentrations Available: Communication; Journalism or Mass Communication; Public Relations; Radio, Television, Broadcasting, or Telecommunications; Speech; *Undergraduate Objectives or Program Emphases*: Broad-based liberal arts education; *Bachelor's Degree Majors*: 100; *Full-Time Faculty*: 7; *Part-Time Faculty*: 2; *Full-Time Professional (non-clerical) Staff Members*: 1.

FACILITIES AND SERVICES

Practical experiences available through: Advertising Agency; Associated Press Wire Service Feed; Audio Recording Laboratory; Community Antenna (Cable) Television Origination; Campus Newspaper (Published Independently); Local Commercial Television Station; Desktop Publishing Facility; Photographic Darkrooms; Video Editing; Electronic Field Production (Video); FM Radio Station (Institutional); Institutional Newspaper; Public Relations Agency; United Press International Feed; Video News and Data Processing.

William Woods College (Private)

Department of Performing Arts/Communication
200 West 12th
Fulton, Missouri 65251
Telephone: (314) 642-2251

Christian O. West, Chair
George Tuit, Coordinator, Fine Arts

CURRICULUM AND INSTRUCTION

Courses or Concentrations Available: Advertising; Radio, Television, Broadcasting, or Telecommunications; Speech; *BFA Degree Majors*: 3; *Full-Time Faculty*: 4; *Part-Time Faculty*: 2.

FACILITIES AND SERVICES

Practical experiences available through: Audio Recording Laboratory; Closed Circuit Television Facility; Campus Newspaper (Published Independently); Local Commercial Television Station; Desktop Publishing Facility; Photographic Darkrooms; Electronic Field Production (Video).

Carroll College (Private)

Department of Communication Studies
North Benton Avenue
Helena, Montana 59625
Telephone: (406) 442-3450

Harold A. Smith, Chair
Jeff Baker, Academic Vice President

CURRICULUM AND INSTRUCTION
Courses or Concentrations
Available: Communication; Public Relations; Speech; *Undergraduate Objectives or Program Emphases*: To create a better understanding of the many aspects of the communicational scene, to include knowledge of self, culture, and the psychological aspects of the interpersonal encounter in business, in the family, and in education; *Bachelor's Degree Majors*: 21; *Full-Time Faculty*: 4; *Part-Time Faculty*: 2.

FACILITIES AND SERVICES
Practical experiences available through: Advertising Agency; Campus Newspaper (Published Independently); Local Commercial Newspaper; Local Commercial Television Station; Photographic Darkrooms; Public Relations Agency.

Eastern Montana College (Public)

Department of Communication Arts
1500 North 30th Street
Billings, Montana 59101
Telephone: (406) 657-2178

Stephen L. Coffman, Chair

CURRICULUM AND INSTRUCTION
Courses or Concentrations
Available: Communication; Journalism or Mass Communication; *Undergraduate Objectives or Program Emphases*: Organizational communication and mass communication; *Bachelor's Degree Majors*: 100; *Full-Time Faculty*: 6; *Part-Time Faculty*: 6.

FACILITIES AND SERVICES
Practical experiences available through: Advertising Agency; Community Antenna (Cable) Television Origination; Campus Newspaper (Published Independently); Local Commercial Newspaper; Local Commercial Television Station; Desktop Publishing Facility; Photographic Darkrooms; FM Radio Station (Institutional); Public Relations Agency.

Miles Community College (Public)

Academic Division
2715 Dickinson Street
Miles City, Montana 59301
Telephone: (406) 232-3031

Larry Torstenbo, Chair
George Bell, Dean of Instruction

CURRICULUM AND INSTRUCTION
Courses or Concentrations
Available: Advertising; Communication; Film or Cinema; Speech; *Program Coordinators*: James Joyce (Advertising); *Undergraduate Objectives or Program Emphases*: Basic course work that will transfer to other four year colleges in region; *Associate's Degree Majors*: 168; *Full-Time Faculty*: 7; *Part-Time Faculty*: 5.

FACILITIES AND SERVICES
Practical experiences available through: Closed Circuit Television Facility; Local Commercial Newspaper; Desktop Publishing Facility; Photographic Darkrooms; FM Radio Station (Institutional).

Montana State University (Public)

Department of Media and Theatre Arts
Bozeman, Montana 59717-0001
Telephone: (406) 994-6224

Paul Monaco, Head
Clifford Shipp, Dean

CURRICULUM AND INSTRUCTION
Courses or Concentrations Available: Film or
Cinema; Video; Television, Photography;
*Undergraduate Objectives or Program
Emphases*: Preparation of students to take
complete artistic and technical control of all
phases of production (full, pre-professional
education in four years); *Bachelor's Degree
Majors*: 150; *Full-Time Faculty*: 13;
Part-Time Faculty: 4; *Full-Time Professional
(non-clerical) Staff Members*: 10.

FACILITIES AND SERVICES
Practical experiences available through: AM
Radio Station (Institutional); Campus
Newspaper (Published Independently);
Local Commercial Newspaper; Local
Commercial Television Station; Television
Broadcast Station (Institutional); Film or
Cinema Laboratory; Video Production
Laboratory or Television Studio.

University of Montana

School of Journalism
PAR 182
Missoula, Montana 59812

Joseph Durso, Jr., Adminstrator

University of Montana (Public)

Department of Interpersonal
Communication
Missoula, Montana 59812
Telephone: (406) 243-4331

William W. Wilmot, Chair

CURRICULUM AND INSTRUCTION
*Courses or Concentrations
Available*: Communication; Speech;
*Undergraduate Objectives or Program
Emphases*: Interpersonal and Organizational
Communication; *Graduate Objectives or
Program Emphases*: Interpersonal and
Organizational Communication; *Bachelor's
Degree Majors*: 175; *Master's Degree
Majors*: 18; *Full-Time Faculty*: 5; *Part-Time
Faculty*: 1; *Full-Time Professional
(non-clerical) Staff Members*: 1.

FACILITIES AND SERVICES
*Practical experiences available
through*: Institutional Newspaper.

Central Community College - Hastings

Business Occupations
P. O. Box 1024
Hastings, Nebraska 68901

Josiah Woodward, Administrator

College of St. Mary (Private)

Department of Creative Arts and
Communication
1901 South 72nd Street
Omaha, Nebraska 68124
Telephone: (402) 399-2400

Evelyn M. Whitehill, Director
Mike Gendler, Division Chair

CURRICULUM AND INSTRUCTION
*Courses or Concentrations
Available*: Communication; *Undergraduate
Objectives or Program Emphases*: Overview of
communication field; *Bachelor's Degree
Majors*: 8; *Full-Time Faculty*: 1; *Part-Time
Faculty*: 2.

FACILITIES AND SERVICES
*Practical experiences available
through*: Advertising Agency; Campus
Newspaper (Published Independently);
Local Commercial Newspaper; Local
Commercial Television Station; Desktop
Publishing Facility; Photographic
Darkrooms; Video Editing.

Creighton University (Private)

Department of Journalism and Mass
Communication
California at 24th Street
Omaha, Nebraska 68178-0119
Telephone: (402) 280-2825

David A. Haberman, Chair
Michael Proterra, Dean

CURRICULUM AND INSTRUCTION
Courses or Concentrations

Available: Advertising; Journalism or Mass
Communication; Public Relations; Radio,
Television, Broadcasting, or
Telecommunications; *Undergraduate
Objectives or Program Emphases*: Preparation
of students for professional careers in four
sequence areas; *Bachelor's Degree Majors*: 62;
Full-Time Faculty: 4; *Part-Time Faculty*: 7;
*Full-Time Professional (non-clerical) Staff
Members*: 1.

FACILITIES AND SERVICES
*Practical experiences available
through*: Advertising Agency; Audio
Recording Laboratory; Community Antenna
(Cable) Television Origination; Closed
Circuit Television Facility; Local
Commercial Newspaper; Local Commercial
Television Station; Desktop Publishing
Facility; Photographic Darkrooms; Video
Editing; Electronic Field Production
(Video); Institutional Magazine;
Institutional Newspaper; Public Relations
Agency; Satellite Uplink Facility (C Band
Transmitter); Video Production Laboratory
or Television Studio.

Creighton University (Private)

Program of Applied Communication
2500 California Street
Omaha, Nebraska 68178
Telephone: (402) 280-2822

John Hollwitz, Major Advisor
Michael Sundermeier, Administrator

CURRICULUM AND INSTRUCTION
*Courses or Concentrations
Available*: Communication; Film or Cinema;
Speech; Organizational Communication;
*Undergraduate Objectives or Program
Emphases*: Organizational communication;
general applied communication; *Bachelor's
Degree Majors*: 50; *Full-Time Faculty*: 6;
Part-Time Faculty: 2; *Full-Time Professional
(non-clerical) Staff Members*: 1.

FACILITIES AND SERVICES
*Practical experiences available
through*: Advertising Agency; Audio
Recording Laboratory; Community Antenna

(Cable) Television Origination; Carrier Current Audio Distribution System; Closed Circuit Television Facility; Local Commercial Newspaper; Local Commercial Television Station; Desktop Publishing Facility; Photographic Darkrooms; Video Editing; Electronic Field Production (Video); ITFS Distribution System; Institutional Magazine; Institutional Newspaper; Video Production Laboratory or Television Studio.

Hastings College

Department of English/Journalism
Box 269
Hastings, Nebraska 68901

Sara Jane Gardner, Administrator

Kearney State College (Public)

Department of Speech Communication and Theatre Arts
905 West 24th
Kearney, Nebraska 68849
Telephone: (308) 236-8406

Maurine C. Eckloff, Chair
Betty Becker-Theye, Dean, School of Fine Arts and Humanities

CURRICULUM AND INSTRUCTION
Courses or Concentrations Available: Communication; Information Science; Public Relations; Speech; *Undergraduate Objectives or Program Emphases*: Organizational Communication; Speech Communication; Teacher Education; Theatre; *Graduate Objectives or Program Emphases*: Speech Communication and Theatre; *Bachelor's Degree Majors*: 90; *BFA Degree Majors*: 30; *Master's Degree Majors*: 40; *Full-Time Faculty*: 11; *Part-Time Faculty*: 15; *Full-Time Professional (non-clerical) Staff Members*: 1.

Kearney State College (Public)

Department of Journalism and Mass Communication
Mitchell Center
Kearney, Nebraska 68849
Telephone: (308) 234-8249

C. Thomas Draper, Chair
Betty Becker-Theye, Dean

CURRICULUM AND INSTRUCTION
Courses or Concentrations Available: Advertising; Journalism or Mass Communication; Public Relations; Radio, Television, Broadcasting, or Telecommunications; *Bachelor's Degree Majors*: 300; *Full-Time Faculty*: 9; *Part-Time Faculty*: 1.

FACILITIES AND SERVICES
Practical experiences available through: Associated Press Wire Service Feed; Audio Recording Laboratory; Community Antenna (Cable) Television Origination; Closed Circuit Television Facility; Local Commercial Newspaper; Local Commercial Television Station; Desktop Publishing Facility; Photographic Darkrooms; Video Editing; Electronic Field Production (Video); FM Radio Station (Institutional); Institutional Newspaper; Video News and Data Processing; Video Production Laboratory or Television Studio.

McCook Community College

Department of Humanities
1205 East Third Street
McCook, Nebraska 69001

Roger Toomey, Administrator

Mid-Plains Community College (Public)

Department of Communications and Drama
State Farm Road
North Platte, Nebraska 69101
Telephone: (308) 532-8980

Colin M. Taylor, Chair
Burton B. Brockney, Dean

CURRICULUM AND INSTRUCTION
Courses or Concentrations

Available: Communication; Speech; Theatre; *Undergraduate Objectives or Program Emphases*: General education requirements and lower division introductory classes in interpersonal communication, public speaking, business communication, and theatre; *Associate's Degree Majors*: 6; *Full-Time Faculty*: 1; *Part-Time Faculty*: 2.

FACILITIES AND SERVICES
Practical experiences available through: Photographic Darkrooms.

Midland Lutheran College (Private)

Division of Journalism
900 N. Clarkson
Fremont, Nebraska 68025
Telephone: (402) 721-5480

Marilyn A. Peterson, Chair
Donald Kahnk, Academic Dean

CURRICULUM AND INSTRUCTION
Courses or Concentrations Available: Advertising; Communication; Film or Cinema; Journalism or Mass Communication; Public Relations; Radio, Television, Broadcasting, or Telecommunications; Photography, color, black and white; *Program Coordinators*: Paul Rehm (Broadcasting); Joyce Gissler (Mass Communication and Desktop Publishing); Neil Schilke (Journalism Law); George Riggle (Advertising Photography); *Undergraduate Objectives or Program Emphases*: Training for professional employment in four sequences, as well as preparation for graduate school and teaching on the secondary level; *Bachelor's Degree Majors*: 67; *Full-Time Faculty*: 2; *Part-Time Faculty*: 11.

FACILITIES AND SERVICES
Practical experiences available through: Local Commercial Newspaper; Local Commercial Television Station; Desktop Publishing Facility; Photographic Darkrooms; Video Editing; Electronic Field Production (Video); Institutional Magazine; Institutional Newspaper.

Midland Lutheran College (Private)

Department of Speech/Theatre Arts
900 N. Clarkson
Fremont, Nebraska 68025
Telephone: (402) 721-5480

Michael A. Daehn, Chair
Donald Kahnk, Dean

CURRICULUM AND INSTRUCTION
Courses or Concentrations Available: Film or Cinema; Speech; Theatre; *Bachelor's Degree Majors*: 10; *Full-Time Faculty*: 1; *Part-Time Faculty*: 3; *Full-Time Professional (non-clerical) Staff Members*: 1.

FACILITIES AND SERVICES
Practical experiences available through: Audio Recording Laboratory; Campus Newspaper (Published Independently); Desktop Publishing Facility; Photographic Darkrooms; Video Editing; Film or Cinema Laboratory.

Nebraska Wesleyan University (Private)

Department of Speech Communication and Theatre Arts
5000 St. Paul Avenue
Lincoln, Nebraska 68504
Telephone: (402) 465-2388

Philip A. Kaye, Chair

CURRICULUM AND INSTRUCTION
Courses or Concentrations Available: Communication; Film or Cinema; Mass Communication; Public Relations; Speech; Persuasion; Internships; Organizational Communication; *Full-Time Faculty*: 5; *Part-Time Faculty*: 2.

Northeast Community College (Public)

Program of Broadcasting, Radio, Television
801 East Benjamin Avenue
Norfolk, Nebraska 68702-0469
Telephone: (402) 644-0482

John M Skogstoe, Director
Larry Godel, Liberal Arts Cluster Manager

CURRICULUM AND INSTRUCTION
Courses or Concentrations Available: Advertising; Journalism or Mass Communication; Radio, Television, Broadcasting, or Telecommunications; Speech; Audio and Recording Technology; *Undergraduate Objectives or Program Emphases*: Prepare two year graduates for entry-level jobs in small market radio and television with heavy emphasis on practical skills, and prepare graduates for transfer to four year college as Juniors in broadcasting major; *Associate's Degree Majors*: 5; *Full-Time Faculty*: 1.

FACILITIES AND SERVICES
Practical experiences available through: Audio Recording Laboratory; Community Antenna (Cable) Television Origination; Video Editing; Electronic Field Production (Video); Video News and Data Processing; Video Production Laboratory or Television Studio.

Northeast Community College (Public)

Department of Speech
801 E. Benjamin Avenue
Norfolk, Nebraska 68702
Telephone: (402) 371-2020

Max E. Keeler, Director
Larry Godel, Administrator

CURRICULUM AND INSTRUCTION
Courses or Concentrations Available: Advertising; Communication; Journalism or Mass Communication; Radio, Television, Broadcasting, or Telecommunications; Speech; Oral Interpretation, Small Group Communication; *Undergraduate Objectives or Program Emphases*: Provide basic course instruction for general education courses for those transferring to four year college; *Associate's Degree Majors*: 150; *Full-Time Faculty*: 1; *Part-Time Faculty*: 3.

FACILITIES AND SERVICES
Practical experiences available through: AM Radio Station (Institutional); Associated Press Wire Service Feed; Audio Recording Laboratory; Community Antenna (Cable) Television Origination; Closed Circuit Television Facility; Campus Newspaper (Published Independently); Photographic Darkrooms; Television Broadcast Station (Institutional); Institutional Newspaper;

United Press International Feed; Video News and Data Processing; Video Production Laboratory or Television Studio.

University of Nebraska - Lincoln (Public)

Department of Speech Communication
432 Oldfather Hall
Lincoln, Nebraska 68588-0329
Telephone: (402) 472-2070

Jack Kay, Chair
John Peters, Dean, College of Arts and Sciences

CURRICULUM AND INSTRUCTION
Courses or Concentrations Available: Communication; Public Relations; Speech; *Undergraduate Objectives or Program Emphases*: Service courses to meet general education requirements or special needs in professional communication; career training for communication related occupations; *Graduate Objectives or Program Emphases*: Research and teaching preparation in Applied Communication; Language and Culture; Rhetorical and Communication Theory; *Bachelor's Degree Majors*: 125; *Master's Degree Majors*: 14; *Doctoral Degree Majors Currently in Residence*: 10; *Additional Doctoral Degree Majors*: 8; *Full-Time Faculty*: 10; *Part-Time Faculty*: 23.

FACILITIES AND SERVICES
Practical experiences available through: Audio Recording Laboratory; Video Editing; Video Production Laboratory or Television Studio.

University of Nebraska - Lincoln (Public)

Department of Broadcasting
206 Avery Hall
Lincoln, Nebraska 68588
Telephone: (402) 472-3051

Larry Walklin, Chair
R. Neale Copple, Dean, College of Journalism

CURRICULUM AND INSTRUCTION
Courses or Concentrations Available: Radio,

Television, Broadcasting, or Telecommunications; *Bachelor's Degree Majors*: 300; *Master's Degree Majors*: 6; *Full-Time Faculty*: 6; *Part-Time Faculty*: 9; *Full-Time Professional (non-clerical) Staff Members*: 2.

FACILITIES AND SERVICES
Practical experiences available through: Associated Press Wire Service Feed; Audio Recording Laboratory; Community Antenna (Cable) Television Origination; Closed Circuit Television Facility; Local Commercial Television Station; Video Editing; Electronic Field Production (Video); Television Broadcast Station (Institutional); Film or Cinema Laboratories; FM Radio Station (Institutional); ITFS Distribution System; Satellite Uplink Facility (Ku Band Transmitter) (C Band Transmitter); Video News and Data Processing; Video Production Laboratory or Television Studio.

University of Nebraska - Lincoln (Public)

College of Journalism
206 Avery Hall
Lincoln, Nebraska 68588-0127
Telephone: (402) 472-3041

R. Neale Copple, Dean
Robert Furgason, Vice Chancellor for Academic Affairs

CURRICULUM AND INSTRUCTION
Courses or Concentrations Available: Advertising; Radio, Television, Broadcasting, or Telecommunications; *Undergraduate Objectives or Program Emphases*: All undergraduate majors are designed to produce beginning professionals with a sound liberal arts background; *Graduate Objectives or Program Emphases*: MA program to provide career development to professionals with five years or more experience; *Bachelor's Degree Majors*: 591; *Master's Degree Majors*: 84; *Full-Time Faculty*: 22; *Part-Time Faculty*: 18; *Full-Time Professional (non-clerical) Staff Members*: 3.

FACILITIES AND SERVICES
Practical experiences available through: Associated Press Wire Service Feed; Audio Recording Laboratory; Community Antenna (Cable) Television Origination;

Closed Circuit Television Facility; Campus Newspaper (Published Independently); Local Commercial Newspaper; Local Commercial Television Station; Desktop Publishing Facility; Photographic Darkrooms; Video Editing; Electronic Field Production (Video); Television Broadcast Station (Institutional); FM Radio Station (Institutional); ITFS Distribution System; Institutional Magazine; Institutional Newspaper; United Press International Feed; Video News and Data Processing; Video Production Laboratory or Television Studio.

University of Nebraska - Lincoln (Public)

Department of Advertising
College of Journalism, 206 Avery Hall
Lincoln, Nebraska 68588-0127
Telephone: (402) 472-3041

Linda J. Shipley, Chair
R. Neale Copple, Dean

CURRICULUM AND INSTRUCTION
Courses or Concentrations Available: Advertising; *Master's Degree Majors*: 5; *Other Degree Majors*: 296; *Full-Time Faculty*: 6; *Part-Time Faculty*: 4.

FACILITIES AND SERVICES
Practical experiences available through: Campus Newspaper (Published Independently); Local Commercial Newspaper; Local Commercial Television Station; Desktop Publishing Facility.

University of Nebraska - Lincoln (Public)

Department of News-Editorial
College of Journalism
206 Avery Hall
Lincoln, Nebraska 68588-0132
Telephone: (402) 472-3047

Jack C. Botts, Chair
R. Neale Copple, Dean

CURRICULUM AND INSTRUCTION
Courses or Concentrations Available: Journalism or Mass Communication; *Undergraduate Objectives or*

Program Emphases: Newspaper and magazine writing, reporting, editing. Also, preparation for entry-level positions, including photography, layout; *Degree Majors*: 250; *Full-Time Faculty*: 6; *Part-Time Faculty*: 2; *Full-Time Professional (non-clerical) Staff Members*: 1.

FACILITIES AND SERVICES
Practical experiences available through: Closed Circuit Television Facility; Campus Newspaper (Published Independently); Local Commercial Newspaper; Desktop Publishing Facility; Photographic Darkrooms; Video Editing; Institutional Magazine; Institutional Newspaper; Public Relations Agency; United Press International Feed; Video News and Data Processing.

University of Nebraska - Lincoln (Public)

Department of English
1223 Oldfather Hall 0321
Lincoln, Nebraska 68588-0329

Frederick M. Link, Chair
John Peters, Dean, College of Arts and Sciences

CURRICULUM AND INSTRUCTION
Courses or Concentrations Available: Film or Cinema; English and American Literature; ESL; *Program Coordinator*: Wheeler Dixon (Film Studies); *Undergraduate Objectives or Program Emphases*: General introduction in reading and writing for all students. Majors and minors in English; *Graduate Objectives or Program Emphases*: MA and Ph.D. in English (does not include film); *Bachelor's Degree Majors*: 350; *Master's Degree Majors*: 50; *Doctoral Degree Majors Currently in Residence*: 60; *Additional Doctoral Degree Majors*: 25; *Full-Time Faculty*: 60; *Part-Time Faculty*: 50; *Full-Time Professional (non-clerical) Staff Members*: 8.

FACILITIES AND SERVICES
Practical experiences available through: Closed Circuit Television Facility; Campus Newspaper (Published Independently); Desktop Publishing Facility; Television Broadcast Station (Institutional); Film or Cinema Laboratory; FM Radio Station (Institutional).

University of Nebraska - Omaha (Public)

Department of Communication
Omaha, Nebraska 68182
Telephone: (402) 554-2600

Hugh P. Cowdin, Chair
John M. Newton, Dean

CURRICULUM AND INSTRUCTION
Courses or Concentrations Available: Advertising; Communication; Film or Cinema; Journalism or Mass Communication; Public Relations; Radio, Television, Broadcasting, or Telecommunications; Speech; Organizational Communication; *Undergraduate Objectives or Program Emphases*: To provide an understanding of the principles and various areas of mass communication, and to develop the necessary skills that the students will need; *Graduate Objectives or Program Emphases*: To provide a broader and deeper understanding of the whole communication process, and to introduce the students to the various research methodologies; *Bachelor's Degree Majors*: 333; *Master's Degree Majors*: 133; *Full-Time Faculty*: 18; *Part-Time Faculty*: 29.

FACILITIES AND SERVICES
Practical experiences available through: Advertising Agency; Community Antenna (Cable) Television Origination; Closed Circuit Television Facility; Campus Newspaper (Published Independently); Local Commercial Newspaper; Local Commercial Television Station; Desktop Publishing Facility; Photographic Darkrooms; Video Editing; Electronic Field Production (Video); Television Broadcast Station (Institutional); FM Radio Station (Institutional); Public Relations Agency; Video Production Laboratory or Television Studio.

Wayne State College (Public)

Division of Humanities
Wayne, Nebraska 68787
Telephone: (402) 375-2200

Jo Taylor, Head
Donald Whisenhunt, Vice President, Academic Affairs

CURRICULUM AND INSTRUCTION

*Courses or Concentrations
Available*: Journalism or Mass
Communication; Radio, Television,
Broadcasting, or Telecommunications;
Speech; *Program Coordinators*: Regis Tucci
(Radio Broadcasting); Maureen Carrigg
(Television Broadcasting); Luigi Manca
(Journalism); Kathryn Carter (Speech
Communication); *Undergraduate Objectives
or Program Emphases*: The programs in
Communication Arts provide preparation for
those who wish to develop communication
skills for teaching, the ministry, drama, law,
public service, journalism and broadcasting;
Bachelor's Degree Majors: 89; *Full-Time
Faculty*: 20; *Part-Time Faculty*: 33;
*Full-Time Professional (non-clerical) Staff
Members*: 1.

FACILITIES AND SERVICES

*Practical experiences available
through*: Associated Press Wire Service Feed;
Audio Recording Laboratory; Community
Antenna (Cable) Television Origination;
Closed Circuit Television Facility; Local
Commercial Television Station;
Photographic Darkrooms; Video Editing;
FM Radio Station (Institutional);
Institutional Magazine; Institutional
Newspaper; Video Production Laboratory or
Television Studio.

Sierra Nevada College

Department of Humanities
Box 4269
Incline Village, Nevada 89450-4269

Laird Blackwell, Administrator

University of Nevada - Las Vegas

Department of Communication Studies
4505 South Maryland Parkway
Las Vegas, Nevada 89154

George Chapel, Administrator

University of Nevada - Reno

Reynolds School of Journalism
Ninth and Center Streets
Reno, Nevada 89557-0040

Sharon Adams, Administrator

Colby-Sawyer College (Private)

Program of Communication
Main Street
New London, New Hampshire 03257
Telephone: (603) 526-2010

Don E. Coonley, Director
Patrick Anderson, Chair, Humanities
Division

CURRICULUM AND INSTRUCTION
*Courses or Concentrations
Available*: Advertising; Communication; Film
or Cinema; Journalism or Mass
Communication; Public Relations; Radio,
Television, Broadcasting, or
Telecommunications; Graphic Design;
Program Coordinators: Gordon Marshall
(Advertising, Business Communication,
Public Relations); Joe Hruby (Graphic
Design); *Undergraduate Objectives or
Program Emphases*: To provide an
interdisciplinary approach to prepare
students to function competently in
communication based careers. To offer a
balance of theory and practice by providing
opportunities to apply classroom knowledge
to community situations; *Bachelor's Degree
Majors*: 20; *Full-Time Faculty*: 2; *Part-Time
Faculty*: 2.

FACILITIES AND SERVICES
Practical experiences available through: Audio
Recording Laboratory; Community Antenna
(Cable) Television Origination; Campus
Newspaper (Published Independently);
Local Commercial Newspaper; Local
Commercial Television Station; Desktop
Publishing Facility; Photographic
Darkrooms; Video Editing; Electronic Field
Production (Video); FM Radio Station
(Institutional); Public Relations Agency;
Video Production Laboratory or Television
Studio.

Franklin Pierce College (Private)

Program of Mass Communication
Rindge, New Hampshire 03461
Telephone: (603) 899-5111

Ray E. Oakes, Coordinator
Nancy Stone, Division Director

CURRICULUM AND INSTRUCTION
Courses or Concentrations Available: Radio,
Television, Broadcasting, or
Telecommunications; *Undergraduate
Objectives or Program Emphases*: An
education leading to a professional
communication career within the liberal arts
tradition; *Bachelor's Degree Majors*: 60;
Full-Time Faculty: 3; *Part-Time Faculty*: 2.

FACILITIES AND SERVICES
*Practical experiences available
through*: Advertising Agency; Associated
Press Wire Service Feed; Audio Recording
Laboratory; Carrier Current Audio
Distribution System; Closed Circuit
Television Facility; Campus Newspaper
(Published Independently); Local
Commercial Television Station; Desktop
Publishing Facility; Photographic
Darkrooms; Electronic Field Production
(Video); Institutional Magazine; Public
Relations Agency; Video Production
Laboratory or Television Studio.

Keene State College (Public)

Department of English
229 Main Street
Keene, New Hampshire 03431
Telephone: (603) 352-1909

Ann Marie Mallon, Chair
Michael Heines, Dean, Arts and Humanities

CURRICULUM AND INSTRUCTION
*Courses or Concentrations
Available*: Journalism or Mass
Communication; Radio, Television,
Broadcasting, or Telecommunications;
*Undergraduate Objectives or Program
Emphases*: To provide a broad background in

print and broadcast journalism; *Bachelor's Degree Majors*: 32; *Full-Time Faculty*: 3.

FACILITIES AND SERVICES
Practical experiences available through: Associated Press Wire Service Feed; Audio Recording Laboratory; Closed Circuit Television Facility; Campus Newspaper (Published Independently); Local Commercial Television Station; Desktop Publishing Facility; Photographic Darkrooms; Video Editing; Electronic Field Production (Video); Film and Cinema Laboratory; FM Radio Station (Institutional); Video Production Laboratory or Television Studio.

New England College

Department of Arts and Communication
Henniker, New Hampshire 03242

Thomas Mickey, Administrator

New Hampshire Technical College - Stratham (Public)

Program of English/Communications
277 R. Portsmouth Avenue
Stratham, New Hampshire 03885
Telephone: (603) 772-1194

Barbara R. Fein, Professor
Barney Share, Chair, Arts and Sciences

CURRICULUM AND INSTRUCTION
Courses or Concentrations Available: Advertising; Communication; Information Science; Journalism or Mass Communication; Public Relations; Speech; Technical writing--processes, manuals; Language; Logic; Rhetoric; Business Correspondence; *Undergraduate Objectives or Program Emphases*: To teach students how to read and write effectively within their technologies; to prepare students for a writing career in a particular area; *Degree Majors*: 168; *Full-Time Faculty*: 3; *Part-Time Faculty*: 2; *Full-Time Professional (non-clerical) Staff Members*: 20.

FACILITIES AND SERVICES
Practical experiences available through: Campus Newspaper (Published Independently); Photographic Darkrooms; Video Editing; Institutional Newspaper.

Notre Dame College (Private)

Division of Arts/Communications
2321 Elm Street
Manchester, New Hampshire 03104
Telephone: (603) 669-4298

Blanche E. Lamaere, Chair
Robert Michael, Administrator

CURRICULUM AND INSTRUCTION
Courses or Concentrations Available: Advertising; Communication; Journalism or Mass Communication; Public Relations; Radio, Television, Broadcasting, or Telecommunications; Speech; *Program Coordinators*: Carl Hausman (Broadcasting, Radio); Raymond Gamache (Communication, Journalism); *Undergraduate Objectives or Program Emphases*: Public relations, mass communication, and broadcast journalism; *Full-Time Faculty*: 2; *Part-Time Faculty*: 2.

FACILITIES AND SERVICES
Practical experiences available through: Advertising Agency; Associated Press Wire Service Feed; Audio Recording Laboratory; Carrier Current Audio Distribution System; Local Commercial Newspaper; Local Commercial Television Station; Desktop Publishing Facility; Photographic Darkrooms; Video Editing; Electronic Field Production (Video); FM Radio Station (Institutional); Institutional Magazine; Video Production Laboratory or Television Studio.

Plymouth State College (Public)

Department of English
Summer Street
Plymouth, New Hampshire 03264
Telephone: (603) 536-5000

Barbara Blaha, Chair
Theo Kalikow, Dean

CURRICULUM AND INSTRUCTION
Courses or Concentrations Available: Communication; Film or Cinema; Journalism or Mass Communication; Speech.

FACILITIES AND SERVICES
Practical experiences available through: AM Radio Station (Institutional); Audio Recording Laboratory; Closed Circuit Television Facility; Campus Newspaper

(Published Independently); Local
Commercial Newspaper; Desktop Publishing
Facility; Photographic Darkrooms; Video
Editing; Educational Television Station

University of New Hampshire

Journalism Program
Durham, New Hampshire 03824

Andrew Merton, Administrator

White Pines College (Private)

Program of Communications
Chester, New Hampshire 03036
Telephone: (603) 887-4401

Edward Meadows, Acting Chair
John B. Hoar, Dean

CURRICULUM AND INSTRUCTION
Courses or Concentrations
Available: Advertising; Journalism or Mass
Communication; Radio, Television,
Broadcasting, or Telecommunications;
Program Coordinators: Calvin Libby
(Advertising); Vincent Cianni (Photography);
*Undergraduate Objectives or Program
Emphases*: Basic training of students in
journalism, photography, or advertising
design to prepare them for the work place or
for continued studies in a four year college;
Associate's Degree Majors: 16; *Full-Time
Faculty*: 5; *Part-Time Faculty*: 3.

FACILITIES AND SERVICES
*Practical experiences available
through*: Advertising Agency; Local
Commercial Newspaper; Local Commercial
Television Station; Photographic
Darkrooms; Institutional Newspaper; Public
Relations Agency.

Bergen Community College

Communication Arts Department
400 Paramus Road
Paramus, New Jersey 07652

M. Ann Cunningham, Administrator

Brookdale Community College (Public)

Department of Telecommunications
Learning Center
Newman Springs Road
Lincroft, New Jersey 07738
Telephone: (201) 842-1900

Paul S. Keating, Chair
Louis Pullano, Dean, Applied Humanities

CURRICULUM AND INSTRUCTION
*Courses or Concentrations
Available*: Communication; Film or Cinema;
Information Science; Journalism or Mass
Communication; Public Relations; Radio,
Television, Broadcasting, or
Telecommunications; Photography;
Graphics; Telephony; *Undergraduate
Objectives or Program Emphases*: To provide
general education requirements and some
career study courses for AA degree students;
general education and enough career study
courses for immediate employment for AAS
degree students; *Associate's Degree
Majors*: 250; *Full-Time Faculty*: 7;
Part-Time Faculty: 7; *Full-Time Professional
(non-clerical) Staff Members*: 3.

FACILITIES AND SERVICES
*Practical experiences available
through*: Associated Press Wire Service Feed;
Audio Recording Laboratory; Community
Antenna (Cable) Television Origination;
Closed Circuit Television Facility; Campus
Newspaper (Published Independently);
Local Commercial Newspaper; Local
Commercial Television Station;
Photographic Darkrooms; Video Editing;
Electronic Field Production (Video);
Television Broadcast Station (Institutional);
FM Radio Station (Institutional); Public
Relations Agency; Video Production
Laboratory or Television Studio.

Camden County College (Public)

Program of Visual and Performing Arts
P.O. Box 200
Blackwood, New Jersey 08012
Telephone: (609) 227-7200

Judith Rowlands, Coordinator
Dean Kazcorski, Administrator

CURRICULUM AND INSTRUCTION
*Courses or Concentrations
Available*: Advertising; Communication; Film
or Cinema; Journalism or Mass
Communication; Public Relations; Speech;
Theatre; *Undergraduate Objectives or
Program Emphases*: Transfer programs;
Associate's Degree Majors: 150; *Full-Time
Faculty*: 7; *Part-Time Faculty*: 8.

FACILITIES AND SERVICES
Practical experiences available through: AM
Radio Station (Institutional); Campus
Newspaper (Published Independently);
Local Commercial Television Station;
Desktop Publishing Facility; Photographic
Darkrooms; Institutional Magazine;
Institutional Newspaper.

Cumberland County College

P. O. Box 517
Sherman Avenue
Vineland, New Jersey 08360

Richard King, Administrator

Fairleigh Dickinson University - Madison (Private)

Department of English/Communications
285 Madison Avenue
Madison, New Jersey 07940
Telephone: (201) 593-8710

Michael B. Goodman, Director
Martin Green, Chair

CURRICULUM AND INSTRUCTION
Courses or Concentrations
Available: Advertising; Communication; Public Relations; Radio, Television, Broadcasting, or Telecommunications; Speech; Business Policy; Organizational Behavior; Problem Solving; Language Theory; *Undergraduate Objectives or Program Emphases*: Develop communication expertise; *Graduate Objectives or Program Emphases*: Develop managerial expertise in all areas of communication; *Bachelor's Degree Majors*: 100; *Master's Degree Majors*: 125; *Full-Time Faculty*: 10; *Part-Time Faculty*: 4; *Full-Time Professional (non-clerical) Staff Members*: 4.

FACILITIES AND SERVICES
Practical experiences available through: Advertising Agency; AM Radio Station (Institutional); Associated Press Wire Service Feed; Audio Recording Laboratory; Community Antenna (Cable) Television Origination; Closed Circuit Television Facility; Campus Newspaper (Published Independently); Local Commercial Newspaper; Local Commercial Television Station; Desktop Publishing Facility; Photographic Darkrooms; Video Editing; Television Broadcast Station (Institutional); Film and Cinema Laboratory; FM Radio Station (Institutional); Institutional Newspaper; New York Times Service Feed; Public Relations Agency; United Press International Feed; Video News and Data Processing; Video Production Laboratory or Television Studio.

Fairleigh Dickinson University - Teaneck (Private)

Department of Communication and Speech
1000 River Road
Teaneck, New Jersey 07430
Telephone: (201) 692-2415

Donald W. Jugenheimer, Chair

CURRICULUM AND INSTRUCTION
Courses or Concentrations
Available: Advertising; Communication; Film or Cinema; Journalism or Mass Communication; Public Relations; Radio, Television, Broadcasting, or Telecommunications; Speech; *Undergraduate Objectives or Program Emphases*: To prepare students for professional careers in media-related positions; *Bachelor's Degree Majors*: 165; *Full-Time Faculty*: 7; *Part-Time Faculty*: 6.

FACILITIES AND SERVICES
Practical experiences available through: Advertising Agency; AM Radio Station (Institutional); Associated Press Wire Service Feed; Audio Recording Laboratory; Community Antenna (Cable) Television Origination; Closed Circuit Television Facility; Campus Newspaper (Published Independently); Local Commercial Newspaper; Local Commercial Television Station; Desktop Publishing Facility; Photographic Darkrooms; Video Editing; Film or Cinema Laboratory; FM Radio Station (Institutional); Public Relations Agency; Video Production Laboratory or Television Studio.

Glassboro State College (Public)

Department of Communications
Glassboro, New Jersey 08028
Telephone: (609) 863-7187 Extension or Alternate: 863-7186

David Cromie, Chair
Minna Doskow, Dean, School of Liberal Arts and Science

CURRICULUM AND INSTRUCTION
Courses or Concentrations
Available: Advertising; Communication; Film or Cinema; Journalism or Mass Communication; Public Relations; Radio, Television, Broadcasting, or Telecommunications; Freshman writing;

Developmental writing; Creative writing; *Program Coordinators*: Jack Gillespie (Journalism); Don Gallagher (Graduate Public Relations); Frank Grazian (Advertising); Ben Resnik (Mass Media); Mike Donovan (Radio); Ned Eckhardt (Television); Richard Gruyenhoff (Film); Don Bagin (Public Relations); Additional coordinators for writing; *Undergraduate Objectives or Program Emphases*: To provide students with a broad general education and to provide them with knowledge and skills needed to pursue and succeed in their chosen career fields; *Graduate Objectives or Program Emphases*: Graduate program in Public Relations only; to expand upon undergraduate foundations and those developed by practicum professionals in Public Relations providing students a chance to grow professionally; *Bachelor's Degree Majors*: 670; *Master's Degree Majors*: 120; *Full-Time Faculty*: 30; *Part-Time Faculty*: 25; *Full-Time Professional (non-clerical) Staff Members*: 4.

FACILITIES AND SERVICES
Practical experiences available through: Advertising Agency; AM Radio Station (Institutional); Associated Press Wire Service Feed; Audio Recording Laboratory; Campus Newspaper (Published Independently); Local Commercial Newspaper; Local Commercial Television Station; Desktop Publishing Facility; Photographic Darkrooms; Video Editing; Electronic Field Production (Video); Film or Cinema Laboratory; FM Radio Station (Institutional); Institutional Magazine; Institutional Newspaper; Public Relations Agency; United Press International Feed; Video News and Data Processing; Video Production Laboratory or Television Studio.

Kean College of New Jersey (Public)

Department of Communication and Theatre
Morris Avenue
Union, New Jersey 07083
Telephone: (201) 527-2349

James R. Murphy, Chair
Ed Weil, Dean, Liberal Arts

CURRICULUM AND INSTRUCTION
Courses or Concentrations Available: Communication; Film or Cinema; Journalism or Mass Communication; Public

Relations; Radio, Television, Broadcasting, or Telecommunications; Speech; Persuasion; Organizational Communication; *Undergraduate Objectives or Program Emphases*: To prepare the students for careers and graduate school; *Bachelor's Degree Majors*: 200; *Full-Time Faculty*: 14; *Part-Time Faculty*: 28.

FACILITIES AND SERVICES
Practical experiences available through: Advertising Agency; Associated Press Wire Service Feed; Audio Recording Laboratory; Community Antenna (Cable) Television Origination; Closed Circuit Television Facility; Campus Newspaper (Published Independently); Local Commercial Newspaper; Local Commercial Television Station; Desktop Publishing Facility; Photographic Darkrooms; Video Editing; Film or Cinema Laboratory; FM Radio Station (Institutional); Public Relations Agency; Video News and Data Processing; Video Production Laboratory or Television Studio.

Mercer County Community College (Public)

Division of Visual and Performing Arts
P. O. Box B
Trenton, New Jersey 08690
Telephone: (609) 586-4800

David Levin, Chair
D. David Conklin, Dean, Academic Affairs

CURRICULUM AND INSTRUCTION
Courses or Concentrations Available: Advertising; Communication; Film or Cinema; Journalism or Mass Communication; Radio, Television, Broadcasting, or Telecommunications; Architecture; Music; Art; Theatre; Photography; *Program Coordinators*: Donna R. Munde (Radio Program); Ralph Tangney (Television Program); *Undergraduate Objectives or Program Emphases*: The Communications Program is primarily a transfer program. The Radio and Television programs are career-oriented; *Associate's Degree Majors*: 220; *Full-Time Faculty*: 15; *Part-Time Faculty*: 6; *Full-Time Professional (non-clerical) Staff Members*: 4.

FACILITIES AND SERVICES
Practical experiences available through: Advertising Agency; AM Radio

Station (Institutional); Associated Press Wire Service Feed; Audio Recording Laboratory; Carrier Current Audio Distribution System; Closed Circuit Television Facility; Campus Newspaper (Published Independently); Desktop Publishing Facility; Photographic Darkrooms; Video Editing; Electronic Field Production (Video); FM Radio Station (Institutional); ITFS Distribution System; Institutional Newspaper; Satellite Uplink Facility (Ku Band Transmitter); United Press International Feed; Video News and Data Processing; Video Production Laboratory or Television Studio.

Monmouth College (Private)

Department of Speech, Communication and Theatre
Cedar Avenue
West Long Branch, New Jersey 07764
Telephone: (201) 571-3449

Robert L. Huber, Chair
Gloria Nemerowicz, Dean

CURRICULUM AND INSTRUCTION
Courses or Concentrations
Available: Communication; Film or Cinema; Journalism or Mass Communication; Public Relations; Radio, Television, Broadcasting, or Telecommunications; Speech; *Undergraduate Objectives or Program Emphases*: Public speaking and interpersonal communication service courses; *Bachelor's Degree Majors*: 90; *Full-Time Faculty*: 7; *Part-Time Faculty*: 9; *Full-Time Professional (non-clerical) Staff Members*: 2.

FACILITIES AND SERVICES
Practical experiences available through: Associated Press Wire Service Feed; Audio Recording Laboratory; Closed Circuit Television Facility; Campus Newspaper (Published Independently); Local Commercial Newspaper; Local Commercial Television Station; Photographic Darkrooms; Video Editing; Electronic Field Production (Video); FM Radio Station (Institutional): Public Relations Agency; Video Production Laboratory or Television Studio.

Montclair State College (Public)

Department of Speech and Theatre
Normal Avenue
Upper Montclair, New Jersey 07043
Telephone: (201) 893-4217

Gerald Lee Ratliff, Chair
Geoffrey Newman, Dean

CURRICULUM AND INSTRUCTION
Courses or Concentrations
Available: Advertising; Communication; Journalism or Mass Communication; Public Relations; Radio, Television, Broadcasting, or Telecommunications; Speech Communication; *Program Coordinators*: Tom Veen Endall (Speech Communication); Jan Hunold (Broadcasting); *Undergraduate Objectives or Program Emphases*: Provide career opportunities in management and production; *Bachelor's Degree Majors*: 205; *Master's Degree Majors*: 40; *Full-Time Faculty*: 7; *Part-Time Faculty*: 4; *Full-Time Professional (non-clerical) Staff Members*: 3.

FACILITIES AND SERVICES
Practical experiences available through: Advertising Agency; AM Radio Station (Institutional); Audio Recording Laboratory; Community Antenna (Cable) Television Origination; Campus Newspaper (Published Independently); Local Commercial Newspaper; Local Commercial Television Station; Photographic Darkrooms; Video Editing; Electronic Field Production (Video); Television Broadcast Station (Institutional); Film or Cinema Laboratories; ITFS Distribution System; Institutional Magazine; Institutional Newspaper; Public Relations Agency; Video News and Data Processing; Video Production Laboratory or Television Studio.

Ocean County College (Public)

Program of Print and Broadcast Journalism
College Drive CN2001
Toms River, New Jersey 08754-2001
Telephone: (201) 255-0400

Karen L. Bosley, Coordinator
James Doran, Assistant Dean, Humanities

CURRICULUM AND INSTRUCTION
Courses or Concentrations
Available: Journalism or Mass Communication; Public Relations; Radio,

Television, Broadcasting, or Telecommunications; Communication Law; Internships; Publications Workshops; Photojournalism; Editing and Reporting; *Undergraduate Objectives or Program Emphases*: Prepare graduates for entry-level work on newspapers or radio stations as journalists or as publicity writers in public-relations firms or other businesses or organizations. Also, prepare students for entry-level television journalism work and magazine or wire-service writing; *Associate's Degree Majors*: 12; *Full-Time Faculty*: 1; *Part-Time Faculty*: 1; *Full-Time Professional (non-clerical) Staff Members*: 1.

FACILITIES AND SERVICES
Practical experiences available through: Advertising Agency; Audio Recording Laboratory; Community Antenna (Cable) Television Origination; Campus Newspaper (Published Independently); Local Commercial Newspaper; Local Commercial Television Station; Desktop Publishing Facility; Photographic Darkrooms; Video Editing; FM Radio Station (Institutional); Institutional Magazine.

Princeton Theological Seminary (Private)

Division of Speech and Communication
CN 821
Princeton, New Jersey 08542
Telephone: (609) 921-8300

Rev. Wayne R. Whitelock, Director
Conrad Massa, Dean, Academic Affairs

CURRICULUM AND INSTRUCTION
Courses or Concentrations Available: Advertising; Communication; Journalism or Mass Communication; Radio, Television, Broadcasting, or Telecommunications; Speech; *Degree Majors*: 460; *Full-Time Faculty*: 4; *Part-Time Faculty*: 34; *Full-Time Professional (non-clerical) Staff Members*: 2.

FACILITIES AND SERVICES
Practical experiences available through: Audio Recording Laboratory; Community Antenna (Cable) Television Origination; Carrier Current Audio Distribution System; Closed Circuit Television Facility; Desktop Publishing Facility; Photographic Darkrooms; Video Editing; Electronic Field

Production (Video); Film and Cinema Laboratory; ITFS Distribution System; Satellite Uplink Facility (Ku Band Transmitter); Video News and Data Processing; Video Production Laboratory or Television Studio.

Ramapo College of New Jersey (Public)

School of Contemporary Arts
Communication Arts Major
505 Ramapo Valley Road
Mahwah, New Jersey 07430
Telephone: (201) 529-7500

James B. Hollenbach, Director and Associate Dean
Robert Hatala, Vice President, Academic Affairs

CURRICULUM AND INSTRUCTION
Courses or Concentrations Available: Communication; Film or Cinema; Journalism or Mass Communication; Radio, Television, Broadcasting, or Telecommunications; Speech; Photography; Computer Graphics; *Program Coordinator*: William Kollock (Communication Arts); *Undergraduate Objectives or Program Emphases*: Professional preparation; Graduate school preparation; *Bachelor's Degree Majors*: 150; *Full-Time Faculty*: 7; *Part-Time Faculty*: 10; *Full-Time Professional (non-clerical) Staff Members*: 1.

FACILITIES AND SERVICES
Practical experiences available through: Associated Press Wire Service Feed; Audio Recording Laboratory; Community Antenna (Cable) Television Origination; Campus Newspaper (Published Independently); Local Commercial Newspaper; Local Commercial Television Station; Desktop Publishing Facility; Photographic Darkrooms; Video Editing; Electronic Field Production (Video); Film or Cinema Laboratory; FM Radio Station (Institutional); Satellite Uplink Facility; Video News and Data Processing; Video Production Laboratory or Television Studio.

Rider College (Private)

Department of Communications
2083 Lawrenceville Road
Lawrenceville, New Jersey 08648
Telephone: (609) 896-5089

Howard Schwartz, Chair
Dominick Iorio, Dean, School of Liberal
Arts and Sciences

CURRICULUM AND INSTRUCTION
Courses or Concentrations
Available: Communication; Journalism or
Mass Communication; Public Relations;
Radio, Television, Broadcasting, or
Telecommunications; Speech; *Undergraduate
Objectives or Program Emphases*: To provide
academic and professional training in speech,
journalism, radio-television and public
relations; *Bachelor's Degree Majors*: 170;
Full-Time Faculty: 8; *Part-Time Faculty*: 4;
*Full-Time Professional (non-clerical) Staff
Members*: 1.

FACILITIES AND SERVICES
*Practical experiences available
through*: Advertising Agency; Audio
Recording Laboratory; Carrier Current
Audio Distribution System; Campus
Newspaper (Published Independently);
Local Commercial Newspaper; Local
Commercial Television Station; Desktop
Publishing Facility; Photographic
Darkrooms; Video Editing; FM Radio
Station (Institutional); Public Relations
Agency; Video News and Data Processing;
Video Production Laboratory or Television
Studio.

Rutgers University - New Brunswick (Public)

Department of Journalism and Mass Media
4 Huntington Street
New Brunswick, New Jersey 08903
Telephone: (201) 932-8587

Roger Cohen, Chair
Richard W. Budd, Dean, School of
Communication, Information/Library

CURRICULUM AND INSTRUCTION
Courses or Concentrations
Available: Journalism or Mass
Communication; Radio, Television,
Broadcasting, or Telecommunications; Mass
Media and Government; Technical Writing;
*Undergraduate Objectives or Program
Emphases*: Writing; News editorial in both
print and broadcasting; *Bachelor's Degree
Majors*: 300; *Full-Time Faculty*: 10;
Part-Time Faculty: 10. See one or more
related entries below.

FACILITIES AND SERVICES
*Practical experiences available
through*: Community Antenna (Cable)
Television Origination; Closed Circuit
Television Facility; Campus Newspaper
(Published Independently); Local
Commercial Newspaper; Desktop Publishing
Facility; Photographic Darkrooms;
Electronic Field Production (Video);
Television Broadcast Station (Institutional);
FM Radio Station (Institutional); ITFS
Distribution System; Institutional Magazine;
Public Relations Agency; Video Production
Laboratory or Television Studio.

Rutgers University - New Brunswick (Public)

Department of Communication
4 Huntington Street
New Brunswick, New Jersey 08903
Telephone: (201) 932-8563

Lea P. Stewart, Chair
Richard W. Budd, Dean, School of
Communication, Information/Library

CURRICULUM AND INSTRUCTION
Courses or Concentrations
Available: Communication; Journalism or
Mass Communication; Public Relations;
Speech; Organizational Communication;
Interpersonal Communication; Intercultural
Communication; *Undergraduate Objectives or
Program Emphases*: The program encourages
a broad, theory-based, general education;
Bachelor's Degree Majors: 650; *Full-Time
Faculty*: 20; *Part-Time Faculty*: 10.

FACILITIES AND SERVICES
*Practical experiences available
through*: Advertising Agency; Campus
Newspaper (Published Independently);
Local Commercial Television Station;
Desktop Publishing Facility; FM Radio
Station (Institutional); Public Relations
Agency.

Rutgers University - Newark (Public)

Program of Journalism
Hill Hall
Newark, New Jersey 07102
Telephone: (201) 648-5431
Alternate: (201) 648-1107

Allan Wolper, Director

CURRICULUM AND INSTRUCTION
Courses or Concentrations
Available: Journalism or Mass
Communication; Public Relations; Radio,
Television, Broadcasting, or
Telecommunications; Photojournalism;
*Undergraduate Objectives or Program
Emphases*: To provide a broad liberal
education through the offering of as many
courses as possible; *Bachelor's Degree
Majors*: 50; *Full-Time Faculty*: 4; *Part-Time
Faculty*: 2; *Full-Time Professional
(non-clerical) Staff Members*: 12.

FACILITIES AND SERVICES
*Practical experiences available
through*: Advertising Agency; Audio
Recording Laboratory; Community Antenna
(Cable) Television Origination; Campus
Newspaper (Published Independently);
Local Commercial Newspaper; Local
Commercial Television Station; Desktop
Publishing Facility; Photographic
Darkrooms; Video Editing; Electronic Field
Production (Video); Television Broadcast
Station (Institutional); Film and Cinema
Laboratory; FM Radio Station
(Institutional); Institutional Magazine;
Public Relations Agency; Video Production
Laboratory or Television Studio.

Seton Hall University

Department of Communication
South Orange, New Jersey 07079

William H. Rockett, Administrator

Trenton State College (Public)

Department of Communication and Theatre
Hillwood Lakes, CN 4700
Trenton, New Jersey 08650
Telephone: (609) 771-2106

Norman A. Heap, Chair
Richard Kamber, Dean, Arts and Sciences

CURRICULUM AND INSTRUCTION
Courses or Concentrations
Available: Communication; Film or Cinema;
Journalism or Mass Communication; Public
Relations; Radio, Television, Broadcasting,
or Telecommunications; Speech;
Interpersonal Communication; Theatre;
*Undergraduate Objectives or Program
Emphases*: BA in Communication with
choice of specializations (Electronic,
Television, Video, Radio, Interpersonal,
Public and Mass Communication); *Bachelor's
Degree Majors*: 120; *Full-Time Faculty*: 12;
Part-Time Faculty: 20; *Full-Time
Professional (non-clerical) Staff Members*: 2.

FACILITIES AND SERVICES
*Practical experiences available
through*: Advertising Agency; Associated
Press Wire Service Feed; Audio Recording
Laboratory; Community Antenna (Cable)
Television Origination; Carrier Current
Audio Distribution System; Closed Circuit
Television Facility; Campus Newspaper
(Published Independently); Local
Commercial Newspaper; Local Commercial
Television Station; Photographic
Darkrooms; Video Editing; Electronic Field
Production (Video); Television Broadcast
Station (Institutional); FM Radio Station
(Institutional); ITFS Distribution System;
Institutional Newspaper; Public Relations
Agency; Satellite Uplink Facility; United
Press International Feed; Video News and
Data Processing; Video Production
Laboratory or Television Studio.

William Paterson College (Public)

Department of Communication
301 Hobart Hall
Wayne, New Jersey 07470
Telephone: (201) 595-2167

Diana N. Peck, Chair
**Jay Ludwig, Dean, School of the Arts and
Communication**

CURRICULUM AND INSTRUCTION
Courses or Concentrations Available: Communication; Film or Cinema; Journalism or Mass Communication; Public Relations; Radio, Television, Broadcasting, or Telecommunications; Speech; Telecommunications-Audio/Data; Interpersonal; *Undergraduate Objectives or Program Emphases*: Broad-based communication program which balances a liberal arts education with professional studies. Students are free to select courses across all areas; *Graduate Objectives or Program Emphases*: Broad-based course of study offered to familiarize students with communication theory, research and practicum; *Bachelor's Degree Majors*: 700; *Master's Degree Majors*: 70; *Full-Time Faculty*: 19; *Part-Time Faculty*: 16; *Full-Time Professional (non-clerical) Staff Members*: 9.

FACILITIES AND SERVICES
Practical experiences available through: Advertising Agency; Associated Press Wire Service Feed; Audio Recording Laboratory; Community Antenna (Cable) Television Origination; Carrier Current Audio Distribution System; Closed Circuit Television Facility; Campus Newspaper (Published Independently); Local Commercial Newspaper; Local Commercial Television Station; Desktop Publishing Facility; Video Editing; Electronic Field Production (Video); Film or Cinema Laboratory; FM Radio Station (Institutional); Public Relations Agency; Satellite Uplink Facility (Ku Band Transmitter) (C Band Transmitter); Video News and Data Processing; Video Production Laboratory or Television Studio.

College of Santa Fe (Private)

Department of Communication Arts
St. Michael's Drive
Santa Fe, New Mexico 87501
Telephone: (505) 473-6400

Joseph E. Dispenza, Chair
James Lawrence, Vice President, Academic and Student Affairs

CURRICULUM AND INSTRUCTION
Courses or Concentrations Available: Advertising; Communication; Film or Cinema; Journalism or Mass Communication; Public Relations; Radio, Television, Broadcasting, or Telecommunications; Speech; *Bachelor's Degree Majors*: 30; *Full-Time Faculty*: 3; *Part-Time Faculty*: 3; *Full-Time Professional (non-clerical) Staff Members*: 1.

FACILITIES AND SERVICES
Practical experiences available through: Advertising Agency; Audio Recording Laboratory; Community Antenna (Cable) Television Origination; Campus Newspaper (Published Independently); Desktop Publishing Facility; Photographic Darkrooms; Video Editing; Electronic Field Production (Video).

Eastern New Mexico University (Public)

Department of Communicative Arts and Sciences
Portales, New Mexico 88130
Telephone: (505) 562-2130

Anthony B. Schroeder, Chair
Patrice Caldwell, Administrator

CURRICULUM AND INSTRUCTION
Courses or Concentrations Available: Communication; Journalism or Mass Communication; Public Relations; Radio, Television, Broadcasting, or Telecommunications; Speech; Communicative Disorders; *Undergraduate Objectives or Program Emphases*: To produce graduates who can construct messages using appropriate print and non-print media, who articulate ideas, positions and arguments in a manner which respects the settings, and who understand the theoretical basis of the communicative process; *Graduate Objectives or Program Emphases*: The student is expected to develop a sound grasp of their discipline, a command of the relevant research findings, the methodology used, along with rhetorical and aesthetic principles of communication; *Bachelor's Degree Majors*: 250; *Master's Degree Majors*: 27; *Full-Time Faculty*: 10; *Part-Time Faculty*: 16.

FACILITIES AND SERVICES
Practical experiences available through: Associated Press Wire Service Feed; Audio Recording Laboratory; Closed Circuit Television Facility; Campus Newspaper (Published Independently); Local Commercial Newspaper; Photographic Darkrooms; Video Editing; Electronic Field Production (Video); Television Broadcast Station (Institutional); FM Radio Station (Institutional); ITFS Distribution System; United Press International Feed; Video News and Data Processing; Video Production Laboratory or Television Studio.

New Mexico Highlands University

Department of English, Speech and Journalism
Las Vegas, New Mexico 87701

Richard J. Panofsky, Administrator

New Mexico Military Institute (Public)

Learning Resource Center
101 W. College
Roswell, New Mexico 88201-5173
Telephone: (505) 622-6250

M. Bruce McLaren, Director
J. Tuso, Dean

CURRICULUM AND INSTRUCTION
Courses or Concentrations Available: Library;
Full-Time Faculty: 2; *Full-Time Professional
(non-clerical) Staff Members*: 8.

FACILITIES AND SERVICES
*Practical experiences available
through*: Community Antenna (Cable)
Television Origination; Closed Circuit
Television Facility; Campus Newspaper
(Published Independently); Desktop
Publishing Facility; Photographic
Darkrooms; Institutional Magazine;
Institutional Newspaper; Video Production
Laboratory or Television Studio.

New Mexico State University
(Public)

**Department of Communication Studies
Department 3W
Las Cruces, New Mexico 88003
Telephone: (505) 646-2801**

**L. Blaine Goss, Head
Thomas Gale, Dean**

CURRICULUM AND INSTRUCTION
*Courses or Concentrations
Available*: Communication; *Undergraduate
Objectives or Program
Emphases*: Interpersonal; Organizational;
Intercultural; Communication Education;
*Graduate Objectives or Program
Emphases*: Interpersonal; Organizational;
Intercultural; Communication Education;
Bachelor's Degree Majors: 50; *Master's
Degree Majors*: 25; *Full-Time Faculty*: 7;
Part-Time Faculty: 3; *Full-Time Professional
(non-clerical) Staff Members*: 1.

FACILITIES AND SERVICES
*Practical experiences available
through*: Desktop Publishing Facility; Video
Production Laboratory or Television Studio.

New Mexico State University
(Public)

**Department of Journalism and Mass
Communication
Center for Broadcasting
Box 3J
Las Cruces, New Mexico 88003
Telephone: (505) 646-1034**

**J. Sean McCleneghan, Director
Rene Casillas, Associate Dean, College of
Arts and Sciences**

CURRICULUM AND INSTRUCTION
*Courses or Concentrations
Available*: Advertising; Journalism or Mass
Communication; Public Relations; Radio,
Television, Broadcasting, or
Telecommunications; *Undergraduate
Objectives or Program Emphases*: To train
students in order to find employment in the
professional media upon graduation;
Bachelor's Degree Majors: 171; *Full-Time
Faculty*: 8; *Full-Time Professional
(non-clerical) Staff Members*: 11.

FACILITIES AND SERVICES
*Practical experiences available
through*: Associated Press Wire Service Feed;
Audio Recording Laboratory; Campus
Newspaper (Published Independently);
Local Commercial Newspaper; Photographic
Darkrooms; Video Editing; Electronic Field
Production (Video); Television Broadcast
Station (Institutional); FM Radio Station
(Institutional).

San Juan College (Public)

**Department of Communications/Media
4601 College Boulevard
Farmington, New Mexico 87401
Telephone: (505) 326-3311**

**James L. Burgess, Director
Robert Hokom, Administrator**

CURRICULUM AND INSTRUCTION
*Courses or Concentrations
Available*: Journalism or Mass
Communication; Radio, Television,
Broadcasting, or Telecommunications;
Speech; Photography; *Undergraduate
Objectives or Program Emphases*: Production
oriented with a philosophy of hands-on
training and field experience; *Associate's
Degree Majors*: 29; *Full-Time Faculty*: 2;

Part-Time Faculty: 3; *Full-Time Professional (non-clerical) Staff Members*: 1.

FACILITIES AND SERVICES
Practical experiences available through: Community Antenna (Cable) Television Origination; Local Commercial Newspaper; Local Commercial Television Station; Photographic Darkrooms; Video Editing; Electronic Field Production (Video); FM Radio Station (Institutional); Institutional Newspaper.

University of New Mexico (Public)

Department of Journalism
Albuquerque, New Mexico 87131
Telephone: (505) 277-2326

Fred V. Bales, Chair

CURRICULUM AND INSTRUCTION
Courses or Concentrations Available: Advertising; Journalism or Mass Communication; Radio, Television, Broadcasting, or Telecommunications; *Program Coordinators*: Charles K. Coates (Broadcasting); Bob Lawrence (News Photography); *Undergraduate Objectives or Program Emphases*: News editorial, broadcast sequences; *Bachelor's Degree Majors*: 180; *Full-Time Faculty*: 6; *Part-Time Faculty*: 8.

FACILITIES AND SERVICES
Practical experiences available through: Advertising Agency; Associated Press Wire Service Feed; Audio Recording Laboratory; Community Antenna (Cable) Television Origination; Campus Newspaper (Published Independently); Local Commercial Newspaper; Local Commercial Television Station; Desktop Publishing Facility; Photographic Darkrooms; Video Editing; Electronic Field Production (Video); Television Broadcast Station (Institutional); FM Radio Station (Institutional); Public Relations Agency; Satellite Uplink Facility (Ku Band Transmitter); Video News and Data Processing; Video Production Laboratory or Television Studio.

University of New Mexico (Public)

Department of Communication
1801 Roma NE
Albuquerque, New Mexico 87131
Telephone: (505) 277-5305

Richard J. Jensen, Interim Chair
Hobson Wildenthal, Dean, Arts and Sciences

CURRICULUM AND INSTRUCTION
Courses or Concentrations Available: Communication; Public Relations; Radio, Television, Broadcasting, or Telecommunications; Speech; *Undergraduate Objectives or Program Emphases*: Rhetoric and public address; interpersonal communication; organizational communication; telecommunications; cross cultural communication; forensics; public relations; *Graduate Objectives or Program Emphases*: MA in rhetoric and public address; interpersonal communication; organizational communication; telecommunications; cross cultural communication; forensics; public relations; *Bachelor's Degree Majors*: 200; *Master's Degree Majors*: 70; *Full-Time Faculty*: 11; *Part-Time Faculty*: 7.

FACILITIES AND SERVICES
Practical experiences available through: Advertising Agency; AM Radio Station (Institutional); Audio Recording Laboratory; Community Antenna (Cable) Television Origination; Local Commercial Television Station; Video Editing; Electronic Field Production (Video); Television Broadcast Station (Institutional); Public Relations Agency; Video Production Laboratory or Television Studio.

Adelphi University

Department of Communications
South Avenue
Garden City, New York 11530

Paul Pitcoff, Administrator

Adirondack Community College (Public)

Division of Technology
Bay Road
Queensbury, New York 12801
Telephone: (518) 793-4491

C. Ronald Pesha, Head
Robert Fox, Chair

CURRICULUM AND INSTRUCTION
Courses or Concentrations
Available: Journalism or Mass
Communication; Radio, Television,
Broadcasting, or Telecommunications;
Speech; *Undergraduate Objectives or Program
Emphases*: Preparation for transfer to four
year institutions for television study;
Associate's Degree Majors: 27; *Full-Time
Faculty*: 1.

FACILITIES AND SERVICES
*Practical experiences available
through*: Community Antenna (Cable)
Television Origination; Campus Newspaper
(Published Independently); Local
Commercial Television Station;
Photographic Darkrooms; Video Editing;
Electronic Field Production (Video); FM
Radio Station (Institutional); Institutional
Newspaper.

Borough of Manhattan Community College - CUNY (Public)

Program of Corporate and Cable
Communication
199 Chambers Street
New York, New York 10007
Telephone: (212) 618-1354

George W. Fleck, Director
Anthony Millili, Chair, Speech,
Communication and Theatre Arts
Department

CURRICULUM AND INSTRUCTION
Courses or Concentrations
Available: Communication; Journalism or
Mass Communication; Speech;
Non-Broadcast Television (Corporate
television); *Program Coordinator*: Anthony
Millili (Mass Media, Communication and
Speech); *Undergraduate Objectives or
Program Emphases*: The corporate and cable
communications program (CCC) prepares
students for entry level videotape production
and operations/management positions in
corporate communications departments,
audio-visual production companies,
industrial videotape production; *Other Degree
Majors*: 400; *Full-Time Faculty*: 2;
Part-Time Faculty: 7.

FACILITIES AND SERVICES
Practical experiences available through: Audio
Recording Laboratory; Community Antenna
(Cable) Television Origination; Closed
Circuit Television Facility; Campus
Newspaper (Published Independently);
Local Commercial Television Station; Video
Editing; Electronic Field Production
(Video); Video News and Data Processing;
Video Production Laboratory or Television
Studio.

Bronx Communication College (Public)

Program of Audiovisual Technology
181st and University Avenue
Bronx, New York 10453
Telephone: (212) 220-6478

Donald J. Canty, Curriculum Supervisor
Jo Ann Graham, Administrator

CURRICULUM AND INSTRUCTION
Courses or Concentrations Available: Communication; Journalism or Mass Communication; Radio, Television, Broadcasting, or Telecommunications; Photography; *Program Coordinators*: Martin Diehl (Photography); A. Cosentino (Mass Communication); Jo Ann Graham (Communication); *Undergraduate Objectives or Program Emphases*: Train students for entry level media positions in the non-broadcast area; *Associate's Degree Majors*: 35; *Full-Time Faculty*: 1; *Part-Time Faculty*: 3.

FACILITIES AND SERVICES
Practical experiences available through: Audio Recording Laboratory; Carrier Current Audio Distribution System; Closed Circuit Television Facility; Campus Newspaper (Published Independently); Desktop Publishing Facility; Photographic Darkrooms; Video Editing; Electronic Field Production (Video); Video Production Laboratory or Television Studio.

Brooklyn College (Public)

Department of Television and Radio
Bedford Avenue and Avenue H
Brooklyn, New York 11210
Telephone: (718) 780-5555

Robert C. Williams, Chair
Christoph M. Kimmich, Provost

CURRICULUM AND INSTRUCTION
Courses or Concentrations Available: Film or Cinema; Information Science; Journalism or Mass Communication; Radio, Television, Broadcasting, or Telecommunications; Speech; *Program Coordinators*: Adrian Meppen (Broadcast Journalism); *Undergraduate Objectives or Program Emphases*: BA includes Television Production, Radio Production, Sales and Management. BS emphasizes Broadcast Journalism; *Graduate Objectives or Program Emphases*: MS includes Program Planning and Management. MFA emphasizes Television Production; *Bachelor's Degree Majors*: 375; *Master's Degree Majors*: 2; *MFA Degree Majors*: 22; *Other Degree Majors*: 40; *Full-Time Faculty*: 15; *Part-Time Faculty*: 28; *Full-Time Professional (non-clerical) Staff Members*: 8; Also, see following related entries.

FACILITIES AND SERVICES
Practical experiences available through: Advertising Agency; Associated Press Wire Service Feed; Audio Recording Laboratory; Community Antenna (Cable) Television Origination; Carrier Current Audio Distribution System; Campus Newspaper (Published Independently); Local Commercial Television Station; Video Editing; Electronic Field Production (Video); Public Relations Agency; Video News and Data Processing; Video Production Laboratory or Television Studio.

Brooklyn College (Public)

Department of Speech
Bedford Avenue and Avenue H
Brooklyn, New York 11210
Telephone: (718) 780-5225

Charles E. Parkhurst, Chair
Christoph M. Kimmich, Provost

CURRICULUM AND INSTRUCTION
Courses or Concentrations Available: Communication; Speech; Speech-Language Pathology; Audiology; Speech and Hearing Science; *Bachelor's Degree Majors*: 50; *Master's Degree Majors*: 160; *Full-Time Faculty*: 22; *Part-Time Faculty*: 12; *Full-Time Professional (non-clerical) Staff Members*: 2.

FACILITIES AND SERVICES
Practical experiences available through: Closed Circuit Television Facility; Campus Newspaper (Published Independently); Video Editing; Video Production Laboratory or Television Studio.

Brooklyn College (Public)

Program of Journalism
Brooklyn, New York 11210
Telephone: (718) 780-5302

Bruce Porter, Director
Ellen Belton, Chair, English Department

CURRICULUM AND INSTRUCTION
Courses or Concentrations
Available: Journalism or Mass
Communication; *Undergraduate Objectives or*
Program Emphases: To provide students the
skills they need to get an entry level job on a
daily newspaper and perform it successfully;
Bachelor's Degree Majors: 80; *Full-Time*
Faculty: 2; *Part-Time Faculty*: 2.

FACILITIES AND SERVICES
Practical experiences available
through: Associated Press Wire Service Feed;
Audio Recording Laboratory; Closed Circuit
Television Facility; Campus Newspaper
(Published Independently); Local
Commercial Newspaper; Local Commercial
Television Station; Photographic
Darkrooms; Video Editing; Electronic Field
Production (Video); Television Broadcast
Station (Institutional); Film or Cinema
Laboratories; FM Radio Station
(Institutional); Video Production Laboratory
or Television Studio.

Broome Community College

Department of Humanities
Binghamton, New York 13902

Broome Community College

Communication and Media Arts
Box 1017
Binghamton, New York 13902

John T. Butchko, Administrator

Buffalo State College (Public)

Department of Communication
1300 Elmwood Avenue
Buffalo, New York 14222-1095
Telephone: (716) 878-6008

W. Richard Whitaker, Chair
Patricia Cummins, Dean

CURRICULUM AND INSTRUCTION
Courses or Concentrations
Available: Advertising; Journalism or Mass
Communication; Public Relations; Radio,
Television, Broadcasting, or
Telecommunications; Speech; *Undergraduate*
Objectives or Program Emphases: To provide
education for the journalists, broadcasters
and PR practitioners of tomorrow with a
blend of professional and academic
coursework; *Bachelor's Degree Majors*: 325;
Full-Time Faculty: 13; *Part-Time Faculty*: 6.

FACILITIES AND SERVICES
Practical experiences available
through: Community Antenna (Cable)
Television Origination; Closed Circuit
Television Facility; Campus Newspaper
(Published Independently); Local
Commercial Newspaper; Local Commercial
Television Station; Video Editing;
Electronic Field Production (Video); FM
Radio Station (Institutional); ITFS
Distribution System; Public Relations
Agency; Video Production Laboratory or
Television Studio.

Canisius College

Department of Communication
2001 Main Street
Buffalo, New York 14208

Marilyn S. G. Watt, Administrator

City College of New York (Public)

Department of Communications, Film and
Video
138th Street and Convent Avenue
New York, New York 10031
Telephone: (212) 690-4167

Mark H. Schulman, Chair
Virginia Red, Dean of the Arts

CURRICULUM AND INSTRUCTION

*Courses or Concentrations
Available*: Advertising; Communication; Film or Cinema; Journalism or Mass Communication; Public Relations; Radio, Television, Broadcasting, or Telecommunications; *Undergraduate Objectives or Program Emphases*: Liberal Arts based, career-oriented programs in Journalism, Advertising/Public Relations, Film-Video production, Communication Studies (BA). Professional Film/Video programs (BFA); *Bachelor's Degree Majors*: 150; *BFA Degree Majors*: 50; *Full-Time Faculty*: 8; *Part-Time Faculty*: 6; *Full-Time Professional (non-clerical) Staff Members*: 2.

FACILITIES AND SERVICES

Practical experiences available through: Advertising Agency; Audio Recording Laboratory; Closed Circuit Television Facility; Campus Newspaper (Published Independently); Local Commercial Newspaper; Local Commercial Television Station; Desktop Publishing Facility; Video Editing; Electronic Field Production (Video); Film or Cinema Laboratory; FM Radio Station (Institutional); Public Relations Agency; Video News and Data Processing; Video Production Laboratory or Television Studio.

College of New Rochelle (Private)

**Department of Communication Arts
New Rochelle, New York 10801
Telephone: (914) 654-5576**

James M. O'Brien, Chair

CURRICULUM AND INSTRUCTION

*Courses or Concentrations
Available*: Advertising; Film or Cinema; Journalism or Mass Communication; Public Relations; Radio, Television, Broadcasting, or Telecommunications; *Undergraduate Objectives or Program Emphases*: Film, aesthetics; Broadcast, professional understanding; Journalism, basic skills; Advertising, pre-professional; Public Relations, pre-professional; *Graduate Objectives or Program Emphases*: Public relations; corporate communications; *Bachelor's Degree Majors*: 40; *Other Degree Majors*: 12; *Full-Time Faculty*: 3; *Part-Time Faculty*: 3.

FACILITIES AND SERVICES

Practical experiences available through: Advertising Agency; Audio Recording Laboratory; Closed Circuit Television Facility; Campus Newspaper (Published Independently); Local Commercial Newspaper; Local Commercial Television Station; Desktop Publishing Facility; Photographic Darkrooms; Video Editing; Public Relations Agency; Satellite Uplink Facility (Ku Band Transmitter); Video News and Data Processing; Video Production Laboratory or Television Studio.

College of Saint Rose (Private)

**Department of Public Communications
Box 79 432 Western Avenue
Albany, New York 12203
Telephone: (518) 454-5265**

**Mary Alice Molgard, Program Coordinator
Catherine Cavanaugh, Division Chair**

CURRICULUM AND INSTRUCTION

*Courses or Concentrations
Available*: Advertising; Communication; Film or Cinema; Journalism or Mass Communication; Public Relations; Radio, Television Production, Broadcasting, or Telecommunications; Communication Law; Media Ethics; Small Group Communication; Internship; *Undergraduate Objectives or Program Emphases*: Combined Liberal Arts and strong technical components give students theoretical background as well as practical training. Writing, production, research emphasized. Internship integral part of program; *Bachelor's Degree Majors*: 60; *Other Degree Majors*: 65; *Full-Time Faculty*: 4; *Part-Time Faculty*: 4.

FACILITIES AND SERVICES

Practical experiences available through: Advertising Agency; Associated Press Wire Service Feed; Audio Recording Laboratory; Campus Newspaper (Published Independently); Local Commercial Newspaper; Local Commercial Television Station; Desktop Publishing Facility; Video Editing; Electronic Field Production (Video); Public Relations Agency; Video News and Data Processing; Video Production Laboratory or Television Studio.

College of Staten Island - CUNY (Public)

Program of Cinema Studies
130 Stuyvesant Place
Staten Island, New York 10301
Telephone: (718) 390-7902

Ella Shohat, Coordinator
Mortimer Schiff, Chair, Department of
Performing and Creative Arts

CURRICULUM AND INSTRUCTION
Courses or Concentrations Available: Film or
Cinema; *Program Coordinators*: George
Custen (Communication Program);
*Undergraduate Objectives or Program
Emphases*: Film Theory, History, Criticism
and Film Production; *Graduate Objectives or
Program Emphases*: Film Theory, History,
Criticism; *Bachelor's Degree Majors*: 50; *BFA
Degree Majors*: 50; *Master's Degree
Majors*: 30; *Full-Time Faculty*: 5; *Part-Time
Faculty*: 10; *Full-Time Professional
(non-clerical) Staff Members*: 5.

FACILITIES AND SERVICES
*Practical experiences available
through*: Photographic Darkrooms;
Television Broadcast Station (Institutional);
Film or Cinema Laboratory; Video
Production Laboratory or Television Studio.

College of Staten Island - CUNY (Public)

Program of Communications
120 Stuyvesant Place
Staten Island, New York 10301
Telephone: (718) 390-7992

George F. Custen, Director
Mortimer Schiff, Chair, Performing and
Creative Arts

CURRICULUM AND INSTRUCTION
*Courses or Concentrations
Available*: Communication; Film or Cinema;
Journalism or Mass Communication; Radio,
Television, Broadcasting, or
Telecommunications; Desktop Publishing;
Publication Design; *Undergraduate Objectives
or Program Emphases*: Media Studies;
Publication Design; Corporate
Communication; Journalism; *Degree
Majors*: 40; *Full-Time Faculty*: 2; *Part-Time
Faculty*: 5; *Full-Time Professional
(non-clerical) Staff Members*: 1.

FACILITIES AND SERVICES
*Practical experiences available
through*: Advertising Agency; Audio
Recording Laboratory; Community Antenna
(Cable) Television Origination; Local
Commercial Newspaper; Local Commercial
Television Station; Desktop Publishing
Facility; Photographic Darkrooms; Video
Editing; Film or Cinema Laboratory; FM
Radio Station (Institutional); Institutional
Magazine; Institutional Newspaper; Public
Relations Agency; Video News and Data
Processing; Video Production Laboratory or
Television Studio.

Columbia University (Private)

Graduate School of Journalism
Journalism Building
New York, New York 10027
Telephone: (212) 854-4150

Stephen D. Isaacs, Associate Dean
Joan Kenner, Dean, School of Journalism

CURRICULUM AND INSTRUCTION
*Courses or Concentrations
Available*: Journalism or Mass
Communication; Radio, Television,
Broadcasting, or Telecommunications;
Degree Majors: 181; *Full-Time Faculty*: 21;
Part-Time Faculty: 80.

FACILITIES AND SERVICES
*Practical experiences available
through*: Associated Press Wire Service Feed;
Audio Recording Laboratory; Campus
Newspaper (Published Independently);
Desktop Publishing Facility; Photographic
Darkrooms; Video Editing; Electronic Field
Production (Video); Institutional Magazine;
Institutional Newspaper; Video News and
Data Processing; Video Production
Laboratory or Television Studio.

Cornell University (Public)

Department of Communication
Roberts Hall
Ithaca, New York 14853
Telephone: (607) 255-2111

Royal D. Colle, Chair
David Call, Dean

CURRICULUM AND INSTRUCTION
Courses or Concentrations

Available: Advertising; Communication; Journalism or Mass Communication; Public Relations; Radio, Television, Broadcasting, or Telecommunications; Organizational Communication; *Undergraduate Objectives or Program Emphases*: Communication Planning and Strategy for Public Communication (Public Relations with advertising); Publications; Electronic Media; Interpersonal Communication; Science Communication; *Graduate Objectives or Program Emphases*: Development Communication; Communication Planning; Science Communication; *Degree Majors*: 239; *Full-Time Faculty*: 23.

FACILITIES AND SERVICES
Practical experiences available through: Advertising Agency; Audio Recording Laboratory; Community Antenna (Cable) Television Origination; Campus Newspaper (Published Independently); Desktop Publishing Facility; Video Editing; Electronic Field Production (Video); Institutional Magazine; Public Relations Agency; Satellite Uplink Facility (Ku Band Transmitter); Video News and Data Processing; Video Production Laboratory or Television Studio.

Dutchess Community College (Public)

Program of Communication and Media Arts
Pendell Road
Poughkeepsie, New York 12601
Telephone: (914) 471-4500

Deborah Jay De Silva, Chair
Eric Somers, Administrator

CURRICULUM AND INSTRUCTION
Courses or Concentrations Available: Radio, Television, Broadcasting, or Telecommunications; Speech; Multi Track Audio Recording; *Undergraduate Objectives or Program Emphases*: AS and AAS degree programs which offer three concentrations: Television production, Audio production, Broadcast News; *Associate's Degree Majors*: 186; *Full-Time Faculty*: 7.

FACILITIES AND SERVICES
Practical experiences available through: Advertising Agency; Associated Press Wire Service Feed; Audio Recording Laboratory; Community Antenna (Cable) Television Origination; Closed Circuit

Television Facility; Campus Newspaper (Published Independently); Local Commercial Television Station; Desktop Publishing Facility; Photographic Darkrooms; Video Editing; Electronic Field Production (Video); Television Broadcast Station (Institutional); FM Radio Station (Institutional); ITFS Distribution System; Public Relations Agency; Satellite Uplink Facility (Ku Band Transmitter) (C Band Transmitter); United Press International Feed; Video News and Data Processing; Video Production Laboratory or Television Studio.

Empire State College - SUNY

Circulation, Marketing and Management Program
Rochester, New York 14607

Scott A. Chisholm, Administrator

Five Towns College (Private)

2165 Seaford Avenue
Seaford, New York 11757
Telephone: (516) 783-8800

Nancy Porretto, Assistant Dean
George Berardinelli, Dean

CURRICULUM AND INSTRUCTION
Courses or Concentrations Available: Advertising; Public Relations; Speech; Video Technology; Audio Recording Technology; *Undergraduate Objectives or Program Emphases*: Associate Degrees are offered in the Business Management area with concentrations in Video Technology, Audio Recording Technology and Music Business. The Music Business concentration offers courses in advertising and public relations; *Associate's Degree Majors*: 500; *Full-Time Faculty*: 24; *Part-Time Faculty*: 19; *Full-Time Professional (non-clerical) Staff Members*: 7.

FACILITIES AND SERVICES
Practical experiences available through: Audio Recording Laboratory; Campus Newspaper (Published Independently); Local Commercial Television Station; Video Editing; Electronic Field Production (Video); Video Production Laboratory or Television Studio.

Fordham University (Private)

Department of Communications
Bronx, New York 10458
Telephone: (212) 579-2533

Donald C. Matthews, Chair
Gerard Reedy, SJ, Dean

CURRICULUM AND INSTRUCTION
*Courses or Concentrations
Available*: Advertising; Communication; Film
or Cinema; Journalism or Mass
Communication; Public Relations; Radio,
Television, Broadcasting, or
Telecommunications; *Undergraduate
Objectives or Program Emphases*: General
communications program with emphasis in
broadcasting, journalism and film; *Graduate
Objectives or Program Emphases*: Masters
program in public communication; *Bachelor's
Degree Majors*: 400; *Master's Degree
Majors*: 40; *Full-Time Faculty*: 11;
Part-Time Faculty: 11.

FACILITIES AND SERVICES
*Practical experiences available
through*: Associated Press Wire Service Feed;
Campus Newspaper (Published
Independently); Local Commercial
Newspaper; Local Commercial Television
Station; Electronic Field Production
(Video); FM Radio Station (Institutional);
ITFS Distribution System; Public Relations
Agency; United Press International Feed.

Friends World College (Private)

North American Center
Plover Lane
Huntington, New York 11743
Telephone: (516) 549-5000

D. R. Nilson, Director
Jane Ann Smith, Administrator

CURRICULUM AND INSTRUCTION
*Courses or Concentrations
Available*: Advertising; Communication; Film
or Cinema; Information Science; Journalism
or Mass Communication; Public Relations;
Radio, Television, Broadcasting, or
Telecommunications; Speech; International
Journalism; *Undergraduate Objectives or
Program Emphases*: All students receive B.A.
in International Interdisciplinary Studies.
Students have area of concentration in video
technology, broadcast journalism. All study

is individualized and project-centered;
internship learning; *Bachelor's Degree
Majors*: 6; *Full-Time Faculty*: 7; *Part-Time
Faculty*: 4.

Fulton-Montgomery Community College

Career Education
Route 67
Johnstown, New York 12095

Robert Kusek, Administrator

Genesee Community College

Department of Humanities
One College Road
Batavia, New York 14020

Paul Schulte, Administrator

Hartwick College

Sociology Department
Oneonta, New York 13820

Otto Sonder, Administrator

Herkimer County Community College (Public)

Division of Telecommunications and
Applied Science
Herkimer, New York 13350
Telephone: (315) 866-0300

David H. Champoux, Chair
Ted D. Spring, Dean

CURRICULUM AND INSTRUCTION
*Courses or Concentrations
Available*: Journalism or Mass
Communication; Radio, Television,
Broadcasting, or Telecommunications;
*Undergraduate Objectives or Program
Emphases*: Successful Transfer; Entry Level
Employment; *Degree Majors*: 100; *Full-Time
Faculty*: 4; *Full-Time Professional
(non-clerical) Staff Members*: 3.

FACILITIES AND SERVICES
Practical experiences available through: Advertising Agency; AM Radio Station (Institutional); Associated Press Wire Service Feed; Audio Recording Laboratory; Community Antenna (Cable) Television Origination; Carrier Current Audio Distribution System; Closed Circuit Television Facility; Local Commercial Television Station; Desktop Publishing Facility; Photographic Darkrooms; Video Editing; Electronic Field Production (Video); Film or Cinema Laboratories; Institutional Magazine; Satellite Uplink Facility (Ku Band Transmitter) (C Band Transmitter); Video News and Data Processing; Video Production Laboratory or Television Studio.

Herkimer County Community College (Public)

**Program of Radio-Television Broadcasting
100 Reservoir Road
Herkimer, New York 13350
Telephone: (315) 866-0300 Extension: 232**

**Kalman A. Socolof, Senior Professor
David H. Champoux, Division Chair**

CURRICULUM AND INSTRUCTION
Courses or Concentrations Available: Journalism or Mass Communication; Radio, Television, Broadcasting, or Telecommunications; Copy writing, Broadcast Sales; *Undergraduate Objectives or Program Emphases*: Preparation for entry level job in broadcast/cable/video, or for transfer to a four year school; *Full-Time Faculty*: 3; *Full-Time Professional (non-clerical) Staff Members*: 2.

FACILITIES AND SERVICES
Practical experiences available through: Associated Press Wire Service Feed; Audio Recording Laboratory; Community Antenna (Cable) Television Origination; Campus Newspaper (Published Independently); Local Commercial Television Station; Video Editing; Electronic Field Production (Video); Video Production Laboratory or Television Studio.

Hofstra University (Private)

**Department of Communication Arts
Dempster Hall
Hempstead, New York 11550
Telephone: (516) 560-5424**

**Peter Haratonik, Chair
Robert C. Vogt, Dean**

CURRICULUM AND INSTRUCTION
Courses or Concentrations Available: Communication; Film or Cinema; Journalism or Mass Communication; Public Relations; Radio, Television, Broadcasting, or Telecommunications; *Program Coordinators*: Jerome Delamater (Film); *Undergraduate Objectives or Program Emphases*: Prepare students for professional careers in areas of radio, television, film, journalism; *Bachelor's Degree Majors*: 271; *Full-Time Faculty*: 9; *Part-Time Faculty*: 7; *Full-Time Professional (non-clerical) Staff Members*: 2.

FACILITIES AND SERVICES
Practical experiences available through: Advertising Agency; Audio Recording Laboratory; Closed Circuit Television Facility; Campus Newspaper (Published Independently); Local Commercial Newspaper; Local Commercial Television Station; Video Editing; Electronic Field Production (Video); Film or Cinema Laboratory; FM Radio Station (Institutional); Institutional Magazine; Public Relations Agency; Video Production Laboratory or Television Studio.

Houghton College (Private)

**Department of Communication
Houghton, New York 14744
Telephone: (716) 567-9200**

**Douglas M. Gaerte, Head
B. Sue Crider, Chair, Division of Languages and Literature**

CURRICULUM AND INSTRUCTION
Courses or Concentrations Available: Advertising; Communication; Journalism or Mass Communication; Public Relations; Radio, Television, Broadcasting, or Telecommunications; Speech; Writing (technical writing, advanced composition, rhetorical patterns); *Program Coordinator*: James Zoller (Writing courses); *Undergraduate Objectives or Program*

Emphases: An interdisciplinary program in the composition and performance of oral and written discourse, examined theoretically and in various practical situations; the nature of decision making, the role of communication in society, and methods of influence; *Bachelor's Degree Majors*: 21; *Full-Time Faculty*: 4; *Part-Time Faculty*: 2.

FACILITIES AND SERVICES
Practical experiences available through: Audio Recording Laboratory; Closed Circuit Television Facility; Campus Newspaper (Published Independently); Desktop Publishing Facility; Photographic Darkrooms; Video Editing; Electronic Field Production (Video); FM Radio Station (Institutional); ITFS Distribution System; Institutional Magazine; Public Relations Agency; United Press International Feed; Video Production Laboratory or Television Studio.

Hudson Valley Community College (Public)

Department of English
80 Vandenburgh Avenue
Troy, New York 12019
Telephone: (518) 283-1100

Vivian A. Tortorici, Chair
James LaGatta, Dean, Liberal Arts and Sciences

CURRICULUM AND INSTRUCTION
Courses or Concentrations Available: Communication; Journalism or Mass Communication; Speech; Composition; Literature; Drama; Creative Writing; *Undergraduate Objectives or Program Emphases*: To develop skills necessary for clear, concise, and effective communication and to foster an appreciation of the aesthetic qualities of the language through literature; *Full-Time Faculty*: 18; *Part-Time Faculty*: 31.

FACILITIES AND SERVICES
Practical experiences available through: Closed Circuit Television Facility; Campus Newspaper (Published Independently); Local Commercial Newspaper; Local Commercial Television Station.

Iona College

Department of Communication Arts
715 North Avenue
New Rochelle, New York 10801
Telephone: (914) 633-2000

George V. Thottam, Chair
Ernst Menze, Dean

CURRICULUM AND INSTRUCTION
Courses or Concentrations Available: Advertising; Film or Cinema; Journalism or Mass Communication; Public Relations; Radio, Television, Broadcasting, or Telecommunications; *Undergraduate Objectives or Program Emphases*: Degree in mass communication with limited specialization in journalism, advertising, broadcasting (radio), public relations and film studies; *Graduate Objectives or Program Emphases*: MS in Communication Arts with specialization in organizational communication or public relations; *Bachelor's Degree Majors*: 2; *Other Degree Majors*: 107; *Full-Time Faculty*: 9; *Part-Time Faculty*: 26; *Full-Time Professional (non-clerical) Staff Members*: 2.

FACILITIES AND SERVICES
Practical experiences available through: Audio Recording Laboratory; Community Antenna (Cable) Television Origination; Closed Circuit Television Facility; Campus Newspaper (Published Independently); Local Commercial Television Station; Desktop Publishing Facility; Video Editing; Electronic Field Production (Video); Video Production Laboratory or Television Studio.

Ithaca College (Private)

Roy H. Park School of Communication
Ithaca, New York 14850
Telephone: (607) 274-3895

Thomas W. Bohn, Dean
Thomas C. Longin, Provost

CURRICULUM AND INSTRUCTION
Courses or Concentrations Available: Advertising; Film or Cinema; Journalism or Mass Communication; Public Relations; Radio, Television, Broadcasting, or Telecommunications; *Undergraduate Objectives or Program Emphases*: To ground students in the theory, history, ethics, economics, practice, and criticism of

communications. The program introduces students to the broad academic and professional traditions of the field, linking them to current communications practices; *Graduate Objectives or Program Emphases*: Prepares graduates to pursue professional careers as communication consultants, media designers and producers, and managers of media and training programs within corporate, medical, and educational settings. Students from all disciplines may apply; *Program Coordinators*: W. Williams (Television-Radio); G. E. Landen (Cinema and Photography); Steve Seidman (Corporate Communication); *Bachelor's Degree Majors*: 840; *BFA Degree Majors*: 75; *Master's Degree Majors*: 25; *Full-Time Faculty*: 35; *Part-Time Faculty*: 5; *Full-Time Professional (non-clerical) Staff Members*: 35. See one or more additional entries below.

FACILITIES AND SERVICES
Practical experiences available through: Advertising Agency; AM Radio Station (Institutional); Associated Press Wire Service Feed; Audio Recording Laboratory; Community Antenna (Cable) Television Origination; Carrier Current Audio Distribution System; Campus Newspaper (Published Independently); Local Commercial Newspaper; Desktop Publishing Facility; Photographic Darkrooms; Video Editing; Electronic Field Production (Video); Film or Cinema Laboratory; FM Radio Station (Institutional); Institutional Newspaper; Public Relations Agency; Video News and Data Processing; Video Production Laboratory or Television Studio.

Ithaca College (Private)

Department of Television/Radio
Roy Park School of Communications
Ithaca, New York 14850
Telephone: (607) 274-3242

Wenmouth Williams, Jr., Chair
Thomas Bohn, Dean

CURRICULUM AND INSTRUCTION
Courses or Concentrations Available: Advertising; Journalism or Mass Communication; Public Relations; Radio, Television, Broadcasting, or Telecommunications; Media Studies; Photography; Corporate Communication;

Video Production, Media Management; *Degree Majors*: 513; *Full-Time Faculty*: 17; *Part-Time Faculty*: 3.

FACILITIES AND SERVICES
Practical experiences available through: Advertising Agency; AM Radio Station (Institutional); Associated Press Wire Service Feed; Audio Recording Laboratory; Community Antenna (Cable) Television Origination; Carrier Current Audio Distribution System; Closed Circuit Television Facility; Local Commercial Newspaper; Local Commercial Television Station; Desktop Publishing Facility; Photographic Darkrooms; Video Editing; Electronic Field Production (Video); Film or Cinema Laboratories; FM Radio Station (Institutional); Institutional Newspaper; Public Relations Agency; United Press International Feed; Video News and Data Processing; Video Production Laboratory or Television Studio.

Ithaca College (Private)

School of Humanities and Sciences
Danby Road
Ithaca, New York 14850
Telephone: (607) 274-3102

Howard S. Erlich, Dean
Thomas C. Longin, Provost

CURRICULUM AND INSTRUCTION
Courses or Concentrations Available: Speech; *Program Coordinator*: Constantine Perialas (Speech Communication); *Bachelor's Degree Majors*: 799; *BFA Degree Majors*: 65; *Other Degree Majors*: 107; *Full-Time Faculty*: 216; *Part-Time Faculty*: 59.

John Jay College - CUNY

Department of Speech and Theatre
New York, New York 10019

Kingsborough Community College (Public)

Program of Journalism
2001 Oriental Boulevard
Brooklyn, New York 11235
Telephone: (718) 934-5237 Extension or
Alternate: 934-5849

John B. Manbeck, Director
Stephen Weidenborner, Chair, English
Department

CURRICULUM AND INSTRUCTION
Courses or Concentrations
Available: Advertising; Journalism or Mass
Communication; Radio, Television,
Broadcasting, or Telecommunications;
Photojournalism; Typography; Layout
Design; *Program Coordinators*: Cliff Hesse
(Broadcast Management); Thomas Nonn
(Photojournalism, Layout, Typography);
Fred Mayerson (Business); *Undergraduate
Objectives or Program Emphases*: To train
students for placement in community and
neighborhood newspapers and/or transfer to
four year liberal arts programs; *Associate's
Degree Majors*: 75; *Full-Time Faculty*: 3;
Part-Time Faculty: 3.

FACILITIES AND SERVICES
*Practical experiences available
through*: Associated Press Wire Service Feed;
Campus Newspaper (Published
Independently); Local Commercial
Newspaper; Desktop Publishing Facility;
Photographic Darkrooms; FM Radio Station
(Institutional); Institutional Newspaper.

Laboratory Institute of Merchandising

12 East 53rd Street
New York, New York 10022

Joseph H. Moskowitz, Administrator

Le Moyne College (Private)

Department of English/Communication
Le Moyne Heights
Syracuse, New York 13214
Telephone: (315) 445-4380

Thomas R. Hogan, Director
Roger Lund, Chair

CURRICULUM AND INSTRUCTION
Courses or Concentrations
Available: Advertising; Communication; Film
or Cinema; Journalism or Mass
Communication; Public Relations; Radio,
Television, Broadcasting, or
Telecommunications; Speech; Theatre;
*Undergraduate Objectives or Program
Emphases*: Liberal Arts training, career
opportunities, preparation for graduate
school; *Bachelor's Degree Majors*: 150;
Full-Time Faculty: 3; *Part-Time Faculty*: 6;
*Full-Time Professional (non-clerical) Staff
Members*: 1.

FACILITIES AND SERVICES
*Practical experiences available
through*: Advertising Agency; Community
Antenna (Cable) Television Origination;
Carrier Current Audio Distribution System;
Closed Circuit Television Facility; Campus
Newspaper (Published Independently);
Local Commercial Newspaper; Local
Commercial Television Station; Desktop
Publishing Facility; Photographic
Darkrooms; Video Editing; Electronic Field
Production (Video); Film or Cinema
Laboratory; Public Relations Agency; Video
News and Data Processing; Video
Production Laboratory or Television Studio.

Lehman College - CUNY (Public)

Department of Speech and Theatre
Bedford Park Boulevard West
Bronx, New York 10801
Telephone: (212) 960-8134

Albert Bermel, Chair
Anne Humpherys, Dean

CURRICULUM AND INSTRUCTION
Courses or Concentrations
Available: Communication; Film or Cinema;
Journalism or Mass Communication; Radio,
Television, Broadcasting, or
Telecommunications; Speech; Theatre;
Speech and Hearing; *Program
Coordinator*: Frank Kahn (Radio/Television,
History, Production); *Undergraduate
Objectives or Program Emphases*: Education
for living and thinking, rather than
vocational, although some students do go
with related professions; *Graduate Objectives
or Program Emphases*: Speech and hearing
only, training as pathologists; *Bachelor's
Degree Majors*: 100; *Master's Degree
Majors*: 50; *Full-Time Faculty*: 18;

Part-Time Faculty: 6; *Full-Time Professional (non-clerical) Staff Members*: 4.

FACILITIES AND SERVICES
Practical experiences available through: Advertising Agency; AM Radio Station (Institutional); Audio Recording Laboratory; Community Antenna (Cable) Television Origination; Closed Circuit Television Facility; Campus Newspaper (Published Independently); Local Commercial Newspaper; Local Commercial Television Station; Desktop Publishing Facility; Photographic Darkrooms; Video Editing; Electronic Field Production (Video); Film or Cinema Laboratory; Public Relations Agency; Video Production Laboratory or Television Studio.

Lehman College - CUNY (Public)

Program of Mass Communication
Bedford Park Boulevard West
Bronx, New York 10468
Telephone: (212) 960-8136

Frank Kahn, Director
Albert Bermel, Chair, Department of Speech and Theatre

CURRICULUM AND INSTRUCTION
Courses or Concentrations
Available: Communication; Film or Cinema; Journalism or Mass Communication; Radio, Television, Broadcasting, or Telecommunications; Speech; *Undergraduate Objectives or Program Emphases*: Multi disciplinary approach in a variety of production and non-production courses; *Bachelor's Degree Majors*: 70; *Full-Time Faculty*: 1; *Part-Time Faculty*: 2; *Full-Time Professional (non-clerical) Staff Members*: 1.

FACILITIES AND SERVICES
Practical experiences available through: Audio Recording Laboratory; Carrier Current Audio Distribution System; Campus Newspaper (Published Independently); Local Commercial Newspaper; Institutional Magazine; Video Production Laboratory or Television Studio.

Long Island University - Brooklyn (Private)

Media Arts Department
Communications Center
1 University Plaza
Brooklyn, New York 11201
Telephone: (718) 403-1052

Joseph W. Slade, Chair
David Cohen, Dean, Arts and Sciences

CURRICULUM AND INSTRUCTION
Courses or Concentrations
Available: Advertising; Communication; Film or Cinema; Journalism or Mass Communication; Public Relations; Radio, Television, Broadcasting, or Telecommunications; Computer Graphics; Photography; *Undergraduate Objectives or Program Emphases*: To turn out production specialists in all phases of media, and to prepare theorists for graduate school; *Bachelor's Degree Majors*: 70; *Full-Time Faculty*: 4; *Part-Time Faculty*: 8; *Full-Time Professional (non-clerical) Staff Members*: 3.

FACILITIES AND SERVICES
Practical experiences available through: AM Radio Station (Institutional); Associated Press Wire Service Feed; Audio Recording Laboratory; Community Antenna (Cable) Television Origination; Carrier Current Audio Distribution System; Closed Circuit Television Facility; Campus Newspaper (Published Independently); Local Commercial Newspaper; Local Commercial Television Station; Desktop Publishing Facility; Photographic Darkrooms; Video Editing; Electronic Field Production (Video); Film or Cinema Laboratory; Reuters News Agency; United Press International Feed; Video News and Data Processing; Video Production Laboratory or Television Studio.

Long Island University - Brooklyn (Private)

Department of Journalism
University Plaza
Brooklyn, New York 11201-9926
Telephone: (718) 403-1053

Donald Allport Bird, Chair
David Cohen, Dean, Arts and Sciences

CURRICULUM AND INSTRUCTION
Courses or Concentrations
Available: Advertising; Journalism or Mass
Communication; Public Relations;
*Undergraduate Objectives or Program
Emphases*: News Editorial; Mass
Communication and Journalism; Advertising;
Public Relations; *Bachelor's Degree
Majors*: 55; *Full-Time Faculty*: 3; *Part-Time
Faculty*: 10.

FACILITIES AND SERVICES
*Practical experiences available
through*: Advertising Agency; AM Radio
Station (Institutional); Associated Press
Wire Service Feed; Audio Recording
Laboratory; Community Antenna (Cable)
Television Origination; Carrier Current
Audio Distribution System; Closed Circuit
Television Facility; Campus Newspaper
(Published Independently); Local
Commercial Newspaper; Local Commercial
Television Station; Desktop Publishing
Facility; Photographic Darkrooms; Video
Editing; Electronic Field Production
(Video); Television Broadcast Station
(Institutional); FM Radio Station
(Institutional); Institutional Magazine;
Institutional Newspaper; Public Relations
Agency; Video News and Data Processing;
Video Production Laboratory or Television
Studio.

Long Island University - Southampton (Private)

Program of Communication Arts
Montauk Highway
Southampton, New York 11968
Telephone: (516) 283-4000

Jon Fraser, Director
**William Peterson, Division Director, Fine
Arts**

CURRICULUM AND INSTRUCTION
Courses or Concentrations
Available: Advertising; Communication; Film
or Cinema; Journalism or Mass
Communication; Public Relations; Radio,
Television, Broadcasting, or
Telecommunications; Photojournalism;
*Undergraduate Objectives or Program
Emphases*: To provide students with a
thorough knowledge of the communications
field, including broadcasting, advertising,
public relations, and photojournalism;
prepare them for graduate study or jobs in

the market place; *BFA Degree Majors*: 50;
Full-Time Faculty: 2; *Part-Time Faculty*: 4.

FACILITIES AND SERVICES
Practical experiences available through: AM
Radio Station (Institutional); Campus
Newspaper (Published Independently);
Local Commercial Newspaper; Local
Commercial Television Station;
Photographic Darkrooms; Video Editing;
Television Broadcast Station (Institutional);
FM Radio Station (Institutional); Video
Production Laboratory or Television Studio.

Marymount Manhattan College (Private)

Department of Communication Arts
221 East 71st Street
New York, New York 10021
Telephone: (212) 517-0400

Arlene Krebs, Professor
Marilyn Massey, Dean

CURRICULUM AND INSTRUCTION
Courses or Concentrations
Available: Advertising; Communication; Film
or Cinema; Public Relations; Speech; Video
Production, Film Production, Organizational
Communication, New Communications
Technologies, Mass Communications;
Program Coordinator: David Linton
(Communication Theory, Speech,
Interpersonal Communications, Mass Media
Effects); *Undergraduate Objectives or
Program Emphases*: Students are required to
complete 34 credits of course work in their
major with a core curriculum of 40 credits;
Full-Time Faculty: 2; *Part-Time Faculty*: 1.

FACILITIES AND SERVICES
*Practical experiences available
through*: Advertising Agency; Photographic
Darkrooms; Video Editing; Electronic Field
Production (Video); Video Production
Laboratory or Television Studio.

Medaille College (Private)

Division of Humanities
18 Agassiz Circle
Buffalo, New York 14214
Telephone: (716) 884-3281

John R. Schedel, Chair
Thomas Rookey, Dean, Academic Affairs

CURRICULUM AND INSTRUCTION
Courses or Concentrations
Available: Communication; Speech;
Undergraduate Objectives or Program
Emphases: Generalized humanities objectives
with emphases offered in art, fine arts,
graphic arts, literature, public address, and
writing; *Bachelor's Degree Majors*: 5;
Full-Time Faculty: 9; *Part-Time Faculty*: 19;
Full-Time Professional (non-clerical) Staff
Members: 1.

FACILITIES AND SERVICES
Practical experiences available
through: Desktop Publishing Facility;
Institutional Magazine.

Medaille College (Private)

Program of Media Communications
18 Agassiz Circle
Buffalo, New York 14214
Telephone: (716) 884-3281

Judith Baker-Martin, Chair
Thomas Rookey, Dean, Academic Affairs

CURRICULUM AND INSTRUCTION
Courses or Concentrations
Available: Advertising; Communication;
Journalism or Mass Communication; Public
Relations; Radio, Television, Broadcasting,
or Telecommunications; Graphics and
Photography; *Undergraduate Objectives or*
Program Emphases: Five minor areas with
general media degree program; students may
specialize or generalize in advertising, public
relations, journalism, broadcasting
(Television or Radio) and
graphics/photography. Require 18 hours in
internships. Others available as electives;
Degree Majors: 67; *Full-Time Faculty*: 3;
Part-Time Faculty: 3.

FACILITIES AND SERVICES
Practical experiences available
through: Advertising Agency; Associated
Press Wire Service Feed; Audio Recording

Laboratory; Community Antenna (Cable)
Television Origination; Campus Newspaper
(Published Independently); Local
Commercial Newspaper; Commercial
Television Facility; Desktop Publishing
Facility; Photographic Darkrooms; FM
Radio Station (Institutional); Public
Relations Agency.

Molloy College

Communication Arts Department
1000 Hempstead Avenue
Rockville Centre, New York 11570

Sister Margaret C. Kavanagh,
Administrator

Monroe Community College (Public)

Department of Communication
1000 East Henrietta Road
Rochester, New York 14623
Telephone: (716) 424-5200

Thomas P. Proietti, Chair

CURRICULUM AND INSTRUCTION
Courses or Concentrations
Available: Communication; Film or Cinema;
Journalism or Mass Communication; Radio,
Television, Broadcasting, or
Telecommunications; Speech; *Undergraduate*
Objectives or Program
Emphases: Photography, Television; Graphic
Arts, Printing; Mass Communication;
Associate's Degree Majors: 380; *Full-Time*
Faculty: 12; *Part-Time Faculty*: 19;
Full-Time Professional (non-clerical) Staff
Members: 2.

FACILITIES AND SERVICES
Practical experiences available
through: Advertising Agency; Audio
Recording Laboratory; Community Antenna
(Cable) Television Origination; Carrier
Current Audio Distribution System; Closed
Circuit Television Facility; Campus
Newspaper (Published Independently);
Local Commercial Newspaper; Local
Commercial Television Station; Desktop
Publishing Facility; Photographic
Darkrooms; Video Editing; Electronic Field
Production (Video); Film or Cinema
Laboratory; Public Relations Agency; Video

News and Data Processing; Video
Production Laboratory or Television Studio.

Mount Saint Mary College

Communication Arts
33 Powell Avenue
Newburgh, New York 12550

Irene W. Nunnari, Administrator

New School for Social Research (Private)

Department of Film/Television
Media Studies Program
66 West 12th Street
New York, New York 10011
Telephone: (212) 741-8903

Gerald Hefoer, Dean

CURRICULUM AND INSTRUCTION
Courses or Concentrations
Available: Advertising; Communication; Film
or Cinema; Journalism or Mass
Communication; Public Relations; Radio,
Television, Broadcasting, or
Telecommunications; *Undergraduate
Objectives or Program Emphases*: The New
School for Social Research offers
undergraduate courses in Film/Television,
Journalism, Communication, and
Advertising.; *Graduate Objectives or Program
Emphases*: M.A. degree in Media Studies;
Master's Degree Majors: 185; *Full-Time
Faculty*: 6; *Part-Time Faculty*: 45; *Full-Time
Professional (non-clerical) Staff Members*: 4.

FACILITIES AND SERVICES
*Practical experiences available
through*: Advertising Agency; Audio
Recording Laboratory; Local Commercial
Television Station; Desktop Publishing
Facility; Photographic Darkrooms; Video
Editing; Electronic Field Production
(Video); Film or Cinema Laboratory;
Public Relations Agency; Video News and
Data Processing; Video Production
Laboratory or Television Studio.

New York University (Private)

Department of Journalism and Mass
Communication
Washington Square
New York, New York 10003
Telephone: (212) 998-7990

Terri Brooks, Chair
C. Duncan Rice, Dean, Faculty of Arts and
Science

CURRICULUM AND INSTRUCTION
Courses or Concentrations
Available: Journalism or Mass
Communication; Public Relations; Radio,
Television, Broadcasting, or
Telecommunications; Ethics; Media
Criticism; *Undergraduate Objectives or
Program Emphases*: Training in practices,
principles, ethics, and traditions of journalism
and non-fiction; *Graduate Objectives or
Program Emphases*: Training in practices,
principles, ethics, and traditions of journalism
and non-fiction; *Bachelor's Degree
Majors*: 315; *Master's Degree Majors*: 235;
Full-Time Faculty: 18; *Part-Time
Faculty*: 21; *Full-Time Professional
(non-clerical) Staff Members*: 3.

FACILITIES AND SERVICES
*Practical experiences available
through*: Associated Press Wire Service Feed;
Audio Recording Laboratory; Carrier
Current Audio Distribution System; Closed
Circuit Television Facility; Campus
Newspaper (Published Independently);
Local Commercial Newspaper; Local
Commercial Television Station; Desktop
Publishing Facility; Video Editing;
Electronic Field Production (Video);
Institutional Magazine; Video News and
Data Processing; Video Production
Laboratory or Television Studio.

New York University (Private)

Program of Speech Communication
50 W. 4th Street, #829
New York, New York 10003
Telephone: (212) 998-5192

Deborah J. Borisoff, Director

CURRICULUM AND INSTRUCTION
Courses or Concentrations
Available: Communication; Public Relations;
Speech; *Program Coordinators*: Terry Moran

(Media Ecology); Terri Brooks (Journalism); *Bachelor's Degree Majors*: 120; *Master's Degree Majors*: 20; *Full-Time Faculty*: 3; *Part-Time Faculty*: 12.

FACILITIES AND SERVICES
Practical experiences available through: Advertising Agency; AM Radio Station (Institutional); Campus Newspaper (Published Independently); Local Commercial Television Station; Desktop Publishing Facility; Photographic Darkrooms; Television Broadcast Station (Institutional); ITFS Distribution System; Public Relations Agency; Video Production Laboratory or Television Studio.

New York University (Private)

Tisch School of the Arts
Washington Square
New York, New York 10003
Telephone: (212) 998-1800

David Oppenheim, Dean
L. Jay Oliva, Chancellor

CURRICULUM AND INSTRUCTION
Courses or Concentrations Available: Communication; Film or Cinema; Radio, Television, Broadcasting, or Telecommunications; Interactive Telecommunications; *Program Coordinators*: Charles Milne (Film and Television); William Simon (Cinema Studies); Red Burns (Interactive Telecommunications); Janet Heipris (Dramatic Writing); Tom Drysdale (Photography); *Undergraduate Objectives or Program Emphases*: Train practicing artists; educate scholars in parallel fields; *BFA Degree Majors*: 650; *Master's Degree Majors*: 150; *MFA Degree Majors*: 90; *Doctoral Degree Majors Currently in Residence*: 20; *Full-Time Faculty*: 105; *Part-Time Faculty*: 200.

FACILITIES AND SERVICES
Practical experiences available through: Associated Press Wire Service Feed; Audio Recording Laboratory; Campus Newspaper (Published Independently); Desktop Publishing Facility; Photographic Darkrooms; Video Editing; Film or Cinema Laboratory; FM Radio Station (Institutional); Video Production Laboratory or Television Studio.

Niagara County Community College (Public)

Department of Communication/Media Arts
3111 Saunders Settlement Road
Sanborn, New York 14120
Telephone: (716) 731-3271

Jon Williams, Coordinator
Rosemary Sweetman, Administrator

CURRICULUM AND INSTRUCTION
Courses or Concentrations Available: Advertising; Communication; Journalism or Mass Communication; Public Relations; Radio, Television, Broadcasting, or Telecommunications; Speech; *Undergraduate Objectives or Program Emphases*: Liberal arts based program to prepare students for either transfer to a four year institution or immediate employment in the communications or media industry; *Degree Majors*: 150; *Full-Time Faculty*: 5; *Part-Time Faculty*: 2.

FACILITIES AND SERVICES
Practical experiences available through: Advertising Agency; Audio Recording Laboratory; Carrier Current Audio Distribution System; Closed Circuit Television Facility; Campus Newspaper (Published Independently); Local Commercial Newspaper; Local Commercial Television Station; Desktop Publishing Facility; Video Editing; Electronic Field Production (Video); Public Relations Agency; Satellite Uplink Facility; Video Production Laboratory or Television Studio.

Niagara University (Private)

Program of Communication Studies
Niagara, New York 14109
Telephone: (716) 285-1212

Robert F. Crawford, Director
Susan Mason, Dean, College of Arts and Sciences

CURRICULUM AND INSTRUCTION
Courses or Concentrations Available: Advertising; Communication; Film or Cinema; Journalism or Mass Communication; Radio, Television, Broadcasting, or Telecommunications; Media Research; *Undergraduate Objectives or Program Emphases*: To provide a comprehensive study of mass

communications forms and technologies to prepare students for entry-level positions through concentrated conceptual and skill-related course work; *Full-Time Faculty*: 3; *Part-Time Faculty*: 4.

FACILITIES AND SERVICES
Practical experiences available through: AM Radio Station (Institutional); Closed Circuit Television Facility; Campus Newspaper (Published Independently); Photographic Darkrooms; Video Editing; Electronic Field Production (Video); Film or Cinema Laboratory; Video Production Laboratory or Television Studio.

Onondaga Community College (Public)

Department of Radio/Television
Route 173
Syracuse, New York 13215
Telephone: (315) 469-7741

Catherine M. Hawkins, Chair
Bernadette Russell, Dean, Center for Arts, Humanities and Social Science

CURRICULUM AND INSTRUCTION
Courses or Concentrations Available: Radio, Television, Broadcasting, or Telecommunications; *Undergraduate Objectives or Program Emphases*: AAS degree in Radio Television; *Degree Majors*: 160; *Full-Time Faculty*: 4; *Part-Time Faculty*: 1; *Full-Time Professional (non-clerical) Staff Members*: 1.

FACILITIES AND SERVICES
Practical experiences available through: Audio Recording Laboratory; Carrier Current Audio Distribution System; Campus Newspaper (Published Independently); Video Editing; Electronic Field Production (Video); Video Production Laboratory or Television Studio.

Orange County Community College

Department of Speech and Theatre
Middletown, New York 10940

Pace University - New York (Private)

Department of Speech Communication Studies
Pace Plaza
New York, New York 10038
Telephone: (212) 346-1510

Jeffrey C. Hahner, Chair
Joseph E. Houle, Dean

CURRICULUM AND INSTRUCTION
Courses or Concentrations Available: Communication; Journalism or Mass Communication; Public Relations; Speech; *Undergraduate Objectives or Program Emphases*: Concentrations provided in Media Studies, Organizational Communication, and Political-Legal Studies. Each area provides a broad understanding of communication and emphasizes skills needed in an increasingly competitive job market. Graduate study preparation; *Bachelor's Degree Majors*: 65; *Full-Time Faculty*: 8; *Part-Time Faculty*: 24; *Full-Time Professional (non-clerical) Staff Members*: 1.

FACILITIES AND SERVICES
Practical experiences available through: Campus Newspaper (Published Independently); Photographic Darkrooms; Video Editing; Television Broadcast Station (Institutional); FM Radio Station (Institutional); Video Production Laboratory or Television Studio.

Pace University - Pleasantville (Private)

Department of Literature and Communications
Bedford Road
Pleasantville, New York 10570
Telephone: (914) 773-3790

Robert M. Klaeger, Chair
Charles Masiello, Vice Dean

CURRICULUM AND INSTRUCTION
Courses or Concentrations Available: Advertising; Communication; Film or Cinema; Public Relations; Radio, Television, Broadcasting, or Telecommunications; Speech; *Undergraduate Objectives or Program Emphases*: Skill oriented communication courses with a traditional liberal arts major (literature);

Bachelor's Degree Majors: 120; *Full-Time Faculty*: 23; *Part-Time Faculty*: 65; *Full-Time Professional (non-clerical) Staff Members*: 4.

FACILITIES AND SERVICES
Practical experiences available through: Advertising Agency; Audio Recording Laboratory; Community Antenna (Cable) Television Origination; Campus Newspaper (Published Independently); Local Commercial Television Station; Desktop Publishing Facility; Photographic Darkrooms; Video Editing; Electronic Field Production (Video); Film or Cinema Laboratory; Video Production Laboratory or Television Studio.

Pace University - White Plains (Private)

Department of Journalism
78 North Broadway
White Plains, New York 10603

Allen Oren, Administrator

Queens College - CUNY (Public)

Department of Communication Arts and Sciences
G Building, Kissena Boulevard
Flushing, New York 11367
Telephone: (718) 520-7353

Stuart E. Liebman, Acting Chair
Susan Rembert, Deputy Chair

CURRICULUM AND INSTRUCTION
Courses or Concentrations Available: Communication; Film or Cinema; Radio, Television, Broadcasting, or Telecommunications; Speech; *Bachelor's Degree Majors*: 300; *Master's Degree Majors*: 30; *Full-Time Faculty*: 12; *Part-Time Faculty*: 14; *Full-Time Professional (non-clerical) Staff Members*: 2.

FACILITIES AND SERVICES
Practical experiences available through: Television Broadcast Station (Institutional); Film or Cinema Laboratory.

Rensselaer Polytechnic Institute (Private)

Department of Language, Literature, and Communication
8th Street
Troy, New York 12180-3590
Telephone: (518) 276-6569

Merrill D. Whitburn, Chair
Thomas Phelan, Dean

CURRICULUM AND INSTRUCTION
Courses or Concentrations Available: Communication; Graphics; Rhetoric; Composition; *Undergraduate Objectives or Program Emphases*: The BS program emphasizes those communication processes involved in the creation and use of technology, but also offers a broad range of applied and theoretical work; preparation for employment in Technical-Professional Communication or advanced study; *Graduate Objectives or Program Emphases*: MS and Ph.D. programs emphasize humanistic and social science approaches to the study of human communication. Programs lead to careers in technical and/or visual communication on both operational and managerial levels in business and government; *Doctoral Degree Majors Currently in Residence*: 23; *Additional Doctoral Degree Majors*: 18; *Other Degree Majors*: 49; *Full-Time Faculty*: 19; *Part-Time Faculty*: 5.

FACILITIES AND SERVICES
Practical experiences available through: Campus Newspaper (Published Independently); Desktop Publishing Facility; FM Radio Station (Institutional); Institutional Newspaper.

Roberts Wesleyan College

Department of Communications
2301 Westside Drive
Rochester, New York 14514

Walter Radzyminski, Administrator

Rochester Institute of Technology

Photojournalism - Applied Photography
1 Lomb Memorial Drive
Rochester, New York 14623

Kathy Collins, Administrator

Rockland Community College - SUNY (Public)

Department of English, Speech, Philosophy,
Foreign Language
145 College Road
Suffern, New York 10901
Telephone: (914) 356-4650

Libby Bay, Chair
Barbara Viniar, Dean of Instructional
Services

CURRICULUM AND INSTRUCTION
Courses or Concentrations Available: Film or
Cinema; Journalism or Mass
Communication; Speech; *Undergraduate
Objectives or Program Emphases*: To provide
written, oral, aesthetic, and intercultural
skills; *Full-Time Faculty*: 30; *Part-Time
Faculty*: 30.

FACILITIES AND SERVICES
*Practical experiences available
through*: Campus Newspaper (Published
Independently); Local Commercial
Newspaper; Desktop Publishing Facility;
Film or Cinema Laboratory; Institutional
Magazine; Institutional Newspaper; Video
Production Laboratory or Television Studio.

Rockland Community College - SUNY (Public)

Program of Speech
145 College Road
Suffern, New York 10901
Telephone: (914) 356-4650

Wilma J. Frank, Coordinator
Libby Bay, Chair, English, Speech,
Philosophy and Foreign Language

CURRICULUM AND INSTRUCTION
*Courses or Concentrations
Available*: Communication; Speech;
*Undergraduate Objectives or Program
Emphases*: General oral/verbal competence

for students. Speech/language development
and proficiency in English for ESL students;
Full-Time Faculty: 3; *Part-Time Faculty*: 5.

St. Bonaventure University (Private)

Department of Mass Communication
Route 417
St. Bonaventure, New York 14778
Telephone: (716) 375-2520

Douglas J. Carr, Chair
Richard Reilly, Dean, School of Arts and
Sciences

CURRICULUM AND INSTRUCTION
*Courses or Concentrations
Available*: Advertising; Communication;
Journalism or Mass Communication; Public
Relations; Radio, Television, Broadcasting,
or Telecommunications; Photojournalism;
Communication Research; *Undergraduate
Objectives or Program Emphases*: To educate
students in the understanding and application
of the principles of mass communication, and
to integrate professional skills with a
background in liberal arts. The emphasis is
on acquiring competence in writing and
editing; *Bachelor's Degree Majors*: 265;
Full-Time Faculty: 7; *Part-Time Faculty*: 6.

FACILITIES AND SERVICES
*Practical experiences available
through*: Associated Press Wire Service Feed;
Audio Recording Laboratory; Campus
Newspaper (Published Independently);
Local Commercial Newspaper; Desktop
Publishing Facility; Photographic
Darkrooms; Video Editing; Electronic Field
Production (Video); FM Radio Station
(Institutional); Institutional Magazine;
Video News and Data Processing; Video
Production Laboratory or Television Studio.

St. Francis College (Public)

College of Communication Arts
180 Remsen Street
Brooklyn, New York 11201
Telephone: (718) 522-2300

Edward Setrakean, Chair
John Harvey, Dean

CURRICULUM AND INSTRUCTION
Courses or Concentrations
Available: Advertising; Communication; Film or Cinema; Journalism or Mass Communication; Radio, Television, Broadcasting, or Telecommunications; Speech; *Undergraduate Objectives or Program Emphases*: A liberal arts approach with some emphasis on professional capabilities; *Bachelor's Degree Majors*: 75; *Full-Time Faculty*: 4; *Part-Time Faculty*: 2.

FACILITIES AND SERVICES
Practical experiences available through: Advertising Agency; Campus Newspaper (Published Independently); Local Commercial Television Station; Video Editing; Film or Cinema Laboratory; Public Relations Agency; Video Production Laboratory or Television Studio.

St. John Fisher College (Private)

Department of Communication/Journalism
3690 East Avenue
Rochester, New York 14618
Telephone: (716) 385-8116

Thomas M. McFadden, Academic Vice President

CURRICULUM AND INSTRUCTION
Courses or Concentrations
Available: Advertising; Communication; Film or Cinema; Journalism or Mass Communication; Public Relations; Radio, Television, Broadcasting, or Telecommunications; Speech; Photography; *Undergraduate Objectives or Program Emphases*: The Communication Journalism Department helps prepare students for advanced studying in communication, and for future careers in both electronic and print media. Areas include journalism, public relations, advertising, political communication, and media criticism; *Bachelor's Degree Majors*: 126; *Full-Time Faculty*: 6; *Part-Time Faculty*: 5; *Full-Time Professional (non-clerical) Staff Members*: 2.

FACILITIES AND SERVICES
Practical experiences available through: Advertising Agency; AM Radio Station (Institutional); Audio Recording Laboratory; Community Antenna (Cable) Television Origination; Carrier Current Audio Distribution System; Campus Newspaper (Published Independently); Local Commercial Newspaper; Local Commercial Television Station; Photographic Darkrooms; Video Editing; Electronic Field Production (Video); Institutional Magazine; Public Relations Agency; Video Production Laboratory or Television Studio.

St. John's University

School of General Studies/Public Relation
Grand Central and Utopia Parkways
Jamaica, New York 11439

Martin J. Healy, Administrator

St. Thomas Aquinas College

Communication Arts
Route 340
Sparkill, New York 10976

Carl Rattner, Administrator

State University of New York - Albany (Public)

Department of English
Albany, New York 12222

Carolyn Yalkut, Administrator

State University of New York - Binghamton (Public)

Department of English
Binghamton, New York 13850
Telephone: (607) 777-2168

Elizabeth Tucker, Director
Norman Burns, Chair

CURRICULUM AND INSTRUCTION
Courses or Concentrations
Available: Communication; Journalism or Mass Communication; Speech; Internships (but not courses) in advertising, public relations, television and radio, newspaper work; *Undergraduate Objectives or Program Emphases*: Quality undergraduate education in five majors: English and general literature, literature and rhetoric, literature and folklore, literature and creative writing,

literature and the English Language; *Bachelor's Degree Majors*: 340; *Full-Time Faculty*: 45; *Part-Time Faculty*: 38; *Full-Time Professional (non-clerical) Staff Members*: 5.

FACILITIES AND SERVICES
Practical experiences available through: Advertising Agency; Closed Circuit Television Facility; Campus Newspaper (Published Independently); Local Commercial Newspaper; Local Commercial Television Station; Photographic Darkrooms; Video Editing; FM Radio Station (Institutional); Institutional Magazine; Public Relations Agency.

State University of New York - Brockport (Public)

Department of Communication
Brockport, New York 14420
Telephone: (716) 395-2511

Bill W. Reed, Chair
Ginny L. Studer, Dean, School of Arts and Performance

CURRICULUM AND INSTRUCTION
Courses or Concentrations Available: Communication; Journalism or Mass Communication; Public Relations; Radio, Television, Broadcasting, or Telecommunications; *Undergraduate Objectives or Program Emphases*: Communication Studies, Business, Organizational, Personal Communication, Mass Media. Communications Applications, Business; Journalism (news editorial, broadcast journalism, public relations). Broadcast, production; *Graduate Objectives or Program Emphases*: General communication; *Bachelor's Degree Majors*: 350; *Master's Degree Majors*: 25; *Full-Time Faculty*: 13; *Part-Time Faculty*: 7; *Full-Time Professional (non-clerical) Staff Members*: 3.

FACILITIES AND SERVICES
Practical experiences available through: Associated Press Wire Service Feed; Audio Recording Laboratory; Community Antenna (Cable) Television Origination; Closed Circuit Television Facility; Campus Newspaper (Published Independently); Video Editing; Electronic Field Production (Video); FM Radio Station (Institutional).

State University of New York - Buffalo (Public)

Department of Media Study
201 Wende Hall
Buffalo, New York 14214
Telephone: (716) 831-2426

Brian R. Henderson, Chair
Thomas E. Headrick, Acting Dean, Faculty of Arts and Letters

CURRICULUM AND INSTRUCTION
Courses or Concentrations Available: Film or Cinema; Video, Digital Arts; *Program Coordinators*: Paul Sharits (Filmmaking); Brian Henderson (Film History/Theory); Sarah Elder (Documentary Film); Tony Conrad (Video); Peter Weibel (Digital Arts); *Undergraduate Objectives or Program Emphases*: Concentrations in Filmmaking, Videomaking, Digital Arts, and Interpretation of Media; *Graduate Objectives or Program Emphases*: Master of Arts in Humanities degree; Interdisciplinary degree in which Media Study is linked with work in another fine art or natural or social science discipline; *Bachelor's Degree Majors*: 56; *Other Degree Majors*: 25; *Full-Time Faculty*: 6; *Part-Time Faculty*: 3; *Full-Time Professional (non-clerical) Staff Members*: 1.

FACILITIES AND SERVICES
Practical experiences available through: Audio Recording Laboratory; Community Antenna (Cable) Television Origination; Campus Newspaper (Published Independently); Local Commercial Television Station; Desktop Publishing Facility; Video Editing; Electronic Field Production (Video); Film or Cinema Laboratory; FM Radio Station (Institutional); Satellite Uplink Facility; Video News and Data Processing; Video Production Laboratory or Television Studio.

State University of New York - Fredonia (Public)

Department of English
Fredonia, New York 14063
Telephone: (716) 673-3111

James Shokoff, Chair
Will Rockett, Dean, Arts and Humanities

CURRICULUM AND INSTRUCTION
Courses or Concentrations Available: Film or Cinema; Journalism or Mass

Communication; Television Criticism; *Undergraduate Objectives or Program Emphases*: A journalism sequence (six courses) and a film sequence (six courses) with objectives to help students think clearly, solve problems and write effectively. Internships are available; *Bachelor's Degree Majors*: 125; *Full-Time Faculty*: 25; *Part-Time Faculty*: 12.

FACILITIES AND SERVICES
Practical experiences available through: Campus Newspaper (Published Independently); Local Commercial Newspaper; Public Relations Agency.

State University of New York - Fredonia (Public)

Department of Communication Media
326 McEwen Hall
Fredonia, New York 14063
Telephone: (716) 673-3410

Ted Schwalbe, Chair
Will Rockett, Dean, Faculty of Arts and Humanities

CURRICULUM AND INSTRUCTION
Courses or Concentrations Available: Communication; Radio, Television, Broadcasting, or Telecommunications; Speech; *Undergraduate Objectives or Program Emphases*: Provide a solid liberal arts education, a background in communication, and a specialized education within communication; *Degree Majors*: 278; *Full-Time Faculty*: 7; *Part-Time Faculty*: 1; *Full-Time Professional (non-clerical) Staff Members*: 4.

FACILITIES AND SERVICES
Practical experiences available through: Associated Press Wire Service Feed; Audio Recording Laboratory; Community Antenna (Cable) Television Origination; Carrier Current Audio Distribution System; Closed Circuit Television Facility; Campus Newspaper (Published Independently); Desktop Publishing Facility; Photographic Darkrooms; Video Editing; Electronic Field Production (Video); FM Radio Station (Institutional); Satellite Uplink Facility (Ku Band Transmitter); Video Production Laboratory or Television Studio.

State University of New York - Genesco (Public)

Department of Communication
Genesco, New York 14454
Telephone: (716) 245-5228

John J. Makay, Chair
Thomas C. Colahan, Vice President, Academic Affairs

CURRICULUM AND INSTRUCTION
Courses or Concentrations Available: Advertising; Communication; Journalism or Mass Communication; Public Relations; *Undergraduate Objectives or Program Emphases*: To prepare students for successful careers in the field of communication or to be fully prepared for graduate study. Five career paths: two in mass media, two in communication and rhetoric, graduate school; *Bachelor's Degree Majors*: 300; *Full-Time Faculty*: 8; *Part-Time Faculty*: 2.

FACILITIES AND SERVICES
Practical experiences available through: AM Radio Station (Institutional); Associated Press Wire Service Feed; Audio Recording Laboratory; Carrier Current Audio Distribution System; Closed Circuit Television Facility; Campus Newspaper (Published Independently); Local Commercial Television Station; Video Editing; Electronic Field Production (Video); FM Radio Station (Institutional); Public Relations Agency; United Press International Feed; Video Production Laboratory or Television Studio.

State University of New York - Morrisville (Public)

Department of Journalism
107 Charlton Hall
Morrisville, New York 13408
Telephone: (315) 684-6169

Gerald A. Leone, Chair
Greg Gray, Dean, School of Business

CURRICULUM AND INSTRUCTION
Courses or Concentrations Available: Journalism or Mass Communication; *Undergraduate Objectives or Program Emphases*: Train entry level reporters and/or photographers for weekly or small-sized daily newspapers; provide

strong basic news skills to transfer students into four year programs; *Degree Majors*: 121; *Full-Time Faculty*: 3.

FACILITIES AND SERVICES
Practical experiences available through: AM Radio Station (Institutional); Closed Circuit Television Facility; Photographic Darkrooms; Institutional Magazine; Institutional Newspaper; Video News and Data Processing.

State University of New York - New Paltz (Public)

Department of Communication
FT 214
New Paltz, New York 12561
Telephone: (914) 257-3450

Adelaide Haas, Chair
Marleigh G. Ryan, Dean

CURRICULUM AND INSTRUCTION
Courses or Concentrations Available: Advertising; Communication; Film or Cinema; Radio, Television, Broadcasting, or Telecommunications; Speech; Interpersonal Communication; Intercultural Communication; Organizational Communication; *Undergraduate Objectives or Program Emphases*: Part of the College of Liberal Arts and Sciences which also offers pre-professional training; *Graduate Objectives or Program Emphases*: Preparation of students to be speech-language pathologists and audiologists; *Bachelor's Degree Majors*: 449; *Other Degree Majors*: 35; *Full-Time Faculty*: 15; *Part-Time Faculty*: 15; *Full-Time Professional (non-clerical) Staff Members*: 1.

FACILITIES AND SERVICES
Practical experiences available through: Advertising Agency; AM Radio Station (Institutional); Audio Recording Laboratory; Campus Newspaper (Published Independently); Video Editing; Electronic Field Production (Video); Film or Cinema Laboratory; Video Production Laboratory or Television Studio.

State University of New York - Oneonta

Department of Speech Communication and Theatre
Oneonta, New York 13820

Brian Holleran, Chair

State University of New York - Oneonta (Public)

Program of Mass Communication Minor
Oneonta, New York 13820
Telephone: (607) 431-3510

Ali R. Zohoori, Coordinator
Brian Holleran, Chair, Speech Communication and Theatre

CURRICULUM AND INSTRUCTION
Courses or Concentrations Available: Film or Cinema; Journalism or Mass Communication; Radio, Television, Broadcasting, or Telecommunications; Speech; *Undergraduate Objectives or Program Emphases*: The Department provides students with excellent opportunities to understand the nature and processes of communicating and the nature and forms of theatre and the elements involved in theatrical expression; *Bachelor's Degree Majors*: 130; *Full-Time Faculty*: 22.

FACILITIES AND SERVICES
Practical experiences available through: Advertising Agency; Audio Recording Laboratory; Closed Circuit Television Facility; Campus Newspaper (Published Independently); Local Commercial Newspaper; Local Commercial Television Station; Desktop Publishing Facility; Photographic Darkrooms; Video Editing; Electronic Field Production (Video); Film or Cinema Laboratory; FM Radio Station (Institutional); Public Relations Agency; Satellite Uplink Facility (Ku Band Transmitter) (C Band Transmitter); Video Production Laboratory or Television Studio.

State University of New York - Oswego (Public)

Department of Communication Studies
2 Lanigan Hall
Oswego, New York 13126
Telephone: (315) 341-2357

Fritz J. Messere, Chair
Paul Morman, Dean, Arts and Sciences

CURRICULUM AND INSTRUCTION
Courses or Concentrations Available: Communication; Information Science; Journalism or Mass Communication; Public Relations; Radio, Television, Broadcasting, or Telecommunications; Speech; *Program Coordinators*: Bette Brindle (Information Science); Nola Heidlebaugh (Rhetoric and Speech); Joe Berry (Public Relations); *Undergraduate Objectives or Program Emphases*: To understand how we interact, exchange ideas and build relationships. To analyze the process of creating and sending and interpreting verbal and non verbal messages; *Bachelor's Degree Majors*: 350; *Full-Time Faculty*: 11; *Part-Time Faculty*: 4; *Full-Time Professional (non-clerical) Staff Members*: 1.

FACILITIES AND SERVICES
Practical experiences available through: Advertising Agency; Audio Recording Laboratory; Community Antenna (Cable) Television Origination; Carrier Current Audio Distribution System; Closed Circuit Television Facility; Campus Newspaper (Published Independently); Local Commercial Newspaper; Local Commercial Television Station; Desktop Publishing Facility; Photographic Darkrooms; Video Editing; Electronic Field Production (Video); FM Radio Station (Institutional); Public Relations Agency; United Press International Feed; Video News and Data Processing; Video Production Laboratory or Television Studio.

State University of New York - Plattsburgh (Public)

Department of Communication
Yokum Community Lecture Hall
Plattsburgh, New York 12901
Telephone: (518) 564-2285

A. R. Montanaro Jr., Chair
H. Z. Liu, Dean, Arts and Sciences

CURRICULUM AND INSTRUCTION
Courses or Concentrations Available: Advertising; Communication; Film or Cinema; Journalism or Mass Communication; Public Relations; Radio, Television, Broadcasting, or Telecommunications; Speech; *Undergraduate Objectives or Program Emphases*: To provide a sound educational experience in communication and mass communication, sufficient to make graduates competitive in job markets and graduate school; *Bachelor's Degree Majors*: 300; *Full-Time Faculty*: 11; *Part-Time Faculty*: 6; *Full-Time Professional (non-clerical) Staff Members*: 1.

FACILITIES AND SERVICES
Practical experiences available through: Advertising Agency; Associated Press Wire Service Feed; Audio Recording Laboratory; Community Antenna (Cable) Television Origination; Carrier Current Audio Distribution System; Closed Circuit Television Facility; Campus Newspaper (Published Independently); Local Commercial Newspaper; Local Commercial Television Station; Desktop Publishing Facility; Photographic Darkrooms; Video Editing; Electronic Field Production (Video); Television Broadcast Station (Institutional); FM Radio Station (Institutional); ITFS Distribution System; Institutional Newspaper; Public Relations Agency; Video News and Data Processing; Video Production Laboratory or Television Studio.

State University of New York - Stony Brook (Public)

Department of Theatre Arts
Staller Center for the Arts
Stony Brook, New York 11794
Telephone: (516) 632-7300

Farley Richmond, Chair
Don Ihde, Dean

CURRICULUM AND INSTRUCTION
Courses or Concentrations Available: Film or Cinema; Radio, Television, Broadcasting, or Telecommunications; Speech; Oral Interpretation; Public Speaking; *Undergraduate Objectives or Program Emphases*: Media minor and individual courses in radio, television, film and speech offered to non-media minors; *Degree Majors*: 15; *Full-Time Faculty*: 2; *Full-Time Professional (non-clerical) Staff Members*: 3.

FACILITIES AND SERVICES
Practical experiences available through: AM Radio Station (Institutional); Audio Recording Laboratory; Campus Newspaper (Published Independently); Desktop Publishing Facility; Photographic Darkrooms; Video Editing; Electronic Field Production (Video); Film or Cinema Laboratory; FM Radio Station (Institutional); ITFS Distribution System; Video Production Laboratory or Television Studio.

State University of New York - Tompkins/Cortland

Division of Instruction and Learning Resources
170 North Street
Dryden, New York 13053

William Demo, Administrator

State University of New York Fashion Institute of Technology (Public)

Department of Advertising and Marketing Communications
227 West 27 Street
New York, New York 10001
Telephone: (212) 760-7705

Arthur A. Winters, Chair
J. Giblin, Acting Dean

CURRICULUM AND INSTRUCTION
Courses or Concentrations Available: Advertising; Communication; Film or Cinema; Journalism or Mass Communication; Public Relations; Radio, Television, Broadcasting, or Telecommunications; Speech; *Program Coordinators*: Jeffrey Buchman

(Broadcasting); *Undergraduate Objectives or Program Emphases*: Career development and placement; advertising (copy and strategy); media planning, media sales; account management, corporate communication; business journalism, public relations; video production; *Associate's Degree Majors*: 150; *Other Degree Majors*: 100; *Full-Time Faculty*: 8; *Part-Time Faculty*: 25; *Full-Time Professional (non-clerical) Staff Members*: 1.

FACILITIES AND SERVICES
Practical experiences available through: Advertising Agency; AM Radio Station (Institutional); Audio Recording Laboratory; Closed Circuit Television Facility; Campus Newspaper (Published Independently); Local Commercial Newspaper; Local Commercial Television Station; Desktop Publishing Facility; Photographic Darkrooms; Video Editing; Electronic Field Production (Video); Television Broadcast Station (Institutional); ITFS Distribution System; Institutional Magazine; Institutional Newspaper; Public Relations Agency; Satellite Uplink Facility; Video News and Data Processing; Video Production Laboratory or Television Studio.

State University of New York Institute of Technology (Public)

Program of Technical Communication
Marcy, New York 13504-3050
Telephone: (315) 792-7100

Walter E. Johnston, Administrator
Theodore Hamley, Dean, Arts

CURRICULUM AND INSTRUCTION
Courses or Concentrations Available: Communication; Speech; *Undergraduate Objectives or Program Emphases*: Technical writing and presentation. A new graduate program begins Fall 1990.; *Full-Time Faculty*: 5; *Part-Time Faculty*: 5.

FACILITIES AND SERVICES
Practical experiences available through: Campus Newspaper (Published Independently); Desktop Publishing Facility; Photographic Darkrooms; Video Editing; FM Radio Station (Institutional); Satellite Uplink Facility; Video Production Laboratory or Television Studio.

Sullivan County Community College (Public)

Program of Communication/Media Arts
Leroy Road
Lock Sheldrake, New York 12759
Telephone: (914) 434-5750

Mike Fisher, Head
Robert Glatt, Chair, Humanities

CURRICULUM AND INSTRUCTION
*Courses or Concentrations
Available*: Communication; Journalism or
Mass Communication; Radio, Television,
Broadcasting, or Telecommunications;
Speech; *Undergraduate Objectives or Program
Emphases*: To provide the student with the
technical and artistic skills against a general
background in the liberal arts; *Associate's
Degree Majors*: 96; *Full-Time Faculty*: 2;
*Full-Time Professional (non-clerical) Staff
Members*: 1.

FACILITIES AND SERVICES
Practical experiences available through: Audio
Recording Laboratory; Community Antenna
(Cable) Television Origination; Carrier
Current Audio Distribution System; Closed
Circuit Television Facility; Photographic
Darkrooms; Video Editing; Electronic Field
Production (Video); Video Production
Laboratory or Television Studio.

Syracuse University (Private)

S. I. Newhouse School of Public
Communications
215 University Place
Syracuse, New York 13244
Telephone: (315) 443-2302

Lawrence Myers, Jr., Dean
Gershon Vindow, Vice Chancellor, Academic
Affairs

CURRICULUM AND INSTRUCTION
*Courses or Concentrations
Available*: Advertising; Film or Cinema;
Journalism or Mass Communication; Public
Relations; Radio, Television, Broadcasting,
or Telecommunications; Magazine;
Photography; Broadcast Journalism; *Program
Coordinators*: John Philip Jones
(Advertising); Samuel Kennedy
(Newspaper); Jake Hubbard (Magazine);
Fred Demarest (Photography); Don Edwards
(Broadcast Journalism); Lawrence Myers

(Radio, Television, Film); William Ehling
(Public Relations); George Comstock (Mass
Communication); *Undergraduate Objectives
or Program Emphases*: To educate young
persons to enter the various communication
professions and eventually assume leadership
positions; *Graduate Objectives or Program
Emphases*: To educate young persons to
enter the various communication professions
and eventually assume leadership positions;
Bachelor's Degree Majors: 1062; *Master's
Degree Majors*: 161; *Doctoral Degree Majors
Currently in Residence*: 27; *Full-Time
Faculty*: 48; *Part-Time Faculty*: 15;
*Full-Time Professional (non-clerical) Staff
Members*: 5.

FACILITIES AND SERVICES
*Practical experiences available
through*: Advertising Agency; Audio
Recording Laboratory; Community Antenna
(Cable) Television Origination; Carrier
Current Audio Distribution System; Closed
Circuit Television Facility; Campus
Newspaper (Published Independently);
Local Commercial Newspaper; Local
Commercial Television Station; Desktop
Publishing Facility; Photographic
Darkrooms; Video Editing; Electronic Field
Production (Video); Film or Cinema
Laboratory; FM Radio Station
(Institutional); Public Relations Agency;
Satellite Uplink Facility; Video News and
Data Processing; Video Production
Laboratory or Television Studio.

Teachers College, Columbia University (Private)

Program of Communication and Education
525 West 120th Street
New York, New York 10027
Telephone: (212) 678-3734

Robert O. McClintock, Professor
Harold Ables, Director, Division of
Instruction

CURRICULUM AND INSTRUCTION
*Courses or Concentrations
Available*: Communication; *Graduate
Objectives or Program Emphases*: To advance
knowledge about communication in ways that
will improve the understanding and practice
of education; *Master's Degree Majors*: 8;
*Doctoral Degree Majors Currently in
Residence*: 11. *Full-Time Faculty*: 2;

Part-Time Faculty: 4; Full-Time Professional (non-clerical) Staff Members: 1.

FACILITIES AND SERVICES
Practical experiences available through: Desktop Publishing Facility; Video Editing.

Tisch School of the Arts, New York University (Private)

Department of Film and Television
721 Broadway, Room 1042
New York, New York 10003
Telephone: (212) 998-1700

Charles Milne, Chair
David Oppenheim, Dean

CURRICULUM AND INSTRUCTION
Courses or Concentrations Available: Film or Cinema; Radio, Television, Broadcasting, or Telecommunications; *Program Coordinators*: Sheril Antonio (Undergraduate Film and Television); Ellie Hamerow (Graduate Film); *Undergraduate Objectives or Program Emphases*: Students receive professional hands-on training in film, television, video, animation, radio and sound. Required studies in both the liberal arts and film/television/radio production. Students, freshmen through seniors, learn in all aspects of production; *Graduate Objectives or Program Emphases*: A production intensive MFA program covering cinematography, editing, writing, directing, sound recording and mixing. A specialization in animation is also available. Curriculum designed to develop creative as well as technical abilities; *BFA Degree Majors*: 970; *MFA Degree Majors*: 136; *Full-Time Faculty*: 40; *Part-Time Faculty*: 85; *Full-Time Professional (non-clerical) Staff Members*: 13.

FACILITIES AND SERVICES
Practical experiences available through: AM Radio Station (Institutional); Associated Press Wire Service Feed; Audio Recording Laboratory; Community Antenna (Cable) Television Origination; Campus Newspaper (Published Independently); Local Commercial Television Station; Photographic Darkrooms; Video Editing; Film or Cinema Laboratory; FM Radio Station (Institutional); Video Production Laboratory or Television Studio.

Ulster County Community College (Public)

Department of Communications and Media Arts/Speech and Theatre
Stone Ridge, New York 12484
Telephone: (914) 687-7621

Helene M. Lehtinen, Chair

CURRICULUM AND INSTRUCTION
Courses or Concentrations Available: Advertising; Communication; Film or Cinema; Journalism or Mass Communication; Public Relations; Radio, Television, Broadcasting, or Telecommunications; Speech; *Undergraduate Objectives or Program Emphases*: Liberal Arts based curriculum for transfer oriented students; *Associate's Degree Majors*: 50; *Full-Time Faculty*: 3; *Part-Time Faculty*: 4.

FACILITIES AND SERVICES
Practical experiences available through: Advertising Agency; Audio Recording Laboratory; Community Antenna (Cable) Television Origination; Local Commercial Newspaper; Local Commercial Television Station; Desktop Publishing Facility; Photographic Darkrooms; Video Editing; Electronic Field Production (Video); Institutional Newspaper; Public Relations Agency; Video Production Laboratory or Television Studio.

Utica College (Private)

Program of Public Relations/Journalism
Burrstone Road
Utica, New York 13502
Telephone: (315) 792-3056

John C. Behrens, Director
Harold Burger, Associate Dean, Business Administration Division

CURRICULUM AND INSTRUCTION
Courses or Concentrations Available: Journalism or Mass Communication; Public Relations; *Bachelor's Degree Majors*: 100; *Full-Time Faculty*: 4; *Part-Time Faculty*: 1; *Full-Time Professional (non-clerical) Staff Members*: 1.

FACILITIES AND SERVICES
Practical experiences available through: Associated Press Wire Service Feed; Audio Recording Laboratory; Closed Circuit

Television Facility; Campus Newspaper
(Published Independently); Local
Commercial Newspaper; Local Commercial
Television Station; Photographic
Darkrooms; Video Editing; FM Radio
Station (Institutional); Institutional
Magazine; Public Relations Agency.

York College - CUNY (Public)

Center for Educational Technology
150-14 Jamaica Avenue
Jamaica, New York 11451

Che-Tsao Huang, Administrator

NORTH CAROLINA

Appalachian State University (Public)

Department of Communication Arts
Boone, North Carolina 28608
Telephone: (704) 262-2221

Charles E. Porterfield, Chair
Ming Land, Dean

CURRICULUM AND INSTRUCTION
Courses or Concentrations
Available: Advertising; Journalism or Mass
Communication; Public Relations; Radio,
Television, Broadcasting, or
Telecommunications; Speech; *Undergraduate
Objectives or Program Emphases*: To prepare
students for careers in Applied
Communication, Radio Television
Broadcasting, Journalism, Advertising, and
Public Relations; *Bachelor's Degree
Majors*: 700; *Full-Time Faculty*: 14;
Part-Time Faculty: 12; *Full-Time
Professional (non-clerical) Staff Members*: 1.

FACILITIES AND SERVICES
Practical experiences available through: Audio
Recording Laboratory; Community Antenna
(Cable) Television Origination; Closed
Circuit Television Facility; Campus
Newspaper (Published Independently);
Desktop Publishing Facility; Photographic
Darkrooms; Video Editing; Electronic Field
Production (Video); Film or Cinema
Laboratory; FM Radio Station
(Institutional); ITFS Distribution System;
Institutional Newspaper; Video News and
Data Processing; Video Production
Laboratory or Television Studio.

Atlantic Christian College (Private)

Department of Communications
ACC Station Box 5250
Wilson, North Carolina 27893
Telephone: (919) 237-3161

Marc A. Krein, Director
Katherine James, Administrator

CURRICULUM AND INSTRUCTION
Courses or Concentrations
Available: Advertising; Communication;
Journalism or Mass Communication; Radio,
Television, Broadcasting, or
Telecommunications; Speech; Desktop
Publishing; Animation; *Undergraduate
Objectives or Program Emphases*: Train for
employment with media organizations,
corporate communications; graduate school
preparation; *Bachelor's Degree Majors*: 75;
Full-Time Faculty: 5; *Part-Time Faculty*: 3;
*Full-Time Professional (non-clerical) Staff
Members*: 2.

FACILITIES AND SERVICES
*Practical experiences available
through*: Advertising Agency; Audio
Recording Laboratory; Community Antenna
(Cable) Television Origination; Closed
Circuit Television Facility; Campus
Newspaper (Published Independently);
Local Commercial Newspaper; Local
Commercial Television Station; Desktop
Publishing Facility; Photographic
Darkrooms; Video Editing; Electronic Field
Production (Video); Television Broadcast
Station (Institutional); Institutional
Magazine; Video News and Data Processing;
Video Production Laboratory or Television
Studio.

Campbell University (Private)

Program of Mass Communication
P. O. Box 130
Buies Creek, North Carolina 27506
Telephone: (919) 893-4111 Extension: 2608

Daniel R. Ensley, Director
**Walter S. Barge, Dean, College of Arts and
Sciences**

CURRICULUM AND INSTRUCTION
Courses or Concentrations
Available: Advertising; Journalism or Mass
Communication; Public Relations; Radio,
Television, Broadcasting, or
Telecommunications; *Program
Coordinators*: Daniel Ensley (Broadcast);
Jack Bridges (Public Relations); Milton
Jordon (Print Media); *Undergraduate
Objectives or Program Emphases*: Offer four

specializations emphasizing skills needed for success in mass media industries: Broadcast, print media, advertising and Public Relations; each designed to develop production, writing and management skills; *Bachelor's Degree Majors*: 120; *Full-Time Faculty*: 3; *Part-Time Faculty*: 3; *Full-Time Professional (non-clerical) Staff Members*: 1.

FACILITIES AND SERVICES
Practical experiences available through: Advertising Agency; Associated Press Wire Service Feed; Audio Recording Laboratory; Community Antenna (Cable) Television Origination; Closed Circuit Television Facility; Campus Newspaper (Published Independently); Local Commercial Newspaper; Local Commercial Television Station; Desktop Publishing Facility; Video Editing; Electronic Field Production (Video); FM Radio Station (Institutional); Institutional Magazine; Institutional Newspaper; Public Relations Agency; Video Production Laboratory or Television Studio.

Catawba College (Private)

Department of Theatre Arts
2300 West Innes Street
Salisbury, North Carolina 28144
Telephone: (704) 637-4343

Karl E. Hales, Advisor
James R. Epperson, Administrator

CURRICULUM AND INSTRUCTION
Courses or Concentrations Available: Communication; Journalism or Mass Communication; Speech; *Program Coordinators*: James Mahood (Journalism); *Undergraduate Objectives or Program Emphases*: Communication Arts; Speech Communication Education; *Bachelor's Degree Majors*: 40; *Full-Time Faculty*: 2; *Full-Time Professional (non-clerical) Staff Members*: 1.

FACILITIES AND SERVICES
Practical experiences available through: Campus Newspaper (Published Independently); Local Commercial Newspaper; Photographic Darkrooms; FM Radio Station (Institutional); Institutional Magazine; Institutional Newspaper.

Coastal Carolina Community College (Public)

Division of English and Humanities
444 Western Boulevard
Jacksonville, North Carolina 28540
Telephone: (919) 455-1221

Patricia L. Fountain, Chair
David Heatherly, Dean of College Transfer

CURRICULUM AND INSTRUCTION
Courses or Concentrations Available: Film or Cinema; Journalism or Mass Communication; Speech; *Undergraduate Objectives or Program Emphases*: To educate students about the specific disciplines; *Full-Time Faculty*: 17; *Part-Time Faculty*: 19.

FACILITIES AND SERVICES
Practical experiences available through: Closed Circuit Television Facility; Desktop Publishing Facility; Photographic Darkrooms;

East Carolina University (Public)

Department of Communication
Greenville, North Carolina 27858
Telephone: (919) 757-4227

Marie T. Farr, Acting Head
Eugene Ryan, Dean, College of Arts and Sciences

CURRICULUM AND INSTRUCTION
Courses or Concentrations Available: Communication; Journalism or Mass Communication; Radio, Television, Broadcasting, or Telecommunications; Speech; *Program Coordinators*: Carlton Benz (Broadcast); James Rees (Speech); William Gonzenbach and Brenda Sanchez (Journalism); *Undergraduate Objectives or Program Emphases*: The Department offers two degrees: BA in Journalism and Mass Communications and BS in Broadcasting; *Bachelor's Degree Majors*: 140; *Full-Time Faculty*: 11; *Part-Time Faculty*: 4.

FACILITIES AND SERVICES
Practical experiences available through: AM Radio Station (Institutional); Closed Circuit Television Facility; Campus Newspaper (Published Independently); Local Commercial Television Station; Desktop Publishing Facility; Photographic

Darkrooms; Institutional Newspaper; Video Production Laboratory or Television Studio.

East Carolina University

Journalism Program
Greenville, North Carolina 27834

Jeanne Scafella, Administrator

Elon College (Private)

Department of Journalism and Communication
Elon College, North Carolina 27244-2010
Telephone: (919) 584-2522

Don A. Grady, Chair
Clair Myers, Associate Dean

CURRICULUM AND INSTRUCTION
Courses or Concentrations Available: Communication; Journalism or Mass Communication; Radio, Television, Broadcasting, or Telecommunications; Corporate Communication; *Bachelor's Degree Majors*: 200; *Full-Time Faculty*: 7; *Part-Time Faculty*: 1.

FACILITIES AND SERVICES
Practical experiences available through: Advertising Agency; Associated Press Wire Service Feed; Audio Recording Laboratory; Community Antenna (Cable) Television Origination; Closed Circuit Television Facility; Campus Newspaper (Published Independently); Local Commercial Newspaper; Local Commercial Television Station; Desktop Publishing Facility; Photographic Darkrooms; Video Editing; Electronic Field Production (Video); FM Radio Station (Institutional); Public Relations Agency; Video Production Laboratory or Television Studio.

Fayetteville State University (Public)

Department of Communication and Fine Arts
Murchison Road
Fayetteville, North Carolina 28301
Telephone: (919) 486-1438

Evelyn H. Burrows, Discipline Coordinator
Robert Owens, Chair

CURRICULUM AND INSTRUCTION
Courses or Concentrations Available: Radio, Television, Broadcasting, or Telecommunications; Speech; *Program Coordinators*: Eric Moore (Mass Communication); *Undergraduate Objectives or Program Emphases*: To provide a liberal arts education for students who wish to major in speech communication and theatre; *Bachelor's Degree Majors*: 25; *Full-Time Faculty*: 5; *Part-Time Faculty*: 3; *Full-Time Professional (non-clerical) Staff Members*: 3.

FACILITIES AND SERVICES
Practical experiences available through: Associated Press Wire Service Feed; Audio Recording Laboratory; Community Antenna (Cable) Television Origination; Closed Circuit Television Facility; Campus Newspaper (Published Independently); Local Commercial Newspaper; Local Commercial Television Station; Photographic Darkrooms; Video Editing; Electronic Field Production (Video); FM Radio Station (Institutional); Public Relations Agency; Video News and Data Processing; Video Production Laboratory or Television Studio.

Gaston College

Broadcasting Department
Box 95
Dallas, North Carolina 28034

Dave Campbell, Administrator

High Point College

Program of Media Communications
Montlieu Avenue
High Point, North Carolina 27262

Gary B. Foster, Coordinator
Marion Hodge, Chair, English Department

CURRICULUM AND INSTRUCTION
Courses or Concentrations
Available: Advertising; Communication; Film or Cinema; Journalism or Mass Communication; Radio, Television, Broadcasting, or Telecommunications; Speech; *Undergraduate Objectives or Program Emphases*: Two tracks, Production and Communication theory, both with heavy emphasis on writing; both taught to acknowledge the relationship between media, writing and literature programs; *Bachelor's Degree Majors*: 60; *Full-Time Faculty*: 3.

FACILITIES AND SERVICES
Practical experiences available through: AM Radio Station (Institutional); Audio Recording Laboratory; Community Antenna (Cable) Television Origination; Local Commercial Newspaper; Local Commercial Television Station; Desktop Publishing Facility; Photographic Darkrooms; Video Editing; Electronic Field Production (Video); FM Radio Station (Institutional); Institutional Magazine; Institutional Newspaper; Video Production Laboratory or Television Studio.

Isothermal Community College (Public)

Division of Vocational/Technical
P. O. Box 804
Spindale, North Carolina 28160
Telephone: (704) 286-3636

Bruce G. Waddingham, Dean
Robert Harrison, Vice President, Academic and Student Affairs

CURRICULUM AND INSTRUCTION
Courses or Concentrations Available: Public Relations; Radio, Television, Broadcasting, or Telecommunications; Speech; *Undergraduate Objectives or Program Emphases*: On-air radio; radio production; video production; industrial video; television production; satellite programs; *Associate's Degree Majors*: 35; *Full-Time Faculty*: 2;

Full-Time Professional (non-clerical) Staff Members: 1.

FACILITIES AND SERVICES
Practical experiences available through: Associated Press Wire Service Feed; Audio Recording Laboratory; Community Antenna (Cable) Television Origination; Carrier Current Audio Distribution System; Closed Circuit Television Facility; Campus Newspaper (Published Independently); Desktop Publishing Facility; Photographic Darkrooms; Video Editing; FM Radio Station (Institutional); Satellite Uplink Facility (Ku Band Transmitter and Mobile C Band Facility); United Press International Feed; Video Production Laboratory or Television Studio.

Johnson C. Smith University (Private)

Department of Communication Arts
Charlotte, North Carolina 28216
Telephone: (704) 378-1173

Albert Kreiling, Head
Anthony M. Camele, Chair, Humanities Division

CURRICULUM AND INSTRUCTION
Courses or Concentrations
Available: Communication; Journalism or Mass Communication; Public Relations; Radio, Television, Broadcasting, or Telecommunications; Speech; *Undergraduate Objectives or Program Emphases*: Three professional programs of study: Journalism, Broadcasting, Public Relations; *Bachelor's Degree Majors*: 103; *Full-Time Faculty*: 4; *Part-Time Faculty*: 6.

FACILITIES AND SERVICES
Practical experiences available through: Advertising Agency; AM Radio Station (Institutional); Audio Recording Laboratory; Community Antenna (Cable) Television Origination; Carrier Current Audio Distribution System; Campus Newspaper (Published Independently); Local Commercial Newspaper; Local Commercial Television Station; Desktop Publishing Facility; Photographic Darkrooms; Video Editing; Electronic Field Production (Video); Institutional Magazine; Institutional Newspaper; Public Relations Agency; Video News and Data Processing;

Video Production Laboratory or Television Studio.

Lenoir Community College (Public)

Program of Broadcast Technology
P. O. Box 188
Kinston, North Carolina 28502-0188
Telephone: (919) 527-6223 Extension or
Alternate: 113

James E. Kelso, Head
William E. Reck, Administrator

CURRICULUM AND INSTRUCTION
Courses or Concentrations
Available: Advertising; Journalism or Mass Communication; Radio, Television, Broadcasting, or Telecommunications; Speech; *Undergraduate Objectives or Program Emphases*: Principal objective is to give graduates sufficient training to enable them to get gainful employment in the broadcasting field. In so doing they are also exposed to general education social sciences and humanities; *Degree Majors*: 25; *Full-Time Faculty*: 1.

FACILITIES AND SERVICES
Practical experiences available through: Associated Press Wire Service Feed; Audio Recording Laboratory; FM Radio Station (Institutional); Institutional Newspaper.

Lenoir-Rhyne College (Private)

Department of Art, Theatre Arts and Communication
Hickory, North Carolina 28601
Telephone: (704) 328-7160

Marion H. Love, Chair
Richard Von Dohlen, Administrator

CURRICULUM AND INSTRUCTION
Courses or Concentrations
Available: Communication; Journalism or Mass Communication; Public Relations; Radio, Television, Broadcasting, or Telecommunications; Speech; Theatre Arts; Visual Arts; *Program Coordinators*: Mary Evanish (Communication); Douglas Burton (Visual Arts); Ray Mills (Theatre Arts); *Undergraduate Objectives or Program*

Emphases: Institution provides professional training and guidance for students in rigorous communication programs designed to challenge and motivate. The primary concern of the college is the development of the whole person intellectually, spiritually, artistically; *Bachelor's Degree Majors*: 38; *Full-Time Faculty*: 6; *Part-Time Faculty*: 5; *Full-Time Professional (non-clerical) Staff Members*: 3.

FACILITIES AND SERVICES
Practical experiences available through: Advertising Agency; Associated Press Wire Service Feed; Audio Recording Laboratory; Community Antenna (Cable) Television Origination; Carrier Current Audio Distribution System; Campus Newspaper (Published Independently); Local Commercial Newspaper; Local Commercial Television Station; Desktop Publishing Facility; Photographic Darkrooms; Video Editing; Electronic Field Production (Video); Institutional Magazine; Institutional Newspaper; Public Relations Agency; Video Production Laboratory or Television Studio.

Mars Hill College (Private)

Program of Communication and Public Relations
Mars Hill, North Carolina 28754
Telephone: (704) 689-1142

C. Earl Leininger, Dean and Director
Donald D. Schmeltekopt, Provost

CURRICULUM AND INSTRUCTION
Courses or Concentrations
Available: Communication; Information Science; Journalism or Mass Communication; Speech; Management and Marketing; Arts Management; *Undergraduate Objectives or Program Emphases*: To prepare graduates for entry-level positions and/or graduate study in a variety of communications oriented fields. The program is built on a solid and demanding general education base with four concentrations within the major; *Bachelor's Degree Majors*: 30; *Full-Time Faculty*: 4; *Part-Time Faculty*: 1; *Full-Time Professional (non-clerical) Staff Members*: 3.

FACILITIES AND SERVICES
Practical experiences available through: Advertising Agency; Audio

Recording Laboratory; Campus Newspaper (Published Independently); Local Commercial Newspaper; Local Commercial Television Station; Photographic Darkrooms; Video Editing; FM Radio Station (Institutional); Public Relations Agency; Video Production Laboratory or Television Studio.

North Carolina State University (Public)

Department of Speech Communication
Box 8104
Raleigh, North Carolina 27695
Telephone: (919) 737-7942

William J. Jordan, Head
William B. Toole, Dean

CURRICULUM AND INSTRUCTION
Courses or Concentrations
Available: Communication; Film or Cinema; Public Relations; Radio, Television, Broadcasting, or Telecommunications; Speech; *Undergraduate Objectives or Program Emphases*: Liberal Arts education with emphases in Public Relations, Radio-Television-Film, and general communication skills; *Bachelor's Degree Majors*: 700; *Full-Time Faculty*: 34; *Part-Time Faculty*: 2; *Full-Time Professional (non-clerical) Staff Members*: 1.

FACILITIES AND SERVICES
Practical experiences available through: Audio Recording Laboratory; Community Antenna (Cable) Television Origination; Campus Newspaper (Published Independently); Local Commercial Television Station; Desktop Publishing Facility; Video Editing; Television Broadcast Station (Institutional); Film or Cinema Laboratory; FM Radio Station (Institutional); Institutional Newspaper; Public Relations Agency; Video Production Laboratory or Television Studio.

Pembroke State University (Public)

Program of Telecommunications
Box 5062
Pembroke, North Carolina 28372
Telephone: (919) 521-4214 Extension or Alternate: 378

Oscar Patterson III, Director
Richard Piseno, Vice Chancellor

CURRICULUM AND INSTRUCTION
Courses or Concentrations
Available: Communication; Journalism or Mass Communication; Public Relations; Radio, Television, Broadcasting, or Telecommunications; *Full-Time Faculty*: 3; *Full-Time Professional (non-clerical) Staff Members*: 2.

FACILITIES AND SERVICES
Practical experiences available through: Community Antenna (Cable) Television Origination; Campus Newspaper (Published Independently); Local Commercial Television Station; Desktop Publishing Facility; Photographic Darkrooms; Video Editing; Electronic Field Production (Video); Television Broadcast Station (Institutional); Institutional Newspaper; Public Relations Agency.

Queens College

Humanities Division
1900 Selwyn Avenue
Charlotte, North Carolina 28274

Paul Newman, Administrator

Shaw University (Private)

Department of Radio and Television
118 East South Street
Raleigh, North Carolina 27611
Telephone: (919) 755-4800

Glenn M. Leshner, Head
Joan Barrax, Administrator

CURRICULUM AND INSTRUCTION
Courses or Concentrations
Available: Journalism or Mass Communication; Radio, Television, Broadcasting, or Telecommunications;

Undergraduate Objectives or Program Emphases: Prepare students for careers in Journalism and/or broadcasting, and to prepare students for graduate school; *Bachelor's Degree Majors*: 90; *Full-Time Faculty*: 3; *Full-Time Professional (non-clerical) Staff Members*: 3.

FACILITIES AND SERVICES
Practical experiences available through: Associated Press Wire Service Feed; Audio Recording Laboratory; Community Antenna (Cable) Television Origination; Local Commercial Television Station; Photographic Darkrooms; Video Editing; Electronic Field Production (Video); FM Radio Station (Institutional)Video Production Laboratory or Television Studio.

Southwestern Community College (Public)

Department of Radio and Television Broadcasting Technology
275 Webster Road
Sylva, North Carolina 28779
Telephone: (704) 586-4091 Extension or Alternate: 322

Roy W. Burnette, Director
Sue Monroe, Division Chair

CURRICULUM AND INSTRUCTION
Courses or Concentrations Available: Advertising; Communication; Film or Cinema; Journalism or Mass Communication; Public Relations; Radio, Television, Broadcasting, or Telecommunications; Speech; Management; Broadcast Law; *Undergraduate Objectives or Program Emphases*: Associate Degree in Applied Science; *Degree Majors*: 11; *Full-Time Faculty*: 1; *Full-Time Professional (non-clerical) Staff Members*: 1.

FACILITIES AND SERVICES
Practical experiences available through: Advertising Agency; Audio Recording Laboratory; Carrier Current Audio Distribution System; Closed Circuit Television Facility; Campus Newspaper (Published Independently); Local Commercial Television Station; Desktop Publishing Facility; Photographic Darkrooms; Video Editing; Electronic Field Production (Video); Video Production Laboratory or Television Studio.

St. Andrews College (Private)

Department of Theatre and Mass Communication
Laurinburg, North Carolina 28352
Telephone: (919) 276-3652

Beverle R. Bloch, Chair
Carl Walters, Division Chair

CURRICULUM AND INSTRUCTION
Courses or Concentrations Available: Advertising; Communication; Film or Cinema; Journalism or Mass Communication; Public Relations; Radio, Television, Broadcasting, or Telecommunications; Speech; Theatre; *Undergraduate Objectives or Program Emphases*: An interdisciplinary program designed to promote a more sophisticated and critical response to the mass media while also preparing students for careers in mass communication; *Bachelor's Degree Majors*: 33; *Full-Time Faculty*: 1; *Part-Time Faculty*: 2.

FACILITIES AND SERVICES
Practical experiences available through: Campus Newspaper (Published Independently); Local Commercial Newspaper; Local Commercial Television Station; Desktop Publishing Facility; Photographic Darkrooms; Electronic Field Production (Video); Film or Cinema Laboratory; FM Radio Station (Institutional); Video Production Laboratory or Television Studio.

University of North Carolina - Asheville (Public)

Department of Mass Communication
University Heights
Asheville, North Carolina 28804-3299
Telephone: (704) 251-6227

Alan M. Hantz, Chair
Lauren Wilson, Vice Chancellor for Academic Affairs

CURRICULUM AND INSTRUCTION
Courses or Concentrations Available: Advertising; Film or Cinema; Journalism or Mass Communication; Public Relations; Radio, Television, Broadcasting, or Telecommunications; *Undergraduate Objectives or Program Emphases*: A Liberal Arts major focusing on the functions of

media in society; *Bachelor's Degree Majors*: 40; *Full-Time Faculty*: 5; *Part-Time Faculty*: 2.

FACILITIES AND SERVICES
Practical experiences available through: Advertising Agency; Audio Recording Laboratory; Campus Newspaper (Published Independently); Local Commercial Newspaper; Local Commercial Television Station; Desktop Publishing Facility; Photographic Darkrooms; Video Editing; Electronic Field Production (Video); Public Relations Agency; Video News and Data Processing; Video Production Laboratory or Television Studio.

University of North Carolina - Chapel Hill (Public)

Department of Radio-Television-Motion Pictures
Swain Hall 004A CB #6235
Chapel Hill, North Carolina 27599-6235
Telephone: (919) 962-2311

Gorham Kindem, Chair
Gillian T. Cell, Dean, Arts and Sciences

CURRICULUM AND INSTRUCTION
Courses or Concentrations Available: Film or Cinema; Radio, Television, Broadcasting, or Telecommunications; Broadcast Journalism; Media Speech; *Program Coordinators*: Richard Elan (Broadcast Journalism); Seth Finn (Graduate Studies and Admissions); *Undergraduate Objectives or Program Emphases*: Develop critical thinking, writing, production and management skills for future media professionals and media users; *Graduate Objectives or Program Emphases*: Develop research, production, and writing skills with an emphasis upon research and upon integrating social scientific and critical/humanistic research perspectives; *Bachelor's Degree Majors*: 380; *Master's Degree Majors*: 15; *Full-Time Faculty*: 12; *Part-Time Faculty*: 12; *Full-Time Professional (non-clerical) Staff Members*: 7.

FACILITIES AND SERVICES
Practical experiences available through: Advertising Agency; AM Radio Station (Institutional); Audio Recording Laboratory; Community Antenna (Cable) Television Origination; Closed Circuit Television Facility; Campus Newspaper;

Local Commercial Newspaper; Local Commercial Television Station; Desktop Publishing Facility; Video Editing; Electronic Field Production (Video); Television Broadcast Station (Institutional); Film or Cinema Laboratory; FM Radio Station (Institutional); Department Published Newspaper; Video Production Laboratory or Television Studio.

University of North Carolina - Chapel Hill (Public)

School of Journalism
Howell Hall
Chapel Hill, North Carolina 27599-3365
Telephone: (919) 962-1204

Richard R. Cole, Dean
Dennis O'Connor, Provost

CURRICULUM AND INSTRUCTION
Courses or Concentrations Available: Advertising; Communication; Journalism or Mass Communication; Public Relations; Broadcast News; *Undergraduate Objectives or Program Emphases*: AB in Journalism; News-editorial sequence; Advertising; Public Relations; Visual Communications; Broadcast; *Graduate Objectives or Program Emphases*: MA and Ph.D. in Mass Communication; *Bachelor's Degree Majors*: 600; *Master's Degree Majors*: 60; *Doctoral Degree Majors Currently in Residence*: 10; *Additional Doctoral Degree Majors*: 10; *Full-Time Faculty*: 23; *Part-Time Faculty*: 15.

FACILITIES AND SERVICES
Practical experiences available through: Associated Press Wire Service Feed; Community Antenna (Cable) Television Origination; Campus Newspaper (Published Independently); Local Commercial Newspaper; Local Commercial Television Station; Desktop Publishing Facility; Photographic Darkrooms; Video Editing; Television Broadcast Station (Institutional); FM Radio Station (Institutional); Institutional Magazine; Institutional Newspaper; Public Relations Agency; Video News and Data Processing.

University of North Carolina - Chapel Hill (Public)

Department of Speech Communication
Campus Box 3285
Chapel Hill, North Carolina 27599-3285
Telephone: (919) 962-1127

Beverly W. Long, Chair

CURRICULUM AND INSTRUCTION
Courses or Concentrations
Available: Communication; Speech; Rhetoric; Cultural Studies; Performance Studies; *Undergraduate Objectives or Program Emphases*: Communication and human relationships, rhetoric and cultural studies, performance studies; *Graduate Objectives or Program Emphases*: Communication and human relationships, rhetoric and cultural studies, performance studies; *Bachelor's Degree Majors*: 300; *Master's Degree Majors*: 40; *Full-Time Faculty*: 16; *Part-Time Faculty*: 30.

FACILITIES AND SERVICES
Practical experiences available through: Campus Newspaper (Published Independently); Desktop Publishing Facility; FM Radio Station (Institutional).

University of North Carolina - Greensboro (Public)

Department of Communication and Theatre
201 Taylor Building
Greensboro, North Carolina 27412
Telephone: (919) 334-5576

Robert C. Hansen, Head
Joanne Creighton, Dean

CURRICULUM AND INSTRUCTION
Courses or Concentrations
Available: Communication; Film or Cinema; Journalism or Mass Communication; Public Relations; Radio, Television, Broadcasting, or Telecommunications; Speech; Theatre; Communication Disorders; *Program Coordinators*: Ethel Glenn (Communication Studies); John Jellicorse (Theatre); Anthony Fragola (Broadcasting, Cinema); Rex Prater (Communication Disorders); *Bachelor's Degree Majors*: 400; *BFA Degree Majors*: 75; *Master's Degree Majors*: 50; *MFA Degree Majors*: 75; *Full-Time Faculty*: 34; *Part-Time Faculty*: 76; *Full-Time Professional (non-clerical) Staff Members*: 5.

FACILITIES AND SERVICES
Practical experiences available through: AM Radio Station (Institutional); Audio Recording Laboratory; Campus Newspaper (Published Independently); Local Commercial Television Station; Desktop Publishing Facility; Video Editing; Electronic Field Production (Video); Television Broadcast Station (Institutional); Film or Cinema Laboratory; ITFS Distribution System; Video Production Laboratory or Television Studio.

University of North Carolina - Greensboro (Public)

Division of Broadcasting and Cinema
Taylor Building
Greensboro, North Carolina 27412
Telephone: (919) 334-5360

Anthony N. Fragola, Director
Robert Hansen, Head, Department of Communication and Theatre

CURRICULUM AND INSTRUCTION
Courses or Concentrations
Available: Communication; Film or Cinema; Journalism or Mass Communication; Radio, Television, Broadcasting, or Telecommunications; *Program Coordinator*: Ethel Glenn (Communication and Public Relations); *Undergraduate Objectives or Program Emphases*: A set of professional writing, production and performance skills, knowledge of mass communication theory and electronic media history within a broad education grounded in liberal arts; *Graduate Objectives or Program Emphases*: To develop professionals in broadcast and film production; *Bachelor's Degree Majors*: 284; *MFA Degree Majors*: 18; *Full-Time Faculty*: 6; *Part-Time Faculty*: 7; *Full-Time Professional (non-clerical) Staff Members*: 1.

FACILITIES AND SERVICES
Practical experiences available through: Audio Recording Laboratory; Community Antenna (Cable) Television Origination; Campus Newspaper (Published Independently); Video Editing; Electronic Field Production (Video); Film or Cinema Laboratory; FM Radio Station (Institutional); Video Production Laboratory or Television Studio.

University of North Carolina - Wilmington

Department of Creative Arts
601 South College Road
Wilmington, North Carolina 28403

Dennis J. Sporre, Administrator

Wake Forest University (Private)

Department of Speech Communication and
Theatre Arts
Box 7347, Reynolda Station
Winston-Salem, North Carolina 27109
Telephone: (919) 759-5405

Donald H. Wolfe, Chair
Thomas E. Mullen, Dean

CURRICULUM AND INSTRUCTION
*Courses or Concentrations
Available*: Communication; Film or Cinema;
Journalism or Mass Communication; Radio,
Television, Broadcasting, or
Telecommunications; Speech; *Program
Coordinators*: Michael D. Hazen
(Communication, Rhetoric); Julian C.
Burroughs (Radio, Television, Film);
*Undergraduate Objectives or Program
Emphases*: Communication,
Rhetoric: Interpersonal, Organizational,
Public Communication, Mass
Communication, Intercultural
Communication. Radio, Television,
Film: Production and Criticism; *Graduate
Objectives or Program Emphases*:
Communication, Rhetoric: Interpersonal,
Organizational, Public Communication, Mass
Communication, Intercultural
Communication; *Bachelor's Degree
Majors*: 141; *Master's Degree Majors*: 18;
Full-Time Faculty: 7; *Part-Time Faculty*: 1;
*Full-Time Professional (non-clerical) Staff
Members*: 1.

FACILITIES AND SERVICES
*Practical experiences available
through*: Advertising Agency; Campus
Newspaper (Published Independently);
Local Commercial Television Station;
Desktop Publishing Facility; FM Radio
Station (Institutional); Public Relations
Agency; Satellite Uplink Facility.

Western Carolina University (Public)

Department of Speech and Theatre Arts
123 Stillwell
Cullowhee, North Carolina 28723
Telephone: (704) 227-7491

Lawrence J. Hill, Head
Clifford Lovin, Dean, School of Arts and
Sciences

CURRICULUM AND INSTRUCTION
*Courses or Concentrations
Available*: Journalism or Mass
Communication; Radio, Television,
Broadcasting, or Telecommunications;
Speech; Theatre Arts; *Undergraduate
Objectives or Program Emphases*: A wide
range of experiences in a liberal arts setting is
expected of each undergraduate before
focusing on a specific communications
discipline; *Bachelor's Degree Majors*: 120;
BFA Degree Majors: 20; *Full-Time
Faculty*: 10; *Part-Time Faculty*: 3.

FACILITIES AND SERVICES
*Practical experiences available
through*: Campus Newspaper (Published
Independently); FM Radio Station
(Institutional).

Wilkes Community College (Public)

Department of Radio-Television
Broadcasting
P. O. Box 120, Collegiate Drive
Wilkesboro, North Carolina 28697
Telephone: (919) 651-8723

Al G. Stanley, Head
Dewey Mayes, Administrator

CURRICULUM AND INSTRUCTION
*Courses or Concentrations
Available*: Advertising; Communication;
Journalism or Mass Communication; Radio,
Television, Broadcasting, or
Telecommunications; Speech; *Degree
Majors*: 20; *Full-Time Faculty*: 2.

FACILITIES AND SERVICES
*Practical experiences available
through*: Associated Press Wire Service Feed;
Audio Recording Laboratory; Community
Antenna (Cable) Television Origination;
Campus Newspaper (Published

Independently); Photographic Darkrooms; Video Editing; Electronic Field Production (Video); FM Radio Station (Institutional) Film or Cinema Laboratory.

Wingate College (Private)

Program of Communication Studies
Wingate, North Carolina 28174
Telephone: (704) 233-8000

Leon Smith, Coordinator

CURRICULUM AND INSTRUCTION
Courses or Concentrations
Available: Advertising; Journalism or Mass Communication; Radio, Television, Broadcasting, or Telecommunications; Speech; *Undergraduate Objectives or Program Emphases*: To offer broad based communication experience (writing, speaking, media communication); *Bachelor's Degree Majors*: 200; *Part-Time Faculty*: 1; *Full-Time Professional (non-clerical) Staff Members*: 1.

FACILITIES AND SERVICES
Practical experiences available through: Community Antenna (Cable) Television Origination; Closed Circuit Television Facility; Local Commercial Newspaper; Local Commercial Television Station; Photographic Darkrooms; Video Editing; Electronic Field Production (Video); Institutional Newspaper.

Winston-Salem State University (Public)

Department of Mass Communications
601 Martin Luther King Drive
Winston-Salem, North Carolina 27110
Telephone: (919) 750-2000

Maurice S. Odine, Chair
Fred Tanner, Division Director

CURRICULUM AND INSTRUCTION
Courses or Concentrations
Available: Advertising; Film or Cinema; Journalism or Mass Communication; Public Relations; Radio, Television, Broadcasting, or Telecommunications; *Undergraduate Objectives or Program Emphases*: To train young men and women to work in advertising and public relations, news-editorial, and

radio-television; *Bachelor's Degree Majors*: 150; *Full-Time Faculty*: 4; *Part-Time Faculty*: 3; *Full-Time Professional (non-clerical) Staff Members*: 2.

FACILITIES AND SERVICES
Practical experiences available through: Advertising Agency; Associated Press Wire Service Feed; Audio Recording Laboratory; Local Commercial Newspaper; Local Commercial Television Station; Desktop Publishing Facility; Photographic Darkrooms; Video Editing; Electronic Field Production (Video); FM Radio Station (Institutional); Public Relations Agency; Satellite Uplink Facility (Ku Band Transmitter) (C Band Transmitter); Video News and Data Processing.

Minot State University (Public)

Department of Communication Arts and Journalism
500 University Avenue NW
Minot, North Dakota 58701
Telephone: (701) 857-3878

Kevin R. Newharth, Coordinator
George Slanger, Division Chair

CURRICULUM AND INSTRUCTION
Courses or Concentrations
Available: Advertising; Communication; Journalism or Mass Communication; Radio, Television, Broadcasting, or Telecommunications; Speech; *Bachelor's Degree Majors*: 20; *Full-Time Faculty*: 6; *Part-Time Faculty*: 2.

FACILITIES AND SERVICES
Practical experiences available through: Associated Press Wire Service Feed; Audio Recording Laboratory; Carrier Current Audio Distribution System; Campus Newspaper (Published Independently); Local Commercial Newspaper; Local Commercial Television Station; Desktop Publishing Facility; Photographic Darkrooms; Video Editing; Institutional Newspaper.

North Dakota State University (Public)

Department of Mass Communication, Speech Communication, Theatre Arts
Box 5462
Fargo, North Dakota 58105
Telephone: (701) 237-7783

Robert S. Littlefield, Chair
Margriet Lacy, Dean

CURRICULUM AND INSTRUCTION
Courses or Concentrations
Available: Advertising; Communication; Film or Cinema; Journalism or Mass Communication; Public Relations; Radio, Television, Broadcasting, or Telecommunications; Speech; *Program Coordinators*: Lou Richardson (Print); Julie Henderson (Public Relations); Bill Chandler (Mass Communication Theory); Sherri Beam (Broadcast Production); C.T. Hanson (Speech Communication); Larry Knowles (Theatre Arts); *Undergraduate Objectives or Program Emphases*: Theory with applications to various contexts; *Graduate Objectives or Program Emphases*: Broad, generalist approach; *Bachelor's Degree Majors*: 10; *BFA Degree Majors*: 4; *Master's Degree Majors*: 15; *Full-Time Faculty*: 18; *Part-Time Faculty*: 19; *Full-Time Professional (non-clerical) Staff Members*: 1.

FACILITIES AND SERVICES
Practical experiences available through: Advertising Agency; Associated Press Wire Service Feed; Audio Recording Laboratory; Community Antenna (Cable) Television Origination; Carrier Current Audio Distribution System; Campus Newspaper (Published Independently); Local Commercial Newspaper; Local Commercial Television Station; Desktop Publishing Facility; Photographic Darkrooms; Video Editing; Electronic Field Production (Video); FM Radio Station (Institutional); Public Relations Agency; United Press International Feed; Video Production Laboratory or Television Studio.

University of Mary

Humanities Division
Apple Creek Road
Bismarck, North Dakota 58501

Scott Prebys, Administrator

University of North Dakota (Public)

College of Fine Arts
Grand Forks, North Dakota 58202
Telephone: (701) 777-4111

Bruce C. Jacobsen, Dean
Alice T. Clark, Vice President, Academic Affairs

CURRICULUM AND INSTRUCTION

Courses or Concentrations Available: Music; Visual Arts; *Undergraduate Objectives or Program Emphases*: Pre-professional and teacher education; *Graduate Objectives or Program Emphases*: Professional and teacher education; *BFA Degree Majors*: 55; *MFA Degree Majors*: 23; *Other Degree Majors*: 16; *Full-Time Faculty*: 32; *Part-Time Faculty*: 25; *Full-Time Professional (non-clerical) Staff Members*: 2.

FACILITIES AND SERVICES

Practical experiences available through: AM Radio Station (Institutional); Audio Recording Laboratory; Campus Newspaper (Published Independently); Photographic Darkrooms; Television Broadcast Station (Institutional); FM Radio Station (Institutional).

University of North Dakota (Public)

School of Communication
Box 8118
Grand Forks, North Dakota 58202
Telephone: (701) 777-2159

John H. Vivian, Interim Director

CURRICULUM AND INSTRUCTION

Courses or Concentrations Available: Advertising; Communication; Journalism or Mass Communication; Public Relations; Radio, Television, Broadcasting, or Telecommunications; Speech; *Undergraduate Objectives or Program Emphases*: Career preparation within a strong liberal arts context; *Graduate Objectives or Program Emphases*: Study of communication as process; *Bachelor's Degree Majors*: 425; *Master's Degree Majors*: 15; *Full-Time Faculty*: 12; *Part-Time Faculty*: 17; *Full-Time Professional (non-clerical) Staff Members*: 17.

FACILITIES AND SERVICES

Practical experiences available through: Advertising Agency; AM Radio Station (Institutional); Associated Press Wire Service Feed; Audio Recording Laboratory; Community Antenna (Cable) Television Origination; Closed Circuit Television Facility; Campus Newspaper (Published Independently); Local Commercial Newspaper; Local Commercial Television Station; Desktop Publishing Facility; Photographic Darkrooms; Video

Editing; Electronic Field Production (Video); Television Broadcast Station (Institutional); FM Radio Station (Institutional); ITFS Distribution System; Institutional Magazine; Public Relations Agency; Satellite Uplink Facility (Ku Band Transmitter) (C Band Transmitter); Video News and Data Processing; Video Production Laboratory or Television Studio.

Ashland University (Private)

Department of Radio and Television
401 College Avenue
Ashland, Ohio 44805
Telephone: (419) 289-4142

Jerry Milam Emmert, Director/Chair
Fred Rafeld, Dean, Business, Economics and Radio/Television

CURRICULUM AND INSTRUCTION
Courses or Concentrations Available: Radio, Television, Broadcasting, or Telecommunications; *Undergraduate Objectives or Program Emphases*: To emphasize theory by hands-on operation; to place student in position of responsibility and expertise in dissemination of broadcast news, information; preparation for career in field of endeavor; *Bachelor's Degree Majors*: 30; *Full-Time Faculty*: 5; *Part-Time Faculty*: 1; *Full-Time Professional (non-clerical) Staff Members*: 2.

FACILITIES AND SERVICES
Practical experiences available through: Audio Recording Laboratory; Community Antenna (Cable) Television Origination; Campus Newspaper (Published Independently); Local Commercial Television Station; Desktop Publishing Facility; Photographic Darkrooms; Video Editing; Electronic Field Production (Video); Television Broadcast Station (Institutional); FM Radio Station (Institutional); Institutional Newspaper; United Press International Feed; Video Production Laboratory or Television Studio.

Bluffton College (Private)

Department of
English/Communication/Language
Bluffton, Ohio 45817
Telephone: (419) 358-8015

Wesley D. Richard, Chair
Burton Yost, Interim Dean of Academic Affairs

CURRICULUM AND INSTRUCTION
Courses or Concentrations

Available: Communication; Journalism or Mass Communication; Speech; *Undergraduate Objectives or Program Emphases*: Program offers a broad foundation in communication studies for students interested in graduate study or specialized vocations; *Bachelor's Degree Majors*: 8; *Full-Time Faculty*: 6; *Part-Time Faculty*: 1.

FACILITIES AND SERVICES
Practical experiences available through: AM Radio Station (Institutional); Campus Newspaper (Published Independently); Local Commercial Newspaper; Local Commercial Television Station; Photographic Darkrooms; Public Relations Agency.

Bowling Green State University (Public)

School of Mass Communication
Bowling Green, Ohio 43403
Telephone: (419) 372-8400

F. Dennis Hale, Director
Andrew Kerek, Dean, College of Arts and Sciences

CURRICULUM AND INSTRUCTION
Courses or Concentrations Available: Film or Cinema; Journalism or Mass Communication; Public Relations; Radio, Television, Broadcasting, or Telecommunications; *Program Coordinators*: R. K. Clark (Radio, Television, Film); Harold Fisher (Journalism); *Undergraduate Objectives or Program Emphases*: Professional programs in journalism and broadcasting; *Graduate Objectives or Program Emphases*: Training in law and public policy, international and developmental communication, theory and methodology, new technology; *Master's Degree Majors*: 25; *Doctoral Degree Majors Currently in Residence*: 12; *Additional Doctoral Degree Majors*: 3; *Full-Time Faculty*: 18; *Part-Time Faculty*: 15; *Full-Time Professional (non-clerical) Staff*

Members: 2. See one or more additional entries below.

FACILITIES AND SERVICES
Practical experiences available through: AM Radio Station (Institutional); Associated Press Wire Service Feed; Audio Recording Laboratory; Carrier Current Audio Distribution System; Closed Circuit Television Facility; Campus Newspaper (Published Independently); Local Commercial Newspaper; Local Commercial Television Station; Desktop Publishing Facility; Photographic Darkrooms; Video Editing; Electronic Field Production (Video); Television Broadcast Station (Institutional); FM Radio Station (Institutional); ITFS Distribution System; Institutional Magazine; Institutional Newspaper; Public Relations Agency; Video News and Data Processing; Video Production Laboratory or Television Studio.

Bowling Green State University (Public)

Department of Radio-Television-Film
West Hall
Bowling Green, Ohio 43403
Telephone: (419) 372-2138

Robert K. Clark, Chair
F. Dennis Hale, Director, School of Mass Communication

CURRICULUM AND INSTRUCTION
Courses or Concentrations Available: Film or Cinema; Radio, Television, Broadcasting, or Telecommunications; *Undergraduate Objectives or Program Emphases*: Television, Radio, Film, Audience Research, Sales/Management; *Full-Time Faculty*: 8; *Part-Time Faculty*: 8; *Full-Time Professional (non-clerical) Staff Members*: 2.

FACILITIES AND SERVICES
Practical experiences available through: Associated Press Wire Service Feed; Audio Recording Laboratory; Community Antenna (Cable) Television Origination; Carrier Current Audio Distribution System; Closed Circuit Television Facility; Campus Newspaper (Published Independently); Local Commercial Television Station; Desktop Publishing Facility; Video Editing; Electronic Field Production (Video); Television Broadcast Station (Institutional); Film or Cinema Laboratory; FM Radio

Station (Institutional); Video News and Data Processing; Video Production Laboratory or Television Studio.

Bowling Green State University (Public)

Department of Interpersonal and Public Communication
Bowling Green, Ohio 43403
Telephone: (419) 372-2823

Michael T. Marsden, Interim Chair
Andrew Kerek, Dean, College of Arts and Sciences

CURRICULUM AND INSTRUCTION
Courses or Concentrations Available: Communication; *Graduate Objectives or Program Emphases*: Interpersonal, Organizational Communication; Rhetorical Theory, Criticism; *Bachelor's Degree Majors*: 400; *Master's Degree Majors*: 10; *Doctoral Degree Majors Currently in Residence*: 10; *Additional Doctoral Degree Majors*: 6; *Full-Time Faculty*: 6; *Part-Time Faculty*: 20.

Bowling Green State University (Public)

Department of Journalism
319 West Hall
Bowling Green, Ohio 43403
Telephone: (419) 372-2077

Harold A. Fisher, Chair
Dennis Hale, Director, School of Mass Communication

CURRICULUM AND INSTRUCTION
Courses or Concentrations Available: Journalism or Mass Communication; Public Relations; *Undergraduate Objectives or Program Emphases*: Broadcast journalism; Print journalism (news editorial); Magazine journalism; Photojournalism; Public Relations; *Graduate Objectives or Program Emphases*: MA Students can specialize in Print Journalism, Broadcast Journalism, or Public Relations. Ph.D. students can specialize in Law and Policy, International and Development Communication, or Social Research related to the media; *Bachelor's Degree Majors*: 96; *Master's Degree*

Majors: 33; *Doctoral Degree Majors Currently in Residence*: 15; *Additional Doctoral Degree Majors*: 2; *Other Degree Majors*: 309; *Full-Time Faculty*: 9; *Part-Time Faculty*: 8; *Full-Time Professional (non-clerical) Staff Members*: 2.

FACILITIES AND SERVICES
Practical experiences available through: AM Radio Station (Institutional); Associated Press Wire Service Feed; Audio Recording Laboratory; Community Antenna (Cable) Television Origination; Carrier Current Audio Distribution System; Closed Circuit Television Facility; Campus Newspaper (Published Independently); Local Commercial Newspaper; Local Commercial Television Station; Desktop Publishing Facility; Photographic Darkrooms; Video Editing; Electronic Field Production (Video); Television Broadcast Station (Institutional); FM Radio Station (Institutional); Film or Cinema Studio; Institutional Magazine; Public Relations Agency; Satellite Uplink Facility; Video News and Data Processing; Video Production Laboratory or Television Studio.

Capital University (Private)

Department of Speech and Communication Arts
2199 E. Main Street
Columbus, Ohio 43209
Telephone: (614) 236-6201

Armin P. Langholz, Chair
Daina McGary, Dean, College of Arts and Sciences

CURRICULUM AND INSTRUCTION
Courses or Concentrations Available: Public Relations; Radio, Television, Broadcasting, or Telecommunications; Speech; *Undergraduate Objectives or Program Emphases*: To develop an appreciation for and understanding of the historical development and relationship of speech communication, the communication media as a social force, and the aesthetic elements of communication; *Bachelor's Degree Majors*: 60; *Full-Time Faculty*: 6; *Part-Time Faculty*: 3.

FACILITIES AND SERVICES
Practical experiences available through: Advertising Agency; Audio Recording Laboratory; Community Antenna

(Cable) Television Origination; Carrier Current Audio Distribution System; Campus Newspaper (Published Independently); Local Commercial Newspaper; Local Commercial Television Station; Desktop Publishing Facility; Photographic Darkrooms; Video Editing; Electronic Field Production (Video); Public Relations Agency; Video Production Laboratory or Television Studio.

Case Western Reserve University

Department of Communication Sciences
University Circle
Cleveland, Ohio 44106
Telephone: (216) 368-2470

Danielle Ripick, Chair
Desh S. Fergusan, Administrator

CURRICULUM AND INSTRUCTION
Courses or Concentrations Available: Communication; Information Science; Journalism or Mass Communication; Radio, Television, Broadcasting, or Telecommunications; Speech; *Undergraduate Objectives or Program Emphases*: To prepare students as generalists in communications; *Bachelor's Degree Majors*: 6; *Full-Time Faculty*: 4; *Part-Time Faculty*: 6; *Full-Time Professional (non-clerical) Staff Members*: 1.

FACILITIES AND SERVICES
Practical experiences available through: Advertising Agency; AM Radio Station (Institutional); Audio Recording Laboratory; Closed Circuit Television Facility; Campus Newspaper (Published Independently); Local Commercial Television Station; Desktop Publishing Facility; FM Radio Station (Institutional); Public Relations Agency.

Cedarville College (Private)

Department of Communication Arts
Box 601
Cedarville, Ohio 45314
Telephone: (513) 766-2211

James R. Phipps, Chair

CURRICULUM AND INSTRUCTION
Courses or Concentrations

Available: Communication; Journalism or Mass Communication; Radio, Television, Broadcasting, or Telecommunications; Speech; Intercultural Communication; Organizational Communication; *Bachelor's Degree Majors*: 149; *Full-Time Faculty*: 8; *Part-Time Faculty*: 5; *Full-Time Professional (non-clerical) Staff Members*: 2.

FACILITIES AND SERVICES
Practical experiences available through: Associated Press Wire Service Feed; Audio Recording Laboratory; Community Antenna (Cable) Television Origination; Carrier Current Audio Distribution System; Campus Newspaper (Published Independently); Desktop Publishing Facility; Photographic Darkrooms; Video Editing; Electronic Field Production (Video); Television Broadcast Station (Institutional); FM Radio Station (Institutional); Satellite Uplink Facility (Ku Band Transmitter); Video News and Data Processing; Video Production Laboratory or Television Studio.

Central Ohio Technical College (Public)

Department of General Studies
University Drive
Newark, Ohio 43055
Telephone: (614) 366-1351

Jim Fullen, Head
Marilyn Tritt, Dean

CURRICULUM AND INSTRUCTION
Courses or Concentrations
Available: Communication; Information Science; Speech; English; Communication Skills; Sociology; Ethics; *Program Coordinator*: Phylis Thompson (Education); *Undergraduate Objectives or Program Emphases*: To help student become a confident and competent listener, leader, writer, speaker and thinker. To become aware of nonverbal skills and group dynamics. To grow lingually; to continue to learn; *Full-Time Faculty*: 8; *Part-Time Faculty*: 25; *Full-Time Professional (non-clerical) Staff Members*: 2.

FACILITIES AND SERVICES
Practical experiences available through: Audio Recording Laboratory; Closed Circuit Television Facility; Campus Newspaper (Published Independently); Desktop Publishing Facility; Video Editing;

Institutional Magazine; Video Production Laboratory or Television Studio.

Central State University (Public)

Department of English, Theatre and Communication
Wilberforce, Ohio 45384
Telephone: (513) 376-6459

Terrence L. Glass, Chair
Melvin Johnson, Administrator

CURRICULUM AND INSTRUCTION
Courses or Concentrations
Available: Communication; Journalism or Mass Communication; Radio, Television, Broadcasting, or Telecommunications; Speech; *Program Coordinator*: Emil Dansker (Communication); *Undergraduate Objectives or Program Emphases*: Three separate degrees offered in the areas of Radio/Television, Journalism, and Speech Communication; *Bachelor's Degree Majors*: 150; *Full-Time Faculty*: 19; *Part-Time Faculty*: 3; *Full-Time Professional (non-clerical) Staff Members*: 2.

FACILITIES AND SERVICES
Practical experiences available through: Audio Recording Laboratory; Closed Circuit Television Facility; Campus Newspaper (Published Independently); Local Commercial Newspaper; Local Commercial Television Station; Desktop Publishing Facility; Photographic Darkrooms; Video Editing; FM Radio Station (Institutional); Institutional Newspaper; Video Production Laboratory or Television Studio.

Cleveland State University (Public)

Department of Communication
Cleveland, Ohio 44115
Telephone: (216) 687-4630

Leo W. Jeffres, Chair
Earl Anderson, Interim Dean, College of Arts and Sciences

CURRICULUM AND INSTRUCTION
Courses or Concentrations
Available: Advertising; Communication; Film or Cinema; Journalism or Mass Communication; Public Relations; Radio,

Television, Broadcasting, or Telecommunications; Speech; Political Communication; Drama; *Program Coordinators*: Reuben Silva (Drama); *Undergraduate Objectives or Program Emphases*: Communication with specialized sequences in film, radio-television, organizational communication, interpersonal communication, journalism, promotional communication, political communication; *Graduate Objectives or Program Emphases*: Master of Applied Communication Theory and Methodology, a social science program; *Bachelor's Degree Majors*: 500; *BFA Degree Majors*: 50; *Full-Time Faculty*: 21; *Part-Time Faculty*: 10; *Full-Time Professional (non-clerical) Staff Members*: 2.

FACILITIES AND SERVICES
Practical experiences available through: AM Radio Station (Institutional); Audio Recording Laboratory; Closed Circuit Television Facility; Campus Newspaper (Published Independently); Desktop Publishing Facility; Photographic Darkrooms; Video Editing; Electronic Field Production (Video); Institutional Newspaper; Video News and Data Processing.

College of Mount St. Joseph (Private)

Department of Humanities
Delhi and Neeb Roads
Mount St. Joseph, Ohio 45051
Telephone: (513) 244-4200

William C. Schutzius, Chair
Ronald Becht, Dean

CURRICULUM AND INSTRUCTION
Courses or Concentrations Available: Advertising; Communication; Film or Cinema; Journalism or Mass Communication; Public Relations; Radio, Television, Broadcasting, or Telecommunications; Speech; *Undergraduate Objectives or Program Emphases*: Writing; broad liberal education; *Associate's Degree Majors*: 8; *Bachelor's Degree Majors*: 60; *Full-Time Faculty*: 11; *Part-Time Faculty*: 15.

FACILITIES AND SERVICES
Practical experiences available through: Advertising Agency; Audio

Recording Laboratory; Community Antenna (Cable) Television Origination; Closed Circuit Television Facility; Campus Newspaper (Published Independently); Local Commercial Newspaper; Local Commercial Television Station; Desktop Publishing Facility; Photographic Darkrooms; Video Editing; Electronic Field Production (Video); Film or Cinema Laboratory; Public Relations Agency; Video Production Laboratory or Television Studio.

College of Wooster (Private)

Department of Communication
Wooster, Ohio 44691
Telephone: (216) 263-2000

Bonnie W. Buzza, Chair
Yvonne Williams, Dean of Faculty

CURRICULUM AND INSTRUCTION
Courses or Concentrations Available: Advertising; Communication; Film or Cinema; Public Relations; Radio, Television, Broadcasting, or Telecommunications; Speech; Rhetoric; *Program Coordinators*: Rod Korba (Advertising, Film, Public Relations, Radio, TV, Broadcasting, Communication, Speech); Amos Kiewe (Rhetoric, Communication, Speech); *Undergraduate Objectives or Program Emphases*: Communication Studies, teaching theoretical and conceptual foundations in the Communication discipline with emphases on research in upper-level courses. Also offer Communication Sciences and Disorders as separate track in the department; *Bachelor's Degree Majors*: 33; *Full-Time Faculty*: 4.

FACILITIES AND SERVICES
Practical experiences available through: AM Radio Station (Institutional); Associated Press Wire Service Feed; Audio Recording Laboratory; Campus Newspaper (Published Independently); Desktop Publishing Facility; Photographic Darkrooms; Video Editing; FM Radio Station (Institutional); Satellite Uplink Facility.

Denison University (Private)

Department of Speech Communication
Knapp Hall 205
Granville, Ohio 43023
Telephone: (614) 587-6289

Suzanne E. Condray, Chair

CURRICULUM AND INSTRUCTION
Courses or Concentrations
Available: Communication; Radio,
Television, Broadcasting, or
Telecommunications; Speech; *Undergraduate*
Objectives or Program
Emphases: Concentrations in General
Speech, Mass Media, and Speech Science;
Bachelor's Degree Majors: 80; *Full-Time*
Faculty: 5; *Part-Time Faculty*: 2.

FACILITIES AND SERVICES
Practical experiences available
through: Campus Newspaper (Published
Independently); FM Radio Station
(Institutional); United Press International
Feed.

Edison State Community College (Public)

Division of Liberal Arts
1973 Edison Drive
Piqua, Ohio 45356
Telephone: (513) 778-8600

Thomas E. Ruddick, Assistant Professor
Mary Harris, Associate Dean

CURRICULUM AND INSTRUCTION
Courses or Concentrations
Available: Communication; Journalism or
Mass Communication; Radio, Television,
Broadcasting, or Telecommunications;
Speech; *Undergraduate Objectives or Program*
Emphases: Transfer programs (AA) in order
to undertake study at a four year school;
Associate's Degree Majors: 28; *Full-Time*
Faculty: 13; *Part-Time Faculty*: 16.

FACILITIES AND SERVICES
Practical experiences available
through: Campus Newspaper (Published
Independently).

Franciscan University of Steubenville (Private)

Department of Communication Arts
Franciscan Way
Steubenville, Ohio 43952
Telephone: (614) 283-6386

James E. Coyle, Jr., Director
Elsie Luke, Chair

CURRICULUM AND INSTRUCTION
Courses or Concentrations
Available: Advertising; Communication;
Journalism or Mass Communication; Public
Relations; Radio, Television, Broadcasting,
or Telecommunications; *Program*
Coordinators: Wayne Lewis (Journalism);
Undergraduate Objectives or Program
Emphases: Radio, Television: Theory and
process of planning and producing for
broadcast and private media; hands-on
experience; computer networking and
communication; Journalism: writing and
computer production in print media;
Bachelor's Degree Majors: 60; *Full-Time*
Faculty: 2; *Part-Time Faculty*: 1.

FACILITIES AND SERVICES
Practical experiences available
through: Advertising Agency; Audio
Recording Laboratory; Campus Newspaper
(Published Independently); Local
Commercial Newspaper; Local Commercial
Television Station; Desktop Publishing
Facility; Video Editing; Electronic Field
Production (Video); Public Relations
Agency; Video News and Data Processing;
Video Production Laboratory or Television
Studio.

Franklin University (Private)

Program of Applied Communication
201 South Grant Avenue
Columbus, Ohio 43215
Telephone: (614) 224-6237

Janice I. Gratz, Director
Bart Schairr, Acting Dean, College of Arts
and Sciences

CURRICULUM AND INSTRUCTION
Courses or Concentrations
Available: Advertising; Communication; Film
or Cinema; Information Science; Journalism
or Mass Communication; Public Relations;
Radio, Television, Broadcasting, or

Telecommunications; Speech; Management Communication; Organizational Communication; *Undergraduate Objectives or Program Emphases*: Communication generalist combining writing, speaking, media communication, and organizational communication; *Degree Majors*: 200; *Full-Time Faculty*: 5; *Part-Time Faculty*: 2.

FACILITIES AND SERVICES
Practical experiences available through: Advertising Agency; Audio Recording Laboratory; Community Antenna (Cable) Television Origination; Closed Circuit Television Facility; Campus Newspaper (Published Independently); Local Commercial Newspaper; Local Commercial Television Station; Desktop Publishing Facility; Video Editing; Electronic Field Production (Video); Public Relations Agency; Video Production Laboratory or Television Studio.

Heidelberg College

Communication and Theatre Arts Department
College Hill
Tiffin, Ohio 44883

Leanne O. Wolff, Administrator

Hocking Technical College (Public)

Program of Broadcast Engineering Technology
3301 Hocking Parkway
Nelsonville, Ohio 45764-9704
Telephone: (614) 753-3591 Extension or Alternate: 2346

Harry L. Tompkins, Lead Instructor
Robert Hawkins, Director

CURRICULUM AND INSTRUCTION
Courses or Concentrations Available: Radio, Television, Broadcasting, or Telecommunications; *Undergraduate Objectives or Program Emphases*: Training in the technical aspects of radio and television broadcasting and telecommunications. Equipment and systems care, maintenance, alignment, design and installation; *Associate's Degree Majors*: 10; *Full-Time Faculty*: 2; *Part-Time Faculty*: 3.

FACILITIES AND SERVICES
Practical experiences available through: Audio Recording Laboratory; Community Antenna (Cable) Television Origination; Closed Circuit Television Facility; Desktop Publishing Facility; Video Editing; Electronic Field Production (Video); Video Production Laboratory or Television Studio.

International College of Broadcasting

6 South Smithville Road
Dayton, Ohio 45431

Linda K. Craft, Administrator

John Carroll University (Private)

Department of Communication
University Heights, Ohio 44118
Telephone: (216) 397-4378

Jacqueline Schmidt, Chair
Fred Travis, Dean, Arts and Sciences

CURRICULUM AND INSTRUCTION
Courses or Concentrations Available: Communication; Journalism or Mass Communication; Public Relations; Radio, Television, Broadcasting, or Telecommunications; Speech; Speech Pathology; *Undergraduate Objectives or Program Emphases*: Provide an understanding of communication from a variety of emphasis; establish the ability to understand and send messages from several media and situations; *Bachelor's Degree Majors*: 160; *Full-Time Faculty*: 13; *Part-Time Faculty*: 6.

FACILITIES AND SERVICES
Practical experiences available through: Advertising Agency; AM Radio Station (Institutional); Audio Recording Laboratory; Closed Circuit Television Facility; Campus Newspaper (Published Independently); Local Commercial Newspaper; Local Commercial Television Station; Desktop Publishing Facility; Photographic Darkrooms; Video Editing; Electronic Field Production (Video); FM Radio Station (Institutional); Public Relations Agency; Video News and Data Processing; Video Production Laboratory or Television Studio.

Kent State University (Public)

School of Speech Communication
Kent, Ohio 44242
Telephone: (216) 672-2659

D. Ray Heisey, Director
Thomas J. Barber, Dean

CURRICULUM AND INSTRUCTION
Courses or Concentrations
Available: Communication; Speech;
*Undergraduate Objectives or Program
Emphases*: Communication Studies;
Rhetorical Studies; *Graduate Objectives or
Program Emphases*: Communication Studies;
Rhetorical Studies; *Bachelor's Degree
Majors*: 100; *Master's Degree Majors*: 12;
*Doctoral Degree Majors Currently in
Residence*: 17; *Additional Doctoral Degree
Majors*: 17; *Full-Time Faculty*: 13;
Part-Time Faculty: 38.

Kent State University (Public)

**School of Journalism and Mass
Communication**
Kent, Ohio 44242-0001
Telephone: (216) 672-2572

Judy VanSlyke Turk, Director
Thomas J. Barber, Dean

CURRICULUM AND INSTRUCTION
Courses or Concentrations
Available: Advertising; Journalism or Mass
Communication; Public Relations; Radio,
Television, Broadcasting, or
Telecommunications; Photography; *Program
Coordinators*: Greg Blase (Advertising);
Joseph Harper (News); Greg Moore
(Photography); E. Zoe McCathrin (Public
Relations); Thomas Olson
(Radio/Television); *Undergraduate Objectives
or Program Emphases*: Professional career
preparation in advertising, news (broadcast,
newspaper, magazine); photography
(photo-illustration, photo-journalism), public
relations and radio-television (corporate
video media sales and promotion,
production); *Graduate Objectives or Program
Emphases*: Professional career preparation in
reporting/editing and media management;
Bachelor's Degree Majors: 1136; *Master's
Degree Majors*: 26; *Full-Time Faculty*: 19;
Part-Time Faculty: 22; *Full-Time
Professional (non-clerical) Staff Members*: 5.

FACILITIES AND SERVICES
*Practical experiences available
through*: Associated Press Wire Service Feed;
Community Antenna (Cable) Television
Origination; Carrier Current Audio
Distribution System; Desktop Publishing
Facility; Photographic Darkrooms; Video
Editing; Electronic Field Production
(Video); Television Broadcast Station
(Institutional); FM Radio Station
(Institutional); ITFS Distribution System;
Institutional Magazine; Institutional
Newspaper; Public Relations Agency;
Satellite Uplink Facility; Video News and
Data Processing; Video Production
Laboratory or Television Studio.

Kent State University (Public)

Media Department
6000 Frank Avenue, Northwest
Canton, Ohio 44720

Roger Davis, Administrator

Lorain County Community College

Language and Humanities Division
1005 North Abbe Road
Elyria, Ohio 44035

Roy M. Berko, Administrator

Malone College (Private)

Department of Communication Arts
515 25th Street, NW
Canton, Ohio 44709
Telephone: (216) 489-0800

Kim S. Phipps, Chair
Ron Johnson, Dean of the College

CURRICULUM AND INSTRUCTION
Courses or Concentrations
Available: Journalism or Mass
Communication; Public Relations; Radio,
Television, Broadcasting, or
Telecommunications; Speech; *Undergraduate
Objectives or Program Emphases*: Theory and
practice. Students take a core of theory
courses and then they select one of four
concentrations in Journalism, Broadcasting,
Speech, or Theatre; *Bachelor's Degree*

Majors: 69; *Full-Time Faculty*: 3; *Part-Time Faculty*: 2.

FACILITIES AND SERVICES
Practical experiences available through: Community Antenna (Cable) Television Origination; Carrier Current Audio Distribution System; Campus Newspaper (Published Independently); Local Commercial Newspaper; Local Commercial Television Station; Photographic Darkrooms; Video Editing; Electronic Field Production (Video); Institutional Newspaper; Public Relations Agency; Video Production Laboratory or Television Studio.

Marietta College (Private)

Department of Mass Media
Marietta, Ohio 45750
Telephone: (614) 374-4802

Ron L. Jacobson, Chair
Gwen Jensen, Dean

CURRICULUM AND INSTRUCTION
Courses or Concentrations Available: Advertising; Journalism or Mass Communication; Public Relations; Radio, Television, Broadcasting, or Telecommunications; *Undergraduate Objectives or Program Emphases*: To offer a professional orientation to radio-television, advertising, public relations, and journalism within a liberal arts context; *Master's Degree Majors*: 113; *Full-Time Faculty*: 3; *Part-Time Faculty*: 3; *Full-Time Professional (non-clerical) Staff Members*: 3.

FACILITIES AND SERVICES
Practical experiences available through: Associated Press Wire Service Feed; Community Antenna (Cable) Television Origination; Closed Circuit Television Facility; Photographic Darkrooms; Video Editing; Electronic Field Production (Video); Television Broadcast Station (Institutional); FM Radio Station (Institutional); Institutional Magazine; Institutional Newspaper; Video Production Laboratory or Television Studio.

Miami University

Department of Communication
162 Bachelor Hall
Oxford, Ohio 45056

Gerald H. Sanders, Administrator

Mount Union College (Private)

Department of Speech, Communication and Theatre Arts
Clark Avenue
Alliance, Ohio 44601
Telephone: (216) 821-5320

William E. Coleman, Chair
Conrad Stanitski, Dean

CURRICULUM AND INSTRUCTION
Courses or Concentrations Available: Communication; Film or Cinema; Journalism or Mass Communication; Public Relations; Radio, Television, Broadcasting, or Telecommunications; Speech; *Program Coordinator*: Charles Monford (Campus Radio Director); *Undergraduate Objectives or Program Emphases*: To offer a broad introduction into the field of communication; *Bachelor's Degree Majors*: 45; *Full-Time Faculty*: 5; *Part-Time Faculty*: 2; *Full-Time Professional (non-clerical) Staff Members*: 1.

FACILITIES AND SERVICES
Practical experiences available through: Associated Press Wire Service Feed; Audio Recording Laboratory; Campus Newspaper (Published Independently); FM Radio Station (Institutional).

Mt. Vernon Nazarene College (Private)

Department of Communication
800 Martinsburg Road
Mt. Vernon, Ohio 43050-9987
Telephone: (614) 397-1244

Mervin Ziegler, Chair
Fordyce Bennett, Administrator

CURRICULUM AND INSTRUCTION
Courses or Concentrations Available: Radio, Television, Broadcasting, or Telecommunications; Speech; *Bachelor's Degree Majors*: 50; *Full-Time Faculty*: 3;

Full-Time Professional (non-clerical) Staff Members: 1.

FACILITIES AND SERVICES
Practical experiences available through: Associated Press Wire Service Feed; Audio Recording Laboratory; Carrier Current Audio Distribution System; Campus Newspaper (Published Independently); Video Editing; FM Radio Station (Institutional).

Muskingum College (Private)

Department of Speech Communication and Theatre
New Concord, Ohio 43762
Telephone: (614) 826-8375

Jeffrey D. Harman, Chair
Dan VanTassel, Vice President for Academic Affairs

CURRICULUM AND INSTRUCTION
Courses or Concentrations Available: Communication; Film or Cinema; Journalism or Mass Communication; Radio, Television, Broadcasting, or Telecommunications; Speech; Theatre; *Program Coordinator*: Don Hill (Theatre); *Undergraduate Objectives or Program Emphases*: Speech Communication degree with emphasis usually in general speech or broadcasting; also, degree available in Theatre; *Bachelor's Degree Majors*: 28; *Full-Time Faculty*: 5; *Part-Time Faculty*: 2; *Full-Time Professional (non-clerical) Staff Members*: 1.

FACILITIES AND SERVICES
Practical experiences available through: Associated Press Wire Service Feed; Audio Recording Laboratory; Community Antenna (Cable) Television Origination; Local Commercial Newspaper; Local Commercial Television Station; Desktop Publishing Facility; Video Editing; Electronic Field Production (Video); FM Radio Station (Institutional); Institutional Magazine; Institutional Newspaper.

North Central Technical College (Public)

Department of English
2441 Kenwood Circle
Mansfield, Ohio 44901
Telephone: (419) 755-4800

Paul A. Sukys, Coordinator
Bruce Sliney, Dean

CURRICULUM AND INSTRUCTION
Courses or Concentrations Available: Communication; Public Relations; Speech; *Undergraduate Objectives or Program Emphases*: To provide students with instruction and practical experience in business communication, technical communication, public relations, legal writing, and speech; *Full-Time Faculty*: 5; *Part-Time Faculty*: 8.

FACILITIES AND SERVICES
Practical experiences available through: Campus Newspaper (Published Independently); Desktop Publishing Facility; Photographic Darkrooms; Institutional Magazine; Institutional Newspaper; Video Production Laboratory or Television Studio.

Notre Dame College of Ohio (Private)

Department of English/Communications
4545 College Road
Cleveland, Ohio 44121
Telephone: (216) 381-1680

Dalma S. Takacs, Chair
Rev. John Crawford, Chair, Humanities Division

CURRICULUM AND INSTRUCTION
Courses or Concentrations Available: Communication; Film or Cinema; Journalism or Mass Communication; Radio, Television, Broadcasting, or Telecommunications; Speech; *Undergraduate Objectives or Program Emphases*: Programs of study leading to BA degree in Communications (49 credits) and Teaching Certification (7-12 credits); in Comprehensive Communications (61 credits) and in Speech Communications (31 credits); *Bachelor's Degree Majors*: 15; *Full-Time Faculty*: 3; *Part-Time Faculty*: 6.

FACILITIES AND SERVICES
Practical experiences available through: Campus Newspaper (Published Independently); Desktop Publishing Facility; Photographic Darkrooms.

Ohio Northern University (Private)

Department of Communication Arts
Main Street
Ada, Ohio 45810
Telephone: (419)-772-2049

Nils Riess, Chair
David Peltier, Dean

CURRICULUM AND INSTRUCTION
Courses or Concentrations Available: Communication; Public Relations; Radio, Television, Broadcasting, or Telecommunications; Speech; Theatre; *Program Coordinators*: G. Richard Gainey (Broadcasting); Jessica Gisclair (Public Relations); *Undergraduate Objectives or Program Emphases*: Public Relations; Broadcasting; Theatre; Speech; *Bachelor's Degree Majors*: 36; *Full-Time Faculty*: 7; *Full-Time Professional (non-clerical) Staff Members*: 1.

FACILITIES AND SERVICES
Practical experiences available through: Advertising Agency; Carrier Current Audio Distribution System; Campus Newspaper (Published Independently); Desktop Publishing Facility; Photographic Darkrooms; Video Editing; Public Relations Agency; United Press International Feed.

Ohio State University (Public)

School of Journalism
242 West 18th Ave.
Columbus, Ohio 43210-1107
Telephone: (614) 292-6291

Walter K. Bunge, Director
Joan Huber, Dean, College of Social and Behavioral Sciences

CURRICULUM AND INSTRUCTION
Courses or Concentrations Available: Advertising; Journalism or Mass Communication; Public Relations; Radio, Television, Broadcasting, or Telecommunications; *Undergraduate Objectives or Program Emphases*: Professional preparation of students committed to serving the public interest through careers in journalism and mass communication. This preparation involves a liberal education, study of journalism in a free society, and practical competence; *Graduate Objectives or Program Emphases*: To achieve a basic competency in graduate level research, an appreciation for the role of media in society, professional skills, and a fluency in an area outside journalism with emphasis on how it relates to journalism; *Bachelor's Degree Majors*: 751; *Master's Degree Majors*: 100; *Full-Time Faculty*: 25; *Part-Time Faculty*: 25; *Full-Time Professional (non-clerical) Staff Members*: 6.

FACILITIES AND SERVICES
Practical experiences available through: AM Radio Station (Institutional); Associated Press Wire Service Feed; Audio Recording Laboratory; Community Antenna (Cable) Television Origination; Carrier Current Audio Distribution System; Campus Newspaper (Published Independently); Desktop Publishing Facility; Photographic Darkrooms; Video Editing; Electronic Field Production (Video); Television Broadcast Station (Institutional); FM Radio Station (Institutional); Institutional Newspaper; Public Relations Agency; Video Production Laboratory or Television Studio.

Ohio State University (Public)

Department of Photography and Cinema
156 W. 19th Avenue
Columbus, Ohio 43137
Telephone: (614) 292-0404

J. Ronald Green, Chair
Donald Harris, Dean, College of the Arts

CURRICULUM AND INSTRUCTION
Courses or Concentrations Available: Film or Cinema; Photography and Video; *Undergraduate Objectives or Program Emphases*: BA presents the study of photography, cinema and video as the emphasis of a liberal arts education; provides a foundation for more advanced study. BFA is designed to develop an understanding of materials, technique, history, theory and aesthetics; *Graduate Objectives or Program Emphases*: MA program that allows for the

integration of theory and practice. Studies in history, theory and criticism; production in the mediums of photography, cinema and video offer a unique environment for graduate studies; *Bachelor's Degree Majors*: 80; *BFA Degree Majors*: 30; *Master's Degree Majors*: 31; *Doctoral Degree Majors Currently in Residence*: 1; *Full-Time Faculty*: 12; *Part-Time Faculty*: 13; *Full-Time Professional (non-clerical) Staff Members*: 2.

FACILITIES AND SERVICES
Practical experiences available through: Audio Recording Laboratory; Community Antenna (Cable) Television Origination; Campus Newspaper (Published Independently); Local Commercial Television Station; Photographic Darkrooms; Video Editing; Electronic Field Production (Video); Television Broadcast Station (Institutional); Film or Cinema Laboratory; FM Radio Station (Institutional); Institutional Magazine; Institutional Newspaper; Satellite Uplink Facility; United Press International Feed.

Ohio State University (Public)

Department of Communication
154 N. Oval Mall
Columbus, Ohio 43210
Telephone: (614) 292-3400

Joseph M. Foley, Chair
Joan Huben, Dean, College of Social and Behavioral Sciences

CURRICULUM AND INSTRUCTION
Courses or Concentrations Available: Communication; Radio, Television, Broadcasting, or Telecommunications; Speech; Critical/Cultural Studies; *Undergraduate Objectives or Program Emphases*: To provide a coherent program which produces graduates who are well versed in the theoretical foundations of communication study, and who are equipped to apply this knowledge and understanding to a wide variety of practical situations; *Graduate Objectives or Program Emphases*: The focus is upon symbolic processes in human communication, distinguished by the varied contributions of scholars in the areas of interpersonal and organizational communication, rhetoric, critical cultural studies, and telecommunications and media;

Bachelor's Degree Majors: 600; *Master's Degree Majors*: 40; *Doctoral Degree Majors Currently in Residence*: 60; *Additional Doctoral Degree Majors*: 30; *Full-Time Faculty*: 25; *Part-Time Faculty*: 60; *Full-Time Professional (non-clerical) Staff Members*: 1.

FACILITIES AND SERVICES
Practical experiences available through: AM Radio Station (Institutional); Audio Recording Laboratory; Community Antenna (Cable) Television Origination; Carrier Current Audio Distribution System; Local Commercial Newspaper; Local Commercial Television Station; Desktop Publishing Facility; Video Editing; Electronic Field Production (Video); Television Broadcast Station (Institutional); FM Radio Station (Institutional); Satellite Uplink Facility (C Band Transmitter); Video Production Laboratory or Television Studio.

Ohio State University (Public)

Division of Biomedical Communications
1583 Perry Street
Columbus, Ohio 43210
Telephone: (614) 292-5517

David S. Stein, Director
Stephen Wilson, Director, School of Allied Medical Professions

CURRICULUM AND INSTRUCTION
Courses or Concentrations Available: Communication; Radio, Television, Broadcasting, or Telecommunications; Photography, Medical Marketing, Medical Illustration; *Program Coordinator*: Steve Moon, (Medical Illustration, Academic Coordinator); *Undergraduate Objectives or Program Emphases*: Generalist positions in medical communications, including video, still media, illustration; *Graduate Objectives or Program Emphases*: PT education, human resource development, instructional design; *Bachelor's Degree Majors*: 50; *Master's Degree Majors*: 6; *Full-Time Faculty*: 4; *Part-Time Faculty*: 2; *Full-Time Professional (non-clerical) Staff Members*: 24.

FACILITIES AND SERVICES
Practical experiences available through: Audio Recording Laboratory; Closed Circuit Television Facility; Photographic Darkrooms; Video Editing; Electronic Field

Production (Video); Satellite Uplink Facility (Ku Band Transmitter) (C Band Transmitter); Video Production Laboratory or Television Studio.

Ohio State University (Public)

Program of Agricultural Communications
208 Ag Admin, 2120 Fyffe Road
Columbus, Ohio 43210
Telephone: (612) 292-6671

Curtis E. Paulson, Coordinator
Kirby Barrick, Administrator

CURRICULUM AND INSTRUCTION
Courses or Concentrations
Available: Communication; Journalism or Mass Communication; Radio, Television, Broadcasting, or Telecommunications; *Undergraduate Objectives or Program Emphases*: To provide training in the theory and skills needed in the print, electronic, and emerging media of agricultural communications. A graduate of this program will have a broad knowledge of the agricultural industry and related methods of communication; *Graduate Objectives or Program Emphases*: Graduate level study and research in areas of agricultural communications; *Degree Majors*: 26; *Full-Time Faculty*: 2; *Part-Time Faculty*: 1.

FACILITIES AND SERVICES
Practical experiences available through: Advertising Agency; AM Radio Station (Institutional); Audio Recording Laboratory; Closed Circuit Television Facility; Local Commercial Newspaper; Local Commercial Television Station; Desktop Publishing Facility; Photographic Darkrooms; Video Editing; Electronic Field Production (Video); FM Radio Station (Institutional); ITFS Distribution System; Institutional Magazine; Institutional Newspaper; Public Relations Agency; Satellite Uplink Facility (C Band Transmitter); Video News and Data Processing; Video Production Laboratory or Television Studio.

Ohio State University (Public)

Program of Instructional Design and Technology
29 W. Woodruff
Columbus, Ohio 43210-1177
Telephone: (614) 292-4872

John C. Belland, Coordinator
Robert Lawson, Chair, Department of Educational Policy/Leadership

CURRICULUM AND INSTRUCTION
Courses or Concentrations
Available: Communication; Information Science; Radio, Television, Broadcasting, or Telecommunications; Instructional Design; Educational Computing; *Graduate Objectives or Program Emphases*: Instructional Design; Computers in Education; Video in Education; Interactive Technologies; School Library, Media; Research and Theory; *Master's Degree Majors*: 55; *Doctoral Degree Majors Currently in Residence*: 13; *Additional Doctoral Degree Majors*: 26; *Full-Time Faculty*: 7; *Part-Time Faculty*: 10.

FACILITIES AND SERVICES
Practical experiences available through: Desktop Publishing Facility; Video Editing; Electronic Field Production (Video).

Ohio State University - Marion (Public)

Communication Department
1465 Mount Vernon Avenue
Marion, Ohio 43302

Robert Cohen, Administrator

Ohio University - Athens (Public)

J. Warren McClure School of Communication Systems Management
Radio-TV-Communication Building
Athens, Ohio 45701
Telephone: (614) 593-4890

Phyllis W. Bernt, Director
Paul E. Nelson, Dean, College of Communication

CURRICULUM AND INSTRUCTION
Courses or Concentrations
Available: Communication; Voice/Data

Systems; *Undergraduate Objectives or Program Emphases*: Interdisciplinary program. Management of voice/data networks; *Bachelor's Degree Majors*: 175; *Full-Time Faculty*: 4; *Part-Time Faculty*: 2.

Ohio University - Athens (Public)

School of Telecommunications
Radio-Television Communication Building 253
Athens, Ohio 45701
Telephone: (614) 593-4870

Drew O. McDaniel, Director
Paul E. Nelson, Dean, College of Communication

CURRICULUM AND INSTRUCTION
Courses or Concentrations Available: Radio, Television, Broadcasting, or Telecommunications; *Undergraduate Objectives or Program Emphases*: Video Production; Audio Production; Management Administration; Comprehensive; *Graduate Objectives or Program Emphases*: MA in Management, Audience Analysis, Policy, Writing, International, Communication and Development. Ph.D. in Management, International, Media Studies; *Bachelor's Degree Majors*: 250; *Master's Degree Majors*: 15; *Doctoral Degree Majors Currently in Residence*: 25; *Additional Doctoral Degree Majors*: 10; *Other Degree Majors*: 400; *Full-Time Faculty*: 17; *Part-Time Faculty*: 5; *Full-Time Professional (non-clerical) Staff Members*: 1.

FACILITIES AND SERVICES
Practical experiences available through: AM Radio Station (Institutional); Associated Press Wire Service Feed; Audio Recording Laboratory; Community Antenna (Cable) Television Origination; Carrier Current Audio Distribution System; Closed Circuit Television Facility; Desktop Publishing Facility; Video Editing; Electronic Field Production (Video); Television Broadcast Station (Institutional); FM Radio Station (Institutional); Video Production Laboratory or Television Studio.

Ohio University - Athens (Public)

E. W. Scripps School of Journalism
Scripps Hall 233
Athens, Ohio 45701-2979
Telephone: (614) 593-1000

Ralph S. Izard, Director
Paul E. Nelson, Dean, College of Communication

CURRICULUM AND INSTRUCTION
Courses or Concentrations Available: Advertising; Journalism or Mass Communication; Public Relations; Radio, Television, Broadcasting, or Telecommunications; Newspapers, Magazines, Visual Communication; *Program Coordinator*: Chuck Scott (Visual Communication on undergraduate level); *Undergraduate Objectives or Program Emphases*: Courses are offered in six sequences, including public relations, broadcasting, advertising, newspapers, magazines, and visual communication. Besides these students get a strong liberal arts education; *Graduate Objectives or Program Emphases*: Master's Program is a combination of research and professional courses. Doctoral Program has a heavy research focus and also emphasizes good teaching; *Doctoral Degree Majors Currently in Residence*: 10; *Additional Doctoral Degree Majors*: 14; *Other Degree Majors*: 149; *Full-Time Faculty*: 24; *Part-Time Faculty*: 16; *Full-Time Professional (non-clerical) Staff Members*: 2.

FACILITIES AND SERVICES
Practical experiences available through: AM Radio Station (Institutional); Associated Press Wire Service Feed; Audio Recording Laboratory; Community Antenna (Cable) Television Origination; Closed Circuit Television Facility; Campus Newspaper (Published Independently); Local Commercial Newspaper; Local Commercial Television Station; Desktop Publishing Facility; Photographic Darkrooms; Video Editing; Electronic Field Production (Video); Television Broadcast Station (Institutional); FM Radio Station (Institutional); Institutional Magazine; Video News and Data Processing; Video Production Laboratory or Television Studio.

Ohio University - Athens (Public)

School of Interpersonal Communication
107 Kantner Hall
Athens, Ohio 45701

Anita James, Administrator

Ohio University - Athens (Public)

School of Film
378 Lindley Hall
Athens, Ohio 45701
Telephone: (614) 593-1323

David O. Thomas, Director
Dova Wilson, Dean, College of Fine Arts

CURRICULUM AND INSTRUCTION
Courses or Concentrations Available: Film or
Cinema; *Undergraduate Objectives or Program
Emphases*: Limited enrollment dual-major
BFA program and honors tutorial program in
motion picture production and scholarship;
*Graduate Objectives or Program
Emphases*: Professional training leading to
MFA degree in film and video; Film history,
theory, criticism; *BFA Degree Majors*: 6;
Master's Degree Majors: 5; *MFA Degree
Majors*: 35; *Full-Time Faculty*: 8; *Part-Time
Faculty*: 11.

FACILITIES AND SERVICES
*Practical experiences available
through*: Desktop Publishing Facility; Video
Editing; Electronic Field Production
(Video); Film or Cinema Laboratory.

Ohio University - Athens (Public)

School of Visual Communication
Lasher Hall
Athens, Ohio 45701
Telephone: (614) 593-4898

Charles L. Scott, Director
Paul E. Nelson, Dean, College of
Communication

CURRICULUM AND INSTRUCTION
Courses or Concentrations Available: Picture
Editing, Newspaper and Magazine Layout
and Design, Informational Graphics, Photo
Communication, Photo Illustration;
*Undergraduate Objectives or Program
Emphases*: To equip students with the
necessary skills, background, and motivation
to be successful in the media and to compete
for leadership roles. To set high standards
for visual integrity and communication ethics
for photographers, artists, and editors;
*Graduate Objectives or Program
Emphases*: The College of Communication
and the College of Fine Arts offer curricula
based on the same objectives for both
undergraduate and graduate programs;
Bachelor's Degree Majors: 82; *BFA Degree
Majors*: 82; *Master's Degree Majors*: 20;
Full-Time Faculty: 5; *Part-Time Faculty*: 1.

FACILITIES AND SERVICES
*Practical experiences available
through*: Campus Newspaper (Published
Independently); Local Commercial
Newspaper; Desktop Publishing Facility;
Photographic Darkrooms.

Ohio University - Zanesville (Public)

Department of Radio-Television
1425 Newark Road
Zanesville, Ohio 43701
Telephone: (614) 453-0762

Reed W. Smith, Director
James Hoefler, Division Coordinator

CURRICULUM AND INSTRUCTION
*Courses or Concentrations
Available*: Advertising; Communication;
Journalism or Mass Communication; Radio,
Television, Broadcasting, or
Telecommunications; Speech; *Undergraduate
Objectives or Program Emphases*: Broadcast
Engineering; Production, Performance;
Associate's Degree Majors: 40; *Full-Time
Faculty*: 3; *Part-Time Faculty*: 2.

FACILITIES AND SERVICES
*Practical experiences available
through*: Community Antenna (Cable)
Television Origination; Local Commercial
Television Station; Photographic
Darkrooms; Video Editing; Electronic Field
Production (Video); FM Radio Station
(Institutional); ITFS Distribution System;
Video Production Laboratory or Television
Studio.

Ohio Wesleyan University (Private)

Department of Journalism
Delaware, Ohio 43015
Telephone: (614) 368-3650

Robert A. Papper, Chair
G. William Benz, Provost

CURRICULUM AND INSTRUCTION
Courses or Concentrations
Available: Journalism or Mass
Communication; Radio, Television,
Broadcasting, or Telecommunications;
*Undergraduate Objectives or Program
Emphases*: Help students understand basic
principles of writing, thinking, and analyses
within broader contexts of strong liberal arts
education; *Bachelor's Degree Majors*: 50;
Full-Time Faculty: 4; *Part-Time Faculty*: 2.

FACILITIES AND SERVICES
*Practical experiences available
through*: Associated Press Wire Service Feed;
Audio Recording Laboratory; Community
Antenna (Cable) Television Origination;
Closed Circuit Television Facility; Campus
Newspaper (Published Independently);
Local Commercial Newspaper; Local
Commercial Television Station; Desktop
Publishing Facility; Photographic
Darkrooms; Video Editing; Electronic Field
Production (Video); FM Radio Station
(Institutional).

Otterbein College (Private)

Department of Speech Communication
Westerville, Ohio 43081
Telephone: (614) 898-1752

John T. Ludlum, Chair
**Ralph Pearson, Vice President, Academic
Affairs**

CURRICULUM AND INSTRUCTION
*Courses or Concentrations
Available*: Communication; Journalism or
Mass Communication; Public Relations;
Radio, Television, Broadcasting, or
Telecommunications; Speech;
Business/Organizational Communication;
Program Coordinators: John Buckles (Radio);
Libby McGlone (Television); *Undergraduate
Objectives or Program Emphases*: Otterbein's
primary mission is to provide students with a
combination of liberal arts background,

professional training and practical experience
in Radio-Television, Public Relations,
Journalism, Business and Speech
Communication; *Bachelor's Degree
Majors*: 100; *Full-Time Faculty*: 5;
Part-Time Faculty: 5; *Full-Time Professional
(non-clerical) Staff Members*: 1.

FACILITIES AND SERVICES
*Practical experiences available
through*: Associated Press Wire Service Feed;
Audio Recording Laboratory; Community
Antenna (Cable) Television Origination;
Campus Newspaper (Published
Independently); Local Commercial
Newspaper; Local Commercial Television
Station; Desktop Publishing Facility;
Photographic Darkrooms; Video Editing;
Electronic Field Production (Video);
Television Broadcast Station (Institutional);
FM Radio Station (Institutional);
Institutional Newspaper; Public Relations
Agency; Video Production Laboratory or
Television Studio.

Otterbein College (Private)

English Department
Westerville, Ohio 43081

James R. Bailey, Administrator

Southern Ohio College (Private)

Department of Audio Video Production
1055 Laidlaw Avenue
Cincinnati, Ohio 45237
Telephone: (513) 242-3791

Mark R. Turner, Chair
Joan L. Krabbe, Administrator

CURRICULUM AND INSTRUCTION
Courses or Concentrations Available: Audio
Production; Video Production;
*Undergraduate Objectives or Program
Emphases*: The Audio Video Production
program is designed to provide the graduate
with the skills necessary to enter traditional
audio and video production fields as well as
the expanding field of corporate and
industrial communications; *Associate's
Degree Majors*: 130; *Full-Time Faculty*: 3;
Part-Time Faculty: 2; *Full-Time Professional
(non-clerical) Staff Members*: 1.

FACILITIES AND SERVICES
Practical experiences available through: Audio Recording Laboratory; Community Antenna (Cable) Television Origination; Campus Newspaper (Published Independently); Local Commercial Television Station; Video Editing; Electronic Field Production (Video); Video Production Laboratory or Television Studio.

United Theological Seminary

Department of Television
1810 Harvard Boulevard
Dayton, Ohio 45406

Aaron Sheaffer, Administrator

University of Akron (Public)

Department of Communication
Akron, Ohio 44325
Telephone: (216) 375-7954

John D. Bee, Chair

CURRICULUM AND INSTRUCTION
Courses or Concentrations Available: Communication; Film or Cinema; Journalism or Mass Communication; Public Relations; Radio, Television, Broadcasting, or Telecommunications; Speech; *Bachelor's Degree Majors*: 830; *Master's Degree Majors*: 35; *Full-Time Faculty*: 14; *Part-Time Faculty*: 30; *Full-Time Professional (non-clerical) Staff Members*: 5.

FACILITIES AND SERVICES
Practical experiences available through: Advertising Agency; Audio Recording Laboratory; Community Antenna (Cable) Television Origination; Campus Newspaper (Published Independently); Local Commercial Newspaper; Local Commercial Television Station; Desktop Publishing Facility; Electronic Field Production (Video); FM Radio Station (Institutional); ITFS Distribution System; United Press International Feed; Video Production Laboratory or Television Studio.

University of Akron (Public)

Television Production Center
106 Kolbe Hall
Akron, Ohio 44325

Thomas M. Ditzel, Administrator

University of Cincinnati (Public)

Department of Communication
McMicken College of Arts and Sciences
Cincinnati, Ohio 45221
Telephone: (513) 556-4455

Cynthia Berryman-Fink, Head
Joseph Caruso, Dean, College of Arts and Sciences

CURRICULUM AND INSTRUCTION
Courses or Concentrations Available: Communication; Speech; *Undergraduate Objectives or Program Emphases*: Interpersonal, Group, Organizational Communication; Rhetoric and Public Communication; *Graduate Objectives or Program Emphases*: Interpersonal Group Organizational Communication; Rhetoric and Public Communication; *Bachelor's Degree Majors*: 300; *Master's Degree Majors*: 25; *Full-Time Faculty*: 13; *Part-Time Faculty*: 19.

FACILITIES AND SERVICES
Practical experiences available through: Advertising Agency; Audio Recording Laboratory; Campus Newspaper (Published Independently); Local Commercial Newspaper; Local Commercial Television Station; Desktop Publishing Facility; FM Radio Station (Institutional); Institutional Magazine; Public Relations Agency.

University of Cincinnati (Public)

Division of Broadcasting
College Conservatory of Music
Cincinnati, Ohio 45221-0003
Telephone: (513) 556-4394

Manfred K. Wolfram, Head
Robert J. Werner, Administrator

CURRICULUM AND INSTRUCTION
Courses or Concentrations

Available: Advertising; Communication; Film or Cinema; Journalism or Mass Communication; Radio, Television, Broadcasting, or Telecommunications; *Undergraduate Objectives or Program Emphases*: Prepare students for a spectrum of career choices in the field of broadcasting as well as in the larger communications sector. These include employment in radio, television, commercial/industrial production, and advertising; *BFA Degree Majors*: 65; *Full-Time Faculty*: 5; *Part-Time Faculty*: 7; *Full-Time Professional (non-clerical) Staff Members*: 2.

FACILITIES AND SERVICES
Practical experiences available through: Advertising Agency; Audio Recording Laboratory; Community Antenna (Cable) Television Origination; Campus Newspaper (Published Independently); Local Commercial Television Station; Desktop Publishing Facility; Video Editing; Electronic Field Production (Video); FM Radio Station (Institutional); Institutional Magazine; Public Relations Agency; Video News and Data Processing.

University of Cincinnati (Public)

Department of Language Arts
Cincinnati, Ohio 45221
Telephone: (513) 556-1699

R. William Vilter, Head
David Hartleb, Administrator

CURRICULUM AND INSTRUCTION
Courses or Concentrations Available: Communication; Speech; Freshman English; Literature, reading and study; *Program Coordinator*: Jim Crocker-Lakness (Speech); *Undergraduate Objectives or Program Emphases*: Competence in public speaking and interpersonal skills. Service courses for technical and transfer programs; *Full-Time Faculty*: 1; *Part-Time Faculty*: 7.

FACILITIES AND SERVICES
Practical experiences available through: Campus Newspaper (Published Independently); Desktop Publishing Facility; Electronic Field Production (Video); FM Radio Station (Institutional).

University of Cincinnati (Public)

Program of Writing
McMichen Hall, M.L. 69
Cincinnati, Ohio 45221
Telephone: (513) 556-3947

Mary Beth Debs, Director
Jim Hall, Acting Head, Department of English

CURRICULUM AND INSTRUCTION
Courses or Concentrations Available: Journalism or Mass Communication; Professional/Technical Writing; *Undergraduate Objectives or Program Emphases*: Writing certificate, 27 hours in Journalism and Professional, Technical Writing; *Graduate Objectives or Program Emphases*: MA in English with emphasis on editing and publishing, or professional writing; *Bachelor's Degree Majors*: 50; *Master's Degree Majors*: 15; *Full-Time Faculty*: 15; *Part-Time Faculty*: 5.

FACILITIES AND SERVICES
Practical experiences available through: Associated Press Wire Service Feed; Campus Newspaper (Published Independently); Local Commercial Newspaper; Local Commercial Television Station; Desktop Publishing Facility; Photographic Darkrooms; Television Broadcast Station (Institutional); FM Radio Station (Institutional); Institutional Magazine.

University of Cincinnati - Clermont College (Public)

Department of Speech Communication and Drama
725 College Drive
Batavia, Ohio 45103
Telephone: (513) 732-5200

Patricia E. Fried, Area Coordinator
Maryl Fletcher DeJong, Chair

CURRICULUM AND INSTRUCTION
Courses or Concentrations Available: Communication; Speech; Theatre; *Undergraduate Objectives or Program Emphases*: Two year programs only, including 26 degree programs and 15 certificates. Speech and Theatre provides a service program and electives only;

Full-Time Faculty: 11; *Part-Time Faculty*: 32.

University of Dayton (Private)

Department of Communication
300 College Park
Dayton, Ohio 45469
Telephone: (513) 229-2028

Donald B. Morlan, Chair
C. J. Chantell, Interim Dean, College of Arts and Sciences

CURRICULUM AND INSTRUCTION
Courses or Concentrations Available: Communication; Journalism or Mass Communication; Public Relations; Radio, Television, Broadcasting, or Telecommunications; Speech; *Undergraduate Objectives or Program Emphases*: Professional; *Bachelor's Degree Majors*: 400; *Master's Degree Majors*: 40; *Full-Time Faculty*: 19; *Part-Time Faculty*: 15; *Full-Time Professional (non-clerical) Staff Members*: 3.

FACILITIES AND SERVICES
Practical experiences available through: AM Radio Station (Institutional); Associated Press Wire Service Feed; Audio Recording Laboratory; Carrier Current Audio Distribution System; Campus Newspaper (Published Independently); Local Commercial Newspaper; Local Commercial Television Station; Desktop Publishing Facility; Video Editing; Electronic Field Production (Video); FM Radio Station (Institutional); Institutional Newspaper; Public Relations Agency; Video News and Data Processing; Video Production Laboratory or Television Studio.

University of Findlay (Private)

Division of Fine Arts
1000 North Main Street
Findlay, Ohio 45840
Telephone: (419) 424-4571

James G. Greenwood, Chair
Edward Erner, Administrator

CURRICULUM AND INSTRUCTION
Courses or Concentrations Available: Advertising; Communication;

Journalism or Mass Communication; Public Relations; Radio, Television, Broadcasting, or Telecommunications; Speech; *Undergraduate Objectives or Program Emphases*: To provide a solid liberal arts background; *Bachelor's Degree Majors*: 25; *Full-Time Faculty*: 3; *Part-Time Faculty*: 2.

FACILITIES AND SERVICES
Practical experiences available through: Advertising Agency; Audio Recording Laboratory; Campus Newspaper (Published Independently); Local Commercial Newspaper; Photographic Darkrooms; FM Radio Station (Institutional); Public Relations Agency; United Press International Feed.

University of Toledo

Department of Communication
2801 West Bancroft Street
Toledo, Ohio 43606

James Benjamin, Administrator

Walsh College (Private)

Program of Communication Arts
2020 Easton Street, NW
Canton, Ohio 44720
Telephone: (216) 499-7090

Mary E. Beadle, Coordinator
David Baxter, Chair

CURRICULUM AND INSTRUCTION
Courses or Concentrations Available: Communication; Journalism or Mass Communication; Radio, Television, Broadcasting, or Telecommunications; Speech; *Undergraduate Objectives or Program Emphases*: The program is based on a liberal arts core. Additionally, the program reflects competencies in the traditional areas the college has to offer, including speech, interpersonal, and theatre with a special emphasis on mass communication; *Bachelor's Degree Majors*: 25; *Full-Time Faculty*: 2; *Part-Time Faculty*: 4.

FACILITIES AND SERVICES
Practical experiences available through: Advertising Agency; Audio Recording Laboratory; Carrier Current Audio Distribution System; Campus

Newspaper (Published Independently);
Local Commercial Newspaper; Local
Commercial Television Station; Video
Editing; Electronic Field Production
(Video); Public Relations Agency.

Wright State University (Public)

Department of Communication
Colonel Glenn Highway
Dayton, Ohio 45435
Telephone: (513) 873-2145

James E. Sayer, Chair
Perry Moore, Dean, College of Liberal Arts

CURRICULUM AND INSTRUCTION
Courses or Concentrations
Available: Communication; Journalism or
Mass Communication; Public Relations;
Radio, Television, Broadcasting, or
Telecommunications; Speech; Organizational
Communication; *Undergraduate Objectives or
Program Emphases*: Understanding,
appreciation of communication; knowledge
and skill development of oral and written
communication; application of
communication skills in a professional
setting; *Bachelor's Degree Majors*: 300;
Full-Time Faculty: 14; *Part-Time Faculty*: 6;
*Full-Time Professional (non-clerical) Staff
Members*: 2.

FACILITIES AND SERVICES
*Practical experiences available
through*: Associated Press Wire Service Feed;
Audio Recording Laboratory; Community
Antenna (Cable) Television Origination;
Campus Newspaper (Published
Independently); Local Commercial
Newspaper; Local Commercial Television
Station; Desktop Publishing Facility;
Photographic Darkrooms; Video Editing;
Electronic Field Production (Video);
Television Broadcast Station (Institutional);
Film or Cinema Laboratory; FM Radio
Station (Institutional); Institutional
Newspaper; Public Relations Agency; Video ·
News and Data Processing; Video
Production Laboratory or Television Studio.

Wright State University (Public)

Telecommunications Department
Dayton, Ohio 45435

William C. Lewis, Administrator

Xavier University (Private)

Department of Communication Arts
B-11 Alter Hall
Cincinnati, Ohio 45207
Telephone: (513) 745-3087

John Eric Anderson, Chair
Stan Hedeen, Dean

CURRICULUM AND INSTRUCTION
Courses or Concentrations
Available: Advertising; Communication; Film
or Cinema; Journalism or Mass
Communication; Public Relations; Radio,
Television, Broadcasting, or
Telecommunications; Organizational
Communication; *Program Coordinators*: Dave
Smith (Television Studies); James King
(Radio Station WVXU-FM); *Undergraduate
Objectives or Program
Emphases*: Pre-professional training offered
within a strong core of liberal arts; *Bachelor's
Degree Majors*: 310; *Full-Time Faculty*: 11;
Part-Time Faculty: 15; *Full-Time
Professional (non-clerical) Staff Members*: 4.

FACILITIES AND SERVICES
*Practical experiences available
through*: Advertising Agency; Associated
Press Wire Service Feed; Audio Recording
Laboratory; Community Antenna (Cable)
Television Origination; Campus Newspaper
(Published Independently); Local
Commercial Newspaper; Local Commercial
Television Station; Desktop Publishing
Facility; Photographic Darkrooms; Video
Editing; Electronic Field Production
(Video); FM Radio Station (Institutional);
Public Relations Agency; Video Production
Laboratory or Television Studio.

Youngstown State University (Public)

Department of Marketing
Youngstown, Ohio 44555
Telephone: (216) 742-3082

E. Terry Deiderick, Chair
James Cicarelli, Dean, Williamson School of Business Administration

CURRICULUM AND INSTRUCTION
Courses or Concentrations
Available: Advertising; Communication; Journalism or Mass Communication; Public Relations; Radio, Television, Broadcasting, or Telecommunications; Speech; *Undergraduate Objectives or Program Emphases*: Career oriented toward Advertising and Public Relations; *Bachelor's Degree Majors*: 52; *Full-Time Faculty*: 14; *Part-Time Faculty*: 6.

FACILITIES AND SERVICES
Practical experiences available through: Advertising Agency; AM Radio Station (Institutional); Campus Newspaper (Published Independently); Local Commercial Newspaper; Local Commercial Television Station; Desktop Publishing Facility; Photographic Darkrooms; Television Broadcast Station (Institutional); FM Radio Station (Institutional); Institutional Newspaper; Public Relations Agency.

Youngstown State University (Public)

Department of Speech Communication and Theatre
410 Wick Avenue
Youngstown, Ohio 44555
Telephone: (216) 742-3631

Alfred W. Owens, Chair
David Sweet Kind, Administrator

CURRICULUM AND INSTRUCTION
Courses or Concentrations
Available: Communication; Radio, Television, Broadcasting, or Telecommunications; Speech; Organizational Communication; *Undergraduate Objectives or Program Emphases*: Liberal Arts education with corresponding skills, attitudes and values. Academic emphases in General Speech, Organization Communication,

Telecommunication Studies, and Theatre; *Bachelor's Degree Majors*: 250; *BFA Degree Majors*: 20; *Full-Time Faculty*: 14; *Part-Time Faculty*: 26; *Full-Time Professional (non-clerical) Staff Members*: 2.

FACILITIES AND SERVICES
Practical experiences available through: Associated Press Wire Service Feed; Audio Recording Laboratory; Carrier Current Audio Distribution System; Campus Newspaper (Published Independently); Local Commercial Newspaper; Local Commercial Television Station; Desktop Publishing Facility; Video Editing; Electronic Field Production (Video); FM Radio Station (Institutional); Institutional Newspaper; Video Production Laboratory or Television Studio.

Youngstown State University (Public)

Program of Journalism
English Department
Youngstown, Ohio 44555
Telephone: (216) 742-3415

Carolyn C. Martindale, Director
Barabara Brothers, Administrator

CURRICULUM AND INSTRUCTION
Courses or Concentrations
Available: Journalism or Mass Communication; *Undergraduate Objectives or Program Emphases*: Journalism minor, or journalism major through individualized curriculum program, or professional writing and editing major. All are BA degrees; *Bachelor's Degree Majors*: 14; *Full-Time Faculty*: 2; *Part-Time Faculty*: 2.

FACILITIES AND SERVICES
Practical experiences available through: Campus Newspaper (Published Independently); Local Commercial Newspaper; Desktop Publishing Facility; Photographic Darkrooms; Video Editing.

Cameron University (Public)

Department of Communication
2800 West Gore Boulevard
Lawton, Oklahoma 73505
Telephone: (405) 581-2425
Alternate: 581-2249

Tony M. Allison, Chair
Jack Bowman, Dean, School of Fine Arts

CURRICULUM AND INSTRUCTION
Courses or Concentrations
Available: Communication; Journalism or
Mass Communication; Public Relations;
Radio, Television, Broadcasting, or
Telecommunications; Speech; *Program
Coordinators*: Ron Price (Public Relations);
Don Evers (Journalism); Tony Allison
(Speech); *Undergraduate Objectives or
Program Emphases*: Communications
Department: Speech Communication; Radio,
Television; Public Relations, Organizational
Communication. Languages and Journalism
Department: Journalism; Public Relations,
Organizational Communication; *Bachelor's
Degree Majors*: 190; *Full-Time Faculty*: 8;
Part-Time Faculty: 1.

FACILITIES AND SERVICES
Practical experiences available through: Audio
Recording Laboratory; Local Commercial
Newspaper; Local Commercial Television
Station; Desktop Publishing Facility;
Photographic Darkrooms; Video Editing;
Electronic Field Production (Video); FM
Radio Station (Institutional); Institutional
Newspaper; Video Production Laboratory or
Television Studio.

Carl Albert Junior College (Public)

Division of Communication and Fine Arts
1507 S. Mc Kenna
Poteau, Oklahoma 74953-5208
Telephone: (918) 647-8660

Brad Garrett, Chair
Jim Jinkins, Vice President

CURRICULUM AND INSTRUCTION
Courses or Concentrations
Available: Communication; Journalism or
Mass Communication; Radio, Television,
Broadcasting, or Telecommunications;
Speech; *Program Coordinators*: Dennis
Meeks (Program Director KFSM-TV);
*Undergraduate Objectives or Program
Emphases*: Journalism; *Associate's Degree
Majors*: 3; *Full-Time Faculty*: 8; *Part-Time
Faculty*: 2.

FACILITIES AND SERVICES
Practical experiences available through: Local
Commercial Television Station.

Central State University (Public)

Department of Oral Communication
100 North University Drive
Edmond, Oklahoma 73034-0197
Telephone: (405) 341-2980 Extension: 5581

Barbara A. Norman, Chair
Clifton Warren, Dean, Liberal Arts

CURRICULUM AND INSTRUCTION
Courses or Concentrations
Available: Advertising; Communication; Film
or Cinema; Journalism or Mass
Communication; Public Relations; Radio,
Television, Broadcasting, or
Telecommunications; Speech; *Program
Coordinators*: Jack W. Deskin (Broadcast);
*Undergraduate Objectives or Program
Emphases*: Career oriented liberal arts
program; *Bachelor's Degree Majors*: 200;
Full-Time Faculty: 11; *Part-Time Faculty*: 4;
*Full-Time Professional (non-clerical) Staff
Members*: 2.

FACILITIES AND SERVICES
*Practical experiences available
through*: Associated Press Wire Service Feed;
Audio Recording Laboratory; Community
Antenna (Cable) Television Origination;
Closed Circuit Television Facility;
Photographic Darkrooms; Video Editing;
Electronic Field Production (Video); Film
or Cinema Laboratory; FM Radio Station
(Institutional); Institutional Magazine;
Institutional Newspaper; Video Production
Laboratory or Television Studio.

Central State University (Public)

Department of Journalism
100 North University Drive
Edmond, Oklahoma 73034-0196
Telephone: (405) 341-2980

Ray Tassin, Chair
Cliff Warren, Dean, College of Liberal Arts

CURRICULUM AND INSTRUCTION
Courses or Concentrations
Available: Advertising; Journalism or Mass
Communication; Public Relations;
Journalism Business and Economics;
Journalism-General, Magazines, Newspaper,
Photo Arts, Professional Writing; Journalism
Education; *Undergraduate Objectives or*
Program Emphases: Professional writing,
news reporting, editing, public relations;
Graduate Objectives or Program
Emphases: Teaching, Journalism education;
Bachelor's Degree Majors: 133; *Master's*
Degree Majors: 4; *Full-Time Faculty*: 5;
Part-Time Faculty: 5.

FACILITIES AND SERVICES
Practical experiences available
through: Advertising Agency; Associated
Press Wire Service Feed; Campus
Newspaper (Published Independently);
Local Commercial Newspaper; Photographic
Darkrooms; Video Editing; Institutional
Magazine; Institutional Newspaper; Public
Relations Agency; Video News and Data
Processing.

East Central University (Public)

Department of
Speech-Theatre-Communications
Ada, Oklahoma 74820
Telephone: (405) 332-8000

Robert A. Payne, Chair
Doug Nelson, Chair, Division of Arts and
Letters

CURRICULUM AND INSTRUCTION
Courses or Concentrations
Available: Advertising; Communication;
Journalism or Mass Communication; Radio,
Television, Broadcasting, or
Telecommunications; Speech; *Program*
Coordinators: Arlie Daniel (Speech
Education); Mary Bishop (News Editorial);
Collin Pillow (Radio Television); *Bachelor's*

Degree Majors: 20; *Other Degree Majors*: 150;
Full-Time Faculty: 9; *Part-Time Faculty*: 2.

FACILITIES AND SERVICES
Practical experiences available
through: Advertising Agency; Audio
Recording Laboratory; Community Antenna
(Cable) Television Origination; Campus
Newspaper (Published Independently);
Local Commercial Newspaper; Local
Commercial Television Station; Desktop
Publishing Facility; Photographic
Darkrooms; Video Editing; Electronic Field
Production (Video); Video Production
Laboratory or Television Studio.

Northeastern Oklahoma A and M College (Public)

Department of Speech and Theatre
Second and I Streets NE
Miami, Oklahoma 74354
Telephone: (918) 542-8441

Brian V. Hauck, Head
Jack Rucker, Chair, Communications/Fine
Arts Division

CURRICULUM AND INSTRUCTION
Courses or Concentrations
Available: Communication; Film or Cinema;
Radio, Television, Broadcasting, or
Telecommunications; Speech; *Program*
Coordinator: Christopher Willard
(Television/Film); *Undergraduate Objectives*
or Program Emphases: Comprehensive
curriculum of freshman-sophomore level
communication courses, leading to the AA
degree and preparing for transfer to the
4-year university; *Associate's Degree*
Majors: 15; *Full-Time Faculty*: 6; *Full-Time*
Professional (non-clerical) Staff Members: 1.

FACILITIES AND SERVICES
Practical experiences available through: Audio
Recording Laboratory; Community Antenna
(Cable) Television Origination; Video
Editing; ITFS Distribution System; Video
Production Laboratory or Television Studio.

Northeastern State University (Public)

Department of Journalism
Tahlequah, Oklahoma 74464

Byron Evers, Administrator

Northeastern State University (Public)

Department of Mass Communications
Tahlequah, Oklahoma 74464
Telephone: (918) 456-5511

Joseph Loftin and Tom Kennedy, Professors
Tom Cottrill, Dean

CURRICULUM AND INSTRUCTION
Courses or Concentrations
Available: Advertising; Film or Cinema; Journalism or Mass Communication; Public Relations; Radio, Television, Broadcasting, or Telecommunications; *Undergraduate Objectives or Program Emphases*: To provide students with a broad liberal arts background while allowing them to specialize in mass communications; *Bachelor's Degree Majors*: 50; *Full-Time Faculty*: 3; *Part-Time Faculty*: 3; *Full-Time Professional (non-clerical) Staff Members*: 2.

FACILITIES AND SERVICES
Practical experiences available through: Desktop Publishing Facility; Photographic Darkrooms; Institutional Magazine; Institutional Newspaper; Public Relations Agency.

Oklahoma Baptist University (Private)

Department of Communication Arts
500 West University
Shawnee, Oklahoma 74801
Telephone: (405) 275-2850

Roger Hadley, Chair
Paul Hammond, Dean

CURRICULUM AND INSTRUCTION
Courses or Concentrations
Available: Communication; Radio, Television, Broadcasting, or Telecommunications; Speech; *Undergraduate Objectives or Program Emphases*: Enhance human relationships through effective communication behavior and to prepare communication students for productive careers; *Bachelor's Degree Majors*: 30; *Full-Time Faculty*: 4; *Part-Time Faculty*: 6; *Full-Time Professional (non-clerical) Staff Members*: 1.

FACILITIES AND SERVICES
Practical experiences available through: Audio Recording Laboratory; Community Antenna (Cable) Television Origination; Local Commercial Television Station; Video Editing; Electronic Field Production (Video); Video Production Laboratory or Television Studio.

Oklahoma Baptist University (Private)

Department of Journalism
500 W. University
Shawnee, Oklahoma 74801
Telephone: (405) 275-2850

Kathryn Jenson White, Chair
Laura Crouch, Division Director, Languages and Literature

CURRICULUM AND INSTRUCTION
Courses or Concentrations
Available: Communication; Journalism or Mass Communication; Public Relations; Radio, Television, Broadcasting, or Telecommunications; *Undergraduate Objectives or Program Emphases*: Journalism and Public Relations. To provide students with current knowledge base, historical perspective, context and practical experience in their chosen fields.; *Bachelor's Degree Majors*: 103; *Full-Time Faculty*: 1; *Part-Time Faculty*: 2.

FACILITIES AND SERVICES
Practical experiences available through: Audio Recording Laboratory; Carrier Current Audio Distribution System; Campus Newspaper (Published Independently); Local Commercial Newspaper; Local Commercial Television Station; Desktop Publishing Facility; Photographic Darkrooms; Video Editing; Electronic Field Production (Video); Public Relations Agency.

Oklahoma Christian University of Science and Arts (Private)

Department of Communication
Box 11000
Oklahoma City, Oklahoma 73136-1100
Telephone: (405) 425-5000

Philip L. Patterson, Chair
Bailey McBride, Dean

CURRICULUM AND INSTRUCTION
Courses or Concentrations
Available: Advertising; Communication;
Journalism or Mass Communication; Public
Relations; Radio, Television, Broadcasting,
or Telecommunications; Speech; *Program
Coordinator*: Michael O'Keefe (Advertising);
*Undergraduate Objectives or Program
Emphases*: Radio/Television,
including broadcast journalism, broadcast
management, corporate communication.
Journalism; Organizational Communication;
Public Relations and Advertising; *BFA
Degree Majors*: 30; *Bachelor's Degree
Majors*: 110; *Full-Time Faculty*: 4;
Part-Time Faculty: 3.

FACILITIES AND SERVICES
*Practical experiences available
through*: Advertising Agency; Associated
Press Wire Service Feed; Audio Recording
Laboratory; Local Commercial Newspaper;
Local Commercial Television Station;
Desktop Publishing Facility; Photographic
Darkrooms; Video Editing; Electronic Field
Production (Video); FM Radio Station
(Institutional); Institutional Newspaper;
Public Relations Agency; Video Production
Laboratory or Television Studio.

Oklahoma City University (Private)

Department of Mass Communications
2501 North Blackwelder
Oklahoma City, Oklahoma 73106
Telephone: (405) 521-5252

Karlie K. Harmon, Chair
Perry Dillon, Division Coordinator

CURRICULUM AND INSTRUCTION
Courses or Concentrations
Available: Advertising; Journalism or Mass
Communication; Public Relations; Radio,
Television, Broadcasting, or
Telecommunications; *Full-Time Faculty*: 3;
Part-Time Faculty: 3.

FACILITIES AND SERVICES
*Practical experiences available
through*: Advertising Agency; Local
Commercial Newspaper; Local Commercial
Television Station; Photographic
Darkrooms; Video Editing; FM Radio
Station (Institutional); Public Relations
Agency.

Oklahoma State University (Public)

School of Journalism and Broadcasting
Stillwater, Oklahoma 74078-0195
Telephone: (405) 744-6354

Marlan D. Nelson, Director
**Smith L. Holt, Dean, College of Arts and
Sciences**

CURRICULUM AND INSTRUCTION
Courses or Concentrations
Available: Advertising; Journalism or Mass
Communication; Public Relations; Radio,
Television, Broadcasting, or
Telecommunications; *Undergraduate
Objectives or Program Emphases*: To provide
a professional education program to prepare
graduates for careers in mass media fields;
*Graduate Objectives or Program
Emphases*: To provide mass communication
research programs for individual planning a
career in mass communication research and
college teaching; *Full-Time Faculty*: 15;
Part-Time Faculty: 4; *Full-Time Professional
(non-clerical) Staff Members*: 3.

FACILITIES AND SERVICES
*Practical experiences available
through*: Advertising Agency; Associated
Press Wire Service Feed; Audio Recording
Laboratory; Community Antenna (Cable)
Television Origination; Closed Circuit
Television Facility; Campus Newspaper
(Published Independently); Local
Commercial Newspaper; Local Commercial
Television Station; Desktop Publishing
Facility; Photographic Darkrooms; Video
Editing; Electronic Field Production
(Video); FM Radio Station (Institutional);
ITFS Distribution System; Institutional
Newspaper; Public Relations Agency; Video
Production Laboratory or Television Studio.

Oklahoma State University

Department of Speech Communication
109 Morrill Hall
Stillwater, Oklahoma 74078
Telephone: (405) 744-6150

Paul D. Harper, Head
Smith Holt, Dean, College of Arts and Sciences

CURRICULUM AND INSTRUCTION
Courses or Concentrations Available: Communication; Speech; *Undergraduate Objectives or Program Emphases*: To train students for the professional role of communication consultants, especially in Interpersonal and Organizational Communication; *Graduate Objectives or Program Emphases*: To train students for the professional role of communication consultants, especially in Interpersonal and Organizational Communication; *Bachelor's Degree Majors*: 36; *Master's Degree Majors*: 21; *Other Degree Majors*: 34; *Full-Time Faculty*: 6; *Part-Time Faculty*: 13; *Full-Time Professional (non-clerical) Staff Members*: 2.

Oral Roberts University (Private)

Department of Communication Arts
7777 South Lewis Avenue
Tulsa, Oklahoma 74171
Telephone: (918) 495-6866

Ray Lewandowski, Chair
Ralph Fagin, Dean

CURRICULUM AND INSTRUCTION
Courses or Concentrations Available: Advertising; Communication; Film or Cinema; Journalism or Mass Communication; Public Relations; Radio, Television, Broadcasting, or Telecommunications; Speech; Drama; Organizational Communication; *Program Coordinators*: Charles Zwick (Telecommunications); Al Morgan (Journalism); Vicki Clark (Organizational Communication); Laura Holland (Drama); *Undergraduate Objectives or Program Emphases*: Entrance to professional field and into graduate studies; *Bachelor's Degree Majors*: 450; *Full-Time Faculty*: 14; *Part-Time Faculty*: 4.

FACILITIES AND SERVICES
Practical experiences available through: Closed Circuit Television Facility; Campus Newspaper (Published Independently); Local Commercial Television Station; Desktop Publishing Facility; Photographic Darkrooms; Video Editing; Electronic Field Production (Video); Film or Cinema Laboratory; FM Radio Station (Institutional); Institutional Magazine; Institutional Newspaper; Video Production Laboratory or Television Studio.

Panhandle State University (Public)

Department of English
Goodwell, Oklahoma 73939
Telephone: (405) 349-2611

Sara J. Richter, Head
Jesse Hankla, Dean, School of Liberal Arts

CURRICULUM AND INSTRUCTION
Courses or Concentrations Available: Communication; Journalism or Mass Communication; Radio, Television, Broadcasting, or Telecommunications; Speech; English; *Program Coordinators*: Donna Ingham (Mass Communication, Journalism); Bill Underwood (Speech); Russ Guthrie (Radio/Television); *Undergraduate Objectives or Program Emphases*: To provide students coursework in English and Speech to prepare them to teach in the public schools or to attend a graduate school. Secondly, to provide general education requirements in English and Speech to the university students; *Bachelor's Degree Majors*: 20; *Full-Time Faculty*: 2; *Part-Time Faculty*: 6.

FACILITIES AND SERVICES
Practical experiences available through: AM Radio Station (Institutional); Community Antenna (Cable) Television Origination; Photographic Darkrooms; Institutional Newspaper.

Phillips University

Languages and Communication
Zollars Library
Enid, Oklahoma 73702

Glenn Doyle, Administrator

Rose State College

Broadcasting Department
6420 S.E. 15th Street
Midwest City, Oklahoma 73110

Noel Leckness, Administrator

Seminole Junior College (Public)

Program of Photojournalism
P.O. Box 351
Seminole, Oklahoma 74868
Telephone: (405) 382-9950

Jeff L. Cox, Instructor
Kay Dotson, Division Chair

CURRICULUM AND INSTRUCTION
Courses or Concentrations
Available: Advertising; Communication;
Information Science; Journalism or Mass
Communication; Public Relations; Radio,
Television, Broadcasting, or
Telecommunications; Speech; *Program
Coordinators*: Jay McAlvain (Speech);
*Undergraduate Objectives or Program
Emphases*: Teach basic news reporter and
photographer skills; *Associate's Degree
Majors*: 17; *Full-Time Faculty*: 1; *Part-Time
Faculty*: 1.

FACILITIES AND SERVICES
*Practical experiences available
through*: Campus Newspaper (Published
Independently); Local Commercial
Newspaper; Local Commercial Television
Station; Desktop Publishing Facility;
Photographic Darkrooms.

Southern Nazarene University (Private)

Department of Speech Communication
6729 NW 39th Expressway
Bethany, Oklahoma 73008-2694
Telephone: (405) 789-6400

Pamela S. Broyles, Chair
Stephen Gunter, College Dean

CURRICULUM AND INSTRUCTION
Courses or Concentrations
Available: Communication; Journalism or
Mass Communication; Public Relations;
Radio, Television, Broadcasting, or
Telecommunications; Speech; *Undergraduate
Objectives or Program Emphases*: Speech
Communication; Mass
Communication/Journalism; Speech
Education; *Graduate Objectives or Program
Emphases*: Speech Communication
Education; *Bachelor's Degree Majors*: 30;
Master's Degree Majors: 3; *Full-Time
Faculty*: 2; *Part-Time Faculty*: 4.

FACILITIES AND SERVICES
*Practical experiences available
through*: Advertising Agency; Audio
Recording Laboratory; Community Antenna
(Cable) Television Origination; Campus
Newspaper (Published Independently);
Local Commercial Newspaper; Local
Commercial Television Station; Desktop
Publishing Facility; Photographic
Darkrooms; Electronic Field Production
(Video); Institutional Newspaper; Public
Relations Agency; Video News and Data
Processing; Video Production Laboratory or
Television Studio.

Southern Nazarene University (Private)

Bethany College of Ministry and the
Humanities
6729 NW 39th Expressway
Bethany, Oklahoma 73008
Telephone: (405) 789-6400 Extension: 6492

James G. Wilcox, Associate Professor
Peggy Poteet, Chair, English Department

CURRICULUM AND INSTRUCTION
Courses or Concentrations
Available: Advertising; Communication;
Journalism or Mass Communication; Public
Relations; Radio, Television, Broadcasting,
or Telecommunications; Speech; *Program
Coordinators*: Professor Mercer
(Advertising); Pam Broyles (Public Relations
and Speech); *Undergraduate Objectives or
Program Emphases*: To develop, within the
liberal arts framework, a knowledge and
understanding of the theoretical issues of
mass communications; *Bachelor's Degree
Majors*: 12.

University of Oklahoma (Public)

Department of Communication
780 Van Vleet Oval #331
Norman, Oklahoma 73019-0250
Telephone: (405) 325-3111

Robert Norton, Chair
Roland Lehr, Interim Dean

CURRICULUM AND INSTRUCTION
Courses or Concentrations
Available: Communication; *Undergraduate Objectives or Program Emphases*: Study the processes that enable people to develop/exchange messages and the results of those message exchanges. In more practical terms, students concentrate on examining events such as the interpersonal communication between friends, spouses, or families; *Graduate Objectives or Program Emphases*: The program offers a wide variety of specialty areas, including cross-cultural, inter-cultural, and international communication; instructional communication; language and social interaction; organizational and small group communication, and political and mass communication; *Master's Degree Majors*: 11; *Doctoral Degree Majors Currently in Residence*: 59; *Other Degree Majors*: 226; *Full-Time Faculty*: 16; *Part-Time Faculty*: 37.

University of Oklahoma (Public)

H. H. Herbert School of Journalism and
Mass Communication
860 Van Vleet Oval
Norman, Oklahoma 73072
Telephone: (405) 325-2721

David A. Dary, Director
Roland Lehr, Interim Dean

CURRICULUM AND INSTRUCTION
Courses or Concentrations
Available: Advertising; Journalism or Mass Communication; Public Relations; Radio, Television, Broadcasting, or Telecommunications; Professional Writing; *Undergraduate Objectives or Program Emphases*: The School offers opportunities in Radio-Television-Film Production, Sales and Management, Electronic Journalism, Public Relations, Professional Writing, News Communication, and Advertising; *Bachelor's Degree Majors*: 597; *Master's Degree Majors*: 95; *Full-Time Faculty*: 23;

Part-Time Faculty: 8; *Full-Time Professional (non-clerical) Staff Members*: 2.

FACILITIES AND SERVICES
Practical experiences available through: Advertising Agency; Associated Press Wire Service Feed; Audio Recording Laboratory; Community Antenna (Cable) Television Origination; Campus Newspaper (Published Independently); Local Commercial Newspaper; Local Commercial Television Station; Desktop Publishing Facility; Photographic Darkrooms; Video Editing; Electronic Field Production (Video); Film or Cinema Laboratory;FM Radio Station (Institutional); ITFS Distribution System; Institutional Newspaper; Public Relations Agency; Satellite Uplink Facility (Ku Band Transmitter); Video Production Laboratory or Television Studio.

University of Tulsa (Private)

Department of Communication
600 South College Avenue
Tulsa, Oklahoma 74104
Telephone: (918) 631-2541

Robert J. Doolittle, Chair
Susan R. Parr, Dean

CURRICULUM AND INSTRUCTION
Courses or Concentrations
Available: Advertising; Communication; Journalism or Mass Communication; Public Relations; Radio, Television, Broadcasting, or Telecommunications; Organizational Communication, Media Analysis; *Undergraduate Objectives or Program Emphases*: General Communication Studies, Organization Communication, Public Relations, Media Analysis, Journalism and Broadcasting; *Bachelor's Degree Majors*: 147; *Full-Time Faculty*: 8; *Part-Time Faculty*: 2; *Full-Time Professional (non-clerical) Staff Members*: 3.

FACILITIES AND SERVICES
Practical experiences available through: Advertising Agency; Audio Recording Laboratory; Community Antenna (Cable) Television Origination; Closed Circuit Television Facility; Campus Newspaper (Published Independently); Local Commercial Newspaper; Local Commercial Television Station; Desktop Publishing Facility; Photographic

Darkrooms; Video Editing; Electronic Field
Production (Video); FM Radio Station
(Institutional); Public Relations Agency;
Satellite Uplink Facility; Video Production
Laboratory or Television Studio.

Blue Mountain Community College (Public)

Department of Radio Broadcasting
2411 N.W. Carden Avenue
Pendleton, Oregon 97801
Telephone: (503) 276-1260 Extension: 280

Blaine T. Hanks, Chair
Larry O'Rourke, Administrator

CURRICULUM AND INSTRUCTION
Courses or Concentrations
Available: Advertising; Journalism or Mass
Communication; Radio, Television,
Broadcasting, or Telecommunications;
Speech; *Program Coordinators*: Robert Clapp
(Speech); *Undergraduate Objectives or
Program Emphases*: Job entry in local radio
stations; News, Air Personality; *Associate's
Degree Majors*: 12; *Full-Time Faculty*: 1;
Part-Time Faculty: 2.

FACILITIES AND SERVICES
Practical experiences available through: AM
Radio Station (Institutional); Associated
Press Wire Service Feed; Audio Recording
Laboratory; Community Antenna (Cable)
Television Origination; Local Commercial
Newspaper; Desktop Publishing Facility;
Electronic Field Production (Video); FM
Radio Station (Institutional); Institutional
Newspaper; Satellite Uplink Facility; Video
Production Laboratory or Television Studio.

Chemeketa Community College (Public)

Department of Humanities and
Communications
4000 Lancaster Drive, NE
P. O. Box 14007
Salem, Oregon 97309
Telephone: (503) 399-5000

Bernard Knab, Director
Gretchen Schuette, Academic Dean

CURRICULUM AND INSTRUCTION
Courses or Concentrations Available: Film or
Cinema; Speech; Communication Skills;
Curricula for Technical Program students;

Program Coordinators: Rob Bibler (Film);
Leonard Held (Film); Vicki Hilgemann
(Speech); *Undergraduate Objectives or
Program Emphases*: Film: Review of film
genre and directors. Sequence
course: Genre, themes, history, technique
and art of film. Speech: Provide first two
years of undergraduate speech curriculum;
Full-Time Faculty: 21; *Part-Time
Faculty*: 22; *Full-Time Professional
(non-clerical) Staff Members*: 2.

FACILITIES AND SERVICES
Practical experiences available through: Audio
Recording Laboratory; Community Antenna
(Cable) Television Origination; Closed
Circuit Television Facility; Campus
Newspaper (Published Independently);
Desktop Publishing Facility; Photographic
Darkrooms; Video Editing; Television
Broadcast Station (Institutional); Film or
Cinema Laboratory; Satellite Uplink
Facility; Video Production Laboratory or
Television Studio.

George Fox College (Private)

Division of Communication and Literature
Newberg, Oregon 97132
Telephone: (503) 538-8383

Richard Engnell, Chair
Lee Nash, Administrator

CURRICULUM AND INSTRUCTION
Courses or Concentrations
Available: Advertising; Communication; Film
or Cinema; Journalism or Mass
Communication; Public Relations; Radio,
Television, Broadcasting, or
Telecommunications; Speech; *Program
Coordinator*: Warren Koch (Television,
Cinema); *Undergraduate Objectives or
Program Emphases*: Through core courses in
communication and rhetorical theory
investigate, practice and celebrate the central
place of symbols in the human experience;
Bachelor's Degree Majors: 40; *Full-Time
Faculty*: 6; *Part-Time Faculty*: 4; *Full-Time
Professional (non-clerical) Staff Members*: 1.

FACILITIES AND SERVICES
Practical experiences available through: Advertising Agency; Audio Recording Laboratory; Community Antenna (Cable) Television Origination; Campus Newspaper (Published Independently); Local Commercial Newspaper; Local Commercial Television Station; Desktop Publishing Facility; Photographic Darkrooms; Video Editing; Electronic Field Production (Video); FM Radio Station (Institutional); Video Production Laboratory or Television Studio.

Lane Community College (Public)

Division of Visual Arts, Performing Arts and Mass Communication
4000 East 30th Avenue
Eugene, Oregon 97405
Telephone: (503) 726-2209

Richard W. Reid, Chair
Jacquelyn M. Belcher, Vice President for Instruction

CURRICULUM AND INSTRUCTION
Courses or Concentrations Available: Film; Journalism or Mass Communication; Public Relations; Radio, Television, Broadcasting, or Telecommunications; *Program Coordinator*: John J. Dunne (Mass Communication); *Undergraduate Objectives or Program Emphases*: Lower-division vocational program to prepare for entry level positions; curricular emphases in broadcast television, video production, radio broadcasting, corporate media, print journalism, film, and photography; *Degree Majors*: 150; *Full-Time Faculty*: 5; *Part-Time Faculty*: 5; *Full-Time Professional (non-clerical) Staff Members*: 1.

FACILITIES AND SERVICES
Practical experiences available through: Advertising Agency; Audio Recording Laboratory; Community Antenna (Cable) Television Origination; Campus Newspaper (Published Independently); Local Commercial Newspaper; Local Commercial Television Station; Desktop Publishing Facility; Photographic Darkrooms; Video Editing; Electronic Field Production (Video); Film or Cinema Laboratory; FM Radio Station (Institutional); Institutional Magazine; Institutional Newspaper; Satellite Uplink Facility (C Band Transmitter); Video Production Laboratory or Television Studio.

Lewis and Clark College (Private)

Department of Communication
Portland, Oregon 97219
Telephone: (503) 293-2774

Peter Christenson, Chair
Clarence Davis, Dean

CURRICULUM AND INSTRUCTION
Courses or Concentrations Available: Communication; Journalism or Mass Communication; Radio, Television, Broadcasting, or Telecommunications; Speech; *Undergraduate Objectives or Program Emphases*: Liberal Arts Degree, Major in Communications; *Bachelor's Degree Majors*: 100; *Full-Time Faculty*: 5; *Part-Time Faculty*: 1.

FACILITIES AND SERVICES
Practical experiences available through: Advertising Agency; Associated Press Wire Service Feed; Audio Recording Laboratory; Community Antenna (Cable) Television Origination; Carrier Current Audio Distribution System; Campus Newspaper (Published Independently); Local Commercial Newspaper; Local Commercial Television Station; Desktop Publishing Facility; Photographic Darkrooms; Video Editing; Electronic Field Production (Video); FM Radio Station (Institutional); Public Relations Agency; United Press International Feed; Video Production Laboratory or Television Studio.

Linfield College (Private)

Department of Communications
900 South Baker Street
McMinnville, Oregon 97128-6894
Telephone: (503) 472-4121 Extension: 521

William M. Lingle, Chair
Kenneth P. Goodrich, Vice President for Instruction and Academic Dean

CURRICULUM AND INSTRUCTION
Courses or Concentrations Available: Film or Cinema; Journalism or Mass Communication; Public Relations; Radio, Television, Broadcasting, or Telecommunications; Speech; *Undergraduate Objectives or Program Emphases*: Mass communications is a pre-professional program that develops liberally educated students who respond to messages critically and deliver them responsibly; Speech is a

support program in interpersonal and public communication for several majors; *Bachelor's Degree Majors*: 45; *Other Degree Majors*: 50; *Full-Time Faculty*: 4; *Part-Time Faculty*: 1.

FACILITIES AND SERVICES
Practical experiences available through: Associated Press Wire Service Feed; Audio Recording Laboratory; Community Antenna (Cable) Television Origination; Campus Newspaper (Published Independently); Local Commercial Newspaper; Desktop Publishing Facility; Photographic Darkrooms; Video Editing; Electronic Field Production (Video); FM Radio Station (Institutional); Video Production Laboratory or Television Studio.

Mount Hood Community College

Department of Communication
2600 Southeast Stark Street
Gresham, Oregon 97030

John Rice, Administrator

Multnomah School of the Bible (Private)

Department of Journalism
8435 NE Glisan Street
Portland, Oregon 97220
Telephone: (503) 255-0332

Ann D. Staatz, Head
Dave Jongeward, Chair, General Education Department

CURRICULUM AND INSTRUCTION
Courses or Concentrations Available: Journalism or Mass Communication; Graphic Design; Photography; *Undergraduate Objectives or Program Emphases*: Coursework trains students to develop and polish their writing for free-lance writing ministry; to master principles of visual design to know and use good graphics; to practice the disciplines of editorial responsibility. Magazine Journalism emphasis; *Graduate Objectives or Program Emphases*: The college offers a one-year program leading to a certificate in Religious Journalism; *Associate's Degree Majors*: 16; *Full-Time Faculty*: 1; *Part-Time Faculty*: 3.

FACILITIES AND SERVICES
Practical experiences available through: Audio Recording Laboratory; Photographic Darkrooms; Video Editing; Institutional Newspaper; Video Production Laboratory or Television Studio.

Oregon Institute of Technology (Public)

Department of Communications
Campus Drive
Klamath Falls, Oregon 97601-8801
Telephone: (503) 882-6992

David L. Dyrud, Chair
Christian Eismann, Dean

CURRICULUM AND INSTRUCTION
Courses or Concentrations Available: Technical Communication; *Undergraduate Objectives or Program Emphases*: The Technical Communications option attached to a BSET degree prepares students for positions as technical writers; *Degree Majors*: 20; *Full-Time Faculty*: 12; *Part-Time Faculty*: 1.

FACILITIES AND SERVICES
Practical experiences available through: Desktop Publishing Facility; Photographic Darkrooms; Video Editing; Electronic Field Production (Video); FM Radio Station (Institutional); Institutional Magazine; Institutional Newspaper; Public Relations Agency; Video Production Laboratory or Television Studio.

Oregon State University (Public)

Department of Speech Communication
104 Shepard Hall
Corvallis, Oregon 97330
Telephone: (503) 737-2461

Victoria O'Donnell, Chair

CURRICULUM AND INSTRUCTION
Courses or Concentrations Available: Communication; Film or Cinema; Radio, Television, Broadcasting, or Telecommunications; Speech; Film Studies; Speech and Hearing; Theatre Arts; *Undergraduate Objectives or Program Emphases*: BA Speech Communication (rhetoric, interpersonal, persuasion); BA Broadcast Media Communication; BA

Theatre Arts; *Graduate Objectives or Program Emphases*: Master of Interdisciplinary Studies (any 3 areas); Master of Scientific and Technical Communication - Journalism; Speech Communication; English; *Bachelor's Degree Majors*: 450; *Master's Degree Majors*: 35; *Other Degree Majors*: 20; *Full-Time Faculty*: 16; *Part-Time Faculty*: 8; *Full-Time Professional (non-clerical) Staff Members*: 2.

FACILITIES AND SERVICES
Practical experiences available through: Advertising Agency; AM Radio Station (Institutional); Associated Press Wire Service Feed; Audio Recording Laboratory; Community Antenna (Cable) Television Origination; Closed Circuit Television Facility; Local Commercial Television Station; Video Editing; Electronic Field Production (Video); Television Broadcast Station (Institutional); Film or Cinema Laboratory; FM Radio Station (Institutional); ITFS Distribution System; Public Relations Agency; Video Production Laboratory or Television Studio.

Oregon State University (Public)

Department of Journalism
Corvallis, Oregon 97403

Fred C. Zwahlen, Administrator

Pacific University (Private)

Department of Communication
2043 College Way
Forest Grove, Oregon 97116
Telephone: (503) 357-6151

David R. Cassady, Chair
Michael Steele, Administrator

CURRICULUM AND INSTRUCTION
Courses or Concentrations Available: Journalism or Mass Communication; Radio, Television, Broadcasting, or Telecommunications; *Undergraduate Objectives or Program Emphases*: Journalism, Mass Communication, Television Production; *Bachelor's Degree Majors*: 27; *Full-Time Faculty*: 3; *Part-Time Faculty*: 3.

FACILITIES AND SERVICES
Practical experiences available through: Audio Recording Laboratory; Community Antenna (Cable) Television Origination; Campus Newspaper (Published Independently); Desktop Publishing Facility; Photographic Darkrooms; Video Editing; Electronic Field Production (Video); FM Radio Station (Institutional); Satellite Uplink Facility (C Band Transmitter).

Portland Community College

Visual and Performing Arts
12000 Southwest 49th Avenue
Portland, Oregon 97219

William Line, Administrator

Portland State University

Television Services
P. O. Box 751
Portland, Oregon 97207

Robert E. Walker II, Administrator

Southern Oregon State College (Public)

Department of Communication
1250 Siskiyou Boulevard
Ashland, Oregon 97520
Telephone: (503) 482-6424

Jonathan I. Lange, Chair
Richard J. Kaough, Director, School of Humanities

CURRICULUM AND INSTRUCTION
Courses or Concentrations Available: Communication; Film or Cinema; Journalism or Mass Communication; Public Relations; Radio, Television, Broadcasting, or Telecommunications; Speech; *Program Coordinators*: Mark Chilcoat (Broadcasting, Radio, Television, Telecommunication, Film, Cinema); Thomas Pyle (Journalism, Mass Communication, Public Relations); *Undergraduate Objectives or Program Emphases*: The department seeks to provide a wide range of applied and theoretical learning opportunities in speech, journalism and broadcasting in the classroom, through research and through on-campus and

off-campus laboratory and internship experience; *Graduate Objectives or Program Emphases*: The graduate program emphasizes research and creative performance, with students choosing which direction to take. Work toward the MA must be in at least one area in addition to Communication; *Bachelor's Degree Majors*: 95; *Master's Degree Majors*: 8; *Full-Time Faculty*: 9; *Part-Time Faculty*: 18; *Full-Time Professional (non-clerical) Staff Members*: 6.

FACILITIES AND SERVICES
Practical experiences available through: Advertising Agency; AM Radio Station (Institutional); Associated Press Wire Service Feed; Audio Recording Laboratory; Community Antenna (Cable) Television Origination; Campus Newspaper (Published Independently); Local Commercial Newspaper; Local Commercial Television Station; Desktop Publishing Facility; Photographic Darkrooms; Video Editing; Electronic Field Production (Video); Television Broadcast Station (Institutional); FM Radio Station (Institutional); Public Relations Agency; Satellite Uplink Facility (C Band Transmitter); Video News and Data Processing; Video Production Laboratory or Television Studio.

University of Oregon (Public)

Department of Speech, Telecommunications and Film
Eugene, Oregon 97403
Telephone: (503) 686-4171

Ronald E. Sherriffs, Head
Donald R. Van Houten, Dean, College of Arts and Sciences

CURRICULUM AND INSTRUCTION
Courses or Concentrations Available: Communication; Film or Cinema; Radio, Television, Broadcasting, or Telecommunications; Speech; Theatre Arts; *Undergraduate Objectives or Program Emphases*: With a liberal arts basis, students study forms and effects of communication with emphasis on aesthetics, structure, criticism and production as they contribute to our cultural, social, economic and political systems; *Graduate Objectives or Program Emphases*: Mastery of functions, effects, and research methods in communication with

goal of becoming producers of new knowledge. MFA program maintained in design and performance; *Bachelor's Degree Majors*: 617; *Master's Degree Majors*: 35; *MFA Degree Majors*: 5; *Doctoral Degree Majors Currently in Residence*: 45; *Additional Doctoral Degree Majors*: 30; *Full-Time Faculty*: 23; *Part-Time Faculty*: 72; *Full-Time Professional (non-clerical) Staff Members*: 1.

FACILITIES AND SERVICES
Practical experiences available through: Community Antenna (Cable) Television Origination; Local Commercial Television Station; Video Editing; Electronic Field Production (Video); FM Radio Station (Institutional); Video Production Laboratory or Television Studio.

University of Oregon (Public)

School of Journalism
Eugene, Oregon 97403
Telephone: (503) 686-3738

Arnold H. Ismach, Dean

CURRICULUM AND INSTRUCTION
Courses or Concentrations Available: Advertising; Journalism or Mass Communication; Public Relations; Radio, Television, Broadcasting, or Telecommunications; Magazine; *Undergraduate Objectives or Program Emphases*: General liberal arts education combined with preparation in five professional fields; *Graduate Objectives or Program Emphases*: Advanced professional preparation, and pre-doctoral studies. MA and MS; *Bachelor's Degree Majors*: 400; *Master's Degree Majors*: 40; *Full-Time Faculty*: 17; *Part-Time Faculty*: 26; *Full-Time Professional (non-clerical) Staff Members*: 2.

FACILITIES AND SERVICES
Practical experiences available through: Advertising Agency; Associated Press Wire Service Feed; Audio Recording Laboratory; Community Antenna (Cable) Television Origination; Campus Newspaper (Published Independently); Local Commercial Newspaper; Local Commercial Television Station; Desktop Publishing Facility; Photographic Darkrooms; Video Editing; Electronic Field Production (Video); FM Radio Station (Institutional);

Institutional Newspaper; Video News and Data Processing; Video Production Laboratory or Television Studio.

University of Portland (Private)

Department of Communication Studies
5000 North Willamette Boulevard
Portland, Oregon 97203
Telephone: (503) 283-7229

Steven A. Ward, Chair
Richard F. Berg, Dean, College of Arts and Sciences

CURRICULUM AND INSTRUCTION
Courses or Concentrations
Available: Advertising; Communication; Journalism or Mass Communication; Public Relations; Radio, Television, Broadcasting, or Telecommunications; Speech; *Program Coordinators*: William F. Seifort (Journalism); Donn L. Pierce (Video); *Undergraduate Objectives or Program Emphases*: All programs provide liberal arts background and professional preparation. Degrees offered are BA in Communications, BS in Communication Management and BS in Journalism; *Graduate Objectives or Program Emphases*: An MA in Communications and an MS in Management Communication; *Bachelor's Degree Majors*: 158; *Master's Degree Majors*: 10; *Full-Time Faculty*: 6; *Part-Time Faculty*: 6.

FACILITIES AND SERVICES
Practical experiences available through: Carrier Current Audio Distribution System; Campus Newspaper (Published Independently); Local Commercial Newspaper; Local Commercial Television Station; Desktop Publishing Facility; Video Editing; Electronic Field Production (Video); Video Production Laboratory or Television Studio.

Willamette University (Private)

Department of Speech Communication
900 State Street
Salem, Oregon 97301
Telephone: (503) 370-6281

Catherine A. Collins, Chair
Julie Ann Carson, Dean, College of Liberal Arts

CURRICULUM AND INSTRUCTION
Courses or Concentrations
Available: Communication; Speech; Media Criticism; *Undergraduate Objectives or Program Emphases*: Rhetorical Theory, Communication Theory, Media Criticism; *Bachelor's Degree Majors*: 30; *Full-Time Faculty*: 4.

FACILITIES AND SERVICES
Practical experiences available through: Advertising Agency; AM Radio Station (Institutional); Audio Recording Laboratory; Campus Newspaper (Published Independently); Local Commercial Newspaper; Local Commercial Television Station; Photographic Darkrooms; Video Editing; Electronic Field Production (Video); Satellite Uplink Facility; Video Production Laboratory or Television Studio.

Willamette University (Private)

Department of English
900 State Street
Salem, Oregon 97301
Telephone: (503) 370-6300

Kenneth S. Nolley, Chair

CURRICULUM AND INSTRUCTION
Courses or Concentrations Available: Film or Cinema; *Undergraduate Objectives or Program Emphases*: Film, film theory and criticism; *Full-Time Faculty*: 1.

Allegheny College (Private)

**Department of Communication
Arts/Theatre
Meadville, Pennsylvania 16335
Telephone: (814) 332-2370**

**John Hanners, Chair
Andrew T. Ford, Provost**

CURRICULUM AND INSTRUCTION
*Courses or Concentrations
Available*: Communication; Film or Cinema;
Journalism or Mass Communication; Radio,
Television, Broadcasting, or
Telecommunications; Speech; Theatre;
Rhetoric; Public Address; *Program
Coordinators*: Michael Keeley
(Broadcasting); Kate Madden (Mass
Communication) Beth Watkins (Theatre);
Nels G. Juleus (Rhetoric and Public
Address); *Undergraduate Objectives or
Program Emphases*: Liberal Arts; *Bachelor's
Degree Majors*: 59; *Full-Time Faculty*: 9;
Part-Time Faculty: 2; *Full-Time Professional
(non-clerical) Staff Members*: 1.

FACILITIES AND SERVICES
Practical experiences available through: AM
Radio Station (Institutional); Audio
Recording Laboratory; Community Antenna
(Cable) Television Origination; Campus
Newspaper (Published Independently);
Local Commercial Newspaper; Local
Commercial Television Station; Desktop
Publishing Facility; Video Editing;
Electronic Field Production (Video);
Institutional Magazine; Video Production
Laboratory or Television Studio.

Allegheny College (Private)

**Department of English
520 North Main Street
Meadville, Pennsylvania 16335
Telephone: (814) 332-4330**

**I. Lloyd Michaels, Chair
Andrew T. Ford, Provost**

CURRICULUM AND INSTRUCTION
*Courses or Concentrations
Available*: Communication; Film or Cinema;
Journalism or Mass Communication; Radio,
Television, Broadcasting, or
Telecommunications; Speech; *Program
Coordinator*: Dennis Johnson (Journalism);
*Undergraduate Objectives or Program
Emphases*: To provide both the foundation
for a liberal arts education and the personal
enrichment that enhances any career. The
program emphasizes mastering techniques of
analytical reading, critical interpretation,
coherent argument, language, and culture
study; *Bachelor's Degree Majors*: 88;
Full-Time Faculty: 17; *Part-Time Faculty*: 2.

FACILITIES AND SERVICES
*Practical experiences available
through*: Associated Press Wire Service Feed;
Campus Newspaper (Published
Independently); Local Commercial
Newspaper; Photographic Darkrooms;
Video Editing; FM Radio Station
(Institutional); Institutional Newspaper;
New York Times Service Feed.

Alvernia College (Private)

**Department of English/Communication
400 Saint Bernardine Street
Reading, Pennsylvania 19607
Telephone: (215) 777-5411**

**Beth DeMeo, Chair
Richard Shechler, Administrator**

CURRICULUM AND INSTRUCTION
*Courses or Concentrations
Available*: Advertising; Communication; Film
or Cinema; Journalism or Mass
Communication; Public Relations; Radio,
Television, Broadcasting, or
Telecommunications; Speech; *Program
Coordinator*: Joseph Swope (Advertising,
Journalism, Public Relations,
Radio-Television); *Undergraduate Objectives
or Program Emphases*: To prepare students in
media-related fields with emphasis on the
written and spoken word; *Bachelor's Degree
Majors*: 50; *Full-Time Faculty*: 3; *Part-Time
Faculty*: 2.

FACILITIES AND SERVICES
Practical experiences available through: Advertising Agency; Local Commercial Newspaper; Photographic Darkrooms; Video Editing; Institutional Newspaper; Public Relations Agency.

Beaver College (Private)

Program of Communications
Church Road
Glenside, Pennsylvania 19038-3295
Telephone: (215) 572-2168

Shekhar A. Deshpande, Director
Hugh Grady, Administrator

CURRICULUM AND INSTRUCTION
Courses or Concentrations Available: Communication; Film or Cinema; Journalism or Mass Communication; Television; *Undergraduate Objectives or Program Emphases*: Print, Video, and Corporate Communications; *Bachelor's Degree Majors*: 65; *Full-Time Faculty*: 1; *Part-Time Faculty*: 2.

FACILITIES AND SERVICES
Practical experiences available through: Video Editing; Electronic Field Production (Video); Institutional Newspaper; Video Production Laboratory or Television Studio.

Bloomsburg University (Public)

Department of Mass Communication
Bloomsburg, Pennsylvania 17815
Telephone: (717) 389-4565

Walter M. Brasch, Chair
John Baird, Dean

CURRICULUM AND INSTRUCTION
Courses or Concentrations Available: Journalism or Mass Communication; Public Relations; Radio, Television, Broadcasting, or Telecommunications; *Undergraduate Objectives or Program Emphases*: Journalism; Public Relations; Telecommunications; *Bachelor's Degree Majors*: 190; *Full-Time Faculty*: 6; *Part-Time Faculty*: 3.

FACILITIES AND SERVICES
Practical experiences available through: AM Radio Station (Institutional); Community Antenna (Cable) Television Origination;

Carrier Current Audio Distribution System; Closed Circuit Television Facility; Campus Newspaper (Published Independently); Local Commercial Television Station; Desktop Publishing Facility; Photographic Darkrooms; Video Editing; Electronic Field Production (Video); Film or Cinema Laboratory; FM Radio Station (Institutional); ITFS Distribution System; Institutional Magazine; Satellite Uplink Facility (C Band Transmitter); Video Production Laboratory or Television Studio.

Bucks County Community College (Public)

Department of Communication
Swamp Road
Newtown, Pennsylvania 18940
Telephone: (215) 968-8086

Douglas B. Rosentrater, Chair
Alice Letteney, Academic Dean

CURRICULUM AND INSTRUCTION
Courses or Concentrations Available: Advertising; Communication; Film or Cinema; Journalism or Mass Communication; Public Relations; Radio, Television, Broadcasting, or Telecommunications; Speech; Theatre; *Undergraduate Objectives or Program Emphases*: Transfer, vocational; *Associate's Degree Majors*: 175; *Full-Time Faculty*: 12; *Part-Time Faculty*: 15; *Full-Time Professional (non-clerical) Staff Members*: 4.

FACILITIES AND SERVICES
Practical experiences available through: Audio Recording Laboratory; Community Antenna (Cable) Television Origination; Carrier Current Audio Distribution System; Closed Circuit Television Facility; Campus Newspaper (Published Independently); Local Commercial Newspaper; Local Commercial Television Station; Desktop Publishing Facility; Photographic Darkrooms; Video Editing; Electronic Field Production (Video); Television Broadcast Station (Institutional); Film or Cinema Laboratory; FM Radio Station (Institutional); ITFS Distribution System; Institutional Newspaper; Video Production Laboratory or Television Studio.

Cabrini College (Private)

Department of English and
Communications
610 King of Prussia Road
Radnor, Pennsylvania 19087-3699
Telephone: (215) 971-8360

Jerome Zurek, Chair
Atoinette Schiesler, Academic Dean

CURRICULUM AND INSTRUCTION
Courses or Concentrations
Available: Advertising; Journalism or Mass
Communication; Public Relations; Radio,
Television, Broadcasting, or
Telecommunications; Speech; Theatre;
*Undergraduate Objectives or Program
Emphases*: Liberal arts education with a
strong professional component in courses
and extensive cooperative-education and
intern experiences; *Bachelor's Degree
Majors*: 160; *Full-Time Faculty*: 7;
Part-Time Faculty: 10; *Full-Time
Professional (non-clerical) Staff Members*: 1.

FACILITIES AND SERVICES
*Practical experiences available
through*: Advertising Agency; Associated
Press Wire Service Feed; Community
Antenna (Cable) Television Origination;
Carrier Current Audio Distribution System;
Local Commercial Newspaper; Local
Commercial Television Station; Desktop
Publishing Facility; Photographic
Darkrooms; Video Editing; Electronic Field
Production (Video); FM Radio Station
(Institutional); Institutional Magazine;
Institutional Newspaper; Public Relations
Agency; Video News and Data Processing;
Video Production Laboratory or Television
Studio.

California University of Pennsylvania

Speech Communication Department
California, Pennsylvania 15419

Dencil K. Backus, Administrator

Carlow College (Private)

Division of Social Sciences
3333 Fifth Avenue
Pittsburgh, Pennsylvania 15213
Telephone: (412) 578-6036

Brenda Carter, Chair

CURRICULUM AND INSTRUCTION
Courses or Concentrations
Available: Advertising; Communication; Film
or Cinema; Journalism or Mass
Communication; Public Relations; Radio,
Television, Broadcasting, or
Telecommunications; Speech; Photography;
*Undergraduate Objectives or Program
Emphases*: Liberal Arts education for
Catholic women with emphases on the
unique roles of women in today's corporate
world; *Bachelor's Degree Majors*: 16;
Full-Time Faculty: 8; *Part-Time Faculty*: 17.

FACILITIES AND SERVICES
*Practical experiences available
through*: Advertising Agency; Associated
Press Wire Service Feed; Community
Antenna (Cable) Television Origination;
Local Commercial Newspaper; Local
Commercial Television Station;
Photographic Darkrooms; Video Editing;
Electronic Field Production (Video); Film
or Cinema Laboratory; Video News and
Data Processing; Video Production
Laboratory or Television Studio.

Central Pennsylvania Business School (Private)

Division of Media Studies
College Hill Road
Summerdale, Pennsylvania 17093-0309
Telephone: (717) 732-0702

Ronald C. Ross, Chair
M. Dale Good, Academic Dean

CURRICULUM AND INSTRUCTION
Courses or Concentrations
Available: Advertising; Journalism or Mass
Communication; Public Relations; Radio,
Television, Broadcasting, or
Telecommunications; Speech; *Undergraduate
Objectives or Program Emphases*: A Mass
media major in a two year ASB degree
program introduces students to all aspects of
mass media and then encompasses
concentrated studies via lab work and on-job

externship; *Full-Time Faculty*: 2; *Part-Time Faculty*: 6.

FACILITIES AND SERVICES
Practical experiences available through: Advertising Agency; AM Radio Station (Institutional); Carrier Current Audio Distribution System; Local Commercial Newspaper; Local Commercial Television Station; Desktop Publishing Facility; Photographic Darkrooms; Video Editing; Electronic Field Production (Video); Institutional Newspaper; Public Relations Agency; Video News and Data Processing; Video Production Laboratory or Television Studio.

Chatham College (Private)

Department of Communication
Woodland Road
Pittsburgh, Pennsylvania 15232
Telephone: (412) 365-1180

Karen F. Dajani, Chair
Thomas Hershberger, Dean

CURRICULUM AND INSTRUCTION
Courses or Concentrations Available: Communication; Information Science; Journalism or Mass Communication; Public Relations; Radio, Television, Broadcasting, or Telecommunications; *Undergraduate Objectives or Program Emphases*: Writing for the media, production methods, research methods, audience function, techniques and technology; *Bachelor's Degree Majors*: 40; *Full-Time Faculty*: 3; *Part-Time Faculty*: 2.

FACILITIES AND SERVICES
Practical experiences available through: Advertising Agency; Campus Newspaper (Published Independently); Local Commercial Newspaper; Local Commercial Television Station; Desktop Publishing Facility; Photographic Darkrooms; Video Editing; Electronic Field Production (Video); FM Radio Station (Institutional); Public Relations Agency; Video Production Laboratory or Television Studio.

Chestnut Hill College (Private)

Program of Communication
Germantown Avenue
Philadelphia, Pennsylvania 19118-2695
Telephone: (215) 248-7177

Beryl S. Gutekunst, Director
S. Kathryn Miller, Academic Dean

CURRICULUM AND INSTRUCTION
Courses or Concentrations Available: Advertising; Communication; Journalism or Mass Communication; Public Relations; Speech; Writing for the Media; *Undergraduate Objectives or Program Emphases*: An interdisciplinary approach to the study of communications systems is offered. Students interested in advertising, public relations, publishing, broadcast or print journalism may complete a communication concentration while perusing any major.; *Part-Time Faculty*: 6.

FACILITIES AND SERVICES
Practical experiences available through: Advertising Agency; Campus Newspaper (Published Independently); Local Commercial Newspaper; Local Commercial Television Station; Desktop Publishing Facility; Photographic Darkrooms; Video Editing; Institutional Magazine; Public Relations Agency.

Community College of Beaver County

Department of Communication
College Drive
Monaca, Pennsylvania 15061

John Shaver, Administrator

Community College of Luzerne County (Public)

Department of Broadcast Communications
Prospect Street and Middle Road
Nanticoke, Pennsylvania 18634
Telephone: (717) 821-0930

Kathryn A. Bozinski, Director
Wes Franklin, Director, Advanced Technology Center

CURRICULUM AND INSTRUCTION
Courses or Concentrations Available: Radio,
Television, Broadcasting, or
Telecommunications; *Undergraduate
Objectives or Program Emphases*: Extensive
theory, hands-on laboratory and professional
experiences in all broadcast related areas
including journalism, radio-television
production, electronic news gathering,
computer graphics, and audio/visual
presentation; *Degree Majors*: 70; *Full-Time
Faculty*: 3; *Part-Time Faculty*: 5.

FACILITIES AND SERVICES
*Practical experiences available
through*: Associated Press Wire Service Feed;
Audio Recording Laboratory; Campus
Newspaper (Published Independently);
Local Commercial Television Station;
Desktop Publishing Facility; Photographic
Darkrooms; Video Editing; Electronic Field
Production (Video); FM Radio Station
(Institutional); Institutional Magazine;
Institutional Newspaper; Video Production
Laboratory or Television Studio.

Community College of Philadelphia

Department of Photography
1700 Spring Garden Street
Philadelphia, Pennsylvania 19130

Allan Kobernick, Administrator

Delaware Valley College (Private)

Department of Media
Route 202
Doylestown, Pennsylvania 18901-2699
Telephone: (215) 345-1500 Extension: 2387

Marilyn L. Vogel, Director
Craig Hill, Dean of Services

FACILITIES AND SERVICES
Practical experiences available through: AM
Radio Station (Institutional); Photographic
Darkrooms.

Drexel University

**Department of Humanities and
Communications**
32nd and Chestnut Streets
Philadelphia, Pennsylvania 19104

Pia Nicolini, Administrator

Duquesne University (Private)

Department of Communication
600 Forbes Avenue
Pittsburgh, Pennsylvania 15282
Telephone: (412) 434-6460

Nancy L. Harper, Chair
Wallace Watson, Dean, Liberal Arts

CURRICULUM AND INSTRUCTION
*Courses or Concentrations
Available*: Advertising; Communication;
Journalism or Mass Communication; Public
Relations; Radio, Television, Broadcasting,
or Telecommunications; Speech; Corporate
Communications; *Undergraduate Objectives
or Program Emphases*: Journalism, mass
communication, media production,
management, public relations, advertising,
and corporate communication are central to
other areas as well as included in a degree
program; *Graduate Objectives or Program
Emphases*: Corporate communication;
Bachelor's Degree Majors: 200; *Master's
Degree Majors*: 60; *Full-Time Faculty*: 13;
Part-Time Faculty: 23; *Full-Time
Professional (non-clerical) Staff Members*: 1.

FACILITIES AND SERVICES
*Practical experiences available
through*: Advertising Agency; AM Radio
Station (Institutional); Audio Recording
Laboratory; Community Antenna (Cable)
Television Origination; Carrier Current
Audio Distribution System; Campus
Newspaper (Published Independently);
Local Commercial Newspaper; Local
Commercial Television Station; Desktop
Publishing Facility; Photographic
Darkrooms; Video Editing; Electronic Field
Production (Video); Public Relations
Agency; Video News and Data Processing;
Video Production Laboratory or Television
Studio.

East Stroudsburg University (Public)

Department of Media Communication and Technology
East Stroudsburg, Pennsylvania 18301
Telephone: (717) 424-3737

David Campbell, Chair
Michael Davis, Dean

CURRICULUM AND INSTRUCTION
Courses or Concentrations
Available: Advertising; Communication; Radio, Television, Broadcasting, or Telecommunications; *Undergraduate Objectives or Program Emphases*: Media production generalist; *Degree Majors*: 150; *Full-Time Faculty*: 6; *Full-Time Professional (non-clerical) Staff Members*: 2.

FACILITIES AND SERVICES
Practical experiences available through: Audio Recording Laboratory; Community Antenna (Cable) Television Origination; Closed Circuit Television Facility; Campus Newspaper (Published Independently); Local Commercial Television Station; Desktop Publishing Facility; Photographic Darkrooms; Video Editing; Electronic Field Production (Video); FM Radio Station (Institutional).

East Stroudsburg University (Public)

Department of Speech Communication
East Stroudsburg, Pennsylvania 18301
Telephone: (717) 424-3759

Joseph G. Ashcroft, Chair
Ann Stuart, Dean

CURRICULUM AND INSTRUCTION
Courses or Concentrations
Available: Communication; Film or Cinema; Journalism or Mass Communication; Radio, Television, Broadcasting, or Telecommunications; Speech; *Undergraduate Objectives or Program Emphases*: BA in Speech Communication with emphasis on performance and rhetorical theory. BA in Media Studies with emphasis on mass communication theory; *Bachelor's Degree Majors*: 100; *Full-Time Faculty*: 7.

FACILITIES AND SERVICES
Practical experiences available through: Audio Recording Laboratory; Community Antenna (Cable) Television Origination; Closed Circuit Television Facility; Campus Newspaper (Published Independently); Photographic Darkrooms; Video Editing; Electronic Field Production (Video); Film or Cinema Laboratory; FM Radio Station (Institutional); Satellite Uplink Facility; Video Production Laboratory or Television Studio.

Edinboro University of Pennsylvania (Public)

Department of Speech Communication
Edinboro, Pennsylvania 16444
Telephone: (814) 732-2000

Richard A. Forcucci, Chair
Robert C. Weber, Dean, Liberal Arts

CURRICULUM AND INSTRUCTION
Courses or Concentrations
Available: Advertising; Communication; Film or Cinema; Journalism or Mass Communication; Public Relations; Radio, Television, Broadcasting, or Telecommunications; Speech; *Undergraduate Objectives or Program Emphases*: The speech communication major is concerned with the study of communication; its theory, substance, techniques, problems, and results; *Graduate Objectives or Program Emphases*: Provide students with a methodological foundation for performance in communication and decision-making roles essential to the operation of human enterprises and institutions of every description; *Bachelor's Degree Majors*: 135; *Master's Degree Majors*: 42; *Full-Time Faculty*: 13; *Part-Time Faculty*: 4; *Full-Time Professional (non-clerical) Staff Members*: 1.

FACILITIES AND SERVICES
Practical experiences available through: Advertising Agency; Associated Press Wire Service Feed; Campus Newspaper (Published Independently); Local Commercial Newspaper; Local Commercial Television Station; Desktop Publishing Facility; Video Editing; Electronic Field Production (Video); FM Radio Station (Institutional); Public Relations Agency; Video Production Laboratory or Television Studio.

Elizabethtown College (Private)

Department of Communications
One Alpha Drive
Elizabethtown, Pennsylvania 17022-2298
Telephone: (717) 367-1151

Robert C. Moore, Chair
Frederick Ritsch, Provost

CURRICULUM AND INSTRUCTION
Courses or Concentrations
Available: Communication; Journalism or Mass Communication; Public Relations; Radio, Television, Broadcasting, or Telecommunications; Speech; Corporate Media; *Undergraduate Objectives or Program Emphases*: Study of theory, concepts, history and impact of communication; develop expertise in production and performance; foster aesthetic awareness, encourage creative expression, develop professional expertise and critical judgement within a liberal arts education; *Bachelor's Degree Majors*: 65; *Full-Time Faculty*: 6; *Part-Time Faculty*: 2; *Full-Time Professional (non-clerical) Staff Members*: 3.

FACILITIES AND SERVICES
Practical experiences available through: Associated Press Wire Service Feed; Audio Recording Laboratory; Community Antenna (Cable) Television Origination; Carrier Current Audio Distribution System; Closed Circuit Television Facility; Campus Newspaper (Published Independently); Local Commercial Newspaper; Local Commercial Television Station; Desktop Publishing Facility; Photographic Darkrooms; Video Editing; Electronic Field Production (Video); FM Radio Station (Institutional); Institutional Magazine; Video News and Data Processing; Video Production Laboratory or Television Studio.

Gannon University

Department of Theatre and Communication Arts
University Square
Erie, Pennsylvania 16541

Anthony J. Miceli, Administrator

Geneva College

Broadcasting Department
College Avenue
Beaver Falls, Pennsylvania 15010

Peter Croisant, Administrator

Indiana University of Pennsylvania (Public)

Department of Communication Media
RD #2 Box 160A
Indiana, Pennsylvania 15701
Telephone: (412) 357-2493

Kurt P. Dudt, Chair
John Butzow, Dean, College of Education

CURRICULUM AND INSTRUCTION
Courses or Concentrations
Available: Communication; Journalism or Mass Communication; Radio, Television, Broadcasting, or Telecommunications; *Undergraduate Objectives or Program Emphases*: Broad based Broadcasting, Product Development, Training and Development program; *Graduate Objectives or Program Emphases*: A Media degree that emphasizes communication and the use of media in education and industry; *Degree Majors*: 435; *Full-Time Faculty*: 11; *Part-Time Faculty*: 2; *Full-Time Professional (non-clerical) Staff Members*: 1.

FACILITIES AND SERVICES
Practical experiences available through: Audio Recording Laboratory; Community Antenna (Cable) Television Origination; Closed Circuit Television Facility; Campus Newspaper (Published Independently); Photographic Darkrooms; Video Editing; Electronic Field Production (Video); Television Broadcast Station (Institutional); FM Radio Station (Institutional); United Press International Feed; Video Production Laboratory or Television Studio.

Indiana University of Pennsylvania (Public)

Department of Journalism
Indiana, Pennsylvania 15705
Telephone: (412) 357-4411

Craig G. Swauger, Chair
Rachel Fordyce, Dean, College of Humanities and Social Sciences

CURRICULUM AND INSTRUCTION
Courses or Concentrations Available: Journalism or Mass Communication; Public Relations; News-Editorial; *Undergraduate Objectives or Program Emphases*: Two sequences offered, News-Editorial and Public Relations, with objective to prepare (through interdisciplinary studies) students to accept entry level positions in communications field; *Bachelor's Degree Majors*: 110; *Full-Time Faculty*: 6.

FACILITIES AND SERVICES
Practical experiences available through: AM Radio Station (Institutional); Campus Newspaper (Published Independently); Local Commercial Newspaper; Desktop Publishing Facility; Television Broadcast Station (Institutional); FM Radio Station (Institutional); Public Relations Agency.

Juniata College (Private)

Program of Communications
1700 Moore Street
Huntingdon, Pennsylvania 16652
Telephone: (814) 643-4310

Catherine O. Merrill, Professor
Karen Wiley Sandler, Dean

CURRICULUM AND INSTRUCTION
Courses or Concentrations Available: Advertising; Communication; Journalism or Mass Communication; Public Relations; Radio, Television, Broadcasting, or Telecommunications; Speech; *Undergraduate Objectives or Program Emphases*: To provide knowledge and skills in the areas of speech and journalism, emphasizing forensics and writing, as well as survey courses in advertising, public relations; *Bachelor's Degree Majors*: 40; *Full-Time Faculty*: 3.

FACILITIES AND SERVICES
Practical experiences available through: Advertising Agency; AM Radio Station (Institutional); Campus Newspaper (Published Independently); Local Commercial Newspaper; Photographic Darkrooms; FM Radio Station (Institutional).

King's College

Mass Communication Department
Wilkes-Barre, Pennsylvania 18702

Anthony J. Mussari, Administrator

King's College

Theatre and Speech Department
Wilkes-Barre, Pennsylvania 18711

Brother John Miller, Administrator

Kutztown University of Pennsylvania

Department of Telecommunication
Rickenbach Building
Kutztown, Pennsylvania 19530

Helen Clinton, Administrator

La Roche College (Private)

Department of Graphic Design and Communication
9000 Babcock Boulevard
Pittsburgh, Pennsylvania 15237
Telephone: (412) 367-9300

Diane E. Foltz, Area Coordinator
Martha Fairchild-Shepler, Chair

CURRICULUM AND INSTRUCTION
Courses or Concentrations Available: Advertising; Communication; Information Science; Journalism or Mass Communication; Public Relations; Radio, Television, Broadcasting, or Telecommunications; Speech; Mass Communication Law; Intercultural Communication; *Undergraduate Objectives or Program Emphases*: To acquaint students

with a wide spectrum of communication behaviors; to develop written and oral communication skills; to provide experience in the planning and development of communication projects; *Degree Majors*: 36; *Full-Time Faculty*: 5; *Part-Time Faculty*: 3.

FACILITIES AND SERVICES
Practical experiences available through: Campus Newspaper (Published Independently); Local Commercial Television Station; Desktop Publishing Facility; Photographic Darkrooms; Video Editing; Electronic Field Production (Video).

La Salle University (Private)

Department of Communication
20th Street at Olney Avenue
Philadelphia, Pennsylvania 19141
Telephone: (215) 951-1000

Gerard F. Molyneaux, Chair
Bro. James Muldoon, Administrator

CURRICULUM AND INSTRUCTION
Courses or Concentrations Available: Advertising; Communication; Film or Cinema; Journalism or Mass Communication; Public Relations; Radio, Television, Broadcasting, or Telecommunications; Speech; Interpersonal Communication; *Program Coordinators*: Richard Goedkeop (Broadcasting); Sidney MacLeod (Production); Sharon Kirk (Interpersonal, Speech); William Wine (Writing, Journalism); Lynne Texter (Advertising, Public Relations); *Undergraduate Objectives or Program Emphases*: Students receive a broad background in the various aspects of communication with opportunities to develop an emphasis in some area; *Bachelor's Degree Majors*: 170; *Full-Time Faculty*: 8; *Part-Time Faculty*: 8.

FACILITIES AND SERVICES
Practical experiences available through: Carrier Current Audio Distribution System; Campus Newspaper (Published Independently); Local Commercial Newspaper; Local Commercial Television Station; Desktop Publishing Facility; Video Editing; Electronic Field Production (Video); Institutional Magazine; Institutional Newspaper; Public Relations Agency; Video News and Data Processing;

Video Production Laboratory or Television Studio.

Lafayette College (Private)

Department of English
Easton, Pennsylvania 18042
Telephone: (215) 250-5000

David R. Johnson, Head
Sarah R. Blanshei, Provost

CURRICULUM AND INSTRUCTION
Courses or Concentrations Available: Film or Cinema; *Bachelor's Degree Majors*: 75; *Full-Time Faculty*: 20; *Part-Time Faculty*: 4.

FACILITIES AND SERVICES
Practical experiences available through: Campus Newspaper (Published Independently); Local Commercial Newspaper; Photographic Darkrooms; FM Radio Station (Institutional); Public Relations Agency.

Lebanon Valley College (Private)

Department of English
Annville, Pennsylvania 17003
Telephone: (717) 867-4428

John P. Kearney, Chair
William McGill, Dean

CURRICULUM AND INSTRUCTION
Courses or Concentrations Available: Advertising; Communication; Journalism or Mass Communication; Public Relations; Radio, Television, Broadcasting, or Telecommunications; Speech; Technical Writing; Creative Writing; *Undergraduate Objectives or Program Emphases*: Communications is a concentration within a literature based English major. The program aims to expose students to literature as sophisticated examples of communication and to introduce them to the principles and practice of communication industries; Internship; *Bachelor's Degree Majors*: 25; *Full-Time Faculty*: 6; *Part-Time Faculty*: 3.

FACILITIES AND SERVICES
Practical experiences available through: Advertising Agency; AM Radio Station (Institutional); Audio Recording

Laboratory; Campus Newspaper (Published Independently); Local Commercial Newspaper; Local Commercial Television Station; Photographic Darkrooms; Public Relations Agency.

Lehigh University (Private)

Department of Journalism
University Center 29
Bethlehem, Pennsylvania 18017
Telephone: (215) 758-4180

Sharon M. Friedman, Chair
James Gunton, Dean

CURRICULUM AND INSTRUCTION
Courses or Concentrations
Available: Communication; Journalism or Mass Communication; Public Relations; Radio, Television, Broadcasting, or Telecommunications; Speech; Science and Environmental Writing; *Undergraduate Objectives or Program Emphases*: To bring majors to a point at which they can gather significant information, organize it quickly and communicate it clearly, accurately and objectively, and to bring them to an understanding of the legitimate role of the mass media in society; *Bachelor's Degree Majors*: 56; *Full-Time Faculty*: 6; *Part-Time Faculty*: 4.

FACILITIES AND SERVICES
Practical experiences available through: Advertising Agency; Campus Newspaper (Published Independently); Local Commercial Newspaper; Local Commercial Television Station; Desktop Publishing Facility; Photographic Darkrooms; FM Radio Station (Institutional); Institutional Newspaper; Public Relations Agency; Video News and Data Processing.

Lehigh University (Private)

Program of Communication Studies
Journalism Department, U.C. 29
Bethlehem, Pennsylvania 18015
Telephone: (215) 758-4178

Carole M. Gorney, Director
James Gunton, Dean, College of Arts and Science

CURRICULUM AND INSTRUCTION
Courses or Concentrations
Available: Communication; Journalism or Mass Communication; Public Relations; Radio, Television, Broadcasting, or Telecommunications; Speech; Management; Graphic Communication (Art); English; Social Psychology; Philosophy; Psychology; Social Relations; *Undergraduate Objectives or Program Emphases*: To provide interdisciplinary communication curriculum with a broad theoretical and practical base.

Lock Haven University (Public)

Department of Journalism
Lock Haven, Pennsylvania 17745
Telephone: (717) 893-2184

Douglas S. Campbell, Chair
Hugh Williamson, Dean

CURRICULUM AND INSTRUCTION
Courses or Concentrations
Available: Advertising; Film or Cinema; Journalism or Mass Communication; Public Relations; Radio, Television, Broadcasting, or Telecommunications; *Undergraduate Objectives or Program Emphases*: Professional preparation; *Bachelor's Degree Majors*: 130; *Full-Time Faculty*: 3; *Part-Time Faculty*: 3; *Full-Time Professional (non-clerical) Staff Members*: 1.

FACILITIES AND SERVICES
Practical experiences available through: AM Radio Station (Institutional); Community Antenna (Cable) Television Origination; Closed Circuit Television Facility; Campus Newspaper (Published Independently); Local Commercial Newspaper; Desktop Publishing Facility; Photographic Darkrooms; Video Editing; Electronic Field Production (Video); FM Radio Station (Institutional); Video News and Data Processing.

Lock Haven University (Public)

Speech Communication and Theatre Department
Lock Haven, Pennsylvania 17745

John B. Gordon, Administrator

Lycoming College (Private)

Department of Mass Communication
Academy Street
Williamsport, Pennsylvania 17701
Telephone: (717) 321-4000

Bradley L. Nason, Chair
Shirley Van Marter, Academic Dean

CURRICULUM AND INSTRUCTION
Courses or Concentrations
Available: Advertising; Journalism or Mass
Communication; Public Relations; Radio,
Television, Broadcasting, or
Telecommunications; *Program
Coordinators*: Fredric M. Wild (Advertising,
Public Relations); Michael Smith
(Journalism); Brad Nason (Broadcast
Journalism); *Undergraduate Objectives or
Program Emphases*: A liberal arts emphasis
with professional sequences requiring courses
in theory, writing and production; *Bachelor's
Degree Majors*: 35; *Full-Time Faculty*: 3;
Part-Time Faculty: 1.

FACILITIES AND SERVICES
Practical experiences available through: Audio
Recording Laboratory; Community Antenna
(Cable) Television Origination; Local
Commercial Newspaper; Desktop Publishing
Facility; Photographic Darkrooms; Video
Editing; Electronic Field Production
(Video); FM Radio Station (Institutional);
Institutional Magazine; Institutional
Newspaper; Public Relations Agency; Video
News and Data Processing; Video
Production Laboratory or Television Studio.

Mansfield University of Pennsylvania

Department of Speech, Communications,
and Theatre
310 South Hall
Mansfield, Pennsylvania 16933

A. Vernon Lapps, Administrator

Marywood College

Department of Communication Arts
2300 Adams Avenue
Scranton, Pennsylvania 18509

George F. Perry, Administrator

Mercyhurst College (Private)

Department of Communications
Glenwood Hills
Erie, Pennsylvania 16546
Telephone: (814) 825-0464

Richard Ragan, Chair
Michael McQuillen, Administrator

CURRICULUM AND INSTRUCTION
Courses or Concentrations
Available: Communication; Film or Cinema;
Journalism or Mass Communication; Public
Relations; Radio, Television, Broadcasting,
or Telecommunications; *Undergraduate
Objectives or Program Emphases*: Offer three
areas of emphasis in Broadcasting,
Journalism, and Public Relations with
particular emphasis on a broad, liberal
education; *Bachelor's Degree Majors*: 65;
Full-Time Faculty: 1; *Part-Time Faculty*: 2;
*Full-Time Professional (non-clerical) Staff
Members*: 1.

FACILITIES AND SERVICES
*Practical experiences available
through*: Advertising Agency; AM Radio
Station (Institutional); Audio Recording
Laboratory; Carrier Current Audio
Distribution System; Closed Circuit
Television Facility; Local Commercial
Newspaper; Local Commercial Television
Station; Desktop Publishing Facility;
Photographic Darkrooms; Video Editing;
Electronic Field Production (Video); FM
Radio Station (Institutional); Institutional
Newspaper; Public Relations Agency.

Messiah College (Private)

Department of Language, Literature and
Fine Arts
Grantham, Pennsylvania 17027
Telephone: (717) 766-2511

Paul W. Nisly, Chair
Harold Heie, Dean

CURRICULUM AND INSTRUCTION
Courses or Concentrations
Available: Communication; Film or Cinema;
Journalism or Mass Communication; Radio,
Television, Broadcasting, or
Telecommunications; Speech; *Undergraduate
Objectives or Program
Emphases*: Communication major with
concentrations in speech, theatre, or

journalism; *Bachelor's Degree Majors*: 110; *Full-Time Faculty*: 18; *Part-Time Faculty*: 6.

FACILITIES AND SERVICES
Practical experiences available through: Advertising Agency; Audio Recording Laboratory; Campus Newspaper (Published Independently); Local Commercial Newspaper; Local Commercial Television Station; Desktop Publishing Facility; Photographic Darkrooms; FM Radio Station (Institutional); Institutional Magazine.

Millersville University of Pennsylvania (Public)

Department of Communication and Theatre
North George Street
Millersville, Pennsylvania 17551
Telephone: (717) 872-3233

James S. Henke, Chair
Christopher Dahl, Dean

CURRICULUM AND INSTRUCTION
Courses or Concentrations Available: Communication; Public Relations; Radio, Television, Broadcasting, or Telecommunications; Speech; Theatre; *Undergraduate Objectives or Program Emphases*: To provide fundamental training in the various disciplines within the area of communication art and science; *Other Degree Majors*: 10; *Full-Time Faculty*: 9; *Part-Time Faculty*: 5; *Full-Time Professional (non-clerical) Staff Members*: 2.

FACILITIES AND SERVICES
Practical experiences available through: Audio Recording Laboratory; Community Antenna (Cable) Television Origination; Campus Newspaper (Published Independently); Video Editing; Electronic Field Production (Video); FM Radio Station (Institutional); Public Relations Agency; Video Production Laboratory or Television Studio.

Muhlenberg College (Private)

Department of Communication Studies
Allentown, Pennsylvania 18104
Telephone: (215) 821-3480

Sue Curry Jansen, Head

CURRICULUM AND INSTRUCTION
Courses or Concentrations Available: Communication; *Undergraduate Objectives or Program Emphases*: To teach critical skills within a broadly based liberal arts tradition; *Bachelor's Degree Majors*: 60; *Full-Time Faculty*: 5; *Part-Time Faculty*: 5.

FACILITIES AND SERVICES
Practical experiences available through: Advertising Agency; AM Radio Station (Institutional); Audio Recording Laboratory; Campus Newspaper (Published Independently); Local Commercial Newspaper; Local Commercial Television Station; Photographic Darkrooms; Video Editing; Film or Cinema Laboratory; FM Radio Station (Institutional); Public Relations Agency; Video Production Laboratory or Television Studio.

Neumann College (Private)

Department of Communication Arts
Convent Road
Aston, Pennsylvania 19014
Telephone: (215) 459-0905

Terence J. Gleeson, Coordinator
Christa Marie Thompson, Chair, Humanities Division

CURRICULUM AND INSTRUCTION
Courses or Concentrations Available: Advertising; Communication; Film or Cinema; Journalism or Mass Communication; Public Relations; Radio, Television, Broadcasting, or Telecommunications; Speech; Photography, Design; *Undergraduate Objectives or Program Emphases*: Generalist Liberal Arts major emphasizing oral and written competence, skill with contemporary production techniques, and familiarity with media. Some specialization possible in performance, production, or writing; *Bachelor's Degree Majors*: 20; *Full-Time Faculty*: 2; *Part-Time Faculty*: 3.

FACILITIES AND SERVICES
Practical experiences available through: Advertising Agency; Audio Recording Laboratory; Community Antenna (Cable) Television Origination; Campus Newspaper (Published Independently); Local Commercial Newspaper; Local Commercial Television Station; Desktop Publishing Facility; Photographic Darkrooms; Video Editing; Electronic Field

Production (Video); Public Relations Agency; Video Production Laboratory or Television Studio.

Northampton Community College (Public)

Program of Radio/Television
3835 Green Pond Road
Bethlehem, Pennsylvania 18017
Telephone: (215) 861-5545

Mario J. Acerra, Program Coordinator
Doreen Smith, Dean

CURRICULUM AND INSTRUCTION
Courses or Concentrations
Available: Communication; Film or Cinema; Journalism or Mass Communication; Radio, Television, Broadcasting, or Telecommunications; Speech; Photography; Aesthetics; *Undergraduate Objectives or Program Emphases*: To provide practical and theoretical information in video, audio and related communications media; *Other Degree Majors*: 70; *Full-Time Faculty*: 1; *Part-Time Faculty*: 1; *Full-Time Professional (non-clerical) Staff Members*: 1.

FACILITIES AND SERVICES
Practical experiences available through: Advertising Agency; Audio Recording Laboratory; Community Antenna (Cable) Television Origination; Carrier Current Audio Distribution System; Campus Newspaper (Published Independently); Local Commercial Newspaper; Local Commercial Television Station; Desktop Publishing Facility; Photographic Darkrooms; Video Editing; Electronic Field Production (Video); Film or Cinema Laboratory; Institutional Newspaper; Public Relations Agency; Video News and Data Processing; Video Production Laboratory or Television Studio.

Pennsylvania College of Technology (Public)

Department of Communication Arts
One College Avenue
Williamsport, Pennsylvania 17701
Telephone: (717) 326-3761

Janie K. Swartz, Lead faculty
Ernie Zebrowski, Director, Integrated Studies

CURRICULUM AND INSTRUCTION
Courses or Concentrations
Available: Advertising; Communication; Film or Cinema; Journalism or Mass Communication; Public Relations; Radio, Television, Broadcasting, or Telecommunications; Graphic Arts; *Program Coordinators*: Patrick Murphy (Advertising Arts); Fred Schaefar (Graphic Arts); Joe Loehr (Public Relations); *Undergraduate Objectives or Program Emphases*: Electronic media, radio broadcasting hands-on experience; *Associate's Degree Majors*: 125; *Full-Time Faculty*: 8; *Part-Time Faculty*: 6; *Full-Time Professional (non-clerical) Staff Members*: 2.

FACILITIES AND SERVICES
Practical experiences available through: Advertising Agency; Associated Press Wire Service Feed; Audio Recording Laboratory; Local Commercial Television Station; Desktop Publishing Facility; Photographic Darkrooms; Video Editing; Electronic Field Production (Video); FM Radio Station (Institutional); Public Relations Agency; Video News and Data Processing; Video Production Laboratory or Television Studio.

Pennsylvania State Harrisburg (Public)

Division of Humanities
U.S. Route 230
Middletown, Pennsylvania 17057
Telephone: (717) 948-6189

Peter F. Parisi, Coordinator
William Mahar, Division Head

CURRICULUM AND INSTRUCTION
Courses or Concentrations
Available: Advertising; Communication; Film or Cinema; Journalism or Mass Communication; Public Relations; Radio,

Television, Broadcasting, or Telecommunications; Cultural and critical studies of communication; *Undergraduate Objectives or Program Emphases*: To offer practical skills with sophisticated understanding of the social and cultural impacts and influences of communications practice; *Bachelor's Degree Majors*: 60; *Full-Time Faculty*: 15; *Part-Time Faculty*: 14.

FACILITIES AND SERVICES
Practical experiences available through: Advertising Agency; Audio Recording Laboratory; Carrier Current Audio Distribution System; Closed Circuit Television Facility; Campus Newspaper (Published Independently); Local Commercial Newspaper; Local Commercial Television Station; Desktop Publishing Facility; Photographic Darkrooms; Video Editing; Electronic Field Production (Video); Public Relations Agency.

Pennsylvania State University (Public)

School of Communications
Carnagie Building
University Park, Pennsylvania 16802
Telephone: (814) 865-6597

Brian N. Winston, Dean
William Richardson, Provost

CURRICULUM AND INSTRUCTION
Courses or Concentrations Available: Advertising; Film or Cinema; Journalism or Mass Communication; Radio, Television, Broadcasting, or Telecommunications; Speech; Cable; *Undergraduate Objectives or Program Emphases*: Pre-professional education within the context of the scholarly study of mass communications; *Graduate Objectives or Program Emphases*: A scholarly MA and Ph.D. in mass communication, film studies; an MFA for graduates of film production programs; *Bachelor's Degree Majors*: 1110; *Master's Degree Majors*: 10; *MFA Degree Majors*: 2; *Doctoral Degree Majors Currently in Residence*: 5; *Full-Time Faculty*: 44; *Part-Time Faculty*: 23; *Full-Time Professional (non-clerical) Staff Members*: 19.

FACILITIES AND SERVICES
Practical experiences available through: Associated Press Wire Service Feed;

Audio Recording Laboratory; Community Antenna (Cable) Television Origination; Closed Circuit Television Facility; Campus Newspaper (Published Independently); Local Commercial Newspaper; Desktop Publishing Facility; Photographic Darkrooms; Video Editing; Electronic Field Production (Video); Television Broadcast Station (Institutional); Film or Cinema Laboratory; FM Radio Station (Institutional); ITFS Distribution System; Institutional Magazine; Satellite Uplink Facility (Ku Band Transmitter); Video News and Data Processing; Video Production Laboratory or Television Studio.

Pennsylvania State University (Public)

Department of Speech Communication
214 Carnegie Building
University Park, Pennsylvania 16802
Telephone: (814) 865-3461

Dennis S. Gouran, Head
Hart M. Nelsen, Dean, Liberal Arts

CURRICULUM AND INSTRUCTION
Courses or Concentrations Available: Speech; *Undergraduate Objectives or Program Emphases*: Rhetorical studies, communication theory and research, communication education, speech science, ESL; *Full-Time Faculty*: 18; *Part-Time Faculty*: 58.

FACILITIES AND SERVICES
Practical experiences available through: Local Commercial Newspaper; Local Commercial Television Station; FM Radio Station (Institutional).

Point Park College (Private)

Department of Journalism and Communication
201 Wood Street
Pittsburgh, Pennsylvania 15222
Telephone: (412) 391-4100

David M. Jones, Chair
Hsien-Tung Liu, Administrator

CURRICULUM AND INSTRUCTION
Courses or Concentrations Available: Advertising; Communication;

Journalism or Mass Communication; Public Relations; Radio, Television, Broadcasting, or Telecommunications; *Undergraduate Objectives or Program Emphases*: Print Journalism, Photojournalism, Public Relations, Advertising, Radio Broadcasting, Television Broadcasting; *Graduate Objectives or Program Emphases*: Print Journalism, Photojournalism, Public Relations, Advertising, Radio Broadcasting, Television Broadcasting; *Bachelor's Degree Majors*: 106; *Full-Time Faculty*: 7; *Part-Time Faculty*: 3.

FACILITIES AND SERVICES
Practical experiences available through: Advertising Agency; AM Radio Station (Institutional); Audio Recording Laboratory; Community Antenna (Cable) Television Origination; Closed Circuit Television Facility; Campus Newspaper (Published Independently); Local Commercial Newspaper; Local Commercial Television Station; Desktop Publishing Facility; Photographic Darkrooms; Video Editing; Electronic Field Production (Video); Television Broadcast Station (Institutional); Institutional Magazine; Institutional Newspaper; Public Relations Agency; United Press International Feed; Video Production Laboratory or Television Studio.

Robert Morris College (Private)

Department of Communication
600 Fifth Avenue
Pittsburgh, Pennsylvania 15219
Telephone: (412) 262-8200
Alternate: 262-8285

Jo Ann M. Sipple, Chair
Jon A. Shank, Dean, School of Communication Arts and Sciences

CURRICULUM AND INSTRUCTION
Courses or Concentrations Available: Advertising; Communication; Film or Cinema; Journalism or Mass Communication; Radio, Television, Broadcasting, or Telecommunications; Speech; English; Secondary Teaching in English and Communication; *Undergraduate Objectives or Program Emphases*: To prepare graduates who have a thorough command of communication/media theories and problem-solving strategies. Graduates know how to apply these to production practices in print, photography, television, sound media,

and film; *Bachelor's Degree Majors*: 60; *Other Degree Majors*: 150; *Full-Time Faculty*: 18; *Part-Time Faculty*: 12; *Full-Time Professional (non-clerical) Staff Members*: 11.

FACILITIES AND SERVICES
Practical experiences available through: Advertising Agency; Audio Recording Laboratory; Community Antenna (Cable) Television Origination; Closed Circuit Television Facility; Campus Newspaper (Published Independently); Local Commercial Newspaper; Local Commercial Television Station; Desktop Publishing Facility; Photographic Darkrooms; Video Editing; Electronic Field Production (Video); Television Broadcast Station (Institutional); Film or Cinema Laboratory; ITFS Distribution System; Institutional Newspaper; New York Times Service Feed; Public Relations Agency; Satellite Uplink Facility; Video News and Data Processing; Video Production Laboratory or Television Studio.

Robert Morris College (Private)

Division of Learning Resources
Narrows Run Road, P. O. Box 15600
Pittsburgh, Pennsylvania 15244
Telephone: (412) 262-8376

William L. Sipple, Dean
V. Ray Alford, Academic Vice President

CURRICULUM AND INSTRUCTION
Courses or Concentrations Available: Communication; Radio, Television, Broadcasting, or Telecommunications; *Program Coordinators*: Todd Kreps and David Phelps (Television Production); John Szwelnis (Engineer--TV); *Undergraduate Objectives or Program Emphases*: Provide hands-on experience with real world projects in all areas of media: television, audio, photography, and print; *Bachelor's Degree Majors*: 260; *Full-Time Faculty*: 1; *Part-Time Faculty*: 1; *Full-Time Professional (non-clerical) Staff Members*: 11.

FACILITIES AND SERVICES
Practical experiences available through: Audio Recording Laboratory; Community Antenna (Cable) Television Origination; Carrier Current Audio Distribution System; Closed Circuit Television Facility; Campus Newspaper (Published Independently);

Local Commercial Television Station; Photographic Darkrooms; Video Editing; Electronic Field Production (Video); Television Broadcast Station (Institutional); ITFS Distribution System; Public Relations Agency; Video News and Data Processing; Video Production Laboratory or Television Studio.

Saint Francis College

English Department
Loretto, Pennsylvania 15940

Rodrigue Labrie, Administrator

Shippensburg University (Public)

Department of Communications/Journalism
Shippensburg, Pennsylvania 17257
Telephone: (717) 532-1521

Pat Waltermyer, Chair
Robert Golden, Dean, College of Arts and Sciences

CURRICULUM AND INSTRUCTION
Courses or Concentrations
Available: Advertising; Communication; Journalism or Mass Communication; Public Relations; Radio, Television, Broadcasting, or Telecommunications; *Undergraduate Objectives or Program Emphases*: Professional emphasis in Public Relations, Radio/Television, and News Editorial; *Graduate Objectives or Program Emphases*: Mass Communication; *Bachelor's Degree Majors*: 400; *Master's Degree Majors*: 60; *Full-Time Faculty*: 10; *Part-Time Faculty*: 10.

FACILITIES AND SERVICES
Practical experiences available through: Audio Recording Laboratory; Campus Newspaper (Published Independently); Local Commercial Newspaper; Desktop Publishing Facility; Photographic Darkrooms; Video Editing; Electronic Field Production (Video); FM Radio Station (Institutional); Institutional Magazine; Video Production Laboratory or Television Studio.

Slippery Rock University of Pennsylvania (Public)

Department of Communication
Slippery Rock, Pennsylvania 16057
Telephone: (412) 794-7263

Theodore J. Walwik, Chair
Frank V. Mastrianna, Dean

CURRICULUM AND INSTRUCTION
Courses or Concentrations
Available: Communication; Film or Cinema; Journalism or Mass Communication; Public Relations; Radio, Television, Broadcasting, or Telecommunications; Speech; *Undergraduate Objectives or Program Emphases*: Prepare students for careers in public and corporate communication, journalism, and broadcasting; prepare selected students for graduate and professional schools; *Bachelor's Degree Majors*: 200; *Full-Time Faculty*: 18; *Part-Time Faculty*: 2; *Full-Time Professional (non-clerical) Staff Members*: 1.

FACILITIES AND SERVICES
Practical experiences available through: Audio Recording Laboratory; Carrier Current Audio Distribution System; Closed Circuit Television Facility; Campus Newspaper (Published Independently); Desktop Publishing Facility; Photographic Darkrooms; Video Editing; Electronic Field Production (Video); FM Radio Station (Institutional); ITFS Distribution System; Public Relations Agency; United Press International Feed; Video News and Data Processing; Video Production Laboratory or Television Studio.

St. Joseph's University

Instructional Media Center
City Avenue and 54th Street
Philadelphia, Pennsylvania 19131

Sandra Buehler, Administrator

Susquehanna University (Private)

Department of Communication and Theatre Arts
Selinsgrove, Pennsylvania 17870-1001
Telephone: (717) 372-4355

Larry D. Augustine, Chair
Henry Diers, Administrator

CURRICULUM AND INSTRUCTION
Courses or Concentrations Available: Communication; Journalism or Mass Communication; Public Relations; Radio, Television, Broadcasting, or Telecommunications; Speech; Theatre Arts; *Program Coordinators*: Beverly Romberger (Speech); Robert Gross (Radio-Television); Bruce Nary (Theatre); *Undergraduate Objectives or Program Emphases*: Liberal Arts approach to teaching and training students with experiences leading to careers in professional, teaching, and allied fields; *Bachelor's Degree Majors*: 160; *Full-Time Faculty*: 5; *Part-Time Faculty*: 4; *Full-Time Professional (non-clerical) Staff Members*: 1.

FACILITIES AND SERVICES
Practical experiences available through: AM Radio Station (Institutional); Associated Press Wire Service Feed; Audio Recording Laboratory; Carrier Current Audio Distribution System; Campus Newspaper (Published Independently); Photographic Darkrooms; Video Editing; Electronic Field Production (Video); FM Radio Station (Institutional).

Temple University (Public)

School of Communication and Theatre
Philadelphia, Pennsylvania 19122
Telephone: (215) 787-8422

Robert R. Smith, Dean
Barbara Brownstein, Provost

CURRICULUM AND INSTRUCTION
Courses or Concentrations Available: Advertising; Communication; Film or Cinema; Journalism or Mass Communication; Public Relations; Radio, Television, Broadcasting, or Telecommunications; Speech; Telecommunications; Theatre; *Undergraduate Objectives or Program Emphases*: Liberal pre-professional program; *Graduate Objectives or Program*

Emphases: Professional MJ and MFA in Radio-Television-Film and Theatre; Certificate in Speech; Ph.D. in Communication; *Bachelor's Degree Majors*: 2400; *Master's Degree Majors*: 30; *MFA Degree Majors*: 70; *Doctoral Degree Majors Currently in Residence*: 20; *Additional Doctoral Degree Majors*: 30; *Full-Time Faculty*: 83; *Part-Time Faculty*: 75; *Full-Time Professional (non-clerical) Staff Members*: 25.

FACILITIES AND SERVICES
Practical experiences available through: Advertising Agency; Associated Press Wire Service Feed; Audio Recording Laboratory; Community Antenna (Cable) Television Origination; Closed Circuit Television Facility; Campus Newspaper (Published Independently); Local Commercial Newspaper; Local Commercial Television Station; Desktop Publishing Facility; Photographic Darkrooms; Video Editing; Electronic Field Production (Video); Film or Cinema Laboratory; FM Radio Station (Institutional); ITFS Distribution System; Institutional Magazine; Satellite Uplink Facility; United Press International Feed; Video News and Data Processing; Video Production Laboratory or Television Studio.

Temple University (Public)

Department of Radio-Television-Film
Annenberg Hall 011-00
Philadelphia, Pennsylvania 19122

Alex Toogood, Administrator

Temple University (Public)

Department of Journalism
Annenberg Hall
Philadelphia, Pennsylvania 19122
Telephone: (215) 787-8346

Thomas E. Eveslage, Chair

CURRICULUM AND INSTRUCTION
Courses or Concentrations Available: Advertising; Journalism or Mass Communication; Public Relations; Radio, Television, Broadcasting, or Telecommunications; Magazine; Photography; *Undergraduate Objectives or*

Program Emphases: Provide solid professional undergraduate training with a strong liberal arts orientation; *Graduate Objectives or Program Emphases*: Provide a 40-credit professional journalism degree program; *Bachelor's Degree Majors*: 950; *Other Degree Majors*: 85; *Full-Time Faculty*: 19; *Part-Time Faculty*: 45; *Full-Time Professional (non-clerical) Staff Members*: 3.

FACILITIES AND SERVICES
Practical experiences available through: Advertising Agency; Associated Press Wire Service Feed; Campus Newspaper (Published Independently); Desktop Publishing Facility; Photographic Darkrooms; FM Radio Station (Institutional); Institutional Magazine.

Thiel College (Private)

Department of English and Communication
75 College Avenue
Greenville, Pennsylvania 16125
Telephone: (412) 589-2161

Jay A. Ward, Chair
John J. Agria, Vice President, Academic Services

CURRICULUM AND INSTRUCTION
Courses or Concentrations Available: Advertising; Communication; Film or Cinema; Journalism or Mass Communication; Public Relations; Radio, Television, Broadcasting, or Telecommunications; Speech; Speech and hearing science; *Undergraduate Objectives or Program Emphases*: To introduce communication theory; to acquaint with sender/receiver responsibilities; to present communication as ethical decision-making; to provide opportunities for practical applications; to prepare for entry-level communication professional roles; *Bachelor's Degree Majors*: 15; *Full-Time Faculty*: 2; *Part-Time Faculty*: 1.

FACILITIES AND SERVICES
Practical experiences available through: Advertising Agency; Audio Recording Laboratory; Campus Newspaper (Published Independently); Local Commercial Newspaper; Local Commercial Television Station; Photographic Darkrooms; Video Editing; Electronic Field Production (Video); FM Radio Station (Institutional); Public Relations Agency; United Press International Feed; Video Production Laboratory or Television Studio.

University of Pennsylvania (Private)

Annenberg School of Communication
3620 Walnut Street
Philadelphia, Pennsylvania 19104-6220
Telephone: (215) 898-7041

Kathleen Hall Jamieson, Dean
Sheldon Hackney, President

CURRICULUM AND INSTRUCTION
Courses or Concentrations Available: Communication; Film or Cinema; Journalism or Mass Communication; Radio, Television, Broadcasting, or Telecommunications; *Program Coordinators*: Carolyn Marvin (Undergraduate Major); Larry Gross (Graduate Studies); *Undergraduate Objectives or Program Emphases*: Broad, liberal arts approach to the understanding of communicative acts and the symbolic environment, combining insights and methods of the social sciences and humanities; *Graduate Objectives or Program Emphases*: Theory and research oriented preparation for academic and other careers focusing on the nature and social role of communications processes, within a social and historical framework; *Bachelor's Degree Majors*: 127; *Master's Degree Majors*: 104; *Doctoral Degree Majors Currently in Residence*: 25; *Additional Doctoral Degree Majors*: 27; *Full-Time Faculty*: 10; *Part-Time Faculty*: 10; *Full-Time Professional (non-clerical) Staff Members*: 16.

FACILITIES AND SERVICES
Practical experiences available through: Audio Recording Laboratory; Closed Circuit Television Facility; Campus Newspaper (Published Independently); Local Commercial Newspaper; Local Commercial Television Station; Desktop Publishing Facility; Video Editing; Electronic Field Production (Video); Film or Cinema Laboratory; FM Radio Station (Institutional); Video Production Laboratory or Television Studio.

University of Pittsburgh

Department of English
Pittsburgh, Pennsylvania 15260

Lee Gutkind, Administrator

University of Pittsburgh

Communication Department
Pittsburgh, Pennsylvania 15260

Thomas Kane, Administrator

University of Pittsburgh - Bradford (Private)

Department of Broadcast Communications
300 Campus Drive
Bradford, Pennsylvania 16701
Telephone: (814) 362-7587

Jeffrey C. Guterman, Director
Samuel Johnson, Administrator

CURRICULUM AND INSTRUCTION
*Courses or Concentrations
Available*: Advertising; Communication;
Radio, Television, Broadcasting, or
Telecommunications; *Undergraduate
Objectives or Program Emphases*: A
message-design emphasis within the realm of
electronic media. The consequences of these
messages are also explored. All students are
brought to an advanced level of production
before graduation; *Bachelor's Degree
Majors*: 40; *Full-Time Faculty*: 1; *Part-Time
Faculty*: 2.

FACILITIES AND SERVICES
Practical experiences available through: Audio
Recording Laboratory; Carrier Current
Audio Distribution System; Campus
Newspaper (Published Independently);
Local Commercial Television Station;
Desktop Publishing Facility; Photographic
Darkrooms; Video Editing; Electronic Field
Production (Video); Video Production
Laboratory or Television Studio.

University of Pittsburgh - Greensburg (Public)

Department of Humanities
Mount Pleasant Road
Greensburg, Pennsylvania 15601
Telephone: (412) 836-9861

Lillian L. Beeson, Associate Professor

CURRICULUM AND INSTRUCTION
*Courses or Concentrations
Available*: Communication; Film or Cinema;
Information Science; Journalism or Mass
Communication; Speech; *Program
Coordinators*: Colelle Levin (Film); Judy
Vollmer (Journalism); *Undergraduate
Objectives or Program Emphases*: Skills
courses; Rhetorical theory; *Full-Time
Faculty*: 10; *Part-Time Faculty*: 5; *Full-Time
Professional (non-clerical) Staff Members*: 1.

FACILITIES AND SERVICES
Practical experiences available through: Audio
Recording Laboratory; Closed Circuit
Television Facility; Desktop Publishing
Facility; Institutional Magazine.

University of Pittsburgh - Johnstown (Public)

Department of Communication
Johnstown, Pennsylvania 15904
Telephone: (814) 266-9661

Merrily K. Swoboda, Chair
Carroll Grimes, Administrator

CURRICULUM AND INSTRUCTION
*Courses or Concentrations
Available*: Communication; *Undergraduate
Objectives or Program Emphases*: Liberal
Arts educational framework for improving
students knowledge of communication
theories, practices and skills; *Bachelor's
Degree Majors*: 50; *Full-Time Faculty*: 2;
Part-Time Faculty: 2.

FACILITIES AND SERVICES
*Practical experiences available
through*: Advertising Agency; AM Radio
Station (Institutional); Audio Recording
Laboratory; Community Antenna (Cable)
Television Origination; Local Commercial
Television Station; Desktop Publishing
Facility; Institutional Magazine;
Institutional Newspaper; Public Relations

Agency; Video Production Laboratory or Television Studio.

University of Scranton (Private)

Department of Communication
Linden Street and Monroe Avenue
Scranton, Pennsylvania 18510-2192
Telephone: (717) 961-6333

Robert P. Sadowski, Chair
Paul F. Fahey, Dean, College of Arts and Sciences

CURRICULUM AND INSTRUCTION
Courses or Concentrations Available: Advertising; Communication; Film or Cinema; Journalism or Mass Communication; Public Relations; Radio, Television, Broadcasting, or Telecommunications; Speech; Organizational Communication; Cable Television; *Program Coordinators*: Roger D. Wallace (Faculty Advisor to Carrier Current Radio Station); Darla R. Germeroth (Public Speaking); Edward F. Warner (Oral Clinic); John J. Clark (Macintosh Journalism Laboratory); *Undergraduate Objectives or Program Emphases*: Humanistic and scientific perspectives are combined with opportunities to acquire on-the-job experiences through internships, as well as individualized study through faculty-directed projects and theses. Preparation for advanced studies and careers; *Bachelor's Degree Majors*: 200; *Full-Time Faculty*: 9; *Part-Time Faculty*: 9.

FACILITIES AND SERVICES
Practical experiences available through: Advertising Agency; Associated Press Wire Service Feed; Audio Recording Laboratory; Community Antenna (Cable) Television Origination; Carrier Current Audio Distribution System; Closed Circuit Television Facility; Campus Newspaper (Published Independently); Local Commercial Newspaper; Local Commercial Television Station; Desktop Publishing Facility; Photographic Darkrooms; Video Editing; Electronic Field Production (Video); Public Relations Agency; Video News and Data Processing; Video Production Laboratory or Television Studio.

University of the Arts (Private)

Department of Photography/Film/Animation
Broad and Pine Streets
Philadelphia, Pennsylvania 19102
Telephone: (215) 875-4800

Alida Fish, Chair
Stephen Tarantal, Dean

CURRICULUM AND INSTRUCTION
Courses or Concentrations Available: Film or Cinema; Communication Design; Graphic Design; *Undergraduate Objectives or Program Emphases*: To enable students to use the full range of media tools and techniques to create their own personal and artistic vision; *Associate's Degree Majors*: 6; *BFA Degree Majors*: 460; *Master's Degree Majors*: 22; *MFA Degree Majors*: 10; *Full-Time Faculty*: 6; *Part-Time Faculty*: 11; *Full-Time Professional (non-clerical) Staff Members*: 3.

FACILITIES AND SERVICES
Practical experiences available through: Desktop Publishing Facility; Photographic Darkrooms; Film or Cinema Laboratory.

Ursinus College (Private)

Department of Communication Arts
Collegeville, Pennsylvania 19426
Telephone: (215) 489-4111

Joyce E. Henry, Chair
William Akin, Dean

CURRICULUM AND INSTRUCTION
Courses or Concentrations Available: Communication; Mass Communication; Radio, Television, Broadcasting, or Telecommunications; Speech; *Undergraduate Objectives or Program Emphases*: A broad liberal arts education with emphases in speech, mass communication and theatre; *Bachelor's Degree Majors*: 40; *Full-Time Faculty*: 3; *Part-Time Faculty*: 3.

FACILITIES AND SERVICES
Practical experiences available through: Advertising Agency; Carrier Current Audio Distribution System; Closed Circuit Television Facility; Campus Newspaper (Published Independently); Local Commercial Newspaper; Local

Commercial Television Station; Video Editing; Electronic Field Production (Video); Institutional Magazine; Public Relations Agency; Video Production Laboratory or Television Studio.

Villanova University (Private)

Department of Communication Arts
St. Mary's Hall
Villanova, Pennsylvania 19085
Telephone: (215) 645-4750

Marguerite M. Farley, Chair
Rev. Kail Ellis, O.S.A., Dean, College of Arts and Sciences

CURRICULUM AND INSTRUCTION
Courses or Concentrations
Available: Communication; Film or Cinema; Journalism or Mass Communication; Public Relations; Radio, Television, Broadcasting, or Telecommunications; Speech; *Undergraduate Objectives or Program Emphases*: Communication focuses on the understanding and use of symbols that create meaning in multiple contexts. The discipline is grounded in ancient rhetorical traditions and is influenced by contemporary intellectual and technological developments.; *Bachelor's Degree Majors*: 170; *Full-Time Faculty*: 12; *Part-Time Faculty*: 12.

FACILITIES AND SERVICES
Practical experiences available through: Advertising Agency; Audio Recording Laboratory; Carrier Current Audio Distribution System; Closed Circuit Television Facility; Campus Newspaper (Published Independently); Local Commercial Newspaper; Local Commercial Television Station; Video Editing; Electronic Field Production (Video); Film or Cinema Laboratory; FM Radio Station (Institutional); Public Relations Agency; Video Production Laboratory or Television Studio.

Waynesburg College

English Department
Waynesburg, Pennsylvania 15370

William L. Sipple, Administrator

Westminster College

Department of Communication Arts
New Wilmington, Pennsylvania 16172

Walter E. Scheid, Administrator

Westmoreland County Community College (Public)

Department of Media Technology
Armbrust Road
Youngwood, Pennsylvania 15697
Telephone: (412) 925-4138

Annette Georgulis, Instructor
Robert Myers, Chair

CURRICULUM AND INSTRUCTION
Courses or Concentrations
Available: Advertising; Film or Cinema; Public Relations; Radio, Television, Broadcasting, or Telecommunications; *Undergraduate Objectives or Program Emphases*: Design, produce and analyze non-broadcast media; application, utilization and management of non-broadcast communication technologies, human communication; evaluate instruction as media; *Associate's Degree Majors*: 30; *Part-Time Faculty*: 5.

FACILITIES AND SERVICES
Practical experiences available through: Audio Recording Laboratory; Desktop Publishing Facility; Photographic Darkrooms; Video Editing; Electronic Field Production (Video); Film or Cinema Laboratory; Institutional Newspaper; Video Production Laboratory or Television Studio.

Wilkes College (Private)

Department of Speech Communication Arts
Arts and Science School
Wilkes-Barre, Pennsylvania 18766
Telephone: (717) 824-4651

Bradford L. Kinney, Chair
James P. Rodeihko, Dean

CURRICULUM AND INSTRUCTION
Courses or Concentrations
Available: Communication; Film or Cinema; Journalism or Mass Communication; Public Relations; Radio, Television, Broadcasting,

or Telecommunications; Speech;
*Undergraduate Objectives or Program
Emphases*: Indepth training and hands-on
experience through textbook, classroom
instruction, extra curricular and professional
internship experience; *Bachelor's Degree
Majors*: 100; *Full-Time Faculty*: 7;
Part-Time Faculty: 1.

FACILITIES AND SERVICES
*Practical experiences available
through*: Associated Press Wire Service Feed;
Audio Recording Laboratory; Closed Circuit
Television Facility; Campus Newspaper
(Published Independently); Local
Commercial Newspaper; Local Commercial
Television Station; Desktop Publishing
Facility; Photographic Darkrooms; Video
Editing; Electronic Field Production
(Video); FM Radio Station (Institutional);
Video Production Laboratory or Television
Studio.

Wilson College (Private)

**Department of Communications
1015 Philadelphia Avenue
Chambersburg, Pennsylvania 17201
Telephone: (717) 264-4141**

**Ann D. Summerall, Head
R. Lynn Kelly, Dean**

CURRICULUM AND INSTRUCTION
*Courses or Concentrations
Available*: Communication; Film or Cinema;
Journalism or Mass Communication; Public
Relations; Radio, Television, Broadcasting,
or Telecommunications; Speech;
*Undergraduate Objectives or Program
Emphases*: Theory and application;
Full-Time Faculty: 1; *Part-Time Faculty*: 7.

FACILITIES AND SERVICES
Practical experiences available through: Audio
Recording Laboratory; Campus Newspaper
(Published Independently); Local
Commercial Newspaper; Local Commercial
Television Station; Desktop Publishing
Facility; Photographic Darkrooms;
Institutional Magazine; Institutional
Newspaper; Public Relations Agency;
Satellite Uplink Facility; Video News and
Data Processing.

York College of Pennsylvania

**Department of Music, Art and Speech
Communication
Country Club Road
York, Pennsylvania 17403
Telephone: (717) 846-7788**

**Thomas V. Hall, Chair
William DeMeester, Academic Dean**

CURRICULUM AND INSTRUCTION
*Courses or Concentrations
Available*: Communication; Journalism or
Mass Communication; Public Relations;
Radio, Television, Broadcasting, or
Telecommunications; Speech; *Undergraduate
Objectives or Program Emphases*: General
Speech, Radio and Television; *Associate's
Degree Majors*: 13; *Bachelor's Degree
Majors*: 87; *Full-Time Faculty*: 8; *Part-Time
Faculty*: 4.

FACILITIES AND SERVICES
Practical experiences available through: AM
Radio Station (Institutional); Associated
Press Wire Service Feed; Audio Recording
Laboratory; Carrier Current Audio
Distribution System; Closed Circuit
Television Facility; Campus Newspaper
(Published Independently); Local
Commercial Newspaper; Local Commercial
Television Station; Desktop Publishing
Facility; Photographic Darkrooms; Video
Editing; Electronic Field Production
(Video); FM Radio Station (Institutional);
ITFS Distribution System; Institutional
Newspaper; Satellite Uplink Facility (Ku
Band Transmitter) (C Band Transmitter);
Video Production Laboratory or Television
Studio.

Brown University (Private)

Center for Modern Culture and Media
Box 1897
Providence, Rhode Island 02912
Telephone: (401) 863-2853

Roger B. Henkle, Director
Thomas Anton, Dean

CURRICULUM AND INSTRUCTION
Courses or Concentrations Available: Film or
Cinema; Journalism or Mass
Communication; Radio, Television,
Broadcasting, or Telecommunications;
Cultural Studies; Post-structuralist Theory;
*Undergraduate Objectives or Program
Emphases*: Training students in the analysis
of media from an historical and cultural
perspective. Theorizing media production.
Also production of film, video, print
journalism; *Bachelor's Degree Majors*: 225;
Full-Time Faculty: 5; *Part-Time Faculty*: 5;
*Full-Time Professional (non-clerical) Staff
Members*: 2.

FACILITIES AND SERVICES
Practical experiences available through: AM
Radio Station (Institutional); Audio
Recording Laboratory; Community Antenna
(Cable) Television Origination; Closed
Circuit Television Facility; Campus
Newspaper (Published Independently);
Local Commercial Newspaper; Local
Commercial Television Station; Video
Editing; Television Broadcast Station
(Institutional); Film or Cinema Laboratory;
FM Radio Station (Institutional);
Institutional Magazine.

Brown University (Private)

Department of Theatre, Speech and Dance
77 Waterman Street
Providence, Rhode Island 02912
Telephone: (401) 863-3283

Nancy R. Dunbar, Instructor
John Emigh, Chair

CURRICULUM AND INSTRUCTION
Courses or Concentrations

Available: Communication; Speech; Theatre,
Dance; *Undergraduate Objectives or Program
Emphases*: Basic instruction in principles of
rhetorical communication.
Intermediate-level course work in
interpersonal communication, rhetorical
theory and criticism; *Full-Time Faculty*: 2;
Part-Time Faculty: 1.

Johnson and Wales College (Private)

8 Abbott Park Place
Providence, Rhode Island 02903
Telephone: (401) 456-4791

David W. Claire, Subject Coordinator

CURRICULUM AND INSTRUCTION
*Courses or Concentrations
Available*: Advertising; Public Relations;
Speech; *Undergraduate Objectives or Program
Emphases*: Basic curriculum in
advertising/public relations and
management; *Full-Time Faculty*: 3;
Part-Time Faculty: 1; *Full-Time Professional
(non-clerical) Staff Members*: 1.

FACILITIES AND SERVICES
*Practical experiences available
through*: Advertising Agency; Campus
Newspaper (Published Independently);
Local Commercial Newspaper; Public
Relations Agency.

Rhode Island School of Design (Private)

Department of Film/Video
2 College Street
Providence, Rhode Island 02903
Telephone: (401) 331-3511

Yvonne Andersen, Head
David Porter, Division Head

CURRICULUM AND INSTRUCTION
Courses or Concentrations Available: Film or
Cinema; Animation; Video; *Undergraduate*

Objectives or Program Emphases: Students learn the technical skills and concepts necessary to produce artistic and professional work in film, video, and animation. Primary emphasis is placed on form, context and structure of images moving in time; *BFA Degree Majors*: 35; *Other Degree Majors*: 30; *Full-Time Faculty*: 2; *Part-Time Faculty*: 6; *Full-Time Professional (non-clerical) Staff Members*: 2.

FACILITIES AND SERVICES
Practical experiences available through: Audio Recording Laboratory; Campus Newspaper (Published Independently); Local Commercial Television Station; Desktop Publishing Facility; Photographic Darkrooms; Video Editing; Electronic Field Production (Video); Film or Cinema Laboratory; Video News and Data Processing; Video Production Laboratory or Television Studio.

Roger Williams College

Film Studies
Ferry Road
Bristol, Rhode Island 02809

Nancy Harlow, Administrator

University of Rhode Island (Public)

Department of Journalism
Kingston, Rhode Island 02881
Telephone: (401) 792-2195

Barbara F. Luebke, Chair

CURRICULUM AND INSTRUCTION
Courses or Concentrations Available: Journalism or Mass Communication; Public Relations; Radio, Television, Broadcasting, or Telecommunications; *Undergraduate Objectives or Program Emphases*: Print and broadcast journalism; *Bachelor's Degree Majors*: 150; *Full-Time Faculty*: 6; *Part-Time Faculty*: 2.

FACILITIES AND SERVICES
Practical experiences available through: AM Radio Station (Institutional); Audio Recording Laboratory; Community Antenna (Cable) Television Origination; Campus

Newspaper (Published Independently); Local Commercial Newspaper; Local Commercial Television Station; Desktop Publishing Facility; Photographic Darkrooms; Video Editing; Electronic Field Production (Video); Public Relations Agency; Video News and Data Processing.

University of Rhode Island (Public)

Speech Communication Department
Kingston, Rhode Island 02881

Judith Anderson, Chair

Anderson College (Private)

Department of Journalism
316 Boulevard
Anderson, South Carolina 29621
Telephone: (803) 231-2000

Lawrence E. Webb, Chair
Frances Mims, Administrator

CURRICULUM AND INSTRUCTION
Courses or Concentrations
Available: Communication; Journalism or
Mass Communication; Radio, Television,
Broadcasting, or Telecommunications;
*Undergraduate Objectives or Program
Emphases*: To provide foundational courses
in mass communications for freshmen and
sophomores, including survey courses and
beginning courses in reporting and television
production; *Associate's Degree Majors*: 20;
Full-Time Faculty: 1; *Part-Time Faculty*: 1.

FACILITIES AND SERVICES
*Practical experiences available
through*: Community Antenna (Cable)
Television Origination; Local Commercial
Newspaper; Desktop Publishing Facility;
Photographic Darkrooms; Video Editing;
Electronic Field Production (Video);
Institutional Newspaper; Video News and
Data Processing; Video Production
Laboratory or Television Studio.

Benedict College

Department of Radio-Television-Film
Harden and Blanding Streets
Columbia, South Carolina 29204

Benedict College

Journalism Department
Columbia, South Carolina 29204

Anna R. Paddon, Administrator

Bob Jones University (Private)

School of Fine Arts
Greenville, South Carolina 29614
Telephone: (803) 242-5100

Dwight Gustafson, Dean
Phillip Smith, Provost

CURRICULUM AND INSTRUCTION
Courses or Concentrations
Available: Advertising; Communication; Film
or Cinema; Journalism or Mass
Communication; Public Relations; Radio,
Television, Broadcasting, or
Telecommunications; Speech; *Program
Coordinators*: Elmer Rumminger
(Radio-Television Broadcasting); Tim
Rogers (Film, Video); Dewitt Jones
(Speech); *Undergraduate Objectives or
Program Emphases*: To equip the student
with a broad liberal arts training that is an
imperative for media work, and at the same
time to provide an intensive major
concentration that prepares one for career
entry or further specialized study on the
graduate level; *Graduate Objectives or
Program Emphases*: To equip the student for
a professional career in the media through a
program balancing relevant academics with
extensive laboratory production and intern
experience in the specific field; *Bachelor's
Degree Majors*: 7; *Master's Degree Majors*: 12;
MFA Degree Majors: 3; *Other Degree
Majors*: 29; *Full-Time Faculty*: 11;
Part-Time Faculty: 27; *Full-Time
Professional (non-clerical) Staff Members*: 8.

FACILITIES AND SERVICES
*Practical experiences available
through*: Advertising Agency; Associated
Press Wire Service Feed; Audio Recording
Laboratory; Carrier Current Audio
Distribution System; Campus Newspaper
(Published Independently); Local
Commercial Newspaper; Local Commercial
Television Station; Desktop Publishing
Facility; Photographic Darkrooms; Video
Editing; Electronic Field Production
(Video); Film or Cinema Laboratory; Video
Production Laboratory or Television Studio.

Clemson University (Public)

English Department
Strode Tower
Clemson, South Carolina 29634-1503

William Koon, Administrator

Clemson University (Public)

Department of Performing Arts
College of Liberal Arts
Clemson, South Carolina 29634-1505
Telephone: (803) 656-3043

Clifton S. M. Egan, Head
Robert A. Waller, Dean

CURRICULUM AND INSTRUCTION
*Courses or Concentrations
Available*: Communication; Speech;
*Undergraduate Objectives or Program
Emphases*: Minor program in speech with
concentrations in public address and
organizational communication; *Full-Time
Faculty*: 16.

FACILITIES AND SERVICES
Practical experiences available through: Audio
Recording Laboratory; Closed Circuit
Television Facility; Campus Newspaper
(Published Independently); FM Radio
Station (Institutional); ITFS Distribution
System; Institutional Magazine.

College of Charleston

Learning Resources
66 George Street
Charleston, South Carolina 29424

Virginia Friedman, Administrator

Converse College

Department of English
580 East Main Street
Spartanburg, South Carolina 29301

Karen Carmean, Administrator

Furman University (Private)

Program of Speech
Greenville, South Carolina 29613
Telephone: (803) 294-3171

Charles DeLancey, Director
Courtlandt Gilmour, Chair, Department of
Drama and Speech

CURRICULUM AND INSTRUCTION
*Courses or Concentrations
Available*: Communication; Speech;
*Undergraduate Objectives or Program
Emphases*: Primarily to provide service
courses in speech to students at a private
liberal arts college. There is no major in
speech communication; *Bachelor's Degree
Majors*: 5; *Full-Time Faculty*: 3.

Lander College

Learning Resources
P. O. Box 6018
Greenwood, South Carolina 29646

Sam B. Davis, Administrator

Tri County Technical College (Public)

Department of Radio and Television
Broadcasting
Box 587
Pendleton, South Carolina 29670
Telephone: (803) 646-8361

Charles H. Jordan, Head
Darrell Rochester, Chair, Business and
Human Services

CURRICULUM AND INSTRUCTION
*Courses or Concentrations
Available*: Advertising; Communication; Film
or Cinema; Journalism or Mass
Communication; Radio, Television,
Broadcasting, or Telecommunications;
Speech; Photography; *Undergraduate
Objectives or Program Emphases*: Job market
production oriented department designed to
provide sufficient training for entry level
positions in broadcast facilities; *Associate's
Degree Majors*: 53; *Full-Time Faculty*: 1;
Part-Time Faculty: 2.

FACILITIES AND SERVICES
Practical experiences available through: Audio
Recording Laboratory; Community Antenna
(Cable) Television Origination; Local
Commercial Television Station;
Photographic Darkrooms; Video Editing;
Electronic Field Production (Video); Video
Production Laboratory or Television Studio.

Trident Technical College
(Public)

Department of Communications
P. O. Box 10367
Charleston, South Carolina 29411
Telephone: (803) 572-6307

Patricia S. Fox, Head
Charles McCloy, Dean, Communications
Division

CURRICULUM AND INSTRUCTION
*Courses or Concentrations
Available*: Advertising; Communication; Film
or Cinema; Radio, Television, Broadcasting,
or Telecommunications; *Program
Coordinators*: Bill Raitt (Broadcasting, Film
Production); Cerise Camille (Advertising);
*Undergraduate Objectives or Program
Emphases*: Two year institution providing the
student with all the necessary skills to obtain
a full time position in their chosen area;
Full-Time Faculty: 3; *Part-Time Faculty*: 5;
*Full-Time Professional (non-clerical) Staff
Members*: 3.

FACILITIES AND SERVICES
*Practical experiences available
through*: Advertising Agency; Audio
Recording Laboratory; Carrier Current
Audio Distribution System; Closed Circuit
Television Facility; Campus Newspaper
(Published Independently); Local
Commercial Newspaper; Local Commercial
Television Station; Desktop Publishing
Facility; Photographic Darkrooms; Video
Editing; Electronic Field Production
(Video); Television Broadcast Station
(Institutional); Film or Cinema Laboratory;
ITFS Distribution System; Satellite Uplink
Facility.

University of South Carolina
(Public)

Department of Media Arts
College of Applied Professional Sciences
Columbia, South Carolina 29208
Telephone: (803) 777-6812

C. R. Brasington, Chair
H. E. Varney, Dean

CURRICULUM AND INSTRUCTION
Courses or Concentrations Available: Film or
Cinema; Audio Recording; Scriptwriting;
Photography; Video; *Program
Coordinator*: Sandra Wertz (Undergraduate
Studies); *Undergraduate Objectives or
Program Emphases*: Audio recording, film
production, photography, multi-image,
scriptwriting, video management, interactive
media holography and 3-D television;
*Graduate Objectives or Program
Emphases*: Conceptual and organization
aspects of media production; *Degree
Majors*: 250; *Full-Time Faculty*: 10;
Part-Time Faculty: 5; *Full-Time Professional
(non-clerical) Staff Members*: 1.

FACILITIES AND SERVICES
Practical experiences available through: Audio
Recording Laboratory; Desktop Publishing
Facility; Photographic Darkrooms; Video
Editing; Electronic Field Production
(Video); Film or Cinema Laboratory; Video
Production Laboratory or Television Studio.

University of South Carolina
(Public)

College of Journalism and Mass
Communication
Columbia, South Carolina 29208
Telephone: (803) 777-4102

Joseph W. Shoquist, Dean
Arthur Smith, Executive Vice President and
Provost

CURRICULUM AND INSTRUCTION
*Courses or Concentrations
Available*: Advertising; Journalism or Mass
Communication; Public Relations; Radio,
Television, Broadcasting, or
Telecommunications; *Undergraduate
Objectives or Program Emphases*: BA in
Journalism, with sequences in
News-editorial, Advertising and Public
Relations. Broadcasting News-editorial

tracks include Newspapers, Photojournalism, or Magazine. Also, Advertising and Public Relations Management, Creative or Public Relations, Broadcast-News, Production or Management; *Graduate Objectives or Program Emphases*: MA or MMC (Master of Mass Communications); *Bachelor's Degree Majors*: 860; *Master's Degree Majors*: 100; *Full-Time Faculty*: 33; *Part-Time Faculty*: 11; *Full-Time Professional (non-clerical) Staff Members*: 2.

FACILITIES AND SERVICES
Practical experiences available through: Associated Press Wire Service Feed; Audio Recording Laboratory; Community Antenna (Cable) Television Origination; Desktop Publishing Facility; Photographic Darkrooms; Video Editing; Electronic Field Production (Video); FM Radio Station; Institutional Magazine; Institutional Newspaper; Video News and Data Processing; Video Production Laboratory or Television Studio.

University of South Carolina (Public)

Theatre and Speech Department
Columbia, South Carolina 29208

Thorne Compton, Chair

Winthrop College (Public)

Department of Mass Communication
Rock Hill, South Carolina 29733
Telephone: (803) 323-2121

J. William Click, Chair
Albert M. Lyles, Dean of the College

CURRICULUM AND INSTRUCTION
Courses or Concentrations Available: Advertising; Film or Cinema; Journalism or Mass Communication; Public Relations; Radio, Television, Broadcasting, or Telecommunications; *Undergraduate Objectives or Program Emphases*: A professional program that prepares graduates for careers in the professions of journalism and broadcasting and other areas of mass communication; *Bachelor's Degree Majors*: 270; *Full-Time Faculty*: 7; *Full-Time Professional (non-clerical) Staff Members*: 2.

FACILITIES AND SERVICES
Practical experiences available through: Audio Recording Laboratory; Carrier Current Audio Distribution System; Campus Newspaper (Published Independently); Desktop Publishing Facility; Video Editing; Electronic Field Production (Video); Video Production Laboratory or Television Studio.

Winthrop College (Public)

Department of Speech
Rock Hill, South Carolina 29733
Telephone: (803) 323-2379

Louis J. Rosso, Chair
Albert M. Lyles, Dean, Arts and Sciences

CURRICULUM AND INSTRUCTION
Courses or Concentrations Available: Communication; Speech; *Undergraduate Objectives or Program Emphases*: The speech major emphasizes human communication and includes tracks in interpersonal communication, public communication, and speech communication development/disorders; *Bachelor's Degree Majors*: 15; *Full-Time Faculty*: 4; *Part-Time Faculty*: 1.

Augustana College (Private)

Department of Speech Communication and Drama
Sioux Falls, South Dakota 57197
Telephone: (608) 336-5483

Michael Pfau, Chair
Gary Olson, Dean

CURRICULUM AND INSTRUCTION
Courses or Concentrations
Available: Communication; Journalism or Mass Communication; Public Relations; Radio, Television, Broadcasting, or Telecommunications; Speech; *Undergraduate Objectives or Program Emphases*: Knowledge and application of communication across a variety of contexts (interpersonal, public address, mass communication, etc.). A functional specialty in social influence; *Bachelor's Degree Majors*: 100; *Master's Degree Majors*: 2.

FACILITIES AND SERVICES
Practical experiences available through: Advertising Agency; AM Radio Station (Institutional); Associated Press Wire Service Feed; Closed Circuit Television Facility; Campus Newspaper (Published Independently); Local Commercial Newspaper; Local Commercial Television Station; Desktop Publishing Facility; Photographic Darkrooms; Video Editing; FM Radio Station (Institutional); Institutional Magazine; Institutional Newspaper; Public Relations Agency; United Press International Feed; Video Production Laboratory or Television Studio.

Black Hills State University (Public)

College of Arts and Humanities
Box 9003
Spearfish, South Dakota 57783
Telephone: (605) 642-6420

Richard E. Boyd, Dean
Larry Landis, Vice President

CURRICULUM AND INSTRUCTION
Courses or Concentrations
Available: Communication; Journalism or Mass Communication; Public Relations; Radio, Television, Broadcasting, or Telecommunications; Speech; Organizational Communication; English; *Program Coordinators*: Stewart Bellman (English Department); Ben Dar (Mass Communication Department); Al Panerio (Speech Department); *Undergraduate Objectives or Program Emphases*: Teaching programs in English, Speech, Theatre, Mass Communication. Also non-teaching programs in English Speech-Theatre, Mass Communication, Radio-Television, Print Journalism. AA programs in Communication Arts, Radio-Television, and Graphics; *Associate's Degree Majors*: 20; *Bachelor's Degree Majors*: 140; *Full-Time Faculty*: 23.

FACILITIES AND SERVICES
Practical experiences available through: Audio Recording Laboratory; Closed Circuit Television Facility; Local Commercial Newspaper; Local Commercial Television Station; Desktop Publishing Facility; Photographic Darkrooms; Video Editing; Electronic Field Production (Video); FM Radio Station (Institutional); Institutional Newspaper; Video News and Data Processing; Video Production Laboratory or Television Studio.

Dakota Wesleyan University (Private)

Department of Communication/Theatre
1200 West University Boulevard
Mitchell, South Dakota 57301
Telephone: (605) 995-2600

Mike Turchen, Head
Lesta U. Turchen, Vice President, Academic Affairs

CURRICULUM AND INSTRUCTION
Courses or Concentrations
Available: Communication; Speech; *Undergraduate Objectives or Program Emphases*: Basic bachelor's degree for Liberal Arts students; *Bachelor's Degree*

Majors: 10; *Full-Time Faculty*: 2; *Part-Time Faculty*: 3.

FACILITIES AND SERVICES
Practical experiences available through: Campus Newspaper (Published Independently); Local Commercial Newspaper; Desktop Publishing Facility; Photographic Darkrooms.

Huron College

Huron, South Dakota 57350

Edwin Tschetter, Administrator

Mount Marty College (Private)

Program of English/Mass Communication
1105 West 8th Street
Yankton, South Dakota 57078
Telephone: (605) 668-1506

Jerry W. Wilson, Director
Jack Lyons, Division Head

CURRICULUM AND INSTRUCTION
Courses or Concentrations Available: Advertising; Communication; Journalism or Mass Communication; Public Relations; Radio, Television, Broadcasting, or Telecommunications; *Program Coordinators*: Jeff Slade (Broadcast); *Undergraduate Objectives or Program Emphases*: Print Journalism; Advertising/Public Relations; Broadcasting; *Bachelor's Degree Majors*: 15; *Full-Time Faculty*: 4.

FACILITIES AND SERVICES
Practical experiences available through: AM Radio Station (Institutional); Audio Recording Laboratory; Photographic Darkrooms; Video Editing; Institutional Magazine; Institutional Newspaper.

Sioux Falls College

Department of Mass Communication
1501 South Prairie Avenue
Sioux Falls, South Dakota 57105-1699

Gerry Schlenker, Administrator

South Dakota State University - Brookings (Public)

Department of Speech
Brookings, South Dakota 57007-1197
Telephone: (605) 688-4389

Michael R. Schliessmann, Head
Rex C. Myers, Dean, Arts and Science

CURRICULUM AND INSTRUCTION
Courses or Concentrations Available: Communication; Film or Cinema; Radio, Television, Broadcasting, or Telecommunications; Speech; Communication Disorders; Theatre; *Program Coordinators*: C. E. Denton (Film); James L. Johnson (Theatre); Edward L. Meyer (Communication Disorders); Jerry Jorgensen (Mass Communication); *Undergraduate Objectives or Program Emphases*: Professional training or preparation for graduate school; *Bachelor's Degree Majors*: 80; *Master's Degree Majors*: 7; *Full-Time Faculty*: 12; *Part-Time Faculty*: 12; *Full-Time Professional (non-clerical) Staff Members*: 1.

FACILITIES AND SERVICES
Practical experiences available through: Associated Press Wire Service Feed; Campus Newspaper (Published Independently); Local Commercial Newspaper; Video Editing; Television Broadcast Station (Institutional); FM Radio Station (Institutional); Video News and Data Processing; Video Production Laboratory or Television Studio.

South Dakota State University - Brookings (Public)

Department of Journalism and Mass Communication
Brookings, South Dakota 57007-0596
Telephone: (605) 688-4171

Richard W. Lee, Head
Rex C. Myers, Dean, College of Arts and Sciences

CURRICULUM AND INSTRUCTION
Courses or Concentrations Available: Advertising; Journalism or Mass Communication; Radio, Television, Broadcasting, or Telecommunications; Ag-Journalism; Science and Technical Writing; *Undergraduate Objectives or Program*

Emphases: To provide professional skills and a liberal education in News-Editorial, Advertising, Broadcast Journalism and Science and Technical Writing sequences in an AEJMC accredited department; *Bachelor's Degree Majors*: 98; *Master's Degree Majors*: 8; *Full-Time Faculty*: 8; *Part-Time Faculty*: 2.

FACILITIES AND SERVICES
Practical experiences available through: Associated Press Wire Service Feed; Audio Recording Laboratory; Campus Newspaper (Published Independently); Desktop Publishing Facility; Photographic Darkrooms; Video Editing; Electronic Field Production (Video); Television Broadcast Station (Institutional); FM Radio Station (Institutional); Institutional Newspaper.

University of South Dakota - Vermillion (Public)

Department of Mass Communication
MCOM Department Room 108
Vermillion, South Dakota 57069
Telephone: (605) 677-5477

George E. Whitehouse, Chair
John A. Day, Dean, College of Fine Arts

CURRICULUM AND INSTRUCTION
Courses or Concentrations Available: Advertising; Journalism or Mass Communication; Public Relations; Radio, Television, Broadcasting, or Telecommunications; *Undergraduate Objectives or Program Emphases*: Provide professional Mass Communication education within a liberal arts environment, deemphasizing obsolete traditional career tracks and emphasizing the emergence of new disciplines resulting from the merging of technologies; *Graduate Objectives or Program Emphases*: Provide professional education within a liberal arts environment for career progression to positions of leadership in the media, government, business or academic disciplines; *Bachelor's Degree Majors*: 112; *Master's Degree Majors*: 9; *Full-Time Faculty*: 6; *Part-Time Faculty*: 7; *Full-Time Professional (non-clerical) Staff Members*: 1.

FACILITIES AND SERVICES
Practical experiences available through: Advertising Agency; Associated Press Wire Service Feed; Audio Recording Laboratory; Community Antenna (Cable) Television Origination; Closed Circuit Television Facility; Campus Newspaper (Published Independently); Desktop Publishing Facility; Photographic Darkrooms; Video Editing; Electronic Field Production (Video); Television Broadcast Station (Institutional); FM Radio Station (Institutional); Institutional Newspaper; Public Relations Agency; Video News and Data Processing; Video Production Laboratory or Television Studio.

Austin Peay State University (Public)

Department of Speech, Communication and Theatre
Clarksville, Tennessee 37044
Telephone: (615) 648-7378

Ellen W. Kanervo, Chair
James D. Nixon, Dean, College of Arts and Sciences

CURRICULUM AND INSTRUCTION
Courses or Concentrations
Available: Communication; Film or Cinema; Journalism or Mass Communication; Public Relations; Radio, Television, Broadcasting, or Telecommunications; Speech; *Program Coordinators*: Paul Shaffer (Radio-Television); Reece Elliott (Speech); *Bachelor's Degree Majors*: 200; *Master's Degree Majors*: 15; *Full-Time Faculty*: 9; *Part-Time Faculty*: 5.

FACILITIES AND SERVICES
Practical experiences available through: Associated Press Wire Service Feed; Audio Recording Laboratory; Community Antenna (Cable) Television Origination; Campus Newspaper (Published Independently); Local Commercial Newspaper; Local Commercial Television Station; Desktop Publishing Facility; Video Editing; Electronic Field Production (Video); FM Radio Station (Institutional); Public Relations Agency; Video News and Data Processing; Video Production Laboratory or Television Studio.

Austin Peay State University (Public)

Program of Mass Communication
College Street
Clarksville, Tennessee 37044
Telephone: (615) 648-7378

Paul D. Shaffer, Director
Ellen W. Kanervo, Chair, Department of Speech/Communication/Theatre

CURRICULUM AND INSTRUCTION
Courses or Concentrations
Available: Communication; Journalism or Mass Communication; Public Relations; Radio, Television, Broadcasting, or Telecommunications; Speech; *Undergraduate Objectives or Program Emphases*: Training for careers in Mass Communication through academic sequences in Print Journalism, Public Relations, and Radio-Television; *Graduate Objectives or Program Emphases*: Proficiency in Broadcast Programming, Media Management, Media Law and Ethics, and Public Relations; thesis required; *Bachelor's Degree Majors*: 150; *Master's Degree Majors*: 20; *Full-Time Faculty*: 3; *Part-Time Faculty*: 2.

FACILITIES AND SERVICES
Practical experiences available through: Advertising Agency; Associated Press Wire Service Feed; Audio Recording Laboratory; Community Antenna (Cable) Television Origination; Local Commercial Newspaper; Local Commercial Television Station; Desktop Publishing Facility; Photographic Darkrooms; Video Editing; Electronic Field Production (Video); FM Radio Station (Institutional); Institutional Newspaper; Video News and Data Processing; Video Production Laboratory or Television Studio.

Belmont College

Department of Communication Arts
1900 Belmont Boulevard
Nashville, Tennessee 37212-3757

Susan W. Richardson, Administrator

Carson-Newman College (Private)

Department of Communication Arts
Russell Street
Jefferson City, Tennessee 37760
Telephone: (615) 475-9061

H. D. Champion, Jr., Chair
M. V. Carter, Academic Dean

CURRICULUM AND INSTRUCTION
Courses or Concentrations
Available: Advertising; Communication;
Journalism or Mass Communication; Public
Relations; Radio, Television, Broadcasting,
or Telecommunications; Speech; Drama;
*Undergraduate Objectives or Program
Emphases*: Liberal Arts orientation plus
professional skills; *Bachelor's Degree
Majors*: 120; *Full-Time Faculty*: 5;
Part-Time Faculty: 3; *Full-Time Professional
(non-clerical) Staff Members*: 2.

FACILITIES AND SERVICES
*Practical experiences available
through*: Advertising Agency; Audio
Recording Laboratory; Community Antenna
(Cable) Television Origination; Campus
Newspaper (Published Independently);
Local Commercial Newspaper; Local
Commercial Television Station;
Photographic Darkrooms; Video Editing;
Electronic Field Production (Video); United
Press International Feed; Video Production
Laboratory or Television Studio.

Christian Brothers College

**Department of Communication and
Performing Arts
650 East Parkway South
Memphis, Tennessee 38104**

Susan-Lynn Johns, Administrator

Cumberland University

**Division of Humanities and Social Sciences
South Greenwood
Lebanon, Tennessee 37087**

John Blackburn, Administrator

David Lipscomb University (Private)

**Department of Speech Communication
Granny White Pike
Nashville, Tennessee 37204-3951
Telephone: (615) 269-1000**

**F. Marlin Connelly, Chair
James T. Arnett, Vice President, Academic
Affairs and Dean of Faculty**

CURRICULUM AND INSTRUCTION
Courses or Concentrations
Available: Advertising; Communication; Film
or Cinema; Journalism or Mass
Communication; Public Relations; Radio,
Television, Broadcasting, or
Telecommunications; Speech; Preaching;
Speech Therapy; Forensics; *Undergraduate
Objectives or Program Emphases*: BA in
Speech Communication, in Public Relations
and in Mass Communication. Minors in
Speech Communication, Public Relations,
Mass Communication, Drama and
Journalism; *Bachelor's Degree Majors*: 60;
Full-Time Faculty: 10; *Part-Time Faculty*: 1.

FACILITIES AND SERVICES
*Practical experiences available
through*: Community Antenna (Cable)
Television Origination; Carrier Current
Audio Distribution System; Closed Circuit
Television Facility; Campus Newspaper
(Published Independently); Desktop
Publishing Facility; Video Editing;
Electronic Field Production (Video);
Institutional Newspaper; Video Production
Laboratory or Television Studio.

East Tennessee State University (Public)

**Department of Communication
Box 22510A
Johnson City, Tennessee 37614
Telephone: (615) 929-4308**

**Thomas F. Headley, Chair
John Ostheimer, Dean**

CURRICULUM AND INSTRUCTION
Courses or Concentrations
Available: Advertising; Communication; Film
or Cinema; Journalism or Mass
Communication; Public Relations; Radio,
Television, Broadcasting, or
Telecommunications; Speech; Theatre;
Program Coordinators: Edward Dunn
(Advertising); Jerry Hilliard (Public
Relations); Jack Mooney (Journalism); Paul
Walwick (Speech Communication); Warren
Robertson (Theatre); *Undergraduate
Objectives or Program Emphases*: To prepare
young people for entry level jobs in the
various professions and provide theory and
information for future growth and career
development in the communication
industries; *Bachelor's Degree Majors*: 380;
Full-Time Faculty: 13; *Part-Time Faculty*: 6;

Full-Time Professional (non-clerical) Staff Members: 1.

FACILITIES AND SERVICES
Practical experiences available through: Advertising Agency; Associated Press Wire Service Feed; Audio Recording Laboratory; Community Antenna (Cable) Television Origination; Carrier Current Audio Distribution System; Closed Circuit Television Facility; Campus Newspaper (Published Independently); Local Commercial Newspaper; Local Commercial Television Station; Desktop Publishing Facility; Photographic Darkrooms; Video Editing; Electronic Field Production (Video); Film or Cinema Laboratory; FM Radio Station (Institutional); ITFS Distribution System; Institutional Magazine; Institutional Newspaper; Public Relations Agency; Video News and Data Processing; Video Production Laboratory or Television Studio.

Johnson Bible College (Private)

Department of Telecommunications
7900 Johnson Drive
Knoxville, Tennessee 37998
Telephone: (615) 573-4517

Richard D. Phillips, Head
William Blevins, Academic Dean

CURRICULUM AND INSTRUCTION
Courses or Concentrations Available: Advertising; Communication; Journalism or Mass Communication; Public Relations; Radio, Television, Broadcasting, or Telecommunications; *Undergraduate Objectives or Program Emphases*: Prepare students to be effective communicators. Students should be able to understand telecommunication systems, work as communicators/producers within these systems, and enter broadcasting and production fields with at least entry level skill and knowledge; *Bachelor's Degree Majors*: 55; *Full-Time Faculty*: 3; *Part-Time Faculty*: 1; *Full-Time Professional (non-clerical) Staff Members*: 2.

FACILITIES AND SERVICES
Practical experiences available through: AM Radio Station (Institutional); Audio Recording Laboratory; Community Antenna (Cable) Television Origination; Carrier Current Audio Distribution System; Closed

Circuit Television Facility; Local Commercial Television Station; Video Editing; Electronic Field Production (Video); Public Relations Agency; Video Production Laboratory or Television Studio.

Knoxville College (Private)

Program of Communications
901 College Street
Knoxville, Tennessee 37921
Telephone: (615) 524-6593

Robert Gwynne, Director
Harriet Broeker, Department Head

CURRICULUM AND INSTRUCTION
Courses or Concentrations Available: Communication; Journalism or Mass Communication; Radio, Television, Broadcasting, or Telecommunications; Speech; Photography; *Undergraduate Objectives or Program Emphases*: To train students in Mass Communication (electronics and print) and liberal arts for employment or graduate school; *Bachelor's Degree Majors*: 32; *Full-Time Faculty*: 2; *Part-Time Faculty*: 1.

FACILITIES AND SERVICES
Practical experiences available through: Campus Newspaper (Published Independently); Local Commercial Newspaper; Local Commercial Television Station; Photographic Darkrooms; Video Editing; Video Production Laboratory or Television Studio.

Maryville College (Private)

Program of Writing/Communication
Maryville, Tennessee 37801
Telephone: (615) 981-8000

Leonard Butts, Coordinator
Charlotte Beck, Chair

CURRICULUM AND INSTRUCTION
Courses or Concentrations Available: Journalism or Mass Communication; *Undergraduate Objectives or Program Emphases*: News writing and news editing; *Bachelor's Degree Majors*: 15; *Full-Time Faculty*: 1; *Part-Time Faculty*: 1.

FACILITIES AND SERVICES
*Practical experiences available
through*: Campus Newspaper (Published
Independently); Local Commercial
Newspaper; Photographic Darkrooms;
Institutional Magazine.

Memphis State University (Public)

College of Communication and Fine Arts
CFA 232, MSU
Memphis, Tennessee 38152
Telephone: (901) 678-2350

Richard R. Ranta, Dean
Victor E. Feisal, Vice President, Academic
Affairs

Memphis State University (Public)

Department of Journalism
Meeman Journalism Building
Memphis, Tennessee 38152
Telephone: (901) 678-2401

Dan L. Lattimore, Chair
Richard Ranta, Dean

CURRICULUM AND INSTRUCTION
*Courses or Concentrations
Available*: Advertising; Journalism or Mass
Communication; Public Relations; Radio,
Television, Broadcasting, or
Telecommunications; *Bachelor's Degree
Majors*: 300; *Master's Degree Majors*: 40;
Full-Time Faculty: 11; *Part-Time
Faculty*: 17; *Full-Time Professional
(non-clerical) Staff Members*: 5.

FACILITIES AND SERVICES
*Practical experiences available
through*: Advertising Agency; Carrier
Current Audio Distribution System; Local
Commercial Newspaper; Local Commercial
Television Station; Desktop Publishing
Facility; Photographic Darkrooms; Video
Editing; Electronic Field Production
(Video); FM Radio Station (Institutional);
Institutional Magazine; Institutional
Newspaper; Public Relations Agency; Video
Production Laboratory or Television Studio.

Memphis State University (Public)

Department of Theatre and Communication
Arts
Memphis, Tennessee 38152
Telephone: (901) 678-2565

John P. Bakke, Chair
John McFadden, Director, Theatre

CURRICULUM AND INSTRUCTION
*Courses or Concentrations
Available*: Communication; Film or Cinema;
Radio, Television, Broadcasting, or
Telecommunications; Theatre; *Full-Time
Faculty*: 32; *Part-Time Faculty*: 18;
*Full-Time Professional (non-clerical) Staff
Members*: 6.

Middle Tennessee State University (Public)

School of Mass Communication
Murfreesboro, Tennessee 37132
Telephone: (615) 898-2813

Alex Nagy, Interim Dean
Robert Corlew, Academic Vice President

CURRICULUM AND INSTRUCTION
*Courses or Concentrations
Available*: Advertising; Journalism or Mass
Communication; Public Relations; Radio,
Television, Broadcasting, or
Telecommunications; Graphics;
Photography; Recording Industry
Management; *Undergraduate Objectives or
Program Emphases*: To provide appropriate
professional training for people entering the
fields of mass communication and recording
industry management, consumer education
for non-majors, and instruction for persons
with highly specialized needs. Liberal arts
and sciences; *Degree Majors*: 1478;
Full-Time Faculty: 27; *Part-Time
Faculty*: 10; *Full-Time Professional
(non-clerical) Staff Members*: 8.

FACILITIES AND SERVICES
*Practical experiences available
through*: Advertising Agency; Associated
Press Wire Service Feed; Audio Recording
Laboratory; Community Antenna (Cable)
Television Origination; Campus Newspaper
(Published Independently); Local
Commercial Newspaper; Photographic
Darkrooms; Video Editing; Electronic Field

Production (Video); FM Radio Station (Institutional); Institutional Magazine; Institutional Newspaper; Public Relations Agency; Satellite Uplink Facility; Video News and Data Processing; Video Production Laboratory or Television Studio.

Nashville Technical Institute (Public)

Program of Audio Visual Technology
120 White Bridge Road
Nashville, Tennessee 37209
Telephone: (615) 353-3467

Duane M. Muir, Head
Fred Oster, Department Head, Audio Visual, Automation-Robotics

CURRICULUM AND INSTRUCTION
Courses or Concentrations Available: Radio, Television, Broadcasting, or Telecommunications; *Undergraduate Objectives or Program Emphases*: Skills for Audio/Video technician; audio recording; basic electronic repair, photography, multi-image, television production, media equipment operation; *Associate's Degree Majors*: 1; *Full-Time Faculty*: 1; *Part-Time Faculty*: 1.

FACILITIES AND SERVICES
Practical experiences available through: Audio Recording Laboratory; Closed Circuit Television Facility; Local Commercial Television Station; Desktop Publishing Facility; Photographic Darkrooms; Video Editing; Electronic Field Production (Video).

Shelby State Community College (Public)

Department of Fine Arts and Speech
P. O. Box 40568
Memphis, Tennessee 38104
Telephone: (901) 528-6841

Anastasia Herin, Head
Virginia Mitchell, Assistant Dean, General Studies

CURRICULUM AND INSTRUCTION
Courses or Concentrations Available: Communication; Radio,

Television, Broadcasting, or Telecommunications; Speech; *Undergraduate Objectives or Program Emphases*: University parallel curriculum for first two years; *Associate's Degree Majors*: 18; *Full-Time Faculty*: 5; *Part-Time Faculty*: 3.

FACILITIES AND SERVICES
Practical experiences available through: Campus Newspaper (Published Independently); Local Commercial Television Station; Photographic Darkrooms; Video Editing; Video Production Laboratory or Television Studio.

Southern College

Department of Journalism and Communication
P. O. Box 370
Collegedale, Tennessee 37315

C. A. Oliphant, Administrator

Southern College of 7th Day Adventists

English and Speech Department
Collegedale, Tennessee 37315

David Smith, Administrator

Tennessee State University (Public)

Department of Communication
3500 John Merritt Boulevard
Nashville, Tennessee 37209-1561
Telephone: (615) 320-3500
Alternate: 320-3228

Lawrence B. James, Head
Bobby L. Lovett, Interim Dean, School of Arts and Sciences

CURRICULUM AND INSTRUCTION
Courses or Concentrations Available: Communication; Journalism or Mass Communication; Public Relations; Radio, Television, Broadcasting, or Telecommunications; Speech; *Program Coordinators*: Donald Page (Mass Communication); Sandra Holt (Speech Communication); *Undergraduate Objectives*

or Program Emphases: Prepare students for careers in broadcasting, speech, journalism, and theatre; prepare teachers; prepare students for allied occupations; *Bachelor's Degree Majors*: 150; *Full-Time Faculty*: 9; *Part-Time Faculty*: 2.

FACILITIES AND SERVICES
Practical experiences available through: AM Radio Station (Institutional); Associated Press Wire Service Feed; Audio Recording Laboratory; Campus Newspaper (Published Independently); Video Editing; Institutional Newspaper.

Tennessee Technological University (Public)

Program of English-Journalism
Dixie Avenue
Cookeville, Tennessee 38505
Telephone: (615) 372-3060

Earl Hutchison and Hix Stubblefield, Coordinators
Steve Tabachnick, Administrator

CURRICULUM AND INSTRUCTION
Courses or Concentrations Available: Advertising; Communication; Journalism or Mass Communication; Public Relations; Radio, Television, Broadcasting, or Telecommunications; *Undergraduate Objectives or Program Emphases*: Public Relations; News Editorial; *Degree Majors*: 69; *Full-Time Faculty*: 3.

FACILITIES AND SERVICES
Practical experiences available through: Associated Press Wire Service Feed; Audio Recording Laboratory; Closed Circuit Television Facility; Campus Newspaper (Published Independently); Desktop Publishing Facility; FM Radio Station (Institutional); Institutional Newspaper.

Tennessee Wesleyan College (Private)

Department of Mass Communication, Speech and Theatre
Box 281 TWC
Athens, Tennessee 37303
Telephone: (615) 745-7504

Maxwell Taylor Courson, Chair

CURRICULUM AND INSTRUCTION
Courses or Concentrations Available: Advertising; Communication; Film or Cinema; Journalism or Mass Communication; Public Relations; Radio, Television, Broadcasting, or Telecommunications; Speech; *Undergraduate Objectives or Program Emphases*: Mass Communications; *Bachelor's Degree Majors*: 25; *Full-Time Faculty*: 2; *Part-Time Faculty*: 1.

FACILITIES AND SERVICES
Practical experiences available through: Advertising Agency; Audio Recording Laboratory; Campus Newspaper (Published Independently); Local Commercial Newspaper; Photographic Darkrooms; Video Editing; Electronic Field Production (Video); Film or Cinema Laboratory; Public Relations Agency.

Trevecca Nazarene College (Private)

Department of Communication Studies
333 Murfreesboro Road
Nashville, Tennessee 37210
Telephone: (615) 248-1200

James A. Knear, Chair
William Strickland, Dean of the College

CURRICULUM AND INSTRUCTION
Courses or Concentrations Available: Communication; Radio, Television, Broadcasting, or Telecommunications; Speech; Communication and Human Relations; Cross Cultural Communication; Drama; *Undergraduate Objectives or Program Emphases*: To provide theory and practical experience to students of communication studies majoring in Mass Communication, Communication and Human Relations, Drama, Speech, or Cross Cultural Communication; *Associate's Degree*

Majors: 3; *Bachelor's Degree Majors*: 67; *Full-Time Faculty*: 6; *Part-Time Faculty*: 1; *Full-Time Professional (non-clerical) Staff Members*: 2.

FACILITIES AND SERVICES
Practical experiences available through: AM Radio Station (Institutional); Audio Recording Laboratory; Campus Newspaper (Published Independently); Local Commercial Television Station; Photographic Darkrooms; Video Editing; Electronic Field Production (Video); FM Radio Station (Institutional); Public Relations Agency.

Tusculum College (Private)

Department of Telecommunications
Greeneville, Tennessee 37743-0069
Telephone: (615) 638-1111

Wess R. duBrisk, Director
Clem Allison, Division Director

CURRICULUM AND INSTRUCTION
Courses or Concentrations
Available: Communication; Film or Cinema; Radio, Television, Broadcasting, or Telecommunications; Speech; *Program Coordinators*: David Morris (Speech and Drama); Ruth Sharp and Becky Booker (English); *Undergraduate Objectives or Program Emphases*: BA in English, with a concentration in Telecommunications.
Bachelor's Degree Majors: 12; *Full-Time Faculty*: 4.

FACILITIES AND SERVICES
Practical experiences available through: AM Radio Station (Institutional); Audio Recording Laboratory; Carrier Current Audio Distribution System; Local Commercial Newspaper; Local Commercial Television Station; Desktop Publishing Facility; Photographic Darkrooms; Video Editing; Electronic Field Production (Video); Film or Cinema Laboratory.

Union University

Communication Arts Department
U. S. Highway 45 Bypass
Jackson, Tennessee 38305

Mike Pollock, Administrator

University of Tennessee - Chattanooga (Public)

Department of Communication
615 McCallie Avenue
Chattanooga, Tennessee 37403
Telephone: (615) 755-4400

Peter K. Pringle, Head
Paul Gaston, Dean, College of Arts and Sciences

CURRICULUM AND INSTRUCTION
Courses or Concentrations
Available: Advertising; Journalism or Mass Communication; Public Relations; Radio, Television, Broadcasting, or Telecommunications; *Undergraduate Objectives or Program Emphases*: Combination of theory, history, law, and practical skills; *Bachelor's Degree Majors*: 149; *Full-Time Faculty*: 6; *Part-Time Faculty*: 2.

FACILITIES AND SERVICES
Practical experiences available through: Advertising Agency; Audio Recording Laboratory; Campus Newspaper (Published Independently); Local Commercial Newspaper; Local Commercial Television Station; Desktop Publishing Facility; Video Editing; Electronic Field Production (Video); FM Radio Station (Institutional); Public Relations Agency; Video Production Laboratory or Television Studio.

University of Tennessee - Knoxville (Public)

Department of Advertising
426 Communications Building
Knoxville, Tennessee 37996-0343
Telephone: (615) 974-3048

Ronald E. Taylor, Head

CURRICULUM AND INSTRUCTION
Courses or Concentrations
Available: Advertising; *Undergraduate Objectives or Program Emphases*: Professional preparation for careers in advertising and related areas; *Graduate Objectives or Program Emphases*: MS: Management of communication organizations.
Ph.D.: Research and teaching in academics; *Bachelor's Degree Majors*: 157; *Master's*

Degree Majors: 9; *Doctoral Degree Majors Currently in Residence*: 3; *Full-Time Faculty*: 5; *Part-Time Faculty*: 2.

FACILITIES AND SERVICES
Practical experiences available through: Advertising Agency; AM Radio Station (Institutional); Campus Newspaper (Published Independently); Local Commercial Newspaper; Local Commercial Television Station; Desktop Publishing Facility; Photographic Darkrooms; Video Editing; Electronic Field Production (Video); FM Radio Station (Institutional); Public Relations Agency; Satellite Uplink Facility (Ku Band Transmitter).

University of Tennessee - Knoxville (Public)

Department of Broadcasting
295 Communications Building
Knoxville, Tennessee 37996
Telephone: (615) 974-4291

Sam Swan, Head
Kelly Leiter, Dean

CURRICULUM AND INSTRUCTION
Courses or Concentrations Available: Radio, Television, Broadcasting, or Telecommunications; *Undergraduate Objectives or Program Emphases*: Broadcast news, broadcast production, broadcast management; *Graduate Objectives or Program Emphases*: Broadcast management; *Bachelor's Degree Majors*: 400; *Master's Degree Majors*: 20; *Doctoral Degree Majors Currently in Residence*: 10; *Full-Time Faculty*: 7; *Part-Time Faculty*: 6; *Full-Time Professional (non-clerical) Staff Members*: 5.

FACILITIES AND SERVICES
Practical experiences available through: AM Radio Station (Institutional); Audio Recording Laboratory; Local Commercial Television Station; Desktop Publishing Facility; Video Editing; Electronic Field Production (Video); Television Broadcast Station (Institutional); FM Radio Station (Institutional); Satellite Uplink Facility (Ku Band Transmitter); United Press International Feed; Video Production Laboratory or Television Studio.

University of Tennessee - Knoxville (Public)

School of Journalism
330 Communications Building
Knoxville, Tennessee 37996-0330
Telephone: (615) 974-5155

James A. Crook, Director
Kelly Leiter, Dean

CURRICULUM AND INSTRUCTION
Courses or Concentrations Available: Journalism or Mass Communication; Public Relations; *Undergraduate Objectives or Program Emphases*: Professional Journalism and Public Relations Courses; *Graduate Objectives or Program Emphases*: Mass Communications Management; *Bachelor's Degree Major*: 150; *Master's Degree Majors*: 25; *Doctoral Degree Majors Currently in Residence*: 6; *Additional Doctoral Degree Majors*: 8;*Full-Time Faculty*: 13; *Part-Time Faculty*: 8.

FACILITIES AND SERVICES
Practical experiences available through: Associated Press Wire Service Feed; Campus Newspaper (Published Independently); Desktop Publishing Facility; Photographic Darkrooms; Video Editing; Institutional Magazine; Institutional Newspaper; Public Relations Agency; United Press International Feed; Video News and Data Processing.

University of Tennessee - Knoxville (Public)

Department of Speech Communication
T-105 McClung Tower
Knoxville, Tennessee 37996-0405
Telephone: (615) 974-0696

Lorayne W. Lester, Head
Larry Ratner, Dean

CURRICULUM AND INSTRUCTION
Courses or Concentrations Available: Communication; Speech; Oral Interpretation; *Bachelor's Degree Majors*: 94; *Full-Time Faculty*: 8; *Part-Time Faculty*: 12; *Full-Time Professional (non-clerical) Staff Members*: 1.

University of Tennessee - Martin (Public)

Department of Communications
305 Gooch Hall
Martin, Tennessee 38238
Telephone: (901) 587-7550

Gary L. Steinke, Acting Chair
Robert Smith, Dean

CURRICULUM AND INSTRUCTION
*Courses or Concentrations
Available*: Advertising; Communication; Film or Cinema; Journalism or Mass Communication; Public Relations; Radio, Television, Broadcasting, or Telecommunications; Speech; *Undergraduate Objectives or Program Emphases*: To provide quality undergraduate programs in communication for careers in broadcasting, journalism, advertising, and public relations. To provide general education courses to the university in speech; *Bachelor's Degree Majors*: 225; *Full-Time Faculty*: 8; *Part-Time Faculty*: 5; *Full-Time Professional (non-clerical) Staff Members*: 1.

FACILITIES AND SERVICES
Practical experiences available through: Advertising Agency; Associated Press Wire Service Feed; Audio Recording Laboratory; Community Antenna (Cable) Television Origination; Campus Newspaper (Published Independently); Local Commercial Newspaper; Desktop Publishing Facility; Photographic Darkrooms; Video Editing; Electronic Field Production (Video); Television Broadcast Station (Institutional); FM Radio Station (Institutional); Public Relations Agency; Video Production Laboratory or Television Studio.

Abilene Christian University (Private)

Department of Journalism and Mass Communication
Abilene, Texas 79699
Telephone: (915) 674-2298

Charles H. Marler, Chair
Dwain Hart, Dean, College of Professional Studies

CURRICULUM AND INSTRUCTION
Courses or Concentrations Available: Advertising; Journalism or Mass Communication; Public Relations; Radio, Television, or Telecommunications; Photojournalism; Corporate Video; *Program Coordinators*: Jeff Warr (Advertising and Public Relations); Larry Bradshaw (Telecommunication); Keith McMillin (Photojournalism); *Full-Time Faculty*: 8; *Part-Time Faculty*: 4; *Full-Time Professional (non-clerical) Staff Members*: 6.

Amarillo College (Public)

Division of Language and Communication
P. O. Box 447
Amarillo, Texas 79178
Telephone: (806) 371-5226

J. Paul Matney, Chair
Gene Byrd, Vice-President and Dean of Instruction

CURRICULUM AND INSTRUCTION
Courses or Concentrations Available: Advertising; Communication; Journalism or Mass Communication; Radio, Television, or Telecommunications; Speech; Photography; *Program Coordinators*: Danita McAnally (Radio-Television, Journalism); Ken Pirtle (Photography); *Undergraduate Objectives or Program Emphases*: AA and AS degrees for entry level positions or to transfer to senior universities in mass communication, radio-television, journalism, speech communication, advertising or photography. AAS in radio-television production and photography; *Associate's Degree Majors*: 120; *Full-Time Faculty*: 9; *Part-Time Faculty*: 6;

Full-Time Professional (non-clerical) Staff Members: 2.

FACILITIES AND SERVICES
Practical experiences available through: Associated Press Wire Service Feed; Audio Recording Laboratory; Closed Circuit Television Facility; Local Commercial Television Station; Photographic Darkrooms; Video Editing; Electronic Field Production (Video); Television Broadcast Station (Institutional); FM Radio Station (Institutional); Institutional Magazine; Institutional Newspaper; Video Production Laboratory or Television Studio.

Angelo State University (Public)

Department of Communication and Drama
2601 Avenue N
San Angelo, Texas 76909
Telephone: (915) 942-2031

Jack C. Eli, Head
E. James Holland, Dean

CURRICULUM AND INSTRUCTION
Courses or Concentrations Available: Radio, Television, Broadcasting, or Telecommunications; Speech; *Undergraduate Objectives or Program Emphases*: Interpersonal Communication, Broadcasting, Speech Education; *Bachelor's Degree Majors*: 28; *Full-Time Faculty*: 7; *Part-Time Faculty*: 1; *Full-Time Professional (non-clerical) Staff Members*: 1.

FACILITIES AND SERVICES
Practical experiences available through: Audio Recording Laboratory; Closed Circuit Television Facility; Local Commercial Television Station; Video Editing; Electronic Field Production (Video); Institutional Newspaper.

Angelo State University (Public)

Department of Journalism and Mass Communications
San Angelo, Texas 76909
Telephone: (915) 942-2322

Judith A. Norwood, Acting Head
Robert K. Hegglund, Dean

CURRICULUM AND INSTRUCTION
Courses or Concentrations
Available: Advertising; Journalism or Mass Communication; Public Relations; Radio, Television, Broadcasting, or Telecommunications; Photojournalism; *Undergraduate Objectives or Program Emphases*: News-editorial; *Bachelor's Degree Majors*: 50; *Full-Time Faculty*: 2; *Part-Time Faculty*: 2.

FACILITIES AND SERVICES
Practical experiences available through: Advertising Agency; Audio Recording Laboratory; Closed Circuit Television Facility; Local Commercial Newspaper; Local Commercial Television Station; Desktop Publishing Facility; Photographic Darkrooms; Video Editing; Electronic Field Production (Video); Institutional Magazine; Institutional Newspaper; Public Relations Agency; Video Production Laboratory or Television Studio.

Austin College (Private)

Department of Communication Arts
900 North Grand Avenue
Sherman, Texas 75091
Telephone: (214) 813-2000

Daniel L. Seiterberg, Chair
Bill Moore, Dean, Humanities Division

CURRICULUM AND INSTRUCTION
Courses or Concentrations
Available: Communication; Journalism or Mass Communication; Radio, Television, Broadcasting, or Telecommunications; Speech; *Undergraduate Objectives or Program Emphases*: Multi-disciplinary program in a liberal arts context emphasizing integrative studies in disciplines of speech, theatre and media studies. Balanced curriculum of theory and performance in all three areas; *Graduate Objectives or Program Emphases*: Only students seeking teacher certification in speech/theatre through fifth year MA in

teaching program; *Bachelor's Degree Majors*: 35; *Full-Time Faculty*: 4; *Part-Time Faculty*: 2; *Full-Time Professional (non-clerical) Staff Members*: 3.

FACILITIES AND SERVICES
Practical experiences available through: Audio Recording Laboratory; Community Antenna (Cable) Television Origination; Closed Circuit Television Facility; Campus Newspaper (Published Independently); Local Commercial Television Station; Photographic Darkrooms; Video Editing; Electronic Field Production (Video).

Baylor University (Private)

Communication Studies Department
Waco, Texas 76798

Lee R. Polk, Administrator

Baylor University (Private)

Department of Journalism
BU Box 7353
Waco, Texas 76798
Telephone: (817) 755-3261

Loyal N. Gould, Chair
John Belew, Vice President, Academic Affairs

CURRICULUM AND INSTRUCTION
Courses or Concentrations
Available: Journalism or Mass Communication; Public Relations; Photo-Journalism; *Undergraduate Objectives or Program Emphases*: News editorial and public relations; *Graduate Objectives or Program Emphases*: Master of International Journalism; *Bachelor's Degree Majors*: 210; *Other Degree Majors*: 11; *Full-Time Faculty*: 7; *Part-Time Faculty*: 1.

FACILITIES AND SERVICES
Practical experiences available through: Associated Press Wire Service Feed; Local Commercial Newspaper; Desktop Publishing Facility; Photographic Darkrooms; Video Editing; Institutional Newspaper; Public Relations Agency.

Central Texas College (Public)

Division of Telecommunications
P. O. Box 1800
Killeen, Texas 76540-9990
Telephone: (817) 526-1176

Edward B. Jasuta, Jr., Director
Don Mikles, Dean of Central Campus

CURRICULUM AND INSTRUCTION
Courses or Concentrations
Available: Communication; Film or Cinema;
Journalism or Mass Communication; Radio,
Television, Broadcasting, or
Telecommunications; Speech; *Undergraduate
Objectives or Program Emphases*: Preparation
for careers in Radio, Television, Film,
Industrial Video; *Degree Majors*: 45;
Full-Time Faculty: 2; *Part-Time Faculty*: 4;
*Full-Time Professional (non-clerical) Staff
Members*: 32.

FACILITIES AND SERVICES
*Practical experiences available
through*: Advertising Agency; Audio
Recording Laboratory; Closed Circuit
Television Facility; Local Commercial
Television Station; Photographic
Darkrooms; Video Editing; Electronic Field
Production (Video); Television Broadcast
Station (Institutional); Film or Cinema
Laboratory; FM Radio Station
(Institutional); ITFS Distribution System;
Video Production Laboratory or Television
Studio.

Collin County Community College (Public)

Program of Speech Communication
2800 E. Springcreek Parkway
Plano, Texas 75074
Telephone: (214) 881-5810
Alternate: 881-5821

Shelley D. Lane, Program Coordinator
Mitchell Smith, Dean, Arts and Humanities

CURRICULUM AND INSTRUCTION
Courses or Concentrations
Available: Communication; Radio,
Television, Broadcasting, or
Telecommunications; Speech; *Undergraduate
Objectives or Program Emphases*: Elementary
understanding of speech communication and
broadcasting concepts; preparation for
successful transfer to a four year university;

Associate's Degree Majors: 60; *Full-Time
Faculty*: 2; *Part-Time Faculty*: 8.

FACILITIES AND SERVICES
*Practical experiences available
through*: Campus Newspaper (Published
Independently); Local Commercial
Television Station; Institutional Newspaper;
Satellite Uplink Facility.

Collin County Community College (Public)

Journalism/Speech Communication
2800 E. Springcreek Parkway
Plano, Texas 75074
Telephone: (214) 881-5906

Kathy Price Lingo, Head/Coordinator
Mitchel Smith, Dean

CURRICULUM AND INSTRUCTION
Courses or Concentrations
Available: Advertising; Communication;
Journalism or Mass Communication; Radio,
Television, Broadcasting, or
Telecommunications; Speech; *Program
Coordinator*: Michael Macgar (Art,
Graphics); *Undergraduate Objectives or
Program Emphases*: Fundamental of Speech
Communication; Public Speaking;
Broadcasting, Television and Radio; Writing
I and II (Newspaper); Mass Communication
(Journalism); Oral Interpretation; *Full-Time
Faculty*: 5.

FACILITIES AND SERVICES
*Practical experiences available
through*: Advertising Agency; Audio
Recording Laboratory; Community Antenna
(Cable) Television Origination; Campus
Newspaper (Published Independently);
Local Commercial Television Station;
Desktop Publishing Facility; Photographic
Darkrooms; Institutional Newspaper; Public
Relations Agency; Satellite Uplink Facility.

Concordia Lutheran College (Private)

Division of Communication
3400 I-35 North
Austin, Texas 78705
Telephone: (512) 452-7661

John H. Frahm, Chair
Clyde Duder, Vice President, Instructional Services

CURRICULUM AND INSTRUCTION
Courses or Concentrations Available: Communication; Journalism or Mass Communication; Radio, Television, Broadcasting, or Telecommunications; Speech; *Undergraduate Objectives or Program Emphases*: To familiarize students with a broad range of interpersonal and mass communication theories and provide some skills in speech, journalism and video production; *Associate's Degree Majors*: 2; *Bachelor's Degree Majors*: 81; *Full-Time Faculty*: 2; *Part-Time Faculty*: 5; *Full-Time Professional (non-clerical) Staff Members*: 2.

FACILITIES AND SERVICES
Practical experiences available through: Advertising Agency; Associated Press Wire Service Feed; Audio Recording Laboratory; Community Antenna (Cable) Television Origination; Closed Circuit Television Facility; Campus Newspaper (Published Independently); Local Commercial Newspaper; Local Commercial Television Station; Desktop Publishing Facility; Photographic Darkrooms; Video Editing; Electronic Field Production (Video); ITFS Distribution System; Public Relations Agency; Video Production Laboratory or Television Studio.

Corpus Christi State University

Department of Communication, Theatre, Television, Film
6300 Ocean Drive
Corpus Christi, Texas 78412

Paul Orser, Administrator

Dallas Baptist University

Communication Arts
7007 West Kiest Boulevard
Dallas, Texas 75211

John Thomas, Administrator

East Texas State University (Public)

Radio-Television Division
P. O. Box BB, E T Station
Commerce, Texas 75428

Robert Sanders, Administrator

East Texas State University (Public)

Department of Journalism and Graphic Arts
Box D
Commerce, Texas 75428
Telephone: (214) 886-5239

Jack L. Hillwig, Head
Robert Houston, Dean

CURRICULUM AND INSTRUCTION
Courses or Concentrations Available: Advertising; Film or Cinema; Information Science; Journalism or Mass Communication; Public Relations; Photography; Printing Management; *Undergraduate Objectives or Program Emphases*: To prepare students for professional work in journalism, photography, printing, public relations and advertising, or for the teaching of journalism; *Graduate Objectives or Program Emphases*: To meet needs of working professionals in mass media and to meet needs of teachers for advanced certification; *Bachelor's Degree Majors*: 200; *Master's Degree Majors*: 50; *Full-Time Faculty*: 6; *Part-Time Faculty*: 7; *Full-Time Professional (non-clerical) Staff Members*: 2.

FACILITIES AND SERVICES
Practical experiences available through: Associated Press Wire Service Feed; Closed Circuit Television Facility; Campus Newspaper (Published Independently); Desktop Publishing Facility; Photographic Darkrooms; Film or Cinema Laboratory; FM Radio Station (Institutional);

Institutional Magazine; Institutional Newspaper; Satellite Uplink Facility.

East Texas State University (Public)

Department of Communication and Theatre
ET Station
Commerce, Texas 75428
Telephone: (214) 886-5336

Gil Clardy, Head
Robert Houston, Dean

CURRICULUM AND INSTRUCTION
Courses or Concentrations
Available: Communication; Radio, Television, Broadcasting, or Telecommunications; Speech; *Bachelor's Degree Majors*: 150; *Master's Degree Majors*: 15; *Full-Time Faculty*: 7; *Part-Time Faculty*: 1; *Full-Time Professional (non-clerical) Staff Members*: 1.

FACILITIES AND SERVICES
Practical experiences available through: AM Radio Station (Institutional); Associated Press Wire Service Feed; Audio Recording Laboratory; Community Antenna (Cable) Television Origination; Closed Circuit Television Facility; Campus Newspaper (Published Independently); Video Editing; Electronic Field Production (Video); FM Radio Station (Institutional); ITFS Distribution System; Satellite Uplink Facility (C Band Transmitter); United Press International Feed; Video News and Data Processing; Video Production Laboratory or Television Studio.

Eastfield College

Communication Division
3737 Motley Drive
Mesquite, Texas 75150

Michael Burke, Administrator

El Paso Community College (Public)

Department of English/Mass Communication
P. O. Box 20500
El Paso, Texas 79998
Telephone: (915) 594-2000

Ted Johnston, Chair
Leila Macdonald, Dean, Arts and Sciences

CURRICULUM AND INSTRUCTION
Courses or Concentrations Available: Advertising; Journalism or Mass Communication; Public Relations; Radio, Television, Broadcasting, or Telecommunications; *Undergraduate Objectives or Program Emphases*: Journalism; Advertising and Public Relations; Broadcasting; *Associate's Degree Majors*: 120; *Full-Time Faculty*: 2; *Part-Time Faculty*: 4.

FACILITIES AND SERVICES
Practical experiences available through: Advertising Agency; Audio Recording Laboratory; Community Antenna (Cable) Television Origination; Carrier Current Audio Distribution System; Closed Circuit Television Facility; Local Commercial Newspaper; Local Commercial Television Station; Photographic Darkrooms; Video Editing; Electronic Field Production (Video); ITFS Distribution System; Institutional Newspaper; Public Relations Agency; Video Production Laboratory or Television Studio.

El Paso Community College (Public)

Division of Communications
P. O. Box 20500
El Paso, Texas 79998
Telephone: (915) 594-2296

Dennis E. Brown, Chair
Leila MacDonald, Dean, Arts and Sciences

CURRICULUM AND INSTRUCTION
Courses or Concentrations Available: Speech; Communication Disorders; *Undergraduate Objectives or Program Emphases*: Speech Communication emphasizes service to other degree programs; Associate of Arts degree program; Communication Disorders is an Associate of Science transfer degree

program; *Associate's Degree Majors*: 10; *Full-Time Faculty*: 7; *Part-Time Faculty*: 55.

FACILITIES AND SERVICES
Practical experiences available through: Audio Recording Laboratory; Video Production Laboratory or Television Studio.

Frank Phillips College (Private)

Department of Instructional Television
Box 5118
Borger, Texas 79008-5118
Telephone: (806) 274-5311

Bob E. Ramsey, Coordinator
Joe Kirkland, Dean of Instruction

CURRICULUM AND INSTRUCTION
Courses or Concentrations Available: Advertising; Communication; Journalism or Mass Communication; Radio, Television, Broadcasting, or Telecommunications; *Associate's Degree Majors*: 10; *Full-Time Faculty*: 1.

FACILITIES AND SERVICES
Practical experiences available through: Audio Recording Laboratory; Community Antenna (Cable) Television Origination; Closed Circuit Television Facility; Local Commercial Newspaper; Local Commercial Television Station; Desktop Publishing Facility; Photographic Darkrooms; Video Editing; Electronic Field Production (Video); Television Broadcast Station (Institutional); Video Production Laboratory or Television Studio.

Galveston College

TV/Radio Department
5001 Avenue U
Galveston, Texas 77550

William Pulido, Administrator

Hardin-Simmons University

Department of Communication
2200 Hickory Street
Abilene, Texas 79698

Rosanna Herndon, Administrator

Hill College

Department of Speech/Drama
Box 619
Hillsboro, Texas 76645

Jack W. Smith, Administrator

Houston Baptist University (Private)

Department of Communications
7502 Fondren Road
Houston, Texas 77074-3298
Telephone: (713) 774-7661 Extension: 2337

James S. Taylor, Chair
Calvin Huckabay, Dean, College of Humanities

CURRICULUM AND INSTRUCTION
Courses or Concentrations Available: Communication; Journalism or Mass Communication; Radio, Television, Broadcasting, or Telecommunications; Speech; Public Relations and Advertising are shared area with Business; *Bachelor's Degree Majors*: 130; *Full-Time Faculty*: 4; *Part-Time Faculty*: 5.

FACILITIES AND SERVICES
Practical experiences available through: Advertising Agency; Community Antenna (Cable) Television Origination; Campus Newspaper (Published Independently); Local Commercial Newspaper; Local Commercial Television Station; Desktop Publishing Facility; Photographic Darkrooms; Video Editing; Electronic Field Production (Video); ITFS Distribution System; Public Relations Agency; Video News and Data Processing; Video Production Laboratory or Television Studio.

Howard Payne University (Private)

Department of Communication
H. P. Station
Brownwood, Texas 76801
Telephone: (915) 646-2502

H. Neil St. Clair, Head
Geraldine Boyd, Administrator

CURRICULUM AND INSTRUCTION
*Courses or Concentrations
Available*: Communication; Journalism or
Mass Communication; Radio, Television,
Broadcasting, or Telecommunications;
Speech; *Program Coordinators*: Mark Baird
(Radio/Television); Steve Evans
(Journalism); Nancy Jo Humfeld (Speech);
*Undergraduate Objectives or Program
Emphases*: A composite degree which
includes radio-television/speech and
journalism which prepares students for a
career in communication or entry into a
graduate program; *Bachelor's Degree
Majors*: 10; *Full-Time Faculty*: 3; *Part-Time
Faculty*: 2.

FACILITIES AND SERVICES
Practical experiences available through: Audio
Recording Laboratory; Community Antenna
(Cable) Television Origination; Campus
Newspaper (Published Independently);
Local Commercial Newspaper; Photographic
Darkrooms; Video Editing; Television
Broadcast Station (Institutional);
Institutional Magazine; Institutional
Newspaper; Video Production Laboratory or
Television Studio.

Huston-Tillotson College (Private)

**Department of Mass Communication
1820 East Eighth Street
Austin, Texas 78702
Telephone: (512) 476-7421**

**Venise T. Berry, Head
Marvin Kimbrough, Chair, Division of
Humanities**

CURRICULUM AND INSTRUCTION
*Courses or Concentrations
Available*: Journalism or Mass
Communication; Radio, Television,
Broadcasting, or Telecommunications;
Speech; Dramatic Arts; *Bachelor's Degree
Majors*: 41; *Full-Time Faculty*: 2; *Part-Time
Faculty*: 4; *Full-Time Professional
(non-clerical) Staff Members*: 2.

FACILITIES AND SERVICES
Practical experiences available through: Audio
Recording Laboratory; Community Antenna
(Cable) Television Origination; Closed
Circuit Television Facility; Local
Commercial Newspaper; Local Commercial
Television Station; Desktop Publishing
Facility; Photographic Darkrooms;

Electronic Field Production (Video);
Television Broadcast Station (Institutional);
ITFS Distribution System; Institutional
Magazine.

Incarnate Word College (Private)

**Program of Communication Arts
4301 Broadway
San Antonio, Texas 78209
Telephone: (512) 828-1261**

**Sean Douglas Cassidy, Director
Mary Beth Swofford, Administrator**

CURRICULUM AND INSTRUCTION
*Courses or Concentrations
Available*: Advertising; Communication; Film
or Cinema; Journalism or Mass
Communication; Public Relations; Radio,
Television, Broadcasting, or
Telecommunications; *Undergraduate
Objectives or Program Emphases*: The BA is
designed to provide students with an
understanding of the role communication
plays in their lives. This includes technical,
theoretical, and aesthetic perspectives on the
field of communications; *Graduate Objectives
or Program Emphases*: MA is designed to
provide a foundation for students and
professionals preparing for a lifetime career
in the communication field; *Bachelor's Degree
Majors*: 80; *Master's Degree Majors*: 20;
Full-Time Faculty: 1; *Part-Time Faculty*: 12.

FACILITIES AND SERVICES
*Practical experiences available
through*: Advertising Agency; Audio
Recording Laboratory; Community Antenna
(Cable) Television Origination; Local
Commercial Newspaper; Local Commercial
Television Station; Photographic
Darkrooms; Video Editing; Electronic Field
Production (Video); Institutional
Newspaper; Public Relations Agency; Video
Production Laboratory or Television Studio.

Lamar University

**Communication Department
P. O. Box 10050
Beaumont, Texas 77710**

John P. Johnson, Administrator

McLennan Community College (Public)

Program of Journalism
1400 College Drive
Waco, Texas 76708
Telephone: (817) 750-3517

Thomas A. Buckner, Director
Lissette Carpenter, Chair, Language Arts Division

CURRICULUM AND INSTRUCTION
Courses or Concentrations
Available: Journalism or Mass
Communication; *Program Coordinator*: Ann
Harrell (Speech); *Undergraduate Objectives
or Program Emphases*: Freshman,
Sophomore level courses; *Associate's Degree
Majors*: 27; *Full-Time Faculty*: 1.

FACILITIES AND SERVICES
*Practical experiences available
through*: Desktop Publishing Facility;
Photographic Darkrooms; Institutional
Newspaper.

McMurry College (Private)

Department of Communication and Theatre
1400 Sayles Boulevard
Abilene, Texas 79697
Telephone: (915) 691-6295

Carrol Haggard, Chair
Paul Jungmeyer, Vice President, Academic
Affairs

CURRICULUM AND INSTRUCTION
Courses or Concentrations
Available: Communication; Film or Cinema;
Public Relations; Speech; *Program
Coordinator*: Marion Castleberry (Cinema);
*Undergraduate Objectives or Program
Emphases*: To provide a broad based liberal
arts background in the areas of Human
Communication, Public Relations, and
Cinema Studies; *Bachelor's Degree
Majors*: 25; *Full-Time Faculty*: 5; *Part-Time
Faculty*: 1.

FACILITIES AND SERVICES
*Practical experiences available
through*: Advertising Agency; Campus
Newspaper (Published Independently);
Local Commercial Television Station; Film
or Cinema Laboratory; Institutional
Magazine; Institutional Newspaper.

Midwestern State University (Public)

Program of Mass Communications
3400 Taft Boulevard
Wichita Falls, Texas 76308
Telephone: (817) 692-6611

Carla P. Bennett, Coordinator
June Kable, Division Director

CURRICULUM AND INSTRUCTION
Courses or Concentrations
Available: Advertising; Communication; Film
or Cinema; Journalism or Mass
Communication; Public Relations; Radio,
Television, Broadcasting, or
Telecommunications; Speech; *Program
Coordinators*: Mitchell Land (Journalism);
*Undergraduate Objectives or Program
Emphases*: Educate undergraduates in
several areas of mass media, including
broadcast, print, and related fields;
Bachelor's Degree Majors: 90; *Full-Time
Faculty*: 5; *Part-Time Faculty*: 2; *Full-Time
Professional (non-clerical) Staff Members*: 1.

FACILITIES AND SERVICES
*Practical experiences available
through*: Advertising Agency; Community
Antenna (Cable) Television Origination;
Closed Circuit Television Facility; Local
Commercial Newspaper; Local Commercial
Television Station; Desktop Publishing
Facility; Photographic Darkrooms; Video
Editing; Electronic Field Production
(Video); Television Broadcast Station
(Institutional); Institutional Newspaper;
Public Relations Agency; Video Production
Laboratory or Television Studio.

Navarro College

Radio/Television
3200 West 7th Avenue
Corsicana, Texas 75110

Danita McAnally, Administrator

Prairie View A and M University (Public)

Department of Communications
P. O. Box 156
Prairie View, Texas 77446-0156
Telephone: (409) 857-2229

Millard F. Eiland, Head
Edward Martin, Dean, College of Arts and Sciences

CURRICULUM AND INSTRUCTION
Courses or Concentrations
Available: Advertising; Communication; Journalism or Mass Communication; Public Relations; Radio, Television, Broadcasting, or Telecommunications; Speech; *Bachelor's Degree Majors*: 200; *Full-Time Faculty*: 6; *Full-Time Professional (non-clerical) Staff Members*: 4.

FACILITIES AND SERVICES
Practical experiences available
through: Associated Press Wire Service Feed; Audio Recording Laboratory; Campus Newspaper (Published Independently); Local Commercial Newspaper; Local Commercial Television Station; Desktop Publishing Facility; Photographic Darkrooms; Video Editing; FM Radio Station (Institutional); Video Production Laboratory or Television Studio.

Ranger Junior College (Public)

Department of Communicative Arts
College Circle
Ranger, Texas 74670
Telephone: (817) 647-3234

Betty E. Parmele, Chair
John Gresham, Chair, Humanities

CURRICULUM AND INSTRUCTION
Courses or Concentrations
Available: Journalism or Mass Communication; Speech; *Undergraduate Objectives or Program Emphases*: To provide experience in extemporaneous public speaking and listener analysis. In Journalism, to provide experience in news gathering and preparation, and to better understand the mass media; *Associate's Degree Majors*: 5; *Full-Time Faculty*: 1.

FACILITIES AND SERVICES
Practical experiences available
through: Photographic Darkrooms; Institutional Newspaper.

Saint Mary's University (Private)

Program of English Communications Arts
One Camino Santa Maria
San Antonio, Texas 78228-8535
Telephone: (512) 436-3107

Christine R. Catron, Director
Ann Semel, Administrator

CURRICULUM AND INSTRUCTION
Courses or Concentrations
Available: Advertising; Communication; Film or Cinema; Journalism or Mass Communication; Public Relations; Radio, Television, Broadcasting, or Telecommunications; Speech; Photography; Photojournalism; Free Lance Writing; *Program Coordinator*: Alan Cirlin (Speech); *Undergraduate Objectives or Program Emphases*: Courses in Liberal Arts, writing, business and speech with career-oriented courses in communication to provide students with critical thinking ability and practical skills needed for careers in communication; *Graduate Objectives or Program Emphases*: Same as above with emphasis on theory and skill development of communication and production techniques; *Bachelor's Degree Majors*: 80; *Master's Degree Majors*: 25; *Full-Time Faculty*: 13; *Part-Time Faculty*: 4; *Full-Time Professional (non-clerical) Staff Members*: 4.

FACILITIES AND SERVICES
Practical experiences available
through: Advertising Agency; Audio Recording Laboratory; Community Antenna (Cable) Television Origination; Campus Newspaper (Published Independently); Local Commercial Newspaper; Local Commercial Television Station; Photographic Darkrooms; Video Editing; Electronic Field Production (Video); Television Broadcast Station (Institutional); Institutional Newspaper; Public Relations Agency.

Sam Houston State University (Public)

Division of Public Communication
Box 2207
Huntsville, Texas 77341
Telephone: (409) 294-1340

Robert E. Eubanks, Chair
Richard Cording, Dean, College of Arts and Sciences

CURRICULUM AND INSTRUCTION
Courses or Concentrations Available: Advertising; Communication; Film or Cinema; Journalism or Mass Communication; Public Relations; Radio, Television, Broadcasting, or Telecommunications; Speech; *Undergraduate Objectives or Program Emphases*: Radio-Television-Film with concentrations in Advertising, Broadcast Journalism, Marketing and Management, Production, and Public Relations. Journalism with emphasis in Advertising and general print Journalism. Speech Communication with emphasis in Education and Organizational Communication; *Bachelor's Degree Majors*: 115; *BFA Degree Majors*: 275; *Full-Time Faculty*: 15; *Part-Time Faculty*: 4; *Full-Time Professional (non-clerical) Staff Members*: 1.

FACILITIES AND SERVICES
Practical experiences available through: Advertising Agency; Associated Press Wire Service Feed; Audio Recording Laboratory; Community Antenna (Cable) Television Origination; Closed Circuit Television Facility; Desktop Publishing Facility; Photographic Darkrooms; Video Editing; Electronic Field Production (Video); Film or Cinema Laboratory; FM Radio Station (Institutional); Institutional Magazine; Institutional Newspaper; Public Relations Agency; Video News and Data Processing; Video Production Laboratory or Television Studio.

San Antonio College (Public)

Department of Radio-Television-Film
1300 San Pedro Avenue
San Antonio, Texas 78284
Telephone: (512) 733-2793

Fredric A. Weiss, Chair
Homer Hayes, Dean

CURRICULUM AND INSTRUCTION
Courses or Concentrations Available: Radio, Television, Film; *Undergraduate Objectives or Program Emphases*: AA degree for transfer to four year institution. AAS professional preparation for careers in Radio-Television-Film and related areas; *Associate's Degree Majors*: 56; *Other Degree Majors*: 300; *Full-Time Faculty*: 5; *Part-Time Faculty*: 10; *Full-Time Professional (non-clerical) Staff Members*: 3.

FACILITIES AND SERVICES
Practical experiences available through: Audio Recording Laboratory; Community Antenna (Cable) Television Origination; Closed Circuit Television Facility; Campus Newspaper (Published Independently); Local Commercial Television; Video Editing; Electronic Field Production (Video); FM Radio Station (Institutional); Public Relations Agency; Video Production Laboratory or Television Studio.

San Antonio College (Public)

Department of Visual Arts and Technology
1300 San Pedro
San Antonio, Texas 78284
Telephone: (512) 733-2894

Tom Willme, Chair
Lewis Goerner, Dean, Arts and Science

CURRICULUM AND INSTRUCTION
Courses or Concentrations Available: Advertising; Communication; Speech; Visual Arts, Electronic Graphics, Production Pottery, Jewelry Repair/Design, Art History; *Undergraduate Objectives or Program Emphases*: AA/AAS degree programs in Art; preparation for BFA-MFA; transfer; Occupational Training in Advertising Art, Electronic Graphics, Jewelry Repair, Production Pottery; *Associate's Degree Majors*: 450; *Full-Time Faculty*: 15; *Part-Time Faculty*: 13; *Full-Time Professional (non-clerical) Staff Members*: 4.

FACILITIES AND SERVICES
Practical experiences available through: Advertising Agency; AM Radio Station (Institutional); Audio Recording Laboratory; Community Antenna (Cable) Television Origination; Closed Circuit Television Facility; Campus Newspaper (Published Independently); Local Commercial Newspaper; Local Commercial

Television Station; Desktop Publishing Facility; Photographic Darkrooms; Video Editing; Electronic Field Production (Video); Television Broadcast Station (Institutional); Film and Cinema Laboratory; FM Radio Station (Institutional); ITFS Distribution System; Institutional Magazine; Institutional Newspaper; New York Times Service Feed.

San Antonio College (Public)

Department of Journalism/Photography
1300 San Pedro
San Antonio, Texas 78284
Telephone: (512) 733-2870

W. B. Daugherty, Chair

CURRICULUM AND INSTRUCTION
Courses or Concentrations
Available: Advertising; Communication; Journalism or Mass Communication; Public Relations; Desk Top Publishing;
Undergraduate Objectives or Program Emphases: To provide basic training in print journalism (photography, reporting, editing); *Associate's Degree Majors*: 25; *Full-Time Faculty*: 6; *Part-Time Faculty*: 2; *Full-Time Professional (non-clerical) Staff Members*: 3.

FACILITIES AND SERVICES
Practical experiences available through: Advertising Agency; Desktop Publishing Facility; Photographic Darkrooms; Institutional Magazine; Institutional Newspaper; Public Relations Agency.

San Jacinto College North (Public)

Division of Fine Arts and Communications
5800 Uvalde
Houston, Texas 77049
Telephone: (713) 458-4050

Timothy W. Fleming, Chair
Everett Schmidt, Academic Dean

CURRICULUM AND INSTRUCTION
Courses or Concentrations
Available: Advertising; Journalism or Mass Communication; Speech; *Program Coordinators*: Royce Ann Walker (Journalism); Daryll N. Vitaska (Speech);

Undergraduate Objectives or Program Emphases: Prepare students to possess academic skills to transfer to senior institutions; provide courses which support general education component of curricula outside the division; serve as information resource for the community; *Associate's Degree Majors*: 94; *Full-Time Faculty*: 8; *Part-Time Faculty*: 9.

FACILITIES AND SERVICES
Practical experiences available through: Desktop Publishing Facility; Photographic Darkrooms; Institutional Newspaper.

South Plains College

Department of Telecommunication
1401 College Avenue
Levelland, Texas 79336

John Sparks, Administrator

Southern Methodist University

Center for Communication Arts
P. O. Box 296
Dallas, Texas 75275

Lynn Gartley, Administrator

Southwest Texas State University (Public)

Department of Journalism
San Marcos, Texas 78666-4616
Telephone: (512) 245-2656

Roger Bennett, Chair
Richard Cheatham, Dean

CURRICULUM AND INSTRUCTION
Courses or Concentrations
Available: Advertising; Communication; Journalism or Mass Communication; Public Relations; Radio, Television, Broadcasting, or Telecommunications; Agriculture Journalism; *Program Coordinators*: Mike McBride (Advertising); Bob Shrader (Broadcasting); Paula Renfro (Magazine); Dave Nelson (News-Editorial); Carolyn Cline (Public Relations); *Bachelor's Degree*

Majors: 426; *Full-Time Faculty*: 16; *Part-Time Faculty*: 5.

FACILITIES AND SERVICES
Practical experiences available through: Advertising Agency; Associated Press Wire Service Feed; Audio Recording Laboratory; Community Antenna (Cable) Television Origination; Carrier Current Audio Distribution System; Closed Circuit Television Facility; Campus Newspaper (Published Independently); Local Commercial Newspaper; Local Commercial Television Station; Desktop Publishing Facility; Photographic Darkrooms; Video Editing; Electronic Field Production (Video); FM Radio Station (Institutional); Institutional Magazine; Public Relations Agency; Video News and Data Processing; Video Production Laboratory or Television Studio.

Southwest Texas State University (Public)

Department of Speech Communication
San Marcos, Texas 78666
Telephone: (512) 245-2165

Steven A. Beebe, Chair
T. Richard Cheatham, Dean

CURRICULUM AND INSTRUCTION
Courses or Concentrations Available: Communication; Speech; *Undergraduate Objectives or Program Emphases*: Organizational Communication; Public Communication; Communication Education; General Speech Communication; *Graduate Objectives or Program Emphases*: Organizational Communication; Public Communication; Communication Education; General Speech Communication; *Bachelor's Degree Majors*: 275; *Master's Degree Majors*: 25; *Full-Time Faculty*: 15; *Part-Time Faculty*: 7; *Full-Time Professional (non-clerical) Staff Members*: 2.

FACILITIES AND SERVICES
Practical experiences available through: Audio Recording Laboratory; Campus Newspaper (Published Independently); Desktop Publishing Facility.

Southwestern Adventist College (Private)

Department of Communication
Keene, Texas 76059
Telephone: (817) 645-3921 Extension: 731

Robert R. Mendenhall, Chair
Herbert Roth, Administrator

CURRICULUM AND INSTRUCTION
Courses or Concentrations Available: Advertising; Communication; Film or Cinema; Journalism or Mass Communication; Public Relations; Radio, Television, Broadcasting, or Telecommunications; Speech; Photography; *Undergraduate Objectives or Program Emphases*: To develop in students both theoretical understanding and practical skills in communication in order to equip them to become communication professionals at all levels; *Bachelor's Degree Majors*: 5; *Other Degree Majors*: 20; *Full-Time Faculty*: 3; *Part-Time Faculty*: 1.

FACILITIES AND SERVICES
Practical experiences available through: Advertising Agency; Associated Press Wire Service Feed; Audio Recording Laboratory; Community Antenna (Cable) Television Origination; Campus Newspaper (Published Independently); Local Commercial Newspaper; Local Commercial Television Station; Desktop Publishing Facility; Photographic Darkrooms; Video Editing; Electronic Field Production (Video); FM Radio Station (Institutional); Institutional Magazine; Video Production Laboratory or Television Studio.

Southwestern Baptist Theological Seminary (Private)

Department of Communication Center
P. O. Box 22000
Fort Worth, Texas 76133
Telephone: (817) 923-1921 Extension: 6220

Darrell Baergen, Chair
Jack Terry, Dean

CURRICULUM AND INSTRUCTION
Courses or Concentrations Available: Advertising; Communication; Journalism or Mass Communication; Public Relations; Radio, Television, Broadcasting, or Telecommunications; Speech; *Graduate*

Objectives or Program Emphases: Train ministers to use media in a variety of church related activities; *Full-Time Faculty*: 2; *Part-Time Faculty*: 8; *Full-Time Professional (non-clerical) Staff Members*: 2.

FACILITIES AND SERVICES
Practical experiences available through: Audio Recording Laboratory; Community Antenna (Cable) Television Origination; Closed Circuit Television Facility; Local Commercial Newspaper; Video Editing; Electronic Field Production (Video); Institutional Newspaper; Public Relations Agency; Video Production Laboratory or Television Studio.

St. Philips College

Fine Arts, Foreign Language and Speech Department
2111 Nevada Street
San Antonio, Texas 78203

Audrey Mosley, Administrator

Stephen F. Austin State University

Department of Communication
Box 13048
Nacogdoches, Texas 75962

Heber Taylor, Administrator

Sul Ross State University (Public)

Department of Communication and Theatre
Box 43
Alpine, Texas 79832
Telephone: (915) 837-8218

George Bradley, Chair
Nelson Sager, Dean, Arts and Sciences

CURRICULUM AND INSTRUCTION
Courses or Concentrations Available: Communication; Journalism or Mass Communication; Public Relations; Radio, Television, Broadcasting, or Telecommunications; Speech; *Undergraduate Objectives or Program Emphases*: To provide communication skills and knowledge for life

and employment; *Bachelor's Degree Majors*: 30; *Full-Time Faculty*: 3.

FACILITIES AND SERVICES
Practical experiences available through: Audio Recording Laboratory; Community Antenna (Cable) Television Origination; Closed Circuit Television Facility; Campus Newspaper (Published Independently); Photographic Darkrooms; Video Editing; Electronic Field Production (Video); Institutional Magazine; Institutional Newspaper; Video Production Laboratory or Television Studio.

Tarrant County Junior College - Northeast (Public)

Program of Media Communication
828 Harwood Road
Hurst, Texas 76054
Telephone: (817) 281-7860

Lawrence W. Baker, Jr., Coordinator
Cordell Parker, Chair, Communication Arts Department

CURRICULUM AND INSTRUCTION
Courses or Concentrations Available: Communication; Film or Cinema; Journalism or Mass Communication; Radio, Television, Broadcasting, or Telecommunications; Speech; *Program Coordinator*: Cordell Parker (Communication Arts); *Undergraduate Objectives or Program Emphases*: Emphasis upon all aspects of producing for electronic media. Training in use of video and audio equipment; design and composition; art and computer graphic, photographic production; producing/directing television; scriptwriting; audio and video production; *Associate's Degree Majors*: 60; *Full-Time Faculty*: 1; *Part-Time Faculty*: 5; *Full-Time Professional (non-clerical) Staff Members*: 1.

FACILITIES AND SERVICES
Practical experiences available through: Audio Recording Laboratory; Community Antenna (Cable) Television Origination; Closed Circuit Television Facility; Local Commercial Television Station; Photographic Darkrooms; Video Editing; Electronic Field Production (Video); Television Broadcast Station (Institutional); Film or Cinema Laboratory; ITFS Distribution System; Video Production Laboratory or Television Studio.

Texas A and I University

Radio/Television Department
Campus Box 178
Kingsville, Texas 78363

James S. McElhaney, Administrator

Texas A and I University

Department of Communications and
Theatre
Kingsville, Texas 78363

Donna R. Tobias, Administrator

Texas A and M University
(Public)

Department of Speech Communication and
Theatre Arts
College Station, Texas 77843-4234
Telephone: (409) 845-5500

Robert L. Ivie, Head
Daniel Fallon, Dean, College of Liberal Arts

CURRICULUM AND INSTRUCTION
Courses or Concentrations
Available: Communication; Speech; Theatre
Arts; Rhetoric; Public Address;
*Undergraduate Objectives or Program
Emphases*: A rounded curriculum in speech
communication, requiring a combination of
performance and theory courses in rhetoric
and communication and offering a number of
additional courses in organizational, political,
and technical communication; *Graduate
Objectives or Program Emphases*: New MA
will offer a research-oriented program
focusing on message analysis in various
contexts; *Bachelor's Degree Majors*: 500;
Full-Time Faculty: 16; *Part-Time Faculty*: 1.

FACILITIES AND SERVICES
Practical experiences available through: AM
Radio Station (Institutional); Community
Antenna (Cable) Television Origination;
Closed Circuit Television Facility; Campus
Newspaper (Published Independently);
Local Commercial Television Station;
Electronic Field Production (Video);
Television Broadcast Station (Institutional);
Film or Cinema Laboratory; FM Radio
Station (Institutional); Public Relations
Agency.

Texas A and M University
(Public)

Department of Journalism
College Station, Texas 77843-4111
Telephone: (409) 845-4611

Robert G. Rogers, Head
Daniel Fallon, Dean, College of Liberal Arts

CURRICULUM AND INSTRUCTION
*Courses or Concentrations
Available*: Advertising; Journalism or Mass
Communication; Public Relations; Radio,
Television, Broadcasting, or
Telecommunications; *Undergraduate
Objectives or Program Emphases*: To deliver a
program of professional education in
journalism and related areas in the context of
a broad liberal arts and sciences degree
program; *Bachelor's Degree Majors*: 495;
Full-Time Faculty: 16; *Part-Time Faculty*: 5;
*Full-Time Professional (non-clerical) Staff
Members*: 1.

FACILITIES AND SERVICES
*Practical experiences available
through*: Associated Press Wire Service Feed;
Audio Recording Laboratory; Community
Antenna (Cable) Television Origination;
Campus Newspaper (Published
Independently); Local Commercial
Newspaper; Local Commercial Television
Station; Desktop Publishing Facility;
Photographic Darkrooms; Video Editing;
Electronic Field Production (Video);
Television Broadcast Station (Institutional);
FM Radio Station (Institutional); Video
News and Data Processing.

Texas Christian University
(Private)

Department of Radio-Television-Film
Box 30793
Fort Worth, Texas 76129
Telephone: (817) 921-7630

R. Terry Ellmore, Chair
Robert Garwell, Dean

CURRICULUM AND INSTRUCTION
Courses or Concentrations Available: Film or
Cinema; Radio, Television, Broadcasting, or
Telecommunications; *Undergraduate
Objectives or Program Emphases*: Production,
management, film studies, performance,
broadcast journalism; *Bachelor's Degree*

Majors: 250; *Other Degree Majors*: 7;
Full-Time Faculty: 7; *Part-Time Faculty*: 1;
*Full-Time Professional (non-clerical) Staff
Members*: 2.

FACILITIES AND SERVICES
*Practical experiences available
through*: Associated Press Wire Service Feed;
Audio Recording Laboratory; Community
Antenna (Cable) Television Origination;
Local Commercial Television Station; Video
Editing; Electronic Field Production
(Video); Film or Cinema Laboratory; FM
Radio Station (Institutional); Video
Production Laboratory or Television Studio.

Texas Christian University (Private)

Department of Journalism
P. O. Box 32939
Fort Worth, Texas 76129
Telephone: (817) 921-7425

Anantha S. Babbili, Chair
Robert Garwell, Dean

CURRICULUM AND INSTRUCTION
*Courses or Concentrations
Available*: Advertising; Journalism or Mass
Communication; Broadcast Journalism;
Program Coordinator: David Barker
(Radio-Television-Film and advisor to
graduate students); *Undergraduate Objectives
or Program Emphases*: To develop skilled
professional communicators who understand
their social, legal, ethical responsibilities;
have a keen sense of career opportunities.
Accredited journalism program which
emphasizes liberal arts education,
professional competence, personal
awareness; *Graduate Objectives or Program
Emphases*: Graduate degree in Media
Studies offered in collaboration with TCU's
Radio-Television-Film Department.
Emphasizes critical/cultural studies approach
and a progressive approach to the study of
film, television and print media; *Bachelor's
Degree Majors*: 173; *Master's Degree
Majors*: 6; *Full-Time Faculty*: 8; *Part-Time
Faculty*: 15; *Full-Time Professional
(non-clerical) Staff Members*: 1.

FACILITIES AND SERVICES
*Practical experiences available
through*: Advertising Agency; Associated
Press Wire Service Feed; Community
Antenna (Cable) Television Origination;

Local Commercial Newspaper; Desktop
Publishing Facility; Photographic
Darkrooms; Video Editing; Electronic Field
Production (Video); Television Broadcast
Station (Institutional); FM Radio Station
(Institutional); Institutional Newspaper;
Public Relations Agency.

Texas Lutheran College (Private)

Department of Communication Arts
1000 West Court Street
Seguin, Texas 78155
Telephone: (512) 379-4161

Daniel R. Mathis, Chair

CURRICULUM AND INSTRUCTION
*Courses or Concentrations
Available*: Communication; Journalism or
Mass Communication; Public Relations;
Radio, Television, Broadcasting, or
Telecommunications; Speech; Theatre;
*Undergraduate Objectives or Program
Emphases*: Local, national, and international
internships in journalism; theatre productions
and two theaters; forensic activities;
Bachelor's Degree Majors: 88; *Full-Time
Faculty*: 3; *Part-Time Faculty*: 1.

FACILITIES AND SERVICES
*Practical experiences available
through*: Advertising Agency; AM Radio
Station (Institutional); Campus Newspaper
(Published Independently); Local
Commercial Newspaper; Local Commercial
Television Station; Desktop Publishing
Facility; Photographic Darkrooms;
Institutional Magazine; Institutional
Newspaper.

Texas Southern University (Public)

School of Communications
3100 Cleburne Avenue
Houston, Texas 77004
Telephone: (713) 527-7360

Clarice P. Lowe, Head
**Bobby Wilson, Dean, College of Arts and
Sciences**

CURRICULUM AND INSTRUCTION
*Courses or Concentrations
Available*: Advertising; Communication; Film

or Cinema; Journalism or Mass Communication; Public Relations; Radio, Television, Broadcasting or Telecommunications; Speech; Broadcast Journalism; Communication Disorders; *Undergraduate Objectives or Program Emphases*: Majors are offered in Communicative Disorders, Journalism (with concentrations in News/Editorial, Advertising and Public Relations, and Broadcast News), Speech Communication, Telecommunications, and Theatre/Cinema; *Bachelor's Degree Majors*: 167; *BFA Degree Majors:* 2; *Master's Degree Majors*: 36; *Full-Time Faculty*: 17; *Part-Time Faculty*: 10; *Full-Time Professional (non-clerical) Staff Members*: 3.

FACILITIES AND SERVICES
Practical experiences available through: Advertising Agency; Closed Circuit TV Facility; Campus Newspaper (Published Independently); Local Commercial Newspaper; Local Commercial Television Station; Desktop Publishing Facility; Photographic Darkrooms; Video Editing; Electronic Field Production; FM Radio Station (Institutional); Institutional Newspaper; Video News and Data Processing; Video Production Laboratory or Television Studio.

Texas Tech University (Public)

School of Mass Communication
Box 4710
Lubbock, Texas 79409-3082
Telephone: (806) 742-3385

Jerry C. Hudson, Director
Joe R. Goodin, Dean, College of Arts and Sciences

CURRICULUM AND INSTRUCTION
Courses or Concentrations Available: Advertising; Journalism or Mass Communication; Public Relations; Radio, Television, Broadcasting, or Telecommunications; Photo communications; *Program Coordinators*: Tommy Smith (Advertising); Roger Saathoff (Journalism); Dennis A. Harp (Telecommunication); *Undergraduate Objectives or Program Emphases*: To graduate students who are well rounded, and who have the knowledge and skills to serve the professional areas of their disciplines; *Bachelor's Degree Majors*: 512; *Master's*

Degree Majors: 36; *Full-Time Faculty*: 17; *Part-Time Faculty*: 18; *Full-Time Professional (non-clerical) Staff Members*: 2.

FACILITIES AND SERVICES
Practical experiences available through: Advertising Agency; Audio Recording Laboratory; Closed Circuit Television Facility; Campus Newspaper (Published Independently); Local Commercial Newspaper; Local Commercial Television Station; Desktop Publishing Facility; Video Editing; Electronic Field Production (Video); FM Radio Station (Institutional); Institutional Magazine; Institutional Newspaper; Public Relations Agency; Video Production Laboratory or Television Studio.

Texas Tech University (Public)

Department of Theatre Arts
Box 4298
Lubbock, Texas 79409
Telephone: (806) 742-3601

Richard A. Weaver, Chair
Joe R. Goodin, Dean, College of Arts and Sciences

CURRICULUM AND INSTRUCTION
Courses or Concentrations Available: Advertising; Film or Cinema; Radio, Television, Broadcasting, or Telecommunications; Theatre.

Texas Tech University (Public)

Department of Speech Communication
P. O. Box 4209
Lubbock, Texas 79409
Telephone: (806) 742-3911

Dan O'Hair, Chair
Joe R. Goodin, Dean, College of Arts and Sciences

CURRICULUM AND INSTRUCTION
Courses or Concentrations Available: Communication; Speech; *Undergraduate Objectives or Program Emphases*: Interpersonal, organizational, rhetoric, cross-cultural, instructional communication; *Graduate Objectives or Program Emphases*: Interpersonal, organizational, rhetoric, cross-cultural,

instructional communication; *Bachelor's Degree Majors*: 80; *Master's Degree Majors*: 12; *Full-Time Faculty*: 7; *Part-Time Faculty*: 9.

FACILITIES AND SERVICES
Practical experiences available through: Closed Circuit Television Facility; Campus Newspaper (Published Independently); Desktop Publishing Facility.

Texas Wesleyan University (Private)

Department of Mass Communication
1201 Wesleyan Street
Fort Worth, Texas 76105
Telephone: (817) 531-4928

Michael Sewell, Chair
Norval Kneten, Interim Dean

CURRICULUM AND INSTRUCTION
Courses or Concentrations Available: Advertising; Journalism or Mass Communication; Public Relations; Radio, Television, Broadcasting, or Telecommunications; *Undergraduate Objectives or Program Emphases*: Advertising, Public Relations Emphasis, Journalism, Radio-Television; *Degree Majors*: 53; *Full-Time Faculty*: 3; *Part-Time Faculty*: 2.

FACILITIES AND SERVICES
Practical experiences available through: Audio Recording Laboratory; Community Antenna (Cable) Television Origination; Campus Newspaper (Published Independently); Local Commercial Newspaper; Local Commercial Television Station; Desktop Publishing Facility; Photographic Darkrooms; Video Editing.

Texas Woman's University (Public)

Program of Mass Communications
P. O. Box 23866
Denton, Texas 76204
Telephone: (817) 898-2181

Mary K. Sparks, Director
Brooke Sheldon, Dean

CURRICULUM AND INSTRUCTION
Courses or Concentrations Available: Advertising; Journalism or Mass Communication; Public Relations; Radio, Television, Broadcasting, or Telecommunications; *Bachelor's Degree Majors*: 100; *Full-Time Faculty*: 3; *Part-Time Faculty*: 3; *Full-Time Professional (non-clerical) Staff Members*: 1.

FACILITIES AND SERVICES
Practical experiences available through: Associated Press Wire Service Feed; Audio Recording Laboratory; Community Antenna (Cable) Television Origination; Campus Newspaper (Published Independently); Desktop Publishing Facility; Photographic Darkrooms; Video Editing; Video Production Laboratory or Television Studio.

Trinity University (Private)

Department of Communication
715 Stadium Drive
San Antonio, Texas 78212
Telephone: (512) 736-8113

Robert O. Blanchard, Chair
William Walker, Jr., Dean

CURRICULUM AND INSTRUCTION
Courses or Concentrations Available: Communication; *Undergraduate Objectives or Program Emphases*: Integrative, foundational communication media program (professional and theory); *Bachelor's Degree Majors*: 95; *Full-Time Faculty*: 8; *Full-Time Professional (non-clerical) Staff Members*: 3.

FACILITIES AND SERVICES
Practical experiences available through: Advertising Agency; Associated Press Wire Service Feed; Audio Recording Laboratory; Community Antenna (Cable) Television Origination; Closed Circuit Television Facility; Campus Newspaper (Published Independently); Desktop Publishing Facility; Photographic Darkrooms; Video Editing; Electronic Field Production (Video); FM Radio Station (Institutional); Institutional Magazine; Institutional Newspaper; Public Relations Agency; Video News and Data Processing; Video Production Laboratory or Television Studio.

Trinity University (Private)

Department of Speech and Drama
715 Stadium Drive
San Antonio, Texas 78212
Telephone: (512) 736-8511

L. Brooks Hill, Chair
William Walker, Jr., Dean

CURRICULUM AND INSTRUCTION
Courses or Concentrations
Available: Communication; Speech;
Undergraduate Objectives or Program
Emphases: To use speech communication as
a basis for a liberal arts and sciences
education; to prepare students for graduate
work in communication; and to prepare
students for careers in communication
related professions; *Bachelor's Degree*
Majors: 10; *Full-Time Faculty*: 8; *Full-Time*
Professional (non-clerical) Staff Members: 2.

Trinity Valley Community College (Public)

Division of Fine Arts
500 S. Prairieville
Athens, Texas 75751
Telephone: (214) 675-6371

Ray G. Williams, Dean
Jan Huffstutler, Administrator

CURRICULUM AND INSTRUCTION
Courses or Concentrations
Available: Communication; Journalism or
Mass Communication; Speech;
Undergraduate Objectives or Program
Emphases: To provide lower level fine arts
classes which freely transfer to four year
institutions and which provide the foundation
for the completion of more advanced
coursework; *Associate's Degree Majors*: 62;
Full-Time Faculty: 9; *Part-Time Faculty*: 6.

FACILITIES AND SERVICES
Practical experiences available
through: Advertising Agency; Campus
Newspaper (Published Independently);
Local Commercial Newspaper; Photographic
Darkrooms; Video Editing; Institutional
Newspaper.

University of Houston (Public)

Department of Radio-Television
School of Communication
Houston, Texas 77204-4062

Robert Musburger, Administrator

University of Houston (Public)

School of Communication
Houston, Texas 77204-3786
Telephone: (713) 749-7444

Raymond Fielding, Director
James Pickering, Dean

CURRICULUM AND INSTRUCTION
Courses or Concentrations
Available: Advertising; Communication; Film
or Cinema; Journalism or Mass
Communication; Public Relations; Radio,
Television, Broadcasting, or
Telecommunications; Speech;
Communication Disorders; *Program*
Coordinators: Robert Musberger
(Radio-Television-Film); Ted Stanton
(Journalism, Advertising, Public Relations);
William Douglas (Speech Communication);
Martin Adams (Communication Disorders);
Undergraduate Objectives or Program
Emphases: Liberal Arts education;
pre-professional educational specializations
in the School's programs; *Graduate*
Objectives or Program
Emphases: Pre-doctoral education;
professional education for careers in the
communication or public service fields;
Bachelor's Degree Majors: 1035; *Master's*
Degree Majors: 86; *Full-Time Faculty*: 29;
Part-Time Faculty: 20; *Full-Time*
Professional (non-clerical) Staff Members: 5.

FACILITIES AND SERVICES
Practical experiences available
through: Advertising Agency; Associated
Press Wire Service Feed; Audio Recording
Laboratory; Community Antenna (Cable)
Television Origination; Campus Newspaper
(Published Independently); Local
Commercial Newspaper; Local Commercial
Television Station; Desktop Publishing
Facility; Photographic Darkrooms; Video
Editing; Electronic Field Production
(Video); Television Broadcast Station
(Institutional); Film or Cinema Laboratory;
FM Radio Station (Institutional); Public
Relations Agency; Video News and Data

Processing; Video Production Laboratory or Television Studio.

University of Houston - Downtown (Public)

College of Humanities and Social Sciences
1 Main Street
Houston, Texas 77002
Telephone: (713) 221-8009

Michael R. Dressman, Dean
Manuel Pacheco, President

CURRICULUM AND INSTRUCTION
Courses or Concentrations
Available: Advertising; Journalism or Mass Communication; Public Relations; Speech; Writing for Special Purposes; Technical Writing; *Program Coordinator*: Barbara Bartholomew (English); *Undergraduate Objectives or Program Emphases*: BS in professional writing includes all communication areas offered; *Bachelor's Degree Majors*: 120; *Full-Time Faculty*: 42; *Part-Time Faculty*: 135.

FACILITIES AND SERVICES
Practical experiences available through: Advertising Agency; Campus Newspaper (Published Independently); Local Commercial Newspaper; Local Commercial Television Station; Desktop Publishing Facility; Photographic Darkrooms; Institutional Magazine.

University of Mary Hardin-Baylor

Department of Communications
Belton, Texas 76513
Telephone: (817) 939-8642

Charles G. Taylor, Director
Nora Stafford, Chair

CURRICULUM AND INSTRUCTION
Courses or Concentrations
Available: Communication; Speech; *Undergraduate Objectives*: General training in effective speaking, vocal training and survey of speech pathology; *Bachelor's Degree Majors*: 6; *Full-Time Faculty*: 1; *Part-Time Faculty*: 2; *Full-Time Professional (non-clerical) Staff Members*: 2.

University of North Texas (Public)

Division of Communication and Public Address
P. O. Box 5266, NT Station
Denton, Texas 76203-5266
Telephone: (817) 565-2588

John S. Gossett, Chair
Thomas Preston, Dean, Arts and Sciences

CURRICULUM AND INSTRUCTION
Courses or Concentrations
Available: Communication; Information Science; Speech; *Undergraduate Objectives or Program Emphases*: Rhetoric, public address, argumentation, performance studies, persuasion, organizational, interpersonal, and intercultural communication; *Graduate Objectives or Program Emphases*: Two concentrations: Critical and Interpretive Studies (rhetoric, public address, performance studies, legal communication, persuasion) and Social Science Studies (interpersonal, organizational communication and network analysis); *Bachelor's Degree Majors*: 200; *Master's Degree Majors*: 50; *Full-Time Faculty*: 10; *Part-Time Faculty*: 35.

FACILITIES AND SERVICES
Practical experiences available through: Audio Recording Laboratory; Video Editing.

University of North Texas (Public)

Division of Radio/Television/Film
P. O. Box 13108
Denton, Texas 76203-3108
Telephone: (817) 565-2537

John B. Kuiper, Chair
Thomas Preston, Dean, College of Arts and Sciences

CURRICULUM AND INSTRUCTION
Courses or Concentrations
Available: Advertising; Communication; Film or Cinema; Radio, Television, or Telecommunications; Video/Film Studies, Broadcasting studies; *Undergraduate Objectives*: A liberal arts emphasis with a major in Radio-Television-Film.
Preparation for work in the media industries and for continued academic research and degrees; *Graduate Objectives or Program*

Emphases: Preparation for the advanced/terminal degree in Radio-Television-Film and in communication studies. Preparation for advanced research and production in industry. (MA, MS); *Bachelor's Degree Majors*: 350; *Master's Degree Majors*: 43; *Other Degree Majors*: 600; *Full-Time Faculty*: 12; *Part-Time Faculty*: 14; *Full-Time Professional (non-clerical) Staff Members*: 2.

FACILITIES AND SERVICES
Practical experiences available through: Advertising Agency; Associated Press Wire Service Feed; Community Antenna (Cable) Television Origination; Closed Circuit Television Facility; Campus Newspaper (Published Independently); Local Commercial Television Station; Desktop Publishing Facility; Video Editing; Electronic Field Production (Video); Film or Cinema Laboratory; FM Radio Station (Institutional); Institutional Newspaper; Public Relations Agency; Satellite Uplink Facility (C Band Transmitter); Video Production Laboratory or Television Studio.

University of North Texas (Public)

Department of Journalism
Box 5278
Denton, Texas 76203
Telephone: (817) 565-2205

Richard H. Wells, Chair
Tom Preston, Dean, College of Arts and Sciences

CURRICULUM AND INSTRUCTION
Courses or Concentrations Available: Advertising; Communication; Journalism or Mass Communication; Public Relations; Broadcast News; Speech; *Undergraduate Objectives or Program Emphases*: Professional emphasis in undergraduate and graduate; *Bachelor's Degree Majors*: 350; *Master's Degree Majors*: 70; *Full-Time Faculty*: 11; *Part-Time Faculty*: 18; *Full-Time Professional (non-clerical) Staff Members*: 3.

FACILITIES AND SERVICES
Practical experiences available through: Advertising Agency; Associated Press Wire Service Feed; Audio Recording Laboratory; Community Antenna (Cable)

Television Origination; Closed Circuit Television Facility; Local Commercial Newspaper; Local Commercial Television Station; Desktop Publishing Facility; Photographic Darkrooms; Video Editing; Electronic Field Production (Video); FM Radio Station (Institutional); ITFS Distribution System; Institutional Newspaper; Public Relations Agency; Video Production Laboratory or Television Studio.

University of Texas - Austin

College of Fine Arts
Austin, Texas 78712

J. Robert Wills, Administrator

University of Texas - Tyler

Department of Drama and Communication
Tyler, Texas 75701

University of Saint Thomas

Department of Communication
3812 Montrose Boulevard
Houston, Texas 77006

Joyce K. Covington, Administrator

University of Texas - Arlington (Public)

Department of Communication
Box 19107
Arlington, Texas 76019
Telephone: (817) 273-2163

Karin E. McCallum, Acting Chair
Tom Porter, Dean

CURRICULUM AND INSTRUCTION
Courses or Concentrations Available: Advertising; Communication; Journalism or Mass Communication; Public Relations; Radio, Television, Broadcasting, or Telecommunications; Speech; *Undergraduate Objectives or Program Emphases*: BA degree offered in advertising, journalism, public relations, radio-television, and speech communication; overview of the role and function of communication in

society; theories and techniques emphasized; specialized options; *Bachelor's Degree Majors*: 538; *Full-Time Faculty*: 16; *Part-Time Faculty*: 14.

FACILITIES AND SERVICES
Practical experiences available through: Audio Recording Laboratory; Campus Newspaper (Published Independently); Desktop Publishing Facility; Photographic Darkrooms; Video Editing; Electronic Field Production (Video); FM Radio Station (Institutional).

University of Texas - Austin (Public)

College of Communication
Austin, Texas 78712
Telephone: (512) 471-5646

Robert C. Jeffrey, Dean
William Cunningham, President

CURRICULUM AND INSTRUCTION
Courses or Concentrations Available: Advertising; Communication; Film or Cinema; Journalism or Mass Communication; Public Relations; Radio, Television, or Telecommunications; Speech; Communication Sciences and Disorders; *Program Coordinators*: Ed Cundiff (Advertising); Max McCombs (Journalism); Tom Schatz (Radio-Television-Film); Mark Knapp (Speech Communication); Gene Powers (Communication Sciences and Disorders); *Undergraduate Objectives or Program Emphases*: To educate students capable of making decisions based on critical thinking in an age where increased importance is placed on communication; to prepare practitioners in a variety of communication fields; *Graduate Objectives or Program Emphases*: To prepare the next generation of scholars in various communication disciplines; to create new knowledge about human communication and a better understanding of global communication processes; to share with the public and the professions research findings and their applications; *Master's Degree Majors*: 320; *Doctoral Degree Majors Currently in Residence*: 141; *Additional Doctoral Degree Majors*: 41; *Other Degree Majors*: 2121; *Full-Time Faculty*: 79; *Part-Time Faculty*: 117; *Full-Time Professional (non-clerical) Staff Members*: 20.

FACILITIES AND SERVICES
Practical experiences available through: Advertising Agency; Associated Press Wire Service Feed; Audio Recording Laboratory; Community Antenna (Cable) Television Origination; Closed Circuit Television Facility; Campus Newspaper (Published Independently); Local Commercial Newspaper; Local Commercial Television Station; Desktop Publishing Facility; Photographic Darkrooms; Video Editing; Electronic Field Production (Video); Film or Cinema Laboratory; FM Radio Station (Institutional); Institutional Magazine; Institutional Newspaper; Public Relations Agency; Video News and Data Processing; Video Production Laboratory or Television Studio.

University of Texas - Austin (Public)

Department of Advertising
CMA 7.142
Austin, Texas 78712
Telephone: (512) 471-1101

Edward W. Cundiff, Chair
Robert Jeffrey, Dean, College of Communication

CURRICULUM AND INSTRUCTION
Courses or Concentrations Available: Advertising; *Undergraduate Objectives or Program Emphases*: Training for professional work in advertising; *Graduate Objectives or Program Emphases*: Training for professional work in advertising; *Bachelor's Degree Majors*: 500; *Master's Degree Majors*: 75; *Doctoral Degree Majors Currently in Residence*: 14; *Full-Time Faculty*: 13; *Part-Time Faculty*: 8; *Full-Time Professional (non-clerical) Staff Members*: 4.

FACILITIES AND SERVICES
Practical experiences available through: Advertising Agency; AM Radio Station (Institutional).

University of Texas - Austin (Public)

Department of Journalism
Austin, Texas 78712
Telephone: (512) 471-5775

Maxwell E. McCombs, Chair
Robert Jeffrey, Dean, College of Communication

CURRICULUM AND INSTRUCTION
Courses or Concentrations Available: Journalism or Mass Communication; Public Relations; *Program Coordinators*: Al Anderson (Broadcast Journalism); Tom Fensch (Magazine); Martin Gibson (News/Public Affairs); J. B. Colson (Photojournalism); Frank Kalaph (Public Relations); Steve Reese (Graduate Program); *Undergraduate Objectives or Program Emphases*: Professional and liberal arts education in five specialty areas; *Graduate Objectives or Program Emphases*: Education in communication theory and methodology; *Bachelor's Degree Majors*: 550; *Master's Degree Majors*: 85; *Doctoral Degree Majors Currently in Residence*: 20; *Additional Doctoral Degree Majors*: 5; *Full-Time Faculty*: 25; *Part-Time Faculty*: 23; *Full-Time Professional (non-clerical) Staff Members*: 5.

FACILITIES AND SERVICES
Practical experiences available through: AM Radio Station (Institutional); Associated Press Wire Service Feed; Audio Recording Laboratory; Carrier Current Audio Distribution System; Closed Circuit Television Facility; Campus Newspaper (Published Independently); Local Commercial Newspaper; Local Commercial Television Station; Desktop Publishing Facility; Photographic Darkrooms; Video Editing; Electronic Field Production (Video); Television Broadcast Station (Institutional); FM Radio Station (Institutional); Public Relations Agency; Satellite Uplink Facility; Video News and Data Processing; Video Production Laboratory or Television Studio.

University of Texas - Austin (Public)

Department of Radio-Television-Film
CMA 6.118
Austin, Texas 78712
Telephone: (512) 471-4071

Thomas G. Schatz, Acting Chair
Robert Jeffrey, Dean, College of Communication

CURRICULUM AND INSTRUCTION
Courses or Concentrations Available: Film or Cinema; Mass Communication; Radio, Television, Broadcasting, or Telecommunications; *Undergraduate Objectives or Program Emphases*: Critical and cultural studies of the media; Mass Communication International/Technology Studies; Production (Film, Video, Television, Radio, Audio) and Screenwriting; *Graduate Objectives or Program Emphases*: Critical and cultural studies of the media; Mass Communication Internationl/Technology Studies; Production (Film, Video, Television, Radio, Audio) and Screenwriting; *Bachelor's Degree Majors*: 550; *Master's Degree Majors*: 80; *Doctoral Degree Majors Currently in Residence*: 45; *Additional Doctoral Degree Majors*: 15; *Full-Time Faculty*: 20; *Part-Time Faculty*: 41; *Full-Time Professional (non-clerical) Staff Members*: 5.

FACILITIES AND SERVICES
Practical experiences available through: Audio Recording Laboratory; Carrier Current Audio Distribution System; Closed Circuit Television Facility; Local Commercial Television Station; Desktop Publishing Facility; Video Editing; Electronic Field Production (Video); Television Broadcast Station (Institutional); Film or Cinema Laboratory; FM Radio Station (Institutional); Video Production Laboratory or Television Studio.

University of Texas - El Paso (Public)

Department of Communication
202 Cotton Memorial
El Paso, Texas 79968
Telephone: (915) 747-5129

Samuel C. Riccillo, Chair
Carl Jackson, Dean, Liberal Arts

CURRICULUM AND INSTRUCTION

Courses or Concentrations Available: Advertising; Communication; Journalism or Mass Communication; Public Relations; Radio, Television, Broadcasting, or Telecommunications; Speech; *Undergraduate Objectives or Program Emphases*: Speech communication, organizational communication, advertising and public relations, journalism, broadcast journalism, speech and journalism education; *Graduate Objectives or Program Emphases*: General program, communication theory; *Bachelor's Degree Majors*: 400; *Master's Degree Majors*: 30; *Full-Time Faculty*: 6; *Part-Time Faculty*: 28; *Full-Time Professional (non-clerical) Staff Members*: 8.

FACILITIES AND SERVICES

Practical experiences available through: Advertising Agency; Associated Press Wire Service Feed; Audio Recording Laboratory; Campus Newspaper (Published Independently); Local Commercial Newspaper; Local Commercial Television Station; Desktop Publishing Facility; Photographic Darkrooms; Video Editing; Electronic Field Production (Video); FM Radio Station (Institutional); ITFS Distribution System; Institutional Magazine; Public Relations Agency; Satellite Uplink Facility (Ku Band Transmitter) (C Band Transmitter); Video Production Laboratory or Television Studio.

University of Texas - Permian Basin (Public)

Department of Faculty of Communication
4901 East University
Odessa, Texas 79762
Telephone: (915) 367-2214

Robert N. Rothstein, Chair
Warren Gardner, Administrator

CURRICULUM AND INSTRUCTION

Courses or Concentrations Available: Journalism or Mass Communication; Radio, Television, Broadcasting, or Telecommunications; Speech; *Undergraduate Objectives or Program Emphases*: Training to work on print or broadcast media in the west Texas area or to teach in local high schools; *Bachelor's Degree Majors*: 40; *Full-Time Faculty*: 1; *Part-Time Faculty*: 5.

FACILITIES AND SERVICES

Practical experiences available through: Desktop Publishing Facility; Photographic Darkrooms; Video Editing; Institutional Newspaper.

University of Texas - Pan American (Public)

Department of Communications
1201 West University Avenue
Edinburg, Texas 78539
Telephone: (512) 381-3583

Edwin Leach, Chair
Ernest J. Baca, Dean

CURRICULUM AND INSTRUCTION

Courses or Concentrations Available: Advertising; Communication; Journalism or Mass Communication; Public Relations; Radio, Television, Broadcasting, or Telecommunications; Speech; Communication Disorders; Theatre; *Undergraduate Objectives or Program Emphases*: Background courses in communications with upper division course tending to specialize in job-related areas, such as public relations, television production, and courses required for teacher certification; *Graduate Objectives or Program Emphases*: Intercultural, interpersonal, and some work in organizational communication; *Bachelor's Degree Majors*: 40; *Master's Degree Majors*: 5; *Full-Time Faculty*: 8; *Part-Time Faculty*: 4; *Full-Time Professional (non-clerical) Staff Members*: 1.

FACILITIES AND SERVICES

Practical experiences available through: Advertising Agency; Audio Recording Laboratory; Campus Newspaper (Published Independently); Local Commercial Newspaper; Local Commercial Television Station; Desktop Publishing Facility; Photographic Darkrooms; Video Editing; Electronic Field Production (Video); Institutional Magazine; Institutional Newspaper; Public Relations Agency; Video News and Data Processing; Video Production or Television Studio.

West Texas State University
(Public)

Department of Art, Communication and Theatre
WT Box 747
Canyon City, Texas 79016
Telephone: (806) 656-2799

Robert A. Vartabedian, Head
Sue Park, Dean, College of Fine Arts and Humanities

CURRICULUM AND INSTRUCTION
Courses or Concentrations Available: Advertising; Communication; Film or Cinema; Journalism or Mass Communication; Public Relations; Radio, Television, or Telecommunications; Speech; Theatre; Art; *Undergraduate Objectives or Program Emphases*: A solid undergraduate foundation in the communicative arts; *Graduate Objectives or Program Emphases*: Advanced preparation in communication arts, especially research and assorted creative activities; *Bachelor's Degree Majors*: 100; *BFA Degree Majors*: 50; *Master's Degree Majors*: 40; *MFA Degree Majors*: 20; *Full-Time Faculty*: 17; *Part-Time Faculty*: 20; *Full-Time Professional (non-clerical) Staff Members*: 2.

FACILITIES AND SERVICES
Practical experiences available through: Advertising Agency; Associated Press Wire Service Feed; Audio Recording Laboratory; Community Antenna (Cable) Television Origination; Carrier Current Audio Distribution System; Campus Newspaper (Published Independently); Local Commercial Newspaper; Local Commercial Television Station; Desktop Publishing Facility; Photographic Darkrooms; Video Editing; Electronic Field Production (Video); FM Radio Station (Institutional); Institutional Magazine; Public Relations Agency; Satellite Uplink; Video News and Data Processing; Video Production Laboratory or Television Studio.

West Texas State University

Department of Language, Literature, and Journalism
Canyon, Texas 79016

Wharton County Junior College
(Public)

Department of Drama Speech
911 Boling Highway
Wharton, Texas 77488
Telephone: (409) 532-4560

Jerry L. Long, Chair
Sandra Coats, Chair, Division of Communication and Fine Arts

CURRICULUM AND INSTRUCTION
Courses or Concentrations Available: Speech; *Undergraduate Objectives or Program Emphases*: Provide language arts leading to teacher's certificate; to help student improve their listening and speaking skills; *Full-Time Faculty*: 3; *Part-Time Faculty*: 2.

FACILITIES AND SERVICES
Practical experiences available through: Audio Recording Laboratory; Closed Circuit Television Facility; Film or Cinema Laboratory; Video Production Laboratory or Television Studio.

Wiley College (Private)

Division of Communication
711 Wiley Avenue
Marshall, Texas 75670
Telephone: (214) 938-8341

A. J. Stovall, Dean

CURRICULUM AND INSTRUCTION
Courses or Concentrations Available: Advertising; Communication; Journalism or Mass Communication; Radio, Television, or Telecommunications; Speech; *Program Coordinators*: Franchiska Jones (Mass Communications); M.B.A. Ekuri (Communication); *Undergraduate Objectives or Program Emphases*: Print Journalism and Radio Broadcasting; *Bachelor's Degree Majors*: 27; *Full-Time Faculty*: 2; *Part-Time Faculty*: 2; *Full-Time Professional (non-clerical) Staff Members*: 2.

FACILITIES AND SERVICES
Practical experiences available through: Advertising Agency; Campus Newspaper (Published Independently); Local Commercial Newspaper; Local Commercial Television Station; Photographic Darkrooms; FM Radio Station.

Brigham Young University (Private)

Department of Communications
E-509 Harris Fine Arts Center
Provo, Utah 84602
Telephone: (801) 378-2077

Gordon Whiting, Chair
James Mason, Dean

CURRICULUM AND INSTRUCTION
Courses or Concentrations
Available: Advertising; Communication; Journalism or Mass Communication; Public Relations; Radio, Television, Broadcasting, or Telecommunications; *Undergraduate Objectives or Program Emphases*: Prepare students for careers in media industries with a particular emphasis on international matters, ethics, and writing. Prepare some for careers as teachers and for post-graduate work; *Graduate Objectives or Program Emphases*: Theory and research in mass communication (thesis program only); *Bachelor's Degree Majors*: 600; *Master's Degree Majors*: 50; *Full-Time Faculty*: 24; *Part-Time Faculty*: 13; *Full-Time Professional (non-clerical) Staff Members*: 6.

FACILITIES AND SERVICES
Practical experiences available through: Advertising Agency; Associated Press Wire Service Feed; Community Antenna (Cable) Television Origination; Photographic Darkrooms; Video Editing; Electronic Field Production (Video); Television Broadcast Station (Institutional); Film or Cinema Laboratory; FM Radio Station (Institutional); Institutional Newspaper; Public Relations Agency.

College of Eastern Utah (Public)

Program of Journalism
451 N. 400 East
Price, Utah 84501
Telephone: (801) 637-2120

Susan A. Polster, Director
Jay Andrews, Dean of Students

CURRICULUM AND INSTRUCTION
Courses or Concentrations
Available: Advertising; Communication; Journalism or Mass Communication; Speech; *Program Coordinator*: Neil Warren (Speech); *Associate's Degree Majors*: 2; *Other Degree Majors*: 16; *Full-Time Faculty*: 40; *Part-Time Faculty*: 30; *Full-Time Professional (non-clerical) Staff Members*: 7.

FACILITIES AND SERVICES
Practical experiences available through: Local Commercial Newspaper; Desktop Publishing Facility; Photographic Darkrooms; Institutional Newspaper.

Southern Utah State College (Public)

Department of Communication
350 West Center Street
Cedar City, Utah 84720
Telephone: (801) 586-7861

Frain G. Pearson, Chair
Harold Hiskey, Dean

CURRICULUM AND INSTRUCTION
Courses or Concentrations
Available: Advertising; Communication; Journalism or Mass Communication; Public Relations; Radio, Television, Broadcasting, or Telecommunications; Speech; *Program Coordinators*: Jon Smith (Broadcasting); Suzanne Larson (Speech-Forensics); *Undergraduate Objectives or Program Emphases*: Broad-based liberal arts background with professional courses geared to providing necessary competencies for professional employment; *Bachelor's Degree Majors*: 140; *Full-Time Faculty*: 6; *Part-Time Faculty*: 3; *Full-Time Professional (non-clerical) Staff Members*: 4.

FACILITIES AND SERVICES
Practical experiences available through: Audio Recording Laboratory; Community Antenna (Cable) Television Origination; Closed Circuit Television Facility; Campus Newspaper (Published Independently); Local Commercial Newspaper; Local Commercial Television Station; Desktop

Publishing Facility; Photographic Darkrooms; Video Editing; Electronic Field Production (Video); FM Radio Station (Institutional); Institutional Magazine; Public Relations Agency; Video Production Laboratory or Television Studio.

University of Utah (Public)

Department of Communication
Salt Lake City, Utah 84112
Telephone: (801) 581-6888

James A. Anderson, Chair
Norman Council, Dean, College of Humanities

CURRICULUM AND INSTRUCTION
Courses or Concentrations
Available: Advertising; Communication; Film or Cinema; Journalism or Mass Communication; Public Relations; Radio, Television, Broadcasting, or Telecommunications; Speech; News Editorial; *Undergraduate Objectives or Program Emphases*: Mass Communication degrees are pre-professional in orientation. Speech Communication degrees are Liberal Arts in orientation; *Graduate Objectives or Program Emphases*: Graduate study in certain Masters of Mass Communication are terminal and professional in orientation. Most Ph.D. degrees are research based and aimed at teaching in higher education; *Bachelor's Degree Majors*: 397; *Master's Degree Majors*: 30; *Doctoral Degree Majors Currently in Residence*: 39; *Additional Doctoral Degree Majors*: 20; *Full-Time Faculty*: 22; *Part-Time Faculty*: 33; *Full-Time Professional (non-clerical) Staff Members*: 1.

FACILITIES AND SERVICES
Practical experiences available through: Advertising Agency; AM Radio Station (Institutional); Audio Recording Laboratory; Community Antenna (Cable) Television Origination; Closed Circuit Television Facility; Campus Newspaper (Published Independently); Local Commercial Newspaper; Local Commercial Television Station; Desktop Publishing Facility; Photographic Darkrooms; Video Editing; Television Broadcast Station (Institutional); FM Radio Station (Institutional); ITFS Distribution System; Public Relations Agency.

Utah State University (Public)

Department of Communication
Logan, Utah 84322-4605
Telephone: (801) 750-3292

James Derry, Head
Robert Hoover, Dean

CURRICULUM AND INSTRUCTION
Courses or Concentrations
Available: Journalism or Mass Communication; Radio, Television, Broadcasting, or Telecommunications; *Undergraduate Objectives or Program Emphases*: Community journalism, an integrated Journalism, Radio, Television curriculum. Students trained in all media, with management area study; *Graduate Objectives or Program Emphases*: Writing and Management, emphasis in analysis; *Bachelor's Degree Majors*: 58; *Master's Degree Majors*: 11; *Full-Time Faculty*: 7; *Part-Time Faculty*: 7; *Full-Time Professional (non-clerical) Staff Members*: 2.

FACILITIES AND SERVICES
Practical experiences available through: Advertising Agency; Community Antenna (Cable) Television Origination; Closed Circuit Television Facility; Campus Newspaper (Published Independently); Local Commercial Newspaper; Desktop Publishing Facility; Photographic Darkrooms; Video Editing; Electronic Field Production (Video); Television Broadcast Station (Institutional); FM Radio Station (Institutional); Institutional Newspaper; New York Times Service Feed; United Press International Feed; Video Production Laboratory or Television Studio.

Weber State College (Public)

Department of Communication
3750 Harrison Boulevard, 1903
Ogden, Utah 84408-1903
Telephone: (801) 626-7120

P. Larry Stahle, Area Coordinator
Randolph J. Scott, Administrator

CURRICULUM AND INSTRUCTION
Courses or Concentrations
Available: Communication; Journalism or Mass Communication; Public Relations; Radio, Television, Broadcasting, or Telecommunications; Speech; *Program*

Coordinators: Raj Kumar (Broadcasting);
Richard Halley (Speech); *Undergraduate
Objectives or Program Emphases*: To prepare
students as professionals in all four areas
through sound academic training mixed with
internship opportunities. Students are
required to take coursework in all aspects of
the department to refine writing and speech
communication skills; *Bachelor's Degree
Majors*: 209; *Full-Time Faculty*: 11;
Part-Time Faculty: 7; *Full-Time Professional
(non-clerical) Staff Members*: 2.

FACILITIES AND SERVICES
*Practical experiences available
through*: Advertising Agency; Campus
Newspaper (Published Independently);
Local Commercial Newspaper; Desktop
Publishing Facility; Photographic
Darkrooms; Video Editing; Electronic Field
Production (Video); FM Radio Station
(Institutional); Institutional Newspaper;
Public Relations Agency.

Castleton State College (Public)

Program of Communications
Fine Arts Center
Castleton, Vermont 05735
Telephone: (802) 468-5611 Extension: 267

Robert W. Gershon, Coordinator
Joseph Mark, Dean

CURRICULUM AND INSTRUCTION
Courses or Concentrations
Available: Communication; Film or Cinema; Journalism or Mass Communication; Public Relations; Radio, Television, Broadcasting, or Telecommunications; *Undergraduate Objectives or Program Emphases*: Generalist communication approach; experiential components through college media and internships. Liberal arts based. Concentrations in journalism, mass media and corporate; *Associate's Degree Majors*: 15; *Other Degree Majors*: 125; *Full-Time Faculty*: 5; *Part-Time Faculty*: 4.

FACILITIES AND SERVICES
Practical experiences available through: Advertising Agency; Associated Press Wire Service Feed; Community Antenna (Cable) Television Origination; Campus Newspaper (Published Independently); Local Commercial Television Station; Desktop Publishing Facility; Photographic Darkrooms; Video Editing; Electronic Field Production (Video); FM Radio Station (Institutional); Public Relations Agency; Video News and Data Processing; Video Production Laboratory or Television Studio.

Norwich University (Private)

Department of Communications
Northfield, Vermont 05663
Telephone: (802) 485-2000

Narain D. Batra, Chair

CURRICULUM AND INSTRUCTION
Courses or Concentrations
Available: Advertising; Communication; Film or Cinema; Journalism or Mass Communication; Public Relations; Radio, Television, Broadcasting, or Telecommunications; Speech; *Undergraduate Objectives or Program Emphases*: The communications department offers a career-oriented curriculum which also stresses the liberal arts and sciences, for the communications professional must develop creative as well as technical skills; *Graduate Objectives or Program Emphases*: Individually designed graduate program in communications is administered by the division of graduate studies; *Degree Majors*: 120; *Full-Time Faculty*: 4; *Full-Time Professional (non-clerical) Staff Members*: 2.

FACILITIES AND SERVICES
Practical experiences available through: Advertising Agency; Associated Press Wire Service Feed; Audio Recording Laboratory; Community Antenna (Cable) Television Origination; Closed Circuit Television Facility; Local Commercial Newspaper; Local Commercial Television Station; Desktop Publishing Facility; Photographic Darkrooms; Video Editing; Electronic Field Production (Video); Television Broadcast Station (Institutional); FM Radio Station (Institutional); Institutional Newspaper; Public Relations Agency.

Southern Vermont College

Communication Department
Monument Road
Bennington, Vermont 05201

Alex Brown, Administrator

St. Michael's College (Private)

Department of Journalism
Winooski Park
Colchester, Vermont 05439
Telephone: (802) 655-2000

Gifford R. Hart, Acting Chair
Ronald H. Provost, Vice President,
Academic Affairs

CURRICULUM AND INSTRUCTION
Courses or Concentrations
Available: Advertising; Journalism or Mass
Communication; Public Relations; Radio,
Television, Broadcasting, or
Telecommunications; Photojournalism, Print
Graphics; *Undergraduate Objectives or*
Program Emphases: News writing, reporting,
editing within a liberal arts context. Mastery
tracks in print journalism, photojournalism,
public relations, radio/television, print
graphics; *Bachelor's Degree Majors*: 50;
Full-Time Faculty: 4; *Part-Time Faculty*: 6.

FACILITIES AND SERVICES
Practical experiences available
through: Advertising Agency; Associated
Press Wire Service Feed; Audio Recording
Laboratory; Local Commercial Newspaper;
Local Commercial Television Station;
Desktop Publishing Facility; Photographic
Darkrooms; Video Editing; FM Radio
Station (Institutional); Institutional
Newspaper; Public Relations Agency; Video
News and Data Processing; Video
Production Laboratory or Television Studio.

Trinity College of Vermont (Private)

Department of Humanities
208 Colchester Avenue
Burlington, Vermont 05401
Telephone: (802) 658-0337

Vernon Lindquist, Chair
Robert Hahn, Academic Dean

CURRICULUM AND INSTRUCTION
Courses or Concentrations
Available: Advertising; Communication;
Journalism or Mass Communication; Public
Relations; Speech; Marketing,
Organizational Theory, Arts and Graphics,
Creative Writing, Modern Design, Criticism,
Interpersonal Relations, Group Dynamics,
Social Psychology; *Program*

Coordinator: Nancy Holland (Writing and
Publishing); *Undergraduate Objectives or*
Program Emphases: Three Communications
tracks include Writing and Publishing,
Corporate Communications and Public
Relations, and Interpersonal
Communications; *Bachelor's Degree*
Majors: 63; *Full-Time Faculty*: 16;
Part-Time Faculty: 8.

FACILITIES AND SERVICES
Practical experiences available
through: Advertising Agency; Community
Antenna (Cable) Television Origination;
Campus Newspaper (Published
Independently); Local Commercial
Newspaper; Local Commercial Television
Station; Desktop Publishing Facility;
Photographic Darkrooms; Public Relations
Agency; Video News and Data Processing.

Averett College

English-Journalism-Communication
Danville, Virginia 24541

David Hoffman, Administrator

CBN University (Private)

College of Communication and the Arts
Virginia Beach, Virginia 23464
Telephone: (804) 424-7000

David W. Clark, Dean
Carle Hunt, Administrator

CURRICULUM AND INSTRUCTION
*Courses or Concentrations
Available*: Advertising; Communication; Film
or Cinema; Journalism or Mass
Communication; Public Relations; Radio,
Television, Broadcasting, or
Telecommunications; Speech; Media
Management; *Graduate Objectives or
Program Emphases*: To produce graduates
who have superior professional skills and a
Biblically-based lifestyle; encourage critical
and creative thought; provide professional
skills training; balance examination of media
content with production and management
skills; *Master's Degree Majors*: 209;
Full-Time Faculty: 14; *Part-Time
Faculty*: 11; *Full-Time Professional
(non-clerical) Staff Members*: 1.

FACILITIES AND SERVICES
Practical experiences available through: Audio
Recording Laboratory; Community Antenna
(Cable) Television Origination; Local
Commercial Newspaper; Local Commercial
Television Station; Desktop Publishing
Facility; Photographic Darkrooms; Video
Editing; Electronic Field Production
(Video); Film or Cinema Laboratory;
Institutional Magazine; Institutional
Newspaper; Satellite Uplink Facility; United
Press International Feed; Video News and
Data Processing; Video Production
Laboratory or Television Studio.

College of William and Mary

Department of Speech and Theatre
Williamsburg, Virginia 23185

Emory and Henry College

Mass Communications Department
Emory, Virginia 24327

John Wright, Administrator

Ferrum College (Private)

Division of Fine Arts
Ferrum, Virginia 24088
Telephone: (703) 365-4354

Jody D. Brown, Chair
Joseph L. Carter, Dean

CURRICULUM AND INSTRUCTION
Courses or Concentrations Available: Radio,
Television, Broadcasting, or
Telecommunications; Speech; *Undergraduate
Objectives or Program Emphases*: Ferrum
College prepares students for entry level
careers in broadcast or print communication
fields or for graduate school through
programs that combine discipline majors with
a liberal arts degree; *Bachelor's Degree
Majors*: 12; *Full-Time Faculty*: 8; *Part-Time
Faculty*: 4.

FACILITIES AND SERVICES
*Practical experiences available
through*: Advertising Agency; Audio
Recording Laboratory; Campus Newspaper
(Published Independently); Local
Commercial Newspaper; Photographic
Darkrooms; FM Radio Station
(Institutional); Video Production Laboratory
or Television Studio.

George Mason University (Public)

Department of Communication
4400 University Drive
Fairfax, Virginia 22030
Telephone: (703) 323-3575

Don M. Boileau, Chair
Paula Gilbert Lewis, Dean of College

CURRICULUM AND INSTRUCTION
Courses or Concentrations
Available: Communication; Journalism or
Mass Communication; Public Relations;
Radio, Television, Broadcasting, or
Telecommunications; Speech; *Full-Time*
Faculty: 12; *Part-Time Faculty*: 37.

FACILITIES AND SERVICES
Practical experiences available
through: Associated Press Wire Service Feed;
Audio Recording Laboratory; Community
Antenna (Cable) Television Origination;
Campus Newspaper (Published
Independently); Local Commercial
Newspaper; Local Commercial Television
Station; Desktop Publishing Facility;
Photographic Darkrooms; Video Editing;
Electronic Field Production (Video);
Institutional Newspaper; Public Relations
Agency; Satellite Uplink Facility;

Hampton University (Private)

Department of Speech Communication and
Theatre Arts
Armstrong Hall
Hampton, Virginia 23668
Telephone: (804) 727-5401

Karen T. Ward, Chair

CURRICULUM AND INSTRUCTION
Courses or Concentrations
Available: Communication; Speech;
Undergraduate Objectives or Program
Emphases: Interpersonal, Organizational,
Small Group, Rhetorical Criticism, Public
Address; *Bachelor's Degree Majors*: 85;
Full-Time Faculty: 6; *Part-Time Faculty*: 7.

FACILITIES AND SERVICES
Practical experiences available
through: Campus Newspaper (Published
Independently); FM Radio Station
(Institutional).

Hampton University (Private)

Mass Media Arts
Hampton, Virginia 23668

Frank W. Render II, Administrator

Hampton University (Private)

Department of Communication Disorders
Hampton, Virginia 23668

Robert M. Screen, Administrator

Hollins College (Private)

Department of Communication Studies
Roanoke, Virginia 24020
Telephone: (703) 362-6438

Jane Tumas-Serna, Chair
Bridget Puzon, Dean of the College

CURRICULUM AND INSTRUCTION
Courses or Concentrations
Available: Communication; Film or Cinema;
Undergraduate Objectives or Program
Emphases: To explore the communication
process for a theoretical, historical and
critical perspective while gaining practical
experience; *Bachelor's Degree Majors*: 16;
Full-Time Faculty: 2; *Part-Time Faculty*: 2.

FACILITIES AND SERVICES
Practical experiences available
through: Campus Newspaper (Published
Independently); Photographic Darkrooms;
Video Editing; Electronic Field Production
(Video); Film or Cinema Laboratory.

Hollins College (Private)

Department of Theatre Arts
P. O. Box 8617
Roanoke, Virginia 24020
Telephone: (703) 362-6000

Carl R. Plantinga, Chair
Bridget Puzon, Dean of College

CURRICULUM AND INSTRUCTION
Courses or Concentrations Available: Film or
Cinema; *Undergraduate Objectives or Program*
Emphases: Study of Drama, film, and dance
with concentration in drama or film. Film

concentration offers the study of film history, theory, and production; *Bachelor's Degree Majors*: 8; *Full-Time Faculty*: 5; *Part-Time Faculty*: 2; *Full-Time Professional (non-clerical) Staff Members*: 1.

FACILITIES AND SERVICES
Practical experiences available through: Audio Recording Laboratory; Campus Newspaper (Published Independently); Local Commercial Newspaper; Local Commercial Television Station; Photographic Darkrooms; Video Editing; Electronic Field Production (Video); Film or Cinema Laboratory; Institutional Magazine; Institutional Newspaper; Satellite Uplink Facility (C Band Transmitter).

James Madison University (Public)

College of Fine Arts and Communication
Harrisonburg, Virginia 22807
(See Additional Entries Below)

Richard F. Whitman, Dean

James Madison University (Public)

Department of Human Communication
Harrisonburg, Virginia 22807
Telephone: (703) 568-6228

Philip Emmert, Head
Richard F. Whitman, Dean, College of Fine Arts and Communication

CURRICULUM AND INSTRUCTION
Courses or Concentrations Available: Communication; Public Relations; Speech; Medical Communication; Conflict Mediation; *Undergraduate Objectives or Program Emphases:* Within broad-based liberal arts curriculum, students select core courses in one of four tracks: alternative dispute resolution, interpersonal communication, organizational communication, and public relations; *Program Coordinators*: Mae M. Frantz (Public Relations); Anne Gabbard-Alley (Medical Communication); William Kimsey (Mediation); *Bachelor's Degree Majors*: 100; *Full-Time Faculty*: 14; *Part-Time Faculty*: 9.

FACILITIES AND SERVICES
Practical experiences available through: Closed Circuit Television Origination Facility; Local Commercial Newspaper; Local Commercial Television Station; Desktop Publishing Facility; FM Radio Station (Institutional); Public Relations Agency; Video News and Data Processing.

James Madison University (Public)

Department of Mass Communication
Harrisonburg, Virginia 22807
Telephone: (703) 568-6228

George A. Wead, Head
Richard F. Whitman, Dean, College of Fine Arts and Communication

CURRICULUM AND INSTRUCTION
Courses or Concentrations Available: Communication; Film or Cinema; Journalism and Mass Communication; Radio, Television, Broadcasting, or Telecommunications; *Undergraduate Objectives or Program Emphases:* Within broad-based liberal arts curriculum, students select core courses in one of four career tracks: corporate media, print journalism, telecommunication, and visual communication; *Bachelor's Degree Majors*: 250; *Full-Time Faculty*: 11; *Part-Time Faculty*: 7; *Full-Time Professional (non-clerical) Staff Members*: 2.

FACILITIES AND SERVICES
Practical experiences available through: Associated Press Wire Service Feed; Audio Recording Laboratory; Community Antenna (Cable) Television Origination; Local Commercial Newspaper; Local Commercial Television Station; Desktop Publishing Facility; Photographic Darkrooms; Video Editing; Electronic Field Production (Video); FM Radio Station (Institutional); Institutional Newspaper; Institutional Magazine; UPI Feed; Video Production Laboratory or Television Studio.

Liberty University (Private)

School of Communication
Box 20000
Lynchburg, Virginia 24506
Telephone: (804) 582-2466

William G. Gribbin, Dean
Earl Mills, Provost

CURRICULUM AND INSTRUCTION
*Courses or Concentrations
Available*: Advertising; Communication;
Journalism or Mass Communication; Public
Relations; Radio, Television, Broadcasting,
or Telecommunications; Speech; English;
Modern Languages; *Program
Coordinators*: H. Poggemiller (English);
David Partie (Modern Languages); Al
Snyder (Journalism); C. Windsor
(Telecommunications); *Undergraduate
Objectives or Program Emphases*: To prepare
effective Christian communicators;
Bachelor's Degree Majors: 220; *Full-Time
Faculty*: 40; *Part-Time Faculty*: 9; *Full-Time
Professional (non-clerical) Staff Members*: 1.

FACILITIES AND SERVICES
*Practical experiences available
through*: Associated Press Wire Service Feed;
Community Antenna (Cable) Television
Origination; Closed Circuit Television
Facility; Campus Newspaper (Published
Independently); Desktop Publishing Facility;
Photographic Darkrooms; Video Editing;
Electronic Field Production (Video);
Television Broadcast Station (Institutional);
FM Radio Station (Institutional); Satellite
Uplink Facility; Video Production
Laboratory or Television Studio.

Liberty University (Private)

Department of Journalism
Box 20000
Lynchburg, Virginia 24506
Telephone: (804) 582-2311
Alternate: 582-2128

Albert W. Snyder, Chair
**William Gribbin, Dean, School of
Communications**

CURRICULUM AND INSTRUCTION
*Courses or Concentrations
Available*: Advertising; Journalism or Mass
Communication; Public Relations; Radio,
Television, Broadcasting, or
Telecommunications; Speech;
News-editorial; Magazine Journalism;
Journalism Graphics; *Degree Majors*: 125;
Full-Time Faculty: 5; *Part-Time Faculty*: 2.

FACILITIES AND SERVICES
Practical experiences available through: Audio
Recording Laboratory; Carrier Current
Audio Distribution System; Closed Circuit
Television Facility; Desktop Publishing
Facility; Photographic Darkrooms; Video
Editing; Electronic Field Production
(Video); FM Radio Station (Institutional);
Institutional Newspaper; Public Relations
Agency; United Press International Feed;
Video Production Laboratory or Television
Studio.

Liberty University (Private)

Department of Telecommunications
P.O. Box 20000
Lynchburg, Virginia 24506-8001
Telephone: (804) 582-2000

Carl D. Windsor, Chair
**William G. Gribbin, Dean, School of
Communication**

CURRICULUM AND INSTRUCTION
Courses or Concentrations Available: Radio,
Television, Broadcasting, or
Telecommunications; *Bachelor's Degree
Majors*: 95; *Full-Time Faculty*: 4; *Part-Time
Faculty*: 3; *Full-Time Professional
(non-clerical) Staff Members*: 1.

FACILITIES AND SERVICES
Practical experiences available through: AM
Radio Station (Institutional); Audio
Recording Laboratory; Carrier Current
Audio Distribution System; Closed Circuit
Television Facility; Local Commercial
Television Station; Desktop Publishing
Facility; Video Editing; Electronic Field
Production (Video); Television Broadcast
Station (Institutional); FM Radio Station
(Institutional); ITFS Distribution System;
Satellite Uplink Facility (Ku Band
Transmitter) (C Band Transmitter); United
Press International Feed; Video Production
Laboratory or Television Studio.

Lynchburg College (Private)

Department of Communication Studies
1501 Lakeside Drive
Lynchburg, Virginia 24501
Telephone: (804) 522-8178

G. Rex Mix, Chair
James F. Traer, Dean of the College

CURRICULUM AND INSTRUCTION
*Courses or Concentrations
Available*: Communication; Journalism or
Mass Communication; Radio, Television,
Broadcasting, or Telecommunications;
Speech; *Program Coordinators*: Heywood
Greenberg (Journalism); William Young
(Mass Media); *Undergraduate Objectives or
Program Emphases*: A common core
curriculum of basic introduction, beginning
news writing, and mass media with four
specialty tracks in print journalism, broadcast
journalism, rhetoric and public address, and
applied communication; *Associate's Degree
Majors*: 60; *Bachelor's Degree Majors*: 95;
Full-Time Faculty: 6; *Part-Time Faculty*: 7.

FACILITIES AND SERVICES
*Practical experiences available
through*: Advertising Agency; Audio
Recording Laboratory; Community Antenna
(Cable) Television Origination; Carrier
Current Audio Distribution System; Local
Commercial Newspaper; Local Commercial
Television Station; Desktop Publishing
Facility; Photographic Darkrooms; Video
Editing; Electronic Field Production
(Video); Institutional Magazine;
Institutional Newspaper; Public Relations
Agency; Video News and Data Processing.

Mary Baldwin College

Mass Communications Program
Frederick Street
Staunton, Virginia 24401

William L. DeLeeuw, Administrator

Mary Washington College (Public)

Department of English, Linguistics and
Speech
Fredericksburg, Virginia 22401
Telephone: (703) 899-4386

Susan J. Hanna, Chair
Philip Hall, Dean and Vice President,
Academic Affairs

CURRICULUM AND INSTRUCTION
*Courses or Concentrations
Available*: Journalism or Mass
Communication; Speech; Debate and
Forensics Program; *Program
Coordinator*: John Morello (Speech);
*Undergraduate Objectives or Program
Emphases*: Journalism (Print emphasis);
Speech (General with a public address
focus); *Full-Time Faculty*: 2.

FACILITIES AND SERVICES
*Practical experiences available
through*: Campus Newspaper (Published
Independently).

Marymount University (Private)

Division of Communications
2807 North Glebe Road
Arlington, Virginia 22091
Telephone: (703) 284-1570

Janet L. Fallon, Program Advisor
Robert Traghi, Dean, Arts and Sciences

CURRICULUM AND INSTRUCTION
*Courses or Concentrations
Available*: Communication; Journalism or
Mass Communication; Public Relations;
Radio, Television, Broadcasting, or
Telecommunications; Speech; Organizational
Communication; *Undergraduate Objectives or
Program Emphases*: To gain an
understanding of human communication
theory. To develop knowledge and
proficiencies in speech communication and
media writing and analysis; *Bachelor's Degree
Majors*: 100; *Full-Time Faculty*: 3;
Part-Time Faculty: 6.

FACILITIES AND SERVICES
*Practical experiences available
through*: Advertising Agency; Campus
Newspaper (Published Independently);
Local Commercial Television Station; Video

Editing; Institutional Newspaper; Public Relations Agency; Video Production Laboratory or Television Studio.

National Business College

Fuqazzi College
P.O. Box 6400
Roanoke, Virginia 24017-0400
Telephone: (703) 986-1800

Bernard Bever, Director
Frank E. Longaker, Administrator

CURRICULUM AND INSTRUCTION
Courses or Concentrations
Available: Advertising; Communication; Journalism or Mass Communication; Public Relations; Radio, Television, Broadcasting, or Telecommunications; Speech; Radio-Television Station Operations; Media Writing; Radio-Television Production; Broadcast Regulation and Communication Law; *Program Coordinator*: William H. Bull (Program); *Undergraduate Objectives or Program Emphases*: Acquire skills and learning necessary to provide employment in the radio and television industry; *Degree Majors*: 40; *Full-Time Faculty*: 3; *Part-Time Faculty*: 20.

FACILITIES AND SERVICES
Practical experiences available through: Audio Recording Laboratory; Local Commercial Television Station; Video Editing; Electronic Field Production (Video); Video News and Data Processing; Video Production Laboratory or Television Studio.

Norfolk State College (Public)

Department of Mass Communications
2401 Corprew Avenue
Norfolk, Virginia 23504

Lenora Brogdon-Wyatt, Administrator

Norfolk State University (Public)

Department of Journalism
2401 Corprew Avenue
Norfolk, Virginia 23504
Telephone: (804) 683-8330

Dianne Lynne Cherry, Chair
Thelma Curl, Dean

CURRICULUM AND INSTRUCTION
Courses or Concentrations
Available: Advertising; Journalism or Mass Communication; Public Relations; Photojournalism; *Bachelor's Degree Majors*: 84; *Full-Time Faculty*: 3; *Part-Time Faculty*: 6.

FACILITIES AND SERVICES
Practical experiences available through: Advertising Agency; Campus Newspaper (Published Independently); Local Commercial Newspaper; Local Commercial Television Station; Institutional Newspaper; Public Relations Agency.

Northern Virginia Community College

Broadcast Engineering Technology
4001 Wakefield Chapel Road
Annandale, Virginia 22003

Edward Montgomery, Administrator

Old Dominion University (Public)

Department of Speech Communication and Theatre Arts
Hampton Boulevard
Norfolk, Virginia 23529
Telephone: (804) 683-3828

Deborah A. Fisher, Departmental Advisor
Erlene Hendrix, Chair of Department

CURRICULUM AND INSTRUCTION
Courses or Concentrations
Available: Communication; Film or Cinema; Journalism or Mass Communication; Public Relations; Radio, Television, Broadcasting, or Telecommunications; Speech; *Undergraduate Objectives or Program Emphases*: Mass communication; public communication; small group interpersonal communication; theatre. Organizational

communication currently being developed; *Bachelor's Degree Majors*: 210; *Full-Time Faculty*: 12; *Part-Time Faculty*: 8.

FACILITIES AND SERVICES
Practical experiences available through: Advertising Agency; AM Radio Station (Institutional); Campus Newspaper (Published Independently); Local Commercial Television Station; Desktop Publishing Facility; Institutional Magazine; Public Relations Agency.

Old Dominion University (Public)

Department of English
Hampton Boulevard
Norfolk, Virginia 23529-0078
Telephone: (804) 683-3927

Charles E. Ruhl, Chair
Charles O. Burgen, Dean, College of Arts and Letters

CURRICULUM AND INSTRUCTION
Courses or Concentrations Available: Journalism or Mass Communication; Public Relations; Technical Writing; Management Writing; *Program Coordinator*: Frederick E. Talbott (Journalism, Public Relations); *Undergraduate Objectives or Program Emphases*: Journalism, Technical Writing, Literature, Linguistics, Creative Writing; *Graduate Objectives or Program Emphases*: Professional Writing, Literature, Creative Writing; *Bachelor's Degree Majors*: 200; *Master's Degree Majors*: 101; *Full-Time Faculty*: 35; *Part-Time Faculty*: 26.

FACILITIES AND SERVICES
Practical experiences available through: Campus Newspaper (Published Independently); Local Commercial Newspaper; Local Commercial Television Station; Desktop Publishing Facility; Public Relations Agency.

Presbyterian School of Christian Education

Video Education Center
1205 Palmyra Avenue
Richmond, Virginia 23227

Jeff Kellam, Administrator

Radford University (Public)

Department of Telecommunication
Radford, Virginia 24142
Telephone: (703) 831-5282

Clayland H. Waite, Chair

CURRICULUM AND INSTRUCTION
Courses or Concentrations Available: Communication; Journalism or Mass Communication; Public Relations; Radio, Television, Broadcasting, or Telecommunications; Speech; *Undergraduate Objectives or Program Emphases*: Speech Communication, Radio-Television, Public Relations, News Editorial; *Graduate Objectives or Program Emphases*: Corporate professional communication; *Associate's Degree Majors*: 250; *Bachelor's Degree Majors*: 232; *Master's Degree Majors*: 15; *Full-Time Faculty*: 21; *Part-Time Faculty*: 4.

FACILITIES AND SERVICES
Practical experiences available through: Associated Press Wire Service Feed; Audio Recording Laboratory; Community Antenna (Cable) Television Origination; Closed Circuit Television Facility; Campus Newspaper (Published Independently); Local Commercial Newspaper; Local Commercial Television Station; Desktop Publishing Facility; Photographic Darkrooms; Video Editing; Electronic Field Production (Video); FM Radio Station (Institutional); Institutional Magazine; Institutional Newspaper; Public Relations Agency; Video News and Data Processing; Video Production Laboratory or Television Studio.

Roanoke College (Private)

Department of English
Salem, Virginia 24153
Telephone: (703) 375-2500

Bobbye Au, Chair
Gerald Gibson, Academic Vice President and Dean

CURRICULUM AND INSTRUCTION
Courses or Concentrations
Available: Communication; Film or Cinema; Journalism or Mass Communication; Speech; *Program Coordinators*: Bruce Swaffield (Journalism); Carolyn Schneider (Speech, Communication); Anita Turpin (Speech); *Undergraduate Objectives or Program Emphases*: Introduction to the area of communication, oral track and written track; *Full-Time Faculty*: 10; *Part-Time Faculty*: 4.

FACILITIES AND SERVICES
Practical experiences available through: Advertising Agency; Campus Newspaper (Published Independently); Local Commercial Newspaper; Local Commercial Television Station; Public Relations Agency.

University of Richmond

Communication, Speech
Richmond, Virginia 23173

Jerry Tarver, Chair

University of Richmond (Private)

Program of Journalism
Richmond, Virginia 23173
Telephone: (804) 289-8324

Michael M. Spear, Coordinator
David Leary, Dean, Arts and Sciences

CURRICULUM AND INSTRUCTION
Courses or Concentrations
Available: Journalism or Mass Communication; Public Relations; Radio, Television, Broadcasting, or Telecommunications; *Undergraduate Objectives or Program Emphases*: Basic preparation for entry level journalists; *Bachelor's Degree Majors*: 20; *Full-Time Faculty*: 2; *Part-Time Faculty*: 5.

FACILITIES AND SERVICES
Practical experiences available through: Advertising Agency; Associated Press Wire Service Feed; Audio Recording Laboratory; Campus Newspaper (Published Independently); Local Commercial Newspaper; Local Commercial Television Station; Desktop Publishing Facility; Photographic Darkrooms; FM Radio Station (Institutional); Public Relations Agency.

University of Virginia - Charlottesville

Department of Rhetoric and Communication Studies
1 Dawson's Row
Charlottesville, Virginia 22903

William Lee Miller, Administrator

Virginia Commonwealth University (Public)

School of Mass Communications
901 W. Main
Richmond, Virginia 23284
Telephone: (804) 367-1260

Thomas R. Donohue, Director
Elske Smith, Administrator

CURRICULUM AND INSTRUCTION
Courses or Concentrations
Available: Advertising; Journalism or Mass Communication; Public Relations; Radio, Television, Broadcasting, or Telecommunications; *Undergraduate Objectives or Program Emphases*: Professional preparation; critical consumer; *Graduate Objectives or Program Emphases*: Media entrepreneurship; *Bachelor's Degree Majors*: 850; *Master's Degree Majors*: 40; *Full-Time Faculty*: 18; *Part-Time Faculty*: 8; *Full-Time Professional (non-clerical) Staff Members*: 2.

FACILITIES AND SERVICES
Practical experiences available through: Advertising Agency; Associated Press Wire Service Feed; Audio Recording Laboratory; Community Antenna (Cable) Television Origination; Carrier Current Audio Distribution System; Closed Circuit Television Facility; Campus Newspaper (Published Independently); Local Commercial Newspaper; Local Commercial

Television Station; Desktop Publishing Facility; Photographic Darkrooms; Video Editing; Electronic Field Production (Video); Institutional Magazine; Institutional Newspaper; Public Relations Agency; Video Production Laboratory or Television Studio.

Virginia Polytechnic Institute and State University (Public)

Department of Communication Studies
11 Agnew Hall
Blacksburg, Virginia 24061
Telephone: (703) 231-7166

Robert E. Denton Jr., Head
Herman Doswald, Dean

CURRICULUM AND INSTRUCTION
Courses or Concentrations
Available: Communication; Film or Cinema; Journalism or Mass Communication; Public Relations; Radio, Television, Broadcasting, or Telecommunications; Speech; *Bachelor's Degree Majors*: 470; *Full-Time Faculty*: 19; *Part-Time Faculty*: 4.

FACILITIES AND SERVICES
Practical experiences available through: Advertising Agency; AM Radio Station (Institutional); Community Antenna (Cable) Television Origination; Closed Circuit Television Facility; Campus Newspaper (Published Independently); Local Commercial Television Station; Desktop Publishing Facility; Photographic Darkrooms; Video Editing; Electronic Field Production (Video); Television Broadcast Station (Institutional); Film or Cinema Laboratory; FM Radio Station (Institutional); Public Relations Agency; Video Production Laboratory or Television Studio.

Virginia Union University

Department of Radio-Television-Film
1500 North Lombardy Street
Richmond, Virginia 23220

Virginia Union University

Department of Journalism
Richmond, Virginia 23220

Archibald H. Benson, Administrator

Virginia Wesleyan College

Wesleyan Drive
Norfolk, Virginia 23502

H. Rick Hite, Administrator

Virginia Western Community College (Public)

Division of Radio/Television Production Technology
3095 Colonial Avenue, S.W.
Roanoke, Virginia 24015
Telephone: (703) 857-7275

Thomas E. Finton, Head
Wayne Michie, Chair, Engineering Division

CURRICULUM AND INSTRUCTION
Courses or Concentrations
Available: Advertising; Radio, Television, Broadcasting, or Telecommunications; Speech; *Undergraduate Objectives or Program Emphases*: Prepare students for entry and medium level position in production operations and/or transfer to a four year degree program in communications or related area; *Associate's Degree Majors*: 30; *Full-Time Faculty*: 2; *Part-Time Faculty*: 2.

FACILITIES AND SERVICES
Practical experiences available through: Audio Recording Laboratory; Photographic Darkrooms; Video Editing; Electronic Field Production (Video); Video Production Laboratory or Television Studio.

Washington and Lee University (Private)

Department of Journalism and Communications
Lexington, Virginia 24450
Telephone: (703) 463-8432

Hampden H. Smith III, Head
John Elrod, Academic Vice President

CURRICULUM AND INSTRUCTION
Courses or Concentrations Available: Journalism or Mass Communication; Radio, Television, Broadcasting, or Telecommunications; *Undergraduate Objectives or Program Emphases*: Broad liberal education with challenging professional preparation. Many majors go to law, advertising and public relations in addition to print and broadcast journalism; *Bachelor's Degree Majors*: 80; *Full-Time Faculty*: 5.

FACILITIES AND SERVICES
Practical experiences available through: Associated Press Wire Service Feed; Audio Recording Laboratory; Community Antenna (Cable) Television Origination; Closed Circuit Television Facility; Campus Newspaper (Published Independently); Local Commercial Newspaper; Desktop Publishing Facility; Photographic Darkrooms; Video Editing; Electronic Field Production (Video); FM Radio Station (Institutional); Satellite Uplink Facility; Video Production Laboratory or Television Studio.

Bellevue Community College (Public)

Department of Communication
3000 Landerholm Circle, SE
Bellevue, Washington 98007
Telephone: (206) 641-2168

M. Craig Sanders, Chair
Larry Reid, Chair, Arts and Humanities Division

CURRICULUM AND INSTRUCTION
Courses or Concentrations Available: Advertising; Communication; Journalism or Mass Communication; Radio, Television, Broadcasting, or Telecommunications; *Undergraduate Objectives or Program Emphases*: Radio performance, production; journalism (editorial); *Associate's Degree Majors*: 130; *Full-Time Faculty*: 1; *Part-Time Faculty*: 3.

FACILITIES AND SERVICES
Practical experiences available through: Community Antenna (Cable) Television Origination; Local Commercial Newspaper; Desktop Publishing Facility; Photographic Darkrooms; Video Editing; FM Radio Station (Institutional); Institutional Newspaper; Video Production Laboratory or Television Studio.

Bellevue Community College (Public)

Department of Speech
3000 Landerholm Drive
Bellevue, Washington 98004
Telephone: (206) 641-2345

Robert Burke, Chair
Larry Reid, Chair, Arts and Humanities Division

CURRICULUM AND INSTRUCTION
Courses or Concentrations Available: Communication; Speech; *Undergraduate Objectives or Program Emphases*: Provide training in basic communication competencies, i.e. speaking, listening, group process, non verbal, persuasion, organizational and critical thinking; *Full-Time Faculty*: 3; *Part-Time Faculty*: 5.

FACILITIES AND SERVICES
Practical experiences available through: Closed Circuit Television Facility; Campus Newspaper (Published Independently); Desktop Publishing Facility; Photographic Darkrooms; FM Radio Station (Institutional).

Central Washington University (Public)

Department of Communications
Ellenburg, Washington 98926
Telephone: (509) 963-1066

Corwin P. King, Chair
Robert H. Brown, Dean, College of Letters, Arts and Sciences

CURRICULUM AND INSTRUCTION
Courses or Concentrations Available: Journalism or Mass Communication; Public Relations; Radio, Television, Broadcasting, or Telecommunications; Speech; *Undergraduate Objectives or Program Emphases*: To offer practical skills training built on a solid theoretical foundation. The emphasis is hands-on learning, with considerable opportunity for practicum work through internships, individual study; *Bachelor's Degree Majors*: 150; *Full-Time Faculty*: 7; *Part-Time Faculty*: 3.

FACILITIES AND SERVICES
Practical experiences available through: Audio Recording Laboratory; Community Antenna (Cable) Television Origination; Closed Circuit Television Facility; Local Commercial Newspaper; Desktop Publishing Facility; Photographic Darkrooms; Video Editing; Television Broadcast Station (Institutional); FM Radio Station (Institutional); Institutional Newspaper; Video Production Laboratory or Television Studio.

Eastern Washington University (Public)

Department of Radio-Television
MS-104
Cheney, Washington 99004
Telephone: (509) 359-2228

David K. Terwische, Chair
Gregory Hawkins, Acting Dean

CURRICULUM AND INSTRUCTION
Courses or Concentrations Available: Radio, Television, Broadcasting, or Telecommunications; *Bachelor's Degree Majors*: 134; *Master's Degree Majors*: 3; *Full-Time Faculty*: 6; *Part-Time Faculty*: 1; *Full-Time Professional (non-clerical) Staff Members*: 2.

FACILITIES AND SERVICES
Practical experiences available through: Advertising Agency; Associated Press Wire Service Feed; Audio Recording Laboratory; Community Antenna (Cable) Television Origination; Carrier Current Audio Distribution System; Closed Circuit Television Facility; Campus Newspaper (Published Independently); Local Commercial Television Station; Video Editing; Electronic Field Production (Video); FM Radio Station (Institutional); Institutional Newspaper; Video Production Laboratory or Television Studio.

Eastern Washington University (Public)

Department of Communication Studies
MS #108
Cheney, Washington 99004
Telephone: (509) 458-6232

Reta A. Gilbert, Chair
Neil T. Zimmerman, Dean, College of Letters and Sciences

CURRICULUM AND INSTRUCTION
Courses or Concentrations Available: Communication; Information Science; Journalism or Mass Communication; Public Relations; Speech; *Program Coordinators*: David K. Terwische (Radio/Television); Steve Blewett (Journalism); Lew L. Wilson (Master of Science in Communications); *Undergraduate Objectives or Program Emphases*: BA in Speech Communication Education, endorsement in Speech Communication Education; BA in Communication Studies emphases in public, interpersonal and organization; BS in organizational and mass communication; *Graduate Objectives or Program Emphases*: Master of Science in Communications; *Bachelor's Degree Majors*: 42; *Other Degree Majors*: 190; *Full-Time Faculty*: 7; *Part-Time Faculty*: 4; *Full-Time Professional (non-clerical) Staff Members*: 1.

FACILITIES AND SERVICES
Practical experiences available through: AM Radio Station (Institutional); Associated Press Wire Service Feed; Audio Recording Laboratory; Campus Newspaper (Published Independently); Desktop Publishing Facility; Photographic Darkrooms; Video Editing; Electronic Field Production (Video); Institutional Magazine.

Everett Community College

Arts and Communications
801 Wetmore Avenue
Everett, Washington 98201

Nicki Haynes, Administrator

Evergreen State College

Expressive Arts Convener
Olympia, Washington 98505

Sally Cloninger, Administrator

Gonzaga University

Department of Communication Arts
502 E. Boone Avenue
Spokane, Washington 99258

Robert V. Lyons, Administrator

Highline Community College (Public)

Program of Journalism/Mass Media
P. O. Box 98000
Des Moines, Washington 98198
Telephone: (206) 878-3710 Extension or
Alternate: 292

Linda M. Baker, Program Coordinator
Carol Wardell-Tausbaro, Division Chair

CURRICULUM AND INSTRUCTION
Courses or Concentrations
Available: Advertising; Journalism or Mass
Communication; Public Relations; Radio,
Television, Broadcasting, or
Telecommunications; Desktop Publishing;
Program Coordinator: Susan Landgraf
(Advisor to student newspaper; writing and
reporting sequence instructor);
*Undergraduate Objectives or Program
Emphases*: AA, college transfer in
communication; AAS, work in advertising,
public relations or desktop publishing fields;
Certificates in television (technical end of
video); *Degree Majors*: 80; *Full-Time
Faculty*: 2; *Part-Time Faculty*: 3.

FACILITIES AND SERVICES
*Practical experiences available
through*: Advertising Agency; Community
Antenna (Cable) Television Origination;
Closed Circuit Television Facility; Local
Commercial Newspaper; Local Commercial
Television Station; Desktop Publishing
Facility; Photographic Darkrooms; Video
Editing; Electronic Field Production
(Video); Institutional Newspaper; Public
Relations Agency; Video News and Data
Processing; Video Production Laboratory or
Television Studio.

Lower Columbia College (Public)

Instruction
1600 Maple
Longview, Washington 98632
Telephone: (206) 577-3424

Phyllis Marble, Dean

CURRICULUM AND INSTRUCTION
Courses or Concentrations
Available: Communication; Journalism or
Mass Communication; Speech; *Program
Coordinators*: Joseph Green (English); Mike
Dugan (Fine Arts/Speech); *Full-Time*

Faculty: 83; *Part-Time Faculty*: 40;
*Full-Time Professional (non-clerical) Staff
Members*: 83.

Olympic College

Division of Humanities
16th and Chester
Bremerton, Washington 98310

North Seattle Community College

Continuing Education
9600 College Way North
Seattle, Washington 98103

Cecile Andrews, Administrator

Pacific Lutheran University (Private)

Department of Communication Arts
Tacoma, Washington 98107-0003
Telephone: (206) 535-7762

Christopher H. Spicer, Chair
Richard Moe, Dean, School of the Arts

CURRICULUM AND INSTRUCTION
Courses or Concentrations
Available: Journalism or Mass
Communication; Public Relations; Radio,
Television, Broadcasting, or
Telecommunications; Speech; Theatre;
Program Coordinators: William Becvar
(Theatre); Cliff Rowe (Journalism);
*Undergraduate Objectives or Program
Emphases*: Broad understanding of
communication as a process within a liberal
arts perspective. Focus on education rather
than technical training; *Bachelor's Degree
Majors*: 160; *BFA Degree Majors*: 20;
Full-Time Faculty: 9; *Part-Time Faculty*: 8;
*Full-Time Professional (non-clerical) Staff
Members*: 1.

FACILITIES AND SERVICES
Practical experiences available through: Audio
Recording Laboratory; Carrier Current
Audio Distribution System; Closed Circuit
Television Facility; Campus Newspaper
(Published Independently); Local
Commercial Newspaper; Local Commercial
Television Station; Video Editing;

Electronic Field Production (Video); Television Broadcast Station (Institutional); FM Radio Station (Institutional); Public Relations Agency; Video Production Laboratory or Television Studio.

Peninsula College (Public)

Division of Humanities/Social Sciences
1502 East Boulevard
Port Angeles, Washington 98362
Telephone: (206) 452-9277

Jack W. Estes, Chair
Francis Prindle, Dean of Instruction

CURRICULUM AND INSTRUCTION
Courses or Concentrations Available: Film or Cinema; Journalism or Mass Communication; Speech; *Program Coordinators*: Robbie Mantooth (Journalism); *Undergraduate Objectives or Program Emphases*: Associate of Arts Degree; *Associate's Degree Majors*: 75; *Full-Time Faculty*: 13; *Part-Time Faculty*: 6; *Full-Time Professional (non-clerical) Staff Members*: 2.

FACILITIES AND SERVICES
Practical experiences available through: Audio Recording Laboratory; Local Commercial Newspaper; Desktop Publishing Facility; Photographic Darkrooms; Video Editing; Electronic Field Production (Video); Institutional Magazine; Institutional Newspaper.

Pierce College (Public)

Department of Journalism
9401 Far West Drive SW
Tacoma, Washington 98498
Telephone: (206) 964-6348

Michael W. Parks, Head
Morrie Pederson, Director, Humanities Division

CURRICULUM AND INSTRUCTION
Courses or Concentrations Available: Journalism or Mass Communication; *Undergraduate Objectives or Program Emphases*: Offer introductory courses in news writing, feature writing, mass communications, and practical experience in news writing through participation in student newspaper; *Full-Time Faculty*: 1.

FACILITIES AND SERVICES
Practical experiences available through: Campus Newspaper (Published Independently); Local Commercial Newspaper; Desktop Publishing Facility; Photographic Darkrooms; Institutional Newspaper.

Seattle Central Community College (Public)

Division of Visual Arts and Applied Technology
1701 Broadway
Seattle, Washington 98008
Telephone: (206) 344-4349

Myrtle Mitchell, Chair

CURRICULUM AND INSTRUCTION
Courses or Concentrations Available: Radio, Television, Broadcasting, or Telecommunications; Video Production; *Undergraduate Objectives or Program Emphases*: AAS degree; *Full-Time Faculty*: 1; *Part-Time Faculty*: 2.

FACILITIES AND SERVICES
Practical experiences available through: Advertising Agency; Community Antenna (Cable) Television Origination; Campus Newspaper (Published Independently); Local Commercial Newspaper; Local Commercial Television Station; Desktop Publishing Facility; Photographic Darkrooms; Video Editing; Video Production Laboratory or Television Studio.

Seattle Pacific University (Private)

Discipline of Communication
3307 Third Avenue, West
Seattle, Washington 98119
Telephone: (206) 281-2095

Robert G. Chamberlain, Chair
Thomas Trzyna, Dean, School of Humanities

CURRICULUM AND INSTRUCTION
Courses or Concentrations

Available: Communication; Public Relations; Speech; *Undergraduate Objectives or Program Emphases*: Liberal education with human communication specializations; employability developed through practical curricular experiences such as internships; *Bachelor's Degree Majors*: 75; *Full-Time Faculty*: 3; *Part-Time Faculty*: 1.

FACILITIES AND SERVICES
Practical experiences available through: Audio Recording Laboratory; Campus Newspaper (Published Independently); Local Commercial Newspaper; Local Commercial Television Station; Photographic Darkrooms; Video Editing.

Seattle University

Journalism Department
Seattle, Washington 98122

Gary L. Atkins, Administrator

Skagit Valley College (Public)

Department of
Drama/Speech/Radio-Television
2405 College Way
Mount Vernon, Washington 98273
Telephone: (206) 428-1261

Andrew J. Friedlander, Chair
Ted Keeler, Associate Dean

CURRICULUM AND INSTRUCTION
Courses or Concentrations
Available: Communication; Film or Cinema; Journalism or Mass Communication; Radio, Television, Broadcasting, or Telecommunications; Speech; *Undergraduate Objectives or Program Emphases*: To provide basic skills and courses on the freshman/sophomore level. Hands-on experience via campus newspaper, radio station and video projects; *Associate's Degree Majors*: 20; *Full-Time Faculty*: 3; *Part-Time Faculty*: 1.

FACILITIES AND SERVICES
Practical experiences available through: Advertising Agency; Campus Newspaper (Published Independently); Local Commercial Newspaper; Desktop Publishing Facility; Photographic Darkrooms; Video Editing; FM Radio

Station (Institutional); Public Relations Agency.

South Seattle Community College - South (Public)

Division of College Transfer
6000 16th Avenue, SW
Seattle, Washington 98106
Telephone: (206) 764-5357

Michael E. McCrath, Chair
Robert Hester, Dean of Instruction

CURRICULUM AND INSTRUCTION
Courses or Concentrations
Available: Journalism or Mass Communication; Speech; *Undergraduate Objectives or Program Emphases*: Two year Liberal Arts curriculum with courses designed to transfer to four-year institution; developmental education program designed to prepare students to pursue college-level work in English and Math; *Associate's Degree Majors*: 1092; *Full-Time Faculty*: 21; *Part-Time Faculty*: 30.

FACILITIES AND SERVICES
Practical experiences available through: Audio Recording Laboratory; Carrier Current Audio Distribution System; Closed Circuit Television Facility; Campus Newspaper (Published Independently); Desktop Publishing Facility; Photographic Darkrooms; Video Editing; Electronic Field Production (Video); Film or Cinema Laboratory; Institutional Newspaper; Satellite Uplink Facility; Video Production Laboratory or Television Studio.

Spokane Community College (Public)

Department of Speech Communication
North 1810 Greene Street
Spokane, Washington 99207-5399
Telephone: (509) 536-7000

Val Clark, Chair
Tony Embrey, Assistant Dean

CURRICULUM AND INSTRUCTION
Courses or Concentrations
Available: Communication; Film or Cinema; Speech; Vocational focus: Job

Communications; *Undergraduate Objectives or Program Emphases*: To provide communication courses that are transferable to four year institutions as well as support courses for vocational programs; *Full-Time Faculty*: 6; *Part-Time Faculty*: 4.

FACILITIES AND SERVICES
Practical experiences available through: Closed Circuit Television Facility; Campus Newspaper (Published Independently); Local Commercial Newspaper; Local Commercial Television Station; Desktop Publishing Facility; Photographic Darkrooms; Video Editing; Electronic Field Production (Video); ITFS Distribution System; Institutional Magazine; Institutional Newspaper; Video Production Laboratory or Television Studio.

University of Puget Sound (Private)

Department of Communication and Theatre Arts
Tacoma, Washington 98416
Telephone: (206) 753-3334

Kristine M. Bartanen, Chair
Thomas A. Davis, Dean

CURRICULUM AND INSTRUCTION
Courses or Concentrations Available: Communication; Journalism or Mass Communication; Speech; *Undergraduate Objectives or Program Emphases*: Broad based liberal arts preparation with emphases in rhetorical studies, communication studies, media criticism, applied communication (business, organizational); *Bachelor's Degree Majors*: 80; *Full-Time Faculty*: 12; *Full-Time Professional (non-clerical) Staff Members*: 1.

FACILITIES AND SERVICES
Practical experiences available through: Campus Newspaper (Published Independently); Desktop Publishing Facility; Photographic Darkrooms; FM Radio Station (Institutional).

University of Washington (Public)

School of Communication
1400 Northeast Campus Parkway
Seattle, Washington 98195

Ed Bassett, Director

University of Washington (Public)

Department of Speech Communication
Seattle, Washington 98195
Telephone: (206) 543-4860

Ann Q. Staton, Chair
Thomas M. Scheidel, Associate Dean, Humanities

CURRICULUM AND INSTRUCTION
Courses or Concentrations Available: Communication; Speech; *Undergraduate Objectives or Program Emphases*: Students acquire an understanding, both theoretical and practical, of speech communication; *Graduate Objectives or Program Emphases*: Students acquire an advanced understanding of speech communication and the capacity to contribute to knowledge in some field of the discipline through independent research in important problem areas; *Bachelor's Degree Majors*: 200; *Doctoral Degree Majors Currently in Residence*: 45; *Additional Doctoral Degree Majors*: 5; *Full-Time Faculty*: 13; *Part-Time Faculty*: 25.

FACILITIES AND SERVICES
Practical experiences available through: Audio Recording Laboratory; Closed Circuit Television Facility; Campus Newspaper (Published Independently); Photographic Darkrooms; Video Editing.

Walla Walla College (Private)

Department of Communications
College Place, Washington 99324
Telephone: (509) 527-2832

Loren Dickenson, Chair
Alden Thompson, Vice President, Academic Administration

CURRICULUM AND INSTRUCTION
Courses or Concentrations Available: Communication; Journalism or Mass Communication; Radio, Television,

Broadcasting, or Telecommunications; Speech; *Undergraduate Objectives or Program Emphases*: Broadcast Media; Journalism, Public Relations; *Bachelor's Degree Majors*: 80; *Full-Time Faculty*: 4; *Part-Time Faculty*: 1.

FACILITIES AND SERVICES
Practical experiences available through: Audio Recording Laboratory; Campus Newspaper (Published Independently); Desktop Publishing Facility; Photographic Darkrooms; Video Editing; Electronic Field Production (Video); FM Radio Station (Institutional); Video Production Laboratory or Television Studio.

Washington State University (Public)

School of Communications
Pullman, Washington 99164-2520
Telephone: (509) 335-1556

Alex S. Tan, Chair
John Pierce, Dean, College of Arts and Sciences

CURRICULUM AND INSTRUCTION
Courses or Concentrations Available: Advertising; Communication; Journalism or Mass Communication; Public Relations; Radio, Television, Broadcasting, or Telecommunications; Speech; *Undergraduate Objectives or Program Emphases*: Professional, Theory and Research; *Graduate Objectives or Program Emphases*: Theory and Research, Professional; *Bachelor's Degree Majors*: 442; *Master's Degree Majors*: 54; *Doctoral Degree Majors Currently in Residence*: 8; *Full-Time Faculty*: 23; *Part-Time Faculty*: 10; *Full-Time Professional (non-clerical) Staff Members*: 4.

FACILITIES AND SERVICES
Practical experiences available through: AM Radio Station (Institutional); Associated Press Wire Service Feed; Audio Recording Laboratory; Community Antenna (Cable) Television Origination; Closed Circuit Television Facility; Campus Newspaper (Published Independently); Local Commercial Newspaper; Local Commercial Television Station; Desktop Publishing Facility; Photographic Darkrooms; Video Editing; Electronic Field Production (Video); Television Broadcast Station

(Institutional); FM Radio Station (Institutional); ITFS Distribution System; Institutional Magazine; Institutional Newspaper; Video News and Data Processing; Video Production Laboratory or Television Studio.

Western Washington University (Public)

Department of Speech and Broadcast
Bellingham, Washington 98225

Larry S. Richardson, Administrator

Western Washington University (Public)

Department of Journalism
Bellingham, Washington 98225
Telephone: (206) 676-3252

Lyle E. Harris, Chair

CURRICULUM AND INSTRUCTION
Courses or Concentrations Available: Advertising; Communication; Journalism or Mass Communication; Public Relations; *Undergraduate Objectives or Program Emphases*: Education in Journalism focused on writing and reporting; *Bachelor's Degree Majors*: 150; *Full-Time Faculty*: 5; *Part-Time Faculty*: 3.

FACILITIES AND SERVICES
Practical experiences available through: Advertising Agency; Closed Circuit Television Facility; Campus Newspaper (Published Independently); Local Commercial Newspaper; Local Commercial Television Station; Desktop Publishing Facility; Photographic Darkrooms; Television Broadcast Station (Institutional); FM Radio Station (Institutional); Institutional Magazine; Institutional Newspaper; Public Relations Agency; Video News and Data Processing.

Whitman College (Private)

Department of Speech
#183 Olin Hall
Walla Walla, Washington 99362
Telephone: (509) 527-5296

Robert A. Withycombe, Director
David Deal, Dean of Faculty

CURRICULUM AND INSTRUCTION
Courses or Concentrations Available: Speech;
*Undergraduate Objectives or Program
Emphases*: Public Address, History and
Criticism, Social Movements, Competitive
forensics, Service program; *Full-Time
Faculty*: 1.

FACILITIES AND SERVICES
*Practical experiences available
through*: Campus Newspaper (Published
Independently); Photographic Darkrooms;
FM Radio Station (Institutional).

Whitworth College (Private)

Department of Communication Studies
Spokane, Washington 99251
Telephone: (509) 466-1000

Gordon S. Jackson, Chair
Darrell Guder, Administrator

CURRICULUM AND INSTRUCTION
*Courses or Concentrations
Available*: Communication; Journalism or
Mass Communication; Public Relations;
Radio, Television, Broadcasting, or
Telecommunications; Speech; *Undergraduate
Objectives or Program Emphases*: To provide
students with a liberal arts education and
some hands-on experience with journalism;
Bachelor's Degree Majors: 50; *Full-Time
Faculty*: 4; *Part-Time Faculty*: 4.

FACILITIES AND SERVICES
Practical experiences available through: Audio
Recording Laboratory; Campus Newspaper
(Published Independently); Desktop
Publishing Facility; Photographic
Darkrooms; Video Editing; FM Radio
Station (Institutional); Institutional
Newspaper; Video News and Data
Processing.

Bethany College (Private)

Department of Communications
Bethany, West Virginia 26032
Telephone: (304) 829-7877

Harold C. Shaver, Head
Richard Bernard, Dean of Faculty

CURRICULUM AND INSTRUCTION
Courses or Concentrations
Available: Advertising; Communication;
Journalism or Mass Communication; Public
Relations; Radio, Television, Broadcasting,
or Telecommunications; Speech;
*Undergraduate Objectives or Program
Emphases*: Liberal Arts focus with balance of
professional and non-professional education;
comprehensive mass communication
background; employer needs; maintenance
on high academic expectations, integrity,
excellence; focus on social and ethical
responsibilities; *Degree Majors*: 155;
Full-Time Faculty: 6; *Full-Time Professional
(non-clerical) Staff Members*: 1.

FACILITIES AND SERVICES
*Practical experiences available
through*: Advertising Agency; Audio
Recording Laboratory; Community Antenna
(Cable) Television Origination; Desktop
Publishing Facility; Photographic
Darkrooms; Video Editing; Electronic Field
Production (Video); Television Broadcast
Station (Institutional); FM Radio Station
(Institutional); Institutional Magazine;
Institutional Newspaper; Public Relations
Agency; United Press International Feed.

Concord College (Public)

Department of Communication Arts
C. C. Box 50
Athens, West Virginia 24712
Telephone: (304) 384-5275

Ronald L. Burgher, Chair
John Carrier, Vice President

CURRICULUM AND INSTRUCTION
Courses or Concentrations
Available: Advertising; Communication;
Journalism or Mass Communication; Public
Relations; Radio, Television, Broadcasting,
or Telecommunications; Speech; *Bachelor's
Degree Majors*: 30; *Full-Time Faculty*: 4;
Part-Time Faculty: 5; *Full-Time Professional
(non-clerical) Staff Members*: 1.

FACILITIES AND SERVICES
*Practical experiences available
through*: Advertising Agency; Associated
Press Wire Service Feed; Audio Recording
Laboratory; Community Antenna (Cable)
Television Origination; Carrier Current
Audio Distribution System; Closed Circuit
Television Facility; Local Commercial
Newspaper; Local Commercial Television
Station; Desktop Publishing Facility;
Photographic Darkrooms; Video Editing;
Electronic Field Production (Video);
Television Broadcast Station (Institutional);
Institutional Newspaper; Public Relations
Agency; Video Production Laboratory or
Television Studio.

Davis and Elkins College (Private)

Department of Communication
Elkins, West Virginia 26241
Telephone: (304) 636-1900

Barbara G. Cox, Chair
Abbott Brayton, Dean of Faculty

CURRICULUM AND INSTRUCTION
Courses or Concentrations
Available: Communication; Journalism or
Mass Communication; Speech; Rhetoric;
Video Production; *Undergraduate Objectives
or Program Emphases*: Theory and practice
designed for students wishing to improve
their interpersonal and organizational
communication skills, enter a career in a
communication intensive area, or begin a
graduate program; *Bachelor's Degree
Majors*: 22; *Full-Time Faculty*: 1; *Part-Time
Faculty*: 3.

FACILITIES AND SERVICES
*Practical experiences available
through*: Advertising Agency; Audio
Recording Laboratory; Campus Newspaper

(Published Independently); Local Commercial Newspaper; Desktop Publishing Facility; Photographic Darkrooms; Video Editing; Electronic Field Production (Video); FM Radio Station (Institutional).

Fairmont State College (Public)

Department of Speech Communication and Theatre
Fairmont, West Virginia 26554
Telephone: (304) 367-4170

Charles H. Swanson, Coordinator
Leta Carson, Division Chair

CURRICULUM AND INSTRUCTION
Courses or Concentrations Available: Communication; Speech; Theatre; *Undergraduate Objectives or Program Emphases*: Performance based skills training with BA in Speech Communication, BA in Theatre and BA in Oral Communication Education; *Full-Time Faculty*: 7; *Part-Time Faculty*: 6.

FACILITIES AND SERVICES
Practical experiences available through: Audio Recording Laboratory; Community Antenna (Cable) Television Origination; Closed Circuit Television Facility; Campus Newspaper (Published Independently); Local Commercial Newspaper; Local Commercial Television Station; Video Editing; Electronic Field Production (Video); ITFS Distribution System; Institutional Newspaper; Video Production Laboratory or Television Studio.

Glenville State College (Public)

Division of Language
200 High Street
Glenville, West Virginia 26351
Telephone: (304) 462-7361

Dennis J. Wemm, Assistant Professor
Craig Etchison, Acting Chair

CURRICULUM AND INSTRUCTION
Courses or Concentrations Available: Advertising; Communication; Film or Cinema; Journalism or Mass Communication; Speech; *Program Coordinators*: Yvonne King (Journalism); Chris Orr (Film, Cinema); *Undergraduate*

Objectives or Program Emphases: Speech Education Major; Speech minors in Communication, Theatre; *Bachelor's Degree Majors*: 4; *Full-Time Faculty*: 2.

FACILITIES AND SERVICES
Practical experiences available through: Audio Recording Laboratory; Campus Newspaper (Published Independently); Local Commercial Newspaper; Desktop Publishing Facility; Photographic Darkrooms; Video Editing.

Marshall University (Public)

Department of Speech
Huntington, West Virginia 25701

Keith Spears, Administrator

Marshall University (Public)

W. Page Pitt School of Journalism
Huntington, West Virginia 25701
Telephone: (304) 696-2360

Dwight Jensen, Acting Director
Deryl Leoming, Dean

CURRICULUM AND INSTRUCTION
Courses or Concentrations Available: Advertising; Journalism or Mass Communication; Public Relations; Broadcast Journalism; *Undergraduate Objectives or Program Emphases*: Liberal arts education and professional journalism preparation; *Graduate Objectives or Program Emphases*: Liberal arts education and professional journalism preparation; *Bachelor's Degree Majors*: 153; *Master's Degree Majors*: 26; *Other Degree Majors*: 392; *Full-Time Faculty*: 8; *Part-Time Faculty*: 6; *Full-Time Professional (non-clerical) Staff Members*: 2.

FACILITIES AND SERVICES
Practical experiences available through: Closed Circuit Television Facility; Local Commercial Newspaper; Local Commercial Television Station; Desktop Publishing Facility; Photographic Darkrooms; Video Editing; Electronic Field Production (Video); FM Radio Station (Institutional); Institutional Newspaper; Video Production or Television Studio.

Ohio Valley College

Department of Communication
College Parkway
Parkersburg, West Virginia 26101

John E. Williams, Administrator

Salem-Teikyo University (Private)

Department of Communication
Valley of Learning
Salem, West Virginia 26426
Telephone: (304) 782-5011

Venita F. Zinn, Chair
Gary McAllister, Dean

CURRICULUM AND INSTRUCTION
Courses or Concentrations
Available: Advertising; Communication;
Radio, Television, Broadcasting, or
Telecommunications; Speech; *Undergraduate
Objectives or Program Emphases*: Prepare
professional broadcasters for entry level
positions. Students are required to become
acquainted with ;radio, television, cable,
media history, management, sales,
programming, production, and performance;
*Graduate Objectives or Program
Emphases*: Communication education;
Associate's Degree Majors: 10; *Bachelor's
Degree Majors*: 25; *Master's Degree Majors*: 2;
Full-Time Faculty: 3; *Part-Time Faculty*: 2.

FACILITIES AND SERVICES
Practical experiences available through: Audio
Recording Laboratory; Closed Circuit
Television Facility; Campus Newspaper
(Published Independently); Local
Commercial Newspaper; Local Commercial
Television Station; Photographic
Darkrooms; Video Editing; Electronic Field
Production (Video); Television Broadcast
Station (Institutional); FM Radio Station
(Institutional); Satellite Uplink Facility;
Video Production or Television Studio.

University of Charleston (Private)

Department of Mass Communications
2300 MacCorkle Avenue, SE
Charleston, West Virginia 25301
Telephone: (304) 357-4800

Timothy L. Ganser, Head
Barbara Yeager, Chair, Humanities

CURRICULUM AND INSTRUCTION
*Courses or Concentrations
Available*: Advertising; Communication; Film
or Cinema; Journalism or Mass
Communication; Radio, Television,
Broadcasting, or Telecommunications;
Speech; *Undergraduate Objectives or Program
Emphases*: A quality liberal arts based
education with hands on production
experience. Faculty/student ratios are low so
the students receive much one-on-one
instruction; *Bachelor's Degree Majors*: 10;
Full-Time Faculty: 1; *Part-Time Faculty*: 2.

FACILITIES AND SERVICES
*Practical experiences available
through*: Community Antenna (Cable)
Television Origination; Campus Newspaper
(Published Independently); Local
Commercial Newspaper; Local Commercial
Television Station; Desktop Publishing
Facility; Photographic Darkrooms; Video
Editing; Electronic Field Production; Video
Production or Television Studio.

West Liberty State College

Department of Communication
Hall of Fine Arts
West Liberty, West Virginia 26074

John Matviko, Administrator

West Virginia Northern Community College (Public)

Division of Humanities/Social Sciences
College Square
Wheeling, West Virginia 26003
Telephone: (304) 233-5900 Extension: 290

Patricia Burns, Chair
John Anderson, Vice President

CURRICULUM AND INSTRUCTION
Courses or Concentrations

Available: Journalism or Mass Communication; Speech; *Undergraduate Objectives or Program Emphases*: Speech Communication includes a study of the elements of oral communication and practice in organizing and delivering short speeches. Emphasis is on the development of effective communication skills and self-confidence; *Full-Time Faculty*: 2; *Part-Time Faculty*: 3.

FACILITIES AND SERVICES
Practical experiences available through: Closed Circuit Television Facility.

West Virginia State College (Public)

Department of Communication
Box 28
Institute, West Virginia 25112
Telephone: (304) 766-3186

David Wohl, Chair
Barbara Oden, Vice President, Academic Affairs

CURRICULUM AND INSTRUCTION
Courses or Concentrations
Available: Advertising; Communication; Film or Cinema; Journalism or Mass Communication; Public Relations; Radio, Television, Broadcasting, or Telecommunications; Speech; Theatre; *Undergraduate Objectives or Program Emphases*: A generalist degree in communications emphasizing hands-on skills in a variety of communications-related areas; *Degree Majors*: 165; *Full-Time Faculty*: 5; *Part-Time Faculty*: 6; *Full-Time Professional (non-clerical) Staff Members*: 3.

FACILITIES AND SERVICES
Practical experiences available through: Advertising Agency; Audio Recording Laboratory; Community Antenna (Cable) Television Origination; Carrier Current Audio Distribution System; Closed Circuit Television Facility; Campus Newspaper (Published Independently); Local Commercial Newspaper; Local Commercial Television Station; Desktop Publishing Facility; Photographic Darkrooms; Video Editing; Electronic Field Production (Video); Television Broadcast Station (Institutional); Film or Cinema Laboratory; ITFS Distribution System; Public Relations Agency; Satellite Uplink

Facility (Ku Band Transmitter); Video Production Laboratory or Television Studio.

West Virginia University (Public)

Department of Radio and Television
Morgantown, West Virginia 26506

West Virginia University (Public)

School of Journalism
112 Martin Hall
Morgantown, West Virginia 26506
Telephone: (304) 293-3505

Emery L. Sasser, Dean
Frank Franz, Provost

CURRICULUM AND INSTRUCTION
Courses or Concentrations
Available: Advertising; Journalism or Mass Communication; Public Relations; Radio, Television, or Telecommunications; *Program Coordinators*: Richard Schreiber (Advertising); Charles F. Cremer (Broadcast News); Robert M. Ours (News-Editorial); R. Ivan Pinnell (Public Relations); *Undergraduate Objectives*: Professional ethics and responsibilities in the broad study of mass communication and society; *Graduate Objectives*: To help persons involved in the various aspects of mass communication better understand and cope not only with the increased complexity of their own field, but also with fields outside mass communication; *Bachelor's Degree Majors*: 251; *Master's Degree Majors*: 31; *Full-Time Faculty*: 15; *Part-Time Faculty*: 12.

FACILITIES AND SERVICES
Practical experiences available through: Advertising Agency; Associated Press Wire Service Feed; Audio Recording Laboratory; Community Antenna (Cable) Television Origination; Closed Circuit Television Facility; Campus Newspaper (Published Independently); Local Commercial Newspaper; Local Commercial Television Station; Desktop Publishing Facility; Photographic Darkrooms; Video Editing; Electronic Field Production (Video); Television Broadcast Station (Institutional); FM Radio Station (Institutional); ITFS Distribution System; Institutional Newspaper; Public Relations

Agency; Video News and Data Processing; Video Production or Television Studio.

West Virginia University (Public)

Broadcast Journalism
Morgantown, West Virginia 26506

Charles F. Cremer, Administrator

West Virginia University (Public)

Department of Communication Studies
130 Armstrong Hall
Morgantown, West Virginia 26506
Telephone: (304) 293-3905

James C. McCroskey, Chair
Gerald E. Lang, Dean, College of Arts and Sciences

CURRICULUM AND INSTRUCTION
Courses or Concentrations Available: Communication; *Undergraduate Objectives or Program Emphases*: Interpersonal and Organizational Communication; Public and Mass Communication; Communication Theory and Research; *Graduate Objectives*: Communication in Instruction; Interpersonal and Organizational Communication; *Bachelor's Degree Majors*: 135; *Master's Degree Majors*: 627; *Doctoral Degree Majors Currently in Residence*: 4; *Additional Doctoral Degree Majors*: 2; *Full-Time Faculty*: 11; *Part-Time Faculty*: 14.

West Virginia Wesleyan College (Private)

Department of Speech Communication and Dramatic Arts
Box 96
Buckhannon, West Virginia 26201
Telephone: (304) 473-8000 Extension: 8258

Larry Reed, Chair
Barbara Richardson, Dean, Academic Affairs

CURRICULUM AND INSTRUCTION
Courses or Concentrations Available: Communication; Journalism or Mass Communication; Public Relations;

Radio, Television, Broadcasting, or Telecommunications; Speech; Forensics; *Undergraduate Objectives or Program Emphases*: To help students achieve effective expression in personal, public and mass communication environments by building one broad liberal arts background in order to develop the knowledge and skills for their field; *Bachelor's Degree Majors*: 40; *Full-Time Faculty*: 7.

FACILITIES AND SERVICES
Practical experiences available through: Advertising Agency; Community Antenna (Cable) Television Origination; Closed Circuit Television Facility; Campus Newspaper (Published Independently); Local Commercial Newspaper; Local Commercial Television Station; Desktop Publishing Facility; Photographic Darkrooms; FM Radio Station (Institutional); Public Relations Agency; Video Production or Television Studio.

Wheeling Jesuit College (Private)

Program of Professional Writing
316 Washington Avenue
Wheeling, West Virginia 26003
Telephone: (304) 243-2247

Richard L. Krause, Coordinator
Joseph Brumble, Department Chair

CURRICULUM AND INSTRUCTION
Courses or Concentrations Available: Advertising; Journalism or Mass Communication; Public Relations; Radio, Television, Broadcasting, or Telecommunications; *Undergraduate Objectives or Program Emphases*: The professional writing major is appropriate for students who want to work in journalism, public relations, advertising, news-editorial, broadcast and related areas; *Bachelor's Degree Majors*: 14; *Full-Time Faculty*: 1.

FACILITIES AND SERVICES
Practical experiences available through: Advertising Agency; Campus Newspaper (Published Independently); Local Commercial Newspaper; Local Commercial Television Station; Desktop Publishing Facility; Photographic Darkrooms; Public Relations Agency.

Beloit College

Department of Theatre Arts
700 College Street
Beloit, Wisconsin 53511
Telephone: (608) 365-3391

Carl G. Balson, Director
Rod Umlas, Chair

CURRICULUM AND INSTRUCTION
Courses or Concentrations
Available: Advertising; Communication;
Journalism or Mass Communication; Radio,
Television, Broadcasting, or
Telecommunications; Speech; *Undergraduate*
Objectives or Program Emphases: To study
communication in a liberal arts context;
Bachelor's Degree Majors: 12; *Full-Time*
Faculty: 1.

FACILITIES AND SERVICES
Practical experiences available
through: Associated Press Wire Service Feed;
Audio Recording Laboratory; Community
Antenna (Cable) Television Origination;
Campus Newspaper (Published
Independently); Desktop Publishing Facility;
Photographic Darkrooms; Video Editing;
Electronic Field Production (Video); FM
Radio Station (Institutional); Video News
and Data Processing; Video Production
Laboratory or Television Studio.

Blackhawk Technical College (Public)

Division of General Education/Service
Occupations
6004 Prairie Road
Janesville, Wisconsin 53547
Telephone: (608) 756-4121

Barabara A. Cannell, Associate Chair
Carol Brunsell, Division Chair

CURRICULUM AND INSTRUCTION
Courses or Concentrations
Available: Communication; Public Relations;
Speech; *Full-Time Faculty*: 11; *Part-Time*
Faculty: 7.

Cardinal Stritch College (Private)

Department of Communication Arts
6801 North Yates Road
Milwaukee, Wisconsin 53217
Telephone: (414) 352-5400

David L. Oswald, Head
Linda Plagman, Administrator

CURRICULUM AND INSTRUCTION
Courses or Concentrations
Available: Communication; Film or Cinema;
Journalism or Mass Communication; Public
Relations; Radio, Television, Broadcasting,
or Telecommunications; Speech;
Undergraduate Objectives or Program
Emphases: Interpersonal Communication,
Public Communication; *Bachelor's Degree*
Majors: 55; *Full-Time Faculty*: 3; *Part-Time*
Faculty: 8; *Full-Time Professional*
(non-clerical) Staff Members: 1.

FACILITIES AND SERVICES
Practical experiences available
through: Community Antenna (Cable)
Television Origination; Campus Newspaper
(Published Independently); Local
Commercial Newspaper; Local Commercial
Television Station; Desktop Publishing
Facility; Photographic Darkrooms; Video
Editing; Film or Cinema Laboratory; Public
Relations Agency.

Carroll College (Private)

Department of Communication
Waukesha, Wisconsin 53186
Telephone: (414) 524-7270

Joseph J. Hemmer, Jr., Chair

CURRICULUM AND INSTRUCTION
Courses or Concentrations
Available: Advertising; Communication; Film
or Cinema; Journalism or Mass
Communication; Public Relations; Radio,
Television, Broadcasting, or
Telecommunications; Speech; *Undergraduate*
Objectives or Program Emphases: To provide
personalized liberal arts education for career
minded individuals; *Bachelor's Degree*

Majors: 120; *Full-Time Faculty*: 4;
Part-Time Faculty: 4.

FACILITIES AND SERVICES
*Practical experiences available
through*: Advertising Agency; AM Radio
Station (Institutional); Campus Newspaper
(Published Independently); Local
Commercial Newspaper; Local Commercial
Television Station; Photographic
Darkrooms; Video Editing; FM Radio
Station (Institutional); Video Production
Laboratory or Television Studio.

Concordia University Wisconsin (Private)

Department of Communication
12800 North Lakeshore Drive
Mequon, Wisconsin 53092-9652
Telephone: (414) 243-5700

M. D. Hilgendorf, Chair
William Chandler, Dean

CURRICULUM AND INSTRUCTION
*Courses or Concentrations
Available*: Advertising; Communication; Film
or Cinema; Journalism or Mass
Communication; Public Relations; Radio,
Television, Broadcasting, or
Telecommunications; Speech; *Undergraduate
Objectives or Program Emphases*: In Speech
Communication, the program meets the
requirements of the Wisconsin Department
of Education for teacher certification for
those majoring in speech. In Mass
Communication, the program assists in job
placement and/or prepares for graduate
work; *Bachelor's Degree Majors*: 25;
Full-Time Faculty: 3; *Part-Time Faculty*: 2;
*Full-Time Professional (non-clerical) Staff
Members*: 1.

FACILITIES AND SERVICES
*Practical experiences available
through*: Advertising Agency; Audio
Recording Laboratory; Community Antenna
(Cable) Television Origination; Carrier
Current Audio Distribution System; Campus
Newspaper (Published Independently);
Local Commercial Newspaper; Local
Commercial Television Station; Desktop
Publishing Facility; Photographic
Darkrooms; Video Editing; Public
Relations Agency.

Edgewood College (Private)

Department of English
855 Woodrow Street
Madison, Wisconsin 53711
Telephone: (608) 257-4861

Winifred A. Morgan, Chair
Judith Wimmer, Academic Dean

CURRICULUM AND INSTRUCTION
*Courses or Concentrations
Available*: Journalism or Mass
Communication; Public Relations;
*Undergraduate Objectives or Program
Emphases*: Writing to communicate;
Bachelor's Degree Majors: 18; *Full-Time
Faculty*: 1.

FACILITIES AND SERVICES
*Practical experiences available
through*: Advertising Agency; Campus
Newspaper (Published Independently);
Desktop Publishing Facility.

Gateway Technical College (Public)

Department of General Education
3520 30th Avenue
Kenosha, Wisconsin 53142-1690
Telephone: (414) 656-6904

Richard S. Wieland, Lead Instructor
Bernard O'Connell, Administrator

CURRICULUM AND INSTRUCTION
*Courses or Concentrations
Available*: Advertising; Communication;
Public Relations; Radio, Television,
Broadcasting, or Telecommunications;
Speech; *Undergraduate Objectives or Program
Emphases*: To prepare student for entry level
positions in radio broadcasting with emphasis
on announcing skills, production, copywriting
and news reporting; *Degree Majors*: 47;
Full-Time Faculty: 20; *Part-Time Faculty*: 5;
*Full-Time Professional (non-clerical) Staff
Members*: 2.

FACILITIES AND SERVICES
*Practical experiences available
through*: Associated Press Wire Service Feed;
Audio Recording Laboratory; Community
Antenna (Cable) Television Origination; FM
Radio Station (Institutional); Video
Production Laboratory or Television Studio.

Marquette University (Private)

College of Communication, Journalism and Performing Arts
1131 W. Wisconsin Avenue
Milwaukee, Wisconsin 53233
Telephone: (414) 288-7074

Sharon M. Murphy, Dean
Michael J. Price, Associate Dean

CURRICULUM AND INSTRUCTION
Courses or Concentrations
Available: Advertising; Communication; Film or Cinema; Journalism or Mass Communication; Public Relations; Radio, Television, Broadcasting, or Telecommunications; Speech; Communication and Rhetorical Studies; Speech Pathology and Audiology, and Performing Arts; *Program Coordinators*: Bill Baxter (Public Relations); Jack Crowley (Advertising); Michael Price (Broadcasting); James Arnold (Film); Robert Shuter (Communication, Speech, Rhetorical Studies); William Thorn (Journalism); Edward Korabic (Pathology); William Grange (Performance); *Undergraduate Objectives or Program Emphases*: In the context of the Jesuit character of Marquette University, the College is dedicated to the study and application of the art and science of human communication at the undergraduate and graduate level. Preparation for leadership roles in the field; *Graduate Objectives or Program Emphases*: At both levels, study includes critical analysis of communication and development of professional skills in the discipline of advertising and public relations, communication and rhetorical studies, journalism, speech pathology and audiology, and the performing arts; *Bachelor's Degree Majors*: 569; *Master's Degree Majors*: 74; *Full-Time Faculty*: 47; *Part-Time Faculty*: 25; *Full-Time Professional (non-clerical) Staff Members*: 4.

FACILITIES AND SERVICES
Practical experiences available through: Associated Press Wire Service Feed; Audio Recording Laboratory; Carrier Current Audio Distribution System; Closed Circuit Television Facility; Desktop Publishing Facility; Photographic Darkrooms; Video Editing; Electronic Field Production (Video); Television Broadcast Station (Institutional); Film or Cinema Laboratory; Institutional Magazine; Institutional Newspaper; Video News and Data Processing; Video Production Laboratory or Television Studio.

Marquette University (Private)

Department of Broadcast and Electronic Communication
1131 West Wisconsin Avenue
Milwaukee, Wisconsin 53233
Telephone: (414) 288-7149

Michael J. Price, Chair
Sharon Murphy, Dean

CURRICULUM AND INSTRUCTION
Courses or Concentrations
Available: Journalism or Mass Communication; Radio, Television, Broadcasting, or Telecommunications; *Undergraduate Objectives or Program Emphases*: Management, production, programming, broadcast news, corporate media, new technologies; *Graduate Objectives or Program Emphases*: Research/theory in mass communication; *Bachelor's Degree Majors*: 240; *Master's Degree Majors*: 13; *Full-Time Faculty*: 8; *Part-Time Faculty*: 3.

FACILITIES AND SERVICES
Practical experiences available through: Associated Press Wire Service Feed; Audio Recording Laboratory; Carrier Current Audio Distribution System; Closed Circuit Television Facility; Local Commercial Television Station; Video Editing; Electronic Field Production (Video); Video News and Data Processing; Video Production Laboratory or Television Studio.

Milwaukee Area Technical College (Public)

Division of Telecasting
700 West State
Milwaukee, Wisconsin 53233
Telephone: (414) 278-6600

David Baule, Chair
Tom Axtell, General Manager

CURRICULUM AND INSTRUCTION
Courses or Concentrations
Available: Communication; Radio, Television, Broadcasting, or Telecommunications; *Associate's Degree*

Majors: 52; *Full-Time Faculty*: 2; *Part-Time Faculty*: 5; *Full-Time Professional (non-clerical) Staff Members*: 75.

FACILITIES AND SERVICES
Practical experiences available through: Associated Press Wire Service Feed; Audio Recording Laboratory; Community Antenna (Cable) Television Origination; Closed Circuit Television Facility; Local Commercial Television Station; Desktop Publishing Facility; Video Editing; Electronic Field Production (Video); Television Broadcast Station (Institutional); ITFS Distribution System; Video News and Data Processing; Video Production Laboratory or Television Studio.

Nashotah House

Nashotah House Media Center
2777 Mission Road
Nashotah, Wisconsin 53058-9990

Norman P. Aldred, Administrator

Northwestern College (Private)

1300 Western Avenue
Watertown, Wisconsin 53094
Telephone: (414) 261-4352

Robert J. Voss, President

CURRICULUM AND INSTRUCTION
Courses or Concentrations Available: Communication; Speech; *Undergraduate Objectives or Program Emphases*: A speech course designed to acquaint the student with the principles of public speaking and to employ those principles in actual practice; *Bachelor's Degree Majors*: 218; *Full-Time Faculty*: 23.

FACILITIES AND SERVICES
Practical experiences available through: Community Antenna (Cable) Television Origination; Campus Newspaper (Published Independently); Desktop Publishing Facility; Photographic Darkrooms; Video Editing.

Ripon College

Department of Speech and Drama
300 Seward Street, Box 49
Ripon, Wisconsin 54971

Jean Fishman, Administrator

Silver Lake College

Professional Studies Division
2406 South Alvero Road
Manitowoc, Wisconsin 54220

Patrick Gagnon, Administrator

University of Wisconsin - Eau Claire (Public)

Department of Communication and Theatre Arts
Eau Claire, Wisconsin 54702
Telephone: (715) 836-3419

W. Robert Sampson, Chair
Lee E. Grugel, Dean, School of Arts and Sciences

CURRICULUM AND INSTRUCTION
Courses or Concentrations Available: Communication; Public Relations; Radio, Television, Broadcasting, or Telecommunications; Organizational Communication, Public Communication, Theatre Arts; *Undergraduate Objectives or Program Emphases*: Organizational communication, public relations, speech communication, telecommunications; *Graduate Objectives or Program Emphases*: An Entitlement to Plan as Master of Arts in Communication. Program will provide coursework from all four areas listed above and emphasize organizational communication; *Bachelor's Degree Majors*: 418; *Full-Time Faculty*: 20; *Part-Time Faculty*: 2; *Full-Time Professional (non-clerical) Staff Members*: 1.

FACILITIES AND SERVICES
Practical experiences available through: Advertising Agency; Associated Press Wire Service Feed; Audio Recording Laboratory; Community Antenna (Cable) Television Origination; Closed Circuit Television Facility; Campus Newspaper (Published Independently); Local

Commercial Television Station; Desktop Publishing Facility; Video Editing; Electronic Field Production (Video); FM Radio Station (Institutional); ITFS Distribution System; Video Production Laboratory or Television Studio.

University of Wisconsin - Eau Claire (Public)

Department of Journalism
Garfield and Park
Eau Claire, Wisconsin 54701
Telephone: (715) 836-2528

James E. Fields, Chair
Lee E. Grugel, Dean, School of Arts and Sciences

CURRICULUM AND INSTRUCTION
Courses or Concentrations
Available: Advertising; Journalism or Mass Communication; Public Relations; Radio, Television, Broadcasting, or Telecommunications; *Undergraduate Objectives or Program Emphases*: Preparation of professional communicators for mass media and information roles including, though not limited to, print and broadcast news, advertising, public relations, and education; *Bachelor's Degree Majors*: 402; *Full-Time Faculty*: 9; *Part-Time Faculty*: 3; *Full-Time Professional (non-clerical) Staff Members*: 1.

FACILITIES AND SERVICES
Practical experiences available through: Advertising Agency; Associated Press Wire Service Feed; Community Antenna (Cable) Television Origination; Closed Circuit Television Facility; Campus Newspaper (Published Independently); Local Commercial Newspaper; Local Commercial Television Station; Desktop Publishing Facility; Photographic Darkrooms; Video Editing; FM Radio Station (Institutional); Public Relations Agency; Video News and Data Processing.

University of Wisconsin - Green Bay (Public)

Department of Communication Processes
2420 Nicolet Drive
Green Bay, Wisconsin 54311
Telephone: (414) 465-2000

Jerry R. Dell, Chair
Donald Larmouth, Dean, Arts and Sciences

CURRICULUM AND INSTRUCTION
Courses or Concentrations
Available: Advertising; Communication; Information Science; Journalism or Mass Communication; Public Relations; Radio, Television, Broadcasting, or Telecommunications; Speech; Photography; Linguistics; Organizational Communications; Teaching English as a second language; *Program Coordinators*: Dean O'Brien (Journalism, Public Relations); Phillip Clampitt (Organizational Communications); Clifford Abbott (Linguistics); Timothy Meyer (Radio-Television, Telecommunications); Helaine Marshall (Teaching English as a second language); *Undergraduate Objectives or Program Emphases*: Communication Processes provides a broad comprehensive examination of the nature of communication and study in depth of a particular form of communication; *Bachelor's Degree Majors*: 99; *Full-Time Faculty*: 10; *Part-Time Faculty*: 5.

FACILITIES AND SERVICES
Practical experiences available through: Advertising Agency; Audio Recording Laboratory; Community Antenna (Cable) Television Origination; Campus Newspaper (Published Independently); Local Commercial Newspaper; Local Commercial Television Station; Desktop Publishing Facility; Photographic Darkrooms; Video Editing; Electronic Field Production (Video); Television Broadcast Station (Institutional); FM Radio Station (Institutional); Institutional Magazine; Public Relations Agency; Video News and Data Processing; Video Production Laboratory or Television Studio.

University of Wisconsin - La Crosse (Public)

Department of Mass Communications
La Crosse, Wisconsin 54601
Telephone: (608) 785-8368

Joseph Zobin, Chair

CURRICULUM AND INSTRUCTION
Courses or Concentrations
Available: Advertising; Film or Cinema; Journalism or Mass Communication; Public Relations; Radio, Television, Broadcasting, or Telecommunications; *Undergraduate Objectives or Program Emphases*: To acquaint students with the media; to prepare students for entry-level positions; *Bachelor's Degree Majors*: 152; *Full-Time Faculty*: 9; *Full-Time Professional (non-clerical) Staff Members*: 4.

FACILITIES AND SERVICES
Practical experiences available through: Associated Press Wire Service Feed; Community Antenna (Cable) Television Origination; Closed Circuit Television Facility; Campus Newspaper (Published Independently); Local Commercial Newspaper; Local Commercial Television Station; Photographic Darkrooms; Video Editing; Electronic Field Production (Video); Television Broadcast Station (Institutional); FM Radio Station (Institutional); Institutional Magazine; Institutional Newspaper.

University of Wisconsin - La Crosse (Public)

Department of Speech and Theatre
Wing Communications Center
La Crosse, Wisconsin 54601

Jack D. Starr, Administrator

University of Wisconsin - Madison (Public)

Department of Communication Arts
6117 Vilas Hall
Madison, Wisconsin 53706
Telephone: (608) 262-2543

Joanne Cantor, Chair
Sargent Bush, Associate Dean, College of Letters and Science

CURRICULUM AND INSTRUCTION
Courses or Concentrations
Available: Communication; Film or Cinema; Radio, Television, Broadcasting, or Telecommunications; Speech; Rhetoric; *Undergraduate Objectives or Program Emphases*: Radio-Television-Film; Communication Theory and Research; Communication and Public Address; *Graduate Objectives or Program Emphases*: Film Studies; Telecommunications; Rhetoric; Communication Studies; Media Effects; *Bachelor's Degree Majors*: 466; *Master's Degree Majors*: 29; *Doctoral Degree Majors Currently in Residence*: 44; *Additional Doctoral Degree Majors*: 15; *Full-Time Faculty*: 21; *Part-Time Faculty*: 53; *Full-Time Professional (non-clerical) Staff Members*: 6.

FACILITIES AND SERVICES
Practical experiences available through: Audio Recording Laboratory; Campus Newspaper (Published Independently); Television Broadcast Station (Institutional); Film or Cinema Laboratory; FM Radio Station (Institutional); Video Production Laboratory or Television Studio.

University of Wisconsin - Madison (Public)

Department of Agricultural Journalism
Madison, Wisconsin 53706
Telephone: (608) 262-1464

Marion R. Brown, Chair
Leo M. Walsh, Dean, College of Agriculture and Life Sciences

CURRICULUM AND INSTRUCTION
Courses or Concentrations
Available: Advertising; Communication; Film or Cinema; Information Science; Journalism or Mass Communication; Public Relations;

Radio, Television, Broadcasting, or Telecommunications; Video Production; Exhibits; *Program Coordinators*: Hernando Gonzalez (Advertising); Larry Meiller (Broadcast); Richard Powers (Information Science); Jeanne Meadowcroft (Video, Film, Exhibits); *Undergraduate Objectives or Program Emphases*: Subject matter options include Social Science, Natural Science, Natural resources, Agriculture Production and Technology, Family and Consumer, Business Law and Industry. Media Specializations include Print, Broadcast, Advertising; *Graduate Objectives or Program Emphases*: MS and Ph.D. (jointly administered with School of Journalism and Mass Communication); Thesis required for both degrees. Subject matter foci include Mass Communication Theory, Communication and Economic Development, Environmental and Science Communication; *Doctoral Degree Majors Currently in Residence*: 15; *Other Degree Majors*: 160; *Full-Time Faculty*: 12; *Part-Time Faculty*: 9; *Full-Time Professional (non-clerical) Staff Members*: 25.

FACILITIES AND SERVICES
Practical experiences available through: Advertising Agency; Audio Recording Laboratory; Campus Newspaper (Published Independently); Local Commercial Newspaper; Local Commercial Television Station; Desktop Publishing Facility; Photographic Darkrooms; Institutional Newspaper; Public Relations Agency; Satellite Uplink Facility (Ku Band Transmitter); Advertising Agencies.

University of Wisconsin - Madison (Public)

Division of Communication Programs
610 Langdon Street
Madison, Wisconsin 53703
Telephone: (608) 262-3888

Barry Orton, Chair
Howard Martin, Dean

CURRICULUM AND INSTRUCTION
Courses or Concentrations Available: Advertising; Communication; Journalism or Mass Communication; Public Relations; Radio, Television, Broadcasting, or Telecommunications; Speech; Communication Disorders; *Full-Time*

Faculty: 6; *Part-Time Faculty*: 2; *Full-Time Professional (non-clerical) Staff Members*: 5.

University of Wisconsin - Madison (Public)

School of Journalism and Mass Communication
821 University Avenue
Madison, Wisconsin 53706
Telephone: (608) 262-3691

James L. Hoyt, Director
Donald Crawford, Dean

CURRICULUM AND INSTRUCTION
Courses or Concentrations Available: Advertising; Communication; Journalism or Mass Communication; Public Relations; Radio, Television, Broadcasting, or Telecommunications; *Undergraduate Objectives or Program Emphases*: Pre-professional education and training in journalism and mass communication, with major emphasis on the liberal arts and sciences; *Graduate Objectives or Program Emphases*: Original research related to professional and academic disciplines appropriate to the field; *Bachelor's Degree Majors*: 650; *Master's Degree Majors*: 70; *Doctoral Degree Majors Currently in Residence*: 20; *Additional Doctoral Degree Majors*: 10; *Full-Time Faculty*: 22; *Part-Time Faculty*: 30; *Full-Time Professional (non-clerical) Staff Members*: 6.

FACILITIES AND SERVICES
Practical experiences available through: Advertising Agency; AM Radio Station (Institutional); Associated Press Wire Service Feed; Audio Recording Laboratory; Community Antenna (Cable) Television Origination; Carrier Current Audio Distribution System; Closed Circuit Television Facility; Campus Newspaper (Published Independently); Local Commercial Newspaper; Local Commercial Television Station; Desktop Publishing Facility; Photographic Darkrooms; Video Editing; Electronic Field Production (Video); Television Broadcast Station (Institutional); FM Radio Station (Institutional); Institutional Magazine; New York Times Service Feed; Public Relations Agency; Video News and Data Processing.

University of Wisconsin - Menomonie (Public)

Speech Department
Menomonie, Wisconsin 54751

R. S. Hayes, Administrator

University of Wisconsin - Milwaukee (Public)

Department of Film
P. O. Box 413
Milwaukee, Wisconsin 53201
Telephone: (414) 229-6015

Richard Blau, Chair
James Sappenfield, Dean, School of Fine Arts

CURRICULUM AND INSTRUCTION
Courses or Concentrations Available: Film or Cinema; Video; Performance; *Undergraduate Objectives or Program Emphases*: Film/video as focus of personal expression, with particular attention to the relation between individuals, groups, and contemporary culture; *BFA Degree Majors*: 49; *MFA Degree Majors*: 8; *Full-Time Faculty*: 10; *Part-Time Faculty*: 3.

FACILITIES AND SERVICES
Practical experiences available through: Video Editing; Film or Cinema Laboratory; Video Production Laboratory.

University of Wisconsin - Milwaukee (Public)

Department of Communication
P. O. Box 413
Milwaukee, Wisconsin 53201
Telephone: (414) 229-4261

Edward A. Mabry, Chair
Jessica Wirth, Associate Dean, College of Letters and Science

CURRICULUM AND INSTRUCTION
Courses or Concentrations Available: Communication; Speech; Organizational; Interpersonal; Small Group; Public and Rhetorical Communication; Communication Research and Rhetorical Analysis; *Program Coordinator*: Barry Brummet (Introduction to Communication Studies and Public Speaking); *Undergraduate Objectives or Program Emphases*: Communication is the study of human symbolic activity. Courses are designed to help students learn to communicate more effectively and to analyze human communication behavior in instructional, interpersonal, group, organizational, and public settings; *Graduate Objectives or Program Emphases*: An interdepartmental M.A. program is designed to provide specialized study in Human Interactive Processes, Public Communication, and Mass Communication. Students are prepared in theory and research in communication as well as professional applications; *Bachelor's Degree Majors*: 122; *Master's Degree Majors*: 43; *Full-Time Faculty*: 15; *Part-Time Faculty*: 22.

FACILITIES AND SERVICES
Practical experiences available through: Audio Recording Laboratory; Closed Circuit Television Facility; Campus Newspaper (Published Independently); FM Radio Station (Institutional); Video Production Laboratory or Television Studio.

University of Wisconsin - Milwaukee (Public)

Department of Mass Communication
P. O. Box 413
Milwaukee, Wisconsin 53201
Telephone: (414) 229-4436

Ruane B. Hill, Chair
Jessica Wirth, Associate Dean, College of Letters and Science

CURRICULUM AND INSTRUCTION
Courses or Concentrations Available: Journalism or Mass Communication; Public Relations; Radio, Television, Broadcasting, or Telecommunications; *Program Coordinators*: Kay Magowan (Print Sequence); George Bailey (Broadcast Sequence); Don Le Duc (Graduate Studies); *Undergraduate Objectives or Program Emphases*: Thorough cultural education, study of the social implications of mass media professionals, understanding of the media processes and effects; *Graduate Objectives or Program Emphases*: The study of mass media theory, research and practice related to broadcasting, print, or other media; *Bachelor's Degree Majors*: 416; *Master's

Degree Majors: 33; *Full-Time Faculty*: 12; *Part-Time Faculty*: 16.

FACILITIES AND SERVICES
Practical experiences available through: Audio Recording Laboratory; Community Antenna (Cable) Television Origination; Closed Circuit Television Facility; Campus Newspaper (Published Independently); Local Commercial Newspaper; Local Commercial Television Station; Desktop Publishing Facility; Video Editing; Electronic Field Production (Video); FM Radio Station (Institutional); ITFS Distribution System; Institutional Magazine; Public Relations Agency; Video News and Data Processing.

University of Wisconsin - Oshkosh (Public)

Department of Speech
800 Algoma Boulevard
Oshkosh, Wisconsin 54901
Telephone: (414) 424-4422

James A. Benson, Chair
James I. Hoffman, Dean, College of Letters and Sciences

CURRICULUM AND INSTRUCTION
Courses or Concentrations
Available: Communication; Film or Cinema; Radio, Television, Broadcasting, or Telecommunications; Speech; Communication Disorders; Speech Education; *Program Coordinators*: Louis Rossetti (Communication Disorders); S. Clay Willmington (Speech Communication, Speech Education); Robert Snyder (Radio, Television, Film); *Undergraduate Objectives or Program Emphases*: Communication Disorders; Radio, Television, Film; Speech Education; Speech Communication; Theatre; *Graduate Objectives or Program Emphases*: Communication Disorders; *Bachelor's Degree Majors*: 390; *Master's Degree Majors*: 24; *Full-Time Faculty*: 28; *Part-Time Faculty*: 13; *Full-Time Professional (non-clerical) Staff Members*: 2.

FACILITIES AND SERVICES
Practical experiences available through: AM Radio Station (Institutional); Audio Recording Laboratory; Community Antenna (Cable) Television Origination; Video Editing; Film or Cinema Laboratory; FM Radio Station (Institutional); Video Production Laboratory or Television Studio.

University of Wisconsin - Oshkosh (Public)

Department of Journalism
Oshkosh, Wisconsin 54901
Telephone: (414) 424-1042

Frank William Biglow, Chair
James I. Hoffman, Dean, College of Letters and Sciences

CURRICULUM AND INSTRUCTION
Courses or Concentrations
Available: Advertising; Journalism or Mass Communication; Public Relations; News/Editorial; *Degree Majors*: 220; *Full-Time Faculty*: 8; *Part-Time Faculty*: 2.

FACILITIES AND SERVICES
Practical experiences available through: Advertising Agency; Audio Recording Laboratory; Community Antenna (Cable) Television Origination; Carrier Current Audio Distribution System; Closed Circuit Television Facility; Local Commercial Newspaper; Local Commercial Television Station; Desktop Publishing Facility; Photographic Darkrooms; Video Editing; Electronic Field Production (Video); Film or Cinema Laboratory; FM Radio Station (Institutional); ITFS Distribution System; Institutional Magazine; Institutional Newspaper; Public Relations Agency; Video News and Data Processing; Video Production Laboratory or Television Studio.

University of Wisconsin - Oshkosh (Public)

Department of Communication and Theatre Arts
165 Fine Arts Building
Oshkosh, Wisconsin 54702

Terry J. Allen, Administrator

University of Wisconsin - Platteville (Public)

Department of Communication
1 University Plaza
Platteville, Wisconsin 53818-3099
Telephone: (608) 342-1627

George E. Smith, Chair
Kahtan Al Yasiri, Dean

CURRICULUM AND INSTRUCTION
Courses or Concentrations
Available: Advertising; Communication; Journalism or Mass Communication; Public Relations; Radio, Television, Broadcasting, or Telecommunications; Speech; Technical Communication Management (printing, publications, photography); *Undergraduate Objectives or Program Emphases*: Broadcast (engineering, operations, production, performance; advertising, sales). Speech (public relations; organizational communication; sales communication). Technical Communication (printing; publications; telecommunications; photography); *Bachelor's Degree Majors*: 175; *Full-Time Faculty*: 9; *Part-Time Faculty*: 4; *Full-Time Professional (non-clerical) Staff Members*: 1.

FACILITIES AND SERVICES
Practical experiences available through: Audio Recording Laboratory; Community Antenna (Cable) Television Origination; Closed Circuit Television Facility; Campus Newspaper (Published Independently); Local Commercial Newspaper; Desktop Publishing Facility; Photographic Darkrooms; Video Editing; Electronic Field Production (Video); FM Radio Station (Institutional); ITFS Distribution System; Institutional Magazine; Institutional Newspaper; Satellite Uplink Facility; United Press International Feed; Video News and Data Processing; Video Production Laboratory or Television Studio.

University of Wisconsin - River Falls (Public)

Department of Journalism
310 North Hall
River Falls, Wisconsin 54022
Telephone: (715) 425-3169

Michael Norman, Chair

CURRICULUM AND INSTRUCTION
Courses or Concentrations
Available: Advertising; Journalism or Mass Communication; Public Relations; Radio, Television, Broadcasting, or Telecommunications; *Undergraduate Objectives or Program Emphases*: To provide education in journalism and related areas; to educate students for entry level positions in the mass media; *Bachelor's Degree Majors*: 117; *Full-Time Faculty*: 4; *Part-Time Faculty*: 3; *Full-Time Professional (non-clerical) Staff Members*: 1.

FACILITIES AND SERVICES
Practical experiences available through: Advertising Agency; AM Radio Station (Institutional); Associated Press Wire Service Feed; Audio Recording Laboratory; Community Antenna (Cable) Television Origination; Campus Newspaper (Published Independently); Local Commercial Newspaper; Local Commercial Television Station; Desktop Publishing Facility; Photographic Darkrooms; Video Editing; Electronic Field Production (Video); FM Radio Station (Institutional); Institutional Newspaper; Public Relations Agency; Video News and Data Processing; Video Production Laboratory or Television Studio.

University of Wisconsin - River Falls (Public)

Department of Speech Communication and Theatre Arts
River Falls, Wisconsin 54022
Telephone: (715) 425-3971
Alternate: 425-3198

James W. Pratt, Chair
Neal Prochnow, Dean, College of Arts and Sciences

CURRICULUM AND INSTRUCTION
Courses or Concentrations
Available: Communication; Film or Cinema; Mass Communication; Radio, Television, Broadcasting, or Telecommunications; Speech; *Bachelor's Degree Majors*: 145; *Full-Time Faculty*: 9; *Part-Time Faculty*: 1.

FACILITIES AND SERVICES
Practical experiences available through: Audio Recording Laboratory; Community Antenna (Cable) Television Origination; Closed Circuit Television Facility; Campus Newspaper (Published Independently);

Video Editing; FM Radio Station; Video Production or Television Studio.

University of Wisconsin - Stevens Point (Public)

Division of Communication
2100 Main Street
Stevens Point, Wisconsin 54481

Roger Bullis, Administrator

University of Wisconsin - Stevens Point (Public)

Department of Mass Communication
2100 Main Street
Stevens Point, Wisconsin 54481

James M. Haney, Administrator

University of Wisconsin - Superior (Public)

Communicating Arts
Superior, Wisconsin 54880

Paul Kending, Administrator

University of Wisconsin - Whitewater (Public)

Department of Communication
800 W. Main Street
Whitewater, Wisconsin 53190
Telephone: (414) 472-1034

Patricia Townsend, Chair
Mary Quinlivan, Dean, College of Letters and Sciences

CURRICULUM AND INSTRUCTION
Courses or Concentrations
Available: Advertising; Communication; Film or Cinema; Journalism or Mass Communication; Public Relations; Radio, Television, or Telecommunications; Speech; Communicative Disorders; *Program Coordinators*: Richard Jentoft (Communicative Disorders); William Weiss (Mass Communication); John Cease (Speech Communication); *Undergraduate Objectives*:

To prepare speech clinicians; to prepare students for work on print or electronic media; to prepare professionals in public relations, organizational communication, broadcasting and general communication; *Graduate Objectives*: To provide advanced training and clinical experience; to develop management, consulting, critical skills for the mass media. In Speech Communication, to develop management and consulting skills for use in organizational communication or public relations; *Associate's Degree Majors*: 233; *Bachelor's Degree Majors*: 348; *Master's Degree Majors*: 28; *Full-Time Faculty*: 31; *Part-Time Faculty*: 4.

FACILITIES AND SERVICES
Practical experiences available through: Audio Recording Laboratory; Community Antenna (Cable) Television Origination; Carrier Current Audio Distribution System; Closed Circuit Television Facility; Campus Newspaper (Published Independently); Photographic Darkrooms; Video Editing; FM Radio Station (Institutional); Institutional Magazine; Video Production Laboratory or Television Studio.

Wisconsin Lutheran College (Private)

College of Communication
8830 W. Bluemound Road
Milwaukee, Wisconsin 53226
Telephone: (414) 774-8620

Mary L. Heins, Head
John E. Bauer, Administrator

CURRICULUM AND INSTRUCTION
Courses or Concentrations
Available: Communication; Journalism or Mass Communication; Public Relations; Speech; *Undergraduate Objectives or Program Emphases*: Broadcasting; Interpersonal; Public Communication; Theatre Arts. Emphasis is on developing understanding and skills for life. (Four year liberal arts college); *Bachelor's Degree Majors*: 14; *Full-Time Faculty*: 2; *Part-Time Faculty*: 1.

FACILITIES AND SERVICES
Practical experiences available through: Campus Newspaper (Published Independently); Institutional Newspaper; Public Relations Agency.

Casper College (Public)

Division of Language and Literature
125 College Drive
Casper, Wyoming 82601
Telephone: (307) 268-2660
Alternate: 268-2110

Gale Alexander, Chair
Al Skillman, Dean

CURRICULUM AND INSTRUCTION
Courses or Concentrations
Available: Communication; Film or Cinema;
Journalism or Mass Communication; Speech;
Program Coordinators: Mike Kent
(Journalism); Gretchen Wheeler (Speech
Communication); Lloyd Agte (Film);
*Undergraduate Objectives or Program
Emphases*: Communication; Journalism;
Associate's Degree Majors: 30; *Full-Time
Faculty*: 22; *Part-Time Faculty*: 8; *Full-Time
Professional (non-clerical) Staff Members*: 2.

FACILITIES AND SERVICES
*Practical experiences available
through*: Associated Press Wire Service;
Campus Newspaper (Published
Independently); Local Commercial
Newspaper; Local Commercial Television
Station; Desktop Publishing Facility;
Photographic Darkrooms; Video Editing;
Institutional Magazine; Institutional
Newspaper.

Central Wyoming College

Radio-Television
2660 Peck Avenue
Riverton, Wyoming 82501

Dale Smith, Administrator

Northwest College (Public)

Program of Journalism
Sixth and Cheyenne
Powell, Wyoming 82435
Telephone: (307) 754-6611

James I. Bly, Head
Robert Koelling, Chair, Humanities Division

CURRICULUM AND INSTRUCTION
Courses or Concentrations
Available: Journalism or Mass
Communication; *Undergraduate Objectives or
Program Emphases*: Two-year transfer
orientation; print news; *Associate's Degree
Majors*: 6; *Full-Time Faculty*: 1.

FACILITIES AND SERVICES
*Practical experiences available
through*: Campus Newspaper (Published
Independently); Desktop Publishing Facility;
Photographic Darkrooms.

Northwest College (Public)

Department of Speech Communication
6th and Cheyenne
Powell, Wyoming 82435
Telephone: (307) 754-6024

Duanne Fish, Head
Robert Koelling, Chair, Humanities Division

CURRICULUM AND INSTRUCTION
Courses or Concentrations
Available: Communication; Speech;
*Undergraduate Objectives or Program
Emphases*: Service to the campus, to provide
a variety of classes to meet humanities
requirements. Majors are provided with the
basics in order to transfer to a four year
institution; *Associate's Degree Majors*: 12;
Full-Time Faculty: 4; *Part-Time Faculty*: 2.

University of Wyoming (Public)

Department of Communication and Mass
Media
Box 3904, University Station
Laramie, Wyoming 82071-3904
Telephone: (307) 766-3122

Keith A. Miller, Head
B. Oliver Walter, Dean, Arts and Sciences

CURRICULUM AND INSTRUCTION
*Courses or Concentrations
Available*: Advertising; Communication; Film
or Cinema; Journalism or Mass
Communication; Public Relations; Radio,
Television, Broadcasting, or
Telecommunications; Speech; *Undergraduate
Objectives or Program Emphases*: General
Communication Studies; Print Journalism;
Broadcasting; Advertising; Public Relations;
*Graduate Objectives or Program
Emphases*: General Communication Studies;
Mass Communication, Communication
Theory (Social Scientific emphasis);
Bachelor's Degree Majors: 130; *Master's
Degree Majors*: 12; *Full-Time Faculty*: 12;
Part-Time Faculty: 21; *Full-Time
Professional (non-clerical) Staff Members*: 1.

FACILITIES AND SERVICES
*Practical experiences available
through*: Advertising Agency; Community
Antenna (Cable) Television Origination;
Closed Circuit Television Facility; Campus
Newspaper (Published Independently);
Local Commercial Newspaper; Desktop
Publishing Facility; Photographic
Darkrooms; Video Editing; FM Radio
Station (Institutional); Institutional
Newspaper; Public Relations Agency; Video
News and Data Processing; Video
Production Laboratory or Television Studio.

University of Wyoming (Public)

Communication Department
Box 3341, University Station
Laramie, Wyoming 82071

Samuel C. Riccillo, Administrator

Western Wyoming College

Division of Humanities and Fine Arts
2500 College Drive
Rock Springs, Wyoming 82901

Lee Roger Taylor, Jr., Administrator

ALBERTA

Athabasca University (Public)

Concentration of Communication Studies
Box 10,000
Athabasca, Alberta T0G 2R0
Telephone: (403) 675-6111

Peter Chiaramonte, Academic Coordinator
Stephen Murgatroyd, Dean, Faculty of
Administrative Studies

CURRICULUM AND INSTRUCTION
*Courses or Concentrations
Available*: Communication; Film or Cinema;
Management Communication,
Organizational Communication; *Program
Coordinators*: Sharon McGuire (Leadership
Communication, Problem-Solving in
Groups); *Undergraduate Objectives or
Program Emphases*: Interpersonal
communications in management; *Bachelor's
Degree Majors*: 300; *Full-Time Faculty*: 2;
Part-Time Faculty: 10.

FACILITIES AND SERVICES
Practical experiences available through: Audio
Recording Laboratory; Canadian Press
Feed; Desktop Publishing Facility;
Photographic Darkrooms; Video Editing;
Institutional Magazine.

University of Calgary (Public)

School of Communication Studies
2500 University Drive
Calgary, Alberta T2N 1N4
Telephone: (403) 220-7575

Thomas L. McPhail, Director
P. Kruger, Vice President, Academic Affairs

CURRICULUM AND INSTRUCTION
*Courses or Concentrations
Available*: Advertising; Communication;
Information Science; Journalism or Mass
Communication; Public Relations; Radio,
Television, Broadcasting, or
Telecommunications; Methods; International
Communication; *Undergraduate Objectives or*

Program Emphases: Theory; *Graduate
Objectives or Program Emphases*: Theory and
Research; Methodologies; *Bachelor's Degree
Majors*: 160; *Master's Degree Majors*: 60;
Full-Time Faculty: 14; *Part-Time
Faculty*: 24; *Full-Time Professional
(non-clerical) Staff Members*: 1.

BRITISH COLUMBIA

Trinity Western University (Private)

Department of Communications
7600 Glover Road
Langley, British Columbia V3A 6H4
Telephone: (604) 888-7511 Extension: 2333

William O. Strom, Head
Phillip Wiebe, Chair, Humanities Division

CURRICULUM AND INSTRUCTION
*Courses or Concentrations
Available*: Communication; Journalism or
Mass Communication; Public Relations;
Radio, Television, Broadcasting,
or Telecommunications; Speech; Rhetoric;
Cross-cultural Communication; Technical
Communication; *Undergraduate Objectives or
Program Emphases*: To offer a critical,
theoretical and research-based
understanding of the way mass media work,
of public address, non-fiction writing, and
various social contexts of communication (i.e.
cross cultural); *Bachelor's Degree Majors*: 7;
Full-Time Faculty: 1; *Part-Time Faculty*: 2.

FACILITIES AND SERVICES
*Practical experiences available
through*: Campus Newspaper (Published
Independently); Photographic Darkrooms.

University of British Columbia (Public)

School of Audiology and Speech Sciences
5804 Fairview
Vancouver, British Columbia V6T 1W5
Telephone: (604) 228-5591

Judith R. Johnston, Director
William Webber, Dean

CURRICULUM AND INSTRUCTION
Courses or Concentrations
Available: Communication; Speech; Speech
Language Pathology; Neurolinguistics;
*Graduate Objectives or Program
Emphases*: Professional training in
speech-language pathology and audiology;
Master's Degree Majors: 50; *Doctoral Degree
Majors Currently in Residence*: 1; *Full-Time
Faculty*: 9; *Part-Time Faculty*: 1; *Full-Time
Professional (non-clerical) Staff Members*: 1.

FACILITIES AND SERVICES
*Practical experiences available
through*: Carrier Current Audio Distribution
System; Campus Newspaper (Published
Independently); Desktop Publishing Facility.

University of Victoria (Public)

Department of Creative Writing Co-op
P.O. Box 1700
Victoria, British Columbia V8W 2Y2
Telephone: (604) 721-7629

Don Bailey, Program Coordinator
Derk Wynand, Chair

CURRICULUM AND INSTRUCTION
Courses or Concentrations
Available: Communication; Information
Science; Journalism or Mass
Communication; Creative Non-fiction;
Publishing; *Undergraduate Objectives or
Program Emphases*: To provide students with
a balanced experience in creative and applied
writing within a co-operative education
model. Emphasis on fiction, drama, poetry,
non-fiction, journalism, publishing; *Graduate
Objectives or Program Emphases*: New
graduate program to begin 1991-92;
Bachelor's Degree Majors: 30; *BFA Degree
Majors*: 90; *Full-Time Faculty*: 8; *Part-Time
Faculty*: 11.

FACILITIES AND SERVICES
*Practical experiences available
through*: Advertising Agency; Audio
Recording Laboratory; Community Antenna
(Cable) Television Origination; Closed
Circuit Television Facility; Campus
Newspaper (Published Independently);
Local Commercial Newspaper; Local
Commercial Television Station; Desktop
Publishing Facility; Photographic
Darkrooms; Electronic Field Production
(Video); FM Radio Station (Institutional);
Institutional Magazine; Institutional
Newspaper; Public Relations Agency; Video
News and Data Processing.

NOVA SCOTIA

Mount Saint Vincent University (Public)

Department of Public Relations
166 Bedford Highway
Halifax, Nova Scotia B3M 2J6
Telephone: (902) 443-4450 Extension: 477

Judith A. Scrimger, Chair

CURRICULUM AND INSTRUCTION
Courses or Concentrations
Available: Advertising; Communication;
Journalism or Mass Communication; Public
Relations; Radio, Television, Broadcasting,
or Telecommunications; Speech;
*Undergraduate Objectives or Program
Emphases*: Four year professional degree in
public relations (BPR) with a co-operative
education option. The goal of the program is
to produce a generalist practitioner with
strong writing skills and management
orientation; *Degree Majors*: 257; *Full-Time
Faculty*: 6; *Part-Time Faculty*: 10.

FACILITIES AND SERVICES
Practical experiences available through: Audio
Recording Laboratory; Community Antenna
(Cable) Television Origination; Closed
Circuit Television Facility; Campus
Newspaper (Published Independently);
Video Editing; Electronic Field Production
(Video); Video News and Data Processing.

ONTARIO

Brock University (Public)

Program of Communication Studies
Merritan Highway
St. Catharines, Ontario L2S 3A1
Telephone: (416) 688-5550

John A. Lye, Director
Lewis Soroka, Dean, Social Science

CURRICULUM AND INSTRUCTION
Courses or Concentrations
Available: Communication; Film or Cinema;
*Undergraduate Objectives or Program
Emphases*: A liberal arts, theory-based
program. A core of communications courses
is supplemented by relevant courses in three
areas: film and television, social and political
policy; management and marketing;
Bachelor's Degree Majors: 90; *Full-Time
Faculty*: 15; *Part-Time Faculty*: 1.

FACILITIES AND SERVICES
*Practical experiences available
through*: Campus Newspaper (Published
Independently); Desktop Publishing Facility.

Brock University (Public)

**Department of Film Studies, Dramatic and
Visual Arts**
St. Catharines, Ontario L2S 3A1
Telephone: (416) 688-5550 Extension: 3214

Berry Keith Grant, Chair
Cecil Abraham, Dean, Humanities

CURRICULUM AND INSTRUCTION
Courses or Concentrations
Available: Communication; Film or Cinema;
Radio, Television, Broadcasting, or
Telecommunications; Popular culture;
*Undergraduate Objectives or Program
Emphases*: Critical, historical and theoretical
understanding of media and culture;
Bachelor's Degree Majors: 150; *Full-Time
Faculty*: 14; *Part-Time Faculty*: 5; *Full-Time
Professional (non-clerical) Staff Members*: 3.

FACILITIES AND SERVICES
*Practical experiences available
through*: Community Antenna (Cable)
Television Origination; Campus Newspaper
(Published Independently); Video Editing.

Canadore College of Applied Arts
and Technology (Public)

School of Applied Arts
100 College Drive -- P.O. Box 5001
North Bay, Ontario P1B 8K9
Telephone: (705) 474-7600

Sid H. Tompkins, Director
William Garrett, Dean, Post-Secondary

CURRICULUM AND INSTRUCTION
Courses or Concentrations
Available: Advertising; Communication;
Journalism or Mass Communication; Public
Relations; Radio, Television, Broadcasting,
or Telecommunications; Speech;
*Undergraduate Objectives or Program
Emphases*: Radio Broadcasting; Television
Broadcasting; Broadcasting Journalism; Print
Journalism; *Degree Majors*: 200; *Full-Time
Faculty*: 40; *Part-Time Faculty*: 15;
*Full-Time Professional (non-clerical) Staff
Members*: 5.

FACILITIES AND SERVICES
*Practical experiences available
through*: Advertising Agency; AM Radio
Station (Institutional); Audio Recording
Laboratory; Community Antenna (Cable)
Television Origination; Closed Circuit
Television Facility; Campus Newspaper
(Published Independently); Local
Commercial Newspaper; Local Commercial
Television Station; Canadian Press Feed;
Desktop Publishing Facility; Photographic
Darkrooms; Video Editing; Electronic Field
Production (Video); ITFS Distribution
System; Institutional Newspaper; Public
Relations Agency; Video News and Data
Processing; Video Production Laboratory or
Television Studio.

Carleton University (Public)

School of Journalism
Ottawa, Ontario K1S 5B6
Telephone: (613) 788-7406

Anthony Westell, Director
J. Yalden, Dean

CURRICULUM AND INSTRUCTION
Courses or Concentrations
Available: Communication; Journalism or
Mass Communication; Radio, Television,
Broadcasting, or Telecommunications;
Program Coordinators: Eileen Saunders

(Mass Communication); G. Stuart Adam (Graduate Studies); J. Scanlon (Undergraduate Studies); G. Frajkor (Television); B. Freeman (Radio); *Undergraduate Objectives or Program Emphases*: BJ degree: prepares students for career in journalism education and training; BA: Communication is focus of a general education; MJ: prepares graduates of other disciplines for a career in journalism; *Bachelor's Degree Majors*: 160; *Other Degree Majors*: 585; *Full-Time Faculty*: 24; *Part-Time Faculty*: 25; *Full-Time Professional (non-clerical) Staff Members*: 10.

FACILITIES AND SERVICES
Practical experiences available through: Community Antenna (Cable) Television Origination; Closed Circuit Television Facility; Campus Newspaper (Published Independently); Canadian Press Feed; Desktop Publishing Facility; Photographic Darkrooms; Video Editing; Electronic Field Production (Video); FM Radio Station (Institutional); Institutional Newspaper; Video Production Laboratory or Television Studio.

Ryerson Polytechnical Institute

School of Journalism
Toronto, Ontario M5B 1E8

John Miller, Administrator

St. Clair College of Applied Arts and Technology

Journalism Department
Windsor, Ontario N9A 6S4

R. L. MacKenzie, Administrator

St. Paul University (Public)

Institute of Social Communication
223 Main Street
Ottawa, Ontario K1S 1C4
Telephone: (613) 236-1393

Pierrette T. Daviau, Director
Pierre Hurtubise, Rector

CURRICULUM AND INSTRUCTION
Courses or Concentrations Available: Communication; Film or Cinema; Journalism or Mass Communication; Radio, Television, Broadcasting, or Telecommunications; Speech; Media-Faith Expression; Ethics; *Undergraduate Objectives or Program Emphases*: To acquaint the student with diverse communication theories and to prepare him for practical analyses concerning the impact of social communications on society and the Church. Introduction to basic communication techniques; *Full-Time Faculty*: 3; *Part-Time Faculty*: 12; *Full-Time Professional (non-clerical) Staff Members*: 2.

FACILITIES AND SERVICES
Practical experiences available through: Audio Recording Laboratory; Photographic Darkrooms; Video Editing; Electronic Field Production (Video); Video Production Laboratory or Television Studio.

University of Ottawa (Public)

Department of Communication
554 King Edward
Ottawa, Ontario K1N 6N5
Telephone: (613) 564-3351

Denis Bachand, Chair
Marcel Hamelin, Dean, Faculty of Arts

CURRICULUM AND INSTRUCTION
Courses or Concentrations Available: Advertising; Communication; Film or Cinema; Journalism or Mass Communication; Public Relations; Radio, Television, Broadcasting, or Telecommunications; Speech; Organizational Communication; *Undergraduate Objectives or Program Emphases*: Media and Culture; Interpersonal/organizational; *Graduate Objectives or Program Emphases*: To begin soon: Communication's strategies; *Full-Time Faculty*: 11; *Part-Time Faculty*: 15; *Full-Time Professional (non-clerical) Staff Members*: 2.

FACILITIES AND SERVICES
Practical experiences available through: Advertising Agency; AM Radio Station (Institutional); Audio Recording Laboratory; Community Antenna (Cable) Television Origination; Campus Newspaper (Published Independently); Local Commercial Newspaper; Local Commercial Television Station; Desktop Publishing

Facility; Photographic Darkrooms; Video Editing; Electronic Field Production (Video); FM Radio Station (Institutional); ITFS Distribution System; Public Relations Agency; Video Production Laboratory or Television Studio.

University of Waterloo (Public)

Department of English
200 University Avenue W
Waterloo, Ontario N2L 3G1
Telephone: (519) 885-1211

Gordon E. Slethaug, Chair
Robin Banks, Dean, Arts

CURRICULUM AND INSTRUCTION
Courses or Concentrations Available: Advertising; Communication; Journalism or Mass Communication; Professional Writing; *Undergraduate Objectives or Program Emphases*: A rhetoric and professional writing program that incorporates writing for all purposes, business, government, media; *Graduate Objectives or Program Emphases*: Ph.D. pending approval at provincial level; *Bachelor's Degree Majors*: 550; *Master's Degree Majors*: 40; *Full-Time Faculty*: 32; *Part-Time Faculty*: 18.

FACILITIES AND SERVICES
Practical experiences available through: Audio Recording Laboratory; Closed Circuit Television Facility; Campus Newspaper (Published Independently); Local Commercial Newspaper; Local Commercial Television Station; Canadian Press Feed; Desktop Publishing Facility; FM Radio Station (Institutional); Public Relations Agency.

University of Waterloo (Public)

Department of Speech Communication
200 University Avenue W
Waterloo, Ontario N2L 3G1
Telephone: (519) 885-1211

Jill P. Tomasson Goodwin, Director
William Chadwick, Chair

CURRICULUM AND INSTRUCTION
Courses or Concentrations Available: Speech; *Undergraduate Objectives or Program*

Emphases: The Speech Communication Minor and Option introduce students to Speech Communication theory, its critical methods, and practical applications; *Full-Time Faculty*: 1; *Part-Time Faculty*: 10.

FACILITIES AND SERVICES
Practical experiences available through: Video Production Laboratory or Television Studio.

University of Western Ontario (Public)

Graduate School of Journalism
London, Ontario N6A 5B7
Telephone: (519) 661-3377

Peter Desbarats, Dean
G. Mogenson, Dean, Faculty of Graduate Studies

CURRICULUM AND INSTRUCTION
Courses or Concentrations Available: Journalism or Mass Communication; Public Relations; Radio, Television, Broadcasting, or Telecommunications; *Program Coordinators*: A. MacFarlane (Print); D. Spencer (Broadcast); *Undergraduate Objectives or Program Emphases*: A one-year certificate program in Journalism for Canadian Native people (Indian and Inuit); *Graduate Objectives or Program Emphases*: A three-year term (12-month) MA program in print and electronic journalism, theoretical and practical; *Master's Degree Majors*: 40; *Other Degree Majors*: 15; *Full-Time Faculty*: 10; *Part-Time Faculty*: 25; *Full-Time Professional (non-clerical) Staff Members*: 2.

FACILITIES AND SERVICES
Practical experiences available through: Closed Circuit Television Facility; Campus Newspaper (Published Independently); Local Commercial Newspaper; Local Commercial Television Station; Canadian Press Feed; Desktop Publishing Facility; Photographic Darkrooms; Video Editing; Electronic Field Production (Video); FM Radio Station (Institutional); Institutional Newspaper; Public Relations Agency; Video News and Data Processing; Video Production Laboratory or Television Studio.

University of Windsor (Public)

Department of Communication Studies
Windsor, Ontario N8X 1P9
Telephone: (519) 253-4232

Mary Gerace Gold, Chair
Z. Fallenbuchl, Dean, Social Science

CURRICULUM AND INSTRUCTION
Courses or Concentrations
Available: Advertising; Film or Cinema;
Journalism or Mass Communication; Public
Relations; Radio, Television, Broadcasting,
or Telecommunications; *Undergraduate
Objectives or Program Emphases*: Theory,
research, policy, production; *Graduate
Objectives or Program
Emphases*: Communication Policy and
Culture; International Communication and
Development; Organizational and
Instructional Communication; *Bachelor's
Degree Majors*: 400; *Master's Degree
Majors*: 27; *Full-Time Faculty*: 14;
Part-Time Faculty: 20; *Full-Time
Professional (non-clerical) Staff Members*: 1.

FACILITIES AND SERVICES
*Practical experiences available
through*: Community Antenna (Cable)
Television Origination; Campus Newspaper
(Published Independently); Desktop
Publishing Facility; Photographic
Darkrooms; Video Editing; Electronic Field
Production (Video); Film or Cinema
Laboratory; Video Production Laboratory or
Television Studio.

QUEBEC

Concordia University (Public)

Department of Communication Studies
7141 Sherbrooke Street West
Montreal, Quebec H4B 1R6
Telephone: (514) 848-2555

William L. Gardiner, Chair
Charles L. Bertrand, Dean, Arts and Science

CURRICULUM AND INSTRUCTION
Courses or Concentrations
Available: Advertising; Communication; Film
or Cinema; Journalism or Mass
Communication; Public Relations; Radio,
Television, Broadcasting, or

Telecommunications; *Full-Time Faculty*: 17;
Part-Time Faculty: 24.

FACILITIES AND SERVICES
Practical experiences available through: Audio
Recording Laboratory; Campus Newspaper
(Published Independently); Photographic
Darkrooms; Video Editing; Television
Broadcast Station (Institutional); Film or
Cinema Laboratory; Institutional Magazine.

Concordia University (Public)

Department of Journalism
7141 Sherbrooke Street West
Montreal, Quebec H4B 1R6
Telephone: (514) 848-2465

Enn Raudsepp, Acting Director
**Charles L. Bertrand, Dean, Faculty of Arts
and Science**

CURRICULUM AND INSTRUCTION
Courses or Concentrations
Available: Journalism or Mass
Communication; Radio, Television,
Broadcasting, or Telecommunications;
*Undergraduate Objectives or Program
Emphases*: To prepare students for careers as
working journalists (in both print and
broadcasting, Radio/Television); *Graduate
Objectives or Program Emphases*: For those
who already have an undergraduate degree
(not in Journalism): To prepare students for
careers as working journalists (in both print
and broadcasting, Radio/Television);
Bachelor's Degree Majors: 155; *Other Degree
Majors*: 20; *Full-Time Faculty*: 5; *Part-Time
Faculty*: 16.

FACILITIES AND SERVICES
Practical experiences available through: Audio
Recording Laboratory; Community Antenna
(Cable) Television Origination; Carrier
Current Audio Distribution System; Campus
Newspaper (Published Independently);
Local Commercial Newspaper; Local
Commercial Television Station; Desktop
Publishing Facility; Video Editing;
Electronic Field Production (Video);
Television Broadcast Station (Institutional);
FM Radio Station (Institutional); Video
News and Data Processing; Video
Production Laboratory or Television Studio.

Concordia University (Public)

Department of Cinema
1455 de Maisonneuve West
Montreal, Quebec H3G 1M8
Telephone: (514) 848-4666

John W. Locke, Chair
Robert Parker, Dean

CURRICULUM AND INSTRUCTION
Courses or Concentrations Available: Film or Cinema; *Undergraduate Objectives or Program Emphases*: Film animation, film production, film studies taught in the context of a faculty of Fine Arts; *Graduate Objectives or Program Emphases*: Film production taught in the context of a faculty of Fine Arts; *BFA Degree Majors*: 200; *MFA Degree Majors*: 5; *Full-Time Faculty*: 12; *Part-Time Faculty*: 32; *Full-Time Professional (non-clerical) Staff Members*: 4.

FACILITIES AND SERVICES
Practical experiences available through: Audio Recording Laboratory; Campus Newspaper (Published Independently); Video Editing; Film or Cinema Laboratory.

McGill University (Public)

Graduate Program in Communication
3465 Peel Street
Montreal, Quebec H3A 1W7
Telephone: (514) 398-4110

Gertrude J. Robinson, Director

CURRICULUM AND INSTRUCTION
Courses or Concentrations Available: Communication; The program deals with theories of communication processes which takes into consideration several communication areas; *Undergraduate Objectives or Program Emphases*: Core faculty of program teach courses at the undergraduate level which deal with such areas as: History of Communications; Television and Society; Mass Communications; *Graduate Objectives or Program Emphases*: Theories of communication processes. The foci are such areas as: History of Communication Studies; The Study of Popular Culture; Communications and Development; Communication and New Technologies; *Master's Degree Majors*: 20; *Doctoral Degree*

Majors Currently in Residence: 20; *Full-Time Faculty*: 3; *Part-Time Faculty*: 3.

Tele-Universite, Universite du Quebec (Public)

Department of Module Communication
4835 Christophe-Colomb
Montreal, Quebec H2J 4C2
Telephone: (514) 522-3540

Kevin G. Wilson, Director
Alain Laramee, Administrator

CURRICULUM AND INSTRUCTION
Courses or Concentrations Available: Communication; Organizational Communications, Social Impacts of Computer Communications; *Undergraduate Objectives or Program Emphases*: Social and organizational analysis of computer-based communications. Media analysis; *Associate's Degree Majors*: 2; *Bachelor's Degree Majors*: 1; *Full-Time Faculty*: 6; *Part-Time Faculty*: 6; *Full-Time Professional (non-clerical) Staff Members*: 4.

Universite du Quebec a Hull (Public)

Program of Module Psycho education et Sciences Sociales
CP1290 Suu B
Hull, Quebec J8X 3X7
Telephone: (819) 595-2288

Marcel Renou, Director
Toussaint Fortin-Duyen, Administrator

CURRICULUM AND INSTRUCTION
Courses or Concentrations Available: Communication; Information Science; Journalism or Mass Communication; Speech; Sciences Sociales.

FACILITIES AND SERVICES
Practical experiences available through: Campus Newspaper (Published Independently); Photographic Darkrooms; Video Editing; Electronic Field Production (Video).

Universite du Quebec en Abitibi-Temiscamingue (Public)

Department of Sciences du comportement Human
42 Mgr Rheaume E
Rouyn-Noranda, Quebec J9X 2X4
Telephone: (819) 762-0971

Jean Caron, Director
Pierre Audy, Administrator

CURRICULUM AND INSTRUCTION
Courses or Concentrations
Available: Advertising; Communication;
Information Science; Speech; *Program
Coordinators*: Michel Marsan
(Organizational Communication);
*Undergraduate Objectives or Program
Emphases*: Acquire basic skills in oral and
written communication. Solve human and
organizational problems of communication;
Full-Time Faculty: 12; *Part-Time
Faculty*: 20; *Full-Time Professional
(non-clerical) Staff Members*: 2.

FACILITIES AND SERVICES
Practical experiences available through: Audio
Recording Laboratory; Campus Newspaper
(Published Independently); Local
Commercial Newspaper; Local Commercial
Television Station; Desktop Publishing
Facility; Video Editing; Electronic Field
Production (Video); Video Production
Laboratory or Television Studio.

SASKATCHEWAN

University of Regina (Public)

School of Journalism and Communication
Regina, Saskatchewan S4S 0A2
Telephone: (306) 585-4420

Satinder Kumar, Director
D. de Vlieger, Dean, Faculty of Arts

CURRICULUM AND INSTRUCTION
Courses or Concentrations
Available: Journalism or Mass
Communication; Radio, Television,
Broadcasting, or Telecommunications;
*Undergraduate Objectives or Program
Emphases*: To educate in basic journalistic
values and skills in all three media, visual
print, radio and television; *Bachelor's Degree
Majors*: 30; *Other Degree Majors*: 15;
Full-Time Faculty: 4; *Part-Time Faculty*: 3;
*Full-Time Professional (non-clerical) Staff
Members*: 1.

FACILITIES AND SERVICES
Practical experiences available through: AM
Radio Station (Institutional); Audio
Recording Laboratory; Community Antenna
(Cable) Television Origination; Closed
Circuit Television Facility; Campus
Newspaper (Published Independently);
Local Commercial Newspaper; Local
Commercial Television Station; Canadian
Press Feed; Desktop Publishing Facility;
Photographic Darkrooms; Video Editing;
Electronic Field Production (Video);
Institutional Magazine; Institutional
Newspaper; Video Production Laboratory or
Television Studio.

Appendix

**INDIANA UNIVERSITY-
PURDUE UNIVERSITY
at INDIANAPOLIS**

ASSOCIATE DEAN
OF THE FACULTIES

Office of Learning Technologies
902 West New York Street
Indianapolis, Indiana 46202-5154
Voice (317) 274-4507
FAX (317) 274-4513

(Date)

Dear Colleague:

A recent issue of the *ACA Bulletin* described an historic meeting in which the Executive Committees of the Association for Communication Administration (ACA), the Association of Schools of Journalism and Mass Communication (ASJMC), and the Broadcast Education Association (BEA) agreed to work toward closer cooperation. This was the first time the leadership of the three associations had met jointly. Presiders at the session were Robert Blanchard, President of ASJMC, Stan McKenzie, President of BEA, and Robert Smith, President of ACA. The officers were joined by the Executive Directors of the three associations.

One decision that came from the meeting was to publish a single directory of all academic programs in the communication disciplines, including advertising, communication, film, information science, journalism, mass communication, public relations, radio-television-film, speech, and related areas. Compiling such a directory, which will include summary statistics and descriptive narratives, is beyond the scope of one professional association but is practical when developed cooperatively. Indiana University - Purdue University at Indianapolis is participating in compiling, analyzing, and publishing this database.

The new directory promises to be the most exhaustive collection of information about the communication disciplines to date. With your help a publication will emerge that you, other administrators, faculty members, and students will find valuable. Please help by including your academic unit in *The Communication Disciplines in Higher Education: A Directory of Academic Programs in the United States and Canada*, to be published jointly by the ACA and ASJMC. Respond by completing the questionnaire as legibly and accurately as possible and returning it to me in the postage-paid envelope provided.

Thank you for contributing to this project. I would appreciate a response within two weeks.

Sincerely,

Garland C. Elmore
Associate Dean

Enclosures

Questionnaire

Please TYPE or PRINT your responses exactly as they should appear in the
Directory. Thank you for making your entry as accurate as possible.

**PART I
Identification and Mailing Information for YOUR Academic Unit**

Note: Communication administrators with two or more separate departments
or programs reporting to them list divisions in Question 16. Proceed to
identify YOUR academic unit below.

1. First Name(s), M.I., and Last
    Name of Chief Program
    Administrator in Your Academic
    Unit (i.e., YOUR NAME): _____

2. Your Title: ( ) Chair   ( ) Director
                                   ( ) Dean   ( ) Head
                                   ( ) Other: _____

3. Name of Your Academic Unit: _____

4. Designation of Your Academic Unit: ( ) College   ( ) Department
                                       ( ) Division   ( ) Program
                                       ( ) School
                                       ( ) Other: _____

5. Name and Title of Next Highest
    Administrator (Your Supervisor): _____

6. Name of Institution: _____

7. Address: _____

8. City: _____

9. State or Province: _____

10. Country: ( ) USA   ( ) Canada

11. Postal Zip Code: _____

12. Telephone Number: _____ _____
                                   Area Code   Primary Number

PART II
Curriculum and Instruction

All of the remaining questions relate to YOUR academic program as
identified in Question 3. If components of the communication curriculum
listed in Question 14 below are administered through other academic
units that do not report to you at your institution, please note these
organizational patterns in your response to Questions 15-16. If there
are no communication courses offered by your campus in any of the areas
listed in Question 14, ignore all remaining questions.

13. Primary Program Funding: ( ) Public   ( ) Private

14. Your Curriculum INCLUDES (Check   ( ) Advertising
     all that apply and list additional   ( ) Communication
     areas except performing arts such   ( ) Film, Cinema
     as theatre and dance, which are   ( ) Information Science
     reported in another publication):   ( ) Journalism, Mass Comm
                                          ( ) Public Relations
                                          ( ) Radio, TV, Brdcst, Telecom
                                          ( ) Speech
                                          ( ) Other:
                                          _____

                                          _____

15. If areas of the general   _____
     communication curriculum listed   _____
     in Question 14 are administered   _____
     by departments or schools other   _____
     than yours, please provide the   _____
     names and addresses of the other   _____
     chief program administrators so   _____
     that additional questionnaires   _____
     may be mailed to your   _____
     institution. (These programs   _____
     will be listed separately in the
     directory.)

16. If areas of the general   _____
     communication curriculum listed   _____
     in question 14 are coordinated   _____
     or directed by persons other   _____
     than yourself but are   _____
     administered within your own   _____
     department or school, please   _____
     provide the names of the   _____
     coordinators and indicate the   _____
     coordinators' respective areas   _____
     (i.e., "broadcasting", etc.).   _____
     (These programs will appear as
     sub-categories under your
     listing in the printed
     directory.)

17. Describe the principal
    objectives or emphases of
    programs offered to
    Undergraduate and Graduate
    students by your academic unit.
    If you administer multiple
    departments or divisions as
    indicated in Question 16,
    include their respective
    objectives or emphases in your
    statement.

    UNDERGRADUATE:_____
    _____
    _____
    _____
    _____
    _____
    _____
    _____

    GRADUATE:_____
    _____
    _____
    _____
    _____

18. Number of Majors currently
    pursuing degrees in each
    category that applies:

    AA: _____
    BA: _____   (Juniors + Seniors)
    BFA: _____   (Juniors + Seniors)
    MA: _____
    MFA: _____
    PhD: _____   (In Residence Only)
    PhD: _____   (Other)
    Other: _____

PART III
Facilities

19. Check the facilities and services which are available to students
    through your academic program (Check all that apply):

    ( ) AdA - Advertising Agency provides work experience.
    ( ) AM   - AM Radio Station operated by educational institution.
    ( ) AP   - Associated Press Feed.
    ( ) AUD - Audio Recording Laboratory.
    ( ) CATV - Local Community Antenna (Cable) TV use student's work.
    ( ) CCAud- Carrier Current or Land Line Audio Distribution System.
    ( ) CCTV - Closed Circuit TV Facility for classroom or campus.
    ( ) CN   - Campus Newspaper published independently of department.
    ( ) ComN - Local Commercial Newspaper provides work experience.
    ( ) ComTV- Local Commercial TV Station provides work experience.
    ( ) CP   - Canadian Press Feed.
    ( ) DESK - Desktop Publishing Facilities, including MAC Labs.
    ( ) DR   - Darkroom Facilities for photography.
    ( ) EDIT - Video Editing Facility.
    ( ) EFP - Electronic Field Production equipment used in classes.
    ( ) ETV - TV Station operated by educational institution.
    ( ) FILM - Film or Cinema Studio and Laboratories.
    ( ) FM   - FM Radio Station operated by educational institution.
    ( ) ITFS - Instructional Television Fixed Service Distribution.
    ( ) JM   - Journalism or other program publishes Magazine.
    ( ) JN   - Journalism or other program publishes Newspaper.
    ( ) NYTS - New York Times Service Feed.
    ( ) PRA - Public Relations Agency provides work experience.
    ( ) RNA - Reuters News Agency Feed.
    ( ) SAT - Satellite Uplink Facility: [ ] Ku Band [ ] C Band.
    ( ) UPI - United Press International Feed.
    ( ) VDT - Electronic News and Data Processing used in classes.
    ( ) VID - Video Laboratory or Television Simulation Studio.

PART IV
Faculty and Staff

20. Total Number of Full-Time faculty in your Academic Unit as defined in Question 3: _____

21. Number of Part-Time (half-time or less) faculty members and/or graduate teaching assistants: _____

22. Number of Full-Time professional, non-clerical staff members employed in your academic program, i.e., reporters, engineers, etc: _____

PART V
Optional Information

Please help the professional associations formulate a statistical summary of minorities and women employed in the communication disciplines in higher education by answering the following question. Institutionally specific data will not be published; discipline summaries only!

23. Of the Full-Time Faculty members noted in Question 20, indicate the number of males and females in each racial/ethnic data category:

Number Male		Number Female
_____	American Indian or Alaskan Native	_____
_____	Asian or Pacific Islander	_____
_____	Black	_____
_____	White	_____
_____	Hispanic	_____

Thank you for including your program in *Communication Disciplines in Higher Education Directory* to be published simultaneously by the ACA, AEJMC, and BEA. Please RETURN your questionnaire within two weeks to:

Garland C. Elmore
Office of Learning Technologies
Indiana University - Purdue University
902 West New York Street
Indianapolis, Indiana 46209-9971
(317) 274-4507

Postage Free Business Reply Envelope Enclosed